The Palgrave Handbook of Consultancy in Health Psychology

Roseanna Brady • Judit Varkonyi-Sepp
Jan Smith
Editors

The Palgrave Handbook of Consultancy in Health Psychology

palgrave
macmillan

Editors
Roseanna Brady
Psychology for Health Associates
Bedford, UK

Jan Smith
Glasgow Caledonian University
Glasgow, UK

Judit Varkonyi-Sepp
Department of Adult Health Psychology
Hampshire and Isle of Wight Healthcare
NHS Foundation Trust
Southampton, UK

ISBN 978-3-031-94528-1 ISBN 978-3-031-94529-8 (eBook)
https://doi.org/10.1007/978-3-031-94529-8

Contributor: Eugene Sergeev / Alamy Stock Photo

This Palgrave Macmillan imprint is published by the registered company Springer Nature Switzerland AG.
The registered company address is: Gewerbestrasse 11, 6330 Cham, Switzerland

Foreword

The field of health psychology consultancy is constantly evolving, where the combination of psychological theory and methods with health and health practices presents significant opportunities for making a real difference. However, there has been little written on the subject so far, which has led to a lack of awareness about its potential and a lack of confidence among those offering the expertise. *The Palgrave Handbook of Consultancy in Health Psychology* aims to help potential clients understand how they could benefit and to show health psychologists the impact they can make and how to do it effectively.

This handbook brings together the knowledge and experiences of leading experts in the field. It is a comprehensive guide designed for both experienced consultants and those new to health psychology consultancy, providing valuable insights into the many aspects of the role.

The book is divided into four parts, each addressing important elements of consultancy. Part I, 'Introductory Chapters', lays the groundwork for the field, covering the definition of consultancy, the reasons for using consultancy in health psychology, and providing a strong framework for practice. Written by the editors—Roseanna Brady, Judit Varkoni-Sepp, and Jan Smith—these chapters offer a clear understanding of the scope and importance of consultancy work. They are especially useful for health psychologists who are already providing consultancy services but have not labelled their work as such, as well as for potential clients who may not have considered how health psychology can support their challenges.

Part II, 'Perspectives on Practice', focuses on the practical and ethical sides of consultancy. This section offers practical advice on how to deliver consultancy and highlights the complexities that come with it. The contributors cover topics like how to start and maintain a consultancy, handling business aspects, building relationships with clients, working in multidisciplinary and international settings, and addressing the needs of vulnerable clients.

Part III, 'Case Studies', presents a series of real-world examples showing health psychology consultancy in action. These case studies cover a range of situations where health psychology principles have been applied in different contexts. Some examples focus on understanding a problem, while others address managing, developing, or evaluating interventions. The cases cover areas like public health messaging, vaccine uptake, cardiac rehabilitation, surgery, and government projects, providing useful examples of how consultancy can make an impact.

Part IV contains the concluding chapter in which the editors summarise the key contributions in the book and reflect on implications for the profession.

Reading through the chapters of this handbook will help you better appreciate the role of health psychology consultants in improving healthcare outcomes. The experiences and insights shared by the authors offer a wealth of knowledge to inspire and guide future consultancy work. The editors have gathered contributions from some of the top experts in the field, especially in the UK, along with lesser-known authors with valuable, diverse experiences.

In the UK, consultancy has been part of the Health Psychology qualification for over 20 years, but there has been no resource to support learning and practice—until now. This handbook fills that gap and should help accelerate the use of health psychology consultancy, leading to positive impacts. Personally, I know this handbook would have been incredibly useful in my own consultancy work, which I provided (without calling it consultancy) to departments at the Royal Free Hospital in London, with Louise Earll in Gloucestershire and later as a consultant to the Scottish Government's Department of Health.

I, along with the editors, hope this handbook serves as a valuable resource for health psychologists wanting to expand their consultancy work and for potential clients seeking to engage with health psychologists. As health psychology consultancy grows in both volume and quality, its benefits to health and healthcare are more likely to be realized.

University of Aberdeen, UK
March 2025

Professor Marie Johnston

Acknowledgements

In curating and editing this book, we have received invaluable support from several people, and we wish to thank them. The original proposal for the book was reviewed by Christine Bundy, Tracy Epton, Kate Greenwell, and Rachel Povey. Their suggestions and encouragement helped us to shape the structure of the book and to identify additional contributions, which have enriched the content. Marie Johnston agreed early in the process to write a Foreword. Marie also gave generously of her time and wisdom, providing hugely valuable advice, supporting us through unexpected challenges, and giving us the confidence to trust in our vision for the book and in our own expertise. Four of our contributing authors, Paul Chadwick, Emma Kirkby-Geddes, Wendy Lawrence, and Jennifer Lunt, reviewed the editors' chapters. Their feedback and suggestions were enormously helpful, enabling us to refine and improve our own writing. Paul helped us to navigate some thorny issues as we edited the book and did so with expertise, good humour, and kindness. Emma was the first to sign up to contribute a chapter to the book, and she helped us to shape and refine the authors' brief, giving generously of her time, feedback, and expertise. Ashlee Mulimba, in addition to contributing a case study, provided feedback on our Conclusion chapter from the perspective of a health psychologist with an established consultancy practice. We are grateful to Clelia Petracca, Keerthana Ramalingham, Connie Li, and Beth Farrow at Palgrave Macmillan who helped us with manuscript preparation and subsequent publication. We originally chose to contract with Palgrave Macmillan largely because of the excellent support and advice provided by commissioning editor, Isobel Cowper Bowles. We offer our heartfelt thanks to our main collaborators, the 42 contributing authors, for their generosity in sharing their work and for their patience and persistence through drafts and revisions. Finally, we would like to thank our families for supporting us and tolerating the early morning, late evening, and weekend work we did to complete this ambitious project.

Contents

Part I Introductory Chapters 1

1 **Introduction** 3
Roseanna Brady, Judit Varkonyi-Sepp, and Jan Smith

2 **The Case for Consultancy in Health Psychology** 19
Judit Varkonyi-Sepp, Roseanna Brady, and Jan Smith

3 **A Framework for Consultancy in Health Psychology** 37
Roseanna Brady and Judit Varkonyi-Sepp

Part II Perspectives on Practice 57

4 **Ethics and the Consultancy Process** 59
Paul Chadwick, Lisa Hodges-Ballard, Alison Killen, and Roseanna Brady

5 **Multidisciplinary Working in Consultancy: The Delicate Balance of Expertise, Confidence, and Humility** 81
Michelle Constable and Jim McManus

6 **Conducting Consultancy with Vulnerable Clients** 101
Alison Killen

7 **The Sustainable Consultant** 123
Jennifer Lunt

8 **Consultancy in Practice: Navigating Boundaries** 143
Emma Kirkby-Geddes

9 **Pricing and Value in Health Psychology Consultancy** 161
Lisa Newson

10 **Don't Fall at the First Hurdle: Responding to Requests for Proposals** 185
Lou Atkinson

11 **Starting Up a Health Psychology Consultancy** 203
Nisha Sharma and Lisa Hodges-Ballard

12 **A 'How To' Guide to Working in the Private Sector** 221
Lina Eliasson and Christina Jackson

13 **Health Psychology Consultancy in Digital Health** 243
Claire Hamlet

14 **Experiences of Health Psychology Consultancy in International Health Partnerships** 267
Rebecca Turner, Lucie Byrne-Davis, Sian Armstrong, Nisha Sharma, and Jo Hart

Part III Case Studies 289

15 **Enquiry: Supporting Vaccine Uptake Decision-making in Residential Services** 291
Suzanne Allen

16 **Enquiry: Why Aren't People Attending? It's Good for Their Health!** 309
Eleanor Bull, Jo Hall, Rachel Mallon, Laura Walton-Taylor, and Neville Scholten

17 **Enquiry: Understanding High Antibiotic Prescribing Rates for Tailoring Public Health Campaigns** 331
Lisa Hodges-Ballard and Nisha Sharma

18 **Consultant-Client Relationships: Increasing Awareness and Detection of Psychological Difficulties in People Undertaking Haemodialysis** 349
Sarah A. Afuwape

19 **Consultant-Client Relationships: Supporting Development of a National Intellectual Disability Memory Service in Ireland** 369
Marianne Fallon and Eimear McGlinchey

20 **Consultant-Client Relationships: Group Intervention for Post-bariatric Surgery Patients** 387
Gillian Smith

21 **Consultant-Client Relationships: Hearts and Minds - Psychological Consultancy in Cardiac Rehabilitation** 407
Eleanor Whittaker

22 **Negotiation and Contracting: Delivering Healthcare Differently** 425
Liz Edwards-Smith

23 **Planning and Managing: Consultancy for Establishing a Multidisciplinary Rehabilitation Outpatient Clinic** 443
Avital Gershfeld-Litvin

24 **Planning and Managing: Co-developing a Framework Addressing Self-stigma in People Living with HIV** 463
Ashlee Mulimba and Puja Patel

25 **Planning and Managing: Providing Health Psychology Expertise in a Local Co-produced Wellbeing Service** 481
Debbie M. Smith

26 **Planning and Managing: Consultancy for Local Government - Behavioural Science in Self-management of Well-being** 499
Rachael Thorneloe, Abigail Millings, and Madelynne Arden

27 **Planning and Managing: Everything Due an Hour Ago - Consultancy with a Government Department** 519
Daniella Watson, Wendy Lawrence, and Mary Barker

28 Evaluation: Improving Employee Health and Wellbeing 539
Joe Gaunt and Lisa Newson

29 Evaluation: Consultancy to a Health Project in Soweto, Johannesburg 559
Delan Naidoo

30 Evaluation: Including Experiences of Transgender People in Health Care 579
Kevin Turner

Part IV Concluding Chapter 597

31 Conclusion 599
Roseanna Brady, Judit Varkonyi-Sepp, and Jan Smith

Index 615

List of Contributors

Dr Sarah A. Afuwape PhD Royal Free London NHS Foundation Trust, London, UK

Suzanne Allen MPsychSc University of Stirling, Stirling, UK

Professor Madelynne Arden PhD Manchester Metropolitan University, Manchester, UK

Dr Sian Armstrong DHealthPsych The Psychology Collective, Glasgow, UK

Dr Lou Atkinson PhD Veasta, Portland, UK

Professor Mary Barker PhD University of Southampton, Southampton, UK

Dr Roseanna Brady DHealthPsych Psychology for Health Associates, Bedford, UK

Dr Eleanor Bull PhD Derbyshire Community Health Services NHS Foundation Trust, Chesterfield, UK

Derbyshire County Council, Derbyshire, UK

Division of Medical Education, University of Manchester, Manchester, UK

Professor Lucie Byrne-Davis PhD Behavioural Science for International Health Workforce Group, University of Manchester, Manchester, UK

Dr Paul Chadwick DClinPsych UCL Centre for Behaviour Change, London, UK

Dr Michelle Constable DHealthPsych The Behavioural Science and Public Health Network, Stevenage, UK

Liz Edwards-Smith MSc (Psychology) Evalesco Consulting, Plymouth, UK

Dr Lina Eliasson PhD Sprout Health Solutions Ltd., London, UK

Marianne Fallon MSc (Health Psych) Trinity Centre for Ageing and Intellectual Disability, Trinity College Dublin, Dublin, Ireland

Joe Gaunt MSc (Health Psych) Zeno Health Group, Bardsey, Leeds, UK

Dr Avital Gershfeld-Litvin PhD The Academic College of Tel Aviv-Yaffo, Tel Aviv, Israel

Dr Jo Hall DClinPsych Derbyshire Community Health Services, NHS Foundation Trust, Chesterfield, UK

Derbyshire County Council, Derbyshire, UK

Dr Claire Hamlet Independent Consultant, Bristol, UK

Professor Jo Hart PhD Behavioural Science for International Health Workforce Group, University of Manchester, Manchester, UK

Dr Lisa Hodges-Ballard DHealthPsych Cognitiva Consultancy Ltd., Southampton, UK

Dr Christina Jackson PhD Sprout Health Solutions Ltd., London, UK

Dr Alison Killen DHealthPsych Newcastle University, Newcastle, UK

Dr Emma Kirkby-Geddes PhD Independent Health Psychologist, Huddersfield, UK

Dr Wendy Lawrence PhD University of Southampton, Southampton, UK

Dr Jennifer Lunt DHealthPsych University of Derby, Derby, UK

Dr Rachel Mallon DEdCPsych Derbyshire Community Health Services NHS Foundation Trust, Chesterfield, UK

Dr Eimear McGlinchey PhD Trinity Centre for Ageing and Intellectual Disability, Trinity College Dublin, Dublin, Ireland

Professor Jim McManus CPsychol The Behavioural Science and Public Health Network, Stevenage, UK

Public Health Wales, Cardiff, UK

Professor Abigail Millings PhD Sheffield Hallam University, Sheffield, UK

Dr Ashlee Mulimba DHealthPsych Healthy Dialogues, London, UK

Dr Delan Naidoo DPsych Mindsightful, Jersey, UK

Professor Lisa Newson DHealthPsych Liverpool John Moore University, Liverpool, UK

Dr Puja Patel DHealthPsych Healthy Dialogues, London, UK

Neville Scholten Derbyshire Community Health Services NHS Foundation Trust, Chesterfield, UK

Dr Nisha Sharma DHealthPsych Cognitiva Consultancy Ltd., Southampton, UK

Dr Debbie M. Smith PhD University of Manchester, Manchester, UK

Dr Gillian Smith DHealthPsych Healthy You Ltd., Huddersfield, UK

Dr Jan Smith PhD Glasgow Caledonian University, Glasgow, UK

Dr Rachael Thorneloe PhD Sheffield Hallam University, Sheffield, UK

Dr Kevin Turner DHealthPsych Dorset HealthCare University, NHS Foundation Trust, Poole, Dorset, UK

Dr Rebecca Turner PhD Behavioural Science for International Health Workforce Group, University of Manchester, Manchester, UK

Judit Varkonyi-Sepp CPsychol Department of Adult Health Psychology, Hampshire and Isle of Wight Healthcare NHS Foundation Trust, Southampton, UK

Laura Walton-Taylor MSc Derbyshire Community Health Services NHS Foundation Trust, Chesterfield, UK

Dr Daniella Watson PhD Imperial College London, London, UK

Dr Eleanor Whittaker PhD Public Health Team North Yorkshire Council, North Yorkshire, UK

List of Figures

Fig. 5.1	A schema of domains of knowledge needed in psychology consulting	85
Fig. 8.1	Boundary relationships of consultants and clients	145
Fig. 12.1	Overview of clinical trial phases and their objectives	222
Fig. 12.2	Opportunities for health psychology consultants and vendors across the drug development pathway	223
Fig. 17.1	Stakeholder communication flow	334
Fig. 24.1	Key relationships in co-production and delivery of the Empowerment Programme Framework	469
Fig. 27.1	The way that participants' experiences informed the COVID-19 programme. (Watson et al., 2022)	523
Fig. 28.1	A Consultancy-to-Practice Model	543

List of Tables

Table 1.1	Health domain focus in chapters	14
Table 4.1	General principles of ethical codes of practice across countries and geographical regions	62
Table 4.2	Actions to achieve ethical practice during enquiry	73
Table 4.3	Actions to achieve ethical practice during negotiation and contracting	74
Table 4.4	Actions to achieve ethical practice during relationship building	75
Table 4.5	Actions to achieve ethical practice during planning and managing delivery	76
Table 4.6	Actions to achieve ethical practice during evaluation	77
Table 6.1	Domains of health inequality (Public Health England, 2021)	103
Table 8.1	Advisor and implementer	151
Table 9.1	Invited consultancy versus a tendered consultancy exercise	167
Table 9.2	Indirect costs	170
Table 9.3	Setting boundaries for pro bono work	176
Table 9.4	Summary of pricing methodology	178
Table 11.1	Questions to reflect on prior to setting up a consultancy	207
Table 11.2	Operating costs for a consultancy practice	210
Table 12.1	Example budget for a literature review	230
Table 12.2	Pharmaceutical industry acronyms	238
Table 14.1	The Global Health Partnership's nine partnership principles	276
Table 15.1	Stakeholder feedback	294
Table 15.2	Application of the Health Belief Model (HBM) (Rosenstock, 1974)	295
Table 20.1	Outline of group sessions	391
Table 22.1	Stakeholders involved in shared medical appointments (SMA) pilot project	428

Table 22.2	Stages of project, negotiation and contracting spaces, and stakeholders	431
Table 27.1	Actionable points for each lesson learned	529
Table 28.1	Examples of questions asked throughout to engage in formative and process evaluation	541
Table 29.1	Stakeholders and aims	562
Table 29.2	Project aims with psychologist input	564
Table 29.3	Significant project outcomes	565
Table 29.4	Models of consultancy mapped to my consultancy for the client	566
Table 29.5	Mapping APEASE criteria (Michie et al., 2014) to significant agreed consultancy activities	568

List of Boxes

Box 8.1	Features of the Consultancy Project	147
Box 9.1	Examples of Direct Costs for Project-Associated Activities	168
Box 9.2	How Much to Charge for Your Time	169
Box 10.1	Top Tip 1: Contact the Client	189
Box 10.2	Example of Challenging a Client's Assumptions	193
Box 10.3	Top tip 2: Offer Options	194
Box 10.4	Questions to Guide Your Response to an RfP	199
Box 10.5	Questions to Help with Writing a Proposal	199
Box 11.1	Questions When Planning to Set Up Your Own Consultancy	217
Box 12.1	Sample Questions to Inform RFP Response	229
Box 13.1	Questions to Explore During Enquiry in UX Projects	256
Box 24.1	A Framework for Empowerment Programmes to Tackle Internalised Stigma (Fast-Track Cities London, 2021)	467
Box 28.1	Recommendations for Client	548

Part I

Introductory Chapters

1

Introduction

Roseanna Brady, Judit Varkonyi-Sepp, and Jan Smith

This handbook provides a new and substantial resource to support health psychologists engaging in consultancy to develop their practice. In commissioning contributions, we invited chapters that would enable readers to understand 'how to do' consultancy. For the past two decades, one of the main resources aimed specifically at health psychologists engaging in consultancy has been the work of Earll and Bath (2004), who provided a structure for consultancy involving several stages with examples of application. Earlier, Michie (1998) had highlighted the value that psychologists' skills could bring to problems in health through engaging in consultancy. Few other resources exist that specifically address the practice of consultancy in health psychology. To help to fill the gap, we present a case for consultancy in health psychology (Chap. 2), we propose a framework for consultancy in health psychology

R. Brady (✉)
Psychology for Health Associates, Bedford, UK
e-mail: bradykbs@msn.com

J. Varkonyi-Sepp
Department of Adult Health Psychology, Hampshire and Isle of Wight Healthcare NHS Foundation Trust, Southampton, UK
e-mail: j.varkonyi-sepp@soton.ac.uk

J. Smith
Glasgow Caledonian University, Glasgow, UK
e-mail: jan.smith@gcu.ac.uk

R. Brady et al. (eds.), *The Palgrave Handbook of Consultancy in Health Psychology*,
https://doi.org/10.1007/978-3-031-94529-8_1

(Chap. 3), and we include 16 case studies demonstrating consultancy practice together with 11 chapters offering perspectives on consultancy practice.

The book is aimed at four main types of readers. First, health psychologists in consultancy practice will find the book helpful in developing and enhancing their practice. Second, trainee and qualified health psychologists new to consultancy will find it a useful guide to enable them to develop skills required for consultancy practice. Third, those responsible for training health psychologists will find the book a valuable resource for teaching and supervision. Fourth, potential commissioners of consultancy from health psychologists will be able to read about practical applications of health psychology theories, models and tools and the benefits of using them in solving problems in health at scale.

With this handbook book we aim to build on the work of Earll and Bath (2004) and Michie (1998). We draw on the extensive literature on consultancy in other specialist disciplines as well as on the experience and expertise of those health psychology professionals engaging in consultancy practice. In this introductory chapter, we describe briefly what consultancy is and we explain our motivations in curating and editing the book. We also guide readers on how best to use the book to inform their own practice, and we include an overview of the health domains in which contributing authors are working.

What is Consultancy?

There are several definitions and descriptions of consultancy. Earll and Bath (2004) defined it as, "a formal relationship where one party seeks help from another, the consultant's role being to facilitate the process whereby both the consultant and client arrive at a mutually acceptable solution" (pp. 230–231). This definition acknowledges the importance of helping and empowering the client in the process of consultation. The definition fits well with the view of social psychologist and consultancy expert Edgar Schein, who emphasises the 'helping' nature of consultancy (Schein, 2016). Earll and Bath include a list of non-linear 'stages' in consultancy that require particular skills on the part of the consultant. The stages include assessing requests for consultancy, planning and negotiating, establishing working relationships, monitoring the consultancy and evaluating impact. The skills required in these stages are common to all practitioners of consultancy, regardless of their core specialisms. As Earll and Bath acknowledged, consultancy is neither exclusive to health psychology, nor is it new. We will explore this further in Chaps. 2 and 3. For our purposes, we exclude consultancy in clinical practice, although we include the work of psychologist clinicians who provide consultancy as part of their wider role in healthcare. Writing mainly about consultation in the context of providing health services (which they describe as a process of 'advisement' that may include offering expert opinion and making recommendations), Falender and Shafranske (2020, p. 11), acknowledge that "increasingly, psychologists are called on to provide consultation … in diverse and ever-expanding professional and interprofessional settings", settings that include consultation in communities, groups and organisations. This wider area of professional practice is represented in the contributions to this book.

Susan Michie (1998) called for greater engagement by psychologists in evidence-based consultancy in health. She outlined:

> areas in which psychologists have expertise relevant to consultancy work: (i) understanding the contextual nature of health problems; (ii) the systematic analysis of problems and potential solutions; (iii) the understanding of change processes that enable recommendations about the best ways of achieving the task or goal identified by the consultee; and (iv) research skills that enable the evaluation of services, interventions, and changes. (p. 155)

We agree with this analysis which highlights specialist knowledge and skills of health psychologists. To be able to conduct consultancy, however, it is important also to identify and clarify the consultancy-specific skills required to engage with clients and stakeholders as Earll and Bath (2004) highlighted. Consultants need to combine their scientific (technical) expertise with what we term *generic consultancy skills* in order to be effective. Chapter 3 aims to provide guidance on what those generic skills are and how they can be embedded in a consultancy framework for health psychologists.

We can learn from consultancy in business in this regard while acknowledging that there are differences in consultancy practice between, for example, management consultancy and consultancy in behavioural science. Health psychology clients in private, public and third sectors, operate in a 'business' environment. Consultants, regardless of their specialist psychology or behavioural science expertise, also deliver their work in that business environment and in a context of professional management, multidisciplinary professionals, budgetary constraints, shareholder and other stakeholder requirements, and within the legal and regulatory frameworks in which organisations operate. Consultants who are mindful of the needs of the organisations to which they provide their services are more able to tie their recommendations to the realities of the world in which the client operates (Scott & Barnes, 2011). As consultants, we are better placed to apply our specialist expertise if we understand how to apply the generic skills involved in consultancy in a business context. Block (2011) identifies three types of skills that a consultant needs: technical skills requiring expertise in a specific area (e.g., in behavioural science), interpersonal skills (to develop effective relationships), and consultancy skills (required for negotiation and contracting, analysing data, presenting findings, working with others in decision-making) (p. 8). Health psychologists gain competence in research, intervention design, teaching and training during their professional training. These competences are all applicable and transferable to consultancy practice. How straightforward and easy it is to apply these in consultancy projects depends on many factors such as the complexity of the work, the characteristics of the client and the experience of the consultant, not necessarily in consultancy per se, but in adapting health psychology skills and knowledge in practice. Reflecting on these processes and how we can adapt our core skills is both necessary and fruitful, as you will read in the contributions to this book.

In the general consultancy literature, Appelbaum and Steed (2005), citing Greiner and Metzger (1983, p.69), point to the advisory role of management consultants as being "truly external to the organization… [with] financial, administrative, political and emotional independence from the client". This definition is useful in highlighting the objectivity that consultants bring to their work, and which is particularly valuable to clients wishing to solve problems (Scott & Barnes, 2011). There are two issues to raise about this definition, however. First, it neglects *internal consultancy* where specialists work within organisations yet are outside the day-to-day operational activities of the organisation (Hodges, 2018). The internal consultant has several advantages over a consultant who is external to the organisation: an insider perspective on the facilitators and barriers to getting things done; the ability to follow progress and to adapt when obstacles to implementation arise; and as an expert 'ready resource' to the organisation (Scott & Barnes, 2011, pp. 6–8). Internal consultancy is a common experience in health psychology and is explored in several chapters in this book.

Second, the requirement to maintain 'emotional independence' does not fit with the experience of all health psychology consultants and certainly not with our own. Nor is it desirable. Indeed, Schein calls on consultants to "overcome professional distance" (Schein, 2016, p. 15) and to develop more personal, trusting and open relationships with clients from the very first encounter. We believe that one can maintain objectivity and independence while still developing an empathetic relationship with the client, provided one has the necessary skills. As scientific practitioners who draw on theory and evidence to inform our work, and who work within our scope of practice while so doing (e.g., British Psychological Society, n.d.; Health and Care Professions Council, n.d.), we have the advantage of professional and ethical standards to protect us and our clients from potential hazards in any 'blurring' of relationships. The boundaries in consultant-client relationships are a focus of several chapters (most notably, Chap. 8) where authors draw particularly on the work of Kitay and Wright (2004) who explore the impact of 'insider' and 'outsider' consultant roles in their Boundary Model of Relationships.

A further point to note from the management consultancy literature relates to implementation. Block (2011) identifies a consultant as someone who "is in a position to have some influence over an individual, a group or an organization, but no direct power to make changes or to implement programs" (p. 2). The goal of the consultant, according to Block, is to influence change. This also fits with the features of (management) consultants listed by Nicolescu and Nicolescu (2016), one of which is that consultants do not directly implement recommendations but can collaborate with staff regarding implementation. This is a feature of consultancy in health psychology. When consultants agree to take on implementation of an intervention, as some health psychologists tell us they do, they need to be aware of the potential dangers of becoming 'surrogate managers' (Block, 2011) where they hold responsibility for implementation, without control of resources or formal authority in relation to staff.

As you can also read in this book, health psychologists are often involved in designing and delivering educational interventions in their role as consultants. In delivering this type of work, the line between consultancy and teaching (two separate competences required for professional practice as health psychologists in the United Kingdom (UK)) may seem a little blurred. Our position is that delivering a standard prewritten teaching or training programme is not, of itself, consultancy. If, on the other hand, the consultant is asked to develop and deliver teaching or training programmes to meet the needs of a specific client and target population, and if the consultant draws on theory and evidence to design or adapt a teaching or training programme, that is consultancy. Ensuring that the learning is acted on, however, or that recommendations are implemented in practice, is often outside the direct control of the consultant.

Health psychologists are not management consultants, nor do they need or aspire to be. Since health psychologists do, however, provide their services within a business context, the management consultancy literature has much to offer us even if it does not quite 'fit' with our practice. Clients, regardless of the sector in which they operate, need to justify their investment in consultancy services. Clients need to know that in commissioning health psychologists to help them to solve problems, the consultants have the necessary skills to work effectively with stakeholders, to plan use of resources, identify risks and mitigate against those risks, to articulate assumptions, to negotiate and agree to roles, responsibilities, boundaries and deliverables, and to monitor, evaluate and adapt to changing circumstances as consultancy projects are carried out. The processes involved in the practice of consultancy in health psychology, and the skills required, are discussed in depth in Chap. 3 of this book.

In the consultancy literature, several authors also specify *knowledge transfer* as an element of consultancy (see Saad, 2017, for example). It is certainly important that we share knowledge of behavioural science with clients and stakeholders through our practice. However, we need to be aware that while as psychologists or as behavioural scientists we transfer knowledge about psychosocial factors impacting on health, or generic skills in facilitation or communication techniques for example, we do not transfer our *expertise* in psychology or behavioural science. In our experience, this sometimes needs to be clarified with clients and their staff who may assume that knowledge alone is sufficient to create change. This assumption was identified by Kelly and Barker (2016) as one of six common errors made by policy-makers in health in attempts to change health-related behaviours.

Definition of Consultancy in Health Psychology

We define consultancy (in health psychology) as

> the application of specialist psychology knowledge, skills and expertise, under contract to a client, to assist in clarifying and resolving problems with a view to improving the health of target groups and populations.

While our focus is primarily on physical health, we recognise that physical and mental health are closely associated (Department of Health, 2011). The term 'mental health' is somewhat ambiguous, however, depending on how and where it is used. It is important to differentiate 'mental health' from 'mental illness' in terms of diagnostic criteria. Designing and delivering interventions for mental illness requires specialist training and is not within the scope of practice of a health psychologist (although some practitioners may have additional specialist training and accredited qualifications in this area). The term 'under contract' can either mean a formal contract between a client and an external consultant or an agreement between internal consultants and their clients. The term 'client' excludes individuals seeking help for their own health since that fits with 'clinical' work. Target groups for consultancy work in health psychology could be healthcare staff, patient or carer groups, staff or partners from other professions who are involved in designing or delivering health interventions, specific sectors of the population or geographical populations.

Consultancy in health psychology may take several forms (e.g., providing expert advice, designing interventions, advising on policy, working with partners on product and service design, and public health messaging) and can vary widely in terms of scope and complexity. However, we believe it will always include the following ingredients.

External perspective: the consultant is not a member of staff of the organisation, or in the case of internal consultants, the consultant is not a member of the department or group to whom the consultancy service is provided.

Contract: the consultant and client reach an agreement, recorded and confirmed in writing, about what the consultancy work will involve and what outcomes are expected, regardless of whether or not a fee is paid directly to the consultant.

Expertise: the consultant offers specialist expertise, in this case in psychology as applied to health and health behaviour, to the client.

Theory-informed and evidence-based: this is central to our professional practice.

Why This Book?

This book is a resource we wished we had access to when we were training as health psychologists. Our initial motivation for undertaking this project was based on the experiences of two of the editors (RB and JV-S) working with the Health Psychology Exchange (HPX), a collaborative of health psychology professionals who volunteered to assist with the response to the coronavirus (Covid-19) pandemic (Health Psychology Exchange, n.d.). During that collaboration, several fellow volunteers asked us for guidance on how to approach key people in the organisations we were offering to support. The volunteers said they lacked the confidence and knowledge of 'how to' discuss the challenges faced by those organisations. Our fellow volunteers had confidence in the theories, models and tools of behavioural science; they were, however, unsure of how to propose interventions to senior executives in large organisations to help them to deal with some of the impacts of Covid-19. Several consultancy projects were undertaken with small teams of health psychology volunteers led by more experienced consultants (Brady et al., 2021). Subsequently, we (RB & JV-S) offered a series of free webinars on consultancy to the health psychology community, all of which were heavily subscribed. Our learning from these experiences was that despite consultancy being a core competence required in the UK for registration as a health psychologist, some members of the profession, both qualified and in training, wanted to learn more about how to practise as they realised that they lacked some of the generic consultancy skills.

We agree in principle with those who advocate for embedding health psychologists and other behavioural scientists in health organisations (e.g., Byrne-Davis et al., 2022). Creating paid roles for health psychologists in health services has been recommended as a way of applying the theories, models and tools of behaviour change in health (Presseau et al., 2022). However, given the size of the health sector (e.g., health spending accounts for 10.9% and 17.3% of gross domestic product of the UK and the USA respectively (Statista, n.d.-a, n.d.-b)), it is unlikely that there are enough health psychologists available to employ directly across health organisations. In addition, outsourcing of specialist/technical services is a common business practice, particularly in the public sector (O'Mahoney & Markham, 2013; Novruzov, 2024). Consultancy (specifically, management consultancy) in health services is not without its critics (e.g., Oliver, 2014); there may be legitimate concerns about cost and effectiveness, and about overreliance on external consultants leading to a 'hollowing-out' of the public sector (Browne, 2021; cited in Novruzov, 2024). On the other hand, concerns that employing external consultants leads to this hollowing out effect, where external consultancy become substitute for internal functions, have not been substantiated. In fact, an examination of practices in 125 hospitals in the National Health Service in the UK found complementary relationships between consultants and internal management and a lower use of external consultants in organisations that employ internal consultants (Kirkpatrick et al., 2023). This last point is important because health psychologists often fulfil the role of internal consultants even if the word 'consultant' is not used, and there are several examples of internal consultancy in this handbook (see Chaps. 5, 7, 15, 16, 18 and 23).

Behavioural scientists (including health psychologists) working in public health organisations are known to experience challenges in having their recommendations implemented, and some report experiencing burnout due to the pressures of colleagues not understanding the complexity of the work needed to influence behaviour change during Covid-19 (Byrne-Davis et al., 2022). Such challenges can be, and often are, overcome as you will be able to read in several chapters in the book. Schein (2016) encourages consultants to help clients to see the "true complexity and messiness of the problem …and help [the client] to abandon quick fixes and/or knee-jerk reactions" (p. 24). Schein advocates for the consultant to become a 'partner and helper' through an attitude of humility, commitment to helping, and genuine curiosity. Reflecting retrospectively on their consultancy practice through the lens of Schein's model of *process consultation* (Schein, 1999), which involves the consultant working with the client to identify and find solutions to problems (rather than simply providing technical expertise or advice), several contributing authors acknowledge the benefits to clients and to themselves of taking this approach in their work. We echo the sentiments expressed by Susan Michie (2025) recently in an article in *The Psychologist* (January/February 2025), where she stated that "UK psychology as a discipline needs to be much more outward-looking and pro-active … more focused on multidisciplinary efforts in public health" (p. 30) and where she encouraged psychologists to "Get out there and make a noise, and keep saying the same thing – 'we're here, we could help you achieve your goals'" (p. 30). That is what the contributing authors in this handbook are doing.

A Note on Contributors

When curating the content of this book, we sought contributors from our professional networks to identify health psychologists who were engaging currently, or recently, in consultancy. We were seeking people who would be willing to either write a case study from their own experience (Part III, Case Studies), or a chapter exploring a topic of relevance to consultancy in health psychology (Part II, Perspectives). We met online with potential contributors, explained the purpose and proposed structure of the book, shared the framework for consultancy in health psychology (Chap. 3) with them, and invited brief written chapter proposals. Prior to accepting the proposals, we asked all contributors to confirm in writing that they had read and understood the consultancy framework document and a detailed authors' brief. We invited contributors' views on whether or not the framework captured all of the processes involved in their consultancy practice. All said they felt that the framework did so, and several contributors expressed the view that they wished they had had a book like this when they were training and starting out in their professional careers.

To widen the representation of contributing authors we asked for recommendations for potential contributors not known to us and we actively set out to find authors outside of the UK. As a result, five of the contributing authors live and work outside the UK: three in Ireland, one in South Africa and one in Israel, and one team of collaborators works with International Health Partnerships delivering teaching and training interventions in several countries. We advertised for contributors through the European Health Psychology Society. While we feel sure there are many health psychologists providing consultancy expertise to clients across mainland Europe, our efforts to recruit were not successful at that time.

It is important to declare that not all contributors are practitioner health psychologists (as defined by the UK Health and Care Professions Council; HCPC, n.d.). Several contributors are academics and/or practitioner consultants specialising in behavioural science and health psychology who provide expert consultancy to external organisations. Lead authors include a clinical health psychologist working in a hospital setting (Chap. 18), an experienced professional consultant with postgraduate training in psychology working with primary care providers (Chap. 22), a medical psychologist working in a hospital outpatient rehabilitation service in Israel (Chap. 23) and a counselling psychologist working in partnership on a community-wide health initiative in Soweto (Chap. 29). Co-authors include a clinical psychologist, assistant psychologists (educational psychology), and an internal client (Chap. 16), and an academic with specialist expertise in dementia (Chap. 19). The handbook is richer for their input and reflects the strength of multidisciplinary working in addressing problems in health.

The contributing authors also represent a wide variation in experience of consultancy. Several authors bring an advanced level of consultancy expertise developed over years of practice including work with international clients. A third of the lead authors have experience in delivering consultancy either from consultancy practices or as independent health psychology consultants. Some of our contributors had several years of experience as professional consultants prior to their training in psychology. This is reflected in several chapters in Part II and Part III. We also invited contributions from people new to consultancy (Chaps. 11, 17, 20 and 30). Those chapters illustrate opportunities that can be found, and indeed created, to take first steps into consultancy and to make a positive impact in so doing. Other contributors work primarily in research or in clinical practice, occasionally offering consultancy services to clients either via their institutions to external clients, or as internal consultants supporting service development. In inviting the authors to contribute, we aimed to illustrate the variety of opportunities available to health psychologists to engage in consultancy, and to develop expertise from their first projects through to running a successful consultancy practice.

How to Use This Handbook

The handbook is in four parts. Part I contains the introductory chapters that provide context to all that follows. Since most of the chapters examine aspects of the proposed framework for consultancy in health psychology, we recommend reading about the framework in Chap. 3 initially. In that chapter, we describe five processes involved in consultancy, drawing on the consultancy literature and building on the work of Earll and Bath (2004). Chapter 2, also in Part I, outlines the case for (more) health psychologists to become involved in consultancy based on the opinions of 11 leading health psychologists, and highlights the advantages to health psychologists and to clients, as well as some of the challenges in engaging in consultancy in the health sector.

In Part II, several topics relevant to the practice of consultancy in health psychology are explored. Ethical practice and multidisciplinary working, both fundamental to effective consultancy practice, are explored in Chaps. 4 and 5, respectively. The remaining nine chapters in Part II explore getting started in consultancy and building a sustainable consultancy career, providing consultancy in the private sector and in digital health, responding to formal invitations to tender for consultancy contracts, costing and pricing consultancy work, working with vulnerable stakeholders, and working in international partnerships. Each chapter in this section ends with questions for reflection. As reflective practitioners, readers will find the questions a rich source to reflect on assumptions, values, prejudices and habitual responses in professional life, observing how they shape relationships with others and how solutions to professional problems are found.

The 16 case studies in Part III follow a consistent structure: first, there is a brief introduction to the consultancy case to provide context; second, authors provide a more detailed description and analysis of one aspect of the framework for consultancy in health psychology applied to the project; finally, the authors reflect on the case, and on their learning from it through the lens of the framework. Readers with an interest in specific health domains will find Table 1.1 helpful in guiding their reading. While most chapters focus on providing consultancy to external clients, of the four case studies describing work with internal clients, two focus on enquiry (Chaps. 15 and 16), one on relationships with internal client and stakeholders (Chap. 18), and one on planning and implementing a new service in an existing health facility (Chap. 23).

Each of the processes in the framework is explored in depth in three or more cases studies (apart from negotiation and contracting). This enables the reader to learn how the authors approached the processes involved in

Table 1.1 Health domain focus in chapters

Author (Chapter No.)	Health domain
Afuwape, S. (18)	Renal Dialysis
Allen, S. (15)	Intellectual Disability
Bull, E. et al. (16)	Type 2 Diabetes
Edwards-Smith, L. (22)	Chronic Pain
Fallon, M. & McGlinchey, E. (19)	Dementia
Gershfeld-Litvin, A. (23)	Physical Rehabilitation
Gaunt, J. & Newson, L. (28)	Employee Wellbeing
Hamlet, C. (13)	Digital Health Apps
Hodges Ballard, L. & Sharma, N. (17)	Antimicrobial Resistance
Killen, A. (6)	Health Inequalities
Kirkby-Geddes, E. (8)	Loneliness in Older Adults
Lunt, J. (7)	Health and Safety in the Workplace
Mulimba, A. & Patel, P. (24)	HIV Self-stigma
Naidoo, D. (29)	Health Behaviour in a Community Setting
Smith, D. (25)	Wellbeing Recovery
Smith, G. (20)	Post-Bariatric Dietary Regimes
Thorneloe, R.et al. (26)	Health Behaviour Change: Exercise, Social Isolation, Self-management of COVID-19 Behaviours
Turner, K. (30)	Trans Health
Turner,R.et al.(14)	Antimicrobial Resistance
Watson, D. et al. (27)	Covid-19 Screening
Whittaker, E. (21)	Cardiac Rehabilitation

consultancy in different setting and with different health challenges. Although we tried to include more than one case study for negotiation and contracting, only one author (an experienced professional consultant) offered to do so, and we reflect on this in the concluding chapter. Negotiation and contracting features strongly in several of the Part II chapters, particularly in Chap. 7 and in Chaps. 10 and 12. The topic of negotiation and renegotiation also features in case studies exploring the enquiry and planning and managing processes. Of particular interest in the case studies are the reflection sections where contributors generously share not only the positive aspects of their work but also their discomfort and their learnings about their practice. Each of the case studies ends with between three and five 'Top Tips' from the authors based on their experience of conducting the consultancy case study.

In Part IV, key themes and learnings from the contributing author chapters are summarised. The editors reflect on implications for practice and present several Calls to Action for the professional health psychology community.

The handbook shows the value that health psychology professionals (and other psychologists working in health) bring to addressing problems and challenges in health through consultancy. The opportunities to make changes to health in real-world settings are there for us to take and the need is great. Our contributors have generously shared their knowledge and experiences to enable us to see 'how to do' consultancy.

References

Appelbaum, S. H., & Steed, A. J. (2005). The critical success factors in the client-consulting relationship. *Journal of management development, 24*(1), 68–93. https://doi.org/10.1108/02621710510572362

Block, P. (2011). *Flawless consulting: A guide to get your expertise used* (3rd ed.). Pfieffer.

Brady, R., Bull, E., Armstrong, S., Lavalle, J., Cross, A., Howells, L., et al. (2021). Translating the guidance on promoting frontline healthcare worker psychological wellbeing during COVID-19 pandemic: Psychological Needs Assessment Tool. *European Health Psychologist, 22*(1), 745–756.

British Psychological Society. (n.d.). Qualification in Health Psychology (Stage 2). https://www.bps.org.uk/qualification-health-psychology-stage-2

Byrne-Davis, L. M. T., Turner, R. R., Amatya, S., Ashton, C., Bull, E. R., Chater, A. M., et al. (2022). Using behavioural science in public health settings during the COVID-19 pandemic: The experience of public health practitioners and behavioural scientists. *Acta Psychologica, 224*, 103527. https://doi.org/10.1016/j.actpsy.2022.103527

Department of Health. (2011). No health without mental health: A cross-government mental health outcomes strategy for people of all ages HMG/DH No health without mental health. https://assets.publishing.service.gov.uk/media/5a7b25d240f0b66a2fc057b1/dh_124058.pdf

Earll, L., & Bath, J. (2004). Consultancy: What is it, how do you do it, and does it make any difference? In S. Michie & C. Abraham (Eds.), *Health psychology in practice* (pp. 230–250). Blackwell Publishing. https://doi.org/10.1002/9780470694008.ch12

Falender, C. A., & Shafranske, E. P. (2020). Consultation in psychology: A distinct professional practice. In C. A. Falender & E. P. Shafranske (Eds.), *Consultation in psychology: A competency-based approach* (pp. 11–35). American Psychological Association. https://doi.org/10.1037/0000153-002

Greiner, L. E., & Metzger, R. D. (1983). Consulting to Management. Prectice.

HCPC. (n.d.). Standards for proficiency: Practitioner psychologists. Health and Care Professions Council. https://www.hcpc-uk.org/standards/standards-of-proficiency/practitioner-psychologists/

Health Psychology Exchange. (n.d.). *Translating health psychology during a pandemic*. University of Manchester. https://www.manchester.ac.uk/coronavirus-response/bmh-coronavirus-projects/health-psychology-exchange/

Hodges, J. (2018). To be or not to be an internal consultant. In G. Manville & O. Matthias (Eds.), *Management consultancy insights and real consultancy projects* (pp. 65–74). Routledge. https://doi.org/10.4324/9781315593425-20

Kelly, M. P., & Barker, M. (2016). Why is changing health-related behaviour so difficult? *Public Health, 136*, 109–116. https://doi.org/10.1016/j.puhe.2016.03.030

Kirkpatrick, I., Sturdy, A. J., Reguera Alvarado, N., & Veronesi, G. (2023). Beyond hollowing out: Public sector managers and the use of external management consultants. *Public Administration Review, 83*(3), 537–551. https://doi.org/10.1111/puar.13612

Kitay, J., & Wright, C. (2004). Take the money and run? Organisational boundaries and consultants' roles. *The Service Industries Journal, 24*(3), 1–18. https://doi.org/10.1080/0264206042000247731

Michie, S. (1998). 8.06 Consultancy. *Comprehensive Clinical Psychology, 8*, 1530169. https://doi.org/10.1016/B0080-4270(73)00276-5

Michie, S. (2025, January/February). We have to be out there, engaging with people in high places and outside of psychology. *The Psychologist*, ISSN, 2398-1598. https://www.bps.org.uk/psychologist/covid-behaviour-matters-psychology-matters

Nicolescu, O., & Nicolescu, C. (2016). Specificity of managerial consultancy for SMEs and its status in Romania. *Procedia-Social and Behavioral Sciences, 221*, 39–48. https://doi.org/10.1016/j.sbspro.2016.05.088

Novruzov, S. (2024). Management consultancy in public sector. *Open Journal of Business and Management, 12*(4), 2606–2620. https://doi.org/10.4236/ojbm.2024.124135

O'Mahoney, J., & Markham, C. (2013). *Management consultancy*. Oxford University Press.

Oliver, D. (2014). Stop wasting taxpayers' money on management consultancy for the NHS. *BMJ, 349*. https://doi.org/10.1136/bmj.g7243

Presseau, J., Byrne-Davis, L. M., Hotham, S., Lorencatto, F., Potthoff, S., Atkinson, L., et al. (2022). Enhancing the translation of health behaviour change research into practice: A selective conceptual review of the synergy between implementation science and health psychology. *Health Psychology Review, 16*(1), 22–49. https://doi.org/10.1080/17437199.2020.1866638

Saad, Y. G. (2017). Deliverable accountability, change management and breach in consultancy contracts: A comparative study of World Bank versus Europeaid funded projects. *Journal of Public Procurement, 17*(4), 525–571. https://doi.org/10.1108/jopp-17-04-2017-b003

Schein, E. (1999). *Process consultation revisited: Building the helping relationship*. Addison-Wesley Publishing.

Schein, E. H. (2016). *Humble consulting: How to provide real help faster*. Berrett-Koehler Publishers.

Scott, B., & Barnes, B. K. (2011). *Consulting on the Inside: A practical guide for internal consultants* (2nd ed.). American Society for Training and Development.

Statista. (n.d.-a). Total healthcare expenditure as a share of GDP in the United Kingdom from 1980 to 2023. https://www.statista.com/statistics/317708/healthcare-expenditure-as-a-share-of-gdp-in-the-united-kingdom/#:~:text=By%202023%2C%20healthcare%20expenditure%20in%20the%20UK%20amounted,healthcare%20spending%20as%20a%20share%20of%20the%20GDP.

Statista. (n.d.-b). U.S. health expenditure as a percent of GDP 1960–2022. https://www.statista.com/statistics/184968/us-health-expenditure-as-percent-of-gdp-since-1960/#:~:text=In%202022%2C%20U.S.%20national%20health%20expenditure%20as%20a,spending%20based%20on%20GDP%20share%20among%20developed%20countries.

2

The Case for Consultancy in Health Psychology

Judit Varkonyi-Sepp, Roseanna Brady, and Jan Smith

Introduction

As editors of this handbook, we believe that health psychologists practising as consultants bring clear benefits to clients who are seeking to solve problems in health. Although the title 'Health Psychologist' is a protected term in the UK and applies only to psychologists who meet specific practitioner requirements (HCPC, n.d.), we use the term 'health psychologists' to denote qualified practitioners, academics and professional trainees in health psychology.

Much of the work of health psychologists who work as consultants is not in the public domain. What is seen in academic peer-reviewed publications is not necessarily representative of what happens in day-to-day practice. The

J. Varkonyi-Sepp (✉)
Department of Adult Health Psychology, Hampshire and Isle of Wight Healthcare NHS Foundation Trust, Southampton, UK
e-mail: j.varkonyi-sepp@soton.ac.uk

R. Brady
Psychology for Health Associates, Bedford, UK
e-mail: bradykbs@msn.com

J. Smith
Glasgow Caledonian University, Glasgow, UK
e-mail: jan.smith@gcu.ac.uk

R. Brady et al. (eds.), *The Palgrave Handbook of Consultancy in Health Psychology*,
https://doi.org/10.1007/978-3-031-94529-8_2

voices of health psychologists who work either exclusively or partially as consultants are, however, strongly represented in this book. Examples of practice from private, public and third sectors are included. Definitions of consultancy and examples of varying complexity in a variety of health sectors and health domains can be seen in Chap. 1. Some contributors to the book had decades of experience in consultancy prior to training as health psychologists. Others demonstrate that even those relatively new to consultancy make important contributions to improving health. To an extent, the examples of consultancy in this book show that the case for engaging health psychologists as consultants is already made.

With the intention to complement the chapters showcasing practical, more focused applications of health psychology consultancy, we invited views on the case for health psychology consultancy from several experienced health psychologists,[1] particularly those who practise consultancy from academic institutions. One of the contributions is from authors who have authored a chapter in this book; the remaining eight are voices that are not represented elsewhere in this book. By the nature of academia, consultancy provided by that sector might differ from some of the applications portrayed throughout the book. At the same time, academic perspectives are expected to be inherently meta-positional (Glăveanu, 2020); that is, taking a symbolic position where elements of complex systems and the relationship between them can be observed at once. This is indeed what is necessary for the development of models and theories that underpin health psychology consultancy. We very much value these perspectives and, in line with our principle for developing this book, we want to offer a balanced resource that includes as wide a range of contributions as was possible for us.

Contributor Perspectives

The contributors to this chapter are well known within the UK-based health psychology profession and across Europe. Several have worked at international level, and all have established reputations in the field of health

[1] Professor Lucie Byrne-Davis (University of Manchester, UK); Professor Diane Dixon (Edinburgh Napier University, UK); Dr Stephan Dombrowski, (University of New Brunswick, Canada); Professor Jo Hart (University of Manchester, UK); Professor Vangelis Karademas (University of Crete, Greece); Dr Wendy Maltinsky (University of Stirling, UK); Professor Hannah McGee (Royal College of Surgeons, Ireland); Professor Susan Michie (Centre for Behaviour Change, University College London, UK); Professor Felix Naughton, (University of East Anglia, UK); Dr Lucy Porter (Centre for Behaviour Change, University College London, UK); Professor Vivien Swanson, (University of Stirling, UK); Dr Jorina von Zimmermann (Centre for Behaviour Change, University College London, UK).

psychology. To inform this chapter, we posed the same three questions to each of the contributors, and we report their responses verbatim:

1. What kind of problems and challenges in health (and other domains) could health psychologists help with through consultancy?
2. What do you think are the benefits to health psychology as a profession from engaging in consultancy?
3. What, in your opinion, are the barriers to (more) health psychologists engaging in consultancy?

We present the responses to these three questions below. We then summarise the responses after which we comment on them offering the reader our perspective.

Question 1

What kind of problems and challenges in health (and other domains) could health psychologists help with through consultancy?

Professor Diane Dixon. I think it is useful for health psychologists to think of themselves as experts in human behaviour. We specialise in behaviours that are related to health and illness but much of our expertise is generic and can be applied to other behaviours. Thus, we can consider consulting on any problem that involves behaviour of individuals, groups, communities or social structures, such as workplaces. I have colleagues who have consulted on projects ranging from vaccination uptake in farmed fish (required behaviour change on the part of the fishermen), control of aquatic pests (required a behavioural analysis of all stages of the pollution problem) through to projects more easily associated with health, such as patient safety projects in community pharmacy. If the problem involves a role for behaviour, then health psychology can make a meaningful contribution.

Professor Vangelis Karademas. In Greece, most consultancy opportunities refer to the following: (a) supporting patient organisations in developing tailored psychological services for their members; (b) informing and guiding hospital units on establishing psychological services for patients within the hospital setting; (c) organising seminars and workshops in the private sector focused on promoting employees' well-being (e.g., stress management, behavioural health); (d) collaborating with local authorities to develop public health promotion programs (e.g., educational campaigns in schools). However, consultancy with the state or major governmental organisations (regarding, for example, the management of health crises) is uncommon. Also, consultancy opportunities in Greece often suffer from a lack of duration and consistency, mainly due to the lack of funding and limited interest and/or knowledge on the part of the potential beneficiaries.

Professor Lucie Byrne-Davis and Professor Jo Hart. Health psychology is growing as a profession, especially in the global north. Much of the research and practice of health psychology is therefore about, and involving, individuals and communities of the global north and health issues that affect them. However, we live in an increasingly globalised world, and health issues on one continent are likely to affect others: pandemic preparedness, antimicrobial stewardship and climate change stand out as key global challenges. Additionally, there is a moral imperative to engage in the issues that affect us as human beings and not to focus on the issues of the privileged global minority. Across much of the global south, there is a push to achieve health for all, with universal health coverage, increased public health and international development that increases, rather than decreases, the health of populations. The ambition of health for all requires large changes in people's behaviour at all levels, from increased infection prevention, changes in how health professionals practice, and changes in how policies for industry are made and implemented.

Professor Hannah McGee. Challenges in health and healthcare are often complex, and solutions are not immediately obvious to teams delivering that healthcare. Consultancy can provide an external view to help identify the types and sources of information needed to inform solutions to complex problems and likely barriers to collecting that information. Consultants can also help to determine how findings from a consultation will increase the chances of effecting change. For illustration, a request to determine how best to invest in improving national stroke care could lead to identifying key services to consider; for example, stroke recognition by the public, access to emergency services, specialist thrombolysis and speech and swallow service delivery, early mobilisation and later hospital discharge, and ongoing rehabilitation, the latter ranging from complex neurological needs and family supports to addressing more standard cardiovascular challenges such as smoking cessation and increasing physical activity.

Professor Susan Michie, Dr Jorina von Zimmermann and Dr Lucy Porter. Health psychologists at the University College London (UCL) Centre for Behaviour Change apply scientific evidence, theories, methods and frameworks to challenges covering prevention, detection/diagnosis, treatment, maintenance and rehabilitation. Customers (including research agencies, charities, service providers, local authorities and national government departments) may also be interested in applying the approach to other domains, including sustainability or culture change. Health psychologists can support patient-focused behaviour change interventions, but also system-wide projects such as those focused on healthcare professional practices, organisational decision-making and the design, implementation and evaluation of entire policy portfolios and strategies.

Professor Felix Naughton. Health psychologists are uniquely placed to address many 'knotty' health-related problems via consultancy. We are typically well trained and demonstrate leadership in key areas of need, including psychological processes, behaviour change and interactions with the physical, social and cultural environment. We focus on rigour and high-quality methodology, while striving for work to be grounded in everyday experience. Where evidence is lacking, we use tools and frameworks that facilitate estimation. Furthermore, our training skills enable us to meet the increasing demands for knowledge in areas such as behaviour change and evaluation. Our 'package', therefore, could be extended to any societal problem where the above elements play a role, providing topic-specific expertise can be obtained.

Professor Vivien Swanson. It's tempting to answer, '*anything health and wellbeing related*'. A positive health psychology approach helps people to see behavioural problems differently and empower change, so is relevant for a range of issues—from climate change to covid. Its strength is its wide applicability. Combining science and practice competence means we can tackle large or small, 'top-down' or 'bottom-up', health problems in a responsive, flexible way. We combine 'academic' analysis of complex behavioural problems with expert behavioural intervention and teaching skills. The Covid pandemic was a great example of an 'agile' science-led intervention response from the health psychology community.

Dr Stephan Dombrowski. Health affects everyone. Health psychology-based knowledge and skills are therefore universally applicable. The area where health psychology expertise is perhaps most apparent, and the potential for impact is immense, is behaviour change.

Dr Wendy Maltinsky. Health psychologists are well placed to bring their behavioural science expertise to practice, development, innovation and intervention. I have been invited as a behavioural consultant to areas as diverse as self-management education, plant health, aquaculture, population-modelling and digital avatars. The tasks I undertake in each consultancy have differed depending on the objectives. In many cases, I employ interactive approaches to broker discussions around current behaviours that might be impacted by a proposed development; how these behaviours might be resistant to change; if change in one individual/group/system could cascade in ways that are intentional or inadvertent. The work in plant health is an example; my remit was to facilitate a workshop with an international group representing a breadth of disciplines to identify specific challenges and potential solutions. The notion of how behaviour might be instrumental to both problems and solutions had not been previously considered. I supported the consortium to specify these behaviours and the influencing factors and develop an intervention proposal based on this new insight.

Question 2

What do you think are the benefits to health psychology as a profession from engaging in consultancy?

Professor Diane Dixon. There are benefits for the consultant and the profession. Working with folk who are not behavioural scientists can pose interesting challenges that generally progress your own thinking and ways of working. But, for me the best thing about consultancy work is the experience of the direct tangible benefits of one's work for the people and organisations one is working with. In the UK, most health psychologists work as academics, and universities are not known for their ability to show gratitude to their staff. In my experience, working as a consultant is a real fillip. The organisations and individuals I have worked with are always grateful for the input from our discipline. Plus, working with a range of different people can be fun.

Professor Vangelis Karademas. Engaging in consultancy can offer several benefits to health psychology as a profession even in countries with a limited tradition in the field, such as Greece. It can provide health psychologists with an opportunity to broaden the visibility and impact of health psychology in real-world settings, facilitate the sharing of knowledge which can lead to more effective psychological interventions, and may improve public health outcomes. Finally, consultancy can attract more funding opportunities.

Professor Lucie Byrne-Davis and Professor Jo Hart. The study and practice of psychology related to health is needed. As a very small field, with a relatively brief history compared to many other fields and areas of practice, consultancy in health psychology is one of the ways that we can support these changes. We must ensure that consultancy doesn't detract from capacity building, by including training as part of the contractual obligations.

Professor Hannah McGee. Health psychology consultants benefit from access to key decision-makers and influencers in healthcare delivery and policy, and from being able to make a difference in health dilemmas identified by others as a priority. In some instances, specific insights of research using health psychology models and concepts may be pertinent; in others, more general methodological skills of psychologists may be most useful. Health psychology consultants also benefit from networking with others involved in consultancy through events organised by their professional bodies.

Professor Susan Michie, Dr Jorina von Zimmermann and Dr Lucy Porter. Consultancy can lead to mutually beneficial interactions and learning exchanges. It can enrich health psychologists' understanding of the priorities and challenges on the ground and enhance the ability to communicate science to a range of audiences. Consultancy enables health psychology expertise to be implemented in 'real-world' settings, directly impacting people's lives. At the same time, this direct application of health psychology's insights allows the field to evaluate the usefulness and relevance of its methods, theories and recommendations, supporting the continual improvement of our own work.

Professor Felix Naughton. Potential benefits to health psychology from consultancy are numerous. One key benefit of consultancy for us as a profession is that it helps us learn new ways of working through exposure to diverse organisations—for example, industry, local and national government, health services, non-governmental organisations (NGOs), charities and social enterprises—by using rapid investigations and varied frameworks, outcomes and processes. An example of a more pragmatic benefit is that consultancy-related funding is typically more accessible than research grants and can help increase capacity, skills and employment.

Professor Vivien Swanson. Consultancy offers unique career opportunities for health psychologists. Being able to shape and develop your own professional identity and expertise, working across different contexts is really rewarding. My career, based in academia, has included consultancies with NHS, local and national government, companies, and third sector clients. For trainees, consultancy competencies include business, leadership and management skills, and opportunities to learn from different contexts. Consultancies build future career linkages with a wide range of people and organisations and showcase the value of a positive health promoting approach—building confidence in trainees and post-qualification colleagues in relation to their health psychology identity.

Dr Stephan Dombrowski. Health psychology-based successful consultancy is of paramount importance for health psychology to improve people's lives.

Dr Wendy Maltinsky. The benefits of consultancies to health psychologists and the health psychology profession are extensive. It raises our profile as behavioural experts. In interdisciplinary work, there can be immense growth of learning and development for each party. It fosters a shared language and strengthens implementation into practice.

Question 3

What, in your opinion, are the barriers to (more) health psychologists engaging in consultancy?

Professor Diane Dixon. The barriers are mainly in our heads. I would say open yourself up to the possibility of consultancy—start with a modest project and grow from there. I have always found it highly rewarding and always thought-provoking.

Professor Vangelis Karademas. The key factors that prevent having (more) health psychologists engaged in consultancy in Greece, besides the relatively low numbers of health psychologists and the lack of funding, refer to the lack of relevant skills, as the training of health psychologists primarily focuses on research and clinical practice rather than on consultancy skills; the low demand for consultancy services provided by health psychologists as our field is not as widely recognised compared to the more traditional branches of psychology; the limited interest of authorities, institutions and organisations due to the lack of awareness of the possibilities and opportunities that health psychology consulting can offer.

Professor Lucie Byrne-Davis and Professor Jo Hart. Lack of clear opportunities and processes which enable us to engage in consultancy can be a barrier. Those who are regularly engaging in consultancy have tended to have learned both *how* to do consultancy and *with whom* to do consultancy by themselves and that can feel difficult for people starting out. Another barrier is that consultancy contracts often require that we generate clear recommendations based on best evidence, but our science requires us to be cautious about overreaching from our data. Learning how to present data honestly but then use our professional skills to make recommendations with appropriate caveats is a skill that is difficult to learn.

Professor Hannah McGee. Engaging in consultancy requires confidence in addressing the needs of the client which may entail working outside the strict domain of models and methods of health psychology. It also requires an understanding of the structures, hierarchies, key attributes and constraints of diverse healthcare settings and the enquiry skills to achieve this understanding. Consultation may identify challenging findings which require the ability to deliver difficult while constructive messages to clients and to avoid any potential client expectation of a predetermined result.

Professor Susan Michie, Dr Jorina von Zimmermann and Dr Lucy Porter. Applying the Capability Opportunity Motivation and Behaviour (COM-B) model of behaviour can help us understand the barriers to consultancy. Firstly, health psychologists may not have the opportunity to engage in consultancy where work roles do not attract or permit consultancy requests, or where access to the relevant professional connections that generate such invitations is poor. In addition, health psychologists may not have access to the appropriate support for arranging contractual and financial agreements, and may lack the capabilities to undertake this themselves. Motivation may also be low where consultancy is perceived as incompatible with the ability to collect and evaluate evidence rigorously. Understanding the interaction between capability, opportunity and motivation and addressing these barriers could support health psychologists to pass on their expertise and help make a difference to people's lives.

Professor Felix Naughton. Underutilisation of consultancy in our field can be due to factors such as discomfort with delivering work with less rigour than our training endorses and underselling our skills due to a lack of confidence. There can also be opportunity costs, where consultancy outcomes may not align with a health psychologist's career incentives or those of their employing organisation. Finally, the required administration, such as contracts, data sharing and service agreements, reports and so on, can be burdensome and off-putting, particularly if support structures are unavailable.

Professor Vivien Swanson. *Breaking the mould*: the 'traditional' expectations about what psychologists do—from clients, employers and often psychologists themselves, often focus on therapeutic working with individuals or families. It can be challenging to make a convincing moral and economic case for a different type of psychology that promotes health and well-being. Confidence in yourself, and a robust knowledge and belief in your health psychology skills is key! *Small scale of working*: We are a small profession and can be individually isolated and often resource poor, making it tricky to work at scale, and to deliver on projects which need rapid responses.

Dr Stephan Dombrowski. Barriers to health psychology consultancy are located outside and inside the profession. *Outside barriers*: A major barrier is low levels of 'health behaviour literacy'—the ability to identify health behaviours and support change in the general population, including health professionals. Behaviour is typically missed as a focal intervention target, as behavioural impacts on health are often imperceptible from moment to moment. When behaviour is targeted for change, people typically employ a limited common-sense approach based on intuition. To support behaviour change, many people reflexively provide information and instructions—two overused and largely ineffective techniques. Collectively, we need to improve 'health behaviour literacy' overall and a recognition that health psychologists add value to behaviour-related challenges. *Inside barriers*: There is limited practical and implementable guidance on how to set up and offer services. 'Selling' health psychology does not come natural to representatives of a young profession where overpromising one's potential for impact is frowned upon. Additionally, the professional tools available can sometimes lack usability within practice-based contexts, with some tools being overused. Health psychology consultancy requires the application of frameworks with layers of depth, which can solve the dual challenge of simplifying complex issues for multidisciplinary contexts, without sacrificing the richness of health psychological insights and accomplishments. In a context of immediacy where fast, simple and bullet point-style answers are desired, it is paramount that health psychologists stay relevant whilst keeping professional integrity without diluting the rich and diverse background that we can draw from.

Dr Wendy Maltinsky. As a relatively young discipline there can be reticence by health psychologists to acknowledge the unique knowledge and skills they bring to a project. However, if we can build our collective confidence to engage, it better allows us to demonstrate the value of our profession to those unfamiliar with health psychology.

Summary of Key Points in Responses

For each question, we present a brief summary of the responses. Since readers have access to verbatim responses, we do not attribute comments to individual respondents in the summary or in the commentary that follows it.

Summary of responses to: *What kind of problems and challenges in health (and other domains) could health psychologists help with through consultancy?*

Respondents identified two main contributions that health psychologists can make through consultancy. Firstly, health psychologists prioritise and understand the critical role of human behaviour in defining and addressing problems in health. Expertise in behaviour has a wide applicability, for example patient safety in community pharmacies and employee well-being, creation of digital avatars, plant health, climate change, sustainability, culture change, healthcare professional practices, organisational decision-making, and design, implementation and evaluation of entire portfolios and strategies. Secondly, clients benefit from health psychologists' approach that can combine scientific rigour using theory, evidence, scientific methodology, tools and frameworks in defining, analysing and designing interventions with grounding the science in everyday experience.

Summary of responses to: *What do you think are the benefits to health psychology as a profession from engaging in consultancy?*

Respondents identified networking with people from other disciplines and across a wide range of organisations as benefitting the health psychology profession in several ways. Working with other professional disciplines offers the opportunity to progress one's own thinking, enables all profession to learn together and from each other, fosters a shared language and strengthens implementation. Working with other organisations brings health psychology consultants into contact with key decision-makers and individuals who influence healthcare policy. Consultants implement psychology in real-world settings and can get satisfaction from seeing improvements in people's lives. Direct application of health psychology insights also enables consultants to evaluate the usefulness of theories and methods, and that supports continuous improvement in application of health psychology in practice.

A further benefit is that consultancy can showcase health psychology, strengthening its identity, raising its profile and even creating opportunities for trainees and for qualified practitioners.

Summary of responses to: *What, in your opinion, are the barriers to (more) health psychologists engaging in consultancy?*

This question attracted the most detailed responses. The main barriers identified are low confidence and lack of skills. Consultancy requires health psychologists to work outside the domain models and methods of health psychology, and this requires confidence, skill and knowledge. Lacking or having low confidence, for example in knowledge of structures and hierarchies of diverse settings, and skills in contracting and negotiating service agreement, writing consultancy reports and working 'at scale', can create barriers to health psychologist engaging in consultancy. In addition to this, health psychology is a young profession, and, as such, its members must raise awareness in the world outside of the profession of its unique knowledge and skillset. Providing consultancy would be a fitting way to do this. However, the idea of 'selling' health psychology is often the barrier itself. Challenges to scientific rigour and pressure to make recommendations based on 'best evidence' when engaging in consultancy are concerning. The challenges include the perception that consultancy is incompatible with the ability to collect and evaluate evidence with rigour, and a requirement to be able to present 'difficult' messages constructively to clients who might have preconceived expectations of outcomes. Concerns about overreaching from the available data, and about the skills required to make recommendations with appropriate caveats, and the impact of discomfort for health psychologists who feel under pressure to work with less rigour were included in the responses.

Low demand through lack of interest and assumptions that providing information and instruction are sufficient to effect behaviour change was identified as a factor. Other barriers identified were the lack of opportunity, both as a consequence of work roles that do not facilitate consultancy practice, and as a consequence of a 'lack of processes' that enable health psychologists to learn how and with whom to engage in consultancy, as well as practical usability of professional tools used by health psychologists.

Reflections and Implications for the Field

The responses to our three questions have added to our understanding of how the professional health psychology community view consultancy. Some of the responses align with our own experiences and with what we have heard in conversations with colleagues. This is particularly so in relation to the benefits for health psychologists from engaging in consultancy, reasons for trepidation about doing so, and the need for more consultancy skills training. We also have different experiences as consultants, and we reflect on the responses in light of our experiences as consultants in health psychology and in light of the contributions to this book.

First, we declare our belief that there is a moral imperative for the health psychology profession to work together with organisations in the health sector to ensure that health interventions of all kinds are based on robust evidence in order to support engagement and to avoid potential harm, waste of resources, and non-sustainability. While scalability, acceptability, sustainability and equity are recognised as vital factors in achieving health behaviour change (Prestwich et al., 2024, p. 422), few publications in health psychology focus on consultancy practice as a means of supporting that change. Given the challenges to health globally and the increasing demands on healthcare services (Lucero-Prisno III et al., 2023; World Health Organisation-WHO, 2024), health psychology can assist in efforts to achieve better population health. It can do this through use of the theory-informed, evidence-based, practical tools developed by health psychologists (D'Lima et al., 2020). We must recognise that since our profession is a young one, knowledge of the potential benefits from engaging health psychologists in health initiatives is not yet widespread (Curtis et al., 2018). Health psychologists must, therefore, be proactive in raising awareness among potential clients and stakeholders of the benefits of including health psychology and behavioural science in improving human health. While the focus of health psychologists is primarily on human health behaviours, respondents' experience of practising consultancy in a wide range of contexts illustrates the potential for the profession to influence behaviours that indirectly impact on human health. The examples of consultancy in plant and marine health, to name but two cited by respondents, demonstrate the wide applicability of expertise in behaviour and behaviour change. Wherever human behaviour is involved, the theories, models and tools developed by health psychologists can be helpful in addressing real-life problems.

As we engage with organisations in consultancy work, we encounter opportunities to liaise with decision-makers and influencers, and we can take these opportunities to raise the profile of health psychology. Both in negotiating and in contracting, in conducting consultancy and in communicating with stakeholders, we usually speak with decision-makers and people who influence decision-making in client organisations. In larger, more complex projects, we may also work with influential partners outside of the commissioning client organisation. This is evidenced in several chapters in this book (e.g., Chaps. 14, 19, 22 and 29). Examples of becoming 'thought leaders' and 'key opinion leaders', where health psychologists influence other professions in large projects, are available in Chaps. 7 and 12.

Aligned with respondents' perspectives, we too have experienced reluctance by some clients to fund evidence-based research to inform projects; and we have perceived pressures to present or interpret findings to suit predetermined client expectations. Our view, however, is that it is the responsibility of the consultant to explain value of employing rigorous methodology and the expertise they have in employing it. This must be done *after* a thorough enquiry to find out what the client and stakeholders need (in line with Schein, 2016). Use of theory, evidence and method distinguishes us from many other consultants, but telling potential clients about the benefits of health psychology and scientific method per se will not necessarily pique their interest. Demonstrating expertise by explaining how the problem can be addressed using evidence-based methods is a powerful way of introducing clients to behavioural science. Clients are interested in how we can help them in practice, and not in promoting our profession. Clients sometimes possess knowledge about behaviour change. What they cannot do, however, without training in scientific method, is to apply that knowledge to defining problems, designing interventions, and evaluating the effectiveness of those interventions in a scientifically rigorous way. It is up to us as consultants to show the client how our evidence-based approach benefits them in terms of effective solutions in light of their objectives for a project.

Clients are not bound by the professional and ethical guardrails which provide clear guidance to us on the scope and boundaries of our practice (see Chap. 4 for a discussion of ethical practice in consultancy). If a client is not interested in our approach, wishing only to claim endorsement for their products or services by engaging with experts, we should be very cautious about engaging with them. For a discussion of client motives and how to discover and respond to them, see Chap. 7. In negotiating with clients, it is vital to be open and honest about what we are prepared to do. This might involve challenging the client's assumptions in order to reach a deep understanding of their needs (Luttig & de Villiers, 2022, cited in Chap. 10) and in order to ensure the solution proposed is robust in terms of evidence. The communication skills and confidence needed to do this while emphasising the benefits to client and stakeholders can indeed be developed and mastered as illustrated in several of the chapters in this book.

Consultancy also offers an opportunity to generate practice-based evidence as a means to test theory (e.g., De Cocker et al., 2018). In order to do so, scientific method and rigour are essential. Consultants, therefore, need to be ready to make a strong case to clients for the benefits of an evidence-based approach in terms of effectiveness of solutions, and opportunities to enhance the client's reputation and gain competitive advantage.

While we lack objective data to explain potential reasons for lack of engagement amongst some health psychologists, based on our professional networking we recognise several potential reasons for low engagement with consultancy. These include health psychologists' (perceived or real) lack of skills and knowledge; for example, practical skills in negotiation and contracting and on presenting complex information to clients in an accessible way. These skills require advanced communication and relationship building skills as well as confidence to apply those skills in a business environment. Other reasons can be unease about being seen as a management consultant in healthcare consultancy (Oliver, 2014; Kirkpatrick et al., 2019), potentially discrediting the unique scientific rigour we bring to consultancy; concerns that use of external consultants might reduce incentives to increase capacity (e.g., through creating in-house opportunities for health psychologists); concerns that clients prioritising validation for commercial decisions in design of health interventions and initiatives risk compromising scientific rigour.

In the UK, consultancy is a core competence of health psychologists since 2001 (Board of Examiners in Health Psycholgy, 2001), and professional standards for health psychologists set out the competences required for qualification (British Psychological Society, 2020). Whilst the professional standards specify *what* health psychologists need to be able to do in consultancy practice, they do not specify *how* the necessary skills are acquired. Accredited training providers provide skills training and assessment. Variability in the quality of the training has, however, been highlighted by trainees (Armstrong et al., 2020). Some health psychologists have very positive experiences of training and supervision in consultancy skills from health psychologists with extensive experience of consultancy practice (Patel, 2015). However, this experience does not seem to be universal. In terms of practice-based supervision, a recent survey of trainee and qualified health psychologists in the UK reported that only 7 of 24 respondents were supervised by health psychology professionals and not all supervisors felt fully prepared to support trainees to meet the competences (White et al., 2024). While the survey report did not specifically ask about consultancy, it does reveal a potential weakness in training (as well as post-qualification supervision). Training and supervision in consultancy require consultancy expertise on the part of trainers and supervisors in the same way that training and supervision in research requires research expertise on the part of those teaching research skills and supervising practice. The profession as a whole might benefit from finding a way to access the expertise of those practitioners who have built successful and sustainable careers in consultancy practice. This book is a step in that direction.

We agree with those respondents who commented that we have much to learn from engaging with other professions and that consultancy provides an opportunity to learn about enablers and barriers to solving health problems on the ground. It is important, therefore, for us as health psychologists to hold a curious and open mindset as we engage with clients and stakeholders (Schein, 2016) rather than believing that we alone hold the answers. No one profession 'owns' the solutions to health problems, and we learn from each other through practice. Multidisciplinary working is often the norm in consultancy projects. It can be intimidating initially to find ourselves in the same room as seemingly confident and assertive people. Imposter syndrome can make it challenging to make ourselves heard. Reframing our role and expertise as facilitators of acquiring shared knowledge and co-developing solutions can be a helpful perspective to strengthen our footing. A balance of confidence (in our specialist knowledge and skills) and humility encourages curiosity and deeper levels of relationships.

Health psychologists can also learn from engaging with wider literature in consultancy. A feature of the majority of the chapters in this book is that authors reflect on their experiences of consultancy through the lens of the consultancy framework for consultants in health psychology (see Chap. 3). Yet, for the majority of authors, this was their first significant engagement with consultancy literature. From our own experience of networking with health psychology colleagues, some have expressed the view that consultancy in health psychology is so different from management or organisational psychology that the wider literature is of little value. Some consultancy processes, however, are shared across disciplines; this is the basis of our proposed framework for consultancy in health psychology. As consultancy expert Block (2011) has pointed out, 'technical skills' alone are not sufficient to be an effective consultant; consultants also need other skills, for example in negotiation and contracting and in communicating with clients and stakeholders. Without knowledge of how to engage in consultancy processes, we will miss out on opportunities to make an impact in real-world problems.

We are not aware of data on levels of health psychology consultancy activity or on how health psychologists practice consultancy (e.g., through owner-managed consultancy practices, as employees of consultancy firms, as internal consultants in public health organisations, from academic institutions, and so on). Certainly, we have encountered a strong interest and appetite for engagement in consultancy in our professional health psychology networks. If we wish to encourage more health psychologists to engage in consultancy, as a profession we will need to work together to build consultancy-specific skills and confidence.

Summary and Conclusion

As a young profession with a broad scope of practice, health psychology is still developing the volumes of evidence of its impact on human health. The breadth of potential applications might make it more challenging for other stakeholders in healthcare to have clarity on the impactful contributions our professions can make. Consultancy is arguably that area of our practice where we can demonstrate the manifold benefits of engaging health psychology in addressing challenges related to people's health. As we highlighted above, it is our moral imperative to raise awareness of our skills and knowledge and to proactively seek engagement with potential clients, decision-makers and other stakeholders where we identify value of our input. We must recognise that many health psychologists might feel they do not have the skills or the detailed knowledge necessary for delivering consultancy and they may not feel confident enough to tackle the world of big business or large organisations. This book is written with them in mind. It is our hope that on the one hand the learnings from this book and on the other hand reaching back to our professional identity as scientist-practitioners who are having a unique set of psychological theories, models and tools applicable to human health with the attitude of humble curiosity and openness to collaborate and learn from other professions will be the impetus for our colleagues to commence or further develop their work in consultancy.

Methodology for the data collection of this chapter. We recruited contributors through our professional network using a snowballing strategy. We aimed to include a maximum of ten contributions to allow space to report responses verbatim. Two of the people we approached declined, and one who initially agreed was unable to meet the deadline agreed. We asked for responses in 300 words or fewer; the word count could be allocated across the three questions as contributors saw fit. Contributors were informed that the chapter would be included in this handbook. The proposed framework for consultancy in health psychology (see Chap. 3) was not shared with contributors to avoid any priming of responses. The responses to each question were presented in order of receipt, and have been included verbatim. Where wording of responses was ambiguous, one of the authors (RB) contacted the contributors by email to clarify meaning prior to the writing of the commentary.

Competing Interests The authors have no competing interests to declare that are relevant to this chapter.

References

Armstrong, S., Watson, D., Byrne, J., Howells, L. M., Ashworth, P., Phillips, E., George, P., Keith, S., Leech, K., Mead, O., Byrne, M., Carvalho, M., Hynes, L., McSharry, J., Molloy, G. J., Morrissey, E., Noone, C., Toome, E., O'Driscoll, L., et al. (2020). Teaching, training, consultancy and practice: Summaries of work relating to health psychology and Covid-19. *Health Psychology Update, 29*(3), 28–40. https://doi.org/10.53841/bpshpu.2020.29.3.28

Block, P. (2011). *Flawless consulting*. Pfeiffer.

Board of Examiners in Health Psychology (BEHP). (2001). *Regulations for the qualification in health psychology (Stage 2)*. British Psychological Society.

British Psychological Society. (2020). *Qualification in health psychology (Stege 2). Candidate Handbook*. British Psychological Society. https://cms.bps.org.uk/sites/default/files/2022-07/QHP%20Candidate%20Handbook.pdf

Curtis, K., Fulton, E., & Brown, K. (2018). Factors influencing application of behavioural science evidence by public health decision-makers and practitioners, and implications for practice. *Preventive medicine reports, 12*, 106–115. https://doi.org/10.1016/j.pmedr.2018.08.012

D'Lima, D., Lorencatto, F., & Michie, S. (2020). The behaviour change wheel approach. In *Handbook on implementation science* (pp. 168–214). Edward Elgar Publishing. https://doi.org/10.4337/9781788975995.00014

De Cocker, K. D., Cardon, G., Bennie, J. A., Kolbe-Alexander, T., Meester, F. D., & Vandelanotte, C. (2018). From evidence-based research to practice-based evidence:

disseminating a web-based computer-tailored workplace sitting intervention through a health promotion organisation. *International Journal of Environmental Research and Public Health, 15*(5), 1049. https://doi.org/10.3390/ijerph15051049

Glăveanu, V. P. (2020). The meta-position. In *The possible: A sociocultural theory* (online edn). Oxford Academic, December 17. https://doi.org/10.1093/oso/9780197520499.003.0005

HCPC. (n.d.). The standards of proficiency for practitioner psychologists. https://www.hcpc-uk.org/standards/standards-of-proficiency/practitioner-psychologists/

Kirkpatrick, I., Sturdy, A. J., Alvarado, N. R., Blanco-Oliver, A., & Veronesi, G. (2019). The impact of management consultants on public service efficiency. *Policy & Politics, 47*(1), 77–95. https://doi.org/10.1332/030557318X15167881150799

Lucero-Prisno, D. E., III, Shomuyiwa, D. O., Kouwenhoven, M. B. N., Dorji, T., Odey, G. O., Miranda, A. V., et al. (2023). Top 10 public health challenges to track in 2023: Shifting focus beyond a global pandemic. *Public Health Challenges, 2*(2), e86. https://doi.org/10.1002/puh2.86

Luttig, L., & de Villiers, R. (2022). Intention to Create Meaningful Outcomes: Tenders, Bids and Client Pitches. In R. de Villiers (Ed.), *The handbook of creativity & innovation in business: A comprehensive toolkit of theory and practice for developing creative thinking skills* (pp. 267–290). Springer Nature. https://doi.org/10.1007/978-981-19-2180-3_13

Oliver, D. (2014). Stop wasting takpayers' money on management consultancy for the NHS. *BMJ, 349*, g7243. https://doi.org/10.1136/bmj.g7243

Patel, N. (2015). Doing consultancy in health psycholoyg – Stage 2 training independent route. *Health Psychology Update, 24*(1), 28–31. https://doi.org/10.53841/bpshpu.2015.24.1.28

Prestwich, A., Kenworthy, J., & Conner, M. (2024). *Health behavior change: Theories, methods and interventions.* Routledge.

Schein, E. H. (2016). *Humble consulting: How to provide real help faster.* Berrett-Koehler Publishers.

White, C., Baraniac, A., Bull, E., & Mavy, T. (2024). Trainee and qualified health psychologists' views and experiences of practice-based supervision: A summary of the full report. *Health Psychology Update, 33*(1). https://doi.org/10.53841/bpshpu.2024.33.18

WHO. (2024). *World Health Statistics 2024.* https://iris.who.int/bitstream/handle/10665/376869/9789240094703-eng.pdf?sequence=1

3

A Framework for Consultancy in Health Psychology

Roseanna Brady and Judit Varkonyi-Sepp

Introduction

The aim of this chapter is to present a framework for consultancy in health psychology. Health psychologists are actively engaged in consultancy practice and are making a positive impact in health; this is evident from the chapters in Part II and Part III of this book. While there are concerns within the health psychology profession about the research-practice gap (Presseau et al., 2022), practical theory-informed, evidence-based tools are in use in real-world situations day-to-day in consultancy. Much of the work undertaken by health psychology consultants is not available in the public domain since publication is not always a priority for clients. This book goes some way to address this gap and will, hopefully, encourage others to publish their work and to generate

Supplementary Information The online version contains supplementary material available at https://doi.org/10.1007/978-3-031-94529-8_3.

R. Brady (✉)
Psychology for Health Associates, Bedford, UK
e-mail: bradykbs@msn.com

J. Varkonyi-Sepp
Department of Adult Health Psychology, Hampshire and Isle of Wight Healthcare NHS Foundation Trust, Southampton, UK
e-mail: j.varkonyi-sepp@soton.ac.uk

R. Brady et al. (eds.), *The Palgrave Handbook of Consultancy in Health Psychology*,
https://doi.org/10.1007/978-3-031-94529-8_3

practice-based evidence through testing evidence-based solutions to health problems (Ammerman et al., 2014).

In our many conversations within the wider health psychology professional network, the discourse has highlighted a lack of clarity about what health psychology consultancy *is*, about what skills and knowledge equip a practitioner to consult, and about how to start providing consultancy in the first place. Definitions of consultancy (see Chap. 1), while helpful, do not explain 'how to do' it. In addition to scientific and technical skills, tools and methods, consultancy practitioners also need consultancy-specific skills (Block, 2011) to enable them to work effectively with clients. For example, consultants need skills in building effective working relationships with clients and stakeholders, in bidding for work and negotiating contracts, and in planning and monitoring the use of resources.

Some of the skills required for consultancy are transferable from other areas of health psychology practice. For example, research skills equip health psychologists to identify, collect and analyse data from a variety of sources; this is a skill which is also required to explore and understand what is already known about 'problems' to be addressed in consultancy. Communication skills required to work effectively with colleagues, with fellow health professionals and with patients are also used in developing relationships with clients, stakeholders and partners in consultancy work. Critical thinking skills required to design, implement and evaluate interventions in research and in clinical work, are also applicable to consultancy problems. Those transferable skills do, however, need to be adapted to a consultancy environment. We asked several experienced health psychologists about their views on potential barriers to (more) engagement in consultancy by health psychologists (see Chap. 2). Their responses indicated that health psychologists would benefit from a clearer structure for setting up and engaging in consultancy as well as further skills training.

The framework for consultancy in health psychology (henceforth, referred to as 'the framework') that we present in this chapter draws on our own consultancy experiences over several decades, as well as several existing consultancy models and frameworks (e.g., Schein, 1990; Michie, 1998; Cope, 2010; Hodges, 2017). It is important to identify and clarify the *generic* consultancy processes that consultants from all professional backgrounds engage in with clients. We can learn from consultancy in business in this regard. Health psychology consultants provide their services in the client context of professional management, multidisciplinary expertise, budgetary constraints, shareholder and other stakeholder requirements, and within the legal and regulatory frameworks in which organisations conduct their activities (O'Mahoney &

Markham, 2013; Adams & Tovey, 2012). We do not suggest that as health psychologists we try to emulate management consultants; management of organisations is not our area of interest or expertise. However, we are better placed to offer and apply our specialist expertise if we also understand the environment in which our clients operate, and if we apply the generic consultancy skills required.

Why a 'New' Framework

There are two main reasons why we propose a 'new' framework. Firstly, existing consultancy frameworks and models either do not include important aspects of health psychology consultancy practice, do not explore them in sufficient depth, or are focused heavily on management consultancy and organisational change. For example, Hodges (2017, 2021) sets out seven clear stages in a Consultancy Cycle for Change. Some of the elements in the cycle fit with health psychology consultancy practice, for example contracting and evaluation. While Hodges acknowledges that the stages are iterative and may need to be revisited, a staged model of consultancy does not fit well with the scientist-practitioner model that requires us to "weave the information we gather into a story (or formulation), grounded in psychological concepts, that has substantive implications for change" (Lane & Corrie, 2007, p. 3). Gathering information, for example, is one of the most important aspects of consultancy. Enquiry underpins our commitment to ensuring that interventions are evidence-based. It is not a stage with a discrete beginning and end. Rather, it continues throughout the life of a consultancy project enabling us to deepen our understanding of a problem and the solutions to it.

Secondly, we wish to clarify how health psychologists apply their specialist knowledge and skills in consultancy practice. There is no special or unique form of consultancy applicable only to health psychologists. However, the specialist knowledge, skills and expertise of our discipline distinguishes us from other consultants—just as it does for all specialists in consultancy. Providing a framework to include those generic consultancy processes, and one that is a good fit with the type of consultancy work we undertake, will enable health psychologists to identify, apply and further develop their consultancy skills. While other frameworks are relevant and we continue to learn from them, none seem to fully capture the way consultancy is practised by health psychologists. In proposing a framework for health psychology consultants, we are aiming both to demystify consultancy and to capture some of the depth and breadth of it for health psychologists.

The Framework

The framework we propose includes five key consultancy *processes*:

1. Enquiry
2. Building and maintaining relationships
3. Negotiating and contracting
4. Planning and managing delivery
5. Evaluation

The five processes, which we describe below, are distinct but not discrete. In practice, there is considerable overlap. Evaluation, for example, is best planned early on during negotiating and contracting and built into every stage of the work. Nor are the elements always sequential. For example, negotiating and contracting often needs to be revisited, either at predetermined stages of larger projects, when circumstances change, or when unforeseen events occur. In describing the five processes, we are offering our interpretation of them based on our own practice and learning.

1. **Enquiry**

Enquiry is fundamental to successful consultancy. Seeking information and asking questions should start even before consultants engage with potential clients. We need to know who the client is, the purpose of their organisation, their values, and the kinds of problems in health they are trying to solve. Being genuinely curious about the nature of the problem to be addressed is vital (Schein, 2016). The purpose of consultancy is to help the client to achieve a desired (and desirable) outcome. The aim of enquiry is to understand how best to do that. We can and should do our homework even before we meet our client to find out about them from publicly available information, and/or through networking. This will give us an idea how the client wishes to present themselves to the world and how they are being seen. Time spent in early enquiry is time well spent. There is a risk of not winning the work and that the time may not be paid for. However, much will be learned that could be useful for securing future work.

Once we meet the client, we need to find out who the stakeholders are (see Nicolescu & Nicolescu, 2024 for an exploration of stakeholder management). We need to learn what the client's desired outcomes are and their expectations with regard to process (Saad, 2017). We might discover that the outcomes expected by the client are not what evidence suggests is the best solution to a problem. We need to assess the resources required and the costs associated with them, and how the work will 'fit' with our values and areas of expertise. If we then contract with a client, we need information to enable us to plan, deliver and evaluate the work. That may involve research, engagement with stakeholders and exploring with others how best to evaluate outcomes, and so on.

Hodges (2021) observes that 'inquiry' (which we term 'enquiry') is a phase that both client and consultant might skip on the assumption that they already have the information they need. For example, a client might request that research be undertaken to answer a predefined question, or a training programme be developed with predetermined learning outcomes. If the brief is accepted without further enquiry, a fee agreed and a contract signed, then what, if any, consultancy occurs? What has been contracted is effectively research or training. But if we take time to understand why the request was made, what problem it is supposed to address, to identify stakeholders and understand their expectations and potential concerns, to assess whether or not the work as proposed will solve the 'problem', to find out what is already known about the problem and evidence-based solutions to it, and to shape the research or the training intervention based on that knowledge, *then* we are engaging in consultancy.

Depending on the nature and complexity of the consultancy, multiple levels of enquiry may be needed. These can include a deeper understanding of the social and political environment in which the client operates, and the opportunities and threats in their business. The need for this approach to enquiry is also true of internal consultancy (when the consultant is employed by the same organisation as the client; Sturdy & Wright, 2011). In internal consultancy, both clients and consultants might assume a shared understanding of context. We, nevertheless, would advocate for the enquiry process in order to establish a degree of distance from the client and the objectivity consultancy requires. It might provide the consultant with new insights and information of relevance to the work. Even if it is simply reiterating all that is already known, the formal enquiry process creates for both client and consultant a perceptual framework of the consultant as an 'outsider within' (Wright, 2009, p. 311).

Evidence-based practice is core to our professional conduct as practitioner psychologists and may distinguish our practice from other consultants. Enquiry will inform the theory, evidence and practice we need to familiarise ourselves with in order to decide whether or not to engage with a client. The consultant also needs to be aware of any potential ethical issues that might arise from the work and potential reputational risks from being associated with the client. Consultancy, therefore, starts and continues with questions, not in any single 'stage' but throughout. It can be helpful to have an initial list of questions and to refine it as our practice develops. A list of questions we have found helpful in our own practice is available in the supplementary material for this chapter (ESM_3.1).

2. **Building and Maintaining Relationships**

Consultants contract with *people* to deliver consultancy, and so the quality of the relationships established and nurtured is vitally important. As health psychologists, we use our knowledge, skills and expertise to *help* the client with a problem or challenge they face. As consultants external to the client organisation (or department), we aim to develop a 'lateral' or more equal relationship with the client (see Block, 2011) rather than a hierarchical one. Sometimes we might be commissioned to act in a surrogate or interim management role with authority to implement and, if so, we need to be clear about these different roles and how they impact on relationships. We expand on this below under 'Boundaries and expectations'.

Relationships with whom? The key relationship is usually with the person with whom we contract for consultancy. Several other relationships are also important. We may work, for example, with staff in the client organisation, with other stakeholders outside the organisation (e.g., service users, patients, healthcare staff) or with partner consultants who offer different expertise to our own. The degree of our engagement with stakeholders varies from one project to another. The perceived value of our work often depends on expectations of, and potential input from, several different stakeholders, and we benefit from considering this before and during any work we undertake.

Trust. At the core of effective consultant-client relationships is trust (Nikolova et al., 2015; Saad, 2017). Trust has been positioned as based on both character and competence (Zheng et al., 2023). Clarifying and aligning expectations of process (*how* things will be done) and outcomes (*what* will be done) is identified as critical to establishing trust in consultant-client relationships (Nikolova et al.). In new consultant-client relationships, trust also requires a 'leap of faith' and acceptance of some level of uncertainty (Nikolova et al.). We can create trust by facilitating psychological safety; this happens when the client feels able to express their vulnerability without fear of negative judgement or exploitation. As several of our contributing authors observed during conversations with us, some of our clients work in 'broken' systems where trust is sometimes abused, and this can make them defensive. If we as consultants are to really help, we need to discover how best to do so by building trust with clients from the outset. As health psychologists, we bring a range of important skills to this process. We know how to apply advanced communication skills in our interactions with others; we have evidence-based insights into patient and health professionals' perspectives and behaviours; we are reflective practitioners. Although we have these knowledge and skill advantages, being a health psychologist does not guarantee that we have highly developed empathetic interpersonal skills. Each of us benefits from reflecting on our approach to others in the context of consultancy work and in identifying areas for our development. We should also be mindful that our clients are not usually psychologists or behavioural scientists, and they may evaluate our performance based on criteria used for other types of consultants.

Boundaries and expectations. In each of these client relationships, it is helpful to think carefully about boundaries. For example, clients may expect us to do more than we are contracted to do. Staff may expect us to transfer expertise rather than skills or information, without realising the potential harms from inexpert application of psychological concepts. Partners (e.g., other consultants) might feel in competition with us, withholding important information in an attempt to protect their competitive advantage. Stakeholders might not welcome our involvement because of misconceptions about our expertise (e.g., assuming that psychologists work in mental health only) and they might therefore be less than cooperative. We have learned from these experiences in our own work, and we appreciate the importance of considering all stakeholder interests and expectations. We have used tools such as stakeholder mapping (NHS Elect, n.d.) to help us to identify who we need to engage with and why. If we understand these risks and engage with people to clarify roles, responsibilities and expectations, greater understanding can be reached and deeper relationships developed.

Clients (and stakeholders) have varying expectations from consultants which can lead to misunderstandings, scope creep (see below) and a host of other pitfalls. For example, a consultant might be commissioned to design an intervention to be implemented by staff (e.g., changing staff communication with patients about vaccine hesitancy; Brady et al., 2022). Blurring of responsibilities relating to the impact of the intervention is a risk if the consultant has no role in ensuring fidelity to the intervention during implementation. During the negotiation and contracting phase, agreeing what action the client will take if staff or partners do not implement the agreed change is important. Relationships with staff and partners can be damaged if consultants either overstep boundaries or fail to raise problems relating to staff or partner performance.

3. Negotiating and Contracting

Before undertaking work with a client, a process of negotiation is needed. The purpose is to clarify the scope and objectives of the work, and the terms of engagement. Following that, the consultant and client agree what the consultant will do. This agreement is the contract (as are subsequent changes or additions to the agreement). Cope (2010, p. 96) describes negotiation as "the point when the undiscussable has to be discussed … discussing issues such as responsibilities, remuneration, risks and results", and he argues for a 'balanced outcome' where client and consultant collaborate to achieve a mutually beneficial result. He also acknowledges that negotiation starts from the initial meeting with the client, where ideas and expectations are first discussed. We have found that preparation for negotiation requires thinking about assumptions, contingencies and risks.

Assumptions, contingencies, and risks. According to Wulf (2020), joint accountability for projects needs to be clear in the scope of any project. During negotiation then, discussions with clients should include clarifying *assumptions* in order to arrive at a shared and agreed understanding. Assumptions include such things as what the consultant's precise role will be, what access the consultant will have to staff, whether or not partners from other specialist professions will also be involved in the work, and so on. A mismatch between client and consultant understanding and expectations can lead to client dissatisfaction with the work (Applebaum & Steed, 2005). The consultant also needs to consider contingencies, such as what the consultant needs from the client (and other stakeholders) in order to do the work. This could include information, approval or sign-off for stages of the work, or input from staff or partners for aspects of the work. Contingencies (dependencies) need to be identified and discussed prior to agreeing a contract to avoid delays. It is also important for the consultant to identify and assess *risks* and to mitigate them during consultancy (Hodges, 2017). Risks include things that could disrupt the planned delivery of the work and jeopardise the expected outcomes. If this arises through lack of planning by the consultant, it could undermine the consultant's reputation with the client (Oade & Oade, 2012). There could also be a risk to the consultant's reputation from undertaking sensitive work with potential to do harm, or risks relating to the client's intended use of outcomes or reports from the work. Risks need careful assessment prior to contracting given their potential impact on the consultant's professional reputation as well as their ability to deliver the contract itself.

Where work can be clearly divided into phases, it may be necessary to revisit the contract depending on delivery of each phase. Recontracting is sometimes necessary as each phase concludes. Certainly, for larger projects, phasing the work (and agreeing payment for each phase) is advisable to allow for unforeseen events and influences. It should be very clear who is responsible for addressing issues that arise.

Responding to Tender Invitations and Request for Proposals (RfPs). In the health sector, much of the work delivered by external suppliers is put out to competitive tender, particularly where organisations are publicly funded. This is true, for example, of the UK National Health Service (Osipovic et al., 2020). Clients need to demonstrate that they have evaluated several tenders to ensure they use public funds wisely. Consultants can register with procurement sites where much of this work is advertised. Competitive tendering enables clients to choose consultants based on the quality of the written proposal (e.g., McLeod & Schapper, 2020). The consultant's proposal in response to an invitation to tender can show understanding of the issues to be addressed and expertise in identifying and delivering solutions. Potential suppliers are also required to submit costs. Consultants can feel pressure to cut costs to appear more competitive, which in turn may impact on quality. This presents several risks for consultants. In our experience, for example, consultancy usually requires us to review literature. Clients are often reluctant to adequately fund this, not understanding how integral research of this nature is to evidence-based practice. As McLeod and Schapper found in their review, "clients may be tempted to purchase lower quotation offers with limited consideration of proposed scope and exclusions" (p. 7).

In competitive tendering, consultants writing proposals are responding to the client's formal documentation often without knowing much about the organisation or having an opportunity to understand the client's needs. Scoping a project is often a 'best guess' (McLeod & Schapper, 2020) based on the tendering document and information available in the public domain. In formal tendering, knowledge of the client, for example through prior consultancy work, is a distinct advantage.

In private industry, and to some extent in the third sector, RfPs are common. RfPs are a form of tendering, usually less onerous than formal public sector tendering, but no less important as a basis for contracting. RfPs are a useful way for organisations to select from potential suppliers and to prepare for negotiations with those suppliers. RfPs may also be used as a basis for negotiation with a preselected or existing supplier, particularly to get ideas on how a problem might be addressed. A risk for consultants is that they share their intellectual property with clients, who then use it to employ others to do the work at less cost. This can create a tension between demonstrating expertise in a topic and holding back information that would be important in terms of intellectual property. Having said that, there are widely used and accepted ways of managing this in the private sector (e.g., confidentiality disclosure agreements) that can aid the consultant to retain their rights over their intellectual property before a formal contract is in place.

Contracting. A contract is an agreement where one party (the consultant) agrees to do something (deliver a specific project) and the other party (the client) agrees to provide something in return (e.g., a fee, access to people and other resources, and information). Consultants should familiarise themselves with the legal requirements applying to contracts in the country(ies) in which they practise. In some cases, contracts are formal standardised documents drawn up by legal advisors. In smaller projects, the contracting process might be less formal, but it is good practice and strongly advisable to always confirm what is agreed, including the scope of the work, in writing. If something goes wrong, the contract is the document that will help to identify who is responsible. Even in the case of internal consultancy, the terms of any agreement should be written and shared between both parties.

Block (2011) sets out a series of steps for navigating contracting. The steps include communicating understanding of the problem, specifying what the client is asking of the consultant, and what the consultant wants from the client in order for the project to be successful. These steps must be taken prior to agreement. Hodges (2017) specifies several important issues to be clarified during contracting: who the client actually is (the person who is initiating the project), the issue(s) to be addressed in the consultancy, the roles and responsibilities that consultant and client and other stakeholders will undertake, outcome expectations, and client readiness to implement any subsequent recommendations or interventions (pp. 99–102).

When circumstances change during a project, it may be necessary to renegotiate and recontract. Having an initial written contract helps to ensure that consultants can show that they have delivered what they initially agreed and give them bargaining power to renegotiate further funding and resources if needed.

4. **Planning and Managing Delivery**

Following initial negotiating and contracting, and depending on the nature of the consultancy, more detailed planning is required. McLeod and Schapper (2020) provide a comprehensive roadmap to assist in planning to achieve high-quality outcomes. Even smaller, more straightforward consultancy projects require thorough planning, and plans require monitoring to ensure they are fit for purpose and adjusted if needed. Revisiting contracts and negotiating changes in scope is common in larger projects. If the consultancy is limited to providing expert advice to enable clients to devise their own solutions/interventions, planning and monitoring is still relevant. It is likely to involve planning time and resources to synthesise research evidence and review client documentation; planning questions for clients to help to clarify problems and identify possible solutions; identifying how and when progress is to be monitored. It may involve assessing whether the expert advice provided is being implemented, whether it is effective, and adjusting accordingly. It requires the consultant to check that they are doing what they are contracted to do.

Including a communication plan to specify what, when and with whom communication will occur helps in ongoing monitoring and evaluation of projects. It is important to ensure that the communication is two-way, and that the client also takes responsibility to keep the consultant informed and included as appropriate. A communication plan should include agreement and details of unexpected and ad hoc communication, and details of what, when, how and to whom issues and problems should be escalated. Some consultants choose to use standardised project planning tools, particularly for large and complex projects. For smaller projects, consultants can develop their own bespoke tools.

Who does the planning? In our experience, health psychologists in consultancy often work alongside staff and other internal and external consultants and partners with specialist expertise. For example, we may work alongside public health consultants with expertise in epidemiology, medical specialists, patient representatives, planning experts, digital health experts, communication teams, and so on. Planning in this context requires us to work collaboratively, being clear on what our role is and how it interacts with the work of others. In that context, planning and monitoring are collaborative activities, although we retain responsibility for our own work and, possibly, for a project overall. Successful collaborations with other consultants are built on trust, identifying synergies and developing a shared understanding of the context for the collaborative work. (Aunger et al., 2021). The quality of collaboration and knowledge integration with experts from other fields is paramount to delivery of quality outcomes (Dietrich et al., 2010).

Larger projects may involve a formal governance and planning phase and use of formal project management tools. Governance is "the use of systems, structures of authority and processes to allocate resources and co-ordinate and control activity in a project" (Pinto, 2014, cited in Too et al., 2017, p. 1126), and there is a clear link between good governance and project success. From the governance structure, plans specify how and by whom the work will be executed and controlled. This will include documentation which must be signed off by multiple stakeholders before plans can be executed (e.g., McLeod & Schapper, 2020; Saad, 2017; Too et al.). Larger projects also involve measurement of ongoing activities at regular intervals and at critical points (expanded further later in this chapter).

Health psychologists working with agencies providing consultancy to private healthcare companies (e.g., providers of pharmaceuticals, digital health technology, medical devices) often collaborate with multiple international business partners. In some of these agencies, account managers manage the business aspects of consultant-client relationships, while psychologist consultants have a vital role in planning resources (often research based), collaborating with key stakeholders, and designing metrics which will be used to measure outcomes during the evaluation and monitoring process. As consultants, we may be overall project lead, or we may lead on a particular aspect of a larger project. Being clear on our role and responsibilities and how they interact with other stakeholders is vital in order to decide what our role in planning and monitoring is. It is also important to ensure that all other stakeholders are clear on our role and responsibilities and that we are on theirs.

What needs to be planned and monitored? Detailed planning is about what, why, by whom, by when and where activities need to be done (e.g., Aunger et al., 2021). It requires ongoing assessment of risks and review of priorities and activities as work unfolds in order to ensure that project goals and outcomes are delivered on time. One way of conceptualising planning and monitoring is to address questions on what exactly needs to be planned and monitored (resources, time, activities, and so on). Good planning also includes considering early in the work how success will be measured. It might be helpful to separate the work into the content, *what* needs to be done and the process, *how* this will be done, and to plan and manage these aspects accordingly. Consultants also need to record their time and activities, however short/small. Logging activities and the time taken facilitates monitoring the resources deployed against what was planned and enables consultants to detect potential scope creep.

Scope creep versus scope change. Scoping the work is a vitally important aspect of planning and monitoring. Scope creep occurs in consultancy when the demands of the project exceed the original contract without prior agreement, and it can impact costs and timelines (Guanci & Bjork, 2019). Scope change, on the other hand, is when the scope of work is changed formally by mutual agreement (Althiyabi & Qureshi, 2021). Scope creep has several potential causes (Ajmal et al., 2019). Amongst other factors, scope creep may occur due to poor initial specification of the work, conflicting priorities or agendas of stakeholders, or unforeseen events. It may also occur because the consultant decides to do more than was contracted for a variety of reasons: interest in a particular aspect of the work, lack of confidence or power-imbalance between consultant and client, poor time logging, and so on. It is important in contracting, therefore, to specify what is in- and what is out-of-scope, as well as agreeing a process for making changes to the original contract. This is usually quite formal in large contracts. With smaller, less-formal contracts, the process for scope change is often not specified and can lead to the consultant taking on a lot of extra work for which they are not paid.

5. **Evaluation**

Some consultancy models appear to suggest that evaluation takes place at the end stage of consultancy (e.g., Block, 2011). However, we would propose evaluation throughout the project which might even occur informally (McLeod & Schapper, 2020). Working with the project end in mind, the timing and methods of evaluation can be planned from the outset. This requires the consultant to engage both with the client to agree the desired outcomes from the work and with stakeholders to understand their perceptions and expectations of success. Following this, consultant and client agree on how those outcomes will be measured and evaluated.

As health psychologists, we bring invaluable skills learned in research and intervention design to this process. We are familiar with models and frameworks that inform evaluation (e.g., Theoretical Domains Framework (Atkins et al., 2017); Acceptability, Practicability, Effectiveness, Affordability, Spillover effects, Equity (APEASE) (West & Michie, 2019)) at each stage of a project. We can make informed selection of existing measurement tools, and/or construct and test new ones, in order to measure outcomes. Clients may also wish to include 'customer satisfaction', 'user experience' or other elements in the evaluation based on standard models in their organisation. These might not have scientific validity and reliability. Therefore, we may need to assess them and be clear with the client about their impact on the overall evaluation of our consultancy. Saad (2017) examines consultancy evaluation including challenges arising, for example, from blurred boundaries between stakeholders and potential bias in evaluation due to a lack of shared expertise. While agreeing evaluation criteria at the start is important, this can be revised as the project progresses. As work develops, it may become clear that in order to achieve the agreed objectives of a project, some aspects of the work need to be adapted. For example, it might not be possible to collect outcome data in the project time frame as originally agreed; thus, any adaptations to the contract might require different methods of evaluation.

Evaluation, therefore, involves identifying what will be evaluated, when it will be evaluated and how that will be done, a process that is familiar to health psychologists. We cannot assume, however, that clients are interested in the same aspects of evaluation as we are, or that they are willing to fund them. Evidence from a range of sectors shows that clients and consultants might apply different evaluation criteria. For example, clients' main criterion might be value for money, whereas consultants put more emphasis on the quality of client-consultant relationships (Fullerton & West, 1996). Tucmeanu et al. (2017) found that professional integrity, competency, and clarity on outcomes were additional key factors in determining a successful consultancy. Project complexity might also influence what clients deem to be successful project delivery. Patterson (2000) reported that in less complex consultancy work, clients evaluated the value of consultants based on actual performance outcomes. A relevant example for a health psychologist might be reviewing/rewriting a patient information leaflet to encourage attendance at pulmonary rehabilitation sessions. While this is skilled work that needs to be informed by behaviour change evidence, the brief might be straightforward and the outcomes easy to measure. If attendance at the sessions increased and this can be shown to be due to the information leaflet, then the consultancy is deemed a success. On the other hand, when the projects were more complex, Paterson reported that the client judged the consultant performance against initial expectations. For example, if a client wished to address vaccine hesitancy during pregnancy, the issues are more complex; clients and stakeholders are likely to have different perspectives on the issue itself, on how it might be addressed in an ethical way, and what success looks like. If the consultant does not meet these often-disparate expectations, the consultancy might be viewed as unsuccessful.

Evaluation of consultant performance. While evaluating projects based on outcomes is crucial, clients also evaluate the performance of consultants themselves. The literature on evaluating consultancy does not yet tell us if health psychology consultants will be judged by the same criteria as management (or information technology or financial) consultants. Evidence-based practice may be seen as expensive compared to alternatives offered by competitors. This could, for example, impact on data collection methods for establishing baseline and outcome data. We may need therefore to make a strong case for a robust methodology, aware of the short- and longer-term implications for the client.

Interviewing key stakeholders (consultants and clients) in the financial sector, Veres and Varga-Toldi (2021) identified five main attributes used to evaluate consulting services: consultants' attributes (integrity, honesty, credibility), the client's adaptation, communication, the consulting process and deliverables. They then developed an evaluation framework with four distinct quality dimensions: expertise, relations, involvement, and performance (ERIP). While health psychologists have their own models for evaluation (e.g., APEASE; West & Michie, 2019), it is worth remembering that clients may use business models such as ERIP to do so, and, therefore, it can be useful to be aware of them.

In choosing what to evaluate, we need to consider what is important to the client (and stakeholders) and what is important to us as health professionals. We might choose to use project management tools for evaluation, particularly when we are engaged in larger projects. As reflective practitioners, we use reflexivity to consider the nature of our relationships and ways of working with clients and stakeholders. We might bring our practice to supervision or seek the views of peers. We might choose to use the consultancy framework itself to evaluate our work, evaluating our approach to enquiry, to relationship building and so on as some of the contributing authors to this book have done. Whichever approach(es) we use, in order to secure future work, we need to understand how clients and stakeholders evaluate our performance and if they are likely to re-engage us or recommend us to others. And to do that we need to ask the client (and stakeholders) for feedback. Applebaum and Steed (2005) note that successful implementation of recommendations from consultants is likely to be a critical factor in the client-consultant relationship. However, implementation is not always a feature of consultancy in health psychology. In that case, what is evaluated is the recommendations themselves. This can be tricky. How can the value of recommendations be evaluated prior to implementation?

Two key points arise here. Firstly, consultancy usually involves writing a report. The quality and clarity of the report, the explanations of the issues to be addressed, the methods used, and the evidence on which the recommendations are based, will used by clients in evaluation. Presenting reports in a format and language that the client can relate to is important. In our experience, having more than one version of a report is often helpful: a brief slide presentation, a short (lay) summary, and a detailed, referenced report. Secondly, if the recommendations are subsequently implemented, and you are not involved in implementation, you may be judged on the outcome of the implementation. It is useful, therefore, to be very clear in your report about the potential impact of making changes to the recommendations during implementation and consider a follow-up with the client after the consultancy is ended to discuss the implications of their implementation.

As reflective practitioners, in addition to evaluating agreed outcomes from consultancy, we also benefit from evaluating our approach to the consultancy process itself and our own performance as consultants. The *what, when, why* and *how* questions are equally relevant to this. What we evaluate needs to include aspects of our performance that are important to clients and stakeholders as well as aspects of professional practice important to us. We can develop our own tools to do this or adapt the tool used with clients.

Finally, where possible, it is also good practice to do a follow-up evaluation with clients at an appropriate timepoint following the consultancy. This might allow ironing out of any issues standing in the way of optimal use of the consultancy output. It can provide good learning for the consultant. It is also a way to maintain good relationships with clients.

Summary

In the field of health, consultancy can take many forms and varies in scope and complexity. Our experience is that the knowledge and skillset of health psychologists are applicable and transferable to consultancy for a broad range of clients and a wide variety of problems. We trust that considering the processes in the framework will prove a valuable scaffolding to this work. We welcome critical perspectives of the framework from consultancy practitioners and look forward to evidence-based evaluations which may lead to further refinements and enhancements of it. Ultimately, we hope that readers who felt insufficiently equipped to undertake consultancy will realise that they have many skills needed to be a competent consultant in health, and that this will take them to their first brave step into this field.

References

Adams, R., & Tovey, W. (2012). *Consultancy in public services: Empowerment and transformation*. Policy Press.

Ajmal, M., Khan, M., & Al-Yafei, H. (2019). Exploring factors behind project scope creep–stakeholders' perspective. *International Journal of Managing Projects in Business, 13*(3), 483–504. https://doi.org/10.1108/IJMPB-10-2018-0228

Althiyabi, T., & Qureshi, M. (2021). Predefined project scope changes and its causes for project success. *International Journal of Software Engineering & Applications (IJSEA), 12(2/3).* https://ssrn.com/abstract=3882594

Ammerman, A., Smith, T. W., & Calancie, L. (2014). Practice-based evidence in public health: Improving reach, relevance, and results. *Annual Review of Public Health, 35*(1), 47–63. https://10.1146/annrev-publhealth-032013-182458

Applebaum, S. H., & Steed, A. J. (2005). The critical success factors in the client-consulting relationship. *Journal of Management Development, 24*(1), 68–93.

Atkins, L., Francis, J., Islam, R., O'Connor, D., Patey, A., Ivers, N., Foy, R., Duncan, E. M., Colquhoun, H., Grimshaw, J. M., Lawton, R., & Michie, S. (2017). A guide to using the theoretical domains framework of behaviour change to investigate implementation problems. *Implementation Science:IS, 12*(1), 77. https://doi.org/10.1186/s13012-017-0605-9

Aunger, J. A., Millar, R., Greenhalgh, J., Mannion, R., Rafferty, A. M., & McLeod, H. (2021). Why do some inter-organisational collaborations in healthcare work when others do not? A realist review. *Systematic Reviews, 10*, 1–22. https://doi.org/10.1186/s13643-021-01630-8

Block, P. (2011). *Flawless consulting* (3rd ed.). Jossey-Bass.

Brady, R., Moore, A., & Kuczynska, P. (2022). Health psychology consultancy: An example of practice during pandemic. *European Health Psychologist, 22*(5), 864–870.

Cope, M. (2010). *The Seven Cs of Consulting* (3rd ed.). Pearson UK.

Dietrich, P., Eskerod, P., Dalcher, D., & Sandhawalia, B. (2010). *The role of project collaboration quality and knowledge: Integration capability in multi-partner projects.* Paper presented at PMI® Research Conference: Defining the Future of Project Management, Washington, DC. Newtown Square, PA: Project Management Institute. https://www.pmi.org/learning/library/project-collaboration-multi-partner-projects-6428

Fullerton, J., & West, M. A. (1996). Consultant and client – working together. *Journal of Managerial Psychology, 11*(6), 40–49. https://doi.org/10.1108/02683949610129749

Guanci, G., & Bjork, C. (2019). An introduction to project management. *Nursing Management, 50*(10), 20–26. https://doi.org/10.1097/01.NUMA.0000580584.07510.9b

Hodges, J. (2017). *Consultancy, organizational development and change: A Practical guide to delivering value.* Kogan Page.

Hodges, J. (2021). A framework for consulting. *Management Consulting, 4*(2), 52–55.

Lane, D. A., & Corrie, S. (2007). *The modern scientist-practitioner: A guide to practice in psychology.* Routledge.

McLeod, S., & Schapper, J. H. (2020). Understanding quality in planning consultancy: A review and synthesis of the literature. *Journal of Planning Education and Research, 0*(0). https://doi.org/10.1177/0739456X20943928.

Michie, S. (1998). Consultancy. In D. W. Johnston, M. Johnston, A. S. Bellack, & M. Hersen (Eds.), *Health psychology, Vol. 8. Comprehensive clinical psychology* (pp. 153–169). Elsevier Science Publishers.

NHS Elect. (n.d.). *Quality improvement: Stakeholder mapping.* https://www.nhselect.nhs.uk/uploads/files/1/Stakeholder%20Mapping.pdf

Nicolescu, O., & Nicolescu, C. (2024). Stakeholders-Based Management: A Company-Relevant Alternative. In *Romanian management theory and practice: Navigating digitization and internationalization in the new global economy* (pp. 39–56). Cham.

Nikolova, N., Möllering, G., & Reihlen, M. (2015). Trusting as a 'leap of faith': Trust-building practices in client–consultant relationships. *Scandinavian Journal of Management, 31*(2), 232–245. https://doi.org/10.1016/j.scaman.2014.09.00

O'Mahoney, J., & Markham, C. (2013). *Management consultancy.* Oxford University Press.

Oade, A., & Oade, A. (2012). Reputational risk: Your client's dilemma. In *Managing challenging clients: Building effective relationships with difficult customers* (pp. 19–39). Palgrave Macmillan.

Osipovic, D., Allen, P., Shepherd, E., Petsoulas, C., Coleman, A., Perkins, N., Williams, L., & Sanderson, M. (2020). 83Commissioning of healthcare through competitive and cooperative mechanisms under the HSCA 2012. In P. Allen, K. Checkland, V. Moran, & S. Peckham (Eds.), *Commissioning healthcare in England: Evidence, policy and practice (pp. 0).* Policy Press. https://doi.org/10.1332/policypress/9781447346111.003.0006

Patterson, P. G. (2000). A contingency approach to modeling satisfaction with management consulting services. *Journal of Service Research, 3*(2), 138–153.

Presseau, J., Byrne-Davis, L. M., Hotham, S., Lorencatto, F., Potthoff, S., Atkinson, L., et al. (2022). Enhancing the translation of health behaviour change research into practice: A selective conceptual review of the synergy between implementation science and health psychology. *Health Psychology Review, 16*(1), 22–49. https://doi.org/10.1080/17437199.2020.1866638

Saad, Y. G. (2017). Deliverable accountability, change management and breach in consultancy contracts: A comparative study of world bank versus europeaid funded projects. *Journal of Public Procurement, 17*(4), 525–571.

Schein, E. H. (1990). Models of consultation: What do organizations of the 1990s need? *Consultation: An International Journal., 9*(4), 261–275.

Schein, E. H. (2016). *Humble consulting: How to provide real help faster.* Berrett-Koehler Publishers.

Sturdy, A., & Wright, C. (2011). The active client: The boundary-spanning roles of internal consultants as gatekeepers, brokers and partners of their external counterparts. *Management Learning, 42*(5), 485–503. https://doi.org/10.1177/1350507611401536

Too, E., Le, T., & Yap, W. Y. (2017). Front-end planning-The role of project governance and its impact on scope change management. *International Journal of Technology, 8*(6), 1124–1133.

Tucmeanu, A. I., Popescu, D. M., Ionescu, E. V., Oprea, C., Mociu, A., & Iliescu, M. G. (2017). Increasing the quality of health management in Romania through specific consultancy services. *ARS Medica Tomitana, 23*(3), 110–114.

Veres, Z., & Varga-Toldi, K. (2021). ERIP: Service quality model of management consulting projects. *Journal of Business & Industrial Marketing, 36*(7), 1090–1102. https://doi.org/10.1108/jbim-05-2020-0226

West, R., & Michie, S. (2019). *Unlocking Bahaviour Change 7. APEASE.* https://www.unlockingbehaviourchange.com/pdfs/5c766be7b6281890464249.pdf

Wright, C. (2009). Inside out? Organizational membership, ambiguity and the ambivalent identity of the internal consultant. *British Journal of Management, 20*(3), 309–322. https://doi.org/10.1111/j.1467-8551.2008.00585.x

Wulf, S. A. (2020). Successful project consulting. *IEEE Engineering Management Review, 48*(2), 12–14. https://doi.org/10.1109/EMR.2020.2978797

Zheng, X., Wang, W., & Pinto, J. (2023). When does competence matter? Character as a moderator in the development of trust. *Personality and Social Psychology Bulletin*, 01461672231167693. https://doi.org/10.1177/01461672231167693

Part II

Perspectives on Practice

4

Ethics and the Consultancy Process

Paul Chadwick, Lisa Hodges-Ballard, Alison Killen, and Roseanna Brady

Introduction

The authors of this chapter on ethics and the consultancy process have significant and varied expertise in ethics within both healthcare and consultancy. Dr Paul Chadwick is a clinical and health psychologist with extensive consulting experience in public, preventative, and acute care; Dr Lisa Hodges-Ballard's academic work explores the ethical and psychosocial issues of implementing new technologies through research, education, policy engagement, and public

Supplementary Information The online version contains supplementary material available at https://doi.org/10.1007/978-3-031-94529-8_4.

P. Chadwick (✉)
UCL Centre for Behaviour Change, London, UK
e-mail: paulmchadwick@gmail.com

L. Hodges-Ballard
Cognitiva Consultancy Ltd., Southampton, UK
e-mail: l.ballard@soton.ac.uk

A. Killen
Newcastle University, Newcastle upon Tyne, UK
e-mail: alison.killen@newcastle.ac.uk

R. Brady
Psychology for Health Associates, Bedford, UK
e-mail: bradykbs@msn.com

R. Brady et al. (eds.), *The Palgrave Handbook of Consultancy in Health Psychology*,
https://doi.org/10.1007/978-3-031-94529-8_4

dialogue; Dr Alison Killen is a researcher working with people with dementia many of whom lack capacity to consent, and sits as an expert member on a National Health Service (NHS) Research Ethics Committee in the UK; Dr Roseanna Brady is a qualified health psychologist with 30 years' experience in consultancy in private, public, and third sectors in the UK and overseas.

Insights and interventions derived from the theories, models, and methods of health psychology can result in significant transformation for individuals, organisations, communities, and populations (Revenson & Gurung, 2018). As with all powerful technologies, their use needs to be deployed in a considered and responsible way to minimise unintentional harms to those who implement, receive, or are affected by them. Ethics are the overarching values that guide the safe and effective practice of applied psychology. Principles of ethical practice are embedded within the operating procedures of research and development institutions in academia and healthcare, and guide health psychologists employed in these environments to work ethically (The Health and Care Professions Council (HCPC), 2016; Emanuel et al., 2000; NHS HRA, 2023). However, health psychologists working independently in consultancy roles operate outside of these institutional guard rails, sometimes with organisations that lack ethical guidelines, and with individuals or institutions blind to the ethical implications of their activity. Like all applied psychologists, health psychologists working in consultancy roles have a professional duty to practise within ethical guidelines. This chapter builds on previous work on ethics and consultancy in psychology (Cooper & Fisher, 2010; Cooper & Lowman, 2018) by providing a framework for health psychologists as consultants to ensure their practice is consistent with ethical principles at each stage of the process.

Ethics and the Consultancy Context

Health psychologists offering consultancy services typically work with organisations rather than individuals. Those organisations may try to influence the health and well-being of those who use their services directly such as through service provision or indirectly through the design or evaluation of products or services. Most guidance on the ethical dimensions of psychological practice is written with direct models of service provision in mind, and often relates primarily to therapeutic work (e.g., American Psychological Association, 2017). Although the 'client' is not a service user receiving direct support from a health psychologist, the requirement to practise in line with ethical principles during the consultancy context remains. The nature and expression of these principles will be shaped by the unique parameters of the consultancy context. To our knowledge, there are no existing guidelines that specifically address the issue of how health psychologists should practice in order to ensure that their consultancy activities are aligned to ethical guidelines set out by their professional bodies.

Principles of Ethical Practice

Ethical practice for most regulated professions is set out as a 'code of practice', which is the set of rules defining how persons or organisations must act in given situations. The ethical codes of practice governing psychologists are set out by the psychological association with responsibility for governing the profession within a country. This means that most ethical codes reflect the culture of a specific country or geographical area and are influenced by its history, laws, public policy, customs, and the nature of its psychological services (Cooper & Fisher, 2010). They may also be explicitly or implicitly influenced by broader statements relating to ethics such as the United Nations Declaration of Human Rights (UN General Assembly, 1948) and the World Medical Association Declaration of Helsinki (World Medical Association, 2013).

Codes of ethical practice may be expressed in the form of principles (broad, aspirational rules of conduct), standards (specific behaviours that psychologists are required to demonstrate), or guidelines (desired behaviours). Many codes contain both principles and standards (e.g., American Psychological Association, 2017). Guidelines are more commonly used where the professional association does not have the infrastructure to enforce the code, for example in countries without a professional body with legislative powers for the regulation of psychology (e.g., India).

There is remarkable consistency in the ethical principles of most codes of ethics, even across geographies that are linguistically and culturally different. For example, the ethical codes of practice for the American Psychological Association (American Psychological Association, 2017) and the Chinese Psychological Society (Chinese Psychological Society, 2018) include the same five general ethical principles: beneficence, responsibility, integrity, justice, and respect. Similarly, the codes of ethical practice for most European countries are based around four general principles of respect for a person's rights and dignity, professional competence, responsibility, and integrity (see Table 4.1).

What constitutes ethical practice is always bound by context (Søndergaard Christensen & Eriksen, 2020). Health psychology consultancy may cross international boundaries. For example, a UK registered health psychologist may be approached to offer consultancy to an organisation based in the

Table 4.1 General principles of ethical codes of practice across countries and geographical regions

American Psychological Association (American Psychological Association, 2017)	Canadian Psychological Association (Canadian Psychological Association, 2017)	British Psychological Society (British Psychological Society, 2021)	Nordic Psychological Associations (Nordic Psychological Associations, 2021)	European Federation of Psychologist Associations (European Federation of Psychologists' Associations, 2023)
Respect Responsibility Integrity Justice Beneficence and non-maleficence	Respect Responsibility Integrity Justice Beneficence and non-maleficence	Respect Responsibility Integrity Justice	Respect Responsibility Integrity Competency	Respect Responsibility Integrity Competency

US. Psychologists should always practise in accordance with the ethical guidance of the professional body that licence them. However, if their work is in or to be implemented within another country, they should familiarise themselves with that country's code of ethics and consider how this might influence practice.

The diversity and continually evolving nature of health psychology consultancy makes it impossible to provide a prescriptive list of behavioural standards that constitute ethical practice. No code of practice can instruct psychologists how to act in every potential situation (British Psychological Society, 2021; Banks et al., 2022). Health psychologists must actively engage with an ongoing process of assessment and decision-making throughout any piece of work to guide its ethical dimensions.

The Four Principles of Ethical Practice

This chapter offers a framework for ethical practice based on the principles outlined and defined in the British Psychological Society (BPS) codes of ethical practice (British Psychological Society, 2021) as these are largely consistent with international standards (see Table 4.1). These are the principles of: respect, competence, responsibility, and integrity. Each principle is described, and the ways in which they can shape ethical practice at each stage of the consultancy process is outlined. A series of vignettes (available in supplementary materials ESM_4.1) illustrate how these principles apply in practice to assist readers to consider how the principles might apply within their own work. The framework described in this chapter seeks to explore the broad ethical principles in order to provide health psychologists with a more detailed guide on how to carry out consultancy activity in an ethical way (see Banks et al., 2022, for a similar approach for applying ethical principles for industrial/organisational psychologists).

Respect

The principle of respect requires that health psychologists should behave in ways that are consistent with, or demonstrate that they value, the dignity and worth of all persons, and show sensitivity to the dynamics of perceived authority or influence arising from their professional status over persons and peoples, and with particular regard to people's rights. In applying the principle of respect, psychologists should consider the following:

Privacy and confidentiality. Psychologists often work with personal and sensitive information. They should take steps to ensure that all information is kept private and confidential, except in those circumstances where safeguarding concerns necessitate disclosure. Although the 'client' in consultancy work is often an organisation rather than an individual, the requirement of confidentiality still applies. Psychologists may be observing services that a client offers, interviewing members of different staff groups, or reading reports containing private and sensitive information.

Breaches of confidentiality could lead to individual distress, conflict between employees, reputational damage, and financial losses for the organisation (Banks et al., 2022). Consultancy often involves work with multiple organisations, some of which may be in direct competition with each other. The requirement of confidentiality should govern what information the consultant shares between organisations, as well as between individuals within an organisation. This may include information on an organisation's performance, operating procedures, policies, and ways of working. Consultants should only collect identifiable personal data necessary to conduct their project and ensure such data is stored securely in line with the relevant legislative framework in their region of practice (e.g., General Data Protection Regulation (GDPR) requirements in the UK).

Power. Psychologists must consider how *personal*, *professional*, and *institutional* power influences their ability to practise ethically (see Johnstone & Boyle (2018) for a description and analysis of power in psychological work, and Greene (2000) for a more comprehensive description of the role of power in organisations). *Personal power* involves those aspects of a psychologist's characteristics, life history, or status that may influence the way that clients respond to them. This includes but is not limited to the ways that gender, ethnicity, ableness, sexuality, and personal relationships with the client or members of the organisation might affect their work. For example, a straight white cis-gendered male psychologist should reflect on how occupying a position of such structural privilege could influence his work with an organisation advocating for non-binary individuals who may have experienced abuse by individuals with a similar background to the psychologist. *Professional power* involves the privileges attached to having the professional status of psychologist and how this may influence the relationship with client(s). For example, clients with expertise from lived experience may feel reluctant to question a recommendation put forward by a psychologist based on a perceived hierarchy of value attached to different forms of expertise. *Institutional power* manifests when a person can influence what occurs in a system or organisation by virtue of their positioning, such as seniority, personal relationships, and reputation.

Consulting psychologists may have low institutional power because they are external to the organisation. However, they may be engaged by individuals with high institutional power which may potentiate their ability to effect change. It is the responsibility of the consultant to analyse how different forms of power may influence their consultancy and to take action to ensure that it does not limit their ethical practice. This could be achieved in a number of ways. For example, meeting with people individually or in small role-based groups may mitigate the unhelpful influence of all forms of power during the consultancy process. Providing assurances for, and enabling anonymity in, feedback can help reduce power imbalances between stakeholders, as can offering a variety of routes to participation (in-person, phone, email, social media, etc.). It is also important to pay attention to the way that dress, body, and verbal language may affect the ways in which personal, professional, and institutional power influence the consultancy process (British Psychological Society, 2021). Individuals who feel respected by, connected to, and who trust the consultant, may be more forthcoming with information critical to addressing the consultancy issue.

Consent. Consent involves seeking permission from a person to engage with an activity. Consent is always task specific, which means that if the consultancy involves multiple activities (i.e., observation, interviewing, intervention delivery), then consent must be sought for each activity. For example, a psychologist may be engaged by the management of a company to advise on how service delivery might be improved. To do this, they may need to observe and interview staff and service users. Consent must be gained from the individuals who are observed and consulted. Consent ensures that the dignity of individuals involved in the consultancy process is respected. It is an important way in which psychologists can mitigate the negative impact of perceived or actual disparities in power (Lyle et al., 2023).

Diversity and inclusion. Respect requires awareness of how one's practice might influence the experience of individuals who encounter exclusion, marginalisation, and other barriers that influence opportunity. All consultancy activity should operate within the legal requirements of the relevant legislative framework in their country of practice. In the UK, the Equality Act 2010 legislates against discrimination based on nine protected characteristics (age, disability, gender reassignment, marriage and civil partnership, pregnancy and maternity, race, religion or belief, sex, and sexual orientation). Practising respectfully involves analysing the potential of one's practice to discriminate on the basis of a protected characteristic. Unintentional discrimination could occur in several ways: for example, in the use of an inaccessible venue, communication strategies which are not inclusive for people with physical or intellectual disabilities, dissemination routes for reports which assume digital access, or interview protocols or questionnaires that make hetero-normative assumptions (British Psychological Society, 2022).

Health psychologists offering consultancy as part of private practice are under no obligation to take on work when approached to do so. They may be approached by organisations whose activity, or implicit or explicitly stated values, are very different to their own. Whilst codes of ethics and guidelines explicitly outline a set of core values, these values are less explicit in the practice of consultancy (Earll & Bath, 2004). Whilst psychologists have a professional duty to operate in ways that do not discriminate, it is also incumbent upon psychologists to ensure that they can operate ethically with any individual or organisation they choose to work with. For example, if a psychologist feels that there is a fundamental and irreconcilable difference between their own value system and that of a potential consultancy client, this might make it difficult for the psychologist to fully enact the principle of *respect* in their dealings with the client. Where value or belief systems are less fundamentally misaligned, it may still be possible to work ethically if the psychologist makes effective use of supervision and support. For example, the opportunity to discuss work with a more experienced professional can help psychologists reflect on the personal impact of work with clients with different values and belief systems and how this could influence their professional activities (see O'Donovan et al., 2011 for an example). Vignette 1 (in supplementary material ESM_4.1) illustrates some considerations where the principle of respect due to misalignment of values between a health psychologist and a potential client may be an issue.

Competence

The principle of competence requires health psychologists to operate to the standards expected by their professional group, within the scope of their knowledge, skills, training, and experience, to refrain from engaging in work beyond this, and to continually update their knowledge and skills in order to practise safely and effectively. In applying the principle of competence, psychologists should consider the following:

Maintaining and developing technical knowledge and skills. Health psychology is an applied science, and all practitioners are required to keep up to date with developments in psychological knowledge, theory, and practice by engaging in continuing professional development. This requirement aims to ensure that psychologists can practise safely and effectively within their given area of expertise. This may involve reading relevant journals, attending and contributing to conferences, joining an appropriate professional organisation, for example a division of the British Psychological Society, and undertaking refresher training. Practitioners should also ensure that they are up to date with relevant legislation and comply with all mandatory training within the organisations and geography within which they work.

Taking on work within scope of competence. Health psychology is a wide-ranging speciality whose boundaries are continually evolving. Health psychologists working in consultancy roles may be approached by individuals and organisations that do not understand the different types of applied psychological practitioner. A client may request services that fall outside of the scope of health psychology, or outside the expertise of a particular practitioner. It is incumbent on the health psychologist to only take on work that is within their current scope of practice, and where they have the knowledge, skills, and training to practise competently (HCPC, 2023). In our view, the boundaries between health, clinical, occupational, and educational psychology are increasingly fluid. The work of organisations, particularly outside of public services such as the NHS and schools, may not reflect the neat divisions that separate the activity of applied psychologists as set out by, for example, the BPS or HCPC. Consider a situation in which a health psychologist with expertise in health-related behaviour change is approached to advise on how to improve lifestyles of children in a specialist unit for children with complex educational needs to support better academic attainment. Although the psychologist has clearly relevant expertise (i.e., health-related behaviour change) there are other fields of applied psychology practice and professional expertise that may be required to deliver effectively on the brief. This might include educational psychology (expertise in learning and management of pupil behaviour), clinical psychology (expertise in child development and mental health), and nutrition (expertise in dietary principles). Any psychologist approached on such a project will need to consider whether they have the knowledge, skills, and training to fulfil the entirety of the brief and to identify how to fill gaps. This might be achieved, for example, by working with other professionals (psychologists and non-psychologists) with relevant expertise.

Developing scope of competence. Health psychologists who wish to work primarily through offering consultancy services may choose to evolve their scope of competence to make this financially viable. There are a number of mechanisms for evolving scope of competence. Additional professional training may be required (e.g., an accredited training in a relevant therapeutic modality such as cognitive behavioural therapy). Supervision is also essential for supporting practitioners to reflect on their knowledge and skills and identify the training and experience required to diversify into new areas. This may be within the profession of psychology or beyond it. For example, if a research psychologist with academic expertise on environmental influences on adult eating behaviour is approached to offer consultancy services to organisations working with children's nutrition, then it may be advisable to seek professional development opportunities to improve their knowledge and skills in child development, parenting support, paediatric behaviour change, but also support from experts in child nutrition.

Responsibility

The principle of responsibility requires health psychologists to understand and accept appropriate responsibility for what is within their power or control. This includes ensuring that the trust of others is not abused, the power of influence is properly managed, and that duty towards others is always paramount (British Psychological Society, 2021). In applying the principle of responsibility, psychologists should consider the following.

Professional accountability. Psychologists have a responsibility to carry out their duties in a way that is consistent with accepted standards of professional practice. This means ensuring that appropriate work records are kept and are held securely, and that communications are timely, accurate, succinct, and tailored to the needs of the recipient. If working in a team, the responsibilities of the consultant providing health psychology expertise needs to be clarified and distinguished from the responsibilities of other members of the consulting team. Ideally, setting out clear roles and responsibilities for the psychologist should be carried out during the contracting process. Psychologists may also be consulting with several organisations simultaneously and so must ensure that they have sufficient time and resources to manage the demands of multiple stakeholders across organisations.

Duty of care. All psychologists have a duty of care to ensure the well-being of those who are affected by their work. Psychologists must take steps to ensure they are aware of the impact of their work on all stakeholders in a project, using appropriate formal and informal feedback processes to assess risk and monitor for signs that their actions may be causing distress or contributing to disadvantage (see Section "Ethics at Multiple Levels" later in this chapter for additional guidance on how to identify and consider those groups who should be considered under the duty of care requirement). It is not always possible to predict and prevent negative responses to the activities or recommendations that emerge from a piece of consultancy work. However, if a psychologist becomes aware of such responses, they are required to take action to address this (see Vignette 2 in supplementary material ESM_4.1).

Potential ways of mitigating such effects include adapting the formulation of the issue and adjusting methods or finding alternative ways to achieve the desired outcomes. Psychologists have a responsibility to the professional bodies who regulate them as well as to their peers, to refrain from using their qualification or expertise in a way which would jeopardise the credibility of the profession. If in doubt about a potential project, supervision and discussion with trusted peers are appropriate routes to explore this. If working as a lone practitioner, it may help to join groups of others in a similar position. The requirement of duty of care applies to all those affected by a psychologist's work, not just to those identified as the target population. Psychologists should routinely consider the potential ethical dimensions of their activity for all affected individuals. See Section "Ethics at Multiple Levels" for more detail.

Integrity

The principle of integrity requires health psychologists to be honest, truthful, accurate, and consistent in their actions, words, decisions, methods, and outcomes. They should set aside self-interest and be objective and open to challenge in a professional context. Vignette 3 (in supplementary material ESM_4.1) illustrates some considerations when the principle of integrity as a health psychologist may be at risk due to the actions of a client. In applying the principle of integrity, psychologists should consider the following.

Commitment to scientific principles. Health psychology practice involves the application of scientifically derived knowledge and methods to improve human health and well-being. Psychologists working in consultancy roles may be contracted by organisations that have limited understanding of the scientific method or the principles of evidence-based practice. Timelines in consultancy projects are often short, and organisations may not have a full understanding of the resources required to produce work that is scientifically defensible. Psychologists must find ways to meet the needs of those they are contracted to work for, whilst also resisting pressures to take short-cuts that would unacceptably jeopardise the reliability and validity of their work. This is best achieved during the contracting process where psychologists should take time to explore the clients understanding and expectations of the work and engage in discussion about what can and cannot be achieved ethically. Discussion about how the work of the psychologist will be disseminated is important at the contracting stage. Psychologists should take steps to ensure that the outcomes of their work are represented accurately, and that organisations do not make claims that cannot be substantiated by the work of the psychologist. This might include discussing options for input or veto in press releases involving work conducted by the psychologist or setting parameters on how and to whom the work will be disseminated.

Conflicts of interest (CoI). Conflicts of interest arise when a psychologist's professional interests and responsibilities are incompatible with personal motives or goals (American Psychological Society, 2018), or when their professional activity in one context (e.g., as a consultant to a commercial organisation) has the potential to compromise their ability to act ethically in another context (e.g., as a research council funded scientist). Psychologists should assess each new project for potential CoI and raise these for discussion with the relevant parties. Psychologists working across several organisations may experience CoI in projects involving commercially sensitive information, or intellectual property. The presence of a CoI does not in itself prevent a psychologist from working with multiple organisations doing similar work. Ways to mitigate any threats to the organisation arising from the CoI can be developed during the contracting process. Conflicts of interest may arise once the project is underway. This is less likely if the consultant has discussed the work with the client in depth and carefully considered whether the project aligns with their values.

Where a consultant feels that to continue with a project would challenge their integrity, they should address this as soon as possible whilst showing respect for the client and other stakeholders. They may even need to withdraw from the project.

Application of Principles into Practice

The application of ethical principles to real world contexts is rarely straightforward in the field of consultancy (Cooper & Lowman, 2018). This section outlines some of the challenges that can emerge during implementation and potential pathways to resolution.

Conflict Between Ethical Principles

There are situations in which the actions required to fulfil one ethical principle may create problems for fulfilment of another (Banks et al., 2022; Cooper & Lowman, 2018). For example, the requirement to act with *integrity*, such as reporting findings in line with best scientific practice, can sometimes conflict with the requirement to act *responsibly* within a given contractual framework (e.g., constraints on communications imposed by the contracting organisation). Vignette 4 (in supplementary material ESM_4.1) explores the conflict between integrity and responsibility in more detail. Conflict between ethical principles can be mitigated by thinking carefully about the potential ethical dimensions of a piece of work before taking it on, and by building ethical safeguards into the contracting process. We define ethical safeguards as the explicit clauses in a contract that help to define the scope of activity for the contracting psychologist. They outline the specific expectations or responsibilities of both parties, and the conditions under which the psychologist may refuse a client request or terminate work on one part of a contract or its entirety.

Ethical decision-making and practice is an ongoing process. Psychologists must continually monitor the consultancy process with an eye to identifying emerging and unanticipated ethical issues and be prepared to take action to achieve the best possible ethical outcome given the evolving context. Labelling actions as 'ethical' or 'unethical' is rarely helpful. Instead, psychologists should aim to be *ethically prepared* (Samuel et al., 2022), which involves continually evaluating their actions and decision-making in terms of a continuum of ethical adequacy to ethical excellence (Knapp et al., 2015). Ethical excellence involves striving for 'the best possible outcome that is anchored in overarching ethical principles and not being satisfied with a solution that meets only minimal legal and ethical requirements' (Knapp et al., 2015, p. 6). It is not always possible to avoid ethical compromises when working in applied settings. Striving for ethical excellence is likely to minimise the negative consequences of any compromises that need to be made (Lyle et al., 2023).

Ethics at Multiple Levels

The work of health psychologists in consultancy may bring about change at multiple levels of a context such as individuals, organisations, communities, and populations (Sallis et al., 2008). When considering the ethical dimensions of their work, health psychologists should routinely consider the impact on both clients and stakeholders who may be potentially affected by the work. It may be helpful to consider the following groupings of clients and stakeholders, illustrated here with reference to the example of a psychologist consulting to the managers of a group home for people with intellectual disabilities:

Individuals directly affected by the activity: for example, an individual client or a group of individuals (e.g., a resident or group of residents with intellectual disabilities living in a group home).

Individuals delivering the intervention: for example, the support workers in a group home who are required to implement a psychologically informed intervention to people with an intellectual disability.

The wider community who may be indirectly affected by the activity: for example, the family members of the individuals to whom an intervention may be directed, the wider staff team (e.g., other health and social care workers), and others in the organisational or cultural ecosystem (e.g., managers and executives responsible for running a group home, advocate groups for people with intellectual disabilities).

The wider discipline and community of psychologists: for example, other psychologists working in the same area (e.g., other psychologists working in the field of intellectual disability), or the impact on public understandings of psychology and psychologists (e.g., public responses to journalistic reports of the intervention).

The health psychologist: for example, the emotional, social, and physical impact on the psychologist carrying out the work.

Consultancy that appears ethical at the level of the individual could potentially violate ethical principles for others within the same context. For example, the implementation of a token economy system to reinforce desirable behaviour in a group home for people with intellectual disabilities might be considered ethical at the level of the individual residents, but it could cause additional and unacceptable work strain on the staff members who are required to implement it (i.e., violating the principle of *responsibility*). It might be considered unacceptable to the advocates and family members of those residents on the grounds that it violates residents right to autonomy which may violate the principles of *respect*. Psychologists should consider the impact of their activity at different levels of the context and the different groups of clients and stakeholders within those levels.

Ethical Principles Applied to the Framework for Consultancy in Health Psychology

The four principles of ethical practice apply to all consultancy processes. The expression of what is required to behave in line with each principle differs with each process, and for different types of work and context. Tables 4.2 to 4.6 provides examples of actions that health psychologists can take during each consultancy process as set out in the consultancy framework (Brady & Varkonyi-Sepp, 2025; see Chap. 3) to achieve ethical practice. Readers are also encouraged to read and reflect on the five vignettes in supplementary material for this chapter (ESM_4.1).

Table 4.2 Actions to achieve ethical practice during enquiry

Ethical Principle	Actions that can be taken
Respect	• Identify all stakeholders and establish how any protected characteristics they have might influence their ability to engage with a prospective work plan • Take time to find out about the client, both the individual(s) you will contract with and the organisation, to gain insights into their values and their practice • Investigate how the work of the client organisation impacts on stakeholders and on the broader environment • Consider how your personal, professional, and institutional power might affect your interactions with each stakeholder group and take steps to mitigate this as part of developing your work plan
Competence	• Consult your client, seek advice from colleagues in your network, and undertake desk research to identify the competences required to undertake the work • Arrange further training or subcontract expertise to address gaps in your knowledge, skills, or professional training • Determine what professional supervision you will need for the work and put this in place
Responsibility	• Take time to consider whether you will have time to fulfil the contract • Think about potential duty of care issues that might arise during or after your involvement
Integrity	• Consider carefully how client and stakeholder values align with your professional standards and with your professional values • Explore the potential for conflicts of interest and plan ways to address this

Table 4.3 Actions to achieve ethical practice during negotiation and contracting

Ethical principle	Actions that can be taken
Respect	• Build inclusive ways of working into the work plan when developing the contract to ensure there is sufficient resource and time for inclusive working
Competence	• Familiarise yourself with the technical requirements of the proposed consultancy and assess your knowledge, skills, and training—and those of your team members and subcontractors—against the technical requirements of the consultancy project • Prior to contracting, identify competence gaps and ways in which they can be addressed • Clearly state your assumptions regarding consultant (you and your team/partners/subcontractors) competence and responsibilities in your negotiations and in your proposal
Responsibility	• Estimate if the client's budget is sufficient to deliver outputs that are consistent with your ethical practice • In your costings, ensure that you include time for research, reflection, and supervision • Identify and discuss client policies which might impact on your consultancy work and on stakeholders. Ensure that any agreement on how this will be managed is included in your contract
Integrity	• Ensure there is sufficient time and resource in your budget to enable you to practice in line with ethical principles

Table 4.4 Actions to achieve ethical practice during relationship building

Ethical principle	Actions that can be taken
Respect	• Build in regular communication with your client to ensure you understand their needs, to obtain input and feedback, and to keep the client updated on progress and any potential delays or difficulties • Be alert to potential power imbalances in your relationships with client and stakeholders and take steps to avoid negative implications • Ensure that you identify where consent is required and that you obtain informed consent from clients and stakeholders before proceeding • Demonstrate respect towards client staff and partners acknowledging their expertise and any contribution to your work • Use inclusive methods of communication in terms of language, access needs, and cultural factors
Competence	• Identify and acknowledge client and stakeholder needs from the project • Develop a communication plan taking account of client and stakeholder preferences for method, frequency, and format/style of communication • Use appropriate psychological knowledge and skills to communicate with clients and stakeholders respectfully
Responsibility	• Maintain professional boundaries in relationships with clients and stakeholders • Back up your suggestions, proposals, and arguments with appropriate theory and evidence when discussing problems and challenges in the work
Integrity	• Highlight any likely delays or threats to completing the work, together with plans to mitigate them • Discuss with the client any potential conflicts of interest that arise during the project and seek to resolve them • Ensure that you maintain your professional standards in relation to any additional client requests • Act in accordance with your own and/or the client organisation's governance policies if you witness problematic behaviour (e.g., bullying, harassment)

Table 4.5 Actions to achieve ethical practice during planning and managing delivery

Ethical principle	Actions that can be taken
Respect	• Clarify roles and responsibilities for yourself (and any colleagues or subcontractors), the client, and any stakeholders involved • Clarify arrangements regarding sharing of documentation and other information during the project • Assess and clarify risks to yourself (and any colleagues or subcontractors), and to the client and stakeholders from undertaking consultancy activities • Acquaint yourself with different ways of working across organisations, being sensitive and adaptable where these are unfamiliar to you while maintaining your own professional standards
Competence	• Identify the full range of knowledge, psychological skills and other skills (such as facilitation skills, project management) required for the project and update your own knowledge and skills if needed • Outsource, partner with others, or undertake training if required to deliver the project
Responsibility	• Identify and report any threats to the delivery of the consultancy (personal or organisational) and seek/suggest/agree solutions as to how these can be managed • Develop a draft work plan to identify how the client's requirements can be met within best practice guidance and existing evidence base • Monitor the project for emerging/evolving duty of care issues • Remain alert to potential scope creep and threats to timely project delivery if the client requests additional input • Be prepared to renegotiate with the client if the project requires additional resource
Integrity	• Ensure that your work is planned and implemented according to the contract • Resist any suggested changes to the plan if they risk compromising your professional standards

Table 4.6 Actions to achieve ethical practice during evaluation

Ethical principle	Actions that can be taken
Respect	• Build evaluation methods into the project from the beginning to enable the impact of your work on the client, stakeholders, and the broader environment to be continually assessed • Use evaluation methods that take account of issues of power and the need for inclusivity • Use different ways to communicate your findings and recommendations to meet the needs of all stakeholders • Ensure that stakeholders who were consulted during the consultancy have the opportunity to be informed of the results of the evaluation
Competence	• Identify and use methods to evaluate your practice as a consultant (i.e., how you conduct consultancy processes) and include ethical principles in the evaluation • Assess the impact of your work using recognised methods in line with best practice for the type of work being carried out
Responsibility	• Schedule sufficient time and resources in the work plan to include evaluation • Use reflective practice to evaluate your own performance • Identify and take action to mitigate against potential bias in your evaluation methods
Integrity	• Present findings objectively, taking care to situate them in context • Acknowledge any limitations in your methodology and in the conclusions that can be drawn • Check the client's understanding of your findings/outcomes and your recommendations • Agree how your findings will be shared by the client on completion of the work and over time • Acknowledge and credit any co-contributors to your work

Summary

Ethical issues are a critical consideration for all health psychologists undertaking consultancy roles. Psychologists should take steps to ensure they are prepared to act in accordance with the four principles of respect, competency, responsibility, and integrity. By considering ethical principles as part of enquiry and negotiating and contracting processes in consultancy, psychologists can ensure that they are likely to act according to their values and their professional standards and will have the resource to practise ethically. Throughout the consultancy process, psychologists will need to be sensitive to emerging ethical issues and act accordingly. Ethical practice can extend beyond the requirement to align to the ethical code of a governing body and be an expression of wider social issues and a psychologist's personal values. For example, psychologists might consider how their activities contribute to such issues such as climate change, global social inequality, and human rights (see Hardcastle et al., 2023; Ledford, 2023; Hill et al., 2016; Lyle et al., 2023). The principles outlined in this chapter should be considered a starting point for the exploration of ethical dimensions of practice, not the final word.

Questions for Reflection

1. What concepts, practices, and materials can you adapt from your current roles to support ethical practice in your independent consultancy work?
2. What are the unique issues for your area of expertise in terms of the four ethical principles?
3. In your consultancy work, which processes do you identify as strong and which could be strengthened further in terms of ethical practice?
4. How would you respond to the ethical dilemmas in the vignettes in supplementary materials?

Competing Interests The authors have no competing interests to declare that are relevant to this chapter.

References

American Psychological Association. (2017). *Ethical principles of psychologists and code of conduct (2002, amended effective June 1, 2010, and January 1, 2017)*. https://www.apa.org/ethics/code/

American Psychological Association. (2018). APA dictionary of psychology: Conflict of interest. https://dictionary.apa.org/conflict-of-interest

Banks, G., Knapp, D., Lin, L., Sanders, C., & Grand, J. (2022). Ethical decision making in the 21st century: A useful framework for industrial-organizational psy-

chologists. *Industrial and Organizational Psychology, 15*(2), 220–235. https://doi.org/10.1017/iop.2021.143
Brady, R., & Varkonyi-Sepp, J. (2025). A framework for consultancy in health psychology. In R. Brady, J. Varkonyi-Sepp, & J. Smith (Eds.), *The Palgrave handbook of consultancy in health psychology*. Palgrave Macmillan.
British Psychological Society. (2021). Code of ethics and conduct. *Code of Ethics and Conduct*. https://doi.org/10.53841/bpsrep.2021.inf94
British Psychological Society. (2022). *Declaration on equality, diversity and inclusion*. BPS. UK. https://cms.bps.org.uk/sites/default/files/2022-07/Declaration%20on%20equality%2C%20diversity%20and%20inclusion.pdf
Canadian Psychological Association. (2017). Canadian code of ethics for psychologists (4th ed.). https://cpa.ca/docs/File/Ethics/CPA_Code_2017_4thEd.pdf
Chinese Psychological Society. (2018). Code of ethics for clinical and counseling psychology of the Chinese Psychological Society. *Acta Psychologica Sinica, 50*(11), 1314–1322.
Cooper, S., & Fisher, M. (2010). Ethical considerations in the consultancy and advisory process. In A. Carol, A. Ireland, & M. J. Fisher (Eds.), *Consultancy and Advising in Forensic Practice: Empirical and Practical Guidelines* (pp. 51–67). John Wiley & Sons, Ltd.
Cooper, S., & Lowman, R. (2018). Ethical issues in psychological consultation. In M. Leach & E. Welfel (Eds.), *The Cambridge handbook of applied psychological ethics Cambridge handbooks in psychology* (pp. 552–574). Cambridge University Press. https://doi.org/10.1017/9781316417287.028
Earll, L., & Bath, J. (2004). Consultancy: What Is it, how do you do it, and does it make any difference? In S. Michie & C. Abraham (Eds.), *Health psychology in practice* (pp. 230–250). Blackwell Publishing. https://doi.org/10.1002/9780470694008.ch12
Emanuel, E. J., Wendler, D., & Grady, C. (2000). What makes clinical research ethical? *Journal of the American Medical Association, 283*(20), 2701–2711.
European Federation of Psychologists' Associations. (2023). Model code of ethics. https://www.efpa.eu/sites/default/files/2023-03/model-code-of-ethics.pdf
Greene, R. (2000). *The 48 laws of power*. Penguin.
Hardcastle, F., Lyle, K., Horton, R., Samuel, G., Weller, S., Ballard, L., Thompson, R., Trindade, L., Gómez Urrego, J., Kochin, D., Johnson, T., Tatz-Wieder, N., Redrup Hill, E., Robinson Adams, F., Eskandar, Y., Harriss, E., Tsosie, K. S., Dixon, P., Mackintosh, M., … Lucassen, A. (2023). The ethical challenges of diversifying genomic data: A qualitative evidence synthesis. *Cambridge prisms: Precision Medicine*, 1–39. https://doi.org/10.1017/pcm.2023.20
HCPC. (2016). *Standards of conduct, and ethics*. The Health and Care Professions Council, 1–17. https://www.hcpc-uk.org/globalassets/resources/standards/standards-of-conduct-performance-and-ethics.pdf
HCPC. (2023). Standards of proficiency – Practitioner psychologists. HCPC. UK. https://www.hcpc-uk.org/standards/standards-of-proficiency/practitioner-psychologists/

Hill, M., Glaser, K., & Harden, J. (2016). A feminist model for ethical decision making. *Learning from Our Mistakes: Difficulties and Failures in Feminist Therapy, 3149*(1998), 101–122. https://doi.org/10.1300/J015v21n03

Johnstone, L., & Boyle, M. with Cromby, J., Dillon, J., Harper, D., Kinderman, P., Longden, E., Pilgrim, D. & Read, J. (2018). *The power threat meaning framework: Overview.* British Psychological Society.

Knapp, S. J., Gottlieb, M. C., & Handelsman, M. M. (2015). *Ethical dilemmas in psychotherapy: Positive approaches to decision making.* American Psychological Association. https://doi.org/10.1037/14670-000

Ledford, H. (2023, November 7). Don't overlook race and ethnicity: New guidelines urge change for psychology research. *Nature.* https://doi.org/10.1038/d41586-023-03458-9

Lyle, K., Weller, S., Samuel, G., & Lucassen, A. M. (2023). Beyond regulatory approaches to ethics: Making space for ethical preparedness in healthcare research. *Journal of Medical Ethics, 49*(5), 352 LP – 356. https://doi.org/10.1136/medethics-2021-108102

NHS Health Research Authority. (2023). UK policy framework for health and social care research. NHS HRA. UK. https://www.hra.nhs.uk/planning-and-improving-research/policies-standards-legislation/uk-policy-framework-health-social-care-research/

Nordic Psychological Associations. (2021). Ethical principles for Nordic psychologists. https://sal.is/wp-content/uploads/2023/04/Ethical-Principles-for-Nordic-Psychologists-EPNP-final-version-Sept-2021B.pdf

O'Donovan, A., Halford, W. K., & Walters, B. (2011). Towards best practice supervision of clinical psychology trainees. *Australian Psychologist, 46*(2), 101–112. https://doi.org/10.1111/j.1742-9544.2011.00033.x

Revenson, T. A., & Gurung, R. A. R. (Eds.). (2018). *Handbook of Health Psychology* (1st ed.). Routledge. https://doi.org/10.4324/9781315167534

Sallis, J. F., Owen, N., & Fisher, E. B. (2008). Ecological models of health behavior. In K. Glanz, B. K. Rimer, & K. Viswanath (Eds.), *Health Behavior and health education: Theory, research, and practice* (4th ed., pp. 465–485). Jossey-Bass.

Samuel, G., Ballard, L. M., Carley, H., & Lucassen, A. M. (2022). Ethical preparedness in health research and care: The role of behavioural approaches. *BMC Medical Ethics, 23*(1), 1–13. https://doi.org/10.1186/s12910-022-00853-1

Søndergaard Christensen, A., & Eriksen, C. (2020). Contextual ethics – developing conceptual and theoretical approaches. *SATS, 21*(2), 81–84. https://doi.org/10.1515/sats-2020-2015

UN General Assembly. (1948). *Universal declaration of human rights. 217 A (III).* Retrieved November 11, 2023, from https://www.refworld.org/docid/3ae6b3712c.html

World Medical Association. (2013). Declaration of Helsinki: Ethical principles for medical research involving human subjects. *JAMA, 310*(20), 2191–2194. https://doi.org/10.1001/jama.2013.281053

5

Multidisciplinary Working in Consultancy: The Delicate Balance of Expertise, Confidence, and Humility

Michelle Constable and Jim McManus

Consultancy in the field of psychology is a practice that is still developing, and in which there is no single model of practice. There are benefits and disbenefits to the lack of a defined approach to consultancy. Among the benefits are that it enables those in practice to be flexible on methods, tools, and approaches used for different commissions. It also allows the consultant flexibility to discover, set out, and consider the various components of the problem, the organisational environment, and the actors involved, in a way which enables this complexity to be understood and addressed. However, there are also challenges, as with no preferred method there is a risk of being unsystematised and, as with all complex projects, it may sometimes be difficult to see where evidence and theory have influenced practice.

M. Constable (✉)
The Behavioural Science and Public Health Network, Stevenage, UK
e-mail: michelle@thebehaviouralscientists.com

J. McManus
The Behavioural Science and Public Health Network, Stevenage, UK

Public Health Wales, Cardiff, UK
e-mail: jim.mcmanus@wales.nhs.uk

R. Brady et al. (eds.), *The Palgrave Handbook of Consultancy in Health Psychology*,
https://doi.org/10.1007/978-3-031-94529-8_5

As psychologists applying health psychology in practice, the importance of multidisciplinary working has been an ongoing thread throughout our 30-plus years of combined experience. Working in the public and charitable sectors, we have experienced many of the challenges of working with clients to understand, develop, and make changes to programmes that are being delivered in the real world rather than a theoretical or laboratory setting. Most of our experience has been through working in the United Kingdom (UK) National Health Service (NHS) and local government, applying health psychology to improve individual-, community-, and population-level outcomes. This is an area we are passionate about and where the synergy between public health and health psychology offers an exciting and dynamic opportunity for change.

The Environment of Consulting in Health Psychology

For some organisations, in both the public and the private sectors, psychologists and other behavioural scientists have become more sought-after partners in projects both before (Martin & Ferrere, 2017) and after the Covid-19 pandemic. This is evidenced by the increased frequency of employed roles and the extablishment of specialist groups (Local Government Association, 2025), as well as recent presentations delivered to the British Psychological Society Senate (Drury, 2024; McManus, 2024), which reflect the growing institutional engagement with behavioural science. Organisations are increasingly recognising that their existing in-house approaches to changing behaviour (e.g., awareness raising campaigns), or change management, are not sufficient to address the complex challenges they face, nor are they delivering the needed outcomes (Errida & Lotfi, 2021; House of Lords, 2022). Consultancy is not new (Begley & Sheard, 2021); occupational and organisational psychology have a long history in applications from ergonomics to recruitment (Bryan & Pickren, 2020). However, consultants specialising in the use of psychology and evidence-based behaviour change methods, beyond what may be seen as core areas of organisational psychology, are a more recent development. Examples of applying health psychology skills include the design of patient pathways (Mather et al., 2022), reducing workplace harassment (Hayes et al., 2020), and applying behavioural theories to improve anti-microbial prescribing (Talkhan et al., 2020). This expands the range of perspectives, theories, and evidence through which one can view organisational challenges. This broader approach to understanding and solving problems reflects a growing demand for innovative solutions. Organisations are seeking new and objective perspectives on challenges that may have seemed intractable (Appelbaum & Steed, 2005; Drucker, 1979; Sturdy, 2021).

To thrive in this environment of changing organisational expectations, consultants must do more than wield their domain expertise; they must also master the delicate art of building relationships (Block, 2011; Schein, 2016; Mosonyi et al., 2019) and navigate the intricate and diverse dynamics of multidisciplinary collaboration. Consultants practise in a world where the business landscape—whether commercial or public sector—moves at pace and where there are pressures to improve outcomes while providing efficacious and cost-effective services. This is where the expertise of psychologists involved in consultancy work is invaluable. Health psychologists can provide fresh perspectives and innovative solutions, from how social cohesion across teams can improve performance to how better use of theory can improve the outcomes of health interventions. In our experience, such perspectives can create opportunities for clients to reassess challenges in a completely different way, providing opportunities for innovative approaches and new ways of working.

Beyond Academic Training

To be successful in navigating the complexity just described, more than traditional academic training is required. Each project will have its own nuances and complex context of interpersonal, political, and cultural dynamics. This is why the art of consultancy transcends mere technical expertise. Consultants often enter organisational environments that are completely new to them and are expected to develop recommendations or interventions in short time frames. The practice of consultancy here requires the use of skills that allow the consultant to understand the organisational context, manage relationships, and navigate new areas of practice, while managing expectations (Block, 2011). The consultant will need to build relationships while communicating effectively and skilfully navigating multidisciplinary collaborations. As consultancy is multifaceted in its nature, having a mindset which is ready to see this complexity, and establish the strengths within the organisation, is imperative for engagement and achieving successful outcomes.

Getting your Bearings: Developing a Schema for Successful Consulting

Traditional management consultancy literature refers to several skills needed for effective consultancy, including knowledge, technical, contextual, personal, and interpersonal skills (Block, 2011; Mosonyi et al., 2019). Within both the public and private sectors, our experience supports the view that these skills are required to be a successful consultant. Whether the consultant is working internally or externally to an organisation, all consultancy commissions require careful consideration and management of the complexities described above if interventions are to be effective. This can be a challenge, particularly since psychologists may have been commissioned as experts in their field and may be working with an organisation or topic that they have no experience of, making them unaware of the internal dynamics. In this situation, how do you know what you don't know? What are the boundaries of your professional expertise in relation to this project? What other support do you need to successfully deliver the project and how will you find it? These are some of the key questions we consider as part of scoping and negotiating new contracts. This is where the consultant can define their involvement, as the contract will form the basis, look, and feel of the project moving forward (Block, 2011; Sturdy et al., 2010). Failure to explore these questions can result in a 'one size fits all' or 'one method fits all' approach, which consultancy is widely criticised for (Mazzucato & Collington, 2023; Kirkpatrick et al., 2019; Ford & Harding, 2020).

In our experience, the questions asked must be sufficient to encompass the real-world complexity that a consultant, bringing psychological expertise to bear, will face. This means that a single set of questions from the consultancy literature, or from the psychological literature, is inadequate. In almost all projects, we have found that no single source suffices. We therefore devised and implemented a 'domains' model, which sets out a schema of the issues in any project. Using this schema enabled us to work with core processes of consulting (e.g., agreeing the scope and terms of a project) and understand the various dynamics of it, including where new knowledge was needed to answer specific questions or commissions. In this way, we resisted a one-size-fits-all model. If the consulting environment and the consulting challenges are heterogenous, then the consulting method must be sufficiently flexible to reckon with this.

Explaining the Domains Model

Methods of inquiry (*Domain 1*) will not be the same in every context. For example, developing an intervention to help nurses to guide patients to join diabetes prevention programmes is similar to encouraging parents to vaccinate their children in terms of acceptability, access, and ease, but there are also clear differences. In the former, we may interview staff and patients and review pathways. In the latter, we may focus more on what parents feel can be done to help them arrive at informed decisions. It follows that in each we may have recourse to different theories and evidence bases (*Domain 2—Psychological science*). This in turn leads us to consider those things that determine or constrain the operation of the organisation, such as legal requirements, policy, and finance (*Domain 3—Policy, legal, technical, and operational context*). We can then move onto the specific cultural and interpersonal contexts; for example: How is leadership conceived? How can staff identify proposals for service improvement that impact on the project (Domain 4—*Organisational, cultural, and interpersonal contexts)*? Finally, all of this must be fitted within the core consultancy processes of agreeing the terms, remuneration, intended outcomes, reporting, duration, and governance of a project (Fig. 5.1).

In this way, consultancy in health psychology should be perceived as a dynamic and complex activity that is responsive to the problem, context, and method to be successful, while using core and additional skills, techniques, and processes. Influencing the client ethically is essential, encompassing how relationships are built, how trust is maintained, and how project outcomes

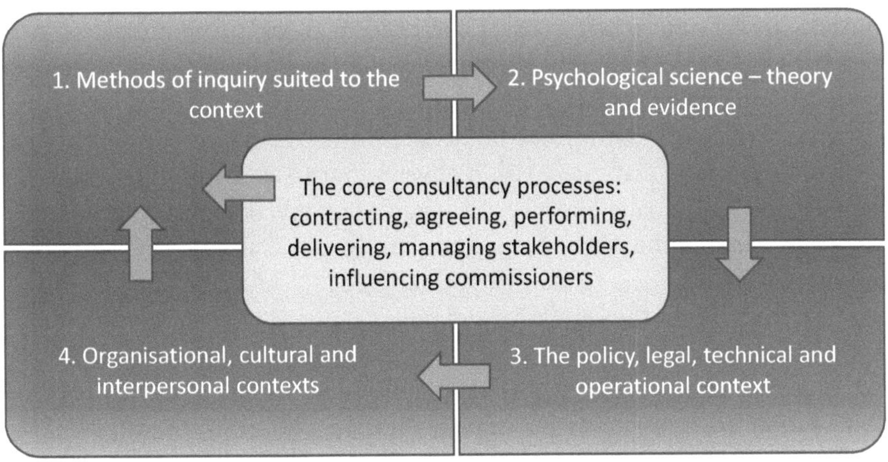

Fig. 5.1 A schema of domains of knowledge needed in psychology consulting

and proposed actions are carried forward after the consultant's work is completed. In our experience, this process is usually iterative and may involve going from one domain to another during the project. It follows that we regard all of these as having ethical dimensions. The use of resources (funding, people's time, and good will) needs to be kept in mind by the consultant as well as how the project will be implemented.

Understanding the Wider Context

Imagine that you have been approached by a potential client from a local authority in the UK. The authority is keen for you to work on an active travel project aiming to increase walking and cycling rates. Active travel forms part of their sustainability agenda and they have recognised that changing people's behaviour will form a key component of their approach. This will be part of their response to the UK Government's Active Travel agenda (Department for Transport, 2023).

While active travel is directly related to health psychology, in terms of increasing physical activity and the wider health and well-being agenda, it also sits within a much larger strategic picture. Firstly, active travel has a similar but distinct policy and legislative context in each of the four devolved nations of the UK. In each nation, this spans the spatial planning, transport infrastructure, sustainability, and health policy agendas (Department for Transport, 2023; Welsh Government, 2021). Secondly, there are roles for a complex network of national and local organisations (Department for Transport, 2023; Welsh Government, 2021). Thirdly, the funding landscape can be complex. A consultant working in active travel will need to consider the impact of local and national strategies and stakeholders (including citizens) in addition to evidence and theory.

In the UK, local authorities hold data on active travel due to national requirements and collaborate with highways, transport, planning, communications, and data analysis teams. Although your psychological expertise is a key component of the project, as a consultant you will also need to work with several key stakeholders to inform your approach. There are three main reasons for this. Firstly, the legislative and policy framework for almost all public services requires some form of stakeholder involvement (Wyard et al., 2023). Secondly, stakeholders have knowledge and power, which can facilitate, or act as a barrier to, the successful implementation of any project (Hooge & Dalmasso, 2015; Bourne, 2016; Miller & Oliver, 2015). This is often critical to success or failure (Aaltonen et al., 2015). The third reason is that there may be strong ethical and legal considerations for stakeholder engagement. For example, if changes to a local service are proposed, then the law may say citizens have a right to be engaged in decision-making (Local Government Association, 2019). In our experience, it is always best to consider that you have gaps in your knowledge, and it is unlikely that you will have expertise in each of the areas forming the larger picture. Therefore, you will need to identify where you can find the information needed to deliver this project. This is one of the reasons why we developed the schema at Fig. 5.1 to help guide us through the work of consulting.

It should be apparent from this that a foundational schema is important to help the consultant navigate this complexity. But that still leaves some gaps in knowledge and skills to be addressed. We suggest three approaches to addressing this, including developing the skills, working with multidisciplinary colleagues in the project team, and acquiring additional expertise.

Developing Complementary Skills

Thriving in the contemporary landscape of consultancy demands the cultivation of a dynamic and adaptable skill set, as well as awareness of where your skills and competencies end. While consultants may enter projects armed with core competencies, the policy and practice of the organisational landscape is constantly changing. As a result, the nature of the policy and organisational environments we work in mandate continuous learning and the acquisition of new skills. Some skills may naturally align with the consultant's existing expertise, such as learning about a new domain of psychological science. Other skill sets, such as change management, the development of clinical pathways, and standard operating procedures, may need to be purposively developed through formal learning, research, or in collaboration with project teams and stakeholders. The benefits of the latter approach are that not everything needs to be undertaken by the consultant. Applying skill sets already available in stakeholder's areas of expertise can build ownership of a project. Using in-house skills can be more efficient for the organisation, allowing the consultant to complete the project and transition to the next one, with resources in place for ongoing support. Among all these skills, we contend, for all the reasons we discuss above, that effective stakeholder management emerges as the linchpin across the project life cycle (Errida & Lotfi, 2021). The literature on consulting strongly emphasises that good stakeholder analysis and management skills are critically important for consultants to develop. A resource such as the *Art of Change Making* (Atkinson et al., 2015), which can be sourced free of charge, provides a range of practical tools to support this. The UK government also provides a brief free online continuous professional development course on effective stakeholder management (Government Communication Service, 2021), which can be a helpful place to start for new consultants.

As part of our formal training in the UK context, future psychologists are taught to develop a rigorous scientific approach from our first lecture as undergraduates. Health psychology trainees are invited to develop important transferrable skills, such as critical thinking, research methods, and academic report writing, among others. For health psychology in particular, as trainees progress through to professional training up to doctoral level, their skills extend into intervention development, undertaking systematic reviews, teaching and training, research design and implementation, and consultancy skills. The consultancy module in professional training aims to develop in trainees the skills necessary to successfully negotiate, undertake, evaluate, and report on consultancy work. But we hope it is evident from the above argument that our skills need to develop further to deal with situations we may not have faced before. Similarly, when learning to drive a car, we are taught the basics, but our learning continues when we drive independently and encounter weather and road conditions that are not familiar to us from our first lessons!

Harnessing Project Management in Consultancy

As part of continuing professional development for psychologists engaged in consulting, it is helpful to review our existing skills, to identify any gaps, and to consider how we can fill them. We use the foundational schema provided in Fig. 5.1 as a way of reflecting on this as we work on projects. For instance, working as a consultant will require you to communicate effectively with people key to the success of your project. That list of people may vary from operational stakeholders to senior managers and board-level executives, including elected representatives, as well as communicating with external stakeholders, laypeople, and service users. In our experience, this is especially the case when working with local municipal authorities and public bodies.

Working with a variety of stakeholders may mean enhancing your communication skills, including delivering presentations (especially if you have not delivered a presentation since you left university). It can also require you to reach out to people who are experts or who specialise in topics where you may have limited experience, such as internal communications and public relations functions. It may be that some of these skills are available through the client's organisation; most large organisations will have a communications lead whose role is to understand how to communicate internally with staff and externally with service users and the public.

It is also worth thinking about developing your skills in other related areas to operate effectively in the world of consultancy. We have found project management methodology to be a particularly complementary skill set. Use of project management tools can help you plan and demonstrate to the client the resources, time, and support you need to deliver a particular piece of work while avoiding scope creep, a common issue in consultancy (Ajmal et al., 2019). This is an approach that we use regularly, especially with large or complex commissions, and especially where we feel the commissioner (client) needs to be clear on the activities being delivered. A good project management approach can protect you from the changes which sometimes come from clients who may not have considered the constraints in changing timelines. Project management includes several skills needed for effective consultancy, such as relationship building and stakeholder analysis (Silacheva, 2019; Wickham & Wilcock, 2016).

The contract or agreement between you and the client should detail the expectations, roles, and responsibilities of each of the parties involved at every stage of the project. This approach is particularly helpful when working on projects with multiple components and deliverables, and those that are large in scale (e.g., needing multiple people delivering different aspects) as it provides a framework for detailing key milestones, risks, and project governance, reducing the chance of the project going off the rails. In our experience, this does not mean you have to become trained to PRINCE2® (Projects In Controlled Environments) standards, which is ideal for very large projects, such as whole-scale organisational change or major construction projects (PRINCE2.com, 2024). Using key project management tools, such as those provided free by The Ohio State University (2025) or undertaking a basic course may well be sufficient. It is important to consider how other key skill sets such as this can enhance your practice and support you to grow your consultancy business.

Working as Part of the Multidisciplinary Team

Collaborating across professional disciplines is a potent catalyst for generating innovative solutions. As the challenges organisations face become increasingly intricate, the limitations of disciplinary boundaries become more evident. The multidisciplinary approach underscores the importance of blending varied perspectives, leading to novel insights and solutions that would otherwise remain obscured within traditional monodisciplinary approaches (Levain, 2023).

Client project teams linking in with consultants are likely to be made up of key stakeholders, each with useful insights, perspectives, and skills that consultants can draw upon. The interpersonal skills of the consultant will be the key to success here. Clients seek support and innovation to tackle their challenges. In our experience, clients rarely (if ever) contact you because things are going well (except possibly for training). Consultants, therefore, need to be sensitive to the challenges clients face and work with them in a non-judgemental way. When exploring an issue with a client, it can be surprising and sometimes shocking to see where the gaps in the data lie. Consultants need to ensure they respond appropriately when they find themselves in this situation. For instance, we were asked to work with a mentoring service for young people not in employment or education, aiming to improve their health, education, and employment prospects. Our discovery/enquiry work revealed no data was being collected on participant demographics or outcomes. While evaluation may come as second nature to trained psychologists, this is not the case for many clients. Gaps in data often stem from historical issues, such as missing key performance indicators, the need to demonstrate impact, and a lack of evaluation and data analysis skills.

The above example demonstrates part of the reason why our skill set is so valuable and, in this case, setting outcomes, and performance indicators helped the mentors demonstrate their impact and undertake quality improvement work. Many organisations do not have the resources to implement quality improvement (Appelbaum & Steed, 2005; Alagoz et al., 2018), or they may have tried but have not seen the desired improvement from their efforts. Psychologists can bring skills to this that complement other disciplines, such as using the evidence to understand the problem, developing interventions, and evaluating their outcomes. In relation to psychologists and the wider behavioural science community, most organisations do not have an in-house resource to draw upon. This creates a gap in the market in which psychologists can add value to organisational outcomes. When we undertake a new project, we need to understand that it forms part of a wider system (e.g., policy contexts, stakeholders, and partner organisations). Part of our work is to understand that system and the dynamics between each part.

Balancing Expertise, Confidence, and Humility

In our experience, a successful consultant needs to strike a delicate balance between expertise, confidence, and humility. Schein (2016) describes this approach as one in which the consultant is genuinely curious, committed to helping the client, and authentically caring about their situation. In our experience, taking a humble approach as a consultant can help you to understand the existing knowledge and skills within the organisation (Anand et al., 2019). Humility can help overcome stakeholder fear or resistance and challenge the assumption that the consultant has all the answers. It can also enable you to reflect on and recognise where your skills and competencies are strong and where they need development. This can result in a more inclusive and rewarding experience for all parties as willingness to consider input from diverse disciplines often leads to richer and more innovative outcomes (Norcross & Manning, 2019). Consultants must be astute in recognising and harnessing the skills that clients, stakeholders, and local experts bring to the table to effectively take the project forward (Carucci & Tetenbaum, 2000). By strategically aligning such diverse skill sets, consultants can amplify their collective impact. As consultants traverse the path towards effective consultancy, appreciating the assets (e.g., knowledge, skills, and connections) within an organisation or project team should be core to their practice.

Trust is the cornerstone of collaborative consultancy work, serving as the foundation for transparent communication and shared responsibility for outcomes. Trust empowers consultants to navigate the intricate landscapes of relationships, inspiring a collective commitment to project success. This approach entails recognising and harnessing the inherent strengths of clients and their teams. By doing so, consultants maximise the potential for collaboration, fostering innovation and effective problem-solving. Humility as part of consulting empowers consultants to acknowledge the expertise of others and view every engagement as an opportunity for mutual learning and growth. This not only nurtures collaborative relationships but also contributes to the creation of solutions that are comprehensive and impactful.

Bridging the Gap: Knowledge Transfer in Consultancy

The sharing of knowledge, skills, or processes from the consultant to the client is the core of any consultancy contract (Block, 2011). That said, wielding expertise, in a way that supports knowledge sharing, requires a delicate touch to avoid unintentionally creating barriers that hinder effective collaboration.

As a scientific discipline, we are evidence-driven, passionate about creating new knowledge, eager to develop innovative solutions, and share best practice. While all of this may be important and exciting for us, in our experience, it may be less so to our clients, who are usually much more outcome focused. Therefore, if we assume an 'expert role', where we are the expert on the task (Schein, 1999), we risk disengaging clients with the technical detail of our discipline rather than empowering them to make the required change. The process of consulting itself, conceptualised in the schema we advocate in Fig. 5.1, is one way of doing this. We should deliver, where possible, a project which enables our client to take the action needed to address the problem they came to us with.

While this process may sound straightforward, language can be a real barrier here. It is surprisingly common, both within and across organisations, for different terminology to be used for the same thing. This can be confusing and create a lack of clarity when trying to define a problem or find a solution! Therefore, a key part of our role is to act as translators, taking the evidence, simplifying it, and explaining in a way that is pertinent to the organisational context. Outside academic contexts, research protocols and academic presentations/reports may provide too much information or be in the wrong format for clients. In such cases, clients may not have the time to absorb a detailed discussion of the literature, or to learn complex psychological theories and frameworks, even if they are interested in them. This is often due to time constraints and other work pressures rather than a lack of engagement. So, it is part of our job to make it easy for the client to understand the evidence behind our proposals and interventions.

Fostering Collaborative Engagement

In our view, balancing expertise, confidence, and humility in a multidisciplinary context in consultancy is achievable; in addition to using the schema in Fig. 5.1, we work to build trust with the client and relevant stakeholders. Schein (2013) reflects on the importance of trust and what he has termed 'humble enquiry'. We believe that this involves respecting the knowledge and power of others in the room. By doing this, we are acknowledging that we do not have all the answers. It may well be that you feel you have a grasp of what the potential issues and solutions could be, but telling people what you know will only take you so far. By respecting others expertise, and hearing what they have to say, we can gather additional information and allow colleagues to share their knowledge and skills as part of the project. Ultimately, you will be reliant on the engagement of others for success, regardless of whether you are an internal or an external consultant.

We have found that the best approach to securing engagement is to start out by openly acknowledging where our expertise sits, and its limitations, as part of introducing yourself to those you will be working with. For instance, when working with NHS clinical colleagues to scope a project on the early identification of urinary tract infections (UTIs), we were very clear that the clinicians had the clinical and operational expertise, and we as health psychologists had the psychological/behaviour change expertise. In other areas, there may be more overlap, but there are always boundaries. Our approach is to map our skill set onto those of others to develop a solution. By opening the conversation in this way, that is, through an open discussion about who has which skill sets and knowledge, it opens the door to a collaborative approach. This approach recognises that you will need the client's input into the process rather than the consultant bringing all the answers. Also, by working with others you can 'grease the wheels' of collaboration, encouraging others to share more information and resources. When people feel devalued or excluded, they may disengage and create barriers, making it harder for us as consultants to obtain the information needed to deliver projects in a timely fashion.

Acquiring Additional Skills and Expertise

If you lack the skills or expertise to deliver aspects of a project, seek additional support. For example, a complex project may require project management skills you do not have. If these skills are not available within the project team, you will need to bring someone in with the necessary expertise and include the cost in your contract. It is important to consider the skills and expertise needed for delivery at the outset, otherwise you can find yourself with an unwieldly project, at risk of failing, and being out of pocket! There are, in addition, times when reaching out to other experts in the field can provide specialist input and supplement your knowledge. In our experience, clients often see consultants as experts with all the answers. However, no one can be an expert in everything! During one of our early projects, we were the consultants on an environmental sustainability project to reduce the impact of climate change on the health of residents. One of the directors said 'here come the experts' as we entered the room. This was unhelpful because it created an impression that we had all the knowledge and skills to address the issue. To staff in the room who were already working on this project, it came across as an implicit statement that their skill set was deficient. This can be terrifying and overwhelming for the consultant in equal measure!

For an early career health psychologist working in consulting, managing others' expectations can be daunting. It took us time to realise that you do not have to be an expert in the client's specific field, only in your own. We have found that mapping our skills on to the clients effectively bridges the gap (well most of it anyway!). Where additional expertise is needed, we have reached out to experts on topics such as stakeholder engagement, digital interventions, environmental science, and sociology to inform our project specification and methods. Where the ask is not great, we have found that experts are very happy to talk to us and offer some guidance. If the 'ask' is more significant, there may be a need to purchase some of their time to ensure you have the required support. These are factors that we budget for across our projects, which gives us the flexibility to bring in additional resource as needed.

Building Client Confidence

If we are aiming to create meaningful change, we need the confidence and support of the client. This can be measured formally through project review meetings and confirming progress, which is where project management tools can be useful. But it can also be measured informally through sense-checking with the client that they are happy and maintaining a good relationship. The client will ultimately influence whether our recommendations are implemented or not. Therefore, there is an art to working with clients rather than 'doing unto them'. We have come across 'experts' saying, 'we have all this fantastic evidence and knowledge, why aren't people banging down the door for us to help them?' The answer here is simple. In general, we have found that clients are not concerned about whether you have a vast portfolio of research and interventions, and they do not generally have time to go searching for experts. The following are the things that they are concerned about when commissioning a project: Do they (the consultants) have the expertise I need? What is their reputation? Will I be able to work with them? Will they save me time? Can I trust them? (Block, 2011); and, of course, how much will this cost? It has been reported that 70% of a consultant's work comes from repeat business or recommendations from others (Kometa et al., 1996; Bennett, 2012). Building positive working relationships with clients is crucial for ongoing and repeat business. Therefore, mapping your skills onto others provides a useful opportunity to acknowledge and work with other experts, while developing your skills and understanding in the process.

From Self-doubt to Strength

Up to this point, we have discussed the importance of collaboration and taking an approach that identifies and utilises the knowledge and skills of others as part of multidisciplinary working. While that is undoubtedly one of the keys to success, it is also useful to note that some health psychologists, particularly those in the early stages of their career, may lack confidence. Experienced health psychologists have also often told us that they feel the same way, particularly in relation to consultancy work. Perceiving these experiences positively as a continual reminder to review and reflect on your skills and competency is, in our experience, a good way of turning this lack of confidence into genuine humility and flexibility. Psychologists are skilled professionals with a sought-after skill set and therefore should be confident in sharing what they can bring to the process. If we are not forthcoming in sharing our skills and experience, clients will not have the confidence to commission us. Therefore, we believe that being underconfident can be just as damaging to the relationship as being overconfident.

Reflective Practice

Taking time to reflect on your practice is part of becoming a high-performing consultant. Consultants should regularly engage in reflective practice, refining their approaches, and taking insights from previous commissions. This process not only nurtures personal growth but also enhances the quality of consultancy services offered. As psychologists, reflective practice is an important pillar of our work. It is an activity that we regularly use when undertaking research, particularly qualitative, or working clinically with clients. It is equally helpful when applied to consultancy work. Ahead of starting a new project, it is worth reflecting on what your assumptions are and how these assumptions will impact on your work (Block, 2011). Taking the time to do this will help you avoid pitfalls and sense check your approach. Clients value consultants who they perceive as genuinely wanting to help them to resolve an issue, and who are not trying to manipulate them or overstate their expertise. If the consultant is trying to be manipulative, or if they are motivated by self-interest, the client will pick up on this and it can undermine the relationship (Carucci & Tetenbaum, 2000). Taking time to consider your approach can help ensure that you can support a positive relationship with the client and the wider project group.

Conclusion

We live in a time where complex systems create pressure on resources and strains on funding are the norm. Organisations are actively looking to psychologists to apply their unique skill set, providing an alternative lens through which to address complex issues. The opportunity for psychologists to undertake consultancy work has never been greater. Our training as health psychologists provides us with a strong basis for starting on this journey, but the skills needed to thrive in this arena extend beyond our formal training. Other skills, from establishing and building relationships to managing clients and project management, will be needed to deliver effective outcomes. These could be skills consultants wish to develop themselves, skills that can be sourced through the client's organisation, or additional expertise that will need to be resourced. Approaching each consultancy commission with the skills and confidence our training provides, along with the humility to recognise the limitations of our knowledge and the respect for others' expertise, will ultimately create transformative change. Learning to navigate the intricacies of working as a consultant is an ongoing process. From our experience, this is an art rather than a science. There is an opportunity for consultant psychologists to position themselves as catalysts for meaningful change outside of the traditional realms of academia and clinical practice. This can be achieved by extending our skill set allowing us to navigate the complex systems we work in, bringing innovation and impact to the organisations and individuals we work with.

Questions for Reflection

1. How can you apply the principles of multidisciplinary collaboration to your professional practice?
2. In what ways can you balance expertise, confidence, and humility in your consultancy work?
3. How can you continuously develop your skills and knowledge to adapt to the evolving demands of consultancy work?

Competing Interests The authors have no competing interested to declare that are relevant to this chapter.

References

Aaltonen, K., Kujala, J., Havela, L., & Savage, G. (2015). Stakeholder dynamics during the project front-end: The case of nuclear waste repository projects. *Project Management Journal, 46*(6), 15–41. https://doi.org/10.1002/pmj.21549

Ajmal, M., Khan, M., & Al-Yafei, H. (2019). Exploring factors behind project scope creep – stakeholders' perspective. *International Journal of Managing Projects in Business, 13*(3), 483–504. https://doi.org/10.1108/ijmpb-10-2018-0228

Alagoz, E., Chih, M., Hitchcock, M., Brown, R., & Quanbeck, A. (2018). The use of external change agents to promote quality improvement and organizational change in healthcare organizations: A systematic review. *BMC Health Services Research, 18*(1). https://doi.org/10.1186/s12913-018-2856-9

Anand, A., Walsh, I., & Moffett, S. (2019). Does humility facilitate knowledge sharing? Investigating the role of humble knowledge inquiry and response. *Journal of Knowledge Management, 23*(6), 1218–1244. https://doi.org/10.1108/jkm-06-2018-0353

Appelbaum, S. H., & Steed, A. J. (2005). The critical success factors in the client-consulting relationship. *Journal of Management Development, 24*(1), 68–93. https://doi.org/10.1108/02621710510572362

Atkinson, J., Loftus, E., & Jarvis, J. (2015). *The art of change making*. The Leadership Centre. https://www.leadershipcentre.org.uk/wp-content/uploads/2016/02/The-Art-of-Change-Making.pdf

Begley, P., & Sheard, S. (2021). From "Honeymoon period" to "Stable marriage": The rise of management consultants in British health Policymaking. *Bulletin of the History of Medicine, 95*(2), 227–255. https://doi.org/10.1353/bhm.2021.0031

Bennett, R. J. (2012). Government advice services for SMEs: recognising and managing expectations-lessons from British experience. In R. A. Blackburn & M. Schaper (Eds.), *Government, SMEs and entrepreneurship development: Policy, practice and challenges*. Routledge.

Block, P. (2011). *Flawless consulting: A guide to getting your expertise used.* John Wiley & Sons.

Bourne, L. (2016). *Advising upwards: A framework for understanding and engaging senior management stakeholders*. CRC Press.

Bryan, L. K., & Pickren, W. (2020). *Historical perspectives in industrial and organizational psychology*. Routledge.

Carucci, R. A., & Tetenbaum, T. J. (2000). *The value-creating consultant: How to build and sustain lasting client relationships*. AMACOM/American Management Association.

Department for Transport. (2023, August 3). *Framework document: Active travel England.* https://www.gov.uk/government/publications/active-travel-england-framework-document-for-working-with-department-for-transport/framework-document-active-travel-england

Drucker, P. F. (1979). Why management consultants? In Z. Melvin & R. G. Greenwood (Eds.), *The evolving science of management: the collected papers of Harold Smiddy and papers by others in his honor*. AMACOM.
Drury, J. (2024, May 15). *Covid – 'behaviour matters, psychology matters'*. British Psychological Society. https://www.bps.org.uk/psychologist/covid-behaviour-matters-psychology-matters
Errida, A., & Lotfi, B. (2021). The determinants of organizational change management success: Literature review and case study. *International Journal of Engineering Business Management, 13*, 184797902110162. https://doi.org/10.1177/18479790211016273
Ford, J., & Harding, N. (2020). Performative seduction: How management consultants influence practices of leadership. *International Journal of Public Leadership, 17*(3), 222–235. https://doi.org/10.1108/ijpl-07-2020-0062
Government Communication Service. (2021, April 23). *Ensuring effective stakeholder engagement*. https://gcs.civilservice.gov.uk/publications/ensuring-effective-stakeholder-engagement/
Hayes, T. L., Kaylor, L. E., & Oltman, K. A. (2020). Coffee and controversy: How applied psychology can revitalize sexual harassment and racial discrimination training. *Industrial and Organizational Psychology, 13*(2), 117–136. https://doi.org/10.1017/iop.2019.84
Hooge, S., & Dalmasso, C. (2015). Breakthrough R&D stakeholders: The challenges of legitimacy in highly uncertain projects. *Project Management Journal, 46*(6), 54–73. https://doi.org/10.1002/pmj.21554
House of Lords Select Committee on the Environment and Climate Change. (2022). *In our hands: Behaviour change for climate and environmental goals*. UK Parliament. https://publications.parliament.uk/pa/ld5803/ldselect/ldenvcl/64/6402.htm
Kirkpatrick, I., Sturdy, A. J., Alvarado, N. R., Blanco-Oliver, A., & Veronesi, G. (2019). The impact of management consultants on public service efficiency. *Policy & Politics, 47*(1), 77–95. https://doi.org/10.1332/030557318x15167881150799
Kometa, S. T., Olomolaiye, P. O., & Harris, F. C. (1996). A review of client-generated risks to project consultants. *International Journal of Project Management, 14*(5), 273–279. https://doi.org/10.1016/0263-7863(96)84510-8
Levain, R. (2023). Embracing the power of the multidisciplinary approach breaking boundaries and fostering innovation. *JBR Journal of Interdisciplinary Medicine and Dental Science, 6*(3), 39–42. https://doi.org/10.37532/2376032X.2023.6(3).39-42
Local Government Association. (2019). *Do I need to consult?* https://www.local.gov.uk/sites/default/files/documents/Do%20I%20need%20to%20consult.pdf
Local Government Association. (2025). *Transformation and Behaviour Change Leads Group*. https://www.local.gov.uk/oursupport/transformation/transformation-and-behaviour-change-leads-group

Martin, S., & Ferrere, A. (2017, December 4). Building behavioral science capability in your company. *Harvard Business Review*. https://hbr.org/2017/12/building-behavioral-science-capability-in-your-company

Mather, M., Pettigrew, L. M., & Navaratnam, S. (2022). Barriers and facilitators to clinical behaviour change by primary care practitioners: A theory-informed systematic review of reviews using the theoretical domains framework and behaviour change wheel. *Systematic Reviews, 11*(1). https://doi.org/10.1186/s13643-022-02030-2

Mazzucato, M., & Collington, R. (2023). *The big con: How the consulting industry weakens our businesses, Infantilizes our governments and warps our economies*. Random House.

McManus, J. (2024, May 15). *Covid – 'behaviour matters, psychology matters'*. British Psychological Society. https://www.bps.org.uk/psychologist/covid-behaviour-matters-

Miller, D., & Oliver, M. (2015). *Engaging stakeholders for project success. PMI White Paper*. Project Management Institute. https://www.pmi.org/learning/library/engaging-stakeholders-project-success-11199

Mosonyi, S., Empson, L., & Gond, J. (2019). Management consulting: Towards an integrative framework of knowledge, identity, and power. *International Journal of Management Reviews, 22*(2), 120–149. https://doi.org/10.1111/ijmr.12218

Norcross, M. A., & Manning, M. R. (2019). *Research in organizational change and development*. (A. B. Shani & D. A. Noumair, Eds.). Emerald Group Publishing.

PRINCE2.com. (2024). *What is PRINCE2? The definition, history & benefits | USA*. https://www.prince2.com/uk/what-is-prince2

Schein, E. H. (1999). *Process consultation revisited: Building the helping relationship*. Process Consultation.

Schein, E. H. (2013). *Humble enquiry: The gentle art of asking instead of telling*. Berrett-Koehler Publishers.

Schein, E. H. (2016). *Humble consulting: How to provide real help faster*. Berrett-Koehler Publishers.

Silacheva, M. (2019). Exploring skills and competencies for consultants. *Management Consulting Journal, 2*(2), 35–42. https://doi.org/10.2478/mcj-2019-0008

Sturdy, A. (2021). The governance of management consultancy Use: Practices, problems, and possibilities. In C. Hurl & A. Vogelpohl (Eds.), *Professional service firms and politics in a global era: Public policy, private expertise*. Springer Nature.

Sturdy, A., Handley, K., Clark, T., & Fincham, R. (2010). *Management consultancy: Boundaries and knowledge in action*. OUP Oxford.

Talkhan, H., Stewart, D., Mcintosh, T., Ziglam, H., Abdulrouf, P. V., Al-Hail, M., Diab, M., & Cunningham, S. (2020). The use of theory in the development and evaluation of behaviour change interventions to improve antimicrobial prescribing: A systematic review. *Journal of Antimicrobial Chemotherapy, 75*(9), 2394–2410. https://doi.org/10.1093/jac/dkaa154

The Ohio State University. (2025). Project Management. Office of Technology and Digital Innovation. https://it.osu.edu/project-management

Welsh Government. (2021). *Policy and strategy: Active travel act guidance.* https://www.gov.wales/sites/default/files/publications/2022-01/active-travel-act-guidance.pdf

Wickham, L., & Wilcock, J. (2016). *Management consulting: Delivering an effective project.* Pearson.

Wyard, M., Hirschmann, J., & Thomas, R. (2023, November 28). *Public sector consultations.* Local Government Lawyer. https://www.localgovernmentlawyer.co.uk/governance/314-governance-a-risk-articles/55748-public-sector-consultations#_ftnref1

6

Conducting Consultancy with Vulnerable Clients

Alison Killen

Introduction

Health psychologists and behavioural scientists working in consultancy undertake projects to improve the health of individuals, groups, or populations. This makes it almost inevitable that they will work directly or indirectly with people who are vulnerable or potentially vulnerable. This chapter guides practitioners towards identifying vulnerable people within their consultancy work and making accommodations to enable their participation.

I am a United Kingdom (UK)-based health psychologist. My interest and expertise concerning vulnerability stem from my work with people living with dementia. This is both as a university researcher designing and evaluating interventions and as a practitioner providing dementia assessments and post-diagnostic support within the National Health Service (NHS). I have conducted a variety of consultancy projects with vulnerable service users, most recently reporting on how people with disabilities experience home care services for a local authority-funded organisation. I have also evaluated a

Supplementary Information The online version contains supplementary material available at https://doi.org/10.1007/978-3-031-94529-8_6.

A. Killen (✉)
NIHR Newcastle Biomedical Research Centre, Newcastle University, Newcastle upon Tyne, UK
e-mail: alison.killen@newcastle.ac.uk

R. Brady et al. (eds.), *The Palgrave Handbook of Consultancy in Health Psychology*,
https://doi.org/10.1007/978-3-031-94529-8_6

university psychoeducational programme for caregivers and worked with an ambulance service to assess the impact of changes to hospital transport.

In this chapter, I explore how vulnerability can be defined in the context of health inequalities. I suggest ways to increase your awareness and understanding of vulnerable people within your consultancy activities and explain why a nuanced approach is needed when identifying any group of people as vulnerable. I then propose accommodations or strategies you can implement for people with specific vulnerabilities. This focuses on ethnicity or race, religion and belief, age, and disability, and includes a case study focused on dementia. Finally, I address the issue of personal vulnerability.

This chapter contains several references to the *consultancy framework for health psychologists* (Brady & Varkonyi-Sepp, 2025) described in Chap. 3. This depicts how consultancy is practised by psychologists and behavioural scientists working in health. It contains five key processes: enquiry, building and maintaining relationships, negotiation and contracting, planning and managing delivery, and evaluation. These processes are distinct, but not sequential or linear; rather, they overlap, being revisited as a project progresses. Identifying vulnerable people and finding ways to accommodate their needs are important considerations throughout each process of the framework.

Within this chapter, I use 'client' to refer to the individual, group or organisation that commissions and approves payment for the consultant's services and 'ultimate client' (Schein, 1997) to denote service users who are the ultimate beneficiaries of consultancy. 'Stakeholders' covers the other individuals or groups with whom a consultant engages, or who may be affected by a project process or outcome (Kerzner, 2017). This chapter predominantly focuses on vulnerable ultimate clients.

Identifying and Understanding the Needs of Vulnerable People in Consultancy

Vulnerability may be apparent by someone's physical presentation, or invisible until disclosed. It has become a significant topic in political and social discussion, used strategically by politicians, charities and social commentators to attract resources, policy interest and public concern (World Health Organisation, 2014). For the purposes of this chapter, health inequalities, which are avoidable, unfair and systematic differences in health between distinct groups of people (King's Fund, 2022), are considered as a proxy for vulnerability.

The Public Health England report '*Addressing health inequalities through collaborative action*' (Public Health England, 2021) built on the influential Marmot reviews (Marmot, 2010, 2020) to identify the features associated with poorer health outcomes. These were categorised into four overlapping domains: socio-economic deprivation, geography, protected characteristics under the UK Equality Act (2010) and vulnerable or inclusion health groups. Inclusion health describes people who are socially excluded and typically experience multiple interacting risk factors for poor health, such as stigma, discrimination, poverty, violence and complex trauma (NHS England, 2023). Examples within each domain are shown in Table 6.1.

Within consultancy, a nuanced approach is essential to avoid making stereotypical assumptions that vulnerability necessarily applies to everyone within a particular domain. For instance, as the Office for Health Improvement and Disparities (2022) highlights, although many protected characteristics are associated with health inequalities, having a protected characteristic is by no means inevitably synonymous with being vulnerable. Such assumptions risk reducing both the perceived and actual agency of the individual or group and depicting them as powerless 'others' in need of protection (Munari et al., 2021). Social context should not be overlooked, including the presence of protective factors and how experiences spanning multiple domains magnify vulnerability. A client in secure employment who self-manages a health condition with their supportive partner is clearly less vulnerable than someone living with a similar condition who is unemployed, insecurely housed and socially isolated.

Identifying the needs of vulnerable individuals and understanding how best to meet them is potentially critical to the success of your project.

Table 6.1 Domains of health inequality (Public Health England, 2021)

Protected characteristics	• Age, disability, gender reassignment, marriage and civil partnership, pregnancy and maternity, race, religion or belief, sex, sexual orientation
Socio-economic deprived population	• Includes impact of wider determinants, for example education, low income, occupation, unemployment, and housing
Inclusion health and vulnerable groups	• For example, Gypsy, Roma, Travellers and Boater communities, people experiencing homelessness, offenders, former offenders, and sex workers
Geography	• Population composition, built and natural environment, levels of social connectedness, features of specific geographies such as urban, rural, and coastal

Neglecting to signify your intention to make appropriate accommodations could result in not being awarded a prospective project, whilst failure to make agreed accommodations could result in the breakdown of a consultancy relationship. In addition, depending on the jurisdiction, making accommodations for vulnerable people may also be a legal necessity, although specific legislation is outside the scope of this chapter.

One key success factor for ideal client-consultant engagement is making 'an investment up front in learning the client's environment' (Applebaum & Steed, 2005, p. 77). Schein (2013, p. 2) views this as taking place through 'humble inquiry'. He describes this as 'the fine art of drawing someone out, of asking questions to which you do not know the answer, of building a relationship based on curiosity and interest in the other person'. This is more than just a way of posing questions, it is an attitude that includes better listening and better responding to what people are telling us.

Vulnerable Clients

Clients commissioning health psychologist consultants are generally based in health and social care. They can be within the private, public and third sector, and vary in size from individuals to large international organisations. Their legal structure includes public or limited companies, charities, public services, social enterprise companies and academic organisations. The focus of their operations is highly variable. It includes healthcare provision, manufacture of healthcare products, healthcare system design, education and training. Any of these commissioning clients could be vulnerable, but in a way which bears no relevance to the work they are commissioning.

Conversely, a client may run a business or charity which aligns with a personal health condition. In this case their lived experience may be key to their work, and relevant to the client consultant relationship. For example, a client with cerebral palsy who runs a charity supporting people with movement disorders and commissions an evaluation of access to public buildings in their city. As a consultant you could use their insights to inform your project planning and gain key information about how best to facilitate stakeholders with similar disabilities to participate.

Vulnerable Ultimate Clients

Many consultants work directly with vulnerable ultimate clients. Examples include programme evaluations of warm spaces for people experiencing homelessness, or a choir for people experiencing poor mental health. Other areas include service design such as creating an activity programme for children with a learning disability and an exercise intervention for new parents. There are also strategic projects such as working with an eating disorder charity to clarify their long-term goals or support their trustees and ultimate clients to identify a shared vision.

In my consultancy practice, I establish whether the vulnerability of ultimate clients is relevant by considering whether I need to adapt my usual working practices to enable their full participation in the project. This could be because they fit one or more of the domains shown in Table 6.1, or have difficult experiences related to the consultancy brief. As an example, when planning my initial engagement, I typically use recruitment methods such as social media, posters and flyers. However, if I were recruiting sex workers to discuss their use of clinical services, this would be unlikely to be effective. Sex workers are vulnerable and invariably socially excluded due to the stigma frequently associated with their work (Martín-Romo et al., 2023). Within this population, finding one person and building their trust and assistance to recruit others through a snowballing effect, street outreach and relevant remuneration are more likely to be successful strategies (Syvertsen et al., 2012).

Accommodations for People with Specific Vulnerabilities

The following section suggests accommodations to consider with ultimate clients who have specific vulnerabilities. These relate to ethnicity or race, religion, or belief, ageing and disability.

Ethnicity, Race, Religion, or Belief

Ethnicity, race, religion or belief do not necessarily make people vulnerable, but often overlap with people who are ethnically marginalised. In the UK, these groups are negatively impacted by institutional racism (Reynolds et al., 2021). They experience significant health and social care disparities, and a greater disease burden (Ekezie et al., 2024). Often simple accommodations can make people feel comfortable and willing to participate in your project.

One factor to consider during your initial enquiry and negotiating processes is that of showing respect to your client. Clothing is a significant factor in first impressions, and complying with any dress code helps gain trust (Sotak et al., 2024). Consider also whether there is a shared understanding of your project language and terminology. If not, this may affect responses. For example, some South Asian languages have no word for 'dementia' (Botsford & Harrison Dening, 2015). Unless this term is explained or reworded, perhaps as 'memory changes', people may fail to self-identify and not respond to requests to share their views. In addition, some members of South Asian and African communities attribute cognitive impairment to divine punishment or curse (Hossain et al., 2020; Kantawala et al., 2023). The stigma can lead to a sense of shame, and concealment. People may be reluctant to become involved unless you provide credible psychoeducation. I have previously done this in conjunction with community leaders.

When delivering consultations or engagement events, familiar environments such as places of worship or community halls can be empowering and increase participation, as can asking stakeholders to shape the format (Cook, 2002). It often works well to fund a member of the community to prepare any refreshments. This ensures they are culturally appropriate.

If you are involving people who have previously lived in countries with less commitment to confidentiality, they may be wary of disclosing health information until they fully understand how you will store or share it (Beck et al., 2016). Formal institutions such as university or hospital settings may have negative connotations and could exacerbate perceived power imbalances between you and your participants (Tembo et al., 2021). If such a venue is essential, then selecting one with a multi-faith prayer room is advisable. Some faiths have particular prayer times which may overlap with your event and could reduce attendance (Gilliat-Ray, 2005).

Awareness of the cultural calendar is important for planning consultancy activities. Within Islam, during Ramadan people fast in daylight hours so are unlikely to participate in a food-based event. Many worshippers attend Friday noon prayers, so Friday lunchtimes are likely to be a poor choice for engaging the Muslim community (Al-Tamimi et al., 2020). Jewish people are unlikely to attend events convened on Saturdays, which are their day of Sabbath observance, a 24-hour period of rest (Fortin, 2020).

Depending on the nature of the consultancy, events may need to be segregated by sex and delivered by facilitators of the same sex. Muslim women may, for example, be unable to discuss sensitive topics such as women's health with a male consultant (Rajaram & Rashidi, 1999). Factor in additional costs for this, both for consultation activities and for any stakeholder feedback.

If English is not the primary language of your stakeholders, it does not necessarily need to be the default language for your activities. At an early stage, enquire whether your client would prefer an alternative language so you can include translation and the additional costs of non-English transcription services in your cost calculations. Registered interpreters on the National Register of Public Service Interpreters in the UK have qualifications and experience and make a confidentiality commitment. Their use avoids the risks of family members translating. These include inaccurate translation, withholding aspects of the response, and adding their own interpretation (van Eechoud et al., 2017). Stakeholders may also give fictitious responses through preferring not to make their views known to their family member or considering a topic unsuitable to discuss, for example, sexual activity or cervical screening. This is particularly likely if the translator is of a different sex or gender (Rimmer, 2020).

Age

Older people, particularly the very elderly, are potentially vulnerable, especially where they have multiple co-morbidities or a life-limiting illness. They are also more likely to have mild cognitive impairment (Petersen, 2004), with the transition phase between normal cognitive ageing and early dementia thought to affect approximately 15% to 30% of older adults (Rosenberg et al., 2006). Using straightforward language for project documents and checking understanding when giving explanations is therefore essential.

Accommodations may also be needed for sensory impairments. Eye diseases that impact vision become more prevalent with age (National Eye Institute, n.d.), as do impairments in visual acuity (Owsley, 2011). Large print documents in a clear font and slide presentations with plain backgrounds will help people access information.

Age is also the strongest predictor of hearing loss, which affects one-third of adults aged 65 to74, and nearly half of those over 75 (National Institute on Deafness and Other Communication Disorders, 2018). Support strategies include encouraging a 'one speaker' principle in groups to reduce distracting or background noise. Speak clearly at a normal speed without exaggerated lip movements (Royal National Institute for Deaf People, n.d.). Talking too slowly affects sound rhythms for those with a hearing impairment. Talking too quickly is difficult for anyone compensating for hearing loss by lip reading.

Consider the impact of frailty in older ultimate clients when planning meetings and engagement events. Frailty describes an accumulation of 'deficits'. This includes the number of diseases and of medications taken, and the frequency of medical interventions (Rockwood et al., 2005). Frailty becomes increasingly common with age and affects around 10% of people aged 65 to 75, and half of those over 80 (Ashfield et al., 2010). Enquire whether people can sit comfortably in standard seating or need adjustments, and timetable regular comfort breaks. Encourage people to get up and walk whenever needed. This reduces restlessness due to low back pain in conditions commonly affecting older people such as osteoarthritis (Gupta et al., 2015), which is exacerbated by sitting for lengthy periods. Older people will benefit from clearly signposted venues which are physically accessible, level without steps, easy to find, are on a public transport route and have toilet facilities close by.

Residential care has a power imbalance which favours the staff and institutional structures of the home (Svanelöv, 2020). If your consultancy involves people with these living arrangements, the impact of the power imbalance may be reduced by involving staff and residents separately. Residents may benefit from assurances regarding the anonymity of their information and your impartiality. If practical, hosting residents at a neutral venue could result in greater willingness to engage.

Disability

The vulnerability of people living with disabilities is hugely variable. Where people are well-supported, including by assistive and digital technology, adjustments to your working practices may be unnecessary. Many ultimate clients, however, will experience the interaction of multiple factors which intensify the effects of their disabilities including social stigma, poverty, unemployment and a lack of access to physical infrastructure, information and enabling environments (Abidi & Sharma, 2014). People with a physical disability may require similar accommodations to those previously described with relation to age, although flexibility around individual needs is essential.

Some mental health conditions could make stakeholders vulnerable during consultation activities. As an example, lack of insight is a widely recognised difficulty in bipolar disorder (Dias et al., 2008). This encompasses being aware of having an illness and able to correctly attribute symptoms to that illness as well as treatment adherence (David, 1990). For a project on improving medication adherence, therefore, many people would need the contribution of a trusted companion. **Psychosis** is a mental health condition typically characterised by people perceiving or interpreting things differently from those around them. Symptoms can be triggered or enhanced by intense emotional reactions to stressful events and daily hassles (Lawlor et al., 2022). You could therefore offer accommodations such as one-to-one discussions rather than larger events. Videoconferencing is often well-received as it avoids the challenges of in-person attendance (Santesteban-Echarri et al., 2020).

In the context of neurodivergence, autistic people may find a quiet space helpful if consultation events are busy. Giving time to prepare can benefit recall and minimise the anxiety caused by unpredictable events (Robertson et al., 2018). Avoid open-ended questions, as autistic people can find these more challenging, perhaps due to difficulties with theory of mind and forming an implicit understanding of the expectations of the questioner (Kenworthy et al., 2008). Written and online tasks reduce social demands, making them less stressful alternatives to speaking (Crane et al., 2013).

Where ultimate clients are vulnerable due to an intellectual disability, consider whether they can consent to their involvement and to your proposed use of their information. A mental health condition or intellectual difficulties are not grounds for deciding that someone does not have capacity, and consent should be assumed to be present (2005 Mental Capacity Act Code of Practice, 2007). Holding an informal conversation about consent and other ethical considerations can help clarify whether someone understands the reason for a proposed activity, knows that taking part is voluntary and is aware of any possible risks and benefits. Consider including a family member or member of their support team. For some ultimate clients, making clear requests in simplified language will be sufficient to enable understanding. A visual grid of pictorial symbols such as 'Talking Mats' (Bunning et al., 2017) may be helpful if someone is familiar with this.

Ultimate clients with intellectual disabilities may take time to become comfortable with you, so consider making familiarisation visits before conducting any activities. Relevant charities are reliable sources of advice about differentiating tasks to suit various levels of understanding. This may include dividing information into smaller segments, with frequent checks of understanding before moving on (Tuffrey-Wijne, 2012). When planning your project, think about your question design. Closed questions requiring 'yes/no' answers are particularly problematic. People may appear to have understood but, instead, appear to have responded to non-verbal cues such as your tone of voice and facial expression and given the response they think is expected (Elliott & Forshaw, 2001). Questions presented in an either/or format are easier than open questions; however, they include some repeat but reversed questions to check that the person is not simply repeating the final option

(Barron & Winn, 2009). Seek advice from group leaders or family members about how best to help ultimate clients with intellectual disabilities understand what is likely to be a short-term relationship with you. This can help ease any feelings of loss they experience when your project finishes.

Case Example

A framework can help you to ensure that you have considered the needs of your vulnerable clients throughout the consultancy process. The supplementary material (ESM_6.1) includes a table of questions for reflection and actions based on the processes identified in the consultancy framework proposed by Brady & Varkonyi-Sepp (2025; see Chap. 3). This can be used to inform your work.

A Consultancy with Ultimate Clients Living with Dementia

The following case example details a consultancy I carried out with ultimate clients who were living with dementia. The accommodations I made are described using the consultancy framework for health psychologists (Brady et al. 2025; see Chap. 3). I was commissioned to evaluate the views of stakeholders who attended a charity-owned dementia hub in a large city. This was a venue where volunteers provided support, information and social activities for people with dementia and family caregivers. The prompt for the consultancy request was a planned expansion by the charity to a neighbouring city. The trustees, who included people with dementia and caregivers, were considering whether to replicate the hub in the new area or to develop new services. The client was the chair of trustees. The ultimate clients were the service users, and the client wanted their voices to be strongly represented in the decision-making.

Enquiry. During the enquiry process, I focused on gathering information about the client, stakeholders and the culture of the charity. I wanted to discover whether I was a good fit for the project and to get a sense of the service and of the client's priorities. I met with the client to establish why they had approached me and to learn about the charity. They shared their personal story of having been a caregiver for their parents who had dementia. The lack of support they had experienced drove their desire to build the charity. I spoke to a local Admiral Nurse (the name for dementia nurses in the UK) about the typical support needs of people she referred to the hub. I also contacted a national dementia charity for background information about third sector work in the city. I learnt that the hub was located in a socio-economically deprived area. Many of the ultimate clients had limited education and had previously had low-income employment. The majority were vulnerable due to poverty as well as their diagnosis or caregiving role. Following my enquiries, I felt that the consultancy would be interesting, within the scope of my practice and a good fit with my values. I therefore agreed to negotiate the work.

Building and maintaining relationships. My clinical role in a memory clinic helped me to establish trust with the client. They valued my expertise and understanding of the concerns of people with dementia and caregivers. It was important to also build trust with the ultimate clients. There could be a power disparity between us if I were viewed as an 'expert', and I wanted them to feel empowered to share their experiences. I therefore visited the dementia hub several times, in order to become familiar to the people attending. On each occasion, I briefly explained who I was and that my aim was to learn about their experiences. I also established the boundaries for my role. I was there to listen and write a report, but the trustees would make the decisions about any new services. I circulated a brief flyer which included my contact details. By my third visit, both the caregivers and people with dementia seemed comfortable, and several initiated conversations with me.

I recognised the reliance that the ultimate clients had on the service and their concerns about any changes. This was unsurprising as people living with dementia frequently experience anxiety (Starkstein et al., 2007) and family caregivers are often under significant stress, even compared with caregivers of people with other disabilities (Sheehan et al., 2021). I passed on the client's assurances that the current service was not threatened by the expansion plans.

Negotiation and contracting. I discussed the scope of the work with the client and made suggestions based on my enquiry and relationship building. As many people attending the hub were socially isolated, I felt they would engage well with an in-person consultation event in the warm and familiar space of the hub. Providing food was another potential incentive. The client assumed that my information gathering during this event would take place in one large group. I, however, negotiated several smaller groups to allow all voices to be heard. I suggested several different feedback methods, aware that people with dementia often develop spelling and writing deficits (Graham, 2000). Furthermore, participants could have physical vulnerabilities common in older adults such as arthritis and visual impairment which might hinder writing. Some participants would have left school at the age of 14 so could have limited literacy skills.

Low levels of literacy and the potential lack of capacity of the people with dementia were two vital issues for me to consider, not just for the consultation event but also for obtaining consent to the use of their feedback. During my familiarisation visits, I had explained my work in a jargon-free way and answered questions. I had encouraged the sharing of my flyer with family members, giving them the opportunity to contact me to discuss any concerns. I therefore felt that people were well-informed and that their attendance at the event would signify their willingness to participate. I intended to use stock images to maintain privacy but on arrival I asked people to complete a brief written consent to the use of their anonymised responses.

Capacity to consent is not a single issue whereby someone has or does not have consent but is specific to the situation in question. I reflected on the benefit of this concept in preventing the unethical exclusion of people with dementia. Having spent time with the group, I felt they understood the purpose of the event and could agree to the intended use of their data. However, I also asked the family member they attended with to sign a simple agreement which stated that participating was congruent with the likely choice that person would have made prior to having dementia. If anyone declined to join in particular activities, a colleague experienced in dementia support was primed to offer support while their family member was occupied.

I suggested to the client that home visits would enable me to involve caregivers unable to leave their care-recipient and anyone who found in-person events overwhelming. The client was keen to conduct these remotely to save costs. I responded that digital engagement rates among older people were still lower than the general population (Kebede et al., 2022) which could exclude people. The client therefore agreed with my home visit plans. They also agreed to payment for a sitting service where caregivers wanted to attend the event alone but could not safely leave the person with dementia. As part of my contingency planning, I developed an interview schedule for phone or digital use in case illness or personal preference required this.

The client suggested attendees arrived for the consultation event independently. Having previously discussed with caregivers the difficulties of public transport, where people with dementia found waiting difficult or were reluctant to stay seated, I explained that this could make caregivers less willing to attend and managed to negotiate for taxi provision.

The client requested feedback via a trustees' report. Three trustees had significant cognitive decline due to dementia. I felt they would be unlikely to understand a report containing the level of detail and complexity the client expected, which risked limiting their capability to fully participate in the decision-making process. The client agreed and we negotiated costs for an additional, shorter report.

Planning and managing delivery. The opportunity to have their views heard within a social gathering in the familiar setting of the hub with refreshments, peer support and reimbursed travel costs proved to be an appropriate incentive. Twenty-one people attended. The format was a two-hour event followed by afternoon tea. The programme comprised three group discussions, each lasting about 20 minutes. This reduced the likelihood of fatigue from prolonged concentration. Discussions were interspersed with brief reminiscence activities including sharing stories prompted by historical photographs of the local town and singing familiar songs. Drinks were available throughout, and there was flexibility to move around, including to a quiet room.

Participants were divided into groups of four to six people, each including a facilitator and an assistant. This small size helped people with dementia to stay involved and not become overwhelmed by multiple voices. People with dementia participated in the same group as their caregiver to minimise any separation anxiety. To support comprehension, questions were short without complex language, acronyms or abbreviations. As word-finding difficulties are characteristic of some forms of dementia, particularly Alzheimer's (Camerer-Waldecker & Supprian, 2019), I reinforced the need for patience and for giving people time to process and respond to questions. I repeated earlier reassurances that responses would be anonymised and would not jeopardise future attendance at the hub. Conversations were recorded with additional notes made by the table assistant to clarify any overlapping voices.

There were several ways to respond including posters, and post-it notes with coloured pens for writing or drawing, laminated cards with choices of facial expressions and response cards with scales to indicate how much people agreed or disagreed over various points. I had sent participants a topic guide to give them the opportunity for prior discussions at home and to make any notes in advance. Two people with dementia found this particularly helpful as they preferred their caregivers to speak for them in public.

Evaluation. Attendees were highly engaged. They offered many, predominantly positive views about the hub and were broadly supportive of expanding the provision. The following day I posted out brief, pictorial feedback. People with most dementia types are impaired in their ability to make new memories (Sabat & Warren, 2023), so I wanted to provide them with this additional prompt. To compile the modified report for the trustees with cognitive impairment I used simplified language checked via a readability tool (NHS, n.d.). This included fully spelling even frequently abbreviated words. I used a larger font, bullet points, bold text, white space and photographic illustrations. After preparing the trustees' reports, I sent further feedback to the participants in newsletter style. As additional feedback, I gave an agreed brief presentation at the start of a Singing for the Brain™ event. This regular hub activity based on group singing was developed by the Alzheimer's Society, UK (Osman et al., 2016). This presentation was attended by the client, other trustees and hub members.

For my own professional development, I requested a feedback meeting with the client. They informed me that my report had been enlightening. It had helped them to understand the most beneficial aspects of the hub and several issues to be mindful of if replicating the service. The trustees with dementia had understood the issues raised in the consultation event and had participated in the decision-making about the future direction of the charity.

Personal Vulnerability

It is crucial to be aware of whether and how personal vulnerabilities impact on your professional and ethical responsibilities as a health psychologist or behavioural scientist undertaking consultancy. In many situations, you will be in a position of strength with a client reliant on your expertise. At other times, however, if a client has several choices over who to appoint, if the extent of the work is unclear, or if you are reliant on securing the revenue-earning business, you may be the one in the vulnerable position (Kitay & Wright, 2004). You may also become temporarily vulnerable due to a physical or mental health condition, bereavement or family concerns, or have ongoing vulnerability from living with a long-term condition or disability.

A vulnerability in common with your client or ultimate client could enhance your project, giving you greater empathy, helping to build trust and generating a personal connection (Bradley et al., 2019). It could, however, reduce your ability to deliver the external perspective in the best interests of your client, which is an essential part of consultancy. It could also be a distraction which jeopardises the professionalism of your work by engendering sympathy from stakeholders or diverting attention towards you (Way & Vosloo, 2016). It is therefore wise to consider the appropriateness of any self-disclosure to your client. Your decision can be guided through supervision, the perspective of trusted peers, and personal reflection.

Reflexive practice can also be used to challenge your beliefs about the impact of a particular vulnerability based on your own value judgements and how this affects your interactions with the person or group. If you recognise these biases, try not to judge yourself harshly or self-censor from working with vulnerable people. Healthcare professionals exhibit the same levels of implicit bias as the wider population (FitzGerald & Hurst, 2017). Reflexivity and training can generate new insight and the potential for transformative actions (McIlveen, 2008; Khanal, 2024). For example, if you recognise a negative evaluation of someone on the basis of race, cultural competency training can broaden your understanding.

As a personal example, I conducted a consultancy for a wheelchair user with a spinal injury. I regarded them as vulnerable due to the limitations caused by their physical disability. Through our interactions and reflexive practice, I developed an understanding of how they perceived themselves as personally strong and resilient, albeit negatively impacted by poor infrastructure in the built environment, and transport networks which favour able-bodied people. This altered my perception.

Before accepting a consultancy with vulnerable stakeholders, consider your competence and confidence as part of your enquiry process. The websites of relevant charities can be helpful for preliminary research. Many include strong representation from people with lived experience, keen to raise awareness of how a condition or social characteristic affects them. While this work may be unremunerated, it can provide invaluable insights.

As your project progresses, working with people who are potentially vulnerable may raise difficult emotions. It may be hard to balance sensitively engaging with vulnerable stakeholders with the other demands of the consultancy. You may experience distress when meeting people living with vulnerabilities of which you had little prior understanding or who share traumatic life stories. This could lead to feelings of inadequacy, imposter syndrome, anxiety or feeling a burden of responsibility. Be reassured, these are feelings commonly experienced by people working in health consultancy and other health-related roles. They can however impact your ability to receive feedback, and affect your resiliency and well-being, (Rivera et al., 2021). It is therefore advisable to discuss them in supervision.

Summary

This chapter has predominantly focused on work with vulnerable 'ultimate clients' who are often the key beneficiaries of health consultancy. Health psychologists and behavioural scientists are ideally placed to deliver an evidence-based, responsive and inclusive service which meets their needs. The predominant learning points to guide your future practice include highlighting the domains of health inequality which will help you to identify people who may be vulnerable and require accommodations to participate. You have been offered suggestions to guide your work in relation to race, religion and belief, older age, and disability. You may also find the dementia-focused case study helpful if your work involves people with this condition. The information in the supplementary material which accompanies this chapter (ESM_6.1) provides questions and actions based around the processes described in the consultancy framework. These will help you to identify and respond to the needs of vulnerable clients. Finally, you have been prompted regarding personal vulnerabilities and situations whereby these may be activated and reminded of the need for self-care.

Conclusion

This chapter offers a guide to practice for working with vulnerable people in health consultancy. It provides vital prompts for health psychologists and behavioural scientists wishing to accommodate the needs of vulnerable clients, ultimate clients and stakeholders within their consultancy cohorts. Following these will help you to ensure that the rightful inclusion and participation of people with vulnerabilities in consultancy projects is not limited in comparison with their non-vulnerable peers.

Questions for reflection

1. What difference will consideration of whether and in what ways my clients, ultimate clients or other stakeholders are vulnerable make to the way I approach my consultancy work?
2. Am I concerned about my competency to work with any particular vulnerable group? How will I address this?
3. Do I find working with any vulnerable client group generates difficult emotions? Who could I discuss this with?
4. How could I adapt my usual working practices to better suit a vulnerable client? How would I evaluate the effectiveness of this?

Competing Interests The author has no competing interests to declare that are relevant to the content of this chapter.

References

Abidi, J., & Sharma, D. (2014). Poverty, disability, and employment: Global Perspectives from the national centre for promotion of employment for disabled people. *Career Development and Transition for Exceptional Individuals, 37*(1), 60–68. https://doi.org/10.1177/2165143413520180

Al-Tamimi, N., Qahtan, A., & Abuelzein, O. (2020). Rear zone for energy efficiency in large mosques in Saudi Arabia. *Energy and Buildings, 223*, 110148. https://doi.org/10.1016/j.enbuild.2020.110148

Applebaum, S. H., & Steed, A. J. (2005). The critical success factors in the client-consulting relationship. *The Journal of Management Development, 24*(1), 68–93. https://doi.org/10.1108/02621710510572362

Ashfield, T. A., Syddall, H. E., Martin, H. J., Dennison, E. M., Cooper, C., & Sayer, A. A. (2010). Grip strength and cardiovascular drug use in older people: Findings from the Hertfordshire Cohort Study. *Age and Ageing, 39*(2), 185–191. https://doi.org/10.1093/ageing/afp203

Barron, D., & Winn, E. (2009). Effective communication. In A. Hassiotis, D. A. Barron, & I. Hall (Eds.), *Intellectual disability psychiatry: A practical handbook* (pp. 3–19). John Wiley & Sons. https://doi.org/10.1002/9780470682968

Beck, E., Gill, W., & De Lay, P. R. (2016). Protecting the confidentiality and security of personal health information in low- and middle-income countries in the era of SDGs and Big Data. *Global Health Action, 9*(1), 1–7. https://doi.org/10.3402/gha.v9.32089

Botsford, J., & Harrison Dening, K. (2015). *Dementia, culture, and ethnicity: Issues for all.* Jessica Kingsley Publishers.

Bradley, S., Tufton, L. R., & Hemmings, B. (2019). Self-disclosure within the sport psychologist-athlete relationship. *Sport & Exercise Psychology Review, 15*(1), 3–12. https://doi.org/10.53841/bpssepr.2019.15.1.3

Brady, R., & Varkonyi-Sepp, J. (2025). A framework for consultancy in health psychology. In R Brady, J. Varkonyi-Sepp & J. Smith *The Palgrave handbook of consultancy in health psychology*. Palgrave Macmillan.

Bunning, K., Alder, R., Proudman, L., & Wyborn, H. (2017). Co-production and pilot of a structured interview using Talking Mats® to survey the television viewing habits and preferences of adults and young people with learning disabilities. *British Journal of Learning Disabilities, 45*(1), 1–11. https://doi.org/10.1111/bld.12167

Camerer-Waldecker, C., & Supprian, T. (2019). Collation of word retrieval disorders in patients with Alzheimer's dementia. *Nervenarzt, 90*(4), 399–407. https://doi.org/10.1007/s00115-018-0572-7

Cook, D. (2002). Consultation, for a change? Engaging users and communities in the policy process. *Social Policy & Administration, 36*(5), 516–531. https://doi.org/10.1111/1467-9515.00300

Crane, L., Lind, S. E., & Bowler, D. M. (2013). Remembering the past and imagining the future in autism spectrum disorder. *Memory, 21*(2), 157–166. https://doi-org.libproxy.ncl.ac.uk/10.1080/09658211.2012.712976
David, A. S. (1990). Insight and psychosis. *The British Journal of Psychiatry, 156*(6), 798–808. https://doi.org/10.1192/bjp.156.6.798
Dias, V. V., Brissos, S., Frey, B. N., & Kapczinski, F. (2008). Insight, quality of life and cognitive functioning in euthymic patients with bipolar disorder. *Journal of Affective Disorders, 110*, 175–183. https://doi.org/10.1016/j.jad.2008.01.010
Ekezie, W., Cassambai, S., Czyznikowska, B., Curtis, F., O'Mahoney, L. L., Willis, A., Chudasama, Y., Khunti, K., & Farooqi, A. (2024). Health and social care experience and research perception of different ethnic minority populations in the East Midlands, United Kingdom (REPRESENT study). *Health Expectations: An International Journal of Public Participation in Health Care and Health Policy, 27*(1), e13944. https://doi.org/10.1111/hex.13944
Elliott, K., & Forshaw, N. (2001). People with borderline-mild learning disability. In J. France & S. Kramer (Eds.), *Communication and mental illness: Theoretical and practical approaches* (pp. 236–250). Jessica Kingsley Publishers. https://uk.jkp.com/products/communication-and-mental-illness
Equality Act 2010 (UK). *Equality Act 2010.* Retrieved May 14, 2024, from https://www.legislation.gov.uk/ukpga/2010/15/contents
FitzGerald, C., & Hurst, S. (2017). Implicit bias in healthcare professionals: A systematic review. *BMC Medical Ethics, 18*, 1–18. https://doi.org/10.1186/s12910-017-0179-8
Fortin, D. (2020). Sabbath rest. *Expository Times, 131*(6), 281–282. https://doi.org/10.1177/0014524620906106
Gilliat-Ray, S. (2005). From 'chapel' To 'prayer Room': The production, use, and politics of sacred space in public institutions. *Culture and Religion, 6*(2), 287–308. https://doi.org/10.1080/01438300500226448
Graham, N. L. (2000). Dysgraphia in dementia. *Neurocase, 6*(5), 365–376. https://doi.org/10.1080/13554790008402708
Gupta, N., Christiansen, C. S., Hallman, D. M., Korshøj, M., Carneiro, I. G., & Holtermann, A. (2015). Is objectively measured sitting time associated with low back pain? A cross-sectional investigation in the NOMAD study. *PloS one, 10*(3), e0121159. https://doi.org/10.1371/journal.pone.0121159
Hossain, M., Crossland, J., Stores, R., Dewey, A., & Hakak, Y. (2020). Awareness and understanding of dementia in South Asians: A synthesis of qualitative evidence. *Dementia, 19*(5), 1441–1473. https://doi.org/10.1177/1471301218800641
Kantawala, B., Zahra, N., Oseili, T., Jawad, A., Ouardouz, S., Nazir, A., Wojtara, M., & Uwishema, O. (2023). Dementia challenges in Africa: Journeying through forgetfulness. *Health Science Reports, 6*(9), e1561. https://doi.org/10.1002/hsr2.1561
Kebede, A. S., Ozolins, L., Holst, H., & Galvin, K. (2022). Digital engagement of older adults: Scoping review. *Journal of Medical Internet Research*, e40192. https://doi.org/10.2196/40192

Kenworthy, L., Yerys, B. E., Anthony, L. G., & Wallace, G. L. (2008). Understanding executive control in autism spectrum disorders in the lab and in the real world. *Neuropsychology Review, 18*(4), 320–338. https://doi-org.libproxy.ncl.ac.uk/10.1007/s11065-008-9077-7

Kerzner, H. (2017). *Project management - A systems approach to planning, scheduling, and controlling* (12th ed.). John Wiley & Sons, Inc.

Khanal, S. (2024). Reflexivity over caste and gender: Disrupting researcher's bias beliefs and habitus. *International Journal of Qualitative Studies in Education, 37*(1), 38–49. https://doi.org/10.1080/09518398.2021.2003896

King's Fund. (2022). *What are health inequalities?* Retrieved May 14, 2024, from https://www.kingsfund.org.uk/insight-and-analysis/long-reads/what-are-health-inequalities

Kitay, J., & Wright, C. (2004). Take the money and run? Organisational boundaries and consultants' roles. *The Service Industries Journal, 24*(3), 1–18. https://doi.org/10.1080/0264206042000247731

Lawlor, C., Vitoratou, S., Duffy, J., Cooper, B., De Souza, T., Le Boutillier, C., Carter, B., Hepworth, C., & Jolley, S. (2022). Managing emotions in psychosis: Evaluation of a brief DBT-informed skills group for individuals with psychosis in routine community services. *British Journal of Clinical Psychology, 61*(3), 735–756. https://doi.org/10.1111/bjc.1235

Marmot, M. (2010). *Fair society, healthy lives: The Marmot Review*. Retrieved January 1, 2025, from Fair Society Healthy Lives full report

Marmot, M. (2020). Health equity in England: The Marmot review 10 years on. *BMJ (Online), 368*, m693–m693. https://doi.org/10.1136/bmj.m693

Martín-Romo, L., Sanmartín, F. J., & Velasco, J. (2023). Invisible and stigmatized: A systematic review of mental health and risk factors among sex workers. *Acta Psychiatrica Scandinavica, 148*(3), 255–264. https://doi.org/10.1111/acps.13559

McIlveen, P. (2008). Autoethnography as a method for reflexive research and practice in vocational psychology. *Australian Journal of Career Development, 17*(2), 13–20. https://doi.org/10.1177/103841620801700204

Mental Capacity Act. (2005). *Code of practice,* (Issued 23 April 2007). Retrieved January 1, 2025, from Mental-capacity-act-code-of-practice.pdf (publishing.service.gov.uk)

Munari, S., Wilson, A. N., Blow, N. J., Homer, C. S. E., & Ward, J. E. (2021). Rethinking the use of 'vulnerable'. *Australian and New Zealand Journal of Public Health, 45*(3), 197–199. https://doi.org/10.1111/1753-6405.13098

National Eye Institute. (n.d.). *Vision and aging resources.* Retrieved January 1, 2025, from https://www.nei.nih.gov/learn-about-eye-health/outreach-resources/vision-and-aging-resources

National Institute on Deafness and Other Communication Disorders. (2018). *Age-related hearing loss.* Retrieved January 1, 2025, from https://www.nidcd.nih.gov/health/age-related-hearing-loss

NHS Document Readability Tool. (n.d.). Retrieved January 1, 2025, from https://newcastlerse.github.io/nhs_readability_react/

NHS England. (2023). *A national framework for NHS – action on inclusion health.* Retrieved January 1, 2025, from https://www.england.nhs.uk/long-read/a-national-framework-for-nhs-action-on-inclusion-health/

Office for Health Improvement & Disparities. (2022). *Health disparities and health inequalities: Applying all our health.* Retrieved January 1, 2025, from https://www.gov.uk/government/publications/health-disparities-and-health-inequalities-applying-all-our-health/health-disparities-and-health-inequalities-applying-all-our-health

Osman, S. E., Tischler, V., & Schneider, J. (2016). 'Singing for the Brain': A qualitative study exploring the health and well-being benefits of singing for people with dementia and their carers. *Dementia, 15*(6), 1326–1339. https://doi.org/10.1177/1471301214556291

Owsley, C. (2011). Aging and vision. *Vision Research (Oxford), 51*(13), 1610–1622. https://doi.org/10.1016/j.visres.2010.10.020

Petersen, R. C. (2004). Mild cognitive impairment as a diagnostic entity. *Journal of Internal Medicine, 256*(3), 183–194. https://doi.org/10.1111/j.1365-2796.2004.01388.x

Public Health England. (2021). *Addressing health inequalities through collaborative action.* PHE publications gateway number: GOV-9224. https://assets.publishing.service.gov.uk/media/615213efe90e077a2db2e804/health_inequalities_briefing.pdf

Rajaram, S. S., & Rashidi, A. (1999). Asian Islamic women and breast cancer screening: A socio-cultural analysis. *Women and Health, 28*(3), 45–58. https://doi.org/10.1300/j013v28n03_04

Reynolds, C., Altmann, R. A., & Allen, D. N. (2021). The problem of bias in psychological assessment. In *Mastering modern psychological testing* (pp. 573–613). Springer International Publishing AG. https://doi.org/10.1007/978-3-030-59455-8_15

Rimmer, A. (2020). Can patients use family members as non-professional interpreters in consultations? *BMJ (Online), 368*, m447–m447. https://doi.org/10.1136/bmj.m447

Rivera, N., Feldman, E. A., Augustin, D. A., Caceres, W., Gans, H. A., & Blankenburg, R. (2021). Do i belong here? Confronting imposter syndrome at an individual, peer, and institutional level in health professionals. *MedEdPORTAL, 17*, 11166–11166. https://doi.org/10.15766/mep_2374-8265.11166

Robertson, A. E., Stanfield, A. C., Watt, J., Barry, F., Day, M., Cormack, M., & Melville, C. (2018). The experience and impact of anxiety in autistic adults: A thematic analysis. *Research in Autism Spectrum Disorders, 46*, 8–18. https://doi-org.libproxy.ncl.ac.uk/10.1016/j.rasd.2017.11.006

Rockwood, K., Song, X., MacKnight, C., Bergman, H., Hogan, D. B., McDowell, I., & Mitnitski, A. (2005). A global clinical measure of fitness and frailty in elderly people. *Canadian Medical Association Journal (CMAJ), 173*(5), 489–495. https://doi.org/10.1503/cmaj.050051

Rosenberg, P. B., Johnston, D., & Lyketsos, C. G. (2006). A clinical approach to mild cognitive impairment. *The American Journal of Psychiatry, 163*(11), 1884–1890. https://doi.org/10.1176/ajp.2006.163.11.1884

Royal National Institute for Deaf People. (n.d.). *Communication tips for people with hearing loss.* Retrieved January 1, 2025, from RNID_CommuicationTips_For_PeopleWithHearingLoss.pdf

Sabat, S., & Warren, A. (2023). Exploring why "memory loss" is a misleading descriptor of people living with dementia and can lead to dysfunctional care. *Dementia, 22*(8), 1819–1832. https://doi.org/10.1177/14713012231200622

Santesteban-Echarri, O., Piskulic, D., Nyman, R. K., & Addington, J. (2020). Telehealth interventions for schizophrenia-spectrum disorders and clinical high-risk for psychosis individuals: A scoping review. *Journal of Telemedicine and Telecare, 26*(1–2), 14–20. https://doi.org/10.1177/1357633X18794100

Schein, E. H. (1997). The concept of "client" from a process consultation perspective: A guide for change agents. *Journal of Organizational Change Management, 10*(3), 202–216. https://doi.org/10.1108/09534819710171077

Schein, E. H. (2013). *Humble inquiry: The gentle art of asking instead of telling.* Berrett-Koehler Publishers.

Sheehan, O. C., Haley, W. E., Howard, V. J., Huang, J., Rhodes, J. D., & Roth, D. L. (2021). Stress, burden, and well-being in dementia and nondementia caregivers: Insights from the caregiving transitions study. *The Gerontologist, 61*(5), 670–679. https://doi.org/10.1093/geront/gnaa10

Sotak, K., Serban, A., Friedman, B. A., & Palanski, M. (2024). Perceptions of ethicality: The role of attire style, attire appropriateness, and context. *Journal of Business Ethics, 189*(1), 149–175. https://doi.org/10.1007/s10551-023-05347-7

Starkstein, S. E., Jorge, R., Petracca, G., & Robinson, R. G. (2007). The construct of generalized anxiety disorder in Alzheimer disease. *American Journal of Geriatric Psychiatry, 15*(1), 42–49. https://doi.org/10.1097/01.jgp.0000229664.11306.b9

Svanelöv, E. (2020). An observation study of power practices and participation in group homes for people with intellectual disability. *Disability & Society, 35*(9), 1419–1440. https://doi.org/10.1080/09687599.2019.1691978

Syvertsen, J., Robertson, A. M., Abramovitz, D., Rangel, M. G., Martinez, G., Patterson, T. L., Ulibarri, M. D., Vera, A., El-Bassel, N., & Strathdee, S. A. (2012). Study protocol for the recruitment of female sex workers and their non-commercial partners into couple-based HIV research. *BMC Public Health, 12*(1), 136–136. https://doi.org/10.1186/1471-2458-12-136

Tembo, D., Hickey, G., Montenegro, C., Chandler, D., Nelson, E., Porter, K., Dikomitis, L., Chambers, M., Chimbari, M., Mumba, N., Beresford, P., Ekiikina, P. O., Musesengwa, R., Staniszewska, S., Coldham, T., & Rennard, U. (2021). Effective engagement and involvement with community stakeholders in the co-production of global health research. *BMJ (Online), 372*, n178. https://doi.org/10.1136/bmj.n178

Tuffrey-Wijne, I. (2012). *How to break bad news to people with intellectual disabilities: A guide for carers and professionals*. Jessica Kingsley Publishers.

Van Eechoud, I., Grypdonck, M., Leman, J., Van Den Noortgate, N., Deveugele, M., & Verhaeghe, S. (2017). Balancing truth-telling: Relatives acting as translators for older adult cancer patients of Turkish or northwest African origin in Belgium. *European Journal of Cancer Care, 26*(5), e12498. https://doi.org/10.1111/ecc.12498

Way, W., & Vosloo, J. (2016). Practical considerations for self-disclosure in applied sport psychology. *Journal of Sport Psychology in Action, 7*(1), 23–32. https://doi.org/10.1080/21520704.2015.1123207

World Health Organisation Consultative Group on Equity and Universal Health Coverage. (2014). *Making fair choices on the path to universal health coverage*. Retrieved January 1, 2025, from https://www.who.int/publications/i/item/9789241507158

7

The Sustainable Consultant

Jennifer Lunt

In the film *Bladerunner* (Scott, 1982), the dying replicant Roy Batty famously recounts their experiences of having 'watched C-Beams glitter near the Tannhäuser Gate' and other outer space experiences. While I might not have undergone space travel, my consultancy experiences have taken me on adventures in Europe, the United States of America (USA) and the Middle East on land and sea. For example, as part of organisational culture assessments, I have delivered focus groups in settings ranging from hulls of ships to US boardrooms. I have presented findings within sight of the White House in Washington, USA, and Middle East Formula One tracks, run co-creation workshops in several European capitals, and attended award ceremonies with clients as one of their team. What I wish to share concerns some of my learning from those adventures so that they don't become the 'moments lost in time' that Roy Batty feared.

First, I start with 'The Consultant' section, in which I outline how health psychology training supported my development as a consultant. Second, I detail career experiences that I believe put me in a position to provide consultancy via 'The History' section. Third, through the subsequent 'Preparation' section, I unpack activities that readied me for independent consultancy. Fourth, in the 'The Contract' section I then focus on learning derived from negotiating and setting up specific contracts. Finally, I conclude with some

J. Lunt (✉)
University of Derby, Derby, UK
e-mail: j.lunt@derby.ac.uk

R. Brady et al. (eds.), *The Palgrave Handbook of Consultancy in Health Psychology*,
https://doi.org/10.1007/978-3-031-94529-8_7

considerations for making consultancy more sustainable under 'Next Contract'. Within this final section, I convey reflections on how to ensure a successful project without compromising business sustainability.

The Consultant

In this section, I elaborate on the nature of the consultancy that I have provided and for whom.

Consultancy on What?

While I now work in academia, most of my time as a qualified health psychologist has been spent applying health psychology to health and safety (H&S). This has meant that I have had to blend health psychology learning with related fields such as organisational and occupational psychology, human factors (Wiggins, 2022) and systems thinking (Stroh, 2015). I have done this to take due account of interactions between organisational influences, job and individual factors upon behaviour. Human Factors help inform the decision-making processes underpinning risk-taking and human error in particular, whereas systems thinking encourages consideration of more complex interactions. Through consultancy and contracted research, I have addressed questions including the following: Why do workers behave unsafely at work; how do behavioural-related factors affect the development of occupational disease; how can the biopsychosocial approach (Engel, 1977) be applied to the full spectrum of health issues that affect health at work; what does the work-relevant stress prevention entail; and how can chronic health conditions at work be managed to prevent avoidable sickness absence? I therefore view health at work not just through the lens of the individual but mainly through the lens of the organisation, and have tended to apply consultancy at the organisational level.

Type of Consultancy

The learning shared is based on nearly fifteen years of undertaking research, training and consultancy within the United Kingdom (UK) Civil Service, and five years working as an independent consultant working either directly for a primary client or indirectly as an associate of other consultancies. Delivered individually, or collaboratively with a team, the consultancy activities that I have been contracted to undertake have served a predominantly diagnostic and strategic role (Ma, 2023), utilising data gathering to drill down to underlying organisational causes and build client rapport. This work has also been delivered as *process consultancy* (Brunning et al., 1990); rather than working independently to provide answers, I have worked with clients to co-create organisational-level problem formulations and solutions. In such situations, the consultant brings their technical and professional expertise inclusive of evidence-based behavioural insights (Brunning et al.). The client brings their understanding of the problem in context.

For me, such work has included undertaking mixed method organisational H&S culture assessments and producing strategic gap analysis to compare a multinational's overall safety management approach against behaviour change good practice. As what might be argued as an example of process consultancy 'on the foot', I have also facilitated 'think-tanks' with industry H&S leaders as a vehicle for collectively considering how to address shared behavioural challenges such as motivating a culturally disparate global workforce or ensuring that health is treated with the same parity as safety. Other work I have undertaken as an independent consultant includes profile-raising through producing and publishing case studies to publicise an organisation's approach to, for example, managing its workforce's well-being. From an intervention perspective, I have designed, delivered and evaluated training interventions on topics such as stress prevention at work, the creation of 'good jobs', and line manager-led approaches for managing chronic health conditions at work.

Consultancy for Whom

The companies for which I have provided consultancy have ranged from small UK businesses to large companies and multinationals within the manufacturing, healthcare, aerospace, construction and maritime sectors. I have also provided internal consultancy within the UK Civil Service on topics such as stress and resilience. The primary clients for my work have tended to be heads of H&S departments, in that it is they who have required a problem resolution (Schein, 1987).

The History

In the following section, I unpack the experiences that put me in the position to deliver consultancy.

Starting Out

Spending several years delivering consultancy-related work as an employee within the UK Civil Service provided me with a safety net for developing consultancy skills. Under these circumstances, personal income was not dependent exclusively on delivering to client satisfaction. Providing consultancy as an employee of a large employer allowed me to 'cut my teeth' within support structures for managing any reputation risks. The consultancy activities that I undertook during this period allowed me to generate case studies and client testimonies that later supported me as an independent consultant. I was able to see first hand the various strategies by which similar organisations addressed similar problems. This included, for example, how a company might motivate a transdisciplinary workforce to work together on H&S. When later operating more independently, I was then able to answer client questions about how organisations that they identified as 'like them' addressed such problems. Such tacit knowledge (Gascoigne & Thornton, 2013) integral to the lived experience of a role cannot be readily gauged from the literature. From my vantage point within the UK Civil Service, I became aware of how future 'competitors' operated, their methods and, to a limited extent, their business models.

Health Psychology Training Benefits

During this time, I also undertook the second stage of my health psychology training. The skills derived from that training that subsequently proved particularly helpful pivoted around critical and analytical thinking. This contributed to my developing consultancy expertise described by Schein (1987) as necessary for empowering clients to robustly understand and solve their problems. Providing proportionate evidence-based claims, accounting for confounding explanations, caveating around generalisability or transferability of interpretations, and advising on process and outcome or impact evaluation seemingly differentiated me from competitors in my field. In my experience, such competitors might understand some psychological theory, but not necessarily the scientific method. For generating a thorough, independent evidence-based diagnosis of an organisational problem, the analytical skills derived from health psychology training have helped me to explain behaviour within a system, and the role of latent or 'root causes' which seemed particularly important in providing reliable organisational consultancy. The ability to synthesise different types of primary and secondary quantitative and qualitative data, from sources ranging from policy documents, existing staff self-report surveys and training material to staff interviews, also enabled me to conduct strategic diagnostic work. This included determining whether, for example, a multinational's corporate approach to managing stress and resilience was sufficiently exhaustive of commonplace work-relevant stressors and sources of resilience. As a form of evidence-synthesis undertaken 'on the foot', the facilitation skills that I developed helped me use group discussions to co-create organisational-level problem formulations and potential solutions. I would also seek second opinions from other consultants on my delivery team to check the soundness of my interpretations. This represents a form of collaborative consultancy (Brunning et al., 1990). The models used in health psychology proved valuable assets for systematically diagnosing patterns in behaviour across an organisation for a range of behaviours, or for highlighting shortcomings with traditional risk management approaches for occupational health. These included Capability, Opportunity, Motivation and Behaviour (COM-B) (Michie et al., 2011), the Theoretical Domains Framework (Atkins et al., 2017) and the biopsychosocial framework (Engel, 1977). The flexibility of these models enabled me to assimilate learning from other fields such as occupational and organisational psychology. Similarly, the models helped ensure that I was more exhaustive when discussing with a client, their organisation's H&S needs. An ability to narrow or drill down into detail and to lift out key messages is another training-derived skill that has helped me provide client-accessible evidence-based reports and presentations. Finally, the thorough grounding in ethics afforded by health psychology training helped me to negotiate later dilemmas surrounding competency boundaries in particular, supported by supervision (British Psychological Society, 2021, 2023). Other skills that I acquired along the way that fall outside of health psychology training, but which became essential for independent consultancy, comprised graphic design, book-keeping, IT literacy and project management.

Thought Leadership

Specialist knowledge that for me proved useful to subsequent professional consultancy (Brunning et al., 1990) evolved from contracted research undertaken while working in the UK Civil Service. The publication of Nudge (Thaler & Sunstein, 2009), with its emphasis on choice architecture and the design of the social and physical context to 'nudge' desired behaviour, provided an opportunity for me to demonstrate the potential relevance of behavioural insights to resolving a widespread safety problem. This concerns controlling the situational determinants of human error (Reason, 2000). Examples include positioning and refreshing point-of-use signage indicating the safe execution of operational tasks. After gathering examples of H&S communications or control methods that could be reframed as nudges, I then tested the premise of nudge as a supplement to extant control measures in presentations to H&S conferences. The resultant interest it attracted escalated into further international speaking opportunities. Spotting and communicating ways by which health psychology-relevant topics could potentially enhance the H&S practitioner's 'toolbox' gave me a platform for building networks within the H&S community. It paved the way for industry article co-authoring with lead H&S practitioners and for further speaking and consultancy opportunities. Through this process, I believe that I built a track record of being 'useful'.

During this time, I also grappled with 'imposter syndrome' (Kar, 2021). I worried whether my experience and training warranted being an *expert.* Focusing on the importance of a moral 'cause', namely to make a difference in improving workers' quality of life, shifted my ruminations from a self-defeating self-orientation (Maister et al., 2001; Markham, 2019), to becoming more intrinsically motivated. I realised that health psychology, and subsequent learning, afforded me channels by which I could affect improvement. Affirmation was provided by the conference invitations and by client feedback. The 'trust equation' (Maister et al., 2001) demonstrates that a client's perceived trustworthiness in a consultant is a function of their perceptions of a consultant's credibility and reliability, and the sense of security inspired by lower self-orientation. In my view, client-centred consultancy unhampered by excessive self-doubt on the part of the consultant appears pivotal in bringing about positive change through consultancy.

The Preparation

Under this section are outlined the activities that I have found useful for setting up as an independent consultant.

Values and Boundaries

The preceding groundwork provided much of the technical expertise, process consultation skills, reputation for thought leadership (Duff, 2015) networks and tacit knowledge that strengthened my potential for working as an independent consultant. Before conducting the consultancy work, some focused preparatory work was important for winning work as a limited company. In addition to triggering the business start-up processes, this stage entailed deliberating the values by which I wanted to conduct consultancy. As a qualified health psychologist, being a scientific practitioner, being ethical and client-centred took priority. At this stage, I also firmed up the range of problems or areas on which I could consult so that I could operate within the boundaries of my expertise.

Alliances and Resources

At this juncture, I also determined the alliances that I needed to establish to be a viable consultancy business. For collaborative consultancy and inter-rater checks on data interpretation and recommendation, I needed to identify fellow psychologists that I could subcontract to provide a second opinion. As a registered UK Health and Care Professions Council (HCPC) health psychologist, I also needed an appropriate HCPC registered health psychologist as a supervisor. Preparation also entailed collating and practising use of a range of preferred software for marketing, survey, analysis, publication activities, and assuring online security to facilitate slicker service delivery. Creating a logo inclusive of a strapline that succinctly captured the nature of the work delivered and 'unique selling point' also helped me to create a coherent consultancy identity or brand. Similarly, developing proposal, report and presentation templates consistent with this branding improved delivery efficiency further down the line. In my experience, the technical credibility afforded by professional training does not offset the need for a strong first impression through a professional look and feel, in person and via written material. Other consultancies seemed adept at getting a foot in the door with the use of infographics, clever imagery, agile project management and client testimonies, even when short on science-based credentials. However, as scientific practitioners steeped in ethical practice and values, health psychologists need to promote themselves on the basis of 'style *and* substance', to get initial client buy-in and maintain credibility.

The Contract

In this section, I provide tips for negotiating the contract, the enquiry process, proposal specification, pricing, unintended consequences and using drafts to negotiate.

Negotiation

Although this section will focus on negotiating a contract, it will also draw on other aspects the framework for consultancy in health psychology proposed by Brady and Varkonyi-Sepp (2025; see Chap. 3) that encompasses enquiry, relationships, negotiating contracts, planning and delivering work, and evaluation. Producing a proposal that is attractive to a client, hinges on managing the enquiry to obtain a reliable understanding of client needs. Unless business is thriving, I discovered that negotiation might not have the parity between consultant and client that the term implies. This seemed notable in initial discussions where the consultant must create a positive first impression. I also found, however, that the power differential can shift once the client feels that they are understood. Consultancy opportunities came my way from promoting consultancy services as an independent consultant to my H&S professional networks, or as an associate responding to opportunities arising via other consultancies.

The Enquiry Process

Skills pertinent to the enquiry process, homework, understanding client motives, structure and budget are now considered.

Key skills. I found that the active listening skills that form part of a health psychologist's training such as open-ended questions, probing and paraphrasing, are particularly valuable tools for narrowing down a problem, its context, client requirements and any actions already undertaken (Schein, 1987). For enquiries made to me directly, prospective clients were already aware of the type of work that I could deliver based on the working relationships previously established with them. The new work would usually involve evidence-based synthesis, contributing to case study production and promotion, or evidence-assessed award applications where my health psychology scientific-practitioner training was a particular advantage. In these instances, the emphasis of my enquiry would not so much be on clarifying the need; this would be clear from the start. Rather, my enquiry moved directly to establishing why the work was being undertaken, and how it would be used. I would also clarify the logistics of the work, such as time scales, sources of data, software compatibility, means of sharing information, any issues around commercial sensitivity, and who I needed to work with both within my client's organisations and amongst their contacts. Process evaluation frameworks (Moore et al., 2015) and the Template for Intervention Description and

Replication framework (TIDieR; Hoffmann et al., 2014) were useful for prompting the exploration of implementation requirements. This included establishing what was required, why, for whom, when, by what delivery mode, how often and for how long. For international data sources, planning translation and back-translation as a reliability check would also be required.

Where opportunities arose via contacts with other independent consultants, I worked with them to generate an interview schedule for scoping client needs. We then worked together to conduct the enquiry to mitigate interpretation bias. For associate work, my client was essentially another larger consultancy. My enquiry was based on my perception of what they expected from me as an associate. I was reliant on their interpretation of the primary client's needs. I might subsequently support them in the enquiry process, particularly around technical aspects of data collection, for example, to ensure balanced workforce sample stratification. In those circumstances, I needed to understand the values and tools of the primary consultancy to act on their behalf, for example, when providing advice on the level of rigour.

Homework. Undertaking homework about the organisation that a prospective client represents, its purpose, mission status within their industry, and scale of operation, usually via their organisation's website, helped to establish my credibility and to convey respect for the client. Such homework could also indicate the relative priority afforded to workforce well-being by, for example, examining company value statements. While some naivety around internal operations might be tolerated by the client, asking naive questions about the organisation's role might indicate a lack of respect and jeopardize subsequent contract negotiation. The consultant needs to be perceived as a serious player by a prospective client, yet it is this is the sort of activity that can get lost in a heavy workload.

Client motives. Consistent with research examining the heterogeneity of client motives (Mattila et al., 2019), I found that there can be both overt and covert motives for undertaking the work. Understanding this can make it easier to address client needs rather than just wants (Andrea, 2005). More subtle motives can surface as the client relationship unfolds. Nonetheless, determining covert motives early on could help make for a more persuasive proposal. A client's stated motive might be to solve a problem, but in some instances it might be to be *seen* to find a fix to their chain of command. If the latter applies, in my experience, a prospective client might be less interested in a more rigorous evidence-based approach than they are in a popular off-the-shelf behavioural solution in the H&S field within which I operated. While this preference might stem from industry normative pressures (Mouzas, 2022), it made gaining a foothold as a consultant harder. Established consultants seemed to be chosen because other companies were choosing them, regardless of whether what was offered was suitably fit for purpose. The relative seniority of the client might also indicate whether being seen to solve or problem, or actual problem-solving applies. Evidence of the former motives might direct the consultant to emphasise their track record over the rigour of their approach.

Obtaining external verification of an existing approach is recognised as a common motive for utilising consultancy (Retna, 2016). In such instances, I found that using the enquiry process to anticipate how a client might respond should they not hear what they wanted to hear could be useful for managing client expectations. This might mean presenting that unwanted scenario as a hypothetical outcome during initial discussions. Covert client motives might also centre on career progression and profile raising. For me, this would become apparent through subsequent feedback on how findings were utilised. Since I was working to affect workforce safety, health and well-being, the realisation that a client might be using the work for career promotion purposes represented less of a concern. The more influence that they had, the more impact that I might have indirectly have on the well-being of their workforce. Nonetheless, understanding this early on can help with the negotiation process by ensuring that any client reputational benefits are addressed by the proposal. Conversely, hearing about experiences that implied staff were exclusively at fault for accidents, for example, would tell me something about the priority genuinely afforded to staff well-being by that organisation. As a health psychologist, raising concerns with a prospective client about the risk that their approach might have for staff well-being in the initial enquiry process could jeopardise prospects of winning that work. However, in the face of such dilemmas, making the client aware of these concerns and recording that this has been done should take precedence. It means that the health psychologist has upheld professional integrity, provided the potential client a chance to immediately address those risks, and helped protect the reputation of client and consultant alike.

Client structure. Using initial discussions to understand the complexity of the 'client structure' informed how I would frame the benefits of undertaking the work within a proposal. Based on Schein's (1987) client classification, the initial 'contact client' raising the consultancy query, and the 'primary client' with ownership of the problem were often the same person. They would typically portray the project as intended to protect workforce well-being, thereby representing the workforce who were the 'ultimate client' (Appelbaum & Steed, 2005). It might not be until later in the enquiry process that I would discover how much interest that indirect clients such as company shareholders had, for example, in maximising profit. This discovery would mean that I would have to make the project's business case (e.g., to avoid costs attributable to sickness absence) crystal clear early on in the proposal.

Budget. Finding out how much budget the client has allocated for the work can feel like a very uncomfortable aspect of the enquiry process. It moves the conversation from more of a hypothetical scenario to forcing your potential client to consider you in investment terms. Doing this, however, should help reveal how serious they are in undertaking the work in the immediate future, whether the scale of their resource matches the scale of the problem and the range of options you might provide within your proposal. For me, it was easier to ask this question once the enquiry process had progressed into the delivery logistics, and once the client had realised from the rigour of my enquiry that my consultancy might be worth the investment.

Proposal

If more speculative enquiry discussions have progressed onto implementation details, then, in my experience, the client is usually receptive to receiving a proposal. Suggesting a proposal prematurely might seem too eager and create the impression of not having listened. The proposal forms the basis of the contract and, therefore, records the enquiry output (Kabeyi, 2020). The proposal represents your understanding of the client's needs and their operational area, the aims and objectives of the work, an approach or methodology, deliverables, a schedule of work, pricing with stated assumptions and caveats upon which they are based, and evidence of a track record of delivery in the form of case studies and/or publications (Markham, 2019). In my view, however, the proposal can still be regarded as part of the enquiry process; it provides the client the opportunity to recalibrate what they need and clarify what they expect to see within the proposal. Before communicating appreciation of the problem that needed addressing, I would put this explanation in context by also outlining my understanding of the organisation, and its purpose and scope of operations. Doing so would imply that my recommendations would take account of that context. I learnt that the detail I gave when explaining my understanding of the problem at hand would need to pivot between creating the impression of having listened, of having an authoritative understanding of the evidence base, and mitigating risks of portraying the client's problem incorrectly. A less-rigorous competitor might win the work by communicating essential understanding only. When explaining the proposed methodology, I also learnt that a commercial client will not necessarily need to know the methodological detail required by grant applications, for example. As a 'lay' client, concerns such as replicability or external validity might have limited sway. What may matter to them more is a track record in having undertaken similar work for other clients 'like them' that can be included in the proposal as case studies. A client with a scientific background might however expect more methodological rigour and justification. Indicating the benefits that you as a provider would bring the work at the start of a proposal can also enhance its persuasive power regardless of how expert your client is in the field.

Rather than communicating the methodology as a fait accompli, I found that providing a prospective client with a suite of options as part of the overall approach can boost a consultant's negotiating position and empower a client to make informed decisions. The options need to provide sufficient detail to indicate variations in methodology and their relative pros and cons. They are likely to build according to rigour and price. Providing options should also convey technical expertise and understanding of the underpinning evidence base. For organisational diagnostic work, options could vary from problem formulation management workshops to staff online surveys, sometimes coupled with face-to-face qualitative work. Each option provides a stepped increase in data triangulation and rigour, all underpinned by the critical thinking afforded by health psychology training. For projects that depend on rigour for successful completion, options may not be necessary. Otherwise, I found that providing such options proved useful where there was any ambiguity surrounding a client's budget. They also helped avoid deterring a client by proffering an unexpectedly high quote. Conversely, it can be all too easy to undertake the extra and perhaps needless work of providing options to avoid the initial discomfort of 'talking prices'.

Pricing

In terms of pricing, the consultant needs to work out their fee based on the direct costs according to activity, and then task breakdown, with an estimation of task duration for each consultant undertaking the work. Expenses and consumables estimates also need to be factored in. Indirect costs, project management time including client update meetings needs to be accounted for, taking care not to underestimate the time required for client communication. Project administration time and associated business housekeeping is also easy to underestimate. Within commercial proposals, revealing too much detail about pricing specifics might weaken negotiating power; it might invite a potential client to question the cost of a hotel or train ticket, for example. A compromise can therefore be to provide a price breakdown by milestone to demonstrate that the pricing has been thought through and is authentic, while providing scope for changes in specific logistics. Thinking through your proposed payment schedule, especially for longer-term work, can protect consultant cash flow. For me, being paid upfront always felt uncomfortable; under such circumstances, I felt more pressure to deliver with less power for negotiating scope creep. Yet clients can prefer to pay for pre-project as way of managing annual budgets. Being paid at regular intervals also helps with consultant business cash flow but potentially places more of an administrative burden on a client. Recording actual hours spent on different tasks will also allow a consultant to develop a more precise gauge of task duration for future proposal development.

Determining any actual consultancy rate (e.g., fees per day) can, in my view, be trickier still. The rate will need to reflect your level of qualification, and to allow for business overheads (Labour Laws, 2024). You will also need to allow for the extent of business utilisation (Markham, 2019), meaning any anticipated downtime over a financial year. You, as the consultant, may also need to consider the 'going rate' for this kind of work. Finding this out for me was made easier through contacts with other consultants. In my experience, this would differ from more academic establishments according to the level of rigour costed into running a project. Quality control strategies within qualitative work in particular, such as transcribing recordings, having a second person take notes, reflexive analysis and allowing for breaks between focus groups or interviews might get overlooked. Collecting lists of related quotes rather than generation of coherent themes seemed commonplace. For quantitative work, quantitative inferential statistics might be omitted. Other consultancies might also cost on the basis of delivery by associates. This might reduce the burden of their direct costs by subcontracting data analysis with conservative estimates of the time required for undertaking that subcontracted work. To compete in such markets, the health psychologist consultant might therefore need to make a judgement call about whether they wish to give away some of their time speculatively and unpaid, whether they wish to compromise on quality and caveat the drawbacks of doing so, or whether they wish to target clients that expect scientific rigour and therefore operate in a more niche market. The consultant might also choose to adopt a sliding scale according to organisational scale so that their services can be accessed by smaller organisations. Pricing for 'like-for-like clients' should, nonetheless, be kept consistent to maintain a reputation of fair practice.

Unintended Consequences

I found it important to specify the assumptions upon which pricing is based. Standard terms usually encompass: the inclusion or exclusion of VAT; payment scheduling; data collection arrangements; data security; location of work; local contacts via which to organise work, overall time scale of work; aspects that might be face-to-face, and the duration for which the current pricing stands. Thinking through potential unintended consequences of each stage of the project would be a worthwhile undertaking at this juncture, right down to the level of determining which logo to use within any survey software—that of the consultant or the client? Overlooking such considerations could cause the client unease further down the line. A risk assessment should be undertaken to prompt consideration of suitable safety arrangements, which for me would include finding out whether I needed to factor in time for safety inductions when arriving on site. Project management risk control typically also involves creating contingency for resource constraints such as time availability.

Drafts

I also found that sending a completed proposal in draft form would convey willingness to continue the negotiation. Usually, for non-associate work the written proposal would offset the need for a presentation. Subsequent negotiation at this juncture would then be minor, could be done via a call or an email, and usually require selecting which methodological options to pursue. For established clients, being invited to write the proposal would usually mean that the work was more or less certain. For new prospective clients, specifying a date by which I would contact them to seek their views would make undertaking that step easier. Reasons for not commissioning this work was in my experience, because a competitor offered less rigour but for a lower fee. This ultimately meant that I migrated towards more science-appreciative clients for direct work.

The Next Contract

In this final section, I share some learning for winning follow-on work around pricing and pride in a client.

Pricing for Quality

In my experience, repeat business from the same client was most likely where I had a long-running working relationship with that client, and where the work aligned with expertise that differentiated me from competitors. For me, that meant repeat work around more strategic data synthesis, or evidence-based case study production. Repeat work would also arise where my work was evidently useful, not just in terms of achieving the project objectives, but in helping clients to influence within their organisation. This might be by their using an analysis of workers' views that I had produced to obtain investment in safety infrastructure, or by providing a client material that allowed them to make a stronger business case for improving workforce well-being. Repeat business did not follow where clients wanted to avoid relying on the same 'opinion' for all stages of a large-scale project. I found that obtaining feedback, not only on whether objectives were met but also on how findings were used, could be profoundly rewarding and help offset any qualms that I might have had about undertaking well-being-related work for financial gain. Nonetheless, achieving project outcomes, and receiving positive feedback from a client, does not guarantee that winning work makes a consultancy sustainable. Profit is harder to achieve where the volume of work required consistently exceeds that which is costed. This can be a particular issue when working as an associate where work is priced on a lean business model that strips resource contingency. Completing work to a high standard is without question integral to upholding professional identity as a health psychologist or a consultant. Continually going 'above and beyond', however, might encourage a client to assume that such working practices are a norm, and mean that the consultant struggles to remain commercially viable. Any sense of self-doubt or sense of imposter syndrome might compound this situation, in that proving your worth as a consultant might dissuade you from seeking compensation for what your project is *actually* worth. On paper, strategies such as marketing to clients that value a more scientific approach, pricing for this accordingly, and having clear and concrete boundaries around the scope of work (e.g., the range of documents or pieces of evidence that you might review) should mitigate such scope creep risks. In practice, there may be a power differential between you and your client that makes it harder to assert your worth relative to the privilege of being asked to do that work in the first instance. Driven by the desire to help in the short term, a consultant may also be tempted to go the extra mile for the sake of the bigger cause. In my experience, reflective practice should prompt consideration of whether over-delivering is also becoming a norm. In the event of such scope creep, and as recommended by Wulf (2020), I found that the proposal can provide leverage for requesting that payment terms be renegotiated. Within it, the consultant should stipulate the circumstances under which they might request additional funding. After all, it is not in your client's interests for your consultancy to be effective in terms of quality, but ineffective in terms of sustainability.

Pride in Your Client

Another strategy for securing repeat work might be to build recommendations into your deliverables that you could undertake as a consultant. There is a risk that the client might perceive your main motive for including such recommendations to stem from self-interest. However, keeping your consultancy client-centred should allow you to develop a reputation of authenticity, which will be apparent in the quality of your work and within interactions with your clients and their stakeholders. It should be unambiguous that you are acting in their best interests. Watching your client go on to make a difference in some way, be that by securing more investment, or improving staff welfare, can then be a huge source of individual pride. If that occurs, reinforce such progress by making it your business to praise them accordingly.

Conclusion

Returning full circle to Ray Batty in the film *Bladerunner*, for me key consultancy-based learning that should not be "lost in time" (Scott, 1982), and which relates to commercial contract negotiation, can be summed up as follows. To be commercially sustainable, the health psychologist should: promote themselves on the basis of their track record as much as they do methodology; occupy a niche market in which technical credentials are valued and sought out; prioritise the wider 'cause' over self-orientation to inspire client confidence; and prioritise business sustainability over proving self-worth to keep operational long-term. If you, as a budding consultant, manage to strike the right balance between all of those considerations, you could find yourself creating a positive and sustainable global health impact.

Questions for Reflection

1. What service options might you provide that play to your strengths as a scientist practitioner but also empowers a client to make informed choices about the trade-off between rigour and price?
2. How might you resist the temptation of telling your client what they want to rather than what they need to hear?
3. What strategies will you use to price your work and its true value, without succumbing to imposter syndrome?

Competing Interests The author has no competing interests to declare that are relevant to the content of this chapter.

References

Andrea, R. (2005). Executing profitable sales negotiations: Selling value, not price. *Industrial and Commercial Training, 37*(1), 18–24. https://doi.org/10.1108/00197850510576448

Appelbaum, S. H., & Steed, A. J. (2005). The critical success factors in the client-consulting relationship. *The Journal of Management Development, 24*(1), 68–93. https://doi.org/10.1108/02621710510572362

Atkins, L., Francis, J., Islam, R., O'Connor, D., Patey, A., Ivers, N., Foy, R., Duncan, E. M., Colquhoun, H., Grimshaw, J. M., Lawton, R., & Michie, S. (2017). A guide to using the Theoretical Domains Framework of behaviour change to investigate implementation problems. *Implementation Science: IS, 12*(1), 77–77. https://doi.org/10.1186/s13012-017-0605-9

Brady, R., Varkonyi-Sepp, J. (2025). A framework for consultancy in health psychology. In R. Brady, J. Varkonyi-Sepp, & J. Smith (Eds.), *The Palgrave handbook of consultancy in health psychology*. Palgrave Macmillan.

British Psychological Society. (2021). *BPS code of conduct and ethics.* https://www.bps.org.uk/guideline/code-ethics-and-conduct

British Psychological Society. (2023). *Code of conduct.* https://www.bps.org.uk/guideline/code-ethics-and-conduct

Brunning, H., Cole, C., & Huffington, C. (1990). *The change directory. key issues in organisational development and the management of change.* British Psychological Society.

Duff, S. (Ed.). (2015). *Thought leadership*. Pearn Kandola Publishing.

Engel, G. L. (1977). The need for a new medical model: A challenge for biomedicine. *Science (New York, N.Y.), 196*(4286), 129–136. https://doi.org/10.1126/science.847460

Gascoigne, N., & Thornton, T. (2013). *Tacit knowledge* (1st ed.). Acumen.
Hoffmann, T. C., Glasziou, P. P., Boutron, I., Milne, R., Perera, R., Moher, D., Altman, D. G., Barbour, V., Macdonald, H., Johnston, M., Lamb, S. E., Dixon-Woods, M., McCulloch, P., Wyatt, J. C., Chan, A.-W., & Michie, S. (2014). Better reporting of interventions: Template for intervention description and replication (TIDieR) checklist and guide. *BMJ (Online), 348*(mar07 3), g1687–g1687. https://doi.org/10.1136/bmj.g1687
Kabeyi, M. J. B. (2020). Project and program evaluation consultancy with terms of reference, challenges, opportunities, and recommendations. *International Journal of Project Management and Productivity Assessment, 8*(2), 47–68. https://doi.org/10.1108/02621710510572362
Kar, P. (2021). Partha Kar: Imposter syndrome is no cause for shame. *BMJ (Online), 373*, n1387–n1387. https://doi.org/10.1136/bmj.n1387
Labour Laws. (2024). Expert guide to consultant contracts in the UK. Expert Guide to Consultant Contracts in the UK
Ma, X. (2023). The diagnostic phase of the consultancy cycle. *Management Consulting Journal, 6*(1), 7–14. https://doi.org/10.2478/mcj-2023-0002
Maister, D. H., Galford, R., & Green, C. (2001). *The trusted advisor*. Simon & Schuster.
Markham, C. (2019). *The art of consultancy*. Legend Business.
Mattila, J., Tukiainen, S., & Kajalo, S. (2019). Heterogeneity in client motives for utilizing management consulting. *Baltic Journal of Management, 14*(2), 250–267. https://doi.org/10.1108/BJM-03-2018-0104
Michie, S., van Stralen, M. M., & West, R. (2011). The behaviour change wheel: A new method for characterising and designing behaviour change interventions. *Implementation Science : IS, 6*(1), 42–42. https://doi.org/10.1186/1748-5908-6-42
Moore, G. F., Audrey, S., Barker, M., Bond, L., Bonell, C., Hardeman, W., Moore, L., O'Cathain, A., Tinati, T., Wight, D., & Baird, J. (2015). Process evaluation of complex interventions: Medical Research Council guidance. *BMJ (Online), 350*(mar19 6), h1258–h1258. https://doi.org/10.1136/bmj.h1258
Mouzas, S. (2022). Behaviour in negotiations: Biases and errors. In *Strategic Negotiations for Sustainable Value* (1st ed., pp. 83–101). Routledge. https://doi.org/10.4324/9781003001010-5
Reason, J. (2000). Human error: Models and management. *BMJ, 320*(7237), 768–770. https://doi.org/10.1136/bmj.320.7237.768
Retna, K. S. (2016). Consultants and their views on changing the mental models of clients. *Journal of Change Management, 16*(3), 184–200. https://doi.org/10.1080/14697017.2015.1121161
Schein, E. H. (1987). *Process consultation, Volume II: Lessons for managers and consultants*. Addison-Wesley.
Scott, R. (1982). *Blade Runner*. Warner Bros.

Stroh, D. P. (2015). *Systems thinking for social change: A practical guide to solving complex problems, avoiding unintended consequences, and achieving lasting results*. Chelsea Green Publishing.

Thaler, R. H., & Sunstein, C. R. (2009). *Nudge*. Penguin.

Wiggins, M. W. (2022). *Introduction to human factors for organisational psychologists*. CRC Press LLC. https://doi.org/10.1201/9781003229858

Wulf, S. A. (2020). Successful project consulting. *IEEE Engineering Management Review, 48*(2), 12–14. https://doi.org/10.1109/EMR.2020.2978797

8

Consultancy in Practice: Navigating Boundaries

Emma Kirkby-Geddes

Introduction

In this chapter I focus on the development of my practice of consultancy in health prior to and during my professional training as a health psychologist. Drawing on my experience of working with a charity dedicated to improving the quality of life of older adults experiencing health and social inequalities, I discuss the status of the consultant as an external contractor and boundaries in the consultant/client relationship. Kitay and Wright's (2004) *Boundary Model of Relationships* is used to explore this further. The complexity of consultant/client relationship boundaries is illustrated through my experience of being both advisor to a client organisation and an implementor of tasks and recommendations.

Key aspects of the consultancy framework for health psychologists (Brady & Varkonyi-Sepp, 2025; see Chap. 3) are also discussed in relation to boundaries. This includes reflections on enquiry, the iterative process of engagement with the client, and how a shared understanding and awareness of boundaries and roles is useful to successful consulting. In my exploration of consultant/client relationships, I draw on the work of experts in management consultancy (i.e., Schein, 1987, 2016; Block, 2011) to discuss how understanding

E. Kirkby-Geddes (✉)
Independent Health Psychologist, Huddersfield, UK
e-mail: emma@emmakgeddes.co.uk

R. Brady et al. (eds.), *The Palgrave Handbook of Consultancy in Health Psychology*,
https://doi.org/10.1007/978-3-031-94529-8_8

the client organisation and the staff working within it requires high levels of interpersonal skills and self-awareness.

Exploring the External Status of the Consultant

In the consultancy literature and in this book (Brady & Varkonyi-Sepp, 2025; see Chap. 3), consultancy is positioned as the consultant being either external to the organisation (external consultancy) or external to the department within the organisation in which the consultant is employed (internal consultancy). The focus of this essay is on consultancy which is external to the organisation.

External Consultancy

External in this context refers to the legal status of consultants as contractors, as distinct from employees. The consultant is the provider of expertise that the organisation lacks in terms of its own internal resources (Jacobson et al., 2005; Becker et al., 2015). This expertise can be in one or more specialisms, for example, business strategy, human resources, or operational efficiency (Kitay & Wright, 2004). In my experience as a consultant, I have drawn upon project management skills in managing community health programmes, as well as skills acquired as a health psychology trainee and academic (e.g., literature reviewing, conducting interviews/focus groups, and more recently as an expert on the psychology of loneliness).

The external nature of consultancy can be understood, therefore, in these terms: the consultant's employment status, and the consultant's role in bringing expertise into the organisation to complete a particular programme of work. Consultants also bring a fresh outside perspective to problems and issues for their clients, and this too is a defining feature of the external status of the role (Brady & Varkonyi-Sepp, 2025; see Chap. 3). This apparently straightforward perspective, however, belies a much more complex experience in practice.

Boundaries

An important distinction to make is that within the external consultant status there is a further boundary that places the consultant as either an insider or outsider. Kitay and Wright (2004) Model of Boundary Relationships, as indicated in Fig. 8.1, illustrate the degree to which a consultant who is external to the organisation can, at the same time, be perceived as either insider or outsider.

Kitay and Wright (2004) frame the outsider consultant role as transactional. The consultant and client are two entirely separate entities with clear role boundaries. For example, the client buys or enlists the consultant's specialist skill or knowledge to help solve a specific problem for the organisation. This is akin to Schein's 'Purchase of Information or Expertise Model' (Schein, 1987) in which the client has already clearly identified the problem and draws on the consultant's expertise to solve the problem.

In contrast, in the insider role, over time the consultant develops a relationship with the client that goes beyond a simple transaction of consultant expertise sought and paid for to solve a problem defined by the client; the boundary between client and consultant is less clear or is "blurred" (Kitay & Wright 2004, p. 12). The importance of building relationships with the client is central also to the "Process Consultation Model" (PC) (Schein, 1987) where the consultant's role, as well as providing expertise, is to understand the "human processes" at play within the organisation (Schein, 1987, p. 2). For Schein, based on his many years as a consultant, the PC model offers the best hope for successful consulting because of the central role of the consultant in understanding "*how* things are done rather than *what* is done" (Schein, 1987, p. 39). Interpersonal relationships and the human processes within organisations are key to understanding how to support change and solve the problems faced by organisations. A point to note and one which I discuss further later

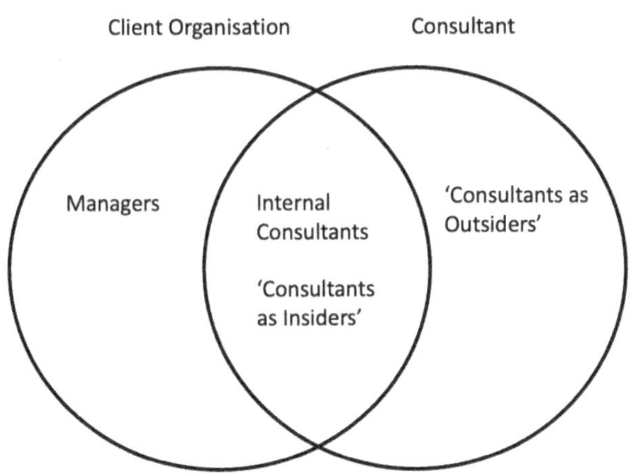

Fig. 8.1 Boundary relationships of consultants and clients

in the chapter is that much of the management consultancy literature is devoted to the importance of a high level of skill in managing *interpersonal* skills (relationships between people) and *intrapersonal* skills (relationship with the self) (Block, 2011; Schein, 1987, 2016). Interpersonal skills include collaboration, negotiation, and dealing with client resistance. Intrapersonal skills include self-awareness and authenticity and being able to manage one's own emotional responses to the client. For Block (2011) this intrapersonal self-awareness facilitates the building of trust with the client that is necessary for effective change and implementation of recommendations.

In addition to the insider and outsider roles of the client/consultant relationship, boundaries can be affected by the nature of day-to-day work undertaken by the consultant. Block (2011) makes a distinction between consultant as advisor where the consultant's role is to influence change without implementing it, and consultant as surrogate manager who becomes involved in implementing their recommendations or carrying out tasks defined by the client. The external employment status of the consultant also means that they work in an advisory capacity, and input stops at the recommendation stage. Kitay and Wright (2004) also make this distinction between advisor and implementor, noting that the consultant role can be "a form of surplus managerial labour which could be hired and dispensed with as needed" (Kitay & Wright, 2004, p. 9), the consultant is drafted in to implement a predetermined project.

In summary, whilst the (external) consultant is legally outside the organisation, the role can vary in the extent to which, in practice, the consultant is truly outside. This is impacted by the boundaries of the relationship between client and consultant (insider/outsider) and by the extent to which the consultant extends their work into implementing recommendations or tasks (advisor/implementor/surrogate manager). Next, I explore my experiences of shifting boundaries from being an outsider to, over time, being an insider. In both of these roles it is also possible to move from advisor to implementor and vice versa. This can impact on the ability to bring a truly fresh perspective to issues, on managing resources to deliver successfully for the client, as well as on one's own well-being.

Boundaries in Consultancy: My Experience

Three months after passing my PhD viva on my research exploring well-being in older adults, I was offered a six-month, part-time contract with a charity as outlined in Box 8.1. The initial aims of the work were to implement a new

Box 8.1 Features of the Consultancy Project

Client—third sector (charity); medium size (100+ employees)

Contractual status—contractor (paid role); 3 days per week

Role description first 6 months—project manager implementing a project exploring older people's experience of living care settings [Residential Care Settings Project]

Role description 6 months to 5 years—(in addition to project management of Residential Care Settings project) I also advised management on a range of issues including strategies and interventions to address loneliness and well-being during coronavirus (COVID-19) pandemic

Client reporting line—Chief Executive Officer

Outcomes delivered

Six short films documenting resident experiences of residential care

Built network of residential care settings regularly receiving input from Key Workers (Years 0–2)

Community-based intervention (Shopping Centre/Supermarkets) to address loneliness (Years 2–5)

programme focusing on improving people's experiences of living in residential care settings and to increase their access to community-based resources. My role had two foci: to co-ordinate a film project which would record the experiences of those in residential care so that their views could contribute and shape the commissioning of services; and to build and then consolidate the working partnerships between the client organisation, residential care organisations, and local health and social care services. The desired outcome was to increase the number of people in residential care accessing community resources to improve their well-being.

Implementor and Advisor

As a contractor my legal status was external to the organisation. I was referred to by the staff team as a consultant. The boundaries were clear: I occupied an outsider position (Kitay & Wright, 2004) delivering a programme of work that had already been designed by the client, within a six-month delivery window. I was not required to advise on the programme but to implement it. The role drew on my previous experience as a project manager in health settings working on health-related community programmes.

The Implementor Role and Its Impact on Relationships with Staff Teams

It was the lack of formal authority over staff that emerged as problematic as the work progressed. This is the common experience in consultancy where the consultant becomes a surrogate manager without having any formal authority over staff (Block, 2011, p. 4). In the initial phase of the project, which was to capture on film people's experiences of living in residential care, it was possible to deliver the programme with no support from the staff team. For example, I was responsible for organising the filming schedule and ensuring participant well-being during filming (i.e., monitoring levels of fatigue and ensuring there were adequate breaks). The focus of the second phase of the project was to build and grow the relationship between the client organisation and residential care settings. To do this, the client organisation's assessment team undertook in-depth quality of life assessment of older people living in the care settings, using an existing quality of life assessment. As the project gained momentum and the partnerships with the care settings began to build and flourish, the demands on staff time also grew as the number of people requiring assessment visits increased and more residential care settings took part in the programme.

Aspects of my work that were manageable at the beginning with a small number of sites became onerous in terms of my time and contracted hours as the project grew; for example, collecting and collating data needed as evidence for project targets such as the number of assessments undertaken. With no formal authority to manage staff and to delegate aspects of this workload, I took this work on in the short term until I could negotiate with the organisation that a member of staff would take this on.

Outsider to Insider and Implementor to Advisor

The project was a success in giving a platform, through the films and the results of the quality-of-life assessments, for the experiences of older people living in residential settings to be heard by those commissioning services. For example, excerpts of the completed films were included at a United Kingdom (UK) National Health Service (NHS) conference attended by health and social care commissioners. The films were also later used in a training tool to improve person-centred care skills of those working within residential care settings.

The second focus for the programme which was to build relationships with care settings was also a success, with many care settings becoming involved and residents benefitting from the support offered by the programme, including increased access to community resources and services. As a result, this part of the programme was recommissioned. I remained involved in the programme for over two years and gained a multi-layered understanding of it. For example, to broker and create relationships between the client organisation and the care settings, I needed to convey the purpose and outcomes of the quality-of-life assessment process. To gain this knowledge, I worked closely with the staff team to learn about their work and the assessment process they used.

In addition, as I built partnerships with the care settings through negotiating their participation, supporting the implementation of filming, and the assessment visits, I came to understand the challenges facing them (e.g., high staff turnover often meant a lack of continuity in engagement with our programme which then resulted in disruption to the assessment team and their work with residents). The close working relationships and working knowledge of the project I developed through implementing the programme meant I was in a unique position to advise the client about how to develop the programme further. This marked the beginning of a change in my role from implementor to that of advisor. For example, I observed that continuity and building relationships was negatively impacted by a high staff turnover in the care settings; it was often the case that no sooner had one of the assessment teams established a working relationship with a care setting manager, than the manager would leave and be replaced. The process of building a relationship with a manager would have to begin over again. To address this, I advised several easy-to-implement changes. First, I advised the client to create a key worker role in which their assessment staff would be paired with only a small number of care settings to better facilitate building interpersonal relationships. Second, I advised that a poster with the photograph of the key worker, including their name and contact details and a short description of the programme, would be displayed on noticeboards in the care settings. This created a way for the client organisation to have a visible and permanent reminder of the key worker and of our programme in the care setting.

My recommendations for the development of the programme were adopted by the organisation and the tasks to implement them were incorporated into the existing assessment team's work. I had moved from being an outsider and implementor to being an insider and advisor. I continued to work for the charity as a part-time contractor for five years in total. As my knowledge and understanding of the organisation deepened, I acted more in an advisory role but at times would also be an implementor. Table 8.1 provides an illustration of how my role could change from implementor to advisor and vice versa sometimes over the course of a working day.

Consultant as Advisor

Hodges (2017) argued that working with an organisation over time allows for the development of an insider's knowledge of the organisation. The longevity of my involvement with the client was a factor in my becoming an insider. Two further factors facilitated the move to advisor. The first was that I was invited to attend the fortnightly leadership team meetings, attended by the Chief Executive Officer (CEO) and senior managers. During the first six months of my contract, my input at these meetings was to provide updated reports on my work with the residential care settings; for example, providing a summary of the data on number of assessments as well as progress on the filming work.

Over time, I witnessed discussions by the leadership team about the strategic direction of the organisation. For example, attending the leadership team meetings I could see that the project I had been working on with care settings was integral to a wider strategic aim to increase the organisation's work reach to all older people in the community, including those living in residential care. I had ideas about how to embed and grow this work; attending the leadership team meetings gave me a platform to discuss my ideas and provide advice. Crucially, as an insider my understanding of the organisation meant I was able to advise based on understanding the practical and resource implications of implementing my advice and recommendations. In reference to Schein's PC model, I had developed an understanding of *how* things got done, not just *what* was done (Schein, 1987, p. 39). For example, having worked closely with the assessment team for almost a year, and seeing the pressures team members were under as demand for their work grew, my recommendations had to be sensitive to this. Implementation of the key worker role meant that staff time could be optimised through the simple intervention of the poster with the key worker photograph to help us build relationships by providing continuity in contact with the residential care sites.

Table 8.1 Advisor and implementer

Time	Activity	Role
Morning	Leadership meeting • Advising on strategy to address loneliness • Advice to hold focus groups (local older people affected by loneliness, local public health professionals, volunteers within organisation) • Advice to develop project steering group	Advisor
Afternoon	Organising focus groups and steering group • Contacting local groups/individuals • Booking venue and organising payment and hospitality	Implementer
Weeks/months later	Running the focus groups	Implementer
	Analysing data from the focus groups and the steering group	Advisor
	Using data to use in my leadership role	

Health Psychology: Bringing a Fresh Perspective

My involvement in leadership meetings, and my own professional development to become a health psychologist, meant that my developing expertise in the psychology of loneliness was key to shaping the organisation's strategy to address a growing problem of loneliness in the local population. Despite increased referrals to the organisation for support, older individuals were only seeking help when in crisis, highlighting that the social activity groups the client organisation provided, to address loneliness, were not effective in providing support and intervention at an early stage. As part of my professional training in health psychology, I undertook a brief review of the literature on interventions addressing loneliness in older adults for the client. The review provided a fresh perspective and was impactful. For example, it stimulated a discussion in the leadership team about a tendency within the organisation to use the terms "loneliness" "and social isolation" interchangeably, when loneliness and social isolation are distinct and separate phenomena: social isolation can be understood as the number of social connections (Rubinstein et al., 1994), whereas loneliness is the perceived quality of those connections (Perlman & Peplau, 1981).

Through this lens, the leadership team recognised that the social activity groups did indeed address social isolation as they increased the number of social connections for participants. However, the team could not be as confident that attending a group would also address loneliness. My reading about loneliness had shown that there was evidence that chronically lonely people are more sensitive to cues of social rejection and, as such, joining a new group could result in feeling lonelier (Hawkley & Cacioppo, 2010). We were then able to ensure going forward that interventions to address loneliness would need to account for the psychological barriers facing older people joining the social activity groups.

I was also able to bring a fresh perspective because I was learning about the theories, models, and tools for behaviour change, such as the Behaviour Change Wheel (BCW) (Michie et al., 2011). The BCW provides a guide to designing behaviour change interventions, in which a key step is to clearly define the problem in behavioural terms. I used the BCW to guide the development of the intervention to address loneliness, beginning with discussions with the leadership team to clearly define the target behaviour for intervention focusing on early help seeking (i.e., not waiting until the crisis). My review of literature had highlighted the importance of including people who considered themselves as lonely in early discussions about their experiences in any intervention design (Michie et al., 2011). This is also a key step included in the BCW toolkit, and I advised that we undertake community engagement work to understand barriers and facilitators to the behaviour of seeking help for loneliness. The community engagement work included six in-depth interviews with local people over 65 years of age who had been identified by the staff assessment team as at risk of loneliness and who were reluctant to attend social activity groups. I designed a semi-structured interview based on these proposed drivers of behaviour change; the BCW includes the COM-B behavioural model (Michie, et al., 2011) in which behaviours (B) are a function of capability (C) which is the skills and knowledge needed to perform the Behaviour; Opportunity (O) which is the physical and social environment that enable the Behaviour; and Motivation (M) which involves the unconscious processes such as habits that may support or work against the Behaviour taking place. The interview questions explored: Capability—whether the older people the client wants to reach have the psychological and physical skills to attend the social activity group; Opportunity—whether the social and physical environment supports older people to attend the social activity group; and Motivation—whether older people have the internal cognitive processes such as habits and beliefs that will support them to attend (i.e., does attending link to important values and personally meaningful goals).

The interviews provided useful insights into the barriers to attending the social events provided by the client organisation. The findings revealed that in terms of Opportunity, a barrier to attending was having to walk into a room or an enclosed space where it was not easy to come and go freely. The need for physical autonomy had not been considered as a barrier by my client. This could help to explain why there was a low uptake with social events, which was that the physical space in which it took place, a room in a community centre, did not allow for enough personal autonomy to be expressed or for control over the activity and participation in it. These findings also helped to explain the huge success of a social event that took place in the open atrium in a large shopping centre. In that setting, people could come and go as they pleased and could observe the event and approach when they felt ready to engage—on their own terms. This then made it possible for the client's organisation to build relationships with those individuals and provide intervention. It was clear that future social activity events aimed at engaging those who found it hard to seek help needed to be in a venue that allowed for personal autonomy. The role of Motivation, and particularly the role of habits, also informed the development of the intervention. Could new social events take place in a venue where older people already had the habit of attending, for example, supermarkets and even pubs?

Further engagement work with older people to develop this approach was undertaken. This included the setting up of a steering group and working with local supermarkets and shopping centres. The project was awarded three years of funding by the UK National Lottery programme. The development of this community-based loneliness intervention has subsequently proven to be very successful and takes place across a number of supermarkets. The data from the programme shows that in providing an event that addressed the barriers to help seeking, it has been possible to build relationships with older people who were not accessing support that could prevent a crisis. Using my skills and knowledge from health psychology, I was able to bring a fresh perspective to what had seemed an intractable issue: how to engage those deemed hard to reach before they were in crisis.

Using the Consultancy Framework to Further Explore Boundaries: Enquiry and Relationships

The shifting boundary from implementor to advisor defines my experience of consultancy with the client. In the next section, with reference to the consultancy framework dimensions of enquiry and relationships (Brady & Varkonyi-Sepp, 2025; see Chap. 3), I discuss how awareness of insider/outsider and advisor/implementor is important in navigating relationships with clients and emphasising the central role of self-awareness (intrapersonal skill) in building and maintaining client relationships.

Consultancy Framework: Enquiry

Enquiry is described by the editors of this book as an iterative process, in which the consultant engages with the client about the work both initially at the start of the relationship but also over time, as the work progresses (Brady & Varkonyi-Sepp, 2025; see Chap. 3). In this section I will focus the role of enquiry in establishing and maintaining role boundaries, particularly on its importance in the initial stages of the relationship.

There is an emphasis in the literature on the benefits gained from investment in the early stages of the relationship with a client. For example, O'Driscoll and Eubanks (1993) state that successful client/consultant projects were much more likely when the consultant had taken time in the initial stages to gather and interpret information about the organisation. Block (2011) also maintains that this information gathering in the first stages of the relationship or "preliminary events" are key to success (Block, 2011, p. 8). Questions such as *Who is the client?* provide an opportunity for you as the consultant, to reflect on whether you have the right expertise and if your values are a good fit with the client.

Hodges (2017) focuses on the importance of the initial meeting with the client as it provides the opportunity to check assumptions, for example, about shared values; the resources available to deliver the work; as well as a discussion about role boundaries. In my experience this happened in an informal way. My initial contact with the organisation was through an informal discussion with the CEO about my PhD research. During this discussion, I learnt about the nature and scope of the organisation's work. Based on this early discussion, I accepted an invitation to meet with members of the leadership team to discuss how I might support the organisation. At that meeting, it was clear that we had shared values and a vision for improving the health and wellbeing of older people. This process of mutual and informal enquiry led to me being offered and my accepting the first six-month contract on the programme with care settings.

The Value of a Shared Understanding About Boundaries

My experience of consultancy with the client would have been improved by having the concepts of insider/outsider and advisor/implementor in mind both at the initial meeting and as the project grew. In initial meetings, having an awareness of the advisor/implementor distinction would have allowed me to discuss managing resources needed to deliver the work and the limitations of being an external contractor. For example, what contingencies were in place, if any, should the work grow beyond the hours I was contracted to work; what was in place given I would have no formal authority to delegate to staff. The lack of this discussion did result in me being slower in asking for support as the residential care project grew, which I discuss below in more detail because of the risk of being seen to be unhelpful or inflexible.

Fresh Perspectives

Kitay and Wright (2004) advise that the consultant should seek clarity about how the client views the insider/outsider dimension. Raising this during initial meetings, framed as a discussion about how the client sees the working relationship (i.e., is there an expectation that the consultant be in close working relationships with senior team members or will the consultant be required to maintain distance from the team), is important. Crucially, establishing this allows for discussion about how the shift to insider could compromise perception of and ability to truly bring a fresh perspective. For example, by regularly attending the leadership team meetings, there were times when I could become enmeshed in the organisation, its politics, and its hierarchies. For those staff who were not in the leadership team, my attending these meetings may have impacted their perceptions of me to be able to bring a fresh perspective. Scott and Barnes (2011) identify that loss, both of the perceived and the real issue of loss, of a fresh perspective is a common issue for consultants occupying an insider role. The authors recommend that to preserve that fresh perspective, cultivating and developing external networks of colleagues can help to ensure alternative perspectives are considered and brought to the work. Indeed, my ability to bring a fresh perspective was facilitated by my professional training, linking me as it did to new ideas and ways of thinking about health issues and to knowledgeable colleagues in academia and health settings.

Consultancy Framework: Relationships

The management consultancy literature is clear that consultancy is as much about emotional and psychological engagement with the client as it is about providing technical expertise (Ben-Gal & Tzafrir, 2011; Bennett, 2007; Covin & Fisher, 1991; Karantinou & Hogg, 2001; Saad, 2017; Schein, 1987). For example, Schein (1987) devotes a large section of his seminal text *Process Consulting: Lessons for managers and consultants Volume 2* (Schein, 1987) and later in *Humble Consulting: How to provide real help faster* (Schein, 2016) to the importance of interpersonal processes: "The relationship existing between consultants and clients is much more than professional and involves a psychological dimension that must be taken into account when exploring the relationship existing between both parties" (Schein, 1987, p. 63). Whilst it seems obvious that the interpersonal aspect of the relationship with the client is central to success in consultancy, of equal importance is the consultant's own psychological processes (intrapsychic or intrapersonal) in the client/consultant relationship. For example, Schein asserts that the consultant must be able to monitor their own perceptual biases and emotional triggers (intrapersonal processes): "the most important thing for consultants to understand is what goes on inside their own heads" (Schein, 1987, p. 63). The importance of this self-awareness is explored next with a focus on its role in building trust with the client and in the psychological well-being of the consultant.

Self-Awareness and Trust

The importance of self-awareness to building trust in relationships is framed by Block in what he terms "authenticity" in each interaction with the client (Block, 2011, p. 37). Authentic interactions are in two parts, the first is self-awareness: knowing what you are feeling during an interaction. The second is expressing this to the client. In practice, managing the relationship with the client and one's own emotional responses, required for authenticity, is challenging.

Outsider and insider—the role of trust. In the literature, trust in consultancy relationships is discussed as being impacted by role boundaries. For example, Kitay and Wright (2004) found that consultants working in an outsider role reported lower trust with clients, and that they were expected to work long hours and could be subject to unreasonable demands from clients. For a client, an outsider consultant whose role is to deliver a project and with whom no interpersonal relationship is built, can result in low levels of trust in the consultant and can make it is easier to make demands on their time. An interviewee (client) for their study of consultant/client boundaries stated: "You won't have to face them [the consultant] over coffee in the office, if you know the task you set them took them all weekend" (Kitay & Wright, 2004, p. 10).

Building trust takes time. Low trust might exist not because the consultant lacks self-awareness, but because voicing reactions and feelings might not be possible or desirable. For example, as the residential care project grew, I needed to delegate scheduling of assessment visits. I was aware of my feelings of being overwhelmed but did not voice my concerns to the client at first. Voicing my concerns felt like a risk: would I be perceived as inefficient and be replaced? However, this feeling changed over time. The concept of experience-based trust is useful here to explain why: "Once established, experience-based trust enables reciprocal and enduring relations and individuals or organizations will tend to transact with trusted partners" (Glückler & Armbrüster, 2003, p. 279). It was time spent in the role and the trust built through delivering on agreed outcomes that enabled me to eventually ask for help and so, to act authentically. Over time, I had proved my value to the organisation, placing me in a good position to be considered for work on future projects.

Self-awareness and well-being. Block (2011) argues that the consultant's ability to be authentic is also a protective factor. In my experience, speaking up about overwhelm and asking for support did impact positively on my mental well-being because I was given support in the form of additional staff who undertook the task of recording the number of visits and assessments in each of the care settings. An awareness of the impact of shifting boundaries, of self-monitoring of advisor/implementor roles, gives a vocabulary with which to be authentic with the client. The words of Lundberg and Young (2001) are helpful here: "Successful consultants need to be in touch with and have ways of dealing with their own anxiety, their own moods and affective reasons, so as to feel reasonably alert, secure, comfortable and centred to interact with their clients" (Lundberg & Young, 2001, p. 536).

Managing the intrapersonal aspects of relationships with clients, in my experience, also benefits from support from peers and from a coach or mentor. For example, when working with the client, there were very few health psychologists working nearby in the charity sector and I was the only psychologist working with the organisation. There were times when I did experience anxiety about bringing my newly found expertise into the organisation. For me, supervision and coaching were crucial in helping me to maintain my focus and in building my confidence to bring my ideas to the client and so, to life.

Summary

In summary, my journey as a health psychologist in consultancy underscores the significance of developing an understanding of the shifts that can happen in the role in terms of boundaries. Developing the skills of self-awareness in monitoring emotional responses to these shifts can support the navigation of the client/consultant relationship for a successful outcome, not just for the client but also for the consultant.

Questions for Reflection

1. How will you discuss with your client, your role as advisor or implementor?
2. At what point in the consultancy contract could you check to address changes to this?
3. Who could provide supervision, coaching, or mentoring during the contract to support your well-being?

Competing Interests The author has no competing interests to declare that are relevant to the content of this chapter.

References

Becker, S. V., Aromaa, E., & Eriksson, P. (2015). Client-consultant interaction: The dynamics of and conflicts in value co-creation and co-destruction. *International Journal of Services Technology and Management, 21*(1–3), 40–54. https://doi.org/10/10.1504/ijstm.2015.071103

Ben-Gal, H. C., & Tzafrir, S. S. (2011). Consultant-client relationship: One of the secrets to effective organizational change? *Journal of Organizational Change Management, 24*(5), 662–679.

Bennett, R. J. (2007). Expectations-based evaluation of SME advice and consultancy: An example of business link services. *Journal of Small Business and Enterprise Development, 14*(3), 435–457.

Block, P. (2011). *Flawless consulting: A guide to get your expertise used* (3rd ed.). Pfieffer.

Brady, R., & Varkonyi-Sepp, J. (2025). A framework for consultancy in health psychology. In R. Brady, J. Varkonyi-Sepp, & J. Smith (Eds.), *The Palgrave Handbook of Consultancy in Health Psychology*. Palgrave Macmillan.

Covin, T. J., & Fisher, T. V. (1991). Consultant and client must work together. *Journal of Management Consulting, 6*(4), 11–20.

Glückler, J., & Armbrüster, T. (2003). Bridging uncertainty in management consulting: The mechanisms of trust and networked reputation. *Organization Studies, 24*(2), 269–297. https://doi.org/10.1177/0170840603242004

Hawkley, L. C., & Cacioppo, J. T. (2010). Loneliness matters: A theoretical and empirical review of consequences and mechanisms. *Annals of Behavioral Medicine, 40*(2), 218–227. https://doi.org/10.1007/s12160-010-9210-8

Hodges, J. (2017). To be or not to be an internal consultant. In G. Manville & O. Matthias (Eds.), *Management consultancy insights and real consultancy projects* (pp. 65–74). Routledge. https://doi.org/10.4324/9781315593425-20

Jacobson, N., Butterill, D., & Goering, P. (2005). Consulting as a strategy for knowledge transfer. *Milbank Quarterly, 83*, 299–321. https://doi.org/10.1111/j.1468-0009.2005.00348.x

Karantinou, K. M., & Hogg, M. K. (2001). Exploring relationship management in professional services: A study of management consultancy. *Journal of Marketing Management, 17*(3–4), 263–286.

Kitay, J., & Wright, C. (2004). Take the money and run? Organisational boundaries and consultants' roles. *The Service Industries Journal, 24*(3), 1–18. https://doi.org/10.1080/0264206042000247731

Lundberg, C. C., & Young, C. A. (2001). A note on emotions and consultancy. *Journal of Organizational Change Management, 14*(6), 530–538. https://doi.org/10.1108/eum0000000006141

Michie, S., Van Stralen, M. M., & West, R. (2011). The behaviour change wheel: A new method for characterising and designing behaviour change interventions. *Implementation science, 6*(1), 1–12. https://doi.org/10.1186/1748-5908-6-42

O'Driscoll, M. P., & Eubanks, J. L. (1993). Behavioural competencies, goal setting and OD practitioner effectiveness. *Group & Organization Management, 18*(3), 308–327. https://doi.org/10.1177/1059601193183004

Perlman, D., & Peplau, L. A. (1981). Toward a social psychology of loneliness. *Personal Relationships, 3*, 31–56.

Rubinstein, R. L., Lubben, J. E., & Mintzer, J. E. (1994). Social isolation and social support: An applied perspective. *Journal of Applied Gerontology, 13*(1), 58–72.

Saad, Y. G. (2017). Deliverable accountability, change management and breach in consultancy contracts: A comparative study of World Bank versus Europeaid funded projects. *Journal of Public Procurement, 17*(4), 525–571. https://doi.org/10.1108/jopp-17-2017-b003

Schein, E. (1987). *Process consultation: Lessons for managers and consultants: Volume 2*. Addison-Wesley.

Schein, E. H. (2016). *Humble consulting: How to provide real help faster*. Berrett-Koehler Publishers.

Scott, B., & Barnes, B. K. (2011). *Consulting on the inside: A practical guide for internal onsultants*. American Society for Training and Development.

9

Pricing and Value in Health Psychology Consultancy

Lisa Newson

There is limited literature that outlines how to price consultancy, especially within health psychology. This chapter integrates evidence from consultancy in legal, business, management, accounting, and healthcare fields to guide health psychology consultancy. It synthesises diverse approaches to highlight the value of health psychology consultancy. It offers pricing strategies, including competition-based (Adesi et al., 2018), cost-based (Buiga et al., 2017), value-based (Guerreiro & Amaral, 2018), and cost-plus-value-based pricing approaches. Competition-based pricing uses market comparisons (Hinterhuber, 2008), cost-based considers expense to formulate the price, value-based relies on client-perceived value, and cost-plus-value-based pricing blends cost, value, and consultant-assessed value. This chapter recommends a process for pricing while prompting reflection on providing pro bono services and ethical considerations for conducting consultancy.

L. Newson (✉)
Liverpool John Moore University, Liverpool, UK
e-mail: l.m.newson@ljmu.ac.uk

R. Brady et al. (eds.), *The Palgrave Handbook of Consultancy in Health Psychology*,
https://doi.org/10.1007/978-3-031-94529-8_9

Health Psychology Consultancy

Health psychology is a diverse field focused on how psychological factors affect health and illness, promoting well-being across the lifespan (Ogden, 2023). Health psychologists apply psychological principles to health promotion and healthcare, which may impact individuals, communities, organisations, and systems (Wallace et al., 2014). Health psychologists typically focus on understanding what influences behaviour and how behaviour influences health, developing strategies to encourage individuals to make healthy choices and manage illness. Health psychologists have expertise in communication, assessment, formulation, intervention design, implementation, and evaluation, which is applicable across various contexts, including clinical settings (Forshaw, 2022), public health and health services (Marks & Estacio, 2018; Newson, 2022, pp. 60–74), policy, global healthcare, training (Turner et al., 2023), and research (Hart et al., 2023). In the United Kingdom (UK), health psychologists work in the National Health Service (NHS), public health, charities, government, academia, independent practice, and industry, supporting environments that promote health (British Psychological Society, 2023). Health psychologists' work may extend into industry and commercial companies, some dedicated to health and others striving to establish healthy environments for their employees or service users (for an example see Gaunt & Newson, Chapter 28 in this book). As health psychologists, we acknowledge the collaborative nature of healthcare and, as such, frequently work with other health professionals to enhance services, care pathways, interventions, policies, practices, and strategies. This broad scope offers varied professional opportunities.

Despite its reach, health psychology is relatively new globally (for a review of the UK development, see Quinn et al., 2020), with only 680 individual registered health psychologists in the UK (Health and Care Professions Council- HCPC, 2023). Many organisations remain unaware of the value health psychologists can bring or have yet to employ them, which presents significant opportunities for consultancy. Health psychology consultants are often commissioned for their specialised expertise, unbiased assessments, and evidence-based practices (e.g., Evans et al., 2022).

Hospital and healthcare settings increasingly recognise the benefits of integrating health psychology into their services (Hissey, 2022, pp. 19–30; Hope-Stone, 2022, pp. 43–57). To offer some examples from my consultancy, I engaged in a Knowledge Transfer Partnership (KTP), a £180,000 project that involved partnering with a housing association to apply health psychology principles for the first time in understanding tenants' needs and improving organisational culture during periods of rapid change. As part of this consultancy, we co-developed and authored several key strategic documents. These documents capture essential consultancy outcomes, including strategic approaches to customer engagement (Awang et al., 2023), sustainability (Chapman et al., 2023), and tenant-centred service delivery (Newson et al., 2023). The project employed evidence reviews, mixed-methods research, workshops, training, and policy changes and secured funding through a competitive Innovate UK application which adopted a cost-based pricing approach (see below for details on pricing methods) and led to spin-off projects and additional consultancy opportunities (Scuotto et al., 2020). Another example is a community-based educational intervention project that evaluated a nature-based educational initiative for vulnerable adolescents. This six-month, £5,000 project utilised a value-based costing approach, which specified a fixed timeframe and budget, with the proposal presented to stakeholders for additional future funding (Gibson et al., 2022).

Engagement Informs Price

Evidence from management consultancy (Dawes et al., 1992) reports the top criteria for selecting consultants: (1) reputation in the specific area; (2) general reputation; (3) known personally; (4) prior experience with the client; and (5) industry experience. Price ranks eighth but is still important. Consultants are often rejected for insufficient or irrelevant experience. Momani and Khirfan (2013, p. 404) reflect on the challenges of hiring external consultants and emphasise the importance of demonstrating project management skills as a key consideration in consultant selection. Success in health psychology consultancy requires professional and technical competence in applying evidence-based health psychology principles and business acumen (Kubr, 2002). As adapted from the management consultancy literature (El Dine & Taher, 2020), professional skills involve sector expertise, a scientific-practitioner approach, and the ability to adapt health psychology to the client's context. As psychologists, we can leverage our communication skills to establish and maintain relationships, employing our professional interactive and analytical behaviours. This chapter focuses on building business competency for consultancy.

To help develop and demonstrate our consultancy competence, I propose breaking down the initial consultancy process into six steps:

Step 1 Understand why a client would engage with you. Clients seek consultants for specific expertise, objectivity, and problem-solving. To effectively engage in consultancy, you must possess a skill set that aligns with their requirements to succeed. Consultants offer an outside perspective, allowing clients to benefit from alternative insights and tailored solutions to their specific challenges (Block, 2011). In this initial step, it is crucial to assess and comprehend your expertise and reflect on the range of skills you might bring to the proposal. Momparler et al. (2015) acknowledge that a consultant's knowledge and professional competencies are the basis of consultancy services. Therefore, the degree of satisfaction that consultants generate highly depends on the person carrying out the work, so reflect on your reputation and ability to convey past achievements.

Step 2 Research the client's needs and establish a good fit. Tailor services to meet the client's objectives. Consider the client's specific aims, objectives, policies, and procedures, ensuring your representation aligns with their interests and goals. For example, private sector work often prioritises return on investment and quick results, while public sector projects focus on long-term impact and policy adherence (Forshaw, 2022). Ensure your background aligns with client goals to assess your suitability for this proposed partnership.

Step 3 Present your expertise. When evaluating a project, it is important to gauge the complexity and challenges and to assess the level of effort, innovation, and problem-solving it demands. Describe and promote your knowledge, skills, and expertise as a health psychologist to match the project needs.

Step 4 Establish credibility. When engaging in the process of pitching and fostering a relationship with a client, it is essential to establish your identity and credibility as a consultant. This task becomes paramount, particularly if you are relatively unknown and new to the consultancy field. Articulate your skills and expertise that resonates with the client's specific needs. Use clear, client-friendly language and share references from previous clients to reinforce your position as a reputable and reliable consultant.

Step 5 Highlight commonalities. Relating past experiences to the client's needs and drawing connections between shared goals can be effective. For instance, if you have a background in public health and the client operates within healthcare services, highlighting commonalities such as population health management, preventive care strategies, health promotion interventions, and the incorporation of evidence-based practices into healthcare delivery can enhance your credibility and relevance to the client's context.

Step 6 Price proposition. While price is not the sole determining factor, it is significant (Dawes et al., 1992). Discussing price can feel uncomfortable, but you must negotiate, present, and justify pricing and state it clearly within your proposal. It can be helpful to present the project in stages or as optional components, for which price elements can be added on. This chunking technique can help justify your pricing proposals, match them to the client's goals, showcase your expertise, and highlight any added value. Stay flexible for potential negotiation.

Pricing Methodology

This section explores how consultancy pricing is determined for health psychology consultants. It then outlines different pricing strategies such as tender-based, competition-based, cost-based, value-based, and cost-plus-value-based pricing. Additionally, it covers methods for calculating costs and considerations for ensuring ethical practice and managing pro bono work.

Pricing determines the charges for services, distinguishing it from costing, which includes direct and indirect costs (covered below). Price sets a monetary value on the consultant's expertise, time, and resources, ensuring fair compensation for services rendered. However, as noted from management consultancy literature, clients (and consultants) "often wrestle with the issues of how to document and communicate value and how to get the pricing of services right" (Ostrom et al., 2010, p. 8).

Published literature on pricing is scarce in health psychology compared to other sectors like management consultancy (see Calabrese & De Francesco, 2014). Michie (1998) was one of the first to discuss consultancy in health psychology, focusing on its purpose and application but not on pricing. In *Health Psychology in Practice* (Michie & Abraham, 2004) several chapters (pages 201–285) offer insight into health psychology consultancy though costing and pricing remain underexplored. For example, Earll and Bath (2004, pp. 230–250) recommend starting with the client's 'ballpark budget' (p. 240) and tailoring pricing to the project's scope, size, and preparation time. They also suggest planning consultancy in stages, treating each stage as a standalone project with its own cost and budget. This staged approach facilitates negotiation for ongoing consultancy and opens avenues for additional funding. I believe this type of chunking approach can also support price negotiation and showcase your expertise across different segments of work. It also helps justify your total price, giving clients a sense of choice and control when investing in your expertise. Walker (2004, pp. 285–307) promoted using a research 'protocol' (akin to a proposal document) as a tool to outline her consultancy research project. Walker (2004) briefly acknowledged the project costs, including expenses for printing, transcription, room hire, intervention costs, and researcher salaries, but did not provide detailed pricing strategies. Brady et al. (2021) describe a pro bono project for which they maintained a log of completed activities. They estimated the final value of the project, based on differing hourly rates, of between £9,450 and £33,750 if it had been billed.

Before finalising the price and submitting a proposal, consultants must consider the client's budget and financial capacity (Earll & Bath, 2004). During pre-contract discussions, the consultant can gather useful information by exploring the following: relevant questions such as who holds the authority to approve financing for the project; what processes are in place for payment and invoice processing; which budget will fund the initiative; what the expected budget or budget range is; who serves as the primary contact (sponsor) for the project; and who can assist in addressing any financial issues that may arise. While these questions should ideally be posed during pre-contract discussions, opportunities to ask them may not always be available and clients may not provide answers even when given the chance. As a health psychology consultant, understanding the client's ability to pay can involve various strategies. For larger consultancies, conducting preliminary research on the client's organisation might be helpful, as well as seeking insights from initial stakeholder conversations or comparing the project scope to industry norms or past experiences. For smaller consultancies, such investigation may not be necessary.

Pricing must be beneficial for the consultant while remaining acceptable to the client. McLachlin (2000) highlights that meeting or exceeding client expectations enhances reputation and builds trust for future projects (Anderson et al., 1994). Limited comprehensive research on pricing structures in consultancy (Ostrom et al., 2010) makes it difficult to establish clear pricing models. Consultants may rely on past experiences or adjust their strategies based on client preferences, especially in tender-based scenarios where the client sets the pricing framework. Table 9.1 contains notes on tender-based scenarios. Before beginning any work, a legal contract should specify the agreed price, but first, consultants must determine their pricing methodology (see Amaral & Guerreiro, 2019, for a full overview of costing approaches also see Lunt, in Chapter 7 of this book, for a personal reflection on pricing processes).

Competition-Based Pricing

Competition-based pricing sets prices by analysing competitors' rates for similar services and adjusting accordingly. This strategy, effective for product

Table 9.1 Invited consultancy versus a tendered consultancy exercise

Tendered exercises follow predetermined engagement and payment methods outlined in the tender documentation, whereas non-tendered engagements offer more flexibility for pricing negotiations based on client needs. (For a review, see Spurgeon & Hicks 2003.)	
Tendered exercises	**Non-tendered engagements**
Engagement and payment methods are specified in the tender documentation, and consultants must adhere to these requirements. Pricing is typically fixed based on the project's specifications, and proposals must align with the outlined criteria.	Pricing is negotiated after discussions with the client, focusing on the scope, deliverables, and timelines. This approach allows for greater flexibility, enabling consultants to tailor the price to the client's specific needs and preferences.

pricing, is also recognised in the service sectors (see Adesi et al., 2018, for a detailed exploration in quantity surveying consultancy). However, I suggest that health psychologists might hesitate to adopt this model for several reasons.

First, service value and uniqueness: health psychology involves specialised expertise and approaches that can be difficult to compare directly. The profession's relative novelty and limited number of practitioners make finding similar services for pricing reference challenging. Competitor-based pricing may not capture the true value of these unique services.

Second, client priorities: for example, clients seeking health psychology often value expertise, quality of care, and consultant rapport over price. Competition-based pricing may overlook these factors, misaligning with client expectations and needs.

Third, ethical considerations: for example, ethical standards in health psychology prioritise client well-being over maximising profits. Competition-based pricing could lead to pricing inconsistencies that undermine service quality or ethical integrity.

In summary, competition-based pricing may not be suitable for health psychologists due to the specialised nature of services, the emphasis on value and quality of care, and ethical considerations. While tender processes might necessitate competitive pricing, other strategies should be considered.

Cost-Based Pricing

Cost-based pricing is the most frequently used and relatively straightforward method (Indounas & Avlonitis, 2011). The consultant using this approach sets a price based on their understanding of the project aims, objectives, and outcomes and estimates the project costs (see cost assessment section), which include resources, materials, and the consultant's time (e.g., hourly/daily/monthly or even project period), and which may also incorporate any pre-contract activities.

Cost-based pricing takes the baseline costs and then adds on a profit (Calabrese & De Francesco, 2014).

$$\text{Formula} : \text{Cost} + \text{Profit} = \text{Price}$$

Profit is typically based on a calculated formula chosen to be applied and assumed to be enough, often calculated as a percentage of the total project cost. In management consultancy, profit typically ranges from 1 to 30%, and in service-based consultancy, it averages around 10% (Guerreiro & Amaral, 2018). This total price aims to satisfy the client and offers enough financial compensation for the consultant to make an acceptable profit. So, cost-based pricing can be calculated as:

$$\text{Formula} : \text{Price} = \text{Cost} + (\text{Cost} \times 10\%)$$

Cost assessment. Conducting a comprehensive cost assessment ensures that consultants avoid unexpected financial losses. Costs (expenses) vary by project type and services offered. Assuming that the health psychology consultant is working independently, for example, as a sole trader, to calculate these costs:

(1) Identify the direct costs, that is, services and resources for project delivery (see Boxes 9.1 and 9.2).
(2) Calculate resource frequency and volume.

Box 9.1 Examples of Direct Costs for Project-Associated Activities

Consultant cost (time/daily rate, as an example).

Additional staff costs.

Supplies (questionnaires, printing, postage, software required for project, intervention supplies, research resources, e.g., interview transcription/language interpretation).

Travel costs to complete the project.

Equipment (rental or purchase).

Office/workshop room hire.

Professional printing/publication or dissemination material.

Contingency measures.

List is not exhaustive.

Box 9.2 How Much to Charge for Your Time

There are no published or standard fees for health psychology consultancy.

In the NHS in England (2024–2025), a trainee psychologist in NHS pay Band 6 earns £19.15–22.99 per hour (£37,338–44,962 annually), while an NHS pay Band 7 qualified psychologist earns £23.60–27.01 per hour (£46,148–52,809 annually). Experienced consultants on NHS pay Band 8c earn £27.99–43.78 per hour (£74,290–85,601 annually) (NHS pay scales, 2024). These figures exclude workplace benefits and indirect costs, so caution is advised when calculating hourly rates based solely on salary.

Brady et al. (2021) found that independent health psychologists reported charging between £70 and £250 per hour. Rates were generally higher in commercial settings, while third-sector clients often received discounted rates.

While hourly rates can be considered, time might be factored in weekly or monthly or even as a project completion period.

(3) Determine the expenses associated with each resource.
(4) Sum all direct costs.
(5) Include overheads (indirect costs). Indirect costs refer to expenses essential for project implementation but are not directly attributable to it due to the inability to determine their exact share in the project (National Institutes of Health, 2020) (see Table 9.2).
(6) Determine the price using the cost-based formula. A major challenge of cost-based pricing is its reliance on fixed or estimated costs. Tzokas et al. (2000) conducted a study evaluating 179 industrial consultancies. They highlighted that cost-based pricing can be rigid, potentially limiting flexibility to adjust prices or capture added value, leading to under-pricing. Health psychology consultancy often requires projecting costs at the proposal stage, but actual costs can fluctuate due to factors like increased expenses for travel, consumables, or unforeseen activities like additional meetings, which increase consultants' costed time. Integrating contingencies into pricing (estimating extra costs for potential risks, as discussed by England and Moreci, 2012) can help manage such changes. Major project adjustments, such as extending timelines or adding new components, may require renegotiation. Clear communication of initial assumptions and agreements is vital for renegotiating effectively. It is important to note that for cost-based pricing to work effectively, the initial negotiation and contracting aspects are critical to successfully implementing the ongoing consultancy process. Proponents' weaknesses often stem not from using

Table 9.2 Indirect costs

Additional costs	Explanation
Professional & Public Liability and Indemnity Insurance	• Consultants should invest in liability insurance to safeguard against potential claims or lawsuits. In the UK, as a registered health psychologist, this is mandatory for professional practice (HCPC, 2014)
Office Space and Equipment	• Renting office space, purchasing supplies, and investing in necessary equipment such as computers, printers and software
Marketing and Advertising	• Costs of promoting the consultancy services, such as creating and maintaining a website, advertising materials, or attending networking events
Professional Memberships and Certifications	• Fees for joining and maintaining professional memberships. Examples include the British Psychological Society (BPS) and HCPC in the UK, the European Federation of Psychologists Associations in Europe, and the Australian Health Practitioner Regulation Agency (AHPRA) in Australia
Training and Development	• Costs for continuous professional development to stay updated with the latest advancements • Professional bodies require evidence of ongoing registration training (e.g., UK HCPC)
Communication and Technology	• The costs of phone plans, internet services, and software subscriptions for communication and data analysis, as well as depreciation costs, are included
Administrative Support	• Hiring administrative staff or outsourcing administrative tasks may incur additional costs. This might be considered within overheads if administrative support covers multiple projects
Tax, banking and accountancy costs	• Costs to hire an accountant, file tax returns, pay national insurance (or equivalent), maintain a business bank account, and cover other liabilities
Holiday and Sick Leave	• Factor in your daily rate for annual holidays or a buffer for unpredicted sickness • According to the Chartered Institute for Personnel and Development (2023), employees take 7.8 sick days annually
Miscellaneous	• Any other cost

Note. You may wish to assign a percentage of the annual cost associated with each overhead to individual projects and explore strategies within your consultancy business to recover these costs.

It is crucial to consider that clients may impose limits on the indirect costs attributed to each contract—this is more common for large consultancies. You must also consider any restrictions, financial or otherwise, that may impact your ability to complete any projects. For instance, the Bill & Melinda Gates Foundation allows 0% for indirect costs USA government agencies (which forces these agencies to pick up the indirect costs elsewhere) but funds up to 15% for non-USA universities and non-government organisations. Horizon Europe, a research funding body, funds indirect costs (overheads) at a flat 25% rate of eligible direct costs (The Austrian Research Promotion Agency, 2022). The UK Government's European Social Fund (2022) specifies a range between 15% and 40%, depending on the project type. Always verify any client-imposed restrictions to determine project feasibility.

cost-based pricing per se but rather from deficiencies in specifying re-negotiating and contracting practices. By addressing these challenges through transparent communication and proactive negotiation, consultants can mitigate risks and ensure that their pricing accurately reflects the evolving nature of any project. The success of the cost-based pricing method is ultimately determined by the project's predicted costs (including contingency costs), the consultants' ability to re-negotiate, and the subsequent desired profit once the work is complete.

Value-Based Pricing

Value-based pricing sets fees according to the perceived *value to the client* rather than focusing solely on the consultant's effort and time, although justifying this price can be challenging (Calabrese & Francesco, 2014). This approach evaluates the service's significance from the client's perspective, encompassing aspects such as business impact, the degree to which the consultant's expertise addresses the client's specific needs, and the overall return on investment experienced because they engage the consultant's services (Hinterhuber, 2008). Essentially, it is about assessing how much the client values the outcomes, benefits, or solutions the consultant provides. This approach acknowledges that different clients may assign different levels of value to the same service based on their unique circumstances, priorities, and perceived benefits. Since price is not the primary reason for initiating a project with a consultant (Dawes et al., 1992; Momani & Khirfan, 2013, p. 404), adopting value-based pricing allows health psychology consultants to reflect the true worth of their services better. This approach cultivates stronger client relationships built on trust and transparency, ultimately optimising pricing strategies to enhance client satisfaction.

Practical Steps for Implementing Value-Based Pricing

Conduct client research: Start by thoroughly understanding the client's business, challenges, and goals. This can be achieved through initial consultations, industry research, and stakeholder interviews. The aim is to gather information that shows how your consultancy aligns with their strategic priorities.

Identify key value drivers. Identify the specific outcomes and benefits that the client values most. For example, this could include improved patient care pathways, enhanced employee training, increased operational efficiency, or improved service outcomes. These value drivers will form the basis of your justification for the proposed pricing. Consultants adopting value-based pricing should assess the client's perspective by asking the following questions. First, is the consultancy designed as a training package to enhance employee skills? If so, what is the impact on their service? Second, does the consultancy streamline care pathways and expedite patient throughput? Third, will the work improve key performance indicators and affect service success or future commissioning (e.g., financial incentives for meeting targets)? Finally, does the project result in a new product or service that yields additional revenue or a competitive advantage for service tendering?

These questions help consultants understand the multifaceted value of their services. As Hinterhuber (2016) notes, consultants should "strive to understand and create customer value as a basis for pricing" (p. 73). Engaging in this exploration with clients while calculating a value-based price helps shape their perception of the service's worth and informs the proposed pricing. Hinterhuber (2016) also asserts the disconnect between the perceived value of consultancy services and its actual costs in value-based pricing. By understanding client value, consultants can set prices that differ from a cost-based approach while maintaining client satisfaction. While costs should be calculated to determine a baseline or lower pricing boundary (see costing assessment above), understanding client value informs the upper pricing limit. Clients facing significant challenges in health, such as those addressed by health psychologists, may be willing to pay higher fees if they perceive a limited pool of qualified consultants.

Develop a value proposition and present financial impact. Differentiating oneself is key to justifying fees and demonstrating added value over competitors. Newton (2019) suggests that specialisation is an effective differentiation strategy. For health psychology consultants, this could involve applying psychological and behavioural theories to address specific health behaviours. For instance, consultants may offer tailored evidence-based interventions for clients seeking to modify behaviours such as smoking cessation or weight management. This specialised focus enhances perceived value by addressing the complex interplay of psychological factors influencing health, setting consultants apart from those without such expertise.

Craft a tailored value proposition. Illustrate how your services address the client's unique needs and lead to measurable benefits. This should convey how your expertise delivers results that the client cannot achieve through other means. Quantify these benefits where possible, showing potential cost savings, time efficiency, additional revenue, productivity improvements, or more specifically, in healthcare, the social value, increase in quality of care, or patient throughflow. For example, if a health psychology intervention to reduce workplace stress helps to reduce employee absenteeism, translate this into monetary terms to illustrate value.

Set the pricing structure. Use the insights gathered from client research and value analysis to determine your pricing structure. Establish a baseline price covering your service costs and set an upper limit informed by the client's perceived value. The formula to guide this could be:

$$\text{Formula : Perceived Value to Client} + \left({}^{3}\text{Baseline Cost}\right) = \text{Price}$$

Communicate your pricing approach. During discussions with the client, emphasise how the proposed fee reflects your services' unique value, focusing on the benefits rather than costs. Outline the strategic advantages, such as specialised knowledge, business impact, and added skills like facilitation and communication, which contribute to overall value (Keränen & Jalkala, 2013).

Solicit feedback from client's post-project. Evaluate whether they feel the value delivered aligns with the client's expectations. This feedback helps refine future pricing strategies and strengthens client trust, showcasing your commitment to value-based service.

It is important to acknowledge that value is ultimately a subjective client perception, and Töytäri et al. (2015) argue that these perceptions can differ and be difficult to predict. Hence, value-based pricing can be difficult to implement. This variability complicates uniform pricing and requires ethical considerations to balance objective service value with client expectations. For smaller practices, assessing client value may be resource intensive, but investing time in understanding client needs fosters rapport and trust, facilitating effective project management. Despite its challenges, value-based pricing can optimise both client satisfaction and profitability. Hinterhuber (2016) notes that only 15–20% of companies use value as their primary pricing strategy, presenting an opportunity for consultants to differentiate themselves by adopting this approach.

Cost-Plus-Value-Based Pricing

Cost-based and value-based pricing concepts are not mutually exclusive; they can be blended approaches, which I believe to be particularly suitable for health psychology consultancy. This method, inspired by Guerreiro and Amaral (2018) in their combined strategy, integrates cost calculations with value assessments to set prices that reflect both internal costs and perceived client value (see Buiga et al., 2017, from the tourism literature; and Guerreiro & Amaral, 2018, from business consultancy). This strategy helps align prices with clients' willingness to pay based on the tangible and social benefits health psychology brings (e.g., improvements in community or health service outcomes).

The process begins with calculating baseline costs, covering all project expenses (as described above). After determining the costs, a value-based approach is integrated. This involves understanding the client's goals, objectives, and expected benefits from the consultancy. Unlike a purely value-based approach focused solely on the client's perception, this combined method also considered the consultant's view of value. The value calculation can adjust the price up or down, depending on the shared benefits. For instance, if there is potential for repeat consultancy and relationship-building, it might be strategic to lower the price by excluding/reducing indirect costs. New consultants may reduce initial prices to gain experience and foster client relationships for future opportunities. In contrast, when a client has high expectations, tight deadlines, or other complexities within a project, these factors may affect the consultant's ability to take on additional work. This could be a reason for the consultant to increase their fee.

Formula: (Costs + Client Perceived Value)
+/– (Consultant's Value) = Final Price

The Value of Pro Bono Work

Pro bono is short for *pro bono publico* derived from the Latin term 'for the public good' and refers to voluntary services offered without payment. Health psychologists may work pro bono to support their communities or individuals facing financial barriers, typically without charge or at a reduced fee (Granfield, 2007). Pro bono work can be a rewarding and impactful way for individual health psychology consultants to contribute to their community or support individuals in need. Unlike general volunteer work, pro bono services require specialised professional skills (Arnold et al., 2011).

Common in sectors such as law, marketing, technology, strategy consulting, and creative industries (Noone & Tomsen, 2001), pro bono work in healthcare may present unique benefits. In law, for instance, pro bono legal clients are unlikely to become future paying clients, minimising financial incentives so there is little potential for a financial reward from this volunteer work. However, this assumption may not be true for those who conduct pro bono work within the healthcare sector or, specifically, for health psychologists. There are, therefore, various circumstances in which one might consider providing pro bono work.

Health psychology consultants may offer pro bono services to individuals, charities, or disadvantaged groups, enhancing access to care. This can be particularly valuable for communities or individuals experiencing challenging circumstances. Consultants may also be motivated to contribute their expertise to social causes, such as health promotion, disaster relief, or community health initiatives. For example, Armstrong et al. (2020) outlined pro bono work conducted by health psychologists during the COVID-19 pandemic. Pro bono work can also enable early-career consultants to gain practical experience, build portfolios, and develop their skills.

Pro bono services foster mutual learning between clients and consultants, potentially developing relationships that lead to future work (Wuyts et al., 2004) or business connections (Price & Arnould, 1999). Since consultancy contracts often favour those with prior experience or established connections (Dawes et al., 1992), pro bono work can be instrumental for new consultants in establishing themselves. Engaging in pro bono projects can also enhance a consultant's reputation and credibility, earning peer recognition (Bekkers & Wiepking, 2011) and signalling expertise, which is especially valuable for those new to consultancy or with limited experience.

While pro bono work can be rewarding, it is important to set clear boundaries to maintain a sustainable and balanced practice (see Table 9.3). By doing so, health psychology consultants can offer pro bono services without compromising the quality of care or the sustainability of their practice. Striking the right balance allows consultants to contribute meaningfully to their community while thriving professionally.

For those new to consultancy or still building a portfolio, pro bono can be valuable for gaining experience and fostering long-term relationships. However, it should not be a default due to a lack of confidence in pricing or fear of rejection. Consultants should be able to create and justify fees, acknowledging the value of the project. Consultants should consider their cost

Table 9.3 Setting boundaries for pro bono work

	Key considerations
Client Eligibility	• Establish specific criteria to identify clients who genuinely need pro bono services and verify their eligibility to avoid potential exploitation.
Limited Scope and Duration	• Set clear limits on the scope and duration of pro bono work to avoid excessive commitments.
Monitor Input and Costs	• Record time, costs, and expenses related to pro bono projects and inform clients of the estimated value. This data can guide future planning.
Preventing Burnout	• Limit pro bono work to maintain energy and enthusiasm for all clients.
Recognising Expertise	• Value your skills appropriately and avoid undervaluing your services, even in pro bono settings.
Transparent Communication	• Clearly communicate the terms of the pro bono agreement, including scope, commitments, and any limitations.
Balancing Paid Work	• Maintain a healthy balance between pro bono work and paid projects to avoid financial strain and prioritise full-fee clients.

assessment and pricing methodology should the work be billed. Pro bono should not stem from embarrassment or fear of being seen as inexperienced. If this is the case, it may be necessary to reassess your expertise and value before offering your services. Upon completion of the work, follow up with an invoice, noting that services were provided 'in-kind' and ensure the client understands the actual costs and price-value of the work.

A Note on Ethical Considerations

Before finalising any proposal, you should consider several ethical considerations in pricing:

Professional responsibility. Pricing in health psychology consultancy involves ethical considerations regarding fairness, transparency, and balancing clients' needs with reasonable income. Health psychologists must navigate these ethical considerations to ensure their pricing practices align with professional and ethical standards.

Determining a 'fair' price. Defining what constitutes a fair price can be subjective and multifaceted. Factors to consider include the value provided, the consultant's expertise and experience, and the client's financial situation. Health psychologists must strive to set reasonable and justifiable prices, avoiding exploitative or opportunistic pricing practices.

Charging the upper limit. While health psychologists have the right to charge fees commensurate with the value offered, charging the upper limit of a client's capacity can raise ethical concerns. This practice could be perceived as taking advantage of clients or prioritising financial gain over ethical principles, such as avoiding harm and fulfilling moral obligations. Pricing decisions should be fair and equitable and uphold ethical standards.

Benchmarking fees. Comparing fees with other consultants, including those in publicly funded organisations, can provide valuable insights into prevailing rates. However, health psychologists should exercise caution in directly mirroring or justifying their fees based solely on what other consultants charge. Instead, they should focus on their unique value proposition, expertise, and client needs.

Adhering to ethical standards. Integrity, professionalism, and client welfare are key principles in health psychology. Pricing must reflect transparency, honesty, and fairness. Health psychologists are accountable for maintaining these ethical standards while navigating pricing complexities. For a more detailed exploration of ethical issues in consultancy see Chadwick et al. in Chapter 4 of this book.

Summary of Pricing Methodology

Determining pricing for health psychology consultants involves selecting appropriate strategies to balance consultant remuneration with client expectations. This chapter has explored key pricing approaches, including tender-based, competition-based, cost-based, value-based, and cost-plus-value-based pricing models. Each strategy presents unique advantages and challenges, particularly in the context of health psychology's specialised services. Pricing involves setting a monetary value on the consultant's expertise, time, and resources, ensuring fair compensation. Unlike costing, which focuses on calculating expenses, pricing strategically communicates the consultant's value proposition to the client. Key considerations for health psychology consultants include understanding client budget constraints, assessing project value, and incorporating contingency measures. Ethical considerations and transparent negotiation practices are essential to maintain service integrity and client trust. Table 9.4 provides a comparative overview of pricing approaches, highlighting their application and relevance for health psychology consultancy.

Table 9.4 Summary of pricing methodology

Pricing strategy	Description	Key characteristics	Strengths	Limitations	Method & formula
Cost-Based	Focus on covering costs and adding a predetermined profit margin	Emphasis on transparency and cost recovery	Simple and clear to apply	Might not reflect the true value of the services provided.	Price = Cost + (Cost × Profit Percentage)
Value-Based	Pricing based on the perceived value of services to the client	Collaborative price setting based on outcomes	Reflects the true value of expertise and the potential for higher fees	Requires strong client relationships and negotiation skills.	Perceived Value to Client + (≥ Baseline Cost) = Price
Cost-Plus-Value-Based	Hybrid approach incorporating cost recovery and value-based considerations	Flexible and adaptable pricing model	Balances fairness and profitability; strengthens relationships	Complexity in determining value metrics and variability.	Costs + Client Perceived Value +/- Consultant's Value = Price
Competition-Based	Prices set according to prevailing market rates	Benchmarking against other consultants' fees	Aligns with market trends; easy to implement	Could lead to price wars and undervaluation of services	No specific formula; relies on market research
Tender-Based	Competitive bidding for contracts based on client specifications	Structured and formal process	Can secure long-term contracts; transparent bidding process	Time-consuming and requires detailed proposals	Competitive offers and client requirements determine price
Ethical/Pro Bono Pricing	Pricing factors in social, ethical, and community benefits	Balances commercial viability and social responsibility	Enhances reputation and community engagement	Might not be financially sustainable	Flexible formula based on pro bono percentage adjustments

Conclusion

Pricing should be based on the consultant's expertise and the complexity of the project. Striking a balance between cost- and value-based pricing and recognising fair compensation for the consultant's skills is important. Ultimately, price should account for the total technical and financial capabilities, reputation, past project experiences, the capacity to deliver services within a specified timeframe, business development, and client value (Perreault & McCarthy, 1996). Value should also be considered within the context of value to the individual consultant.

Pro bono work can be rewarding, allowing consultants to give back to the community and support underserved populations. Benefits include building a positive reputation, gaining experience, and contributing to social causes. However, pro bono work can lead to burnout and undervaluing expertise. To mitigate these risks, health psychology consultants should set clear boundaries and manage the amount of pro bono work to maintain a sustainable and balanced practice. Finally, when setting prices, we should work within our professional boundaries and consider ethical and moral implications.

Competing Interests The author has no competing interests to declare that are relevant to this chapter.

References

Adesi, M., Owusu-Manu, D. G., & Murphy, R. (2018). Strategic competences for pricing quantity surveying consultancy services. *Engineering, Construction and Architectural Management, 25*(3), 458–474. https://doi.org/10.1108/ECAM-12-2016-0264

Amaral, J. V., & Guerreiro, R. (2019). Factors explaining a cost-based pricing essence. *Journal of Business & Industrial Marketing, 34*(8), 1850–1865. https://doi.org/10.1108/JBIM-12-2018-0373

Anderson, E. W., Fornell, C., & Lehmann, D. R. (1994). Customer satisfaction, market share, and profitability: Findings from Sweden. *Journal of marketing, 58*(3), 53–66. https://doi.org/10.1177/002224299405800304

Armstrong, S., Watson, D., Byrne, J., Howells, L. M., Ashworth, P., Phillips, E., et al. (2020). Teaching, training, consultancy and practice: Summaries of work relating to health psychology and Covid-19. *Health Psychology Update, 29*(3), 28–40. https://doi.org/10.53841/bpshpu.2020.29.3.28

Arnold, S., Nguyen, D., & Hartley, N. (2011). Pro bono service sheds new light into commercial friendship. *Journal of Strategic Marketing, 19*(4), 381–394. https://doi.org/10.1080/0965254X.2011.586717

Awang, M., Sewell, R., Bridge, L., Newson, L., Armstrong-Gibbs, F., & Kostopoulos, I. (2023). *Customer engagement strategy*. Cobalt Housing.

Bekkers, R., & Wiepking, P. (2011). A literature review of empirical studies of philanthropy: Eight mechanisms that drive charitable giving. *Nonprofit and Voluntary Sector Quarterly, 40*(5), 924–973. https://doi.org/10.1177/0899764010380972

Block, P. (2011). *Flawless consulting: A guide to get your expertise used.* John Wiley & Sons, Inc. ISBN 978-0-7879-4803-0

Brady, R., Varkonyi-Sepp, J., & Byrne, J. (2021). Consultancy case study: Piloting online group reflective practice for health professionals during the coronavirus pandemic. *Health Psychology Update, 30*(1). https://doi.org/10.53841/bpshpu.2021.30.1.41

British Psychological Society. (2023). Health psychologist job profile. Retrieved May 7, 2024, from https://www.bps.org.uk/health-psychologist-job-profile

Buiga, A., Stegerean, R., Chis, A., & Lazar, D. (2017). Pricing of the tourism product: A tool for entrepreneurs to adapt to a flexible market. *E+M. Ekonomie a Management, 20*, 172–186. ISSN 2336-5604.

Calabrese, A., & De Francesco, F. (2014). A pricing approach for service companies: Service blueprint as a tool of demand-based pricing. *Business Process Management Journal, 20*(6), 906–921. https://doi.org/10.1108/BPMJ-07-2013-0087

Chapman, S., Bridge, L., Newson, L., Armstrong-Gibbs, F., & Kostopoulos, I. (2023). *Sustainability strategy and associated policies*. Cobalt Housing.

Chartered Institute for Personnel and Development. (2023). Health and wellbeing at work. Survey Report. https://www.cipd.org/uk/knowledge/reports/health-well-being-work/

Dawes, P. L., Dowling, G. R., & Patterson, P. G. (1992). Criteria used to select management consultants. *Industrial Marketing Management, 21*(3), 187–193. https://doi.org/10.1016/0019-8501(92)90015-L

Earll, L., & Bath, J. (2004). Consultancy: What is it, how do you do it, and does it make any difference? In S. Michie & C. Abraham (Eds.), *Health psychology in practice* (pp. 230–250). Blackwell Publishing Ltd.. ISBN:9781405110891.

El Dine, N. A. A., & Taher, A. (2020). Knowledge transfer and management consulting: The effect of consultant and client characteristics. *Management, 8*(3), 215–231. https://doi.org/10.17265/2328-2185/2020.03.003

England, K., & Moreci, J. (2012). Contingency—are you covered? Paper presented at PMI® Global Congress 2012—North America, Vancouver, British Columbia, Canada. Newtown Square, PA: Project Management Institute.

Evans T, Ells L, & Newson L. (2022). *National Health Service England Obesity Programme Team. Describing theory in programme designs: A Toolkit.* Leeds Beckett University, UK.

Forshaw, M. (Ed.). (2022). *Health psychology in clinical practice.* Routledge.

Gibson, B., Ashworth, E., & Newson, L. (2022). Research Report. Community by Nature: An examination of an outdoor learning intervention for young people at risk of exclusion. A collaboration between Liverpool John Moores University & Community by Nature. Sept 2022. http://www.communitybynature.org.uk/uploads/6/3/3/7/63379781/cbn_full_report_final.pdf

Granfield, R. (2007). The meaning of pro bono: Institutional variations in professional obligations among lawyers. *Law & Society Review, 41*(1), 113–146. https://doi.org/10.1111/j.1540-5893.2007.00293.x

Guerreiro, R., & Amaral, J. (2018). Cost-based price and value-based price: Are they conflicting approaches? *Journal of Business & Industrial Marketing, 33*(3), 390–404. https://doi.org/10.1108/JBIM-04-2016-0085

Hart, J. K., Michael, P., Hawkins, R., Bull, E. R., Farrar, A., Baguley, C., et al. (2023). 'We just need to find space for them to practice so that we can help to make a stronger society': Perceived barriers and facilitators to employing health psychologists in UK public health and clinical health settings. *British Journal of Health Psychology, 28*(4), 1206–1221. https://doi.org/10.1111/bjhp.12680

Health and Care Professions Council. (2014). Professional indemnity and your registration. https://hcpc-uk.org/resources/guidance/professionalindemnity-and-your-registration/

Health and Care Professions Council (HCPC). (2023). Diversity data: Practitioner psychologists - July 2023. https://hcpc-uk.org/resources/data/2023/diversity-data-practitioner-psychologists-2023

Hinterhuber, A. (2008). Customer value-based pricing strategies: Why companies resist. *Journal of Business Strategy, 29*(4), 41–50. https://doi.org/10.1108/02756660810887079

Hinterhuber, A. (2016). The six pricing myths that kill profits. *Business Horizons, 59*(1), 71–83. https://doi.org/10.1016/j.bushor.2015.09.002

Hissey, L. (2022). Health Psychology in an NHS pain management service. In M. Forshaw (Ed.), *Health psychology in clinical practice*. Routledge. https://doi.org/10.4324/9781003120469

Hope-Stone, L. (2022). Delivering an NHS health psychology service for patients with eye cancer. In M. Forshaw (Ed.), *Health psychology in clinical practice*. Routledge. https://doi.org/10.4324/9781003120469

Indounas, K. A., & Avlonitis, G. J. (2011). New industrial service pricing strategies and their antecedents: Empirical evidence from two industrial sectors. *Journal of Business & Industrial Marketing, 26*(1), 26–33. https://doi.org/10.1108/08858621111097184

Keränen, J., & Jalkala, A. (2013). Towards a framework of customer value assessment in B2B markets: An exploratory study. *Industrial Marketing Management, 42*(8), 1307–1317. https://doi.org/10.1016/j.indmarman.2013.06.010

Kubr, M. (2002). *Management consulting: A guide to the profession* (4th ed.). International Labour Office.

Marks, M., & Estacio, V. (2018). *Health psychology. Theory-research-practice* (5th ed.). Sage. ISBN 9781526412065.
McLachlin, R. (2000). Service quality in consulting: What is engagement success? *Managing Service Quality: An International Journal, 10*(3), 141–150. https://doi.org/10.1108/09604520010336669
Michie, S. (1998). Consultancy. In D. W. Johnston & M. Johnston (Eds.), *Health Psychology. Comprehensive clinical psychology* (Vol. 8, pp. 153–169). Elsevier Science.
Michie, S., & Abraham, C. (Eds.). (2004). *Health psychology in practice.* Blackwell Publishing Ltd. ISBN 9781405110891.
Momani, B., & Khirfan, L. (2013). Explaining the use of planning consultants in Ontario cities. *Canadian Public Administration, 56*(3), 391–413. https://doi.org/10.1111/capa.12027
Momparler, A., Carmona, P., & Lassala, C. (2015). Quality of consulting services and consulting fees. *Journal of Business Research, 68*(7), 1458–1462. https://doi.org/10.1016/j.busres.2015.01.033
National Institute of Health. (2020). The Office of Acquisition Management and Policy (OAMP) Division of Financial Advisory Services (DFAS): Indirect Cost: Definition and Example. https://oamp.od.nih.gov/division-of-financial-advisory-services/indirect-cost-branch/indirect-cost-submission/indirect-cost-definition-and-example
Newson, L. (2022). A spectrum of applied Health Psychology: Across public health and healthcare practice. In M. Forshaw (Ed.), *Health psychology in clinical practice* (pp. 60–74). Routledge. https://doi.org/10.4324/9781003120469
Newson, L., Stenton, G., Armstrong-Gibbs, F., & Kostopoulos, I. (2023). *"More than a rent": Moving toward a tenant-centred approach.* Cobalt MKTP Research Report.
Newton, R. (2019). *The management consultant: Mastering the art of consultancy* (2nd ed.). Pearson Education.
NHS Pay Scales 2024/2025 (predicted – updated May 2024). https://nhspayscales.co.uk/nhs-pay-scales-2024-25-predicted/
Noone, M., & Tomsen, S. (2001). Service beyond self-interest? Australian lawyers, legal aid and professionalism. *International Journal of the Legal Profession, 8*, 251–273. https://doi.org/10.1080/09695950220141043
Ogden, J. (Ed.). (2023). *Health psychology.* McGraw-Hill. ISBN 9780335251865.
Ostrom, A. L., Bitner, M. J., Brown, S. W., Burkhard, K. A., Goul, M., Smith-Daniels, V., & Rabinovich, E. (2010). Moving forward and making a difference: Research priorities for the science of service. *Journal of Service Research, 13*(1), 4–36. https://doi.org/10.1177/1094670509357611
Perreault, W. D., & McCarthy, E. J. (1996). *Basic marketing: A global-managerial approach* (12th ed.). Irwin. https://cir.nii.ac.jp/crid/1130282273093292032
Price, L. L., & Arnould, E. J. (1999). Commercial friendships: Service provider –client relationships in context. *Journal of Marketing, 63*(4), 38–56. https://doi.org/10.1177/002224299906300405

Quinn, F., Chater, A., & Morrison, V. (2020). An oral history of health psychology in the UK. *British Journal of Health Psychology, 25*(3), 502–518. https://doi.org/10.1111/bjhp.12418

Scuotto, V., Garcia-Perez, A., Nespoli, C., & Petruzzelli, A. M. (2020). A repositioning organizational knowledge dynamics by functional upgrading and downgrading strategy in global value chain. *Journal of International Management, 26*(4), 100795. https://doi.org/10.1016/j.intman.2020.100795

Spurgeon, P., & Hicks, C. (2003). The tendering process: Flaws and all. *Health Services Management Research, 16*(3), 188–193. https://doi.org/10.1258/095148403322167942

The Austrian Research Promotion Agency (FFG). (2022). Overview of legal and financial aspects in Horizon Europe: Project proposal. Cost eligibility aspects (presentation). https://www.ffg.at/en/europe/heu/legal-financial/theme_proposal

Töytäri, P., Rajala, R., & Alejandro, T. B. (2015). Organizational and institutional barriers to value-based pricing in industrial relationships. *Industrial Marketing Management, 47*, 53–64. https://doi.org/10.1016/j.indmarman.2015.02.005

Turner, R. R., Epuru Reddy, S., Byrne-Davis, L. M., Bull, E. R., & Hart, J. (2023). An interview study to explore applied psychologists' experiences of implementing health psychology in global health partnerships: The Change Exchange. *British Journal of Health Psychology, 28*(4), 1076–1096. https://doi.org/10.1111/bjhp.12669

Tzokas, N., Hart, S., Argouslidis, P., & Saren, M. (2000). Strategic pricing in export markets: Empirical evidence from the UK. *International Business Review, 9*(1), 95–117. https://doi.org/10.1016/S0969-5931(99)00031-1

UK Government. (2022). Department for Work & Pensions and Ministry of Housing, Communities & Local Government. *Simplified Cost Options Guidance.* https://www.gov.uk/government/publications/european-social-fund-programme-guidance/simplified-cost-options

Walker, A. (2004). Studying and changing healthcare professionals' behaviour. In S. Michie & C. Abraham (Eds.), *Health psychology in practice* (1st ed., pp. 285–307). Blackwell Publishing Ltd..

Wallace, L. M., Brown, K. E., & Hilton, S. (2014). Planning for, implementing and assessing the impact of health promotion and behaviour change interventions: A way forward for health psychologists. *Health Psychology Review, 8*(1), 8–33. https://doi.org/10.1080/17437199.2013.775629

Wuyts, S., Dutta, S., & Stremersch, S. (2004). Portfolios of interfirm agreements in technology intensive markets: Consequences for innovation and profitability. *Journal of Marketing, 68*(2), 88–100. https://doi.org/10.1509/jmkg.68.2.88.27787

10

Don't Fall at the First Hurdle: Responding to Requests for Proposals

Lou Atkinson

Introduction

When people choose to pursue health psychology as a profession, they may imagine themselves undertaking a wide range of tasks and activities in their mission to improve health. However, few individuals are likely to relish the idea of having to compete with other professionals to be given the chance to undertake this important work. Yet, as many of the chapters in this book will demonstrate, consultancy offers some unique opportunities for health psychology practitioners and trainee health psychologists to make real world impact. Thus, mastering the often-uncomfortable process of tendering or 'pitching' for contracts is a very worthwhile pursuit.

There is limited, but insightful, scholarly literature around the process of responding to tenders in consultancy. Much of the literature aims to elucidate the potential pitfalls for both supplier and vendor. For example, Spurgeon and Hicks (2003) critiqued the normalisation of the tendering process as a means of allocating research and consultancy projects from the perspective of academics bidding for public sector projects, such as National Health Service (NHS) research. They argue that rather than providing value for money for the public purse, the hidden cost of the significant time taken to prepare bids and proposals by academics is absorbed by their institutions, whose research

L. Atkinson (✉)
Veasta, Portland, UK
e-mail: lou@veasta.co.uk

R. Brady et al. (eds.), *The Palgrave Handbook of Consultancy in Health Psychology*,
https://doi.org/10.1007/978-3-031-94529-8_10

budget is also publicly funded. Thus, they argue that any savings made through a competitive tender are outweighed by the resources spent on the tendering process. Lack of transparency and impartiality on behalf of the buyer are also highlighted. Spurgeon and Hicks suggest that decisions regarding who will be awarded the contract are "often made on the basis of a 'gentleman's agreement'" (p. 191) where members of the panel making the decision may have assurances of reciprocity from the person or institution chosen. The authors cite the common experiences of invitations to tender being issued with extremely tight deadlines for submission, and/or inadequate information about the project's aims, budget, or timescales, as evidence that someone without prior knowledge of the opportunity would be unable to submit a high quality and competitive proposal. Additionally, they assert that ideas and intellectual property within unsuccessful proposals have later been plagiarised. The authors contend that this ultimately leads to poorer quality project outcomes, as many of those with the best expertise, skills, and ideas will simply not apply.

Others have argued that dissatisfaction with the tendering process has significant consequences for buyers (clients) and their projects, including a reduced pool of potential applicants, barriers to the creation of longstanding and productive relationships, and a mismatch between the client's requirements and the service actually delivered (Kelly et al., 2021). In their survey of suppliers, exploring satisfaction with public sector competitive tendering processes, Kelly et al. identified perceptions of fairness and a comparison of expectations (either related to past experience, or an ideal scenario) together with experience were the key drivers of supplier dissatisfaction. The authors use this evidence to argue for tendering to become a more two-way process, or risk higher costs and poorer outcomes. Although related to the construction sector, Whang et al. (2022) present evidence that costs can actually be elevated as a result of the tendering process. They highlight that poor quality tender documents, lacking detail or clarity, increases uncertainty for the supplier, which in turn can lead to an increase in prices as suppliers attempt to mitigate the risk of taking on a poorly defined project.

Another focus of the literature is exploring the pathways to success. Tucmeanu et al. (2017) surveyed managers of both public and private health units in Romania. The study authors identified that when selecting a consultant, the most important factors were the consultant's professional integrity and competency. However, managers highlighted that correctly defining the consultancy mission and having the necessary financial resources available were equally important, thus highlighting the role of the manager/buyer in success. Osipovic et al. (2020) conducted a longitudinal study of NHS commissioners' and providers' use of competition and cooperation. They highlight a recent move towards more cooperation within the NHS, aimed at reducing the cost of commissioning and fostering long-term collaborations which support strategic planning and align with integrated care models. Yet, competitive procurement remains a statutory requirement, and the authors aimed to explore the intersection of these two approaches. Their findings identified that while commissioners used a range of criteria to assess applications, they particularly focused on whether suppliers were financially sustainable, and capable of delivering the required service. Providers identified the lack of experience of many commissioners as a source of frustration, highlighting that it was common for commissioners to use the procurement process to help them specify and cost a service, often resulting in a protracted and iterative process where details are slowly thrashed out rather than clear requirements being specified up front (Osipovic et al.).

This literature provides some useful critique of the process to the consultant engaging in the world of competitive tenders, and it identifies some key areas for the consultant to attend to. This essay will go on to provide some real-world examples of these challenges and opportunities in the realm of health psychology consultancy.

My Background and Experience

Entering the world of health psychology in my thirties, with an undergraduate degree in psychology and management, managerial experience in a multinational corporate, and several years' experience as a self-employed coach and consultant, I was familiar with writing business cases, preparing budgets, and communicating my skills and expertise in order to attract clients. I had written successful proposals to provide health and wellbeing-related services to businesses as a self-employed health coach. Nevertheless, my initial experiences of writing tenders and proposals as a health psychology consultant were extremely daunting. I experienced self-doubt, and a sense of heading into the unknown. Over 15 years later, I have not only written and submitted many proposals (with a good amount of success), I have taught health psychology students and trainees about the bidding process and spent time learning from those who invite and review proposals. I certainly do not have a magic formula for writing a winning proposal or securing contracts. However, I aim to help readers identify and avoid potential pitfalls. I also offer my experiences as a means to highlight some potential strategies for success, by highlighting my own failures.

What *Is* the First Hurdle?

For the purpose of this chapter, the 'first hurdle' refers to the preparation or submission of a written proposal, as the first step towards being able to deliver a consultancy project. There are several ways a consultant may encounter an opportunity to offer their services. Open competitions are commonly used by the public sector and large organisations and are advertised in the public domain. Organisations often have a list of past and/or preferred suppliers who receive direct invitations to bid for the work, usually called an 'Invitation to Tender (ITT)', the 'tender' being the documents outlining the supplier's approach to the work and associated costs. 'Request for proposal (RfP)' is another common term and I will use this going forward for simplicity. In some cases, there is a pre-qualification process which can be quite arduous, requiring the provision of detailed documentation relating to the bidder's business and previous work. However, the advantages of being alerted directly to opportunities and competing against a smaller pool of suppliers can make this worthwhile. While open competitions offer equal opportunity, they carry uncertainty, as consultants do not know who they are competing against or the content of other proposals.

Aside from open competitions, there are varying degrees of competition involved in other types of RfPs. This ranges from a client approaching a large number of suppliers to approaching a single supplier, and everything in between. Where the potential supplier pool is limited, this can sometimes afford the opportunity to work collaboratively with the client to discuss and even shape the brief for the work. This pre-contracting discussion can be mutually beneficial for both parties, ensuring that the final project both achieves the client's goals and plays to the consultant's strengths. It can also be seen as a way for consultants to demonstrate competence and expertise and to promote their practice (Nicolescu & Nicolescu, 2016). However, this process can also be time-consuming and costly, and it does not always produce satisfactory outcomes for the consultant (Osipovic et al., 2020; Spurgeon & Hicks, 2003).

Given the variety of opportunities, levels of competition and transparency a consultant may be presented with, this begs the question of whether the approach to responding should differ. Certainly, an experienced consultant working in a specific field may make an educated guess at who else is submitting to an open or limited competition. They can potentially then use this knowledge to ensure they explicitly differentiate themselves and their ideas within their proposal. Some consultants may adapt their proposals to reduce the risks associated with high levels of uncertainty, by adding additional time or cost contingencies. On the other hand, when the client indicates there are no competing suppliers, the consultant may focus more attention on the suggested approach and project design, feeling less need to emphasise their track record on the assumption the client already believes they are competent to do the work. All of these can be sensible adaptations to responding to the specific circumstances of an RfP. Yet to my mind, these are relatively subtle differences and overall, the major challenges, pitfalls, and strategies discussed within this chapter are universal, regardless of the exact route by which an RfP has presented itself.

Reducing the Risk of Falling

While the following issues are neither exclusive to working as a consultant, nor do they encompass all of the potential pitfalls of the process of securing consultancy work through RfP, they reflect my experience and that of many colleagues and clients. This section also includes some key areas that should be considered by both new and experienced consultants in health psychology.

What Does the Client Actually Want?

As a consultant, I've encountered wide variations in how clients communicate their needs. Some RfPs are highly detailed, outlining project aims, methods, timelines, and budgets, while others provide clear aims but allow freedom in design. Some are so vague that even the project aims are open to interpretation. In any case, I always recommend reaching out to the client for clarification to better understand their goals. As highlighted in the consultancy framework for health psychologists (Brady & Varkonyi-Sepp 2025; see Chap. 3), the process of 'enquiry' which includes exploring the client, their organisation, and the purpose of the work is integral to successful consultancy; assuming that the brief contains all necessary information could be a damaging misstep. However, aside from gaining vital clarity, there are several other benefits to this contact, summarised in Box 10.1.

Box 10.1 Top Tip 1: Contact the Client

Pitfalls avoided

- Time spent guessing at the client's needs and preferences
- Submitting a proposal that is unnecessarily costly, complex, or time consuming
- Damaging your reputation by misinterpreting the client's intentions

Benefits reaped

- Able to more accurately assess whether you have the capacity, skills, and desire to undertake the project
- Producing the best possible proposal to align with the client's wants and needs
- Identify and mitigate potential risks
- Make a great first impression and begin building the relationship

Given the potential value of this communication with the client, I would advise the following. First, speak with the client by phone rather than send an email. When we consider research methods, we understand that richer data is usually derived from speech-based methods such as interviews, as they offer opportunities for expanding and clarifying answers, and for building the trust and rapport that encourages openness (see, e.g., Marks & Yardley, 2004 and Miles & Gilbert, 2005, for detailed exploration of qualitative and quantitative research methods). Hence a telephone (or face-to-face) conversation will likely not only elicit details that might not be forthcoming in a reply to an email, it also provides the opportunity to build a meaningful relationship with the client (Nikolova et al., 2009). This can be invaluable in establishing yourself as someone the client feels comfortable or even excited about working with. If a phone number is not provided in the RfP, email the contact asking if you can arrange to speak with them on the phone or by video call.

Second, prepare thoroughly. Before making contact, do some research to inform your conversation. The proposed consultancy framework for health psychologists (Brady & Varkonyi-Sepp, 2025; see Chap. 3) includes key questions for the enquiry process in consultancy, which involves gathering information to understand and meet client needs effectively. When contacting the client, establish clear objectives; know what information you need and what you want to communicate. This approach maximises efficiency for both parties. Carefully examine the brief and list the information you have, to show you've done your homework, while also prompting deeper discussion. Use phrases like, "I see that the brief specifies … …; is that correct?" Identify any missing information and prepare open and closed questions. As in qualitative research, open questions can yield detailed responses and minimise bias (Marks & Yardley, 2004; Miles & Gilbert, 2005). For example, "How does this project fit into your organisation's broader strategic objectives?" or "What are the key outcomes you are aiming to achieve through this work?" Closed questions can clarify specifics, like "Is there any flexibility in the timescales?" Also similar to using a semi-structured interview guide in qualitative research, be prepared that the conversation may flow naturally between topics, and you will need to both avoid repetition, and ensure that important questions haven't been missed.

Third, accept that some information may not be forthcoming. Clients may withhold key details, such as a maximum budget, either to encourage competitive bids or due to uncertainty about reasonable costs. Other project details might be unclear at the time the brief is issued, allowing bidders to leverage their expertise in project design. Regardless, consultants must navigate some level of uncertainty when responding to an RfP. Brashers (2001) notes that emotional responses to uncertainty can vary from anxiety to optimism, and individuals may experience mixed emotions, such as fear and excitement. Drawing from Lazarus and Folkman (1984) on stress and coping, reframing uncertainty as a creative opportunity or focusing on factors within one's control can help mitigate negative feelings. For a discussion of uncertainty in management consulting, please see Gluckler and Armbruster (2003).

Alternative options for information gathering. Direct communication with the client can be hugely informative, but this is by no means the only method for gathering information about the client and their needs. Many organisations have information about their mission and vision, their strategic aims and their past achievements in the public domain; for example, in websites, press releases, and so on. Reading these can be helpful in ensuring your proposal aligns with their wider objectives and organisational values. In fact, Luttig and de Villiers (2022) recommend a process of *capture planning*, where the aim is to get into the client's mind and develop a deep understanding of their needs by considering a range of questions: what is the project about, who are the decision makers, and how do they view you and/or your competition? Luttig and de Villiers suggest that the ultimate question that should be asked is "What does this mean for the client—how will it benefit them?" (p. 9).

Designing the Solution

Once you have gathered as much information about the client's needs as possible, the next challenge is to design a solution for them that meets those needs. However, before getting excited about doing the work, I encourage myself to take an objective look at whether this is the right opportunity for me. One of the hardest skills I had to learn as a consultant was knowing when NOT to submit a proposal. Yet, there are sometimes very clear red flags. The proposed consultancy framework for health psychologists (Brady & Varkonyi-Sepp, 2025; see Chap. 3) contains some very useful advice on 'boundaries and expectations' that is relevant here and provides some areas to consider. Ultimately, there are key questions I ask myself to establish whether I should pursue an opportunity or not.

First, *do I have all the knowledge, skills, time, and resources to fulfil the brief?* A 'no' answer doesn't mean the project isn't right for you. Consider bringing in others to provide missing expertise or share the workload or use it as a chance to develop new skills. Larger projects may require additional staff, resources, or software, which can be acquired if within budget and timeline. However, it's crucial to be realistic about whether you can meet the project's needs. Taking on work beyond your capabilities can lead to stress, increase the risk of failure, and harm your professional reputation and finances.

Second, *will I be adequately rewarded for completing the work?* This question primarily concerns whether you'll be paid adequately for the project. It's crucial not to undervalue your expertise by accepting much less than the standard rate, as this can make clients perceive you as less competent and harm the field of health psychology by lowering expectations for fair rates. Accepting low fees can also make the project more stressful and less rewarding due to an imbalanced effort/reward ratio (Siegrist, 2016). However, rewards aren't only financial—building relationships and enhancing your track record may justify a smaller profit margin.

Third, *are the client's expectations realistic?* I've walked away from many opportunities where the timelines, budget, or outcomes seemed unachievable—lessons I learned the hard way! With years of experience, I now trust my judgment to spot when there's insufficient time or budget. Clients may also request unrealistic outcomes, for example, assessing an intervention's effectiveness without adequate data. However, identifying these issues doesn't mean the opportunity is lost; it may open the door for negotiation and collaboration to adjust the requirements based on your expertise.

Preparing the Proposal

Once you've confirmed the opportunity is suitable, the next step is to design a solution that closely meets the client's needs. Here, your core skills as a health psychologist—advanced enquiry, evidence synthesis, and systematic problem-solving—are invaluable. Since every project is unique, I will not provide a step-by-step guide (for detailed guidance, see Samuels, 2022). Instead, I focus on highlighting potential pitfalls to be aware of.

You can (and perhaps should) challenge the client's ideas. Clients sometimes have quite firm ideas about what needs to be done to achieve a certain outcome but lack the expertise to deliver these activities internally. Preconceived ideas about what is required are often formed from past experience and can be influenced by a desire for risk reduction, as well as other political and cultural factors (Curtis et al., 2018). This leads to similar services being commissioned

Box 10.2 Example of Challenging a Client's Assumptions

The request

Within a wide-ranging scope of work aimed at understanding and increasing engagement in family weight management services, the client specifically requested that qualitative data be gathered from local parents using focus groups.

The challenge

Parents of primary school age children are usually incredibly busy throughout the week, balancing work, childcare, and other activities. Additionally, parents from certain groups such as single parents and those on a low income tend to have less flexible working hours and less childcare support. These factors would severely limit participant recruitment and likely bias the findings.

The proposal

Based on extensive experience we proposed telephone interviews with parents instead of focus groups, as these are more convenient for most and would likely increase the amount and diversity of parents recruited.

The outcome

We were commissioned to deliver the majority of the work but not the element where focus groups had been requested. We later learned the consultants chosen to deliver the focus groups had not been successful in recruiting sufficient parents, despite offering significant financial incentives.

The learning

Experience matters, we had good reason for challenging the requested methods and presented our case clearly. By not acquiescing to the client's request, we avoided failing to achieve the desired outcomes and potential damage to our reputation.

repeatedly, even though it risks stifling innovation and limiting the potential for real change. Accordingly, I have always endeavoured to challenge clients' assumptions where appropriate. Luttig and de Villiers (2022) argue that bidding pitches should be considered a creative endeavour, where a deep understanding of client needs is the starting point for the determination of the optimal solution. Viewing the task of proposal writing in this way has certainly increased my enjoyment of the process. An example of challenging client assumptions can be seen in Box 10.2.

You can propose more than one solution. There are several valid reasons to offer only a single solution to a client's request. For example, you may have good evidence to support only one possible method for achieving the desired outcome, the budget may be very limiting, or you may be offering a pre-packaged and proven service that closely fits the client's needs. Nevertheless, in my experience it is often beneficial to propose more than one option to the client, with a few key reasons summarised in Box 10.3.

Box 10.3 Top tip 2: Offer Options

Pitfalls avoided

- Reduces the chance of the proposal being rejected because you have incorrectly assessed the client's needs, preferences, or budget.
- Demonstrating traits which might be viewed as negative within some settings, for example, academic detachment, narrow or authoritarian thinking.

Benefits reaped

- More likely to have offered something the client likes—effectively you are giving yourself multiple opportunities to hit the right buttons.
- Able to clearly demonstrate how available budget affects what can be achieved, for example, by comparing different options with different costs, which could lead to more budget being made available.
- Make clearer arguments for deviating from the client's suggested solution by comparing this to an alternative solution.
- Demonstrates valuable competences as a consultant, for example, flexibility/adaptability, lateral thinking, creativity.
- Provides the client with additional agency and an opportunity to shift the relationship from transactional to collaborative.

In my experience clients often appreciate exploring different solutions, and in some cases, budgets have been increased when options show added value. However, offering too many options can overwhelm the client or suggest uncertainty on your part. In most circumstances I suggest limiting options to three, ranked in order of preference. This way, you clearly recommend the best solution, projecting your expertise, while offering alternatives that could work within (unknown) budget or other constraints.

Always propose a fair price. There can be significant pressure to offer a low-cost solution, especially when participating in a competitive tendering process or if cost is more heavily weighted in the assessment criteria. This is increasingly common practice among commissioners of public services, despite recent moves to give more priority to other aspects such as social value and collaboration (Department of Health & Social Care, 2023). However, this can lead to compromises in the quality of the work that is proposed and eventually conducted. Additionally, costing a solution can be a complex task, and few resources exist to guide you through the process (see Newson, 2025, Chap. 9, and Lunt, 2025, Chap. 7, for more detailed information on costing and pricing). Consultants may under-cost their proposed solution as a result of underestimating the time and resources required to complete the work. The proposed consultancy framework for health psychologists (Brady & Varkonyi-Sepp, 2025; see Chap. 3) highlights the example of literature reviewing being undervalued and a task that clients may be reluctant to pay for. Similarly, 'project management' involving activities such as planning, organising, monitoring progress, co-ordinating team members, and communicating with stakeholders is integral to the successful delivery of a high-quality solution. It is therefore vital to account for project management in the costing process. Training in project management such as the PRINCE2 methodology is available from accredited providers (PRINCE2, n.d.), and guidebooks such as Dwyer et al. (2020) can be helpful. As an inexperienced consultant, I undervalued my work. However, I now ensure that I account for all tasks and include contingencies when calculating costs. Once the true cost is known, it is up to the consultant to decide if discounts should be applied, for example, to stay competitive, or if there are other potential benefits such as repeat business or positive publicity. However, be cautious about setting a pricing precedent with clients. Most importantly, never take on work that doesn't cover your costs or reflect your true value.

Get the client's attention. Your proposal may be one of ten, twenty or more that hit your potential client's desk. Regardless of how excited the client is to select a consultant and get started on the project, assessing a raft of proposals represents a significant workload, and the client may be under considerable pressure to make a decision quickly. Reading several similar documents can lead to a lack of attention to the task, and important points may be missed and/or not recalled later (Smallwood & Schooler, 2006). Even if yours is the only proposal on the table, it should be *enjoyable* and *easy* to read, or there is a risk that it will not make enough of an impression for the client to offer the work.

I suggest setting a few simple, clear goals when presenting a proposed solution, which I will outline shortly. First, I share some reflections. As a consultant and teacher of health psychology trainees, I have found that writing and presenting proposals is often the most challenging part of the consultancy process for psychologists. This may be due to the way psychology students are trained to write—primarily in standardised formats such as research reports and case studies, with little focus on business-oriented writing. Additionally, the emphasis on 'constructive alignment' in higher education (Biggs, 1996), which promotes clear learning outcomes and aligned assessment criteria, may inadvertently narrow students' focus, making them less prepared for real-world proposal writing. Consequently, trainees can struggle when faced with little guidance. To address this, I assign my students the task of writing a proposal for an intervention they have designed. Though most succeed, many initially have difficulty describing their intervention in non-scientific terms and advocating for it effectively. While each proposal is unique, I hope the following suggestions will help.

First, *it's a sales pitch*. The purpose of a proposal is to sell your solution and service to the client by explaining both the 'what' and the 'why' behind your approach, showing how it aligns with the client's desired outcomes. It is important not only to describe what you plan to do but to justify why you have chosen that method. The proposal should highlight the strengths of your solution while acknowledging, but not overemphasising, any potential risks or limitations. Ethically, we cannot ignore the downsides, but demonstrating an awareness of them also shows your expertise in critical evaluation and decision-making. However, extensive focus on the negatives can lead to a negativity bias, where the reader is more influenced by the negative aspects (Baumeister et al., 2001). In line with good project management practices (The Stationery Office, 2017), any identified risks should come with proposed actions to mitigate them. For example, in projects involving key gatekeepers such as healthcare professionals or public sector organisations, changes in personnel or policy could jeopardise the project. Outlining contingency plans reassures the client that the project will still be delivered, even if unexpected challenges arise.

Second, *know your audience and make the complex simple*. In the consultancy proposal assignment, students often presented information like an academic assignment rather than a sales pitch and they assumed too much understanding of key principles and terminology on the part of the reader. However, it is also important not to patronise a reader who may be very familiar with the concepts being presented. As much as possible, try to establish who will be reading and assessing your proposal. Be aware that this may not be the person you contacted at the start of the process, and it can often be more than one person, and get a sense of their background and expertise. This should give you a sense of what needs to be explained and what is likely to be commonly understood by the reader(s). When explaining ideas, models, and especially evidence, do not rely on providing references. Even if your client has access to the scientific articles you have cited (which many will not), they are unlikely to have the time or inclination to search them out and read them. The onus is on the consultant to provide all the information necessary for the proposal to be understood, ideally on its first reading. Similarly, avoid jargon and terminology that is not widely used or understood outside of psychology. There is a body of work that explores communicating with non-academic/scientific audiences (e.g., Orritt & Powell, 2020; Pappas, 2021) that can provide helpful guidance. Requesting feedback from someone without a psychology background before you submit your proposal can be very insightful as to whether you are getting your point across.

Third, *don't use two words when one will do.* Regardless of the space permitted for your proposal, the less time it takes to get your points across the easier it will be for the client to read and absorb what you are proposing. It can be tempting to try to showcase all the hard work you have done in preparing the solution, such as writing multiple paragraphs on the background to the problem, or describing in great detail the step by step intervention design process. Ask yourself, does the client need or want this information? Can you demonstrate your knowledge and expertise without including all this detail in the proposal? In most cases it is likely sufficient to provide only a short overview of the 'how', to demonstrate that the necessary work has been done to derive a well informed and appropriate solution that will reliably deliver the desired outcomes.

Fourth, *a picture paints a thousand words.* Using images in your proposal can make it much more visually appealing to read. More importantly, the picture superiority effect suggests that information presented in pictures and text are processed differently, and that images have an advantage in memory due to an interaction of encoding and retrieval processes (McBride & Anne Dosher, 2002). Hence, your proposal should be more memorable with the judicious use of images.

Finally, *emphasise your track record.* In addition to presenting an appealing solution it is vital that the proposal gives the client confidence that you, and possibly your team, possess the necessary competence, skills, and abilities to deliver the work. In my experience, and in speaking with those who make the decisions on proposals, this is best achieved by including tangible examples of work previously delivered rather than simple assurances. Experience is usually much more highly valued than a long list of qualifications. In the early years of a consultancy career, we may not always have a directly relevant or comparable experience to showcase. Instead, consider the core competences required for the work and draw out your experience of using these, even if the nature of the work was quite different to the present requirement. This can be presented as a list of previous relevant work but may be better woven into the narrative of the proposal, referring to other projects and what you learned from those as part of your rationale for the chosen approach.

Finishing Strong

I will conclude by highlighting a few more pitfalls that could trip you up before you get your proposal safely across the line. The aim of this section is to help you avoid the mistakes I, and some of my colleagues, have made over the years that motivated me to write this chapter.

1. Make a checklist

   Since client briefs and requirements vary, I always create a checklist of what the client wants and does not want, as well as any specific proposal details. This helps me stay focused and avoid straying into irrelevant areas. For example, I once titled a proposal "Investigating the feasibility of…" despite the client explicitly stating they would not fund feasibility studies. A checklist also ensures I do not forget key documents or information, like a Curriculum Vitae or cost breakdown, which could lead to rejection.
2. Pressure points

   It is usual to receive requests or invitations to tender with tight deadlines and strict word limits, making it difficult to include all necessary information. This gets easier with experience, and strategies like repurposing previous proposals can save time. Just be sure to check for any errors or references to the wrong client or project. You might also consider using generative Artificial Intelligence (AI), which can create new content from data (Martineau, 2024). Although still evolving and with potential issues (Hafke, 2023), generative AI will become a common tool in the near future.
3. One final read

   Never underestimate the value of a final proofread before submission. Attention to detail is crucial for consultants. Typos, poor formatting, and minor errors can undermine your proposal and raise doubts about your work quality. While word processing tools may help those living with intellectual disabilities or neurodivergence, they cannot ensure clarity, and autocorrect can create new problems. Ideally, have someone else review your work and allow time to incorporate their feedback.

While these are my personal reflections, it may be helpful to also consider the 3Cs defined by Luttig and de Villiers (2022) as key to successful proposals. These are *Compliance*, *Compellingness*, and *Competitiveness*. Compliance relates to whether the proposal complies with any specific instructions provided by the client, such as word count, font size, inclusion of specific documents. It also relates to whether the content fully meets requirements, addressing both stated and implicit client needs and whether or not the proposal provides the projected return on investment. Compellingness is about whether or not the proposal is framed in a way that will resonate with the client's needs and values.

The proposal needs to clearly differentiate you from the competition, and it needs to convey not just what you will deliver, but that working with you will be a positive experience. Competitiveness relates to whether the proposal clearly indicates value for money in the current market and whether the innovations, cost savings, and specific benefits you will bring are clearly communicated.

Over to You

If you have had some experience of responding to requests for proposals, can you relate to any of the experiences and suggestions in this chapter? If you are new to this aspect of consultancy, do you now feel well prepared, or quite terrified at the prospect of that first request? Regardless of your level of experience, I hope you will take the opportunity now to consider how you respond to future requests and ideally begin to develop your own systematic processes for these. In Box 10.4 there are several questions which might help you to consider the best approach for you.

The questions in Box 10.5 can also be helpful to consider when planning the writing of your proposal.

Box 10.4 Questions to Guide Your Response to an RfP

How will you assess whether the opportunity is right for you?

At what stage will you contact the client, and what will you ask them?

What strategies will you employ when dealing with uncertainty or incomplete information?

How will you employ any systematic methodologies; for example, PRINCE2 (PRINCE2, n.d.), the Behaviour Change Wheel approach (Michie et al., 2014), or other methods to enhance the quality of your proposed solution, and how much time do you need to apply this?

How will you realistically cost the proposal, and how will you identify and quantify potential risks and hidden costs?

Box 10.5 Questions to Help with Writing a Proposal

What are the specific benefits or value of your proposed solution, and how will you communicate these effectively to the client?

What previous work and specific skills are relevant to this work, and how will you communicate these effectively to the client?

Is the proposal easy and enjoyable to read, that is, free from jargon, explained in appropriate detail and language, visually appealing, and so on?

Does the proposal meet all of the client's explicit requirements?

In conclusion, while the process of preparing and submitting a proposal can be daunting, it also gives us as psychologists the opportunity to not only apply our expertise to a problem, by researching and formulating some potential solutions, it allows us to showcase our unique skills and expertise. Preparing a proposal is a vital element of the consultancy process, and ultimately it is a hurdle we must jump to be able to do the work we are all driven to do. I sincerely hope that the advice offered in this chapter enables you to develop an approach that makes that hurdle somewhat easier to clear.

Questions for Reflection

1. What pitfalls have you fallen into when responding to RfPs and how can you avoid them next time?
2. How does your training in health psychology prepare you for the process of responding to RfPs?
3. How can you increase your confidence and competence in responding to RfPs?

Competing Interests The author has no competing interests to declare that are relevant to the content of this chapter.

References

Baumeister, R. F., Bratslavsky, E., Finkenauer, C., & Vohs, K. D. (2001). *Bad is stronger than good.* Educational Publishing Foundation. https://doi.org/10.1037/1089-2680.5.4.323

Biggs, J. (1996). Enhancing teaching through constructive alignment. *Higher education, 32*(3), 347–364. https://doi.org/10.1007/BF00138871

Brady, R., & Varkonyi-Sepp, J. (2025). A framework for consultancy in health psychology. In R. Brady, J. Varkonyi-Sepp, & J. Smith (Eds.), *The Palgrave handbook of consultancy in health psychology*. Palgrave Macmillan.

Brashers, D. E. (2001). Communication and uncertainty management. *Journal of Communication, 51*(3), 477–497. https://doi.org/10.1111/j.1460-2466.2001.tb02892.x

Curtis, K., Fulton, E., & Brown, K. (2018). Factors influencing application of behavioural science evidence by public health decision-makers and practitioners, and implications for practice. *Preventive Medicine Reports, 12*, 106–115. https://doi.org/10.1016/j.pmedr.2018.08.012

Department of Health & Social Care (2023). *Consultation outcome: Preview of proposals for the Provider Selection Regime.* https://www.gov.uk/government/consultations/provider-selection-regime-supplementary-consultation-on-the-detail-of-proposals-for-regulations/preview-of-proposals-for-the-provider-selection-regime#decision-making-criteria

Dwyer, J., Liang, Z., & Thiessen, V. (2020). *Project management in health and community services; getting good ideas to work* (3rd edn). Routledge. https://www.routledge.com/Project-Management-in-Health-and-Community-Services-Getting-good-ideas-to-work/Liang-Stanton/p/book/9781760632816?source=shoppingads&locale=en-GBP&gad_source=1&gclid=CjwKCAjwxLKxBhA7EiwAXO0R0M1h_XgqwwFP3groCXoKJ96ZsRmY2dvWDPBmIXIIK721s1v5QzTphxoC-D4QAvD_BwE

Gluckler, J., & Armbruster, T. (2003). Bridging uncertainty in management consulting: The mechanisms of trust and networked reputation. *Organization Studies, 24*, 269–297. https://doi.org/10.1177/0170840603242004

Hafke, T. (2023). Generative AI in consulting. *Alphasense*. Retrieved April 27, 2024 from https://www.alpha-sense.com/blog/trends/generative-ai-consulting/

Kelly, S., Marshall, D., Walker, H., & Israilidis, J. (2021). Supplier satisfaction with public sector competitive tendering processes. *Journal of Public Procurement, 21*(2), 183–205. https://doi.org/10.1108/JOPP-12-2020-0088

Lazarus, R. S., & Folkman, S. (1984). *Stress, appraisal, and coping*. Springer Publishing Company.

Lunt, J. (2025). The sustainable consultant. In R. Brady, J. Varkonyi-Sepp, & J. Smith (Eds.), *The Palgrave handbook of consultancy in health psychology*. Palgrave Macmillan.

Luttig, L., & de Villiers, R. (2022). Intention to create meaningful outcomes: Tenders, bids and client pitches. In R. de Villiers (Ed.), *The handbook of creativity & innovation in business: A comprehensive toolkit of theory and practice for developing creative thinking skills* (pp. 267–290). Springer Nature. https://doi.org/10.1007/978-981-19-2180-3_13

Marks, D. F., & Yardley, L. (Eds.). (2004). *Research methods for clinical and health psychology*. SAGE Publications Ltd..

Martineau, K. (2024). *What is generative AI?*. Retrieved April 27, 2024 from https://research.ibm.com/blog/what-is-generative-AI

McBride, D. M., & Anne Dosher, B. (2002). A comparison of conscious and automatic memory processes for picture and word stimuli: A process dissociation analysis. *Conscious Cogn, 11*(3), 423–460. https://doi.org/10.1016/s1053-8100(02)00007-7

Michie, S., Atkins, L., & West, R. (2014). *The behaviour change wheel: A guide to designing interventions*. Silverback Publishing.

Miles, J., & Gilbert, P. (Eds.). (2005). *A handbook of research methods for clinical and health psychology*. Oxford University Press. https://doi.org/10.1093/med:psych/9780198527565.001.0001

Newson, L. (2025). Pricing and value in health psychology consultancy. In R. Brady, J. Varkonyi-Sepp, & J. Smith (Eds.), *The Palgrave handbook of consultancy in health psychology*. Palgrave Macmillan.

Nicolescu, O., & Nicolescu, C. (2016). Specificity of managerial consultancy for SMEs and its status in Romania. *Procedia - Social and Behavioral Sciences, 221*, 39–48. https://doi.org/10.1016/j.sbspro.2016.05.088

Nikolova, N., Reihlen, M., & Schlapfner, J. F. (2009). Client–consultant interaction: Capturing social practices of professional service production. *Scandinavian journal of management, 25*(3), 289–298.

Orritt, R., & Powell, P. (2020). Getting the word out: How to talk to the public about your research. *Breathe (Sheff), 16*(2), 200008. https://doi.org/10.1183/20734735.0008-2020

Osipovic, D., Allen, P., Shepherd, E., Petsoulas, C., Coleman, A., Perkins, N., Williams, L., & Sanderson, M. (2020). 83Commissioning of healthcare through competitive and cooperative mechanisms under the HSCA 2012. In P. Allen, K. Checkland, V. Moran, & S. Peckham (Eds.), *Commissioning healthcare in England: Evidence, policy and practice* (p. 0). Policy Press. https://doi.org/10.1332/policypress/9781447346111.003.0006

Pappas, S. (2021). *How to write for a non-academic audience*. American Psychological Association. Retrieved April 27, 2024 from https://www.apa.org/monitor/2021/01/career-write

PRINCE2. Retrieved April 27, 2024 from https://www.prince2.com/uk

Samuels, P. (2022). *Proposal writing for business research projects*. Routledge. https://www.routledge.com/Proposal-Writing-for-Business-Research-Projects/Samuels/p/book/9781032258126?source=shoppingads&locale=en-GBP&gad_source=1&gclid=CjwKCAjwxLKxBhA7EiwAXO0R0IHZJNbVsKguS7amrtexam9jSc3HnH2UeNxbPKRy_X5r3a_OHpCMxhoCqQcQAvD_BwE

Siegrist, J. (2016). Effort-reward imbalance model. In *Stress: Concepts, cognition, emotion, and behavior* (pp. 81–86). Elsevier.

Smallwood, J., & Schooler, J. W. (2006). The restless mind. *Psychological Bulletin, 132*(6), 946–958. https://doi.org/10.1037/0033-2909.132.6.946

Spurgeon, P., & Hicks, C. (2003). The tendering process: Flaws and all. *Health Serv Manage Res, 16*(3), 188–193. https://doi.org/10.1258/095148403322167942

The Stationery Office (2017). *Managing successful projects with PRINCE2*. Crown Copyright. https://books.google.co.uk/books?id=oE2dtAEACAAJ

Tucmeanu, A. I., Popescu, D. M., Ionescu, E. V., Oprea, C., Mociu, A., & Iliescu, M. G. (2017). Increasing the quality of health management in Romania through specific consultancy services. *ARS Medica Tomitana, 23*(3), 110–114. https://doi.org/10.1515/arsm-2017-0019

Whang, S. W., Donyavi, S., Flanagan, R., & Kim, S. (2022). Balanced approach for tendering practice at the pre-contract stage: The UK practitioner's perspective. *Journal of Civil Engineering and Management, 28*(5), 338–348. https://doi.org/10.3846/jcem.2022.16580

11

Starting Up a Health Psychology Consultancy

Nisha Sharma and Lisa Hodges-Ballard

Introduction

This chapter outlines our experiences of setting up a health psychology consultancy in the United Kingdom (UK). In addition to consultancy services, our practice offers teaching, training, research, and one-to-one therapeutic interventions. Since we practise in the UK, our experiences reflect this context. The chapter is aimed at individuals considering setting up their own psychology consultancy practice. When we navigated through the process of setting up our practice, we found there was little guidance specifically tailored to health psychologists. By sharing our experiences and reflections, we hope to inspire others. We do not position ourselves as experts in setting up a consultancy and it is essential for readers to verify the legal, financial, and other regulatory requirements when starting a new business. When we set up our practice, we had little prior experience in providing health psychology consultancy beyond what was required for the British Psychological Society's (BPS) health psychology stage 2 doctoral training. We begin by sharing our motivations for setting up our own practice and then discuss key considerations and actions involved in setting up a psychology-based consultancy.

N. Sharma (✉) • L. Hodges-Ballard
Cognitiva Consultancy Ltd., Southampton, UK
e-mail: info@cognitivaconsultancy.co.uk; l.ballard@soton.ac.uk

R. Brady et al. (eds.), *The Palgrave Handbook of Consultancy in Health Psychology*,
https://doi.org/10.1007/978-3-031-94529-8_11

How It All Started

Our story begins during our doctoral training days daydreaming about qualifying and securing roles that would allow us to apply our diverse skills in behaviour change interventions and research. We imagined having our own practice, sketching potential logos, and considering business names. We believe this helped us get through long study days, keeping us focused and driven to achieve our goal of qualifying as health psychologists. In 2020, while meeting for a socially distanced walk during the COVID-19 pandemic, we discussed our job roles. One of us worked as a practitioner psychologist but felt limited by the lack of variety and flexibility within the role to engage in research or project work. The other worked in an academic setting and, after a few years, missed undertaking practitioner work. As we reflected on our shared feelings, we realised we both needed more professional flexibility and growth. This conversation reignited the idea of setting up our own consultancy practice; a possibility that we began to seriously explore.

Before Setting up a Consultancy Practice

If you are considering setting up a consultancy practice, we suggest you ask yourself why, what, who, and how questions. We will discuss each of these and what they meant for us in the context of setting up a consultancy practice.

The Why

When considering why you want to set up a consultancy, it is important to reflect on your personal, professional, and financial motivations for doing so, as each will come with its own set of costs and benefits. One advantage of setting up your own consultancy practice is the opportunity to be your own boss. This can give you greater control over your schedule and the projects you undertake. You may choose to focus on projects that align with your values, that allow you to make a positive impact, and that you are passionate about. However, there are also potential disadvantages, including financial risk, particularly for initial start-up costs (discussed later in the chapter), uncertainty, and the time commitment. Additionally, there are potential stresses involved in establishing and maintaining a successful business, especially if you are employed while setting up your consultancy. We recommend conducting a cost/benefit analysis, to help guide your decision-making process.

In our case, we were determined to maintain and expand our professional skills in alignment with our values. Reflecting individually and together on our professional values, we identified equality, fairness, and social justice; values that are also shared with other psychologists (Hailes et al., 2021; Montgomery et al., 2011). Through discussions about our work to date, we agreed to focus our consultancy on addressing health inequalities. For example, our initial consultancy project focused on synthesising qualitative research to inform a public health campaign on antimicrobial resistance, which was tailored towards underserved groups (Hodges-Ballard & Sharma, 2025; see Chap. 17). We reflected on how our values were shaped by our experiences of working within the National Health Service (NHS), where we delivered public health interventions to support underserved communities and those in areas of high deprivation. Interestingly, one of us worked as a health trainer, a role introduced in the 2004 UK Department of Health White Paper (Department of Health, 2004). The health trainer role was informed by an evidence-based intervention, which was designed, implemented, and evaluated by a team of health psychologists (Gardner et al., 2012). Through this work, we witnessed first-hand how public health interventions can significantly improve both individual and community wellbeing.

Setting up a consultancy practice offered an opportunity to integrate our broader professional skills into our work, while also supplementing our income. In the practitioner role, although undertaking audit and research was part of the job description, the reality of working in an under-resourced service meant that clinical work had to take priority, leaving no time to undertake research. This is consistent with the findings of Williams et al. (2020), who identified clinical pressures, lack of protected time, and organisational support as the primary barriers to research engagement for health care professionals working in an NHS mental health trust in London. In the academic role, the insecurity of fixed-term contracts, and needing a 'plan B' was a concern; almost 70% of researchers in higher education are on fixed-term contracts and 61% hold more than one position at a time (University and College Union, 2019). We saw the potential to increase our income through growing a consultancy practice over time.

After deciding to go ahead, we immediately began brainstorming potential names for the consultancy practice and thinking about where to start with setting up. We chose to name the consultancy as a first step as it allowed us to complete essential business-related tasks, such as registering the consultancy as a limited company and creating a website. Without a name, it would have been difficult to move forward with these tasks. We also thought it was important to set up a website so that potential clients could learn about our services.

On reflection, starting with our consultancy name was naive on our part. We may have benefited from taking the time to reflect on more important considerations, which we discuss below.

The What

Once you know why you want to set up a consultancy, the next step is to consider the products or services you can offer. Health psychologists are well-positioned to use their knowledge and skills to promote general wellbeing across the population and understand physical illness (The British Psychological Society, n.d.). Health psychologists can work in diverse settings, including hospitals, community health settings, local authorities, universities, and many more. Researching existing psychology services can help increase understanding regarding the current market to identify gaps and assess how your knowledge, skills, and experience can fill those gaps. Start broadly by identifying areas in healthcare where health psychology expertise can be applied (e.g., addressing high rates of smoking or obesity). You might focus on specific populations (e.g., ethnicity, age, gender, socioeconomic status), health domains (e.g., chronic pain, diabetes, renal care), or health sectors (e.g., primary, community, secondary, or tertiary care). Aligning these areas with your expertise, values, and interests is crucial. Stay informed by reading academic papers, reports, current affairs, and social media to guide your research. Additionally, taking the opportunity to speak with colleagues or professionals from different fields can help identify areas where you might provide valuable insight or expertise. As health psychologists, our training focuses our skills in research, teaching, training, and behaviour change, which can form part of the consultancy work that you offer. We have created a list of questions in Table 11.1 to help identify potential services you might wish to offer. There are no set answers to these questions, and they are likely to change over time. You may wish to do a SWOT analysis to assess your Strengths, Weaknesses, Opportunities, and Threats (Benzaghta et al., 2021). It may also be helpful to research examples of similar businesses or to reach out to a business professional, coach, or mentor to guide you through the questions and the SWOT analysis.

Answering the questions in Table 11.1 will inform your business plan, which we discuss later in this chapter. It is also valuable to reflect on your personal values and what is most important to you (Talbot, 2003). Your values will guide your mission statement and serve as a framework for making decisions about the work you pursue and who you choose to work with. For

Table 11.1 Questions to reflect on prior to setting up a consultancy

Consultancy services	Market analysis
• What services can you offer? • What is your niche or unique selling point? • What are your strengths and weaknesses? • What is your business mission? • What are your business values? • What are your key objectives/business goals? • What will success look like, and in what time frame?	• What health psychology consultancy services are already available in the market? • Who are your competitors, and what do they offer? • What gaps exist in the market for health psychology consultancy?

instance, our shared values of equality and fairness are reflected in various aspects of our consultancy, such as the types of projects we undertake (e.g., Hodges-Ballard & Sharma, 2025; see Chap.17) and how we divide the workload fairly between us. When considering new opportunities, we are motivated by our commitment to addressing health inequalities, which leads us to prioritise projects that align with this goal.

The Who

Once you understand the current market, and the products and services you will offer, there are two important questions to reflect on: who are your potential clients, and who else will you be working with? Addressing these questions will help guide your approach to 'the how'.

Firstly, it is essential to network with professionals working in your area(s) of interest. Networking offers a valuable opportunity to share ideas, gather insights, build peer support, and market your consultancy. Networking can be achieved by seeking out pre-existing or special interest groups and attending relevant meetings, events, and conferences. Presenting or exhibiting at events can further increase your visibility. If no established networks exist, it may be an ideal opportunity to create one. Additionally, online platforms and professional networks can be leveraged to connect with potential clients and foster meaningful relationships. Identifying potential clients involves assessing both the needs of the individual or organisation and your area of expertise and skills. It is important to evaluate if there is an alignment between the challenges the client is facing and the services you offer. By identifying your potential clients, you can tailor your approach and the language you use when reaching out to them. For example, when advertising your work and how you can offer support, using keywords or industry-specific terminology in social media posts, marketing materials, and communications can make your message resonate more effectively. Word of mouth recommendations can also help you to connect with potential clients. Our mentor advised us to identify a list of people known to us and encouraged us to reach out to them. We contacted former colleagues informing them that we had set up a consultancy practice and asked them to keep us in mind for any upcoming work.

Secondly, consider whether you will work as a sole practitioner or in a partnership, and whether your consultancy practice includes other professionals. If so, how will they be involved? For example, will the individual(s) work as an employee? The answers to these questions will influence your decision about the type of business structure you need to form, which we discuss further in 'the how' section. Your decision may impact financial considerations; for example, how much revenue is needed to cover staffing costs. As with any decision, there are pros and cons to consider when setting up a consultancy practice with others. Benefits may include having shared decision-making responsibility (if setting up your consultancy with a partner), support with undertaking business tasks, sharing workload, and having greater capacity. Equally, however, challenges can arise, such as differences of opinions on business decisions, conflicting priorities, or varying work styles. If you choose to set up a consultancy practice involving others who do not share business ownership with you (whether as partners or as employees) do ensure you have appropriate legal agreements (i.e., a contract) in place. These agreements should clearly outline responsibilities, duties, payment terms, and other essential details. It is always advisable to consult with a legal representative to ensure your agreement is thorough and meets legal requirements.

We decided to set up a consultancy together for several reasons. Having worked for the same organisation for many years and completed our doctoral studies together, we knew each other well and understood how each other worked. This familiarity provided several advantages in setting up the consultancy together, such as having complementary strengths, skills, and expertise, as well as the ability to share the workload and responsibilities. Additionally, working together meant we could motivate each other, discuss ideas, and avoid feeling isolated. Entrepreneurs can experience an extremely high burden of responsibility, lack of co-worker support, social maladaptation, a lack of resources, and isolation including social, cognitive, and physical (Cardon & Arwine, 2023). We were aware of the risks in entering a business relationship with a friend in terms of blurring personal and professional boundaries and power dynamics. For example, one individual assuming seniority over the other person could create tension and a power imbalance. Before setting up our consultancy practice, we took the time to discuss how we could effectively work together as business partners and friends. We talked about how to separate our friendship from business matters and how we would handle potential conflicts. Fortunately, we share similar values, and we are able to maintain clear boundaries. For instance, when discussing business matters, we set up meetings with agendas, keep a record of the meetings, and prioritise open and honest communication.

The How

Once you have thought about why and what, you will be in a better position to write a business plan, consider the legal form of the business, assess the financial considerations, and manage the administrative tasks.

Writing a business plan. In our view, developing a business plan is vital. It is an essential document that provides a description and overview of your business (Ekanem, 2017; McKeever, 2018). A business plan includes your objectives, market analysis, strategies (e.g., for sales and marketing), and financial forecasts. A business plan helps to clarify your business idea, establish your vision and goals, identify any potential problems, have a clear strategy to follow, and measure your progress. A meta-analysis of 46 studies reported that business planning is beneficial, increasing performance in small businesses (Brinckmann et al., 2010). There are many resources and templates available online to guide you with your business plan, for example, via the UK government website (GOV.UK, n.d.-e). Failing to have a business plan can lead to significant consequences for your consultancy, including a lack of direction, wasted resources, and missed opportunities for growth (Ekanem, 2017).

The legal form of consultancy business. There are several ways to legally operate as a business in the UK. For a new consultancy practice, these options include operating as a sole trader, a limited company, or a partnership (GOV.UK, n.d.-d). How you choose to set up the consultancy has implications for the personal liability of the founders and owners, as well as financial factors, such as tax liabilities. Hill (2015, p. 212) outlines the most common legal forms for businesses within the UK, including their key features, advantages and disadvantages, and further resources. In the UK, sole trader and company limited by shares are the most common forms of business structures (Hill, 2015). In our case, while continuing to work as full-time employees, we decided to set up a limited company. This seemed like the most sensible and pragmatic decision, as it involved the least amount of personal risk. By choosing a limited company, our business finances would be kept separate from our personal finances, and the consultancy would be legally separate from us as individuals.

Financial considerations. Once you decide on the legal form for the practice, it is important to consider the associated costs of setting up and running your consultancy, and how you will generate income. If you plan to rely solely on your consultancy for income (rather than alongside other employment), you will need to estimate the minimum income required to cover personal expenses and costs of operating the business. Costs may include administrative time, equipment, premises, utilities, professional fees, and staff costs (if applicable). Table 11.2 outlines some of the potential operating and running costs involved in setting up and running a consultancy practice. If you decide to run your consultancy practice from your home, you may also need to inform your home insurance provider to ensure adequate coverage for business-related activities.

Pricing your services. As you identify the services you will offer, determining how to price them can be challenging. There are several pricing models that you can consider. For example, you may choose to charge a standard hourly or daily rate or opt to price each individual project. Whatever pricing structure you select, it should cover your costs and include a profit margin.

Table 11.2 Operating costs for a consultancy practice

Some costs to consider[a]	
Time[b]	• Administration • Consultancy
Equipment and consumables	• Stationery • Books and other resources • Computer or laptop • Equipment maintenance/replacement
Overheads	• Utility costs (e.g., energy, rent, water) • Website domain and email subscription service costs • Software licenses and online meeting facilities • Phone charges • Travel costs
Professional fees and insurances	• Professional registration/memberships • Insurances (e.g., public liability, professional indemnity) • Accountancy and other financial fees • Data protection fee • Professional training and supervision
Staff/subcontractors	• Staff salaries • Fees to associates or subcontractors

[a]Based on our experience and thinking in regard to our own consultancy
[b]You could choose to charge a different rate for administration and service delivery to reflect different levels of expertise required for each

Setting competitive prices for a consultancy practice requires assessing your training, expertise, and experience, as well as understanding your clients and their ability to pay for your services. Public and third sector organisations, for example, may have strict budget limits due to reliance on public funds or donations. To address this, you might set a standard price for your services, which can be adjusted based on the client's sector or budget. For instance, you could offer a sliding scale of fees for different sectors, or you may have a standard price and choose to apply discounts or concessions for different sectors and circumstances. It is also possible to adjust the scope of the services you provide depending on the client's budget. Pricing strategies should be reviewed periodically to account for changes in demand, market dynamics, and your evolving expertise. Finding the right balance between appropriately valuing your services and expertise while remaining competitive is key. One challenge we experienced with our initial consultancy project was determining our value and setting fees that aligned both with our worth and the client's budget and expectations. Newson (2025; see Chap. 9) provides more detailed guidance on pricing consultancy in health consultancy.

Record keeping. Maintaining accurate accounting records is essential for any business. This includes keeping copies of receipts, invoices, and bank statements. Proper record-keeping helps with costing projects, tracking cash flow, and ensuring accurate records for tax returns. You can use tools like spreadsheets or a bookkeeping system to document your business's income and expenditure. For UK businesses, HM Revenue and Customs (HMRC) offers a webinar on record-keeping targeted at sole traders and partnerships (HM Revenue & Customs, 2024). Alternatively, you can choose to hire an accountant to prepare your annual accounts and tax returns. It is important to select an accountant registered with a professional regulatory body such as the Association of Chartered Certified Accountants (ACCA), the Chartered Institute of Management Accounting (CIMA), the Institute of Chartered Accountants in England and Wales (ICAEW), or the Institute of Chartered Accountants of Scotland (ICAS). An accountant can also advise you on what qualifies as a business expense, including expenses you might not typically consider, such as electricity, Internet, stationery, printing, travel costs, and tax efficiency strategies.

Choosing a business name. The name of a business is the first thing a client will pay attention to and is an important element for establishing a brand identity (Eskiev, 2021). To get inspiration, consider how well-known companies have chosen their business names. When selecting a name, aim for something simple, easy to pronounce, and memorable. It might be helpful to ask a few friends or colleagues for their feedback to ensure the name resonates well.

The rules for naming your business can vary depending on whether you are operating as a sole trader, limited company, or partnership. You can check the relevant guidance via the UK government website. Before finalising your business name, you will need to ensure that it has not been registered elsewhere. Within the UK, you can easily search company name availability (GOV.UK, n.d.-a). Be aware that there might be similar options to search for available names in other countries. If your business name consists of multiple words and you decide to use an acronym, ensure the abbreviation is not offensive to any individuals or groups.

Registering the consultancy with appropriate authorities. If you choose to set up a limited company or limited liability partnership in the UK, you must register your consultancy practice with Companies House within three months of starting to trade. It is important to be aware of and to comply with the legislative requirements of the country in which your consultancy operates. If you decide to operate in another country, other than where your consultancy is registered, you will need to familiarise yourself with the relevant legislation of that country.

Check what insurance you may need. Depending on the service(s) you provide, we strongly advise taking out additional insurance coverage, such as professional indemnity insurance, public liability insurance, and/or employer liability insurance. Professional indemnity insurance is designed to protect you against claims resulting from your practice as a psychologist. For example, if you are alleged to have provided inadequate advice or services, this insurance can cover legal fees and compensation costs. Within the Code of Ethics and Conduct (British Psychological Society, 2021), the BPS strongly recommends that the professional indemnity insurance includes legal cover and clarifies that the professional indemnity insurance is a legal requirement for members who are registered with the Health and Care Professionals Council (HCPC). Public liability insurance is designed to protect your business from financial risk, for example, if a client or member of the public claims that they have been injured as a result of your business activities. If you employ staff, it is a legal requirement to have employers' liability insurance (GOV.UK, n.d.-c), which protects employees if they experience injury or illness as a result of working for your business. Some clients might request that you have certain insurances in place as a condition of working with them. For any insurance, you need to check whether it should be under your own name or as your business name. Carefully assess your own business risk and choose an appropriate policy with comprehensive cover.

Check if you need to register with the Information Commissioner's Office or equivalent body in other countries. In the UK, if you process personal data, you need to register online and pay a data protection fee to the Information Commissioner's Office (ICO). Personal data refers to any information that relates to an identified or identifiable living individual (Information Commissioner's Office, n.d.-b). If you are setting up your consultancy with more than one person, you need to designate one individual to act as your data protection officer. In the UK, if you have access to personal data, you must comply with 'data protection principles' and act in accordance with data protection laws (GOV.UK, n.d.-b). The ICO provides useful guidance for small businesses about data protection (Information Commissioner's Office, n.d.-a). If you collect or store data from clients, you need secure storage space such as a lockable filing cabinet. If you use an Internet storage facility, you must ensure it is compliant with data protection legislation. Other countries may have their own regulations, which consultants must be familiar with and abide by.

Open a business bank account. If you have set up a limited company or partnership, you will need to open a business bank account. As a sole trader, it is not a legal requirement, but it is considered best practice. Having a separate account for personal and business transactions is important for tracking income and expenses, as well as for preparing annual tax returns as a self-employed individual. When choosing a business bank account, there are several factors to consider, such as: service preferences (e.g., in-person banking at a branch or online banking), credit options and access to a business credit card; fees and benefits, banking fees, and other additional benefits. In line with our values, we made a point of selecting a bank that practices ethical banking. Some banks are more transparent about their investments, for instance, avoiding sectors such as animal testing or fossil fuels. Additionally, we chose a bank that aligns with fair working conditions and pay practices. This was an important consideration, ensuring that the financial institution supports values that reflect our commitment to ethical business practices.

Set up an email account and website. Separating your personal emails from your business email is essential for maintaining professionalism and keeping your communication organised. Renting a unique domain name for a website and email provides several advantages, including increased business credibility, brand consistency, and a memorable email address and website. When handling and emailing personal client information, you may wish to consider using an encrypted email service. This will typically incur an additional cost but is highly recommended to protect client confidentiality. If you choose to set up a website, carefully consider the content and layout to encourage potential clients to contact you. Potential clients are likely to visit your website to learn about your services and assess your suitability for their needs.

It is helpful to include a brief introduction about yourself and any staff (with their permission), the services you offer and how they can benefit potential clients, and clear contact details with a contact form for inquiries. If your budget permits, you may choose to outsource the setup and design of your website.

Getting Started

With the practical elements in place, the next step involves finding work. You might start by researching local or national grants, funding opportunities, and tenders, or reaching out to your existing network or contacts. Once your consultancy is up and running, there are some factors to consider in order to help your business grow, including engaging a mentor and marketing your business. Additionally, we will discuss the importance of establishing client contracts and agreements to ensure clarity and protect your business.

Engaging a Mentor

A mentor is an experienced and trusted advisor who can help you develop and grow your consultancy by sharing their skills, expertise, experience, and contacts. When you are new to consultancy, having access to a mentor is invaluable. A review of 151 business mentoring articles highlights that while mentoring generally has positive outcomes, challenges such as time constraints, lack of training, or poor mentor–mentee matching can lead to negative results (Hansford et al., 2002). To find a suitable mentor, consider who you admire or aspire to in the industry and reach out to them with a clear request. Be specific about your goals, how often you wish to meet, and the duration of the mentorship. It is important to be prepared for the possibility that a potential mentor might decline your request. Mentorships should be optional, not an obligation, and some mentors may charge for their time. You can find both free and paid mentoring options through online searches or networks within the UK. Alternatively, a business coach can offer support, training, and coaching to help you start and grow your consultancy. Additionally, organisations such as the Federation of Small Businesses (Federation of Small Businesses, n.d.) offer legal, financial, and business support.

Our mentorship opportunity came to us by chance. We initially contacted our mentor through a paid opportunity advertised via an email network that we were both part of. Although we both interviewed for the position, we were unsuccessful in securing the opportunity. Despite that, we stayed in touch with the individual, built rapport, and developed a supportive relationship. Our mentor asked us thought-provoking questions that helped us reflect on and clarify our consultancy aims and identify our likely target clients. This process enabled us to pinpoint the types of work we would be excited to undertake and how we could find opportunities aligned with those goals. In hindsight, it would have been beneficial for us to reflect on our values, objectives, and target clients earlier in the process. Our mentor also encouraged us to consider the problems our potential clients might be facing and how we could offer solutions or benefits to them. This exercise proved invaluable, as it allowed us to tailor our communication and use industry-specific language when engaging with potential clients.

Marketing

As part of your business plan, you will need to consider how to market yourself to reach potential clients. This could include information about target clients you wish to approach (i.e., type of organisation, size, geographical areas of operation, values, services offered and to which groups, organisation aims and objectives, health domains of interest, and so on). Much of this information can typically be obtained from the organisation's website. Your marketing plan should also include key contacts, such as the people who make decisions about contracting services or individuals who might introduce you to decision makers. Additionally, it is important to outline the service(s) and product(s) you would offer, the specific populations you wish to work with, and your areas of expertise. These considerations will guide your approach, helping you determine what methods of contact to use, what content to include, and which media channels to utilise when engaging with potential clients.

Consider developing a marketing plan for how you promote your consultancy services (Chernev, 2020). Within this you should think about your branding and online presence. When it comes to branding, you will need to consider elements such as your logo. It can be worthwhile hiring a designer to create one for you, or alternatively, you can use customisable logo templates available online. You will also need to decide on the style of your branding, choosing fonts and colours that look professional. Research suggests that logos that include an icon and the brand name are perceived as more attractive compared to logos made of one component, and black logos are perceived as more attractive than coloured logos (Bresciani & Del Ponte, 2017). You might wish to consider whether having a social media presence is important for your consultancy, and if so, which social media platform(s) to use, and which platform(s) potential clients engage with. The answers to these questions will guide how much time, resources, and energy you invest. If you decide that using social media is part of your strategy, you will need to decide how often and when to post content and engage with your audience. You may also want to review analytic data to track whether people are engaging with your posts, and ultimately whether this leads to new business or clients. You might decide to outsource social media management to an external person, which can give your consultancy a professional look while relieving you of the workload. However, this will likely come at a cost, and so it is important to weigh the benefits against the costs. It is easy to assume that having a website or social media presence is imperative for a successful consultancy. However, in our experience, word of mouth and strong network connections have been effective ways of generating business.

Establishing Client Contracts and Agreements

Agreements between the consultant and client are often reached in meetings and should always be followed up in writing. It is a good idea to have a draft consultancy agreement or contract prepared that can be tailored to each client. This agreement should clearly outline the terms and conditions of your services, deliverables, fees, confidentiality, intellectual property ownership, non-disclosure clauses, and any other relevant provisions. It is essential to consult with a lawyer to ensure legal compliance. Additionally, some clients and organisations may have a contract or agreement. In these cases, it is important to carefully read the terms and negotiate any clauses you are not comfortable with before signing. You can read about contracting with clients in more detail from the perspective of experienced health psychology consultants elsewhere in this book (Lunt, 2025; see Chap. 7, Atkinson, 2025; see Chap. 10, and Edwards-Smith, 2025; see Chap. 22).

Summary and Conclusion

In this chapter, we have shared our experiences of setting up a health psychology consultancy. We discussed how our consultancy practice began, the challenges we experienced in taking the first steps, and the lack of practical and relevant guidance available. To address these challenges, we have shared practical suggestions to consider when setting up your own health psychology consultancy, focusing specifically on the why, what, who, and how. In Box 11.1, we provide a summary of key questions that may act as a checklist to help guide you through the essential considerations when setting up a consultancy practice in the UK.

Box 11.1 Questions When Planning to Set Up Your Own Consultancy

Why do you want to set up a consultancy practice?

What does your market research tell you about demand for consultancy and gaps in the market?

What particular expertise can you offer?

What services/products can you offer?

What professional values will you bring to a consultancy business?

Who are the potential clients?

Will you work alone, with a partner(s), or will you employ people?

What are the practical tasks involved in setting up a consultancy practice—legal, financial, etc.?

What needs to be included in your business plan?

What are the set-up costs involved?

What will your operating costs be?

What income/revenue will you need to generate?

What needs to be included in your marketing plan?

Who can you learn and get advice from—mentor, other consultants, etc.?

Questions for Further Reflection

1. What opportunities for career development could I gain by setting up a consultancy practice?
2. How could I make a difference in the field of health psychology through a consultancy practice?
3. What further learning or support would I need in order to set up a consultancy practice?

Acknowledgements We would like to thank Richard Munday for his advice and support in preparing this chapter.

Competing Interests The authors have no competing interests to declare that are relevant to this chapter.

References

Atkinson, L. (2025). Don't fall at the first hurdle: Responding to requests for proposals. In R. Brady, J. Varkonyi-Sepp, & J. Smith (Eds.), *The Palgrave handbook of consultancy in health psychology*. Palgrave Macmillan.

Benzaghta, M. A., Elwalda, A., Mousa, M. M., Erkan, I., & Rahman, M. (2021). SWOT analysis applications: An integrative literature review. *Journal of Global Business Insights, 6*(1), 55–73. https://doi.org/10.5038/2640-6489.6.1.1148

Bresciani, S., & Del Ponte, P. (2017). New brand logo design: Customers' preference for brand name and icon. *Journal of Brand Management, 24*, 375–390. https://doi.org/10.1057/s41262-017-0046-4

Brinckmann, J., Grichnik, G., & Kapsa, D. (2010). Should entrepreneurs plan or just storm the castle? A meta-analysis on contextual factors impacting the business planning–performance relationship in small firms. *Journal of Business Venturing, 25*(1), 24–40. https://doi.org/10.1016/j.jbusvent.2008.10.007

Cardon, M. S., & Arwine, R. P. (2023). The many faces of entrepreneurial loneliness. *Personnel Psychology, 77*(1), 225–277. https://doi.org/10.1111/peps.12614

Chernev, A. (2020). *The marketing plan handbook*. Cerebellum Press.

Department of Health. (2004). *Choosing health: Making healthy choices easier.* https://webarchive.nationalarchives.gov.uk/ukgwa/+/dh.gov.uk/en/publicationsandstatistics/publications/publicationspolicyandguidance/dh_4094550

Edwards-Smith, L. (2025). Delivering healthcare differently: Formal and informal negotiation and contracting. In R. Brady, J. Varkonyi-Sepp, & J. Smith (Eds.), *The Palgrave handbook of consultancy in health psychology*. Palgrave Macmillan.

Ekanem, I. (2017). *Writing a business plan: A practical guide*. Routledge.

Eskiev, M. (2021). Naming as one of the most important elements of brand management. *SHS Web of Conferences, 128*. https://doi.org/10.1051/shsconf/202112801028

Federation of Small Businesses. (n.d.). *Resources*. Retrieved February 21, 2024, from https://www.fsb.org.uk/knowledge.html

Gardner, B., Cane, J., Rumsey, N., & Michie, S. (2012). Behaviour change among overweight and socially disadvantaged adults: A longitudinal study of the NHS Health Trainer Service. *Psychology & Health, 27*(10), 1178–1193. https://doi.org/10.1080/08870446.2011.652112

GOV.UK. (n.d.-a). *Company name availability checker*. Retrieved February 21, 2024, from https://find-and-update.company-information.service.gov.uk/company-name-availability

GOV.UK. (n.d.-b). *Data protection*. Retrieved February 21, 2024, from https://www.gov.uk/data-protection

GOV.UK. (n.d.-c). *Employers' liability insurance*. Retrieved February 21, 2024, from https://www.gov.uk/employers-liability-insurance

GOV.UK. (n.d.-d). *Set up a business.* Retrieved February 21, 2024, from https://www.gov.uk/set-up-business

GOV.UK. (n.d.-e). *Write a business plan.* Retrieved February 21, 2024, from https://www.gov.uk/write-business-plan

Hailes, H. P., Ceccolini, C. J., Gutowski, E., & Liang, B. (2021). Ethical guidelines for social justice in psychology. *Psychology: Research and Practice, 52*(1), 1–11. https://doi.org/10.1037/pro0000291

Hansford, B., Tennent, L., & Ehrich, L. C. (2002). Business mentoring: Help or hindrance? *Mentoring & Tutoring: Partnership in Learning, 10*(2), 101–115. https://doi.org/10.1080/1361126022000002428

Hill, I. (2015). *Start-Up: A practice based guide for new venture creation.* Bloomsbury Publishing.

HM Revenue & Customs. (2024, June 23). *Guidance.* https://www.gov.uk/guidance/help-and-support-if-youre-self-employed

Hodges-Ballard, L., & Sharma, N. (2025). Understanding high antibiotic prescribing rates for tailoring public health campaigns. In R. Brady, J. Varkonyi-Sepp, & J. Smith (Eds.), *The Palgrave handbook of consultancy in health psychology.* Palgrave Macmillan.

Information Commisioner's Office. (n.d.-a). *Find the right resource.* Retrieved February 21, 2024, from https://ico.org.uk/for-organisations/advice-for-small-organisations/find-the-right-resource/

Information Commisioner's Office. (n.d.-b). *What is personal data?* Retrieved February 21, 2024, from https://ico.org.uk/for-organisations/uk-gdpr-guidance-and-resources/personal-information-what-is-it/what-is-personal-data/what-is-personal-data/

Lunt, J. (2025). The sustainable consultant. In R. Brady, J. Varkonyi-Sepp, & J. Smith (Eds.), *The Palgrave handbook of consultancy in health psychology.* Palgrave Macmillan.

McKeever, M. P. (2018). *How to write a business plan* (14th ed.). NOLO.

Montgomery, A., Michie, S., Baban, A., McIntyre, T., Kok, G., Lawrence, W., Murray, M., & Johnston, M. (2011). Social justice: What has health psychology contributed? *The European Health Psychologist, 13*(1), 3–12.

Newson, L. (2025). Pricing and value in health psychology consultancy. In R. Brady, J. Varkonyi-Sepp, & J. Smith (Eds.), *The Palgrave handbook of consultancy in health psychology.* Palgrave Macmillan.

Talbot, M. (2003). *Make your mission statement work: Identify your organisation's values and live them every day* (2nd ed.). How To Books.

The British Psychological Society. (2021). *Code of ethics and conduct.* https://doi.org/10.53841/bpsrep.2021.inf94

The British Psychological Society. (n.d.). *Health psychologist job profile.* Retrieved June 24, 2024, from https://www.bps.org.uk/health-psychologist-job-profile

University and College Union. (2019). *Counting the costs of casualisation in higher education.* https://www.ucu.org.uk/media/10336/Counting-the-costs-of-casualisation-in-higher-education-Jun-19/pdf/ucu_casualisation_in_HE_survey_report_Jun19.pdf

Williams, J., Craig, T. J., & Robson, D. B. (2020). Barriers and facilitators of clinician and researcher collaborations: A qualitative study. *BMC Health Service Research, 20*(1), 1126. https://doi.org/10.1186/s12913-020-05978-w

12

A 'How To' Guide to Working in the Private Sector

Lina Eliasson and Christina Jackson

Introduction

This chapter presents a 'how to' guide to working in the private sector. It focuses on working with pharmaceutical (pharma) companies, although much of our advice and experience applies to other private sectors where a health psychologist may consult. This chapter is loosely structured according to the framework for consultancy in health psychology outlined in Brady and Varkonyi-Sepp (2025; see Chap. 3). The framework includes five distinct but overlapping elements of the process of consultancy: Enquiry, Relationships, Negotiating and contracting, Planning and managing delivery, and Evaluation. We have focused on the first three elements in this chapter and provide a concise overview of the final two elements in the last section, which will explore project delivery from the start of the consultancy to evaluation.

The consultancy approach we apply has evolved over nearly twenty years of working within the pharma sector. As we have grown our company and established in-house training for our consultants, we have found that the general consultancy literature is limited and lacks applicability for our work. The existing literature is aimed mainly at management consultants and does not reflect the complexities of working and conducting research within a highly

L. Eliasson (✉) • C. Jackson
Sprout Health Solutions Ltd., London, UK
e-mail: lina.eliasson@sprout-hs.com

R. Brady et al. (eds.), *The Palgrave Handbook of Consultancy in Health Psychology*,
https://doi.org/10.1007/978-3-031-94529-8_12

regulated healthcare industry with a very broad range of stakeholders to consider at a local, regional, and global level. We hope this chapter will help close this gap. Two resources that we have found helpful, however, are the Harvard Business Review (Harvard Business Review, n.d.) and Forbes (Forbes, n.d.). These journals can be accessed online and frequently publish relevant articles on consulting and business management.

Health Psychology and the Pharmaceutical Industry

Health psychology has many potential benefits for pharma throughout the clinical trial phases and in launch and post-marketing settings of health technologies (see Fig. 12.1); in particular, in areas related to elevating the patient's voice to understand and guide the work. Health technology is a broad term used to describe products that improve health, including drugs and pharmaceuticals, medical devices, and software applications. Health psychology is valuable across this health technology spectrum, although our work has focused mainly on drugs and pharmaceuticals. For ease of reading, we will mainly refer to drugs throughout this chapter.

As a health psychologist, you possess a diverse skill set that enables you to understand, promote, and optimise health and wellbeing. You can offer valuable contributions to the pharma industry in several ways (see Fig. 12.2). Behaviour change work (in our case informed by Michie et al., 2011a, 2011b; Michie et al., 2013) has been successful in bridging the gap between the academic and real-world settings. Indeed, our highly cited paper applying the COM-B framework (Capability Opportunity Motivation—Behaviour; Michie et al., 2011b) to medication adherence (Jackson et al., 2014) has

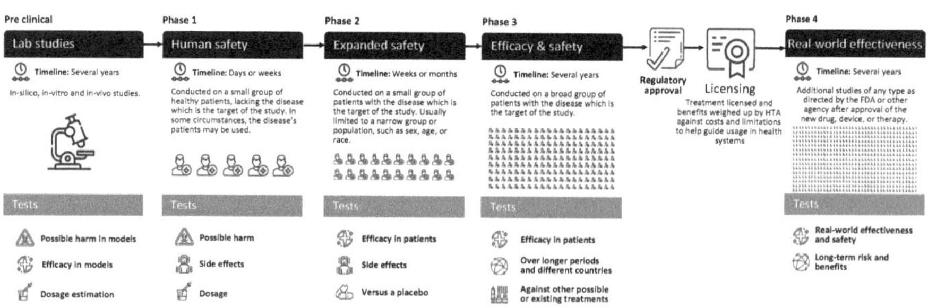

Fig. 12.1 Overview of clinical trial phases and their objectives

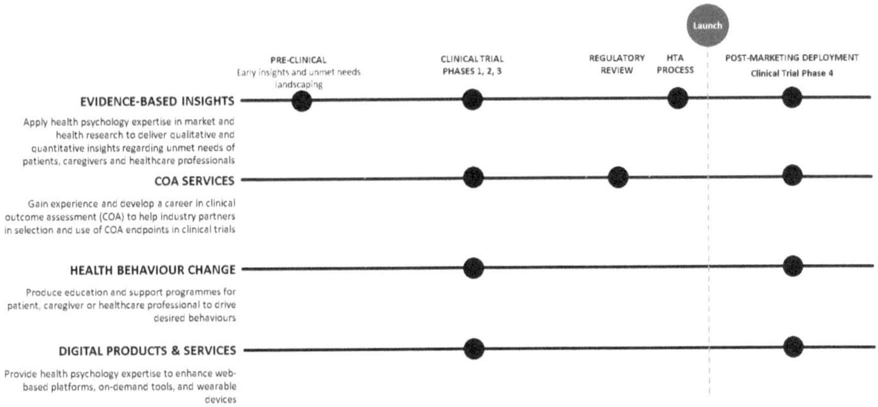

Fig. 12.2 Opportunities for health psychology consultants and vendors across the drug development pathway

generated many business opportunities for us within pharma. For example, health psychologists can apply the principles of behaviour change to provide a deep understanding of behaviours that impact health such as medication adherence, lifestyle change, and coping from the viewpoint of the patient and caregiver. Our understanding of behaviour change can also be applied to healthcare professionals; for example, identifying the barriers and facilitators to prescribing according to guidelines. Health psychology can reach as far as national and international healthcare policy through input on disease awareness campaigns, patient advocacy work, and healthcare guidance; all are areas where pharma companies have a stake.

Another specialist area suitable for health psychologists is clinical outcomes assessment (COA), also known as patient reported outcomes (PRO). This area usually requires on the job training to develop a deep understanding of what is required for tools and questionnaires to be considered fit-for-purpose for clinical trials by regulators such as the United States Food and Drug Administration (FDA) (U.S. Food and Drug Administration, 2009). It is important to acquire robust industry experience to advise pharmaceutical companies on their clinical trials outcome strategies and regulatory interactions.

There are different ways in which health psychologists can work with pharma companies including: as an individual expert consultant (although you may still be registered as a business); or as a vendor, which is a registered business that sells services, typically with a team of more than one. The bulk of this chapter assumes that you are working as a vendor. We (the authors) have worked for pharma both as expert consultants and as vendors, primarily in the United Kingdom (UK). Today our company delivers services to enable our clients to understand the experiences and health-related behaviours of patients, caregivers, and healthcare professionals. We also develop COA endpoint strategies and select, develop, and validate fit-for-purpose COAs for clinical trials. Our team includes health psychologists as well as a range of experts from social sciences and public health, and a project management team.

Structure of Pharmaceutical Companies

Pharma companies vary in size. We work with small to medium sized organisations such as biotechnology (biotech) companies which traditionally focus on pre-clinical and early phase development. At the other end of the spectrum, we work with large multinational organisations that, in addition to early phase development, introduce medical technologies through pivotal trials, commercialisation, and launch (also known as 'big pharma').

Biotech companies may have a global team only, whilst big pharma organisations tend to have global functions, as well as functions overseeing geographical regions such as Europe, for example. Finally, there are country level affiliates or local operating companies. The structure and jargon differ between companies, but they typically have three key strategic areas of responsibility: research and development (R&D), medical affairs, and commercial. As implied in the name, R&D leads the development of new medical technologies. Medical affairs concern themselves with evidence generation; that is, defining and producing the data that are needed to satisfy different stakeholders. These stakeholders include regulators such as the FDA assessing safety and efficacy data and approving the drug for use; health technology assessors (HTAs) such as NICE (National Institute for Health and Care Excellence) in the UK assessing the cost-effectiveness and approving the drug for reimbursement; healthcare providers prescribing medicines; and patients ultimately expected to adhere to treatment recommendations. Commercial makes the drug marketable, including the development of brand and marketing strategies, launch preparations, and wrap around services and training for prescribers, allied health professionals, patients, and caregivers. Campbell (2024) provides a comprehensive overview of the inner workings of pharma.

We find that requests for insights research and COA projects come from big pharma or biotech companies; however, our health behaviour change projects come exclusively from big pharma companies who bring drugs to the market. This is because until a drug is close to being approved and licensed for use, pharmaceutical companies do not invest in developing services to support it. Projects related to digital therapeutics and applications typically come from big pharma that invest in such development in-house, or from health technology companies such as decentralised clinical trial platform providers and health app developers. You will find a thorough description of the opportunities for health psychology within digital health in Hamlet (2025; see Chap. 13).

Enquiry and Establishing Relationships

How do you find your first pharma client? A good place to start is to investigate companies where there is an overlap between their experience or pipeline and your research experience. Essentially, all the publications that we have authored have led to work with industry partners, including in areas such as chronic myeloid leukaemia (Eliasson, 2011a, 2012; Eliasson et al., 2011; Ibrahim et al., 2011), inflammatory bowel disease (Jackson et al., 2010), and the application of the COM-B to adherence (Jackson et al., 2014).

Pharma companies' websites list their pipelines and often provide a section with recent press releases and news. ClinicalTrials.gov is a helpful resource to explore clinical trials sponsored by specific companies. We recommend you take some time to look for publicly facing materials such as videos and blog posts published by the company. These resources can provide insights into how the company communicates with their stakeholders and their priorities. You may also wish to explore their geographical footprint to understand countries they may invest in and where they are located. Your previous experience combined with an understanding of the target company's priorities will provide a great resource to initiate a conversation with a prospective client.

Building Your Brand as a Consultant

It takes time and effort to build strong relationships and a personal brand as an expert in the pharma industry. It involves establishing credibility, visibility, and trust with potential clients. Networking is vital. We recommend the use of online professional networks to connect with potential clients and engage with your audience by sharing resources like blogs and templates that demonstrate your expertise. There are also good online, free resources for learning about sales, marketing, and brand strategies.

Peer-reviewed publications are invaluable in building your presence as an expert and are likely to open doors for networking and new business leads. We continuously publish in scientific journals to strengthen our reputation and generate business opportunities, including writing publications with our clients (Eliasson et al., 2017a, 2017b) and publications we fund internally (Eliasson et al., 2020).

Conferences are great places for networking. Ensure you are confident in what you have to offer because having a clear focus makes it easier for you to position yourself and talk to potential clients. Consider whether there is an opportunity for you to submit an abstract or a poster or speaker engagement at the conference which will increase your chances of making fruitful business connections. We have presented at meetings such as ISPOR US (Petit et al., 2024), ISPOR EU (Patel et al., 2023), BOPA Symposium (Duncan et al., 2023), ISOQOL Annual Conference (Haberland et al., 2019), DIA Global Annual Meeting (Clifford & Eliasson, 2019), and ESPACOMP Conference (Prieto-Merino et al., 2020; Eliasson et al., 2023) (see Table 12.2 for full forms of acronyms).

Many of these associations and societies which host annual conferences also have specialist interest groups and committees you can join, which will offer further opportunities for showcasing your expertise (e.g., Eliasson, 2024). There may also be conferences that align with your area of expertise. One of the authors of this chapter curated early career opportunities in industry whilst still working in academia through pharma-sponsored speaker events at disease-specific conferences (e.g., Eliasson, 2011a, 2011b).

It can be expensive to attend events and conferences, so before deciding to attend, scrutinise who is going to be there. The organisers will often make the list of sponsors or attendees available. Try to identify attendees who may be in a role that involves commissioning projects, for example, role titles that include Lead, Director, Head, and so on. Online announcements and professional profiles may provide information about potential commissioners' work, and you can try to connect with them. Use a brief introductory note about why you are connecting and ask if they have time for a quick meet and greet. Do not get put off by people ignoring you. Many will not respond, and you need to be resilient in order to be successful in building your company and brand.

Working as an Expert Consultant

You might support pharma as an expert consultant (Schein, 1978). For example, you might speak at a conference, sit on a steering committee, or take part in an advisory board (a group of experts who lend their skills, knowledge, and guidance to an organisation). Your role in this sort of consultancy project may fall into pharma's classification of Key Opinion Leader (KOL); that is, a respected person with expertise in an area. These opportunities are dependent on your visibility; you need to be seen as a leader within your field of expertise. In this field, it would normally be expected that you have relevant peer-reviewed publications. Chapter 7 of this book also has suggestions for demonstrating thought leadership to raise your profile (Lunt, 2025). Working as a KOL is a great opportunity to build relationships with potential clients that may generate business downstream.

Finding a Strategic Partner

Whether you are an independent health psychology consultant or a vendor, you may wish to offer your services to other vendors that do not have your skillset in-house. Partnering with another vendor can be a strategic move for both parties. Initiate contact through your existing network or by connecting with their business development or partnership teams. You will need to outline how partnering will enhance their value proposition, adapting your messaging and jargon so that it makes sense to them. If you plan to develop a proposal or start working on a project together, it is essential that you formalise a partnership agreement, which we discuss later in this chapter. Suitable strategic partners may include agencies offering services around patient engagement, medical communications, and clinical research organisations. It is good business development practice to know who your potential partners and competitors are, so we recommend researching such organisations online.

Invitation to Bid for a Project

When you receive an invitation for an engagement with a pharma company, it is essential to consider all elements of the consultancy framework as proposed by Brady and Varkonyi-Sepp (2025; see Chap. 3). For example, engage in robust enquiry to understand the bidding process and the proposal requested, identify the type of clients you may engage with and attempt to build strong relationships, carefully plan how to manage the delivery including scope and timelines, consider how the project will be evaluated, and prepare for the negotiation and contracting process.

Formal Bidding Process

Pharma companies often use a formal bidding process. The invitation to bid typically goes out to an existing pool of vendors that the company is aware of. You may initially receive a Request For Information (RFI) which asks about your general capabilities, following which you may receive a Request for Proposal (RFP). You are likely to be competing against other companies, including an incumbent company, and the process will be managed by the company's procurement department. The process normally includes several stages including:

- Submitting questions
- Responding to a survey capturing company information
- Pitching, for example, presenting a question-and-answer session with the prospective client following proposal submission
- Revising the proposal as part of negotiation and contracting

Informal Bidding Process

As a vendor, you may also hear about potential projects by word-of-mouth. This type of introduction may give rise to a less formal proposal process where your chance of winning the business is higher. Typically, there is a budget ceiling for these projects. For example, primary clients within pharmaceutical companies will normally have autonomy to sign off projects up to a certain value, above which a formal procurement process is required. Even with a less formal process, you need a well-documented scope and a contract. As a small to medium sized consultancy with a limited budget for marketing and business development, we find that 90% of our projects come from our existing network. New work can be with the primary client or their colleagues, or it might be someone within our wider network who has reached out due to word-of-mouth.

Understanding the Brief

Before embarking on the proposal, familiarise yourself with the client company. The next step is to contact the person who distributed the RFP and arrange a meeting, if possible. This is your first opportunity to showcase

Box 12.1 Sample Questions to Inform RFP Response

1. What is the disease and/or treatment area?
2. What is the target patient population?
3. What are the target markets (countries)?
4. Has any prior work been conducted by the pharma company?
5. How will the project output be used by the pharma company?
6. Are there any critical milestones or hard deadlines?
7. What are the budget constraints?
8. Is the RFP competitive (how many other vendors are bidding for the work)?

expertise and build rapport. Ahead of the meeting, form a list of questions to clarify the RFP. You need to have a deep understanding of the client's aims and objectives to define your scope. Aligned with the consultancy framework (Brady and Varkonyi-Sepp, 2025) presented in Chap. 3, we work with a template RFP questionnaire aligned to our services. Examples are included in Box 12.1. In our experience, potential clients are usually responsive through email to questions in situations where a meeting has not been possible.

Choosing Your Team

Several questions need to be asked when assembling the project team that will be named in the proposal. First, what is the project aiming to do? Second, to meet the project aims, what functions and skillsets are needed? To explore this second question, consider the following supplementary questions: Can you deliver those in-house? Who will take on different tasks? What additional third-parties or subcontractors will you need? For example, you may need to work with a specialist recruitment company to recruit research participants; a specialist statistician for a complex dataset; a user experience (UX) specialist to support user optimisation for a digital programme; a copy editor to support content development; or a graphic designer to ensure deliverables are visually engaging and in an appropriate format, and so on.

Putting together an appropriate and experienced team is the best way to win business. We have strategic partnerships with other companies of a similar size, but with different areas of expertise, to ensure successful business development and project delivery.

Scope and Budgeting

Detailed budget planning must be done at the proposal stage. Estimating the time required for a project involves analysing the scope, complexity, available resources, and potential risks to project delivery. As researchers, we tend to underestimate the hours we need to complete a project, which is detrimental to our profit margin. Breaking the project down into tasks and subtasks will help you develop a budget and estimate how many people will be needed to deliver the project. You will also need to estimate time for project management, internal and client meetings, and client-provided training, such as adverse event (AE) reporting. Lastly, remember to include any out-of-pocket expenses you will need to pay, for example, copyright fees for journal articles. Using a literature review as an example, the scope and budget can be broken down by the subtasks and the number of hours needed by varying experience levels. Table 12.1 illustrates a budget, with example hours.

Table 12.1 Example budget for a literature review

Task assumptions	Senior oversight	Mid-level researcher	Junior researcher	Cost
Search strategy development and database search *Assumptions*: 1 database search	1 hour × hourly rate	5 hours × hourly rate		
Abstract review Assumptions: 720 abstracts taking 1 minute each to review		2 hours × hourly rate	12 hours × hourly rate	
Full-text review *Assumptions*: 15 full-text papers for review for inclusion @ 30 minutes each		2 hours × hourly rate	7.5 hours × hourly rate	
Data extraction *Assumptions*: 10 full-text papers @ 1.5 hours each to extract		4 hours × hourly rate	15 hours × hourly rate	
Write up *Assumptions*: 15-page word report and PowerPoint deck with <20 slides	4 hours × hourly rate	10 hours × hourly rate	22.5 hours × hourly rate	
Revisions following review by client *Assumptions*: Minor edits to content	1 hour × hourly rate	2 hours × hourly rate	4 hours × hourly rate	
Total				

You must describe each task sufficiently so that you and the client can agree on what is expected (usually referred to as 'scope assumptions'). Investing time in clearly defining the scope assumptions will facilitate negotiation and contracting and will help to manage delivery. Below are examples of other assumptions that may be relevant for a literature review:

- Number of papers included: reviewing 500 paper titles and abstracts is drastically different to 2,500, so it is important that the time budgeted reflects this.
- Cost of copyright fees (if applicable): we usually calculate a ballpark based on a reasonable upper limit charge for one download multiplied with the number of full text articles to be reviewed.
- Number and size of deliverables being produced: for example, a publication ready literature review report in Microsoft Word or a summary presentation-based report in Microsoft PowerPoint.
- Number of rounds of client review of a deliverable: each round of review requires additional time and resources from both your project team and the client.

What is the deadline and how many people do you need to get the project completed in that timeframe? We are frequently approached by clients with short timeframes meaning that multiple tasks may need to run in parallel or multiple team members might need to work on the same task to get it finished in time. For example, we completed two COA strategy projects for one client within twelve weeks, from contract signing to report delivery. The project involved two targeted literature reviews to identify PROs in two conditions, an analysis of the relevant PROs used for clinical trials, an evaluation of the measure development and validation, and recommendations for the client on which measures to select for their upcoming clinical trials. We were able to achieve this by having several team members of mixed experience levels dedicated to the project.

For the above method of budgeting, you will need to set your hourly rate(s). Your rate covers salary, overhead costs (such as equipment, insurance, legal counsel, bookkeeper) and a profit margin. To calculate your rate, you can estimate your total costs for the year, including your salary, divided by the hours you feasibly have available to work in a year. Consider that not all your working time can be spent on delivering projects as you also need time for winning business and dealing with company administration.

Creating a Convincing Proposal and Pitching

Your proposal must show a deep understanding of the client's needs. Clearly present your solution by describing and defining what you will do to achieve the project's aim and objectives. Be selective with what you include and make sure it is relevant to the proposal. Your experience and capabilities must be demonstrated. This can be done by sharing your publication history, case studies of previous work, and thought leadership such as speaking engagements.

You need to define your unique selling points to differentiate your proposal from other vendors. Why should the pharma client choose your company? If the process is managed by the client's procurement department, you need to persuade both the potential end client, that is, the person or team with a problem that needs solving, and procurement, whose job is to get the best quality vendor at the lowest price.

The client may request a specific proposal format, or you may choose one yourself. Consider which format best communicates your approach and aligns with the submission method, whether by email, a client portal, or in a meeting. Be aware that your proposal will implicitly communicate your professionalism and attention to detail, and it will set expectations about the quality of your project deliverables. Working with a graphic designer can ensure your proposal is professional and engaging.

In the pitch meeting you may encounter a range of clients, as outlined in the Building and Maintaining Relationships section of Chap. 3 (Brady & Varkonyi-Sepp, 2025), including the contact client, the primary client, and a range of intermediate clients (see Schein, 1997, for a description of different categories of client). They may all have different questions and opinions related to their specific role within the pharma company. The pitch is your most important meeting to showcase your experience and expertise and ultimately win over the client with your proposed approach.

Negotiating and Contracting

Negotiating the Project Scope

There will likely be a period of negotiation after the pitch and before the project scope is signed off. This is a process of adjusting and adapting your proposal to meet the prospective client's needs more closely so that both sides can agree the final scope of work to be delivered. Conversations during this period may relate to clarifying project objectives, the tasks or constituent subtasks to meet those objectives, the number and type of deliverables to be produced, the frequency and length of meetings with the client and other project stakeholders, invoicing schedule and fees. Negotiation relating to fees is common at this stage. Companies will rarely tell you the amount of budget available at the initial proposal stage, and they may not have sufficient budget to run the project the way you originally proposed. If the client does not have sufficient budget, you need to think about ways to streamline, simplify, or phase the project to make cost savings. These decisions require honest discussions between you and the client. One of our principles is to provide valid and useful solutions to clients regardless of the size of their budget. This is not the same as saying we will run projects at a loss or without an acceptable margin. Instead, it is about working with the client to truly understand their problem and then being selective about the steps we will take to get to a solution (Block, 2000). A useful consideration is whether the project would stand up to external scrutiny. Would the proposed research be acceptable to an ethics review board? Does it comply with regulatory requirements? Be smart about how to solve a problem but do not compromise ethical and regulatory requirements. Once you get to a point where both sides are in agreement the project can go into contracting.

Contracting and Insurance

A word of caution. We strongly recommend using professional legal services to review all contracts that you sign to ensure you are fully aware of your contractual obligations and risks. It is always acceptable to ask for revisions to a contract, which the other party may or may not accept. You may not be able to mitigate all your financial and legal risks, but you should be aware and take an informed decision about what is acceptable to you. One common financial risk you can mitigate is ensuring that the client is contractually obligated to cover any non-refundable out-of-pocket expenses you incur if the project is cancelled. For example, a proportion of research participant recruitment costs are often paid upfront and will not be reimbursed if the recruitment does not go ahead due to a cancelled project. We also recommend you ensure that the payment terms (such as how long it will take from you submitting your invoice until you get paid) are manageable for you financially.

It may be helpful to have some key contract templates on file; for example, a mutual non-disclosure agreement (NDA), as well as subcontractor and client contracts. These should be drafted by a lawyer who understands your services and needs. It is essential also that you procure the appropriate insurance cover to provide your services, including professional liability insurance. Insurance requirements are often stipulated in client contracts so it is important to review this and negotiate as necessary to ensure you can comply.

Contracting as an expert consultant or KOL. A contract for an expert consultancy or KOL engagement is usually significantly simpler than a vendor contract, and your overall legal and financial risk will typically be less. Your contract is likely to use a pharma company template and cover key aspects such as confidentiality, data privacy, and intellectual property, and include a brief description of expectations of your involvement and key deadlines. When you are operating as a KOL, you typically get paid a Fair Market Value (FMV) rate, which the pharma company calculates. In our experience, these types of contracts are between an individual and the pharmaceutical company. If you are also an employee, for example, of a university, you would need to be sure that your contract with your employer allows you to take on consulting work. You may be able to contract through a company or institution with you as the named person, if necessary.

Contracting as a vendor. For your first project with a new client, you are likely to have a single-project contract. In almost every case, the contract will be based on templates provided by the pharma company, although smaller companies may agree to using your template. The contract must include a section that lists the scope of the work involved. For example, an outline of tasks, assumptions, deliverables and timelines, project fees, and invoicing schedule. Your contract will also outline the legal provisions for the two parties and requirements in terms of insurance, liability, data security, and data protection, among other things. It is important to review your contractual obligations regarding compliance with the pharma company's Standard Operating Procedures (SOPs), and request to read any that are relevant to your project. Subject to contract, the client may choose to audit your processes therefore you must be confident that you can meet their requirements. Over time you may be able to negotiate a Master Service Agreement (MSA), which is a long-standing agreement covering broad legal principles that can cover multiple projects. The MSA is accompanied by a statement of work (SOW) used for individual projects which includes the deliverables, timeline, scope assumptions, and costs.

Contracting with your subcontractors. Be aware that you will usually be legally responsible for the conduct of any subcontractors you use on a project. You can work with your lawyer to ensure that the agreement with the subcontractor matches any legal obligations you have to your client. Unless the subcontractor is a large vendor, you are typically expected to use your templates for the contracting.

Contracting with strategic partners. When entering a relationship with a strategic partner, it is essential to carefully manage negotiation and contracting to establish a balanced partnership. Key considerations include clearly defined roles and responsibilities, financial arrangements, intellectual property rights, non-solicitation, confidentiality, and dispute resolution. In this type of arrangement, one of the strategic partners would typically contract with the pharma company and the other party would be a subcontractor. It is less common that both parties contract directly with the pharma client. This is something to be clarified at the outset. For strategic partners you may either use their template or yours to contract.

Project Delivery from Kick-off to Evaluation

Getting Started

A comprehensive kick-off meeting will set your project up for success. It is an opportunity to realign on objectives, deliverables, and timelines (especially if there has been an extended period between negotiating the contract and kicking off), establish procedures for approval of project deliverables, and agree to a communication plan. Ideally your primary client will invite their colleagues with a stake in the project to the meeting so that you can understand how their role and priorities may impact the project. Be prepared to reassure the wider team of your expertise as a health psychologist and the rationale for the project.

Legal and regulatory compliance is paramount for the pharma industry. As a consultant and a vendor, you must demonstrate an understanding of the legal, regulatory, and ethical requirements that apply to your work. There are helpful resources on this from organisations such as the British Healthcare Business Intelligence Association (BHBIA) (British Healthcare Business Intelligence Association, n.d.), the Association of the British Pharmaceutical Industry (ABPI) (Association of the British Pharmaceutical Industry, n.d.), and the Collaborative Institutional Training Initiative (CITI Program) (CITI Program, n.d.).

Managing Timelines and Budget

A detailed and up-to-date project plan ensures deadlines are adhered to and helps you identify risks of delay. Key risks to timelines include delays in the client submitting feedback from their reviews of your deliverables, as well as delays in contracting with third parties and recruitment. Delays can lead to out-of-scope work, however timely communication and a solution-focused mindset will set you apart from other vendors.

Financial risks include reduced profitability by delivering out-of-scope work without pay. It can be challenging finding the right balance between providing an excellent service and making the profit margin needed to keep the business going. You may decide to absorb a small change in scope as a way of maintaining a good client relationship, but you may want to negotiate a contract amendment to cover a more substantial change. Another financial risk is a reduction in the client's budget or a change in priorities leading to the cancellation of your project. The client contract will typically allow them to cancel for convenience without notice. Monthly project reconciliations where you estimate what proportion of the project tasks have been completed will help you manage financial risks. It ensures accurate invoicing, and you would typically be paid for the work that has been completed to date in the event of cancellation.

Providing Expertise and Quality Deliverables

In an industry setting, you are typically hired for your expertise, and you will be expected to have a professional opinion on matters relating to your areas of expertise (e.g., research approaches, health psychology). In line with professionalism, it is important to keep good records, including meeting minutes, so that you can explain why particular actions or decisions were taken throughout the project. Your deliverables may be read by a wide audience from different backgrounds. Ensure the important information is clearly presented up front. To facilitate reading and comprehension, we make use of an executive summary and appendices in addition to the main body of the report to accommodate a range of readers, from those who want to skim to those who want to understand the detail.

There are several key 'soft' skills that are essential to clients perceiving you as a great consultant (Debevoise, 2023). Clients need someone who takes ownership of their work, and who can deliver work on time, within budget and to a high standard. Having excellent attention to detail is also crucial to building trust and increases the likelihood of you winning follow-on work.

Evaluating Your Project

Within the pharma industry you may find you are highly restricted in the type of evaluation you can implement. The pharma company will have key performance indicators for their project. However, the evaluation may not go ahead, or you may not be given access to the metrics. Your internal key performance indicators may include whether the project was delivered on time and within budget, and to the client's satisfaction. A project close-down process will facilitate reflections on how the project went and as part of this you can seek feedback from your client. Be sure to follow-up with the client a few months after the project has ended to enquire about further work. As mentioned earlier, connecting on online business network platforms can also help you build and maintain a network.

Conclusion

The pharmaceutical industry offers numerous opportunities for health psychology consultants to apply their skills and expertise to ultimately improve health outcomes. We love the fast pace and diverse projects we work on, and we see challenges as opportunities to innovate and grow. You will set yourself up for success by curating a strong personal brand as an expert, paying close attention to contractual, ethical, and regulatory requirements, and providing high-quality deliverables on time and to budget.

Questions for Reflection

1. What are your specific areas of expertise and experience that can benefit private sector clients, like pharma companies?
2. What skills do you already have that you could use in these types of consultancy projects versus skills you need to learn or team up with someone else to provide?
3. How would you balance the challenge of pleasing a client by exceeding their expectations whilst keeping a project profitable?
4. How could you go about building your network and visibility to attract projects from pharmaceutical companies?
5. Who do you have in your network who may introduce you to prospective clients?

Competing Interests The authors are directors and shareholders of Sprout Health Solutions Ltd., a company that provides consulting and research services to pharmaceutical and biotechnology companies.

Acronyms

Table 12.2 provides a list of acronyms used in the pharmaceutical industry.

Table 12.2 Pharmaceutical industry acronyms

AE	Adverse Event
ABPI	Association of the British Pharmaceutical Industry
BHBIA	British Healthcare Business Intelligence Association
BOPA	British Oncology Pharmacy Association
COA	Clinical Outcome Assessment
CITI	Collaborative Institutional Training Initiative
DIA	Drug Information Association
EMA	European Medicines Agency
ESPACOMP	The International Society for Medication Adherence
FDA	United States Food and Drug Administration
FMV	Fair Market Value
HTA	Health Technology Assessment
ISOQOL	International Society for Quality of Life Research
ISPOR	International Society for Pharmacoeconomics and Outcomes Research
KEE	Key External Expert
KME	Key Medical Expert
KOL	Key Opinion Leader
KOM	Kick off meeting
MSA	Master Services Agreement
NDA	Non-Disclosure Agreement
NICE	National Institute for Health and Care Excellence
PRO	Patient Reported Outcome
R&D	Research and Development
RFI	Request for Information
RFP	Request for Proposal
SA	Service Agreement
SOP	Standard Operating Procedure
SOW	Statement of Work
UX	User experience

References

Association of the British Pharmaceutical Industry. (n.d.). *Homepage*. https://www.abpi.org.uk/

Block, P. (2000). The contracting meeting. In P. Block & A. Markowitz (Eds.), *The flawless consulting fieldbook and companion: A guide to understanding your expertise* (2nd ed., pp. 69–106). John Wiley & Sons.

Brady, R., & Varkonyi-Sepp, J. (2025). A framework for consultancy in health psychology. In I. R. Brady, J. Varkonyi-Sepp, & J. Smith (Eds.), *The Palgrave handbook of consultancy in health psychology*. Palgrave Macmillan.

British Healthcare Business Intelligence Association. (n.d.). *Homepage*. https://www.bhbia.org.uk/

Campbell, J. J., Dunham, J., Nicholson, S., & Jones, D. (2024). *Understanding pharma: The professional's guide to how pharmaceutical and biotechnology companies really work* (4th ed.). Syneos Health Learning Solutions.

CITI Program. (n.d.). *Homepage*. https://about.citiprogram.org/

Clifford, S., & Eliasson, L. (2019, June). Assessing medical adherence in a clinical trial setting: Challenges and solutions. *Presentation at the DIA 2019 Global Annual Meeting*, San Diego, CA, United States. Contributors: A. Mulick & B. Vrijens.

Debevoise, N. D. (2023). *Why Soft Skills Are All That Matter And What To Do About It.* Forbes. https://www.forbes.com/sites/nelldebevoise/2023/04/04/why-soft-skills-are-all-that-matter-and-what-to-do-about-it/

Duncan, N., Eliasson, L., Hirsch, C., Pratt, G., & Cox, A. (2023). Barriers to and drivers of adherence to oral therapies in patients with multiple myeloma: The ATOMM study. *Journal of Oncology Pharmacy Practice, 29*(1S), 1–94. Poster Abstract 32 presented at the BOPA Symposium 2022.

Eliasson, L. (2011a). *Improved patient choices in CML: Integrating treatment options in 2011* [Satellite symposium]. European Group for Blood and Marrow Transplantation (EBMT), Paris, France.

Eliasson, L. (2011b). *Optimizing patient outcomes through maximizing adherence* [Satellite symposium]. European School of Haematology Annual Congress, Estoril, Portugal.

Eliasson, L. (2012). Treatment adherence in chronic myeloid leukaemia: A systematic review. *Clinical Practice, 9*(1), 87–100.

Eliasson, L. (2024, May). Establishing the criteria for the value assessment of medication adherence-enhancing interventions. *Medication Adherence and Persistence Special Interest Group Forum at ISPOR 2024*, Atlanta, GA, United States. Panelists: T. Agh, B. Borah, D. Nayak, & A. Turcu-Stiolica.

Eliasson, L., Bewley, A. P., Mughal, F., Johnston, K. M., Kuznik, A., Patel, C., & Lloyd, A. J. (2017b). Evaluation of psoriasis patients' attitudes toward benefit–risk and therapeutic trade-offs in their choice of treatments. *Patient Preference and Adherence, 11*, 353–362. https://doi.org/10.2147/PPA.S121838

Eliasson, L., Clifford, S., Barber, N., & Marin, D. (2011). Exploring chronic myeloid leukemia patients' reasons for not adhering to the oral anticancer drug imatinib as prescribed. *Leukemia Research, 35*, 626–630. https://doi.org/10.1016/j.leukres.2010.10.017

Eliasson, L., Clifford, S., Mulick, A., Jackson, C., & Vrijens, B. (2020). How the EMERGE guideline on medication adherence can improve the quality of clinical trials. *British journal of clinical pharmacology, 86*(4), 687–697. https://doi.org/10.1111/bcp.14240

Eliasson, L., Cooper, V., Vrijens, B., & Mulick, A. (2023, November). Assessing medication adherence in clinical trials: Challenges and solutions. *Round table session at the ESPACOMP 2023 Annual Meeting*, Budapest, Hungary.

Eliasson, L., de Freitas, H. M., Dearden, L., Calimlim, B., & Lloyd, A. J. (2017a). Patients' preferences for treatment of metastatic castrate-resistant prostate cancer: A discrete choice experiment. *Clinical Therapeutics, 39*(4), 732–737. https://doi.org/10.1016/j.clinthera.2017.02.009

Forbes. (n.d.). *Forbes: Business news, financial news, and more.* https://www.forbes.com/

Haberland, C., Moshkovich, O., Eliasson, L., Doll, H., Filonenko, A., Seitz, C., & Gerlinger, C. (2019, October). A qualitative study exploring patients' perspectives on ease of understanding, interpretation and completion of the Uterine Fibroid Daily Bleeding Diary. *Poster presented at the ISOQOL 26th Annual Conference*, San Diego, CA, United States. Abstract published in *Quality of Life Research, 28*(Suppl 1), S1–S190.

Hamlet, C. (2025). Health psychology consultancy in digital health. In R. Brady, J. Varkonyi-Sepp, & J. Smith (Eds.), *The Palgrave Handbook of consultancy in health psychology*. Palgrave Macmillan.

Harvard Business Review. (n.d.). *Homepage*. https://hbr.org/

Ibrahim, A., Eliasson, L., Apperley, J. F., Milojkovic, D., Bua, M., Szydlo, R., et al. (2011). Poor adherence is the main reason for loss of CCyR and imatinib failure for CML patients on long-term imatinib therapy. *Blood, 117*(14), 3733–3736. https://doi.org/10.1182/blood-2010-10-309807

Jackson, C. A., Clatworthy, J., Robinson, A., & Horne, R. (2010). Factors associated with non-adherence to oral medication for inflammatory bowel disease: A systematic review. *American Journal of Gastroenterology, 105*(3), 525–539. https://doi.org/10.1038/ajg.2009.685

Jackson, C. A., Eliasson, L., Barber, N., & Weinman, J. (2014). Applying COM-B to medication adherence: A suggested framework for research and interventions. *European Health Psychologist Bulletin, 16*(1), 7–17.

Lunt, J. (2025). The sustainable consultant. In R. Brady, J. Varkonyi-Sepp, & J. Smith (Eds.), *The Palgrave handbook of consultancy in health psychology*. Palgrave Macmillan.

Michie, S., Hyder, N., Walia, A., & West, R. (2011a). Development of a taxonomy of behaviour change techniques used in individual behavioural support for smoking cessation. *Addictive Behaviors, 36*(4), 315–319. https://doi.org/10.1016/j.addbeh.2010.11.016

Michie, S., Richardson, M., Johnston, M., Abraham, C., Francis, J., Hardeman, W., Eccles, M. P., Cane, J., & Wood, C. E. (2013). The behavior change technique taxonomy (v1) of 93 hierarchically clustered techniques: Building an international consensus for the reporting of behavior change interventions. *Annals of Behavioral Medicine, 46*(1), 81–95. https://doi.org/10.1007/s12160-013-9486-6

Michie, S., van Stralen, M. M., & West, R. (2011b). The behaviour change wheel: A new method for characterising and designing behaviour change interventions. *Implementation Science, 6*, 42. https://doi.org/10.1186/1748-5908-6-42

Patel, C., de la Motte, A., Eliasson, L., Xia, A., Gervas-Arruga, J., & Clifford, S. (2023). PCR137 Understanding the signs, symptoms and impacts of metachromatic leukodystrophy (MLD). *Value in Health, 26*(12), S475.

Petit, I., Eliasson, L., Romero, B., Patel, C., Rosa, A. D., & Quinn, J. (2024). PCR76 Exploring the content and psychometric validity of clinical outcome assessments in renal cell carcinoma versus the patient-reported symptoms and impacts. *Value in Health, 27*(6), S309. https://doi.org/10.1016/j.jval.2024.03.1955

Prieto-Merino, D., Mulick, A., Armstrong, C., Hoult, H., Fawcett, S., Clifford, S., & Eliasson, L. (2020, November). A new proportion-of-days-covered (PDC) algorithm to measure implementation adherence in real-world datasets. *Presentation at the 24th ESPACOMP Conference*. Online.

Schein, E. H. (1978). The role of the consultant: Content expert or process facilitator? *The Personnel and Guidance Journal, 56*(6), 339–343.

Schein, E. H. (1997). The concept of "client" from a process consultation perspective: A guide for change agents. *Journal of Organizational Change Management, 10*(3), 202–216. https://doi.org/10.1108/09534819710171077

U.S. Food and Drug Administration. (2009). *Guidance for industry patient-reported outcome measures: Use in medical product development to support labeling claims.* https://www.fda.gov/media/77832/download

13

Health Psychology Consultancy in Digital Health

Claire Hamlet

The digital health sector has expanded rapidly in recent years, introducing various innovative technologies to enhance healthcare delivery, such as mobile health apps, wearable devices, and portals for patients to manage their care (Imison et al., 2016). Direct-to-consumer mobile health apps have seen significant growth, in part due to accessibility. While many health apps aim to support health behaviour change, many struggle to deliver a user experience that fosters sustained engagement and adherence, limiting their potential health benefits (Dennison et al., 2013; Yardley et al., 2016).

Health psychologists are uniquely positioned to address these challenges. Our behavioural science knowledge, research skills, and practical experience creating user-centred, evidence-based interventions align closely with user experience (UX) principles. Through stepping into consultancy roles, health psychologists can bridge the gap between academia and industry, guiding the development of scientifically robust, user-centred digital health products that resonate with diverse user groups.

This chapter explores the digital health landscape and associated challenges, highlighting the value health psychologists can bring in enhancing user experience through consultancy. It will examine the opportunities and challenges of consulting in this fast-evolving field, providing practical guidance for those looking to begin.

C. Hamlet (✉)
Independent Consultant, Bristol, UK
e-mail: drclairehamlet@gmail.com

R. Brady et al. (eds.), *The Palgrave Handbook of Consultancy in Health Psychology*,
https://doi.org/10.1007/978-3-031-94529-8_13

The Digital Health Landscape

The United Kingdom (UK) National Institute for Health and Care Excellence (NICE) define Digital Health Technologies (DHTs) as

> ... digital products intended to benefit people or the wider health and social care system. This may include: smartphone apps, standalone software, online tools for treating or diagnosing conditions, preventing ill health, or improving system efficiencies, and programmes that can be used to analyse data from medical devices such as scanners, sensors or monitors. (NICE, 2022, p. 5)

The digital health industry has experienced rapid growth over the past several years with a key catalyst being the coronavirus (COVID-19) pandemic (Hyzy et al., 2023). Health systems, such as the UK National Health Service (NHS) are looking to harness the benefits of digital health to enhance patient health, reduce clinician workload, lower costs, and reduce health disparities (Greaves et al., 2019; Brezing & Brixner, 2022). The NHS Long Term plan (NHS, 2019) focuses on technology as part of the future. It outlines NHS improvement goals for the coming decade, focusing on essential priorities that will drive digital transformation across health and social care services. Key objectives include providing simple digital access to NHS services and empowering individuals to engage actively by accessing, managing, and interacting with digital resources, information, and services (NHS, 2019).

NICE (2022) has classified DHTs according to their influence on patient care. The first category includes those that enhance healthcare system efficiency without directly impacting patient outcomes. The second category consists of clinical decision support systems and predictive models that may assist in treatment decisions, enable active health monitoring, and that are integral to diagnostic and therapeutic processes. The final category encompasses Internet or web and mobile health applications designed for basic monitoring, health information dissemination, and the promotion of behaviour change and self-management, which will be the focus of this chapter.

Mobile health interventions have shown promise for enhancing the accessibility and efficiency of health due to the widespread adoption of mobile phones (Marcolino et al., 2018; Magrabi et al., 2019). Mobile health interventions are effective across diverse conditions, populations, and environments, and are increasingly designed to facilitate health-related behaviour change efficiently and affordably (Pagoto & Bennett, 2013). In 2021, over 350,000 mobile health apps were available to download globally by the public in app stores. Although many of these apps focus on general wellness or fitness, almost 47% specifically aim to manage conditions like diabetes, heart disease, and mental health (IQVIA, 2021).

Digital Health: The Challenges

While the rapidly evolving digital health industry offers exciting opportunities for innovation and advancements in healthcare delivery, it also introduces challenges that must be addressed to achieve significant and sustainable improvements to health on a broader scale (Kasoju et al., 2023)

Lack of safety and regulation. Regulatory agencies play a critical role in controlling the entry of new products into the healthcare sector by managing approval processes for pharmaceuticals and medical devices. Currently no regulatory framework exists for digital health (Iqbal & Biller-Andorno, 2022). In the UK, only digital therapeutics (DtX)—applications with diagnostic or therapeutic functions, such as symptom checkers or platforms delivering psychological therapy—must undergo rigorous clinical and regulatory review by the Medicines and Healthcare Products Regulatory Agency (MHRA) (Sheppard, 2020).

Mobile apps are particularly hard to regulate, as they are easy to develop and deploy (Magrabi et al., 2019). Most mobile apps are not classified as a medical device—that is, a healthcare product or equipment that a person uses for a medical purpose (e.g., a blood pressure monitor) (MHRA, 2019). As a result, apps can avoid regulatory oversight (Magrabi et al.). Regulatory ambiguity surrounding apps means that some developers may not realise their products need to be formally regulated if they could be categorised as medical devices (Mathews et al., 2019). This means that a significant number of mobile health apps can reach consumers without undergoing rigorous evaluation for safety, efficacy, or data protection standards. As a result, users may be exposed to unregulated tools that could provide misleading health information or lack adequate safeguards (Kasoju et al., 2023). A recent study highlights the scope of this issue, finding that only 20% of the 350,000 digital health apps available on major platforms meet standards for clinical assurance, data privacy, and usability (Hyzy et al., 2023).

In response to these challenges, additional checks are being introduced for DHTs seeking adoption within the NHS in the UK. The NHS Digital Technology Assessment Criteria (NHSX, 2021) mandates specific standards around safety, data protection, technical reliability, system interoperability, and user-friendliness for DHTs. In the UK, NICE has developed an evidence standards framework (ESF) specifically for digital health technologies. This framework ensures that new DHTs not only meet clinical standards but also contribute tangible value to the healthcare system. The ESF acknowledges its limitations, highlighting that it is "less relevant to those that are downloaded or purchased directly by users (such as through app stores)" (NICE, 2022, p. 3). Consequently, the regulatory landscape remains inconsistent, with DHTs that are not intended for NHS integration or that do not qualify as 'medical devices' often operating with minimal oversight (Sheppard, 2020).

Lack of evidence-based design. Many DHTS aim to change behaviours to improve health outcomes, such as increasing physical activity or enhancing medication adherence. Often referred to as digital health interventions (DHIs), these tools are more likely to succeed in promoting behaviour change when they are designed based on established behaviour change theories and incorporate specific behaviour change techniques (BCTs) (Nikolaou & Lean, 2017; McKay et al., 2019; Webb et al., 2010).

Most DHI innovators lack expertise in the social and behavioural sciences, making collaboration with professionals in these fields essential (Pagoto & Bennett, 2013). Additionally, partnerships with clinicians who understand the target patient population and the clinical environment where the DHI will be implemented are crucial (Gilbert, 2022). Despite the benefits, many innovators do not engage with behavioural science or with clinical experts, likely due to factors such as the rapid pace of development, time constraints, cost, and a lack of awareness of their value (Gilbert; Cohen et al., 2020). With over 90,000 digital health apps launched in 2020, concerns have emerged that many companies rely on trial-and-error approaches. While DHIs are being developed rapidly, they often lack intentional, user-centred design and a clear strategy to achieve specific healthcare outcomes (Voorheis et al., 2022). The risk is that these DHIs are disconnected from the clinical realities and nuances of the conditions they aim to address (Cohen et al., 2020). Additionally, app developers without a clinical background may not share the same professional duty of care as healthcare professionals, which has potential implications for safety and efficacy (Silven et al., 2022).

Lack of evaluation and effectiveness research. Across various health conditions, DHIs often lack support from rigorous efficacy or effectiveness studies (Simon et al., 2023). The rapid pace of digital health innovation frequently outstrips the capacity of traditional research methodologies to keep up (Guo et al., 2020). Additionally, the financial and logistical challenges of conducting long-term trials and outcome studies pose substantial barriers, particularly for start-ups (Guo et al., 2020). As a result, many direct-to-consumer apps enter the market without sufficient evidence to support their claims of achieving intended health outcomes (Cohen et al., 2020).

While randomised controlled trials (RCTs) are often depicted as the gold standard for evaluating medical interventions, the level of clinical validation required should be proportional to the risk associated with the intervention (Magrabi et al., 2019). For example, apps designed for tracking daily habits or logging symptoms may not necessitate the same level of rigorous evaluation as those addressing more complex health conditions. DHIs targeting more serious conditions, however, are more likely to be adopted and trusted by healthcare professionals and systems, such as the NHS, if they undergo comprehensive clinical evaluation (Greaves et al., 2019). A notable example is the cognitive behavioural therapy app Sleepio (Big Health., n.d.), which, following high-quality RCTs, became the first digital therapeutic recommended by NICE for treating sleep issues (Espie et al., 2019).

Lack of user adoption and engagement. While DHIs often see strong initial uptake, retention rates and duration of engagement are low. Research has found that over 71% of users abandon health-related apps within 90 days of download, and engagement often steeply drops significantly after the first few weeks of use (Amagai et al., 2022; Baumel et al., 2019). This greatly reduces the potential impact of these apps to achieve their aims and significantly impacts behavioural and health outcomes (Yardley et al., 2016; Schueller et al., 2020). Several factors have been found to influence adoption and engagement, including low digital literacy, a lack of trust, minimal endorsement or involvement from health professionals, and privacy concerns (Weik et al., 2024). The overall user experience is also a critical influence. If an app has a cumbersome or confusing interface or lacks personalisation, users are likely to disengage (Dennison et al., 2013). A DHI can only make a meaningful impact if users consistently interact with it; when abandoned, the potential health benefits are lost (Dennison et al., 2013).

What Are the Roles for Health Psychologists in Digital Health?

Health psychologists bring valuable skills to address many key challenges in digital health. Health psychologists' expertise in health behaviour change theory can ensure that DHIs are evidence-based and more likely to improve health outcomes. Our research and data analysis skills can support rigorous evaluations of effectiveness, enhancing trust among healthcare providers. One key strength of health psychologists is our person-centred approach to intervention development, which closely aligns with industry concepts of UX. Given that poor UX is a common barrier to engagement with behavioural content (Dennison et al., 2013), health psychologists are uniquely positioned to make a significant impact. This will be the focus of the remainder of this chapter.

User-Centred Design

The overall experience someone has with a product or service is what UX refers to (Norman, 2013). It encompasses factors such as usability, accessibility, design aesthetics, functionality, emotional resonance, and the ease with which users can achieve their objectives (International Organization for Standardization [ISO], 2019). User-centred design (UCD), or human-centred design, is a framework for iteratively researching, designing, and evaluating products, services, and systems by involving end users and other stakeholders throughout (Norman, 2013). Involving users supports the creation of more effective designs and allows for continuous improvements, enhancing their usability, acceptance, and potential success when implemented (Ben-Zeev et al., 2015).

UX designers and user researchers play distinct yet complementary roles. UX designers focus on crafting the overall design and product layout to ensure it is both visually appealing and functionally efficient, incorporating user feedback into the iterative design process (Interaction Design Foundation). User researchers, on the other hand, are responsible for gathering insights directly from users through research methods such as interviews, usability tests, and surveys, to understand users' needs, preferences, and behaviours (Interaction Design Foundation). Books, academic articles, and other resources can provide accessible, in-depth guidance on both the overall UCD process and specific UCD techniques (e.g., Norman, 2013; Allen & Chudley, 2012; Gothelf & Seiden, 2021).

Importance of User Experience in Digital Health Interventions

Delivering a positive user experience is essential in digital health, particularly as end-users may face physical or psychological vulnerabilities (Sartori et al., 2022). Well-designed digital health tools that align with user needs and usability standards are more likely to be trusted, adopted, and consistently used, which is critical for achieving meaningful health outcomes (Bucher et al., 2024). A well-constructed UX can also prevent user errors, such as incorrect data entry or misinterpretation of feedback, which can have serious safety implications in healthcare (Magrabi et al., 2019).

Digital health interventions can integrate behaviour change techniques within the overall user experience, supporting the effectiveness of the primary intervention. For example, personalisation—tailoring content, features, or experiences to user needs and preferences—and goal-setting features may help users to define and pursue meaningful health objectives at the outset to increase motivation (Yardley et al., 2016; Perski et al., 2017). Features such as progress tracking and timely feedback reinforce positive behaviours, enhancing motivation by visibly demonstrating improvements towards health goals (Dennison et al., 2013). Social support mechanisms such as virtual communities foster accountability and encouragement, acknowledging the social aspects crucial to behaviour change (Schueller et al., 2017). Behavioural prompts, including reminders and notifications, act as cues to action, promoting habit formation by encouraging app engagement at optimal times (Baumel et al., 2019). Clear navigation minimises cognitive load, facilitating sustained engagement by making interactions intuitive and less demanding (Bakker et al., 2016). Additionally, gamification elements, such as rewards and badges, may add enjoyment and a sense of achievement, motivating users to remain committed to their health behaviour change activities (Edwards et al., 2016). In summary, user experience and health behaviour change cannot be treated in isolation; a well-designed UX enhances engagement and adherence, directly supporting the impact of behaviour change techniques.

The Product Development Process

Product development should follow structured stages that prioritise user understanding, iterative testing, and continuous refinement to create a product that delivers maximum user value (Norman, 2013). Research is critical in this process, providing insights that inform each stage and ensure alignment with user needs and expectations. The UX research methods used in product development often mirror those in academic psychology, but the differences in terminology may obscure the relevance of psychologists' skills to this field. For instance, qualitative interviews are often referred to as 'discovery' or 'generative research' in UX, while 'think-aloud' methods is called 'usability testing'. Furthermore, although research in both academic and UX is often centred on users, the application of research diverges significantly.

Academic research generally aims to advance theoretical knowledge, emphasising rigorous methodologies and publications. In contrast, UX research in industry focuses on delivering timely, actionable insights to guide product decisions and reduce business risks (Lazar et al., 2017). Rather than striving for publication, the primary objective in UX research is to ensure products meet user needs and succeed in the market. This approach prioritises the principle of 'do no harm' while also minimising risks of user disengagement and financial losses due to ineffective design (Johnson et al., 2005).

Design Thinking

Design Thinking is a popular user-centred methodology comprising five stages: Empathise, Define, Ideate, Prototype, and Test (Voorheis et al., 2022).

Empathise. This stage typically uses qualitative methods such as semi-structured interviews, focus groups, and ethnographic studies, to understand end users' needs. This is like the assessment stage in 1-1 client work, where data is gathered from clients to understand their experiences. The foundational insights in this phase help shape the product concept, ensuring it addresses actual user needs (Lazar et al., 2017; Norman, 2013). An example is a sleep app that offers digital, personalised cognitive behavioural therapy to help users manage poor sleep and insomnia; the research team would most likely have sought to understand direct behaviours affecting sleep and underlying emotional and environmental factors, gathering a holistic view of users' sleep habits and challenges.

Define. Insights gathered from the Empathise phase are synthesised to identify core user challenges, informing recommendations that shape the product and its features. For instance, in the development of a sleep app, interview findings would have allowed the team to communicate users' primary sleep challenges to the broader team, which could be framed as key problems for the app to address.

Ideate and Prototype. Researchers and designers brainstorm solutions and develop early prototypes based on user needs identified from the research. This stage may include ideation sessions and co-design workshops with end-users, health professionals, and other key stakeholders to maintain a user-centred approach (Johnson et al., 2005; Norman, 2013). Collaboration with clinicians (e.g., medical doctors) may occur to ensure that content aligns with healthcare standards and addresses clinical requirements (Gilbert, 2022). Initial concepts might be presented to end users or key stakeholders at this stage before more formal research is conducted.

Test and iterate. The Test phase involves evaluating prototypes by mimicking real-world conditions as much as possible. Usability testing, such as think-aloud methodology, is common at this stage as it allows users to interact with prototypes, enabling researchers to gather feedback, identify usability issues, and optimise the design (Norman, 2013). Observing user interactions facilitates continuous refinement, ensuring alignment with user expectations and healthcare standards before full-scale deployment (Norman, 2013). Evaluation should continue after launch and user researchers may collect data through analytics, surveys, and behaviour-tracking software to assess the product's effectiveness over time. This feedback loop is essential for making evidence-based and data-driven improvements, ensuring the product continues to meet user needs and adapts to evolving healthcare contexts (Kuniavsky, 2012; Lazar et al., 2017).

Health Psychologists' Value as User Researchers in Digital Health

Health psychologists with expertise in behaviour change intervention design are well-suited to lead user research for DHIs. There is growing demand for collaboration with health psychologists in the digital health industry to apply their expertise more broadly (Jaworski et al., 2023; Marvel et al., 2018).

Firstly, health psychologists have expertise in involving patients and other end users, such as health professionals, in intervention development. Many health psychologists have demonstrated leadership in user-centred design approaches. One such example is Yardley's *Person-Based Approach* which advocates for iterative design, co-production, and a qualitative exploration of user needs before developing digital interventions. Insights from this approach inform the creation of 'guiding principles' that define the intervention's objectives and essential features, ensuring alignment with user needs and intended outcomes (Yardley et al., 2015). Commercial design teams often fail to effectively involve patient and public partners in the product development process, and when they do, involvement can be a 'check-box' exercise (Noorbergen et al., 2021). Health psychologists can work in commercial design teams to provide clear guidance on meaningful user involvement, bridging gaps in design processes where teams may lack the resources or knowledge to engage end users effectively (Bjerkan et al., 2020).

Secondly, health psychologists are behavioural scientists, and there is growing industry interest in applying behavioural science to digital health. This is evidenced by the success of well-known apps that deliver guided meditation or a behavioural approach to weight management which draw on behavioural science theories from health psychology; for example, the COM-B model, which identifies three essential elements for behaviour change: Capability, Opportunity, and Motivation (Michie et al., 2011). By leveraging these principles, UX practitioners can design experiences that address user engagement barriers effectively. The trend of engaging behavioural scientists in digital health reflects an increased awareness that DHIs informed by behaviour change theory are more likely to succeed than those lacking such theoretical grounding (Webb et al., 2010). Similarly, the Behaviour Change Technique (BCT) taxonomy (Michie et al., 2011) combines evidence-based behavioural strategies with user-centred principles, providing a structured approach to embed techniques such as goal setting, self-monitoring, and feedback into the user experience (Pagoto & Bennett, 2013). Integrating BCTs into DHIs has great potential for improving usability, and therefore the intervention's impact on behaviour change (Milne-Ives, et al., 2023).

While behaviour change theories and frameworks can be helpful, they must be applied correctly to have an impact. Although well-funded organisations may have dedicated behavioural science teams, many smaller companies and individual developers lack guidance on applying theory to digital health products (Voorheis et al., 2022) leaving the potential for scientific and practical contributions unrealised. Health psychologists can bridge the gap by translating theoretical models into practical, actionable strategies that enhance the effectiveness of digital health products. Collaborating with digital health teams allows health psychologists to ensure interventions are both user-centred and grounded in evidence-based methods, maximising their potential for positive impact.

Thirdly, in addition to theoretical knowledge, many health psychologists have practical experience developing digital health products from concept to evaluation across numerous health conditions including hypertension, asthma, and weight management, with a consistent focus on user needs (Bradbury et al., 2015; Greenwell et al., 2021; Remskar et al., 2024; Yardley et al., 2022). This practical experience is especially valuable for innovators with less experience in developing digital health interventions.

Fourthly, health psychologists bring a strong foundation in ethics (Chadwick et al., 2025; see Chap. 4) and patient-centred care, which is crucial for navigating the complexities of DHIs. Health psychologists' expertise in human research ethics (e.g., in obtaining informed consent) guided by a code of ethics and conduct (British Psychological Society, 2020, p. 29; British Psychological Society, 2021) supports rigorous standards. The code is particularly valuable in commercial settings where ethical review processes may not always be required, adding an extra layer of accountability and safeguarding.

Finally, health psychologists possess essential 'soft' skills that are highly relevant to user research. For example, empathy is central to user-centred design. Health psychologists' training and experience enables them to address sensitive topics authentically, capturing the perspectives of vulnerable populations who are often the intended users of DHIs (British Psychological Society, 2020, p. 32). Advocacy for these users is crucial in crafting digital health solutions that are accessible, inclusive, and respectful of diverse needs. Skills such as reflective listening, which involves close attention to users' needs and confirming understanding, are core to user research and are areas where health psychologists, particularly those with patient experience, excel (Braillon & Taiebi, 2020).

In summary, health psychologists' foundational and specialised skills are well-suited for user research in commercial digital health, helping innovators develop evidence-based, user-centred products that enhance health outcomes.

Opportunities and Challenges for Health Psychologists

Opportunities

In my view, health psychologists must establish a more prominent presence within the digital health industry. In personal conversations with professionals interested in transitioning to this field, health psychologists indicate concerns about adapting to a different and faster-paced environment, leaving behind long-standing academic or clinical careers, and uncertainty about finding relevant roles. Working in digital health, however, offers health psychologists the opportunity to make a significant impact outside of traditional clinical or academic roles. The digital health field can be both intellectually stimulating and financially rewarding, appealing to professionals who thrive in fast-paced environments and who enjoy cross-disciplinary collaboration (American Psychological Association, 2024). For those who value variety and teamwork, the digital health industry provides a dynamic setting to apply psychological expertise in innovative and impactful ways. For those concerned about transitioning to industry digital health roles, consulting may offer a less intimidating entry point than a full-time position. Consultancy allows those interested to explore the field and assess the 'fit' without committing to a permanent role.

Consultancy also offers professional autonomy. As independent consultants, we have the flexibility to work with clients whose values align with our own and to exit partnerships when we feel those values no longer align. In a fast-paced technology industry, shifts can happen quickly due to factors such as changing investor priorities or strategic pivots in product direction (Baumel et al., 2019). Working as a consultant enables health psychologists to maintain their professional integrity more easily than in full-time roles, as they are not bound to a single company's evolving agenda (Appelbaum & Steed, 2005).

Furthermore, consultancy allows health psychologists to work across a range of projects, fostering adaptability and a broad understanding of different organisational cultures, practices, and problem-solving approaches (Schein, 2019). This is particularly valuable in healthcare UX research, where each project, whether focused on mental health, weight management, or chronic disease management, presents unique user needs, contexts, and challenges. The diversity in project topics and user populations means that research methods, communication styles, and strategies must be tailored accordingly, providing consultants with continuous learning opportunities. With growing industry interest in behavioural science, consulting allows us to disseminate behavioural science and health psychology across organisations, fostering greater awareness and appreciation for the field.

Consultancy also benefits the end users. Assumptions by developers and teams about user needs can significantly impact product design, potentially leading to ineffective products that waste time and resources. With an external perspective, consultants could conduct research that truly focuses on the needs of end users, rather than being influenced by client assumptions. For instance, a sleep app development team may assume users want detailed sleep cycle data to improve their habits. User research, however, might reveal that excessive sleep data overwhelms users, increasing anxiety and worsening sleep. This insight could lead the team to exclude or modify this feature, creating a product better aligned with user needs and saving development time.

Digital health companies also benefit significantly from the consultancy model. They gain access to specialised, on-demand expertise without long-term commitment. For start-ups with limited resources, this model provides a cost-effective way to incorporate behavioural science expertise into their projects. This model allows companies to scale consultant involvement based on project needs, which could be valuable in the resource-constrained environments often found in the digital health field. Additionally, consultancy allows companies to assess the value of integrating health psychology expertise into their projects before committing to a long-term partnership.

Potential Challenges

The framework for consultancy in health psychology (Brady & Varkonyi-Sepp, 2025; see Chap. 3) outlines a structured approach to consultancy. The framework components—enquiry, relationship-building, negotiation and contracting, planning and managing delivery, and evaluation—align well with the requirements of digital health consultancy. Using this consultancy framework is likely to offer a robust foundation for those entering the field. Working in UX, particularly within the fast-paced commercial digital health environment, does present unique and nuanced demands and there are further challenges that consultants must be aware and considerate of.

Finding consultancy opportunities. While some companies specifically seek user or UX researchers, others may label these roles differently, for example, design researcher, product researcher, and patient experience expert. Moreover, some companies may embed user research responsibilities within broader roles, such as behavioural scientist. This variation in titles can make finding relevant consultancy opportunities more challenging. Health psychologists, however, are accustomed to adapting their skills to roles without a dedicated 'health psychologist' title and looking to the job description instead. This will be the same for identifying roles where you can apply DHI user-centred expertise.

Relationship building and promoting our expertise is essential to identify opportunities, as clients may not understand the relevance of user research, let alone behavioural science, in building better digital health products. Word-of-mouth recommendation and networking can be effective strategies for client acquisition. Active participation in digital health conferences, industry-specific meetups, and professional networking events enables health psychologists to establish connections and stay informed about emerging trends. For example, significant investments were made into women's health technology in 2023. Professional networking platforms also host vibrant digital health communities where consistent engagement and thought leadership can greatly enhance one's visibility and credibility.

One potential approach is to reach out to digital health companies of interest to explore available opportunities. Additionally, several recruitment agencies specialise in user experience or product-related roles and establishing a presence with these agencies could lead to promising prospects. For those who prefer a consultancy-style role while maintaining permanent employment, consultancies may be a suitable option. Many consultancies focus on delivering digital health projects for commercial companies, the charity sector, or the

NHS. You will find helpful information on creating consultancy opportunities in Eliasson and Jackson (2025; see Chap. 12) and in Lunt (2025; see Chap. 7) among other chapters in this book.

Aligning research activities to the product development process. In fast-paced industry settings, product teams follow structured roadmaps, guiding development timelines and milestones (Allen & Chudley, 2012). User research must align with these schedules, often within tight deadlines, potentially limiting scope of exploration and depth of insights. Defining research goals, understanding required insights, and clarifying deadlines are essential in planning. Consultants should agree to deliverables and timelines during negotiation and contracting to meet client expectations and project milestones effectively.

Contextual factors can significantly impact the feasibility and speed of delivering user research and may introduce risks as the research progresses. Identifying and addressing these factors helps manage expectations and ensures effective consultancy (Kometa et al., 1996). While many questions may align with those in the consultancy framework and broader consultancy literature, additional industry-specific questions could include those in Box 13.1.

Working in cross-functional teams. In DHIs you will most likely work as part of a 'cross-functional team', a group of professionals from different disciplines. This could include individuals from software development, design, product management, and marketing, each with distinct contributions and priorities. For instance, a product manager focuses on aligning the product

Box 13.1 Questions to Explore During Enquiry in UX Projects

What previous user research has been conducted on this product? Can you have access to it?

Has the company worked with a user researcher before, and what were their experiences?

What is the plan for recruiting participants? Are there established channels, or will external recruitment agency be necessary? If so, is there a willingness to invest in recruitment agencies?

Is there a budget for participant incentives?

Are there specific in-house tools or software required for conducting and analysing research? If not, are they open to investing in additional resources (e.g., transcription software, survey tools)?

What facilities are available for user interviews or usability testing, such as dedicated spaces or remote testing platforms?

Who are the key stakeholders in this research, and should they be involved in sessions or consulted when communicating research findings?

with business objectives and user needs to drive growth, while a software developer's goal is to write, test, and debug code to create reliable, user-friendly software (Allen & Chudley, 2012). A healthcare background is not often a prerequisite for working in digital health and team members may lack familiarity with healthcare-specific challenges. Consultants must use relationship-building and influencing skills to foster team collaboration and build trust with key stakeholders (Fullerton & West, 1996). Building trust is essential, especially as research findings may challenge the team's assumptions or shift the product's direction (Allen & Chudley). Understanding each team member's role and the team's shared goals is essential. Discussions with stakeholders can offer insights into objectives, success metrics, and constraints, helping external consultants align research with business goals, build trust, and facilitate collaboration (Yip et al., 2014).

During the enquiry process, it is also helpful to understand the team's composition and their previous exposure to user research. Common ground between user research consultants and other team members can often be found in recognising that a user-centred approach to development benefits everyone. For example, software developers avoid building unnecessary features, marketers gain insights into users' challenges, and designers can base their work on evidence rather than assumptions (Norman, 2013).

Many DHI team members will not have expertise in user-centred design, psychology, or behavioural science. Consultants play a critical role in educating stakeholders about the value of these disciplines. Activities such as educational sessions, collaborative research planning, and participatory activities (where team members can join as note-takers or even contribute to data analysis) can help foster a shared understanding of user needs. This increases the likelihood that your research findings and recommendations will be embraced and effectively implemented in the product development process.

Heightened risk of scope creep. Many DHIs requiring consultancy support will be from start-ups or scale-ups. While scope creep, when project demands exceed the original agreement without further discussion (Ajmal et al., 2020; Wulf, 2020), is common in consultancy, it can be particularly heightened in digital health. These environments often involve high levels of uncertainty, rapid shifts in priorities, and resource constraints, while DHIs try to get their product off the ground and generate revenue. The passion, excitement, and dedication to the company's mission can result in an 'all hands on deck' mentality whereby employees are expected to take on multiple roles to drive progress.

Due to the applicability of health psychologists' expertise to many aspects of a digital health product, including behaviour change advice and outcomes research, there may be an increased likelihood of requests to engage in activities beyond a contracted user research role. Establishing clear boundaries as a user research consultant is essential. Outlining specific tasks in the initial contract helps create a foundation for engagement. If requests arise that deviate from the agreed responsibilities, it provides an opportunity to revisit the contract and engage in further discussions to realign expectations. Lunt (2025; see Chap. 7) provides useful advice on clarifying the assumptions on which work will be undertaken during negotiation and contracting.

Maintaining integrity and patient focus. In digital health, profit-driven motives, often fuelled by investor pressures or tight timelines, can push companies to rush products to market, potentially compromising user needs for speed or reduced costs (Cortez et al., 2014). Effective consulting in this context starts with a thorough understanding of the client's motivations and the background of their product's development as part of the enquiry process. Have efforts been made to consider and involve end-users so far? Reviewing the product critically helps you assess its content and understand any areas for improvement. While the product may have limitations, a client's genuine commitment to user-centred changes, even if it challenges their assumptions, can make it feasible to work together even if the current product does not yet fully prioritise user needs.

While some research recommendations may be unfeasible due to time, budget, or technical limitations, consistently ignored recommendations or advice without valid reasons may require a more decisive stance. This could mean stepping back from the project or, if necessary, terminating your contract. Sometimes, user research may appear genuine but is merely performative, a fact that may only become clear once the project is underway. Additionally, consulting may not include overseeing the implementation of recommendations. If asked to deliver more work, it can be helpful to verify if previous recommendations were implemented. Awareness of 'dark patterns' in UX (design strategies that subtly manipulate users into specific actions, such as consenting to data-sharing or making unintended purchases) is crucial (Alsebayel et al., 2024). In the healthcare sector, these practices can undermine user trust and present ethical dilemmas for consultants as the practices prioritise exploitation over user support. For instance, during a competitor analysis for a client, one app required users to complete an extensive personal questionnaire on mental health, only to place results and recommendations behind a paywall. If consultants encounter such practices in client products, it is imperative to raise concerns and advocate for ethical design choices. Should these concerns be disregarded, consultants may need to reconsider their professional engagement with the client to avoid ethical conflicts. For a discussion on ethical principles applied to consultancy in health psychology, see Chadwick et al. in Chap. 4.

Consulting in this field requires directing product development with integrity and prioritising user interests. Consultants must remain mindful of potential reputational risks associated with client partnerships. Maintaining open, respectful dialogue is essential for voicing ethical concerns. For example, a client once asserted that their product was 'co-designed' with users, based solely on a single usability study I conducted post-development. This exaggerated the extent of user involvement, and as the user researcher, I perceived a threat to my professional integrity, particularly given that the NHS was a prominent client. I respectfully challenged this claim, clarifying the concept of co-design and highlighting the associated reputational risks. This led to the client revising their marketing. Had they refused, I would have reconsidered the continuation of our professional relationship.

Ultimately, by applying a structured consultancy framework, health psychologists can navigate the complex, fast-paced digital health environment with greater confidence and effectiveness. This approach not only enhances the quality of the consultancy process but also reinforces the alignment of digital health solutions with user-centred principles, ensuring that products serve both the needs of users and the broader goals of healthcare improvement.

Conclusion

Unquestionably, the future of healthcare involves digital health, but there are significant challenges ahead for its potential to be realised. Health psychologists, with skills in behaviour change, research methodology, and ethics, are well-suited to address these challenges, and we need more of us working in the digital health space. As digital health products shape the future of healthcare, scientifically grounded, user-centred design is essential to ensure that these tools are effective, accessible, and truly engaging. Health psychologists bring user-centred expertise that enables DHIs to resonate with diverse user populations, helping to bridge the gap between behavioural science theory and commercial application.

The journey to effective collaboration within digital health is complex and requires a deep understanding of the field's unique demands, adaptability to fast-paced environments, and a commitment to professional values. Yet the potential rewards are profound. Through consultancy, health psychologists offer a flexible, impactful way for digital health companies to incorporate behavioural insights without requiring long-term commitments. Our involvement fosters a future for digital health in which products are technologically advanced and grounded in evidence-based practices, prioritising user well-being and engagement. By working as external consultants, health psychologists contribute to establishing a trusted ecosystem of digital health solutions, ensuring that these tools genuinely support better health outcomes and empower users to engage with their health in meaningful ways.

Questions for Reflection

1. How can health psychologists better communicate their value as behavioural scientists in a way that resonates with industry?
2. What skills or experiences do you already have, such as conducting qualitative research, applying behavioural theories, or engaging with diverse stakeholders, that align with UX?
3. How comfortable are you with adapting your research approach to incorporate scientific rigour within the practical demands of a fast-paced commercial environment?
4. What strategies can health psychologist consultants employ to navigate the fast-paced, commercially focused digital health sector while maintaining ethical standards and a focus on end-users?

Competing Interests The author has no competing interests to declare that are relevant to the content of this chapter.

References

Ajmal, M., Khan, M., & Al-Yafei, H. (2020). Exploring factors behind project scope creep – Stakeholders' perspective. *International Journal of Managing Projects in Business, 13*(3), 483–504. https://doi.org/10.1108/IJMPB-10-2018-0228

Allen, J. J., & Chudley, J. J. (2012). *Smashing UX design: Foundations for designing online user experiences* (Vol. 34). John Wiley & Sons.

Alsebayel, G., Troiano, G., & Harteveld, C. (2024, May 12). "Not Nice!": Towards understanding dark patterns in commercial health apps [Conference session]. CHI conference on Human Factors in Computing Systems, Honolulu, Unites States. https://ceur-ws.org/Vol-3720/paper2.pdf

Amagai, S., Pila, S., Kaat, A. J., Nowinski, C. J., & Gershon, R. C. (2022). Challenges in participant engagement and retention using mobile health apps: Literature review. *Journal of Medical Internet Research, 24*(4), e35120. https://doi.org/10.2196/35120

American Psychological Association. (2024, January). *Psychologists finding roles in the health tech sector. Monitor on Psychology*. https://www.apa.org/monitor/2024/01/psychology-health-tech-sector

Appelbaum, S. H., & Steed, A. J. (2005). The critical success factors in the client-consulting relationship. *Journal of Management Development, 24*(1), 68–93. https://doi.org/10.1108/02621710510572362

Bakker, D., Kazantzis, N., Rickwood, D., & Rickard, N. (2016). Development and pilot evaluation of smartphone-delivered cognitive behavior therapy strategies for mood- and anxiety-related problems: MoodMission. *Cognitive and Behavioural Practice, 23*(4), 499–510. https://doi.org/10.1016/j.cbpra.2018.07.002

Baumel, A., Muench, F., Edan, S., & Kane, J. M. (2019). Objective user engagement with mental health apps: Systematic search and panel-based usage analysis. *Journal of Medical Internet Research, 21*(9), e14567. https://doi.org/10.2196/14567

Ben-Zeev, D., Schueller, S. M., Begale, M., Duffecy, J., Kane, J. M., & Mohr, D. C. (2015). Strategies for mHealth research: lessons from 3 mobile intervention studies. Administration and Policy in Mental Health and Mental Health Services Research, 42(2), 157-167. https://doi.org/10.1007/s10488-014-0556-2

Big Health. (n.d.). *Sleepio* [Mobile application]. https://www.sleepio.com

Bjerkan, J., Kane, B., Uhrenfeldt, L., Veie, M., & Fossum, M. (2020). Citizen-patient involvement in the development of mhealth technology: Protocol for a systematic scoping review. *JMIR Research Protocols, 9*(8), e16781. https://doi.org/10.2196/16781

Bradbury, K., Dennison, L., Little, P., & Yardley, L. (2015). Using mixed methods to develop and evaluate an online weight management intervention. *British Journal of Health Psychology, 20*(1), 45–55. https://doi.org/10.1111/bjhp.12125

Brady, R., & Varkonyi-Sepp, J. (2025). A framework for consultancy in health psychology. In R. Brady, J. Varkonyi-Sepp, & J. Smith (Eds.), *The Palgrave handbook of consultancy in health psychology*. Palgrave Macmillan.

Braillon, A., & Taiebi, M. (2020). Reflective listening and care. *Patient Education and Counseling, 103*(5), 1866–1867. https://doi.org/10.1016/j.pec.2020.03.024

Brezing, C. A., & Brixner, D. I. (2022). The rise of prescription digital therapeutics in behavioral health. *Advances in Therapy, 39*(12), 5301–5306. https://doi.org/10.1007/s12325-022-02320-0

British Psychological Society. (2020). *Qualification in health psychology. Handbook for candidates.* https://cms.bps.org.uk/sites/default/files/2022-07/QHP%20Candidate%20Handbook.pdf

British Psychological Society. (2021). *Code of ethics and conduct.* https://explore.bps.org.uk/binary/bpsworks/bf9d9fead1dfec7c/3acfadeebe810a324dde720ea7b34b6e87a80cad1de5471be0810935dac0415b/inf94_2021.pdf

Bucher, A., Chaudhry, B. M., Davis, J. W., Lawrence, K., Panza, E., Baqer, M., Feinstein, R. T., Fields, S. A., Huberty, J., Kaplan, D. M., & Kusters, I. S. (2024). How to design equitable digital health tools: A narrative review of design tactics, case studies, and opportunities. *PLOS Digital Health, 3*(8), e0000591. https://doi.org/10.1371/journal.pdig.0000591

Chadwick, P., Hodges-Ballard, L., Killen, A., & Brady, R. (2025). Ethics and the consultancy process. In R. Brady, J. Varkony-Sepp, & J. Smith (Eds.), *The Palgrave handbook of consultancy in health psychology*. Palgrave Macmillan.

Cohen, A. B., Mathews, S. C., Dorsey, E. R., Bates, D. W., & Safavi, K. (2020). Direct-to-consumer digital health. *The Lancet Digital Health, 2*(4), e163–e165. https://doi.org/10.1016/S2589-7500(20)30057-1

Cortez, N. G., Cohen, I. G., & Kesselheim, A. S. (2014). FDA regulation of mobile health technologies. *New England Journal of Medicine, 371*(4), 372–379. https://doi.org/10.1056/NEJMhle1403384

Dennison, L., Morrison, L., Conway, G., & Yardley, L. (2013). Opportunities and challenges for smartphone applications in supporting health behavior change: Qualitative study. *JMIR mHealth and uHealth, 3*(1), e23. https://doi.org/10.2196/jmir.2583

Edwards, E. A., Lumsden, J., Rivas, C., Steed, L., Edwards, L. A., Thiyagarajan, A., Sohanpal, R., Caton, T., Griffiths, C. J., Munafo, M. R., Taylor, S., & Walton, R. T. (2016). Gamification for health promotion: Systematic review of behaviour change techniques in smartphone apps. *BMJ open, 6*(10), e012447. https://doi.org/10.1136/bmjopen-2016-012447

Eliasson, L., & Jackson, C. (2025). A how to guide to working in the private sector. In R. Brady, J. Varkony-Sepp, & J. Smith (Eds.), *The Palgrave handbook of consultancy in health psychology*. Palgrave Macmillan.

Espie, C. A., Emsley, R., Kyle, S. D., Gordon, C., Drake, C. L., Siriwardena, A. N., Cape, J., Ong, J. C., Sheaves, B., Foster, R., Freeman, D., Costa-Font, J., Marsden, A., & Luik, A. (2019). Effect of digital cognitive behavioral therapy for insomnia on health, psychological well-being, and sleep-related quality of life: A randomized clinical trial. *JAMA psychiatry, 76*(1), 21–30. https://doi.org/10.1001/jamapsychiatry.2018.2745

Fullerton, J., & West, M. A. (1996). Consultant and client-working together? *Journal of Managerial Psychology, 11*(6), 40–49. https://doi.org/10.1108/02683949610129749

Gilbert, R. (2022). Reimagining digital healthcare with a patient-centric approach: The role of user experience (UX) research. *Frontiers in Digital Health, 4*, 899976. https://doi.org/10.3389/fdgth.2022.899976

Gothelf, J., & Seiden, J. (2021). *Lean UX: Designing great products with agile teams* (3rd ed.). O'Reillmy Media.

Greaves, F., Joshi, I., Campbell, M., Roberts, S., Patel, N., & Powell, J. (2019). What is an appropriate level of evidence for a digital health intervention? *The Lancet, 392*, 2665–2667. https://doi.org/10.1016/S0140-6736(18)33129-5

Greenwell, K., Sereda, M., Coulson, N. S., Geraghty, A. W., Bradbury, K., & Hoare, D. J. (2021). 'That's just how I am': A qualitative interview study to identify factors influencing engagement with a digital intervention for tinnitus self-management. *British Journal of Health Psychology, 26*(3), 727–747. https://doi.org/10.1111/bjhp.12486

Guo, C., Ashrafian, H., Ghafur, S., Fontana, G., Gardner, C., & Prime, M. (2020). Challenges for the evaluation of digital health solutions—A call for innovative evidence generation approaches. *NPJ Digital Medicine, 3*(1), 110. https://doi.org/10.1038/s41746-020-00314-2

Hyzy, M., Bond, R., Mulvenna, M., Bai, L., Dix, A., Daly, R., Frey, A., & Leigh, S. (2023). Quality of digital health interventions across different health care domains: Secondary data analysis study. *JMIR mHealth and uHealth, 11*(1), e47043. https://doi.org/10.2196/47043

Imison, C., Castle-Clarke, S., Watson, R., & Edwards, N. (2016). *Delivering the benefits of digital health care* (pp. 5–6). Nuffield Trust.

Interaction Design Foundation. (n.d.). *User experience (UX) roles*. Interaction Design Foundation. Retrieved October 29, 2024, from https://www.interaction-design.org/literature/topics/ux-roles

International Organization for Standardization. (2019). *Ergonomics of human-system interaction – Part 210: Human-centred design for interactive systems* (2nd ed.). https://www.iso.org/standard/77520.html

Iqbal, J. D., & Biller-Andorno, N. (2022). The regulatory gap in digital health and alternative pathways to bridge it. *Health Policy and Technology, 11*(3), 100663. https://doi.org/10.1016/j.hlpt.2022.100663

IQVIA Institute for Human Data Science. (2021). Digital health trends: What is the market telling us? https://www.iqvia.com/locations/united-states

Jaworski, B. K., Webb Hooper, M., Aklin, W. M., Jean-Francois, B., Elwood, W. N., Belis, D., Riley, W. T., & Hunter, C. M. (2023). Advancing digital health equity: Directions for behavioral and social science research. *Translational Behavioral Medicine, 13*(3), 132–139. https://doi.org/10.1093/tbm/ibac088

Johnson, C. M., Johnson, T. R., & Zhang, J. (2005). A user-centred framework for redesigning health care interfaces. *Journal of Biomedical Informatics, 38*(1), 75–87. https://doi.org/10.1016/j.jbi.2004.11.005

Kasoju, N., Remya, N. S., Sasi, R., Sujesh, S., Soman, B., Kesavadas, C., Muraleedharan, C. V., Varma, P. H., & Behari, S. (2023). Digital health: Trends, opportunities and challenges in medical devices, pharma and bio-technology. *CSI Transactions on ICT, 11*(1), 11–30. https://doi.org/10.1007/s40012-023-00380-3

Kometa, S. T., Olomolaiye, P. O., & Harris, F. C. (1996). A review of client-generated risks to project consultants. *International Journal of Project Management, 14*(5), 273–279. https://doi.org/10.1016/0263-7863(96)84510-8

Kuniavsky, M. (2012). *Observing the user experience: A practitioner's guide to user research*. Morgan Kaufmann.

Lazar, J., Feng, J. H., & Hochheiser, H. (2017). *Research methods in human-computer interaction*. Morgan Kaufmann.

Lunt, J. (2025). The sustainable consultant. In R. Brady, J. Varkony-Sepp, & J. Smith (Eds.), *The Palgrave handbook of consultancy in health psychology*. Palgrave Macmillan.

Magrabi, F., Habli, I., Sujan, M., Wong, D., Thimbleby, H., Baker, M., & Coiera, E. (2019). Why is it so difficult to govern mobile apps in healthcare? *BMJ Health & Care Informatics, 26*(1), e100006. https://doi.org/10.1136/bmjhci-2019-100006

Marcolino, M. S., Oliveira, J. A. Q., D'Agostino, M., Ribeiro, A. L., Alkmim, M. B. M., & Novillo-Ortiz, D. (2018). The impact of mHealth interventions: Systematic review of systematic reviews. *JMIR mHealth and uHealth, 6*(1), e8873. https://doi.org/10.2196/mhealth.8873

Marvel, F. A., Wang, J., & Martin, S. S. (2018). Digital health innovation: A toolkit to navigate from concept to clinical testing. *JMIR Cardio, 2*(1), e7586. https://doi.org/10.2196/cardio.7586

Mathews, S. C., McShea, M. J., Hanley, C. L., Ravitz, A., Labrique, A. B., & Cohen, A. B. (2019). Digital health: A path to validation. *NPJ Digital Medicine, 2*(1), 38. https://doi.org/10.1038/s41746-019-0111-3

McKay, F. H., Slykerman, S., & Dunn, M. (2019). The app behavior change scale: Creation of a scale to assess the potential of apps to promote behavior change. *JMIR mHealth and uHealth, 7*(1), e11130. https://doi.org/10.2196/11130

Medicines and Healthcare products Regulatory Agency. (2019). *Medical devices: Information for users and patients.* https://www.gov.uk/guidance/medical-devices-information-for-users-and-patients

Michie, S., Van Stralen, M. M., & West, R. (2011). The behaviour change wheel: A new method for characterising and designing behaviour change interventions. *Implementation science, 6*, 1–12.

Milne-Ives, M., Homer, S. R., Andrade, J., & Meinert, E. (2023). Potential associations between behavior change techniques and engagement with mobile health apps: A systematic review. *Frontiers in Psychology, 14*. https://doi.org/10.3389/fpsyg.2023.1227443

National Health Service. (2019). *The NHS long term plan.* https://www.england.nhs.uk/wp-content/uploads/2022/07/nhs-long-term-plan-version-1.2.pdf

National Institute for Health and Care Excellence. (2022). Evidence standards framework for digital health technologies. https://www.nice.org.uk/corporate/ecd7/resources/evidence-standards-framework-for-digital-health-technologies-pdf-1124017457605

NHSX. (2021). Digital Technology Assessment Criteria (DTAC). https://transform.england.nhs.uk/key-tools-and-info/digital-technology-assessment-criteria-dtac/

Nikolaou, C. K., & Lean, M. E. (2017). Mobile applications for obesity and weight management: Current market characteristics. *International Journal of Obesity, 41*(1), 200–202.

Noorbergen, T. J., Adam, M. T., Teubner, T., & Collins, C. E. (2021). Using co-design in mobile health system development: A qualitative study with experts in co-design and mobile health system development. *JMIR mHealth and uHealth, 9*(11), e27896. https://doi.org/10.2196/27896

Norman, D. A. (2013). *The design of everyday things*. Basic Books.

Pagoto, S., & Bennett, G. G. (2013). How behavioral science can contribute to digital health. *Journal of Behavioral Medicine, 36*(4), 396–407. https://doi.org/10.1007/s13142-013-0234-z

Perski, O., Blandford, A., West, R., & Michie, S. (2017). Conceptualising engagement with digital behaviour change interventions: A systematic review using principles from critical interpretive synthesis. *Translational Behavioral Medicine, 7*(2), 254–267. https://doi.org/10.1007/s13142-016-0453-1

Remskar, M., Western, M. J., & Ainsworth, B. (2024). Mindfulness improves psychological health and supports health behaviour cognitions: Evidence from a pragmatic RCT of a digital mindfulness-based intervention. *British Journal of Health Psychology, 29*, 1031–1048.

Sartori, F., Savi, M., & Talpini, J. (2022). Tailoring mHealth apps on users to support behavior change interventions: Conceptual and computational considerations. *Applied Sciences, 12*(8), 3782. https://doi.org/10.3390/app12083782

Schein, E. H. (2019). Models of consultation: What do organizations of the twenty-first century need? In Handbook of organizational consultation, second editon (pp. 1153–1164). Routledge

Schueller, S. M., Tomasino, K. N., & Mohr, D. C. (2017). Integrating human support into behavioral intervention technologies: The efficiency model of support. Clinical Psychology: *Science and Practice, 24*(1), 27–45. https://doi.org/10.1037/h0101740

Schueller, S. M., & Torous, J. (2020). Digital mental health and mHealth. *JAMA Psychiatry, 77*(10), 1021–1030. https://doi.org/10.1037/amp0000654

Sheppard, M. K. (2020). mHealth apps: Disruptive innovation, regulation, and trust—a need for balance. *Medical Law Review, 28*(3), 549–572. https://doi.org/10.1093/medlaw/fwaa019

Silven, A. V., van Peet, P. G., Boers, S. N., Tabak, M., de Groot, A., Hendriks, D., van Os, H. J., Bonten, T. N., Atsma, D. E., de Graaf, T. J., Sombroek, M. P., Chavannes, N. H., & Villalobos-Quesada, M. (2022). Clarifying responsibility: Professional digital health in the doctor-patient relationship, recommendations for physicians based on a multi-stakeholder dialogue in the Netherlands. *BMC Health Services Research, 22*(1), 129. https://doi.org/10.1186/s12913-021-07316-0

Simon, L., Reimann, J., Steubl, L. S., Stach, M., Spiegelhalder, K., Sander, L. B., Baumeister, H., Messner, E., & Terhorst, Y. (2023). Help for insomnia from the app store? A standardized rating of mobile health applications claiming to target insomnia. *Journal of Sleep Research, 32*(1), e13642. https://doi.org/10.1111/jsr.13642

Voorheis, P., Zhao, A., Kuluski, K., Pham, Q., Scott, T., Sztur, P., Khanna, N., Ibrahim, M., & Petch, J. (2022). Integrating behavioural science and design thinking to develop mobile health interventions: Systematic scoping review. *JMIR mHealth and uHealth, 10*(3), e35799. https://doi.org/10.2196/35799

Webb, T., Joseph, J., Yardley, L., & Michie, S. (2010). Using the internet to promote health behavior change: A systematic review and meta-analysis of the impact of theoretical basis, use of behavior change techniques, and mode of delivery on efficacy. *Journal of medical Internet Research, 12*(1), e1376. https://doi.org/10.2196/jmir.1376

Weik, L., Fehring, L., Mortsiefer, A., & Meister, S. (2024). Understanding inherent influencing factors to digital health adoption in general practices through a mixed-methods analysis. *NPJ Digital Medicine, 7*(1), 47. https://doi.org/10.1038/s41746-024-01049-0

Wulf, S. A. (2020). Successful project consulting. *IEEE Engineering Management Review, 48*(2), 12–14. https://doi.org/10.1109/EMR.2020.2978797

Yardley, L., Morrison, L., Bradbury, K., & Muller, I. (2015). The person-based approach to intervention development: Application to digital health-related behavior change interventions. *Journal of Medical Internet Research, 17*(1), e30. https://doi.org/10.2196/jmir.4055

Yardley, L., Spring, B. J., Riper, H., Morrison, L. G., Curtis, K., Merchant, G. C., Naughton, F., & Blandford, A. (2016). Understanding and promoting effective engagement with digital behavior change interventions. *American Journal of Preventive Medicine, 51*(5), 833–842. https://doi.org/10.1016/j.amepre.2016.06.015

Yardley, L., Morton, K., Greenwell, K., Stuart, B., Rice, C., Bradbury, K. Ainsworth, B., Band, R., Murray, E., Mair, F., May, C., Michie, S., Richards-Hall, S., Smith, P., Bruton, A., Raferty, A, Zhu, S., Thomas, M., McManus, R., & Little, P. (2022). Digital interventions for hypertension and asthma to support patient self-management in primary care: The DIPSS research programme including two RCTs. *Programme Grants for Applied Research*. https://doi.org/10.3310/BWFI7321

Yip, M. H., Phaal, R., & Probert, D. R. (2014). Stakeholder engagement in early stage product-service system development for healthcare informatics. *Engineering Management Journal, 26*(3), 52–62. https://doi.org/10.1080/10429247.2014.11432020

14

Experiences of Health Psychology Consultancy in International Health Partnerships

Rebecca Turner, Lucie Byrne-Davis, Sian Armstrong, Nisha Sharma, and Jo Hart

Introduction

The process of consultancy in psychology can be applied across many contexts. In this chapter, we discuss integrating consultancy theory into International Health Partnerships (IHPs), including development of a project, processes and key considerations, and evaluation of those consultancy

Supplementary Information The online version contains supplementary material available at https://doi.org/10.1007/978-3-031-94529-8_14.

R. Turner (✉) • L. Byrne-Davis • J. Hart
Behavioural Science for International Health Workforce Group, University of Manchester, Manchester, UK
e-mail: rebecca.turner@manchester.ac.uk; lucie.byrne-davis@manchester.ac.uk; jo.hart@manchester.ac.uk

S. Armstrong
The Psychology Collective, Glasgow, UK
e-mail: sian@thepsychologycollective.co.uk

N. Sharma
Cognitiva Consultancy Ltd, Southampton, UK
e-mail: info@cognitivaconsultancy.co.uk

R. Brady et al. (eds.), *The Palgrave Handbook of Consultancy in Health Psychology*,
https://doi.org/10.1007/978-3-031-94529-8_14

projects. There are several consultancy models and theories which can guide the practice of consultancy in health psychology. In our view, these models can also support a consultant to develop a 'way of being' or a 'consultancy stance' to guide their approach to consultancy. The consultancy work discussed in this chapter intersects the literature both in positionality and project development. There are several ways to position yourself in interactions with clients (Schein, 1999). As *expert*, the consultant provides answers, positioning themselves as having the knowledge to solve a problem, and instructing clients how they should change. In a *doctor-patient* stance, the consultant diagnoses a problem and makes recommendations for treatment (solutions). *Process* consultation positions the client as the expert in their context and as the owners of the problem to be addressed. The process consultant's role is to guide the client to solve problems themselves, rather than providing answers. Sacks and Loon (2016) describe the former three consultant positions in addition to guidance on defining, planning, and carrying out a consultancy project. This involves defining key relationships, identifying stakeholders, developing communication strategies, defining project goals, and providing feedback through an iterative process. It could be said that the process of becoming a psychologist, and the competences required for professional practice, encourage us to be reflective, to collaborate with others, and to communicate effectively in a way that aligns with *process* consultation.

In our international consultancy projects in health partnerships discussed below, it can be said that both Schein's (1999) definition of a process consultant and Sacks and Loon's (2016) process of 'doing' consultancy were used. However, the consultancy processes and the consultant position were applied implicitly rather than explicitly. The projects were delivered by behavioural scientists (who study human behaviour), health psychologists (who develop interventions to improve human health), and/or practitioner psychologists (particularly those who work clinically to support people to improve mental or physical health challenges), as behaviour change intervention is the area where these disciplines intersect. In the partnerships described, the focus was mainly on the processes and 'evaluation' of consultancy projects, rather than the position of the individual delivering the intervention (e.g., health psychologist). Literature on the use of behaviour change and behaviour change intervention in the context of IHPs is limited. The consultancy process within and across projects has therefore been iterative, involving learning about which position, processes, and evaluations work well, and what improvement can be made in future. The specific 'process' of how and when to implement change, and with which groups, was developed collaboratively during the consultancy project and in the field. The health psychologists involved in our

IHPs projects did not explicitly decide to position themselves in a particular role but adapted flexibility during projects, redefining key relationships as we met healthcare professionals 'on the ground' and adapting communication methods to the context. As psychologists, we are able to look back on our work, reflect on it, and understand how it fits with the literature in order to guide future projects.

What Is an International Health Partnership?

International Health Partnerships are arrangements between high-income countries (HIC) and low-to-middle-income countries (LMICs) which aim to strengthen healthcare capacity and improve health in LMICs. IHPs were established to improve health worldwide by responding to global health challenges such as malaria and acquired immune deficiency syndrome (AIDS), drawing on multiple organisations to achieve such goals (WHO, 2023). Typically, health partnerships include activities such as supporting research, providing financial resources and staff, training and educating clinical teams, and/or providing technical support (Plamondon et al., 2021).

Health partnerships fall between academic and medical organisations and are made up of various 'partners' such as multidisciplinary healthcare professionals (e.g. medical/surgical consultants, pharmacists and nurses), academics, policymakers, government agencies, and charities from partner countries (Tropical Health and Education Trust, 2023). Health partnerships are typically funded and delivered by global health organisations including National Institute of Health Research (NIHR), World Health Organisation (WHO), and Global Health Partnerships, formerly known as Tropical Health and Education Trust (THET), with aims ranging from improving medication safety in Mozambique (Bull et al., 2017) to improving neonatal mortality rates in Uganda (Royal College Midwives, 2015).

How Health Psychology and Behavioural Science Can Support International Health Partnerships

Training and education are often the mainstay interventions used to upskill workers (EPOC, 2015) especially in IHPs, to encourage the adoption of new practices to improve healthcare across the world. Training and education are intervention functions as stated in the Behaviour Change Wheel (Michie et al., 2011) and often include workshops (Reale et al., 2021; Turner et al., 2023), online training (Chisholm et al., 2020), use of educational materials (Pearson et al., 2018), and outreach educational visits (Chhina et al., 2013). Following training and education, health workers must then translate their knowledge into practice, but in some instances, they are unable to do so (Byrne-Davis et al., 2017). Whilst training and education are often developed to change a person's or clinical team's practice, they tend to focus solely on changing knowledge rather than on skills development, opportunity barriers, enhancing motivation, and implementation planning; knowledge focus alone is unlikely to change behaviour (Byrne-Davis et al., 2017; Michie et al., 2011). For example, in some of our previous work, we identified that guidelines were provided to healthcare professionals within health partnerships on hand-washing but there was little focus on making plans to follow such guidelines or providing feedback on such behaviours being achieved (Hawkins et al., 2022). Although within these health partnerships, whilst the focus is often training and education, there are other techniques or strategies included within these interventions. For example, 23 different behaviour change techniques, active ingredients within interventions (Michie et al., 2013), were identified within health partnerships specifically aiming to optimise use of antimicrobials by healthcare professionals (Hawkins et al., 2022). Within these interventions, the theory of change, how the training and education will elicit practice change, is implicit. For example, behaviour change techniques '*4.1 Instructions on how to perform the behaviour*' and '*6.1 Demonstration of the behaviour*' were most used to target hand hygiene behaviours, but the interventions were not based on a theoretical underpinning (Hawkins et al., 2022). Within health partnerships, activities target more than skill and knowledge; applying evidence-based behavioural science and health psychology explicitly, systematically, and rigorously could optimise current and future health partnerships (Bartholomew et al., 1998; Byrne-Davis et al., 2017; Michie et al., 2011).

A collaborative antimicrobial stewardship project is one example where consultancy processes were used in IHPs. While not an explicit decision to follow Schein's (1999) process consultancy model, our psychologist 'way of being' fit well with it. In November 2022, behavioural scientist volunteers, working with the authors visited Nepal to approach an antimicrobial stewardship project from a stance of *humble enquiry*, the art of asking questions you do not know the answer to, to build understanding and relationships based on curiosity (Schein, 1999). The project involved working with the Commonwealth Pharmacist Association and with Nepali health professionals to improve their antibiotic prescribing. The volunteers' naivety in the healthcare context of Nepal, our first collaboration with pharmacists, meant that we easily adopted the stance of humble enquiry. We avoided the role of 'saviour,' as we were very aware of our lack of knowledge in this environment. Both internal and external consultants were used; psychologists from the UK, knowledgeable of behaviour change and behaviour change interventions, and pharmacists from Nepal, knowledge able of prescribing practices and healthcare contexts in Nepal. As such, a large part of the consultancy project involved perceiving and understanding the healthcare context, the prescriber role and the patient journey in the proscription of antibiotics. The project involved asking many open questions such as 'Can you explain to me how this process works?' We attempted to position the Nepali healthcare workers as experts, to encourage self-efficacy and ownership over developing quality improvement projects. In one instance of this, we met a hospital pharmacist who adopted an open stance and asked reflective questions, challenging their own colleagues, this individual, while not originally involved in the project, became integral to it. The pharmacist was invited to a training day, shared their knowledge and experience of challenging their colleagues, and provided an example of existing good practice. Involving this individual allowed us to position them as the expert, in the knowledge that an internal colleague would facilitate engagement and build a bridge between our questions and potential resistance. These conversations formed a large part of the consultancy, allowing pharmacist experts who were aware of context-specific barriers to integrate behaviour elements into planned future prescribing interventions such as challenging hierarchy and timing patient prescription review.

There is a plethora of theories of behaviour within the field of health psychology and behavioural science which has caused confusion within and outside of the fields of health psychology and behavioural science (Michie et al., 2014). The 'Capability, Opportunity, Motivation = Behaviour model' (COM-B model) (Michie et al., 2011) has attempted to synthesise behaviour change theories to improve the adoption of health psychology and behavioural science within and outside of its field. The COM-B model proposes that behaviour is part of an interacting system and includes internal and external factors (Michie et al., 2011). *Capability* includes knowledge and skills, *opportunity* includes factors external to use such as environment and social norms, and *motivation* incorporates attitudes and beliefs as well as the influence of habit and automaticity in behaviour. The simplicity of the model can help health partnerships and healthcare professionals/workers to access behaviour change theory. In practice, COM-B provided a way of defining complex theory and provided a shared language that allowed in-country experts and visiting psychologists to share an understanding of behavioural problems and potential solutions.

Strengthening research capacity in LMICs has been a long-term goal of sustainable development efforts (Fosci et al., 2019). This is due to key issues identified within research systems in LMICs including research not being prioritised or funded by governments, and a lack of translation of research findings from LMICs into practice. Both health psychology and behavioural science continue to flourish and grow as fields. For example, expertise of health psychologists has been recently recognised by the WHO and other leading international organisations, and the need to build capacity for research and practice is recognised (Dharni et al., 2023). Strengthening and capacity building for health psychology, behavioural science, and health psychology research within LMICs is a key priority for many large organisations such as the World Health Organisation (WHO) and the Organisation for Economic Co-operation and Development (OECD). As health psychologists, behavioural scientists, and practitioner psychologists, we are at the vanguard of change and recognition of the importance of the field of health psychology and behavioural science within global health.

The Change Exchange: An Example of Health Partnerships

The Change Exchange (TCE) was co-founded by Professor Jo Hart and Professor Lucie Byrne-Davis in 2013. It was initially funded by Health Education England Global Health Exchange, and the Department for International Development funded Health Partnership Scheme managed by the Global Health Partnerships. TCE is a volunteer programme for health psychologists, behavioural scientists, and practitioner psychologists, with the aim of supporting capacity building in IHPs. TCE key principles are: a co-development approach to practice, we get the psychology of behaviour into places where it can make a difference, we research what happens when people educate healthcare professionals, and we influence health education policy. We work with project teams in health partnerships, to support the translation of health psychology and behavioural science to better support and sustain change using participatory approaches and action research (TCE, 2016). Furthermore, the work from TCE drives evidence forward, collating findings to answer research questions about the determinants of healthcare professional practice.

Often, healthcare professionals from HICs are sent to LMICs by large health partnership organisations or charities to deliver training and education to improve health outcomes. Sadly, either the training or education does not stick, changes to practice seem difficult to make, or, if changes are made, they are not sustained when volunteers leave. An example of an early TCE project was a health partnership between a professional association in the UK that addresses global issues in women's healthcare and a private community hospital in Uganda (Byrne-Davis et al., 2015). The aim of the partnership was to improve obstetric care (including pregnancy, childbirth, and up to around six weeks after birth), and to reduce the incidence of obstetric fistula (a condition where a hole develops in the birth canal, which can result in incontinence). The partnership coordinated and delivered a three-day course, which included a mixture of lectures, workshops, and skills-based clinics. For long-term sustainability, the course incorporated a train-the-trainer approach, whereby a select number of delegates were given further training to train other in-country healthcare professionals.

From their monitoring and evaluation data, the UK association found that knowledge retention of the Ugandan healthcare professionals declined over time; they wished to understand what could be done to address this. Across three in-country visits, TCE volunteers (health psychologists and/or behavioural scientists) initially carried out a needs assessment. They recorded field notes on how the course was delivered observing how delegates put learning into practice within their health centres, observing and coding behaviour change techniques, undertaking focus groups, undertaking quantitative questionnaire feedback and delegating course feedback. TCE volunteers made suggestions to improve the content of the course and how it was delivered based on what was observed. Using the COM-B model, TCE volunteers made recommendations around opportunity and motivation (e.g., incorporating SMART goals within action planning, developing posters to be displayed in health centres to act as a reminder, and encouraging a social support network post programme through using common instant messaging platforms or a buddying system).

Identifying the Problem

TCE disseminate their work at global health and other conferences, at policy and strategic meetings, for example, with government agencies and ministers, professional bodies, and through peer-reviewed papers and policy briefing documents and reports. Through this, partnerships and partnership funders contact TCE. The partnerships all aim to enhance their projects through inclusion of behaviour change theory and principles to achieve health worker practice change. We work with partnerships/organisations to understand their theory of change, and to discuss options in terms of ways of working. Part of this inquiry involves identifying the specific client or clients. Partnerships involve teams from different countries. Preliminary meetings involve understanding the role of the partnership, the relationship between partners and the joint deliverables. At this stage we identify key stakeholders, and what specifically will be delivered by TCE. We often place a behaviour change volunteer with a partnership. Behaviour change volunteers are psychologists with experience of working in applied settings, some with previous consultancy experience, who are familiar with behaviour change theory.

Relationships

Health psychologists and behavioural scientists often work in multidisciplinary teams, both within the United Kingdom (UK) and globally. Multidisciplinary teams in IHPs are typically made up of the two health partnership teams, the local team (in the country where the health partnership work is taking place) and the UK team. Both teams are often led by healthcare professionals such as pharmacists, medical consultants, medical doctors, and nurses. The types of healthcare professionals that make up the team will depend upon the aim of the health partnership. For example, if the aim of the IHPs is to raise awareness of antimicrobial resistance, then healthcare professionals within this field will likely make up the health partnership. In addition to healthcare professionals, project managers often work within these partnerships to ensure the project aims are met and delivered on time.

The role of health psychologists and behavioural scientists, and the contribution they can make to health partnerships, is not widely understood (Turner et al., 2023). This poses a challenge for TCE team members and can act as a barrier to building relationships. Our interviews with TCE volunteers revealed a frequent lack of understanding of the role of practitioner psychologists within health partnerships. This presented a barrier to embedding health psychology principles in the work. A common misconception is that psychologists work only in mental health. Explaining the role of health psychologists and behavioural scientists explicitly at the formation of the health partnership and showcasing the value is, therefore, recommended.

A key challenge for health psychologists working in HICs is understanding and having sensitivity about colonialism. For example, there is a risk that multidisciplinary team members and other stakeholders drive projects based on their own priorities rather than those of the host country, leading them to impart their 'superior' Western knowledge on to team members in LMICs (Kulesa & Brantuo, 2021). This can lead to a hierarchy with HIC teams often referred to as 'donors', and the hosting country known as the 'recipient', leading to further issues between the partners and building relationships (Ackers & Ackers-Johnson, 2017). The TCE approach, in attempting to position the in-country healthcare worker as an 'expert', and supporting health workers to develop their own solutions, was aimed at removing this unhelpful hierarchy. In some health partnerships, English was not widely spoken, and volunteers were reliant on translators to communicate and interact with others in-country. This at times was a barrier in terms of knowing if what had been communicated had been correctly translated and understood and not lost in translation.

Negotiating and Contracting

Negotiating can be through two routes, usually through a higher education institution with support from contracting and business engagement teams: (1) a standard agreement with a partnership funder with whom we have discussed and agreed on activities (e.g., general behaviour change training to all partnerships, comment and input into overall evaluation, plus recruitment and supervision of a behaviour change expert, including travel/subsistence/costs if international travel is required); (2) meetings with a partnership to understand their aims, needs, and budget. Following this TCE suggests activities and the charges for each. This is then further discussed if needed.

Planning and Manging Delivery: The Principles of Health Partnerships

Establishing, managing, and nurturing effective health partnerships is crucial to improve the quality of the partnership and its sustainability. This is a complex intervention in itself. Health partnerships aim to work together collaboratively, with mutual respect towards a common aim. However, challenges can come from health partnerships encompassing a diverse and complex intersection of individuals, clinical teams, professions and vast health and social inequities between countries across the world (Plamondon et al., 2021).

WHO and Global Health Partnerships are leading organisations within IHPs. WHO is a specialised agency of the United Nations responsible for international public health and Global Health Partnerships is an international organisation with a key aim to improve health in Asia and Africa via health partnerships. Both organisations, and other key leaders, recognise the importance of effective and sustainable health partnerships and the challenges health partnerships may face. Principles of partnerships have been developed from such organisations to support effective health partnerships. Global Health Partnerships have developed nine key principles for health partnerships to improve the quality and effectiveness of global HPs; please see Table 14.1. These principles are to aid health partnerships teams in starting, nurturing and maintaining effective HPs, although how these principles are enacted into practice is unclear.

Table 14.1 The Global Health Partnership's nine partnership principles

Principles	Definition as provided by Global Health Partnerships
Harmonised and aligned with national plans	• Health partnerships' work is consistent with local and national plans and complements the activities of other development partners.
Effective and sustainable	• Health partnerships operate in a way that delivers high-quality projects that meet targets and achieves long-term results.
Strategic	• Health partnerships have a shared vision, have long-term aims and measurable plans for achieving them and work within a jointly agreed framework of priorities and direction.
Respectful and reciprocal	• Health partnerships listen to one another and plan, implement and learn together.
Organised and accountable	• Health partnerships are well-structured, well-managed and efficient and have clear and transparent decision-making processes.
Responsible and build trust with partners	• Health partnerships conduct their activities with integrity and cultivate trust in their interactions with stakeholders.
Flexible, resourceful and innovative	• Health partnerships proactively adapt and respond to altered circumstances and embrace change.
Committed to joint learning	• Health partnerships monitor, evaluate and reflect on their activities and results, articulate lessons learned and share knowledge with others.
Embed equity and inclusion	• Health partnerships consider unequal power relations and inequalities experienced by individuals as a result of their social identities and conduct GESI activities and analysis to ensure GESI is mainstreamed into organizations, programmes, interventions and activities.

Global Health Partnerships (n.d.) Global Health Partnerships: Principles of Partnership [Available from: https://www.thet.org/]

These principles should be considered by all members of the partnership team, focusing on how they could potentially incorporate them into the partnership working. Sharing examples of practice with other health partnerships teams can also help people understand what works well and what does not. As well as enacting the key principles of IHPs, the following practicalities and expectation setting in planning and managing delivery need to be considered.

Safety and Risk Assessments

Managing the safety of the volunteers or future consultants abroad is an essential aspect to planning IHP visits. In TCE consultancy work, a risk assessment is needed for each trip undertaken outside of the UK on behalf of TCE. Using detailed guidance from TCE, volunteers carry out and record a risk assessment ahead of the visit. The risk assessment form covers general information, risk assessment and management, rescue checklist, and action plan. A summary of the content of the Risk Assessment form can be found at (ESM_14.1). In our agreements with volunteers, we discuss risk and responsibility. All those collaborating in TCE are required to take out travel insurance and professional indemnity insurance and, as they are not employees, they carry responsibility for their own risk. Sometimes, if they are employed by organisations who support their volunteering with TCE, their organisations carry the risk. In these cases, the volunteers complete a risk assessment for themselves and TCE, and also for their employing organisation.

Managing Expectations, Timelines, and Setting Clear Boundaries

Managing expectations, timelines, and setting clear boundaries is an important part of working within a global health partnership. This helps to build relationships, improve communication, and ensures that all parties involved have the same understanding. TCE volunteers are expected to have regular conversations within their partnerships to agree on what they can and cannot deliver within their projects, any output from the work they undertook (e.g. outcome reports, research papers), and the timelines that these would be delivered within. Setting clear boundaries about TCE remit can require ongoing discussion between TCE volunteers and TCE/IHP leadership. For example, during one project, it became clear that national prescribing guidelines were dictated by one group of healthcare professionals, which felt exclusionary and open to bias. TCE volunteers discuss the best course of action with leadership when such issues arise as they are unlikely to be covered in this detail in IHP contracts. Other challenges include, volunteers being motivated to support change outside of the health partnerships because often they were faced with environmental barriers that challenged the ability to deliver planned elements of the proposed interventions. Since these environmental barriers (e.g., lack of clean water) could not be addressed, some volunteers reported emotional difficulties in facing this (Turner et al., 2023). Part of the process of delivering consultancy in IHPs meant adjusting expectations, resizing potential behavioural changes, or turning to solutions more easily addressed within the presented constraints. However, according to the delivery of process consultancy (Schein, 1999) “everything you do is an intervention” (p.17). For example, even discussions about lack of clean water or governmental policy could have the potential to prompt further discussion and future change.

Evaluation

Within IHPs you are typically working in fast-paced, ever-changing environments, often with many challenges such as variable access to resources (electricity and medical equipment), multilingualism, and resistance to outside influence. When designing and delivering interventions we usually aim to change a specific behaviour. To understand if the intervention was successful, we need to evaluate both the change in knowledge and whether the behaviour change has been enacted. We will now discuss our key recommendations for evaluating and assessing behaviours within IHPs from our experience and expertise.

Evaluating and Assessing Behaviour

We can identify and assess the change in healthcare provider behaviour such as hand washing or prescribing practices by measuring the behaviour at different time points. For example, we may assess how many antibiotics clinical teams and/or individual healthcare professionals prescribe. This is followed by delivering a behaviour change intervention, which is then assessed to see if there has been any change in the prescribing of antibiotics following the intervention (Sneddon et al., 2020). Behaviours can be measured in several different ways, directly and indirectly. Direct measures include observation by a trained observer and video or audio recordings that are subsequently coded using a behavioural checklist. The people developing and using the behavioural checklists should understand the clinical situation, so they can make the appropriate clinical judgement against the standard. The checklist must be completed ethically, with full knowledge of those being observed. Sometimes these can be completed as part of a supportive visit, where people are offered feedback and support after the checklist with any practices they found challenging.

To create a behavioural checklist with each of the intended behaviours (e.g., hand washing), you should add three columns (a) if the behaviour was expected; (b) if it was observed and (c) if it met the appropriate standard. Ideally, these observations should take place before and after interventions to fully understand any impact that interventions are having on clinical practice. Observations of behaviour, generally represent a 'gold standard' measure of behaviour (Hrisos et al., 2009), with multiple researchers rating the behavioural checklist (Lorencatto et al., 2013). However, this might not always be possible due to time or resource constraints. Indirect measures can include self-report, review of medical records or interviewing the people whose behaviour the intervention is targeting (Hrisos et al., 2009; Walton et al., 2017).

An important aspect of evaluation of behaviour change is assessing how people feel impacted by change and understanding how they contribute to sustained behaviour change (Sacks & Loon, 2016). With the joint development of a quality improvement (QI) workbook (Hart et al., 2022), practitioners are encouraged to develop their own plans for behaviour change. During the consultancy process, volunteers and TCE bring health behaviour and behaviour change expertise whereas individuals from the partnership bring context-specific healthcare expertise. It is then the role of the volunteer to bring these two knowledge bases together to enable the clients to build context-specific interventions. The QI workbook then allows practitioners in each country to be specific about who will be involved, the determinants of behaviours involved, when and how change will be enacted and how practitioners will know whether an intervention has been successful. The development and use of these plans on the ground or in follow-up support is a further measurement of impact of the visits. According to Schein (1999), we are encouraging the client to own the problem and solution for behaviour change. At times, this has involved staying in touch with practitioners to provide support for ongoing change.

Assessing Determinants of Behaviour

In-depth qualitative data collection and analysis following education, training, or other interventions can help us understand the participants' experiences, any changes to the determinants of behaviour (e.g., beliefs, knowledge, or routines), and how participants have put learning into practice; or, if they have not managed to put their learning into practice, why not. In one TCE project, volunteers explored the impact and implementation of obstetric anaesthesia education and training in Tanzania, Nepal, and Bangladesh via qualitative interviews (Dharni et al., 2023). The three-day interactive course (Safer Anesthesia From Education—SAFE) was developed by the World Federation of the Societies of Anesthesiologists (WFSA) and Association of Anaesthetists, UK (Grewal & Bhatia, 2018), and had previously been evaluated (Lilaonitkul et al., 2020; Livingston et al., 2014; Moore et al., 2020; White et al., 2019). There was, however, a lack of understanding of whether the course led to clinical practice change. The TCE team carried out interviews based on the Theoretical Domains Framework (TDF) (Cane et al., 2012; Michie et al., 2005) with 78 participants who had accessed the SAFE course. The TDF is a comprehensive theoretical framework systematically synthesised from 128 theoretical constructs and 33 theories which contains 14 domains of behaviour and provides a framework for understanding barriers and facilitators of specific behaviours (e.g., hand-washing). All 14 domains were explored within the interviews. Five of the TDF domains were identified as facilitators to implementing SAFE course clinical practices; Behavioural regulation, Beliefs about consequences, Knowledge & skills, Social influences, and Social/professional role and identity (Dharni et al., 2023). By identifying what domains influence implementation, the TDF can allow us to identify potential mediators of behaviour change (Francis et al., 2012), which can help when developing further interventions and reporting what works and what does not work.

Challenges in Evaluation

Health psychology in global health is still a new concept. Whilst the methodologies, theories, and frameworks from the field of health psychology and behavioural science can aid our practice and evaluation, these have typically been developed in HICs and not in LMICs. Psychological research has been, and continues to be, carried out in Western Educated Industrialised Rich and Democratic (WEIRD) societies (Muthukrishna et al., 2020). TCE volunteers reported difficulties in using psychological methodologies, theories, and frameworks in Health partnerships in their everyday practice in HICs (Turner et al., 2023). Theories and frameworks have different meanings in different cultures and countries, and some of the measures used do not make sense to others in health partnership teams. This often leads to volunteers improvising and adapting (Turner et al., 2023). For example, TCE volunteers felt that there was an inherent discordance with some of the theories of behaviour change, due to their individualistic approach with concepts such as 'self-efficacy' not having the same meaning in cultures that are not individualistic as such. When TCE volunteers faced these challenges in the past, they have often been required to 'think on their feet' and adapt how they were planning to carry out the evaluation. This has involved rephrasing questions and/or using observations instead of structured questionnaires or interviews. When recruiting volunteers to TCE projects, ensuring that volunteers have experience in different evaluation methodologies, in different contexts, including outside of formal academic research, is very important.

Despite meticulous planning and organisation, the delivery of consultancy in IHPs is ever changing and fast paced. The context for projects discussed initially in virtual meetings and emails, can be different once volunteers land in a country. The planned intervention may not be possible or may need considerable adaptation to meet the needs of the client. On one occasion, the consultancy process involved a re-diagnosis of need. TCE volunteers had planned to use a data set of prescribing behaviour to illustrate a baseline of behaviours to implement change. On arrival to the host country, the dataset did not exist. TCE volunteers needed to conduct further inquiry to establish what help they could provide in the timeframe agreed for the project as such, the evaluation of behaviour change was more difficult to establish and moved from understanding which behaviours had changed in prescribing practices to understanding the change in behaviours in relation to collecting data on prescribing practices. The TCE volunteers therefore underwent a reflective process to adapt the planned intervention to developing something new in response to client need. This process involved personal, introspective reflection and flexibility to move from the comfort of an established training plan to something novel developed in response to the specific need. TCE volunteers felt comfortable when delivering the planned intervention which had been successfully delivered in other contexts. In this instance, the challenge was to respond and adapt the intervention to meet the need on the ground.

Impact on Health Psychologists and Behavioural Scientists

Another key aspect of evaluation is the impact that IHPs work has on TCE volunteers and other health psychologists, behavioural scientists, and practitioner psychologists. Being a part of IHPs as a health psychologist or behavioural scientist is a novel role, providing new opportunities for applied psychology work. TCE volunteers have expressed feeling like they can see the benefit of their skills in action and this has provided them with the motivation to keep working in the area/field. They have reported the feeling of satisfaction of seeing the individuals they have trained applying key principles of behaviour change to their practice. Furthermore, previous TCE volunteers have reported further developing their skills in applying their knowledge in practice in different contexts. For example, volunteers gained new skills of working in contexts where private healthcare is standard, in rural and remote locations and in multilingual environments. Despite education and training in the multicultural environment of the UK, the language of healthcare is English. Whereas volunteering as part of the TCE saw volunteers adapting to environments where different languages were normal as part of one healthcare journey. For example, in Timor-Leste doctors were trained in Spanish, ordered medication in English, and spoke to patients in the native language of Tetum, all of which could be part of one patient journey from assessment through diagnosis to treatment. Adapting to the implications of this multilingualism for communication and translation in this context meant volunteers had to work creatively to implement consultancy projects. Volunteers discussed reflecting on their current practices such as the use of methods and theories and the applicability of these outside of the countries that have historically contributed to health psychology and behavioural science (e.g., Northern American and Northern Europe).

Summary

Providing health psychology consultancy within health partnerships has some similar and some different challenges to providing consultancy in the UK context. We have presented the case study of The Change Exchange and our attempts over the last decade to increase the quality and quantity of health psychology consultancy in global health partnerships. We have experienced many challenges but also found an abundance of theoretical and practical evidence, guidelines, and models to support the development of this type of consultancy, and how to position yourself as a health psychology consultant in international partnerships. We have learned that relationship building is important in all consultancy work, is both more of a challenge in global health partnerships and more important, due to multiple cross-national partners working together and the time and expense involved in face-to-face interactions. The impact on health psychology consultant themselves seems to be profound, as can the impact they have in the partnerships. For this reason, continuing development in the processes and procedures for ethical health psychology consultancy across international borders is important.

Questions for Reflection

1. How might my consultancy position/stance affect my collaboration with practitioners in partnerships in other countries?
2. When carrying out evaluations and assessments of behaviours, do I have the correct tools? Are they acceptable and understandable to others? Do I need to make any adaptations or explore this further?
3. How might my competencies in one country/region be applied in a different culture/context?
4. What further learning or support would I need in order to be able to practice in a different country?

Competing Interests Lucie Byrne-Davis and Jo Hart are co-founders of The Change Exchange. No other authors have any competing interests to declare that are relevant to the content of this chapter.

References

Ackers, H. L., & Ackers-Johnson, J. (2017). *Mobile professional voluntarism and international development: Killing me softly?* Springer Nature.

Bartholomew, L. K., Parcel, G. S., & Kok, G. (1998). Intervention mapping: A process for developing theory- and evidence-based health education programs. *Health Education & Behavior, 25*(5), 545–563. https://doi.org/10.1177/109019819802500502

Bull, E. R., Mason, C., Junior, F. D., Santos, L. V., Scott, A., Ademokun, D., Simião, Z., Oliver, W. M., Joaquim, F. F., & Cavanagh, S. M. (2017). Developing nurse medication safety training in a health partnership in Mozambique using behavioural science. *Global Health, 13*(1), 45. https://doi.org/10.1186/s12992-017-0265-1

Byrne-Davis, L., Slattery, H., Whiteside, S., Moro, E., Jackson, M., Onyachi, N., Stevens, A., Hart, J., Surgenor, M., Byrne, G., & on behalf of the Manchester Optimising Health through Training, E., & Research, C. (2015). Efficacy and acceptability of an acute illness management course delivered to staff and students in Uganda by staff from the UK. *International Health, 7*(5), 360–366. https://doi.org/10.1093/inthealth/ihu078

Byrne-Davis, L. M. T., Bull, E. R., Burton, A., Dharni, N., Gillison, F., Maltinsky, W., Mason, C., Sharma, N., Armitage, C. J., Johnston, M., Byrne, G. J., & Hart, J. K. (2017). How behavioural science can contribute to health partnerships: The case of The Change Exchange. *Globalization and Health, 13*(1), 30. https://doi.org/10.1186/s12992-017-0254-4

Cane, J., O'Connor, D., & Michie, S. (2012). Validation of the theoretical domains framework for use in behaviour change and implementation research. *Implementation Science, 7*, 37. https://doi.org/10.1186/1748-5908-7-37

Chhina, H. K., Bhole, V. M., Goldsmith, C., Hall, W., Kaczorowski, J., & Lacaille, D. (2013). Effectiveness of academic detailing to optimize medication prescribing behaviour of family physicians. *Journal of Pharmaceutical Sciences., 16*(4), 511–529.

Chisholm, A., Byrne-Davis, L., Peters, S., Beenstock, J., Gilman, S., & Hart, J. (2020). Online behaviour change technique training to support healthcare staff 'Make Every Contact Count'. *BMC Health Services Research, 20*(1), 390. https://doi.org/10.1186/s12913-020-05264-9

Dharni, N., Byrne-Davis, L. M. T., Sanga, E., Hart, J., Shrestha, A. B., Gurung, T., Shrestha, R. R., Vaidya, P. R., Hossain, A., Lilaonitkul, M., Snell, D., Barrett-Chapman, A., Walker, I., & Bull, E. R. (2023). Using behavioural science to explore impact and implementation of obstetric anaesthesia training in Tanzania, Nepal and Bangladesh: A qualitative evaluation study with obstetric anaesthesia providers. *Psychology & Health, 1–15.* https://doi.org/10.1080/08870446.2022.2160472

EPOC. (2015). *Effective practice and organisation of care. EPOC resource for review authors.* https://epoc.cochrane.org/sites/epoc.cochrane.org/files/uploads/taxonomy/epoc_taxonomy.pdf

Fosci, M., Loffreda, L., Velten, L., & Johnson, R. (2019). *Research Capacity strengthening in LMICs: A rapid evidence assessment.* Research Consulting.

Francis, J. J., O'Connor, D., & Curran, J. (2012). Theories of behaviour change synthesised into a set of theoretical groupings: Introducing a thematic series on the theoretical domains framework. *Implementation Science, 7*, 35. https://doi.org/10.1186/1748-5908-7-35

Grewal, A., & Bhatia, N. (2018). Training initiatives for safe obstetric anesthesia care. *Journal of Obstetric Anaesthesia and Critical Care, 8*(2), 63–63.

Hart, J., Weston, S., Nabiryo, M., Garraghan, F., & Byrne-Davis, L. (2022). Quality improvement tool. Commonwealth Pharmacists Association and The Change Exchange internal document (available on request)

Hawkins, R., Michael, P., Byrne-Davis, L., Bull, E., Skone-James, R., & Hart, J. (2022). The behaviours identified and the behaviour change techniques planned in health partnerships for antimicrobial stewardship. *Applied Psychology: Health and Well-Being, n/a*(n/a). https://doi.org/10.1111/aphw.12421

Hrisos, S., Eccles, M. P., Francis, J. J., Dickinson, H. O., Kaner, E. F. S., Beyer, F., & Johnston, M. (2009). Are there valid proxy measures of clinical behaviour? a systematic review. *Implementation Science, 4*(1), 37. https://doi.org/10.1186/1748-5908-4-37

Kulesa, J., & Brantuo, N. A. (2021). Barriers to decolonising educational partnerships in global health. *BMJ Global Health, 6*(11), e006964.

Lilaonitkul, M., Mishra, S., Pritchard, N., Andhoga, J., Olang', P., Kibet, E., Walker, I., Hart, J., & Byrne-Davis, L. (2020). Mixed methods analysis of factors influencing change in clinical behaviours of non-physician anaesthetists in Kenya following obstetric anaesthesia training. *Anaesthesia, 75*(10), 1331–1339.

Livingston, P., Evans, F., Nsereko, E., Nyirigira, G., Ruhato, P., Sargeant, J., Chipp, M., & Enright, A. (2014). Une anesthésie obstétricale plus sécuritaire grâce à l'éducation et au mentorat: un modèle de transfert des connaissances au Rwanda. *Canadian Journal of Anesthesia/Journal canadien d'anesthésie, 61*, 1028–1039.

Lorencatto, F., West, R., Christopherson, C., & Michie, S. (2013). Assessing fidelity of delivery of smoking cessation behavioural support in practice. *Implementation Science, 8*(1), 40. https://doi.org/10.1186/1748-5908-8-40

Michie, S., Atkins, L., & West, R. (2014). *The behaviour change wheel: A guide to designing interventions*. Silverback.

Michie, S., Johnston, M., Abraham, C., Lawton, R., Parker, D., Walker, A., & Psychological Theory, G. (2005). Making psychological theory useful for implementing evidence based practice: A consensus approach. *Quality and Safety in Health Care, 14*(1), 26–33. https://doi.org/10.1136/qshc.2004.011155

Michie, S., Richardson, M., Johnston, M., Abraham, C., Francis, J., Hardeman, W., Eccles, M. P., Cane, J., & Wood, C. E. (2013). The behavior change technique taxonomy (v1) of 93 hierarchically clustered techniques: Building an international consensus for the reporting of behavior change interventions. *Annals of Behavioral Medicine, 46*(1), 81–95. https://doi.org/10.1007/s12160-013-9486-6

Michie, S., van Stralen, M. M., & West, R. (2011). The behaviour change wheel: A new method for characterising and designing behaviour change interventions. *Implementation Science, 6*, 42. https://doi.org/10.1186/1748-5908-6-42

Moore, J. N., Morriss, W. W., Asfaw, G., Tesfaye, G., Ahmed, A. R., & Walker, I. A. (2020). The impact of the Safer Anaesthesia from Education (SAFE) Obstetric Anaesthesia training course in Ethiopia: A mixed methods longitudinal cohort study. *Anaesthesia and Intensive Care, 48*(4), 297–305.

Muthukrishna, M., Bell, A. V., Henrich, J., Curtin, C. M., Gedranovich, A., McInerney, J., & Thue, B. (2020). Beyond Western, Educated, Industrial, Rich, and Democratic (WEIRD) psychology: Measuring and mapping scales of cultural and psychological distance. *Psychological Science, 31*(6), 678–701.

Pearson, E., Byrne-Davis, L., Bull, E., & Hart, J. (2018). Behavior change techniques in health professional training: Developing a coding tool. *Translational Behavioral Medicine*. https://doi.org/10.1093/tbm/iby125

Plamondon, K. M., Brisbois, B., Dubent, L., & Larson, C. P. (2021). Assessing how global health partnerships function: An equity-informed critical interpretive synthesis. *Globalization and Health, 17*(1), 73. https://doi.org/10.1186/s12992-021-00726-z

Reale, S., Turner, R. R., Sutton, E., Taylor, S. J. C., Bourke, L., Morrissey, D., Brown, J., Rosario, D. J., & Steed, L. (2021). Towards implementing exercise into the prostate cancer care pathway: Development of a theory and evidence-based intervention to train community-based exercise professionals to support change in patient exercise behaviour (The STAMINA trial). *BMC Health Services Research, 21*(1), 264. https://doi.org/10.1186/s12913-021-06275-w

Royal College Midwives. (2015). Global midwifery twinning project: Supporting midwifery beyond our borders. https://www.rcm.org.uk/media/2389/supporting-midwifery-beyond-our-borders.pdf

Sacks, R., & Loon, M. (2016). *Developing and using consultancy skills: Professional practice in learning and development: How to design and deliver plans for the workplace*. Kogan Place.

Schein, E. H. (1999). *Process consultation revisited. Building the helping relationship*. Addison-Weley Publishing Company.

Sneddon, J., Cooper, L., Afriyie, D. K., Sefah, I., Cockburn, A., Kerr, F., Cameron, E., Goldthorpe, J., Kurdi, A., & Seaton, R. A. (2020). Supporting antimicrobial stewardship in Ghana: Evaluation of the impact of training on knowledge and attitudes of healthcare professionals in two hospitals. *JAC-Antimicrobial Resistance, 2*(4), dlaa092.

TCE. (2016). *The change exchange key principles*. https://www.mcrimpsci.org/the-change-exchange/

THET. (2023). *The tropical health and education trust health partnership scheme*. Retrieved July 28, from https://www.thet.org/our-work/health-partnership-scheme/

Turner, R. R., Reddy, S. E., Byrne-Davis, L., Bull, E., & Hart, J. (2023). An interview study to explore applied psychologists' experiences of implementing health psychology in global health partnerships: The Change Exchange. *British Journal of Health Psychology, 28*(4), 1076–1096.

Walton, H., Spector, A., Tombor, I., & Michie, S. (2017). Measures of fidelity of delivery of, and engagement with, complex, face-to-face health behaviour change interventions: A systematic review of measure quality. *British Journal of Health Psychology, 22*(4), 872–903. https://doi.org/10.1111/bjhp.12260

White, M. C., Rakotoarisoa, T., Cox, N. H., Close, K. L., Kotze, J., & Watrous, A. (2019). A mixed-method design evaluation of the SAFE obstetric anaesthesia course at 4 and 12–18 months after training in the Republic of Congo and Madagascar. *Anesthesia and Analgesia, 129*(6), 1707.

WHO. (2023). *Global health partnerships.* https://www.who.int/europe/about-us/partnerships/partners/global-health-partnerships

Part III

Case Studies

15

Enquiry: Supporting Vaccine Uptake Decision-making in Residential Services

Suzanne Allen

Introduction

This chapter is divided into three sections. After first providing information on context, I describe an internal consultancy project undertaken with a colleague in a service for adults with intellectual disabilities (ID) in Ireland in 2021. This is followed by a deeper look at the enquiry process, including questioning and researching to discover client and stakeholder needs while studying the implications of pending decision-making capacity legislation. While the project pre-dated the framework for consultancy in health psychology (Brady and Varkonyi-Sepp, 2025; see Chap. 3) proposed in this book, I will reflect on how the steps taken in this project align with that framework.

Context

A practitioner health psychologist with 27 years' experience in the Irish healthcare sector, I am the principal psychologist in a state-funded health and social care service for people with ID, physical disabilities, acquired brain injury, and mental health needs. The organisation provides day and residential services, rehabilitation, and training and I am responsible for a nationwide

Supplementary Information The online version contains supplementary material available at https://doi.org/10.1007/978-3-031-94529-8_15.

S. Allen (✉)
University of Stirling, Stirling, UK
e-mail: sua4@stir.ac.uk

R. Brady et al. (eds.), *The Palgrave Handbook of Consultancy in Health Psychology*,
https://doi.org/10.1007/978-3-031-94529-8_15

psychology service comprising 23 psychologists (including counselling, educational, and health psychologists). Over 4,500 people attend our care services delivered by 1,500 healthcare staff in over 210 locations in Ireland, where this work took place.

The consultancy project took place during the Covid-19 national vaccine roll-out. At the time, new legislation in Ireland, called the Assisted Decision Making (Capacity) Act (2015) (or ADMA) was pending. Although it was signed into law on 30 December 2015 it came into effect fully on 26 April 2023. Prior to this, when in doubt about a person's capacity (which can be defined as our ability to understand when a decision is being made and the consequences of the decision in the context of the options available to us (Citizens Information, 2023), healthcare workers or families could decide to accept or decline a vaccine in the 'best interests' of the person. However, under ADMA, *everyone* is presumed to have capacity, and a person cannot be presumed to lack capacity by virtue of making a decision that others consider unwise. Therefore, healthcare workers (and families) must firstly assume that everyone has capacity. Where there is doubt about capacity, ADMA sets out a functional test, as follows:

1. Can the person understand the options they have about the decision to be taken?
2. Can the person weigh up the pros and cons, retaining the information long enough to make a decision?
3. Can the person communicate their decision (verbally or non-verbally)?

According to ADMA, capacity is dynamic; if a person can meet all three criteria, they are deemed to have capacity *for this decision at this time*. If they cannot meet the criteria, consequently they are deemed to lack capacity *for this specific decision at this time*. Furthermore, the principle of 'best interests' decision-making was replaced by the principle of 'will and preference', which considers the person's values, goals, and preferences (Donnelly, 2016). New procedures, training and practices would be required to enable healthcare staff to implement this functional test of capacity and the principle of will and preference.

The Consultancy Project

In 2021, the internal client, the director of the department in the service where I was employed, requested that my colleague (the lead behaviour therapist) and I consult on a project to respond to requests from staff for guidance on how to support people with ID (henceforth referred to as residents) living in residential services who were undecided about the vaccine. There was a lack of accessible information to support those residents who required pictorial information. Also, staff needed guidance on *how* to provide decision-making support. The client asked us to explore what was required and recommend solutions. We received this brief verbally at a meeting with the internal client. Given the urgency of supporting residents to decide on a vaccine during a pandemic, my colleague and I needed to respond quickly. We met frequently to share information and develop a proposal, which we did by undertaking training in ADMA, reading widely about assisted decision-making, consulting with experts, and listening to stakeholders.

Stakeholder Engagement

Recognising the importance of identifying stakeholders and their needs (e.g., Schein & Schein, 2018), we identified people who would be affected by the project. Because the work had to be completed quickly, we asked the psychologists, behaviour therapists, and service managers to gather feedback from residents, healthcare staff and families, as they encountered them within a two-week timeframe. We did not specify questions but asked for broad feedback on what was important to each stakeholder regarding the residents' decision-making about the vaccine. We also sought feedback from the client about the organisational implications of ADMA. While our method of collecting feedback was not systematic, that was unavoidable given the urgency and limited resources available. This, together with the feedback, displayed in Table 15.1, will be reflected on later in the chapter.

Proposal and Agreed Outcomes

In a meeting to discuss these initial findings, the client specified two desired outcomes: first, vaccine information in pictorial format for residents; and second, a staff guide with easy-to-follow steps on providing decision-making support. We described to the client how ADMA required organisations to retain records of decision-making support provided, so that would need to be built into the process. Following this preliminary work, we proposed the following: templates aligned with ADMA's functional test of capacity to guide staff through each step in providing decision-making support, and the development of a social story aimed at residents who communicate differently and who can experience anxiety when facing unfamiliar health appointments. Social stories are short descriptions of a particular situation or activity which includes specific information about what to expect and why (Gray, 2010).

Table 15.1 Stakeholder feedback

Stakeholder	Feedback
Residents	• Wanted support to make the decision about the vaccine • Had questions about what the vaccine appointments would be like
Families	• Wanted their loved ones to be protected from Covid-19 • Most wanted 'best interests' decision-making applied • A few wanted their loved one to decide
Frontline healthcare staff	• Wanted help to provide decision-making support • Were concerned they might contract Covid-19 at work and pass it to a family member • Advocated for non-verbal residents who became distressed at appointments
The client	• Was concerned about the health and safety of residents and staff • Needed to understand the impact on resources

Each resource would have an inbuilt record-keeping mechanism. This will be elaborated on in the enquiry section of this chapter.

We advised the client that we needed to engage the clinical teams to assist in circulating the resources to staff teams nationwide. Finally, we outlined that we would be making recommendations around staff training, policy reviews, and the establishment of an implementation group. The client agreed to our proposal, and we moved to the planning and development phase.

Planning and Developing Resources

We began by developing the resources for staff. We knew from the literature on implementing capacity legislation that staff would require clear procedures (Davies et al., 2019). Therefore, we specified the actions that staff needed to take at each step of the ADMA functional test of capacity. For example, for step 1 (*Can the person understand the options available*?), we identified that staff would need help selecting the relevant information to present, and so we developed resources to guide them in how to do this. These comprised: first, a checklist of ways to present information about the vaccination decision and second, a social story to demonstrate how to receive a vaccine. Each resource doubled as a record-keeping mechanism. In this way, the ADMA three-step functional assessment naturally formed the *structure* of the staff component of the intervention. (The resources are available in supplementary material ESM_15.1).

Table 15.2 Application of the Health Belief Model (HBM) (Rosenstock, 1974)

HBM component	Associated pros and cons statements[a]
Susceptibility	• Covid-19 is highly contagious
Severity	• A very small number of people get sick after receiving the vaccine (allergic reaction)
Costs	• The vaccine involves two injections given by a doctor or nurse • After receiving the vaccine, they may have a sore arm or fever
Benefits	• If they take the vaccine, they can access the community safely
Cues to action	• Internal cue: Wanting to stay well • Internal cue: The vaccine is a medicine that will prevent sickness from Covid-19 • External cue: Role-play of receiving a vaccine
Health motivation	• Opportunity to practice receiving the vaccine via the social story role play • The vaccine is a medicine that will prevent sickness from Covid-19
Perceived control	• Knowing how to receive the vaccine (from role play)

[a]Resource 15.1a (words) and 15.1b (pictures) in supplementary material (ESM_15.1)

Next, we developed the component of the intervention aimed at residents. To do this we populated the *content* of the resources with the relevant information that people require when making health decisions such as receiving a vaccine. Although several theories inform us of the salient constructs in health decision-making, research particularly supports the usefulness of the Health Belief Model (HBM) (Rosenstock, 1974) in vaccine uptake (e.g., Limbu et al., 2022). Table 15.2 illustrates how we applied the components of the HBM to the resources.

To be clear, the desired outcome was *not* to persuade residents to take the Covid-19 vaccine; rather it was to enable residents to make informed decisions, through the behaviour of the staff. As a health psychologist, I wanted to enhance the effectiveness of staff by providing them with evidence-based templates to follow in supporting informed health decision-making by residents. This two-pronged intervention is consistent with Michie's description of health psychology consultancy as the use of psychological expertise and skills to enhance the effectiveness of others in the promotion of health (Michie, 1998).

The next step was to deliver the resources to staff and ensure they were utilised in an ADMA-aligned way. Therefore, we recommended that healthcare staff complete an available online module on ADMA awareness (from a private provider) *prior* to implementing the resources. We also briefed the clinicians on the resources and explained how each was to be used. Regarding families who wanted best interests' decision-making to be applied, we recommended that the clinicians involve families in multidisciplinary meetings, as studies show this improves families' engagement with supported decision-making (Donnelly et al., 2019). Regarding staff who were anxious they would contract Covid-19 at work and pass it on to others, we advised the clinicians to remind staff about the available supports within the organisation such as the Employee Assistance Programme and psychologist-led wellness workshops. The clinicians then demonstrated to staff how to use the templates, and they supported staff to implement them.

Evaluation and Further Recommendations

We did not formally evaluate the intervention, which I reflect on later in the chapter. However, due to the wide-ranging implications of ADMA, we viewed this consultancy project as a distinct piece within a broader ADMA implementation body of work. We agreed with the client, therefore, that an implementation group be formed with representation from all relevant departments, to consider the following:

A. That the organisation invest in further training for staff and service users, as evidence shows that lack of training is a barrier to ADMA implementation by healthcare staff (Davies et al., 2019; Donnelly et al., 2019).
B. Organisational policy that supports ADMA (Cronin et al., 2018; Davies et al., 2019) is a facilitator to healthcare practitioners' implementing ADMA, therefore we recommended a review of relevant policies and procedures.
C. A further barrier to ADMA implementation identified in the literature is lack of time (Donnelly et al., 2019), therefore we recommended to the client that consideration be given to this. (The work of this implementation group continues to this day.)

Enquiry: Managing Multiple Levels of Enquiry in the Context of Emerging Legislation

The area of the consultancy framework (Brady and Varkonyi-Sepp, 2025; see Chap. 3) that I will now focus on is the enquiry process. Specifically, I will describe the challenge of managing multiple levels of enquiry in the context of new legislation. Essentially, enquiry is the process of exploring and discovering a thorough understanding of the clients' needs. Consultancy projects such as ours often require multiple levels of enquiry: establishing client needs and agreeing outcomes, enquiry into stakeholder's needs, studying the legislative context, and reviewing the literature on similar capacity legislation implementation internationally.

Exploring Enquiry

Researchers describe the enquiry process as the need for the consultant to be able to initiate effective communication with the client, from the outset, to holistically study the issues within the complex system of the organisation it exists within (Heifetz et al., 2009). Social psychologist and consultancy expert Edgar Schein (2016) argues that the enquiry process commences *before* we meet the client; he recommended preparing in advance of the first meeting, by researching the organisation (in external consultancy) or the department (in internal consultancy) so that you can consider what questions to ask about the consultancy request before accepting it. Drawing comparisons to my work as a practitioner psychologist, when I receive a referral for one-to-one therapeutic work, there are many questions I ask before agreeing to accept the referral. In my experience, the enquiry process in consultancy is like the rapport building, assessment and formulation elements of psychological therapy. A further comparison I draw with practitioner work is Schein's recommendation of being mindful of the '3 Cs' which are: commitment to helping, caring for the client, and most important, curiosity. You must 'get personal' as quickly as possible in a way that is similar, in my experience, to the process of creating a therapeutic relationship in psychological therapy.

Establishing Client Needs and Agreeing Outcomes

In this case, our first contact with the client was at a briefing meeting where she outlined the need for staff to be informed on how to provide decision-making support to residents. In these first meetings with a client, Schein (2016) advocates that we try to bypass the professional distance between colleagues and aim to develop 'empathy two' skills while building a closer, more honest relationship with the client; 'empathy one' being when we listen for the situation or problem, and 'empathy two' being when we listen for what is *really* bothering the client about this situation. At that first meeting with the client, being an internal consultant was advantageous in that we already had a rapport and a level of trust that was helpful in achieving empathy two skills. As consultants we must become a partner and a helper to the client, from that first meeting. That first meeting is also about getting to know the brief. In our case, we received the brief verbally from the client. In hindsight, a summary document of the work to be done would have been beneficial in order to track progress. Wulf (2020) advocates that before implementing the project the consultant must create a document that outlines the scope of the project or task, the function of which is to clarify expectations. Wulf insists that if you are finding it difficult to complete this document, you must have incomplete information and recommends asking the client directly, how they will know that their objective has been achieved. The client was clear about the outcomes expected when we asked this question. However, we now believe that we were hasty in agreeing to these outcomes as they required adjustment following review of ADMA, which I will explore later.

According to Schein (1988) I am not alone in having the urge to jump to solutions before fully exploring the problem. In fact, Schein (2016) argues that the larger part of the work *is* the dialogue with the client. Schein goes on to advise against hastily offering proposals without having thoroughly examined not only the issues but the *organisational system* they reside in, such as, the practices of frontline healthcare staff, management structures, values and so on. Comparing this to my practitioner work, often the solutions lie in systemic work such as listening to and working through the staff rather than direct interventions with the residents.

As internal consultants, we have knowledge of the practices of frontline staff, the management structures, and the values of equality and advocacy that drive the service. So, our sense of implementing a rights-based approach to vaccine decision-making was that it matched the values of the organisation, as well as our own. This is a key part of the enquiry process: ensuring that the work matches your values, as well as your area of expertise.

Identifying the Stakeholders and Their Needs

Schein describes the notion of 'genuine curiosity' (2016) and being authentic in trying to understand the brief. To achieve this, we set out to identify and listen to the people most affected: the stakeholders. Failure to identify all the stakeholders is a common pitfall in consultancy, as is failure to communicate with them in a timely manner (Wulf, 2020). One approach in identifying stakeholders, is Block's *whole system approach* meaning the whole system is involved or at least represented which involves having sufficient representatives from all parts of a system who will be acting on the recommendations, to help create them (Block, 2011). In this approach, the people making the decisions are the ones who must make it work. While I see the rationale for this whole system approach, it would have been challenging to follow it in our project because some of the people acting on the recommendations were unaware of the legislation and how it impacted their practice and there was a lack of time to address this.

We identified stakeholders using the Wulf (2020) method of listing all the people and groups who might be impacted by the work. This involved listing all the relevant people internal and external to the organisation. A further step identified in the literature as being effective in internal consultancy is to then ask a colleague to check this list (Sacks & Loon, 2016). We asked our client to check a drafted list to ensure it included all the stakeholders. Liaising with the client is a practice recommended by Hodges (2021) who suggests discussing contracting any time a client meeting takes place – the function of which is to acknowledge progress, clarify any misunderstandings and agree next steps.

Enquiry into the Legislative Context

Block (2011) argued that as consultants our goal should be to split our time evenly between relationship building and the technical issue to be solved. However, the complex technical issues in this consultancy project called for a deep understanding of the legislative context during the enquiry process. We were aware of ADMA as a piece of pending legislation from our practice of scanning the legislative and regulatory environment for developments that could impact on disability services. In fact, in recognition of this complexity, Schein (2016) coined the term 'humble consulting' to reflect the awe he felt of the problems his clients faced. The next layer of the enquiry process we worked through, therefore, was studying the legislation. Nilsson (2012) advocates for the rights of people with disabilities to make their own decisions in life and to be afforded equal legal capacity with the rest of the population. He argued that this was one of the biggest human rights issues in Europe.

These human rights issues as identified by Nilsson (2012) depict the capacity landscape in Ireland, pre-ADMA. One of the challenges was to get to know the principles of ADMA quickly. We familiarised ourselves with ADMA by attending four days of intensive training with a specialist training company, and by consulting with an expert in legal capacity. Learning about the complexity of ADMA, it became clear that the consultancy needed to be rooted within its principles. However, this was challenging as the service users, families, and frontline staff had not previously been given an opportunity to learn about ADMA, which was not yet enshrined in law, but which we were acutely aware was pending. Low awareness of ADMA amongst health professionals has been identified in Ireland. In a study by Curtis et al. (2022), only 2% of doctors had received any training on ADMA, 5% were unsure of their role and 45% were unsure of a patient's role in decision-making; 37% believed that the 'best interests' principle was retained in decision-making. The researchers concluded that further training was urgently required for healthcare staff if ADMA is to be successfully implemented. If healthcare staff were mostly unfamiliar with ADMA, we could reasonably assume that most families would be too.

We realised, therefore, that our approach to consent for the COVID-19 vaccine would be perceived as novel, especially the presumption of capacity in the context of an unwise decision. What we did not want, was for family members or staff to use the resources we produced *to persuade* service users to take the vaccine, removing their right to choose. In fact, during the enquiry process we emphasised with the client that we were not aiming to persuade residents to take the vaccine. Persuasion would be directly opposed to our values as consultants and to ADMA legislation, in that everyone, staff and residents alike, has the right to choose for themselves. The client agreed that the project was more complex than initially anticipated and agreed that we proceed with a rights-based approach which was consistent with the organisation's values. This aligns with a concept Schein writes about, which is that usually the primary assistance a consultant can offer a client is to facilitate their total awareness of the extent of the issue at hand (Schein, 2016).

Reviewing the Literature on Capacity Legislation Implementation Internationally

Since health psychologists are evidence-based practitioners, another important part of the enquiry process for me was to find out what evidence exists for potential solutions. Where we skip to the technical work too soon and rush the enquiry process, it can lead to change being implemented that addresses the symptoms rather than the underlying causes of the problem (Hodges, 2021). To seek evidence-based solutions we searched for studies on the implementation of capacity legislation in healthcare settings. As ADMA was relatively new, few papers had been published. We sourced post-implementation studies about capacity legislation in Scotland (the Adults with Incapacity Act, 2000) and in England and Wales (the Mental Capacity Act, 2005). This reading was helpful in that we learned about the barriers and facilitators to implementing similar capacity legislation in other nations. Relevant barriers included lack of ready-to-use templates (Killeen et al., 2004) and facilitators included the use of social stories (Cronin et al., 2018). This reading informed the evidence base for the resources we developed.

Feedback from residents indicated many were undecided about whether to accept a vaccine and wanted support to make the decision, indicating that they required more information, see Table 15.1. This is consistent with findings from a study by Killeen et al. (2004) who found that there was a lack of information aimed at the relevant person, and this is a barrier to assisted decision-making in relation to capacity legislation in Scotland. Based on this, we developed resources to assist staff in providing the relevant information to the resident. Feedback from residents also indicated they would like to know what would happen during a vaccine appointment. This is consistent with a study conducted by Cronin et al. (2018) which found that effective communication, including the use of social stories, was a facilitator to supported decision-making, as well as the use of assistive technology and communication aides (Davies et al., 2019). We therefore developed a social story to meet this need. Other facilitators of engagement by service users in supported decision-making include having a good relationship with the decision supporter and involving the service user early in the process (Davies et al.). We recommended, therefore, that the resident's keyworker provide the decision-making support, from the outset.

Feedback from families indicated that a majority wanted the 'best interests' principle, which predated ADMA, to be applied. This lack of awareness that best interests' decision-making would no longer be legally sound is consistent with findings by Killeen et al. (2004), who found that lack of investment in public awareness is a barrier to family implementation of the Scottish capacity legislation (Adults with Incapacity Act, 2000). In response, we recommended that multidisciplinary meetings fully involve the resident and their family, from an early stage, because this had been found to be a facilitator to family and service user engagement with supported decision-making (Donnelly et al., 2019).

Feedback from healthcare staff indicated they wanted help in knowing how to provide decision-making support to residents. This need for good practice guidance for healthcare staff is consistent with Killeen et al.'s (2004) findings (in Scotland) which indicated that clear guidance is required on several issues: how to communicate with adults with severe communication difficulties, understanding the impact of different neurological conditions on ability to make decisions, and assessing capacity in relation to a specific decision. Staff feedback at our organisation highlighted a concern that residents without verbal communication skills sometimes became visibly distressed at non-routine health appointments. Developing social stories to meet this need would align with evidence that they are effective tools to aid familiarisation and reduce anxiety about non-routine health appointments (Cronin et al., 2018).

Feedback from the client indicated they were concerned about staff carrying out due diligence in relation to ADMA. Our research in response to this identified organisational facilitators of effective capacity legislation implementation which included fostering a culture of change (Cronin et al., 2018; Davies et al., 2019; Donnelly et al., 2019) and having policies which support ADMA (Cronin et al.; Davies et al.). Consequently, we made recommendations that went beyond the original scope of this consultancy project, such as recommending that record keeping mechanisms are built into each resource. The client was concerned about the impact of supported decision-making work on resources. This is consistent with Cronin et al. (2018) research, which found that heavy documentation associated with ADMA acts as a barrier to implementation for healthcare staff. With record keeping also being identified as a barrier to implementing capacity legislation in healthcare settings (Alonzi et al., 2009), we responded by building in record keeping mechanisms into our resources to minimise the record keeping burden.

Reflection

Schön (1995) wrote about a dilemma of 'rigour versus relevance', which I really connected with. He describes the high ground where researchers apply rigour to solve manageable problems. However, these problems tend to be mostly irrelevant to society. Meanwhile, in 'the swampy lowlands' of everyday practice, the problems most worrying to people exist. Therefore, the practitioner faces a choice – do they remain on the high ground and attempt to solve relatively unimportant problems with scientific rigour? Or do they sink to the swamp where they can attempt to resolve genuinely impactful problems but cannot apply scientific rigour to the same extent?

I relate to this concept of being in the 'swamp' of practitioner work and doubting my own standards of rigour. Schön (1995) calls for us to consider not only how practitioners can better apply academic research results, but what kinds of knowing are already embedded in our practice. Tacit knowledge or 'knowing-in-action' embodies what we know how to do, in everyday life. Schön speaks about the intuitive performance of these actions and says this is how we show ourselves to be knowledgeable. Often, we cannot describe what we know; our knowing is tacit and 'implicit in our patterns of action'. When writing this chapter and reflecting on my work, I found it hard to decipher my contribution from that of my colleague. The reading on tacit knowledge illustrated that knowledge is 'in our action'. For instance, I did not pause to consider why I chose the Health Belief Model (HBM) (Rosenstock, 1974). The HBM is a theoretical framework I often utilise, and, in this case, I applied its constructs without explaining to my colleague what I was doing. Looking back, I can see my approach is consistent with Schön's knowing-in-action.

My experience is that internal consultancy does not come with a written contract. It is a verbal agreement between departments about a project. Michie (1998) explained the importance of contracting highlighting that a lot of consultancy projects carried out by health psychologists take place outside of a formal contract arrangement. This means that it may go unrecognised as consultancy, both by the client and the consultant. To grow consultancy within health psychology, Michie advocated encouraging health psychologists to create formal contracts, to evaluate the consultancy and to publish the report. When practising internal consultancy, I have never requested a written contract. However, informal unwritten contracts in consultancy can lead to misinterpretation. Brady and Varkonyi-Sepp (2025; see Chap. 3) also emphasise the importance of written agreements, advocating for a concise summary of the consultancy as a minimum—a practice I plan to adopt.

Given our lack of formal evaluation at the time of this consultancy, I will reflect on that here. Evaluation is important to evidence the effectiveness or otherwise of the intervention carried out and should be a feature of the work throughout consultancy. We successfully delivered the resources to the client within the agreed eight-week timeframe. These resources were required urgently because the Covid-19 vaccine roll out programme, prioritising the medically vulnerable people in society first, was underway in Ireland. Some residents fell into this category. As a result, staff and residents faced real-life challenges. Some residents who remained undecided about the vaccine had received vaccination appointments. Staff were asking questions, such as: 'How will we know that the service user has consented to the vaccine?' and 'How will we know they have understood the information about the pros and cons of taking the vaccine?' We needed to get the guidance on decision-making support to staff fast. I can see that we handed over the resources without pausing to plan an evaluation because of the urgency of the situation. However, while time can constrain what you do, as a professional I knew that the resources we were handing over were underpinned by evidence: that is, the guiding principles of ADMA and the HBM, as well as research on international capacity legislation implementation.

Urgency aside, other barriers to implementing formal evaluations in health and social care organisations are tight budgets and the reluctance to divert busy healthcare staff in residential services, to involve them in evaluation. However, value *is* placed on evaluation in our organisation and on reflection, we could have garnered an agreement that an evaluation would be carried out post-implementation. However, this reflects real life in the world of internal consultancy whereby as clinicians, we do not have the opportunity to formally measure the impact of our work 100% of the time. Some solutions to this, when formal standardised measures cannot be used, might be: adding an evaluation question at the bottom of the resource for the resident to answer, for example, 'Was this helpful?' or 'What would have helped more?' or further involving residents in the co-production of resources in the first place. Another idea is to ask psychology and behaviour therapy colleagues to test the resources with a resident. Building an evaluation phase into the *disengagement plan* described by Hodges (2021), as the way in which we hand back to clients the responsibility for overseeing the change, can be helpful too.

Another learning point for me was that *scope creep* can be invisible to the client. Scope creep refers to how consultancy projects can grow outside of the original terms of reference. Wulf (2020) identifies scope creep as one of the most common pitfalls in consultancy, and advocates for carefully documenting and communicating the goals, roles, and boundaries of the project. Had we realised the potential for scope creep in this consultancy project, in hindsight we would have clarified the peripheral impact of the work on our other duties. Instead, we interspersed this work between our clinical and supervisory duties by synchronising our diaries. I would not advise this approach because it becomes a scheduling nightmare, although in my experience many senior clinicians operate in this way as our expertise is frequently sought, with high workloads and low resources being an issue across psychology services in Ireland (Joyce & Ryan, 2020). What motivates us to comply is our desire to include the voice of psychology, but I recommend negotiating 'protected time' for projects like this. Working in a caring profession, the drive to care is so strong that saying no (or postponing projects) is very difficult. But boundaries are essential. It is only by managing our boundaries that a project like this can be given the full attention it deserves. After more than 25 years practising as a psychologist, this is one of the biggest learning curves for me and has impacted my growth as a practitioner recently. In terms of our health psychology general professional competency (Allen et al., 2014), learning the valuable lesson of how to manage my professional boundaries and contain my workload is vital if I am to effectively clinically supervise other psychologists to do the same.

To sum up, I would slow down when estimating the amount of time consultancy will take. This step takes time and is important to get right. I tended to rush into agreeing to carry out consultancy without taking care to carefully assess the time or resources it would take. I also consider the framework for consultancy in health psychology proposed by Brady and Varkonyi-Sepp (2025; see Chap. 3) to be an effective tool to help map out the time and resources required to complete work. Considering the resources and time required for each process within the consultancy framework could produce a more accurate estimation. Using a Gantt chart to present this might also give the client a clearer insight into the work required and make it more likely that the requested resources (and/or associated fee) would be met.

Conclusion

For me, consultancy is where all my health psychology competencies (Allen et al., 2014) are activated concurrently: assessing and formulating, designing and implementing interventions, educating and researching, with our general professional competency at its foundation. With health psychology consultancy's inherent ability to reach large numbers of beneficiaries quickly, it is a cost-effective way of providing interventions to improve health outcomes, especially in the context of tight budgets. I hope this chapter encourages other health psychologists to recognise the consultancy they are carrying out, and to evaluate and publish it.

Client Testimony

> It was very important to me that the decision-making support being provided to residents about vaccine uptake, was underpinned by the pending ADMA. Following a rights-based approach is central to what we do in this organisation and is aligned with our core values of equality and advocacy. Drawing on multidisciplinary resources at a strategic and organisational level, is essential to ensure that best practice is upheld, throughout our services nationally. I have no doubt that these resources made a positive impact on the lives of the people who use our services, in that they were supported to make their own health decisions in this regard. We are grateful to our psychology and behaviour therapy colleagues for their efforts in this consultancy (internal client).

Top Tips

1. In internal consultancy always estimate the resources required and negotiate protected time.
2. Use the consultancy framework for health psychologists and a Gantt chart to map out your project.
3. Watch out for scope creep as it will impact you but may be invisible to the client.
4. Involve stakeholders early in the project.
5. Always add on 10–15% of extra time, to allow for unforeseen circumstances.

Acknowledgements First, I wish to acknowledge my consultancy colleague, Darragh O'Regan, who was in the role of Lead Behaviour Therapist at the time of this case study. It was a pleasure to contribute to this interdisciplinary consultancy alongside my learned colleague. Thank you also to our quality improvement colleague, (who assisted with turning our ideas into user-friendly resources) and especially to the support teams in services who took this guidance on board and implemented it. I also thank Shona Logan-King for supporting the publication of this chapter. I am pleased at how much psychology's voice is valued by the organisation.

Competing Interests The author has no competing interests to declare that are relevant to the content of this chapter.

References

Allen, S., Byrne, M., Coughlan, P., Darker, C., & Doyle, F. (2014). *The psychological society of Ireland guidelines for accreditation of postgraduate programmes for health psychology practitioners (Stage 2)*. https://www.psychologicalsociety.ie

Alonzi, A. Sheard, J., & Bateman, M.. (2009). Assessing staff needs for guidance on the Mental Capacity Act 2005. *Nursing Times, 105* (3), 24–27. https://pubmed.ncbi.nlm.nih.gov/19248375/

Block, P. (2011). *Flawless consulting: A guide to getting your expertise used* (3rd ed.). Jossey-Bass. ISBN: 978-1-394-17730-1.

Brady, R., & Varkonyi-Sepp, J. (2025). A Framework for consultancy in health psychology. In R. Brady, J. Varkonyi-Sepp, & J. Smith (Eds.), *The Palgrave handbook of consultancy in health psychology*. Palgrave Macmillan.

Citizens Information. (2023). *Assisted decision making (capacity) act (2015)*. https://www.citizensinformation.ie/en/health/legal-matters-and-health/assisted-decision-making-act/#6e1b65

Cronin K., Greaney A.-M., & Farrell, D. (2018, November 29). Readiness for assisted decision-making: An exploratory qualitative study. [Conference session] 18th Annual Nursing and Midwifery Research Conference, University College Cork, Cork city, Ireland https://sword.cit.ie/allthe/755

Curtis C., Fatoki O., McGuire E., & Cullen A. (2022, April 29). Moving from 'best interests' to 'will and preference': A study of doctor's level of knowledge relating to the assisted decision-making (capacity) act 2015. *Irish Medical Journal, 115* (4), 585, https://pubmed.ncbi.nlm.nih.gov/35695800/

Davies, C., Fattori, F., O'Donnell, D., Donnelly, S., Shé, É. N., Shea, M. O., Prihodova, L., Gleeson, C., Flynn, Á., Rock, B., Grogan, J., O'Brien, M., O'Hanlon, S., Cooney, M. T., Tighe, M., & Kroll, T. (2019). What are the mechanisms that support healthcare professionals to adopt assisted decision-making practice? A rapid realist review. *BMC Health Services Research, 19, 960.* https://bmchealthservres.biomedcentral.com/articles/10.1186/s12913-019-4802-x

Donnelly, M. (2016, August). Best interests in the mental capacity act: Time to say goodbye? *Medical Law Review, 24*(3), 318–332. https://doi.org/10.1093/medlaw/fww030

Donnelly, S., Begley, E., & O'Brien, M. (2019, October–November). How are people with dementia involved in care-planning and decision-making? An Irish social work perspective. *Dementia (London), 18* (7–8), 2985–3003. Epub 2018 Mar 15. https://pubmed.ncbi.nlm.nih.gov/29544346/

Gray, C. (2010). *the new social story book: Over 150 social stories that teach everyday social skills to children with autism or Aspergers syndrome and their peers.* Future Horizons. ISBN: 978-1-935274-05-4.

Heifetz, R. A., Linsky, M., & Grashow, A. (2009). *The practice of adaptive leadership: Tools and tactics for changing your organization and the world.* Harvard Business School Press. ISBN: 978-1-4221-0576-4.

Hodges, J. (2021, June). A framework for consulting. *Management Consulting Journal, 4(2)*, 52–55. https://doi.org/10.2478/mcj-2021-0009

Joyce, R., & Ryan, L. (2020, August). *Psychological society of Ireland working conditions survey.* https://www.psychologicalsociety.ie/source/psi%20working%20conditions%20survey%20report%20(august%202020).pdf

Killeen J., Myers, F., Brisbane, A., Coulson, K., Fearnley, K., Gordon, J., Keith, D., Maclean, J., Thom, M., & Woodhouse, A. (2004) Adults with incapacity (Scotland) Act: Learning from experience, *Legal Studies.* The Scottish Executive. https://www.gov.scot/publications/adults-incapacity-scotland-act-2000-learning-experience/

Limbu Y. B., Gautam, R. K., & Pham, L. (2022, June 18). The health belief model applied to COVID-19 vaccine hesitancy: A systematic review. *Vaccines (Basel), 10* (6), 973. https://pubmed.ncbi.nlm.nih.gov/35746581/

Mental Capacity Act. (2005). *Social care and support guide.* https://www.nhs.uk/conditions/social-care-and-support-guide/making-decisions-for-someone-else/mental-capacity-act/

Michie, S. (1998). *Consultancy 8.06*. Copyright 1998 Elsevier Science Ltd.
Nilsson, A. (2012). *Who gets to decide? The right to legal capacity for people with intellectual and psychosocial disabilities.* Commissioner for Human Rights paper, Strasbourg, February 20th, Comm DH/Issue Paper (2012) 2 Original version ISBN 39912GBR
Rosenstock, I. M. (1974). The Health belief model and preventive health behaviour. *Health Education Monographs, 2*(4), 354–386. https://journals.sagepub.com/doi/abs/10.1177/109019817400200405
Sacks, R., & Loon, M. (2016). Developing and using consultancy skills. In M. Loon (Ed.), *Professional practice in learning and development: How to design and deliver plans for the workplace* (pp. 151–206). Kogan Page. ISBN 9780749477424.
Schein, E. H. (1988). *Process consultation - Vol. 1: Its role in organization development* (2nd ed.). Addison Wesley. ISBN-13: 978-0201067361.
Schein, E. H. (2016). *Humble consulting*. Berrett-Koehler. ISBN 978-1-62656-721-4
Schein, E. H., & Schein, P. A. (2018). Chapter 2: The power of relationships, openness, and trust. In *Humble leadership*. ISBN: 978-1-5230-9538-4
Schön, D. A. (1995). Knowing-in-action: The new scholarship requires a new epistemology. *Change, 27*, 10544673. 6, November/December p26, 9p, 4c https://doi.org/10.1080/00091383.1995.10544673
Scottish Government Factsheet. (2000). *Adults with incapacity act, Scotland (2000).* https://www.gov.scot/publications/adults-with-incapacity-act-principles/
Wulf, S. A. (2020, June) Successful project consulting. *IEEE Engineering Management Review 48 No. 2, Second Quarter*. https://ieeexplore.ieee.org/document/9033995

16

Enquiry: Why Aren't People Attending? It's Good for Their Health!

Eleanor Bull, Jo Hall, Rachel Mallon, Laura Walton-Taylor, and Neville Scholten

Introduction

Service satisfaction scores were high, almost perfect. The programme was a national health priority, enshrined in best practice guidance and policy. The health economic case was robust. Indeed, local General Practitioners (GPs) were referring patients in droves, supported by the Quality and Outcomes Framework (QOF) (NICE, 2024), a mechanism which financially rewards

E. Bull (✉)
Derbyshire Community Health Services NHS Foundation Trust, Chesterfield, UK

Derbyshire County Council, Derbyshire, UK

Division of Medical Education, University of Manchester, Manchester, UK
e-mail: eleanor.bull@derbyshire.gov.uk

J. Hall
Derbyshire Community Health Services NHS Foundation Trust, Chesterfield, UK

Derbyshire County Council, Derbyshire, UK
e-mail: jo.hall@derbyshire.gov.uk

R. Mallon • L. Walton-Taylor • N. Scholten
Derbyshire Community Health Services NHS Foundation Trust, Chesterfield, UK
e-mail: rachel.mallon@nottscc.gov.uk; laura.walton-taylor@nhs.net; n.scholten@nhs.net

R. Brady et al. (eds.), *The Palgrave Handbook of Consultancy in Health Psychology*,
https://doi.org/10.1007/978-3-031-94529-8_16

referrals to Diabetes Education Services (DES) (NHS Digital, 2022a). However, many people were still not 'opting in' for this self-management support offer, an all-too-common scenario in healthcare settings (Henshall et al., 2020).

Opt-in rates at one DES in the UK was the topic for this consultancy case study. Consultancy involved a year-long collaborative project between an National Health Service (NHS) Trust, a Psychological Insights Team (PI team), and DES, focused on an enquiry into the stories behind opt-in data, with findings leading to significant transformations within and beyond this project. This case study firstly introduces the national and local type 2 diabetes education picture, then covers the nature of the request for consultancy, an introduction to the consultancy team, the client and DES, and the key stakeholders. Next, there is a description of how the enquiry aspect of the consultancy work was shaped and conducted by an internal consultancy team and how theory underpinned enquiry activities within this work. Lastly, there are reflections on the work, and key recommendations for psychology consultants undertaking enquiry in consultancy projects.

The Case Study

Type 2 Diabetes: Setting the Scene

Diabetes is a long-term health condition affecting people's ability to regulate their blood glucose (World Health Organization, 2023). Approximately 90% of the five million people living with diabetes in the UK have type 2 diabetes (T2D) (Diabetes UK, 2023). Self-management is essential for people with T2D to stay well and avoid life-threatening health complications. This can include dietary changes, physical activity, weight management, taking medications, attending frequent health appointments and, in some cases, self-injection with insulin.

Structured diabetes education programmes support people diagnosed with T2D with their self-management knowledge and skills (Diabetes UK, 2016). Typically, programmes include information about nutrition, and the psychology of eating, food shopping, and physical activity. A systematic review of randomised control trials investigating diabetes education (k = 21) found positive outcomes in favour of diabetes education; clinically, psychosocially, and in terms of improved health behaviours (Steinsbekk et al., 2012). With this evidence in mind, National Institute for Clinical Excellence (NICE) Guidance (2023) recommends structured education as an integral part of diabetes care. However, the National Diabetes Audit Quarterly Report 2021–2022 (NHS Digital, 2022b) suggests that in the UK in 2020, only 5.6% of people newly diagnosed with T2D attended structured diabetes education within 12 months of their diagnosis.

Our Local Picture

The Diabetes Education Service (DES) is situated within a large community NHS Trust hereafter referred to as the 'Trust', serving a population of one million, in an area with significant pockets of geographical deprivation. The DES team is composed of the service manager (NS the client), administrative staff, and several diabetes educators. Following GP referral, people with T2D are sent an opt-in letter by DES, offering either a one-day course, or a nationally recognised 6-week education programme, according to their preference. Both programmes consist of talks, activities, and group discussions (see Benton et al., 2022). The one-day course covers the same topics as the 6-week programme, but in significantly less detail. During the COVID-19 pandemic, both options had been paused for three months, and from then onwards were being delivered online.

The Call...

Through discussions with the client, we understood that between July 2020 and April 2021 the DES had recorded an opt-in rate of only 25%, indicating that only a quarter of people referred booked onto either education course (fewer still going on to complete their course). The client (NS) and the DES team wished to understand more to inform remedial action. The client contacted a cross-disciplinary Psychological Insights (PI) team who apply psychological and behavioural sciences on a range of health and social care issues. NS and his team had collected data during 2021 on the reasons patients had not opted into the DES, through telephone calls to patients who had not opted into the service (N=1036). The client was keen for consultancy support to analyse this data, and to suggest potential interventions to increase diabetes education attendance rates.

The Psychological Insights (PI) Team

Our PI team provides consultancy within the Trust and to the other health and social care organisations forming the local integrated care system. The PI team is hosted and employed within the Trust's Health Psychology Service and is embedded into partnership local health and social care organisations, thus providing 'internal consultancy' (although we do not tend to use this term, see below). The PI team includes a clinical psychologist (JH), a health psychologist (EB, also a trained CBT therapist), assistant psychologists (APs), and a behavioural science researcher. We consider the PI team's breadth of training and experience a key strength, enabling us to respond to a wide range of consultancy requests with sensitivity, flexibility, and agility. The work herein was largely carried out by the team's two APs (RM and LWT), supervised by JH. EB supported the project team in applying psychological theory and methods and facilitated dissemination.

Who Cared (and Cares) About This?

There were multiple local stakeholders, the stakes were high! DES was seeking to meet the needs of potential patients; their voices were therefore key to this psychological consultancy. There were several professional stakeholders. The clinical director of the host Health Psychology Service was invested in demonstrating the value of psychologists engaging in consultancy. GPs were key stakeholders since all referrals to diabetes education came via primary care. The final stakeholder was the client (NS), the DES manager, who was committed to increasing service uptake rates to improve population health and ensure good value-for-money to NHS England, the funder. Helpfully, the professional stakeholders shared priority to increase DES opt-in rates brought a clear focus to this consultancy ask.

The Agreement

In initial meetings JH and NS agreed that the project would run over the 12-month period for which funding was available from DES to employ to two APs to support this project. The APs would support DES in data analysis and interpretation, and in intervention development. This enabled the psychologist consultants to focus on steering the project. Monthly review meetings with the DES manager, the two APs, and JH were set up, with the project also being discussed at wider monthly PI team meetings. The aims of the consultancy were:

(a) To help DES understand the reasons for people not opting into their service, by triangulating available local data, UK national data, and other evidence.
(b) To support DES implement interventions for increasing service opt-in rates, by using the findings to co-develop psychologically informed interventions with DES workforce and patients.

The intended outcome of the consultation was increased opt-in rates for the local DES courses from 25% to 30%.

Understanding Opt-Out: From Large Data Sheets to Intervention Proposals

Fortunately, we had a large existing anonymised data set to explore in order to understand opt-in behaviours in DES. Alongside referral and service activity data, feedback from those that had not opted in was purposively obtained by the DES workforce through follow-up structured telephone calls to all patients who had not opted in (N = 1036). Questions had included, '*What information and support do you feel that you need at this time to help you better manage your diabetes?*', and '*What if anything stopped you from opting into one of the courses?*'. APs analysed the data recorded by staff using content analysis to understand reasons for non-attendance. The first of three main reasons for not opting in was recorded as 'not sure relevant', which suggested patients lacked knowledge about the diabetes education offer. Second, 'I don't have diabetes/no one has told me I have diabetes' suggested perceived communication difficulties with GPs about diagnosis. Finally, 'unable to access the technology required' indicated low confidence in and/or understanding of use of digital technology. A content analysis of the recorded reasons for not opting in indicated a common theme that service opt-in was impacted by service users' health literacy. Health literacy is defined as "the personal characteristics and social resources needed for individuals and communities to access, understand, appraise and use information and services to make decisions about health" (NHS Library and Knowledge Services, 2020). Further substantiating the hypothesised link between low opt-in rates to DES and lower health literacy, quantitative data analyses showed that people from more economically deprived communities were statistically less likely to opt in to DES. Aligned to this finding, research suggests lower health literacy is more common in more deprived areas (GeoData, n.d.).

The APs presented the findings of the analyses to NS and other DES colleagues in a team meeting. This included a visual summary of the data, a case for action, tailored complementary findings in the literature to DES, and invited discussion to increase DES ownership of the work. The DES team and the APs considered reasons for not opting in which would be potentially amenable to service-level interventions. For example, reasons included lack of knowledge about the relevance of the service offer, and technology barriers.

Co-developing Interventions

JH and EB provided expertise in understanding the analysed data and intervention development through a psychological lens. We supported the DES to make adjustments to enable easier access for people with lower health literacy. This included simplifying their online booking system forms, and we supported the APs in developing a health literacy friendly DES website with input from DES staff and support from the Trust's communications team. We provided guidance on patient video script to increase service accessibility for those with less confidence about attending an education offer, especially online. The APs also developed health literacy friendly course materials drawing upon health literacy literature and guidelines (Health Education England, n.d.). The consultants advised the administrative team on verbal health literacy approaches to conversations about diabetes and the DES as part of their first telephone contact with those referred to the DES. Broader interventions delivered by the consultancy team included GP health literacy awareness sessions to enhance patient understanding of diabetes education.

The Outcome(s)

Opt-in rates increased by 10%, from 25% to 35% in the six months following the project. In addition, there was sustained workforce engagement in ongoing activities to reduce health literacy barriers to DES, illustrated by the following quotes from DES team members:

> For me it's about having health literacy awareness that enables me to tailor my approach to patients. Mindful of my type of language and forming of sentences. Taking time to engage and discuss fully the options which allows patients to make an informed decision about our service offer. (DES administrative staff member)

It's all your fault, all this health literacy, I can't think about anything the same again! (NS, service manager)

Evaluation

This work was evaluated through a peer-led health literacy audit using an adapted version of a health-literacy-friendly audit tool developed by the Community Health and Learning Foundation for Stoke-on-Trent City Council (n.d.). The tool considers how health-literacy-friendly aspects of service or organisations, support an audit of written and verbal communications, physical building accessibility and policies. Post-consultation, the DES scored 104 (excellence in being a health-literacy-friendly organisation), up from a score of 53 (working towards becoming a health-literacy-friendly organisation).

Consultancy work was also evaluated informally through discussions with the client, DES workforce and the Health Psychology Service director, who said they were impressed by the value added by the consultancy project. The work was positively received at an organisational level and investment in a substantive health literacy officer post was secured. Building on this consultancy project, LWT who took up the post of health literacy officer has drawn on a similar model with approximately 18 other teams, across health and social care organisations within just over six months of the role starting. In addition, further Trust services have invested in AP roles to address similar public health-focussed projects through consultancy approaches. The PI's consulting psychologists have become involved in a wider range of activities such as developing of the host Trust's Organisational Strategy, exploring stakeholder needs and perceptions for the strategy through enquiry.

Analysis of Enquiry in Action

In this section, we use the lens of the proposed consultancy framework (Brady & Varkonyi-Sepp, 2025; see Chap. 3) to reflect further on enquiry in how we approached and carried out this internal consultancy project. Enquiry is typically about seeking information and asking questions to help the consultancy work well for all its key stakeholders. Some have suggested enquiry to be a discrete stage or phase in the process of consultancy. Scott and Barnes (2011), for example, prosed an 'information and assessment' phase, where interviews and surveys are used to gather information on areas such as an organisation's strengths, weaknesses and 'problem areas'. Similarly, Zipursky (2022), suggested using enquiry in an 'assess/discovery' phase to understand 'what is going on' in the organisation, opportunities, threats, and 'what can be done'.

As proposed by the editors of this book, we would argue that enquiry is core to most of the interactions psychological professionals have at work. We feel this should be in evidence throughout the lifecycle of a project. For instance, consultants in health psychology may use enquiry to understand the needs of the client and stakeholders, and also to learn about influences on current practice behaviours and stakeholder perspectives of barriers and facilitators to change, to explore the feasibility of different intervention options, to discuss ways of implementing these, and to help evaluate their impact. Enquiry is also fundamental to making the other elements of the consultancy framework work well, such as in building relationships, as discussed below.

In this case study, enquiry started from the moment we received the request for consultancy, when we asked for more information about the client's request for help. Enquiry continued within the initial meetings held with the DES lead and in subsequent communications helping to shape the aims and objectives of the work, which are questions in themselves. For example, 'What is going on here?' 'What has already been explored?' 'How can we best add to the good work of the service?'. In phase one of the work, our team's APs made enquiries of the available data alongside theory and evidence, to ask 'What is influencing decisions to opt-out?' guided by support from the team lead. Later, enquiry focused on understanding which interventions could be most helpful and feasible, involving constant information gathering and sharing with other team members. Throughout, we used enquiry skills to build and shape our relationship with the service team, taking time to ask about and find common ground in other areas of work and life which mattered to our project colleagues. Below we reflect on some of the team values, theoretical frameworks and skills which shape how we approach psychological enquiry within our team's work more generally and this case study specifically.

A Values-Based Approach

Our PI team approach to consultancy in general, and enquiry in particular, is led by our shared values and principles. Firstly, whilst not all chartered psychologists, we are all guided by the four primary ethical principles within the British Psychological Society's Code of Ethics and Conduct (BPS, 2021) of respect, competence, responsibility, and integrity. Asking timely explorative questions and seeking information helps us maintain these principles in our work, and equally the principles helped shape our enquiry. For instance, we explored the desired focus in initial project meetings, and we reflected that service engagement is a health behaviour issue, and that we would be practising within our sphere of competence. Being mindful of our integrity led us to spend time on data cleaning, in order to ensure valid conclusions from our enquiry of the opt-out data. We mapped key stakeholders and tried to ensure we invited and showed respect and appreciation for everyone's inputs during project meetings. We were also mindful of our responsibility to deliver the project to a high standard and of our accountability to our clients as well as to our own service leads.

Relatedly, and more specifically, we aim towards practising in line with our values of partnership working and equality in all that we do. We draw on ideas from person-centred care (Stewart et al., 2003) and co-production (Whitaker, 1980; Israel et al., 1998) in 'collaborating with' rather than 'providing for' the staff, volunteers and citizens we work with, being curious and open to new ideas and perspectives. We try to draw from strengths/asset-based approaches (Brunetto et al., 2020; Foot & Hopkins, 2010), ways of working originally derived from community development and social work approaches which emphasise and focus on people's self-determination and strengths. We try to value our stakeholders' experiences and ideas to build on areas of good practice and existing strengths. We view our role as adding theory and best-available evidence, if and where useful, to help explore influences on people's behaviour and in co-developing/co-producing interventions. We are mindful that our clients/stakeholders have the best understanding of what would work for their particular situation. So core is this partnership working and co-production that we would rarely use the word 'consultant' and 'client' in our work as we find this can unfortunately conjure images of imbalance of power, expertise, and status, as discussed in the management consultancy literature (Bouwmeester Stiekema, 2015). Just as person-centred, collaborative care improves diabetes self-management outcomes (Titchener, 2014), we find taking a partnership approach to our work helps us build positive long-term relationships, improves communication in projects, builds psychological and behavioural science capacity. This supports teams to build sustainable changes, ultimately improving outcomes for our local population. Capacity building feels a particularly important aim, reflected in ongoing debates about use of management consultancy in the public sector, with concerns that over reliance on outsourced expertise can ultimately weaken organisations (Mazzucato & Collington, 2023).

In this case study, this values-based approach helped inform the questions we asked throughout the project. For example, instead of assuming that we would need to gather data to understand the issue of opt-outs, which included the following questions: 'What's your understanding of what's going on here?' and 'What have you been able to do so far?' helped us discover that the team had already made an enormous start with their own telephone enquiries to over 1000 people. Assuming that no actions had been taken, or insisting that we gather our own data, could have led to duplication of effort and wasting service user time, as well as risking rupturing relations with the DES.

The Insider View

Kitay and Wright (2004) reflect on the diversity and complexity of client-consultant relationships in management consultancy, including "the extent to which the consultant is clearly external to the client organisation, with the transaction primarily based on market principles" (p. 4). Since the PI team is hosted by the same NHS trust as the DES and the team are NHS employees, Kitay and Wright, along with authors such as Buono and Subbiah (2014) would likely view this case study as an example of 'internal consultancy'.

Being internal consultants employed by the NHS, had several advantages for our enquiry. As organisational 'insiders' we already had a shared understanding of the local Diabetes care pathway, key stakeholders, other ongoing projects, and the values of the DES, and we were already a trusted team. This accelerated our enquiry as we could progress more quickly onto questions surrounding possibilities for interventions.

Working within the organisation, and governed by its data protection policies and UK General Data Protection Regulation (GDPR) (Information Commissioner's Office, 2022), meant we were able to access the service user data set and to ask questions of the data quickly, without needing the extra permissions that would be required for data to cross organisational boundaries. As 'insiders', we were able to go beyond offering recommendations by supporting implementation, a secondary role of consultants according to Morris (2000). We could provide sustained support over time, leading to further enquiries. In this case, therefore, being internal consultants seemed highly beneficial for the enquiry. However, it is important to reflect that our existing knowledge and relationships may have led us to make assumptions and miss asking questions that seemed 'obvious' to us but may have been valuable in leading an external consultant to shape the enquiry in a different direction.

Psychological and behavioural insights are a relatively new kind of expertise for public health and NHS systems (Byrne-Davis et al., 2022). Recent research suggests potential employers, clients, and collaborators of health psychologists and other behavioural scientists, have varied views about their fit within existing structures and teams and preference for internal versus external consultancy (Hart et al., 2023). For the reasons outlined above, we feel that being 'embedded within', as in Kitay and Wright (2004) model, is the right place for our PI team to do meaningful consultancy within our local NHS Trust and facilitated our enquiry in this case.

Psychological Theories and Models

In approaching enquiry, we tend to draw on several kinds of psychological theories and models flexibly to enhance our sense-making in the consultancy, applying a formulation-based approach (Dale & Bull, 2022). Psychologically informed, person-centred communication skills in active listening, asking open questions and reflections are extremely valuable to consultancy enquiry and as such are also widely applied in management consultancy. One basic example included "So what are our next steps?" towards the end of meetings, to invite collaborative discussion, and help summarise and facilitate moving forward to meet the project goals. Others have discussed applying motivational interviewing skills, such as questions to elicit change talk, for example, "Suppose you took forward this new approach—how could that change things for you, your team or organisation?" (Arbuckle et al., 2020, p. 11) to help enhance organisations' readiness for change and facilitate quality improvement within services.

We viewed opting in to diabetes education as a health-related behaviour. The invitation often comes at a critical period in the diabetes journey and one element of our consultancy expertise was applying our understanding of factors influencing health-related behaviours after a health diagnosis. For instance, the Common-Sense Model (Leventhal et al., 2003), explores how people make sense of health threats and distinguishes between problem-focussed and emotion-focussed coping responses. We considered a person's diabetes diagnosis and invitation to the DES as a potential health threat and explored factors that can lead to emotion-focussed avoidance-based coping responses (e.g., opting out of a DES programme) such as beliefs that an illness is not controllable. This also helped us enquire whether accessible, reassuring health information could reduce fear and increase the likelihood of people responding with problem-focussed coping (such as opting into a DES programme). We were also influenced by socio-ecological models of public health (Sallis et al., 2008) which view health at various interlinking levels and highlight the importance of socio-structural health inequalities, which we explored and reflected on in the enquiry.

When exploring interventions, we drew from models that emphasise the importance of health literacy such as Sørensen et al. (2012) and Ley's classic work on communication of health information (Ley, 1982) which, for example, stresses the importance of clarity and avoiding jargon. It was important to understand that we are all limited in our insight into our own behaviour (Pligt & De Vries, 1998) and we discussed with the team that social desirability (Edwards, 1953) may have influenced people's responses to staff enquiring about why they didn't engage in the service. Triangulating the quantitative and qualitative data and considering theories helped give us confidence that we could answer our psychological enquiry in the fullest sense possible.

In this and other projects in public health, we also apply the Cognitive Behavioural Model (Beck, 1967), Compassion Focussed Therapy (Gilbert, 2014), Acceptance and Commitment Therapy (Hayes et al., 2011), systemic (Hedges, 2005) and psychodynamic approaches (Abrams, 1987) in our enquiry work to inform exploratory questions and make sense of different situations. These have been traditionally used in a therapeutic context but their use with teams and systems are well documented (Hanley et al., 2017). This breadth of psychological approaches was useful in this consultancy enquiry, by enabling the consultancy team to enquire about a multitude of factors that might be impacting on opt-in behaviours, such as anxiety, the influence of their family system or the impact of self-stigma.

Also key to this project was theory-based supervision, since this project was one of the first undertaken by the newly appointed APs (LWT and RM) in a health context. In supervising the APs, JH applied psychological enquiry to help the APs to build their own enquiry skills and confidence, and to explore, reflect on, and manage anxiety and uncertainty, others' expectations, taking time to explore the data and detail, and 'pulls' from different stakeholders, such as requests to expand the project focus to include engagement in other services. Supervision models such as the Seven-eyed Model of Supervision (Hawkins & Shohet, 2012) helped the assistant psychologists explore the process of consultancy by enquiring about what was happening from different relational perspectives, known as the 'Seven Eyes'. These 'Seven Eyes' include 'the client', 'the supervisee's interventions', the 'supervisee-client relationship', 'the supervisee', 'the supervision relationship', 'the supervisor', and 'the wider context'. In this project, within 'the wider context', for example, this meant that supervision was used as a time to reflect on the ethical, organisational, social, and cultural facets of the project. These reflections in supervision prompted the assistant psychologists to enquire around some of the organisational aspects of the project such as the role of the GP referral process.

In summary, we would see enquiry skills as critically linked to the values and principles guiding the work of our local PI team. We find that our position working internally to the organisation, drawing flexibly on a range of psychological theories and approaches and engaging in reflective supervision helps us make informed, helpful psychological enquiries. In this case study, we started with the question 'Why do people not engage?' and from collaboratively exploring the data we had, other key questions emerged which took us forward towards positive outcomes, like 'How can this service become more inclusive and accessible?' and eventually 'What difference does this make?' and 'How can we share and grow such approaches?'

Reflections

The breath of training and experience of the PI team brought a great strength to the work, enabling the project team to draw on the strengths of each team member. For example, the strategic experience and collaborative leadership approach of the clinical psychologist and the health behaviour change knowledge and applied academic expertise of the health psychologist were highly complementary for the present project. JH was able to bring strengths in using psychological approaches to formulate how the psychological responses of patient to diagnosis and education offers might impact on engagement with DES, whilst the EB added significant value to the work through bringing a range of health behaviour models to intervention planning. Through this project, and other work, JH and EB have been able to collaborate to optimise outcomes of behaviour change projects through confident and critical application of a wide range of psychology models and approaches pertaining to both psychology disciplines and other disciplines such as Public Health.

Recruitment of APs as part of consultancy teams offered the potential of expanding the capacity that can be offered to consultancy projects. LWT and RM provided support with detailed data analyses, carrying out work directly with teams (e.g., team focus sessions) and patients/public interactions (e.g., time speaking to patients in clinics), and other activities that require significant time and capacity often unavailable to an internal consultant. Further, working with APs enabled us to increase the pace of change, which may have felt motivating and led to a 'buzz of activity' around the project, improving buy-in. Since the APs were the key link between the consultant and the client, it was important that they could handle large data sets and communicate clearly with the client and the client's team. The recruitment process therefore weighted understanding how potential candidates might handle situations likely to be faced in this role as more important than their topic experience. It was also paramount to consider the motivation of LWT and RM given this was a largely remote, lengthy consultancy project, where indications of success would not be immediate, compared to other AP roles where positive feedback after clinical sessions may be more immediate.

Ongoing motivation of the consultancy team was supported through investing in the relationship with the APs, valuing their work, discussing their professional development opportunities, and ensuring sufficient job role variety, challenge, and tailoring. Effective and multifaceted supervision of in-training psychology colleagues has been recently discussed in work exploring health psychology supervisee experiences by the BPS Division of Health Psychology (White et al., 2024). This suggests that some supervisors struggle to understand their supervisees' relational support needs, which may be a particular challenge when working on longer-term projects and more remotely (White et al.).

Working with a wider consultancy team, largely through online communications, presents potential challenges for the relationship with the client. It was important to have shared and well-labelled files for collaboration, stored in secure file spaces with anonymised information. Weekly updates on progress needed to be digestible and accessible, for example, brief with bullet points. Given this consultancy took place within a local NHS Trust, and the client and consulting psychologists were part of a multifaceted broader service, there was an ongoing relationship in terms of wider Trust activities, irrespective of project outcomes. However, it was important to approach this work as standalone, as one would approach externally requested consultancy work, to help keep focus on this project, and the client's priorities. This included ensuring update meetings were prioritised and summary notes taken, as opposed to slipping into less boundaried and structured approaches, a challenge discussed by Kitay and Wright (2004).

As part of internal consultancy, it was key to provide the client with confidence in the work. It was vital to ensure that there was time for the APs to freely discuss their professional development and work challenges away from the client through weekly 1:1 meetings and group AP supervision provided by JH. For example, the APs had learning needs in relation to quantitative analysis which, had they shared with the client, might have impacted on the client's confidence. As consultants, we retained responsibility for the quality of the analysis, and we were able to ensure that quality by providing supportive supervision in data analysis. In meetings with the client, it was considered key to balance updates, with clear indications of progress and problem-solving, so that the client remained confident in the piece of work.

Further, it was important to ask for, and listen to, the client's feedback on the project to understand whether it was meeting expectations in terms of pace and depth, for example. This was achieved through project update meetings, and it was important to the consultancy team to have reflective discussions with the client, as opposed to written (one-way) updates. The project was by its nature emergent: neither the psychology team nor the client knew the outcome of the enquiry and subsequent intervention development, in terms of DES opt-in rates. As such, it was exciting to be working together to make sense of the data, and to decide on what the next steps would be, reflecting the role of the consultant as process facilitator as discussed by Schein (1978).

A wider obstacle for psychological consultancy in a multidisciplinary context is often 'naming' the additional value of psychological consultancy over and above the contributions of other colleagues. The PI team was aware of the importance of isolating the impact of psychologists in this consultancy project; it was key for learning and for future investment in psychology consultancy projects. The emphasis we placed on relationship-building, partnership working, and capacity building as part of this internal consultancy amplified this challenge. Claiming ownership of outcomes felt counter to the work the consultancy team had put into the 'process' and the 'how' of consultancy. It is suggested that it is helpful for the dilemma of ownership and contribution to be discussed openly at the outset, and revisited regularly, to ensure that the framing of project findings and attribution of contribution/s are agreed upon by parties involved, and prior to dissemination (Owens, 2016). We have found it useful to reflect on this and have put into place regular opportunities for team discussions around this important aspect in our team development days going forward.

Challenges

There were several challenges as part of this work. Firstly, when we were asked to lead this initiative, we were unsure about whether it would 'work', and if the service would achieve the desired result; namely, an increase in opt-in rates. Enquiry is key in a consultancy project. By its nature the outcome was not pre-defined. The road map for the work was uncertain, as was the impact of it. This relates to work by Schein (1978) on process consultation; in that consultants may face a dilemma while helping clients to come up with their own solutions, yet the consultant may also be held accountable for the quality of those solutions. Our enthusiasm and drive meant at times team members experienced anxious thoughts such as 'What if we can't help the DES?' We found it helpful to use evidence-based approaches to ground and guide the work. For example, drawing on Acceptance and Commitment Therapy (Hayes et al., 2011) which emphasises 'psychological flexibility' in the face of life challenges, helped us notice and respond usefully to some of the understandable emotions and unhelpful thoughts which may arise in working on new collaborative enquiries.

A further challenge was the large data sets we were starting with. There was anxiety in the consultancy team that this work involved numerous large data sheets that had not been designed with data analysis in mind, and so would require significant data cleaning. As consultants leading the project, it was important to normalise this situation with the client, ensuring the client's expectations were managed and the important step of data cleaning was explained alongside the time commitments this would entail. This was an important step in developing a relationship with the client which was built on openness and on having conversations as needed about boundaries and expectations.

Lastly, the coronavirus (COVID-19) pandemic cannot be underestimated as a challenge, both in terms of adapting to new ways of working, (a virtual team undertaking this project) and in the impact of remote DES delivery on opt-in rates. There were advantages to working remotely for the project team as meetings were easier to organise at short notice, and with high frequency when needed. However, there were multiple factors to consider in terms of remote education, alongside a continually altering context of education delivery as pandemic restrictions eased. Nonetheless, an enquiry into equity of access at a point in time where many NHS services were considering longer-term hybrid delivery models was timely and drew interest from across the NHS Trust. In fact, this project drew considerable interest, locally, regionally, and nationally, and there have been significant opportunities to share the process and the findings to support further work on service uptake and health literacy.

Conclusion

This case study is an example of how, when questions are asked and answers are truly listened to, there is the potential to unlock new ways of looking at health problems and to reduce health inequalities. The case study illustrates the importance of the 'how' and the 'what' of consultancy, and describes a consultancy project underpinned by theory, and guided by collaboration, relationships, and values. The challenges and learning discussed in applying enquiry to this case study made it an invaluable project in shaping our way of working and informing the ongoing health literacy consultancy work across our organisation.

Top Tips

1. Prepare carefully: peer and team support, supervisions, contracts, shared files, organisation systems, and communications.
2. Stay curious: protect time and space for reflection to ensure interventions are meaningfully informed by local insights.
3. The process counts: recognise the importance of communication, power-sharing, and relationship-building; the 'how' of consultancy.
4. Value-based work: a team led by values has a clear compass direction, and a route through times when consultancy work/contexts feel more 'stuck' or 'messy'.
5. Share generously: much of what was gained from this project has occurred through dissemination of learning.

Competing Interests The authors have no competing interests to declare in relation to this chapter.

References

Abrams, S. (1987). The psychoanalytic process: A schematic model. *The International Journal of Psycho-analysis, 68*, 441–452.

Arbuckle, M. R., Foster, F. P., Talley, R., Covell, N. H., & Essock, S. M. (2020). Applying motivational interviewing strategies to enhance organizational readiness and facilitate implementation efforts. *Quality Management in Health Care, 29*(1), 1. https://doi.org/10.1097/qmh.0000000000000234

Beck, A. T. (1967). *Depression: Causes and treatment*. University of Pennsylvania Press.

Benton, J. S., Cotterill, S., Hawkes, R. E., Miles, L. M., & French, D. P. (2022). Changes in a digital Type 2 diabetes self-management intervention during national rollout: Mixed methods study of fidelity. *Journal of Medical Internet Research, 24*(12), e39483. https://doi.org/10.2196/39483

Bouwmeester, O., & Stiekema, J. (2015). The paradoxical image of consultant expertise: A rhetorical deconstruction. *Management Decision, 53*(10), 2433–2456. https://doi.org/10.1108/md-11-2014-0653

British Psychological Society. (2021). BPS Code of Ethics and Conduct. Retrieved May 15, 2023, from https://www.bps.org.uk/guideline/code-ethics-and-conduct

Brunetto, Y., Dick, T., Xerri, M., & Cully, A. (2020). Building capacity in the healthcare sector: A strengths-based approach for increasing employees' well-being and organisational resilience. *Journal of Management & Organization, 26*(3), 309–323. https://doi.org/10.1017/jmo.2019.53

Buono, A. F., & Subbiah, K. (2014). Internal consultants as change agents: Roles, responsibilities and organizational change capacity. *Organization Development Journal, 32*(2), p.35–53.

Byrne-Davis, L. M., Turner, R. R., Amatya, S., Ashton, C., Bull, E. R., Chater, A. M., et al. (2022). Using behavioural science in public health settings during the COVID-19 pandemic: The experience of public health practitioners and behavioural scientists. *Acta Psychologica, 224*, 103527. https://doi.org/10.1016/j.actpsy.2022.103527

Dale, H., & Bull, E. R. (2022). Formulation in health psychology clinical practice. In M. Forshaw (Ed.), *Health psychology in clinical practice* (1st ed., pp. 117–158). Routledge. https://doi.org/10.4324/9781003120469-9

Diabetes UK (2016). Diabetes education: The big missed opportunity in diabetes care. Retrieved July 2, 2023, from https://diabetes-resources-production.s3-eu-west-1.amazonaws.com/diabetes-storage/migration/pdf/Diabetes%2520UK_Diabetes%2520education%2520-%2520the%2520big%2520missed%2520opportunity_updated%2520June%25202016.pdf

Diabetes UK. (2023, April 13). *Number of people living with diabetes in the UK tops 5 million for the first time*. Retrieved July 2, 2023, from https://www.diabetes.org.uk/about_us/news/number-people-living-diabetes-uk-tops-5-million-first-time

Edwards, A. L. (1953). The relationship between the judged desirability of a trait and the probability that the trait will be endorsed. *Journal of Applied Psychology, 37*, 90–93. https://doi.org/10.1037/h0058073

Foot, J., & Hopkins, T. (2010). *A glass half full: How an asset approach can improve community health and wellbeing*. Improvement and Development Agency.

GeoData. (n.d.). *Health literacy*. GeoData. Retrieved July 2, 2023, from https://healthliteracy.geodata.uk/

Gilbert, P. (2014). The origins and nature of compassion focused therapy. *British Journal of Clinical Psychology, 53*(1), 6–41. https://doi.org/10.1111/bjc.12043

Hanley, B., Scott, H., & Priest, H. (2017). The impact of organisational change on professionals working within a Community Mental Health Team (CMHT): A psychodynamic perspective. *Psychoanalytic Psychotherapy, 31*(2), 176–194. https://doi.org/10.1080/02668734.2017.1315338

Hart, J. K., Hawkins, R., Panayiotis, M., Bull, E. R., Farrar, A., Baguley, C., Turner, R. R., & Byrne-Davis, L. (*2023*). 'We just need to find space for them to practice so that we can help to make a stronger society': Perceived barriers and facilitators to employing Health Psychologists in UK public health and clinical health settings. *British Journal of Health Psychology, 28*, 1206–1221. https://doi.org/10.1111/bjhp.12680

Hawkins, P., & Shohet, P. (2012). *Supervision in the helping professions* (4th ed.). Open University.

Hayes, S. C., Strosahl, K. D., & Wilson, K. G. (2011). *Acceptance and commitment therapy: The process and practice of mindful change*. Guilford Press.

Health Education England. (n.d.). *Improving health literacy*. Retrieved July 2, 2023, from https://hee.nhs.uk/

Hedges, F. (2005). *An introduction to systemic therapy with individuals: A social constructionist approach*. Bloomsbury Publishing. https://doi.org/10.7748/nm.14.7.7.s10

Henshall, C., Potts, J., Walker, S., Hancock, M., Underwood, M., Broughton, N., Ede, R., Kernot, C., O'Neill, L., Geddes, J. R., & Cipriani, A. (2020). Informing National Health Service patients about participation in clinical research: A comparison of opt-in and opt-out approaches across the United Kingdom. *Australian & New Zealand Journal of Psychiatry, 55*(4), 400–408. https://doi.org/10.1177/0004867420973261

Information Commissioner's Office. (2022, October 14). *The UK GDPR*. Retrieved July 2, 2023, from https://ico.org.uk/for-organisations/guide-to-data-protection/guide-to-the-general-data-protection-regulation-gdpr

Israel, B. A., Shulz, A. J., Parker, E. A., & Becker, A. B. (1998). Review of community-based research: Assessing partnership approaches to improve public health. *Annual Review of Public Health, 19*, 173–202. https://doi.org/10.1146/annurev.publhealth.19.1.173

Kitay, J., & Wright, C. (2004). Take the money and run? Organisational boundaries and consultants' roles. *The Service Industries Journal, 24*(3), 1–18. https://doi.org/10.1080/0264206042000247731

Leventhal, H., Brissette, I., & Leventhal, E. A. (2003). The common-sense model of self-regulation of health and illness. In L. D. Cameron & H. Leventhal (Eds.), *The self-regulation of health and illness behaviour* (pp. 42–65). Routledge.

Ley, P. (1982). Satisfaction, compliance and communication. *British Journal of Clinical Psychology, 21*(4), 241–254. https://doi.org/10.1111/j.2044-8260.1982.tb00562.x

Mazzucato, M., & Collington, R. (2023). *The big con: How the consulting industry weakens our businesses, infantilises our governments and warps our economies*. Allen Lane. https://doi.org/10.1080/14767333.2023.2218134

Morris, T. (2000). From key advice to execution? Consulting firms and the implementation of strategic decisions. In P. Flood, T. Dromgoole, S. Carroll, & L. Gorman (Eds.), *Managing strategic implementation: An organizational behaviour perspective*. Blackwell.

National Institute for Health and Care Excellence. (2023, March 2). *Type 2 diabetes in adults: Quality standard [QS209]*. NICE. https://www.nice.org.uk/guidance/qs209

NHS Digital. (2022a, August 30). *Quality and Outcomes Framework (QOF)*. NHS Digital. https://digital.nhs.uk/data-and-information/data-tools-and-services/data-services/general-practice-data-hub/quality-outcomes-framework-qof

NHS Digital. (2022b, August 11). *National Diabetes Audit (NDA) 2021–22 quarterly report for England, Clinical Commissioning Groups and GP practices.* https://digital.nhs.uk/data-and-information/publications/statistical/national-diabetes-audit/nda-core-e4-21-22/nda-core-e4-21-22

NHS Library and Knowledge Services. (2020). *Health literacy 'how to' guide.* NHS. https://library.nhs.uk/wp-content/uploads/sites/4/2020/08/Health-literacy-how-to-guide.pdf

NICE. (2024, May). *Diabetes—Type 2: QOF indicators.* NICE Clinical Knowledge Summaries. https://cks.nice.org.uk/topics/diabetes-type-2/goals-outcome-measures/qof-indicators/

Owens, R. R. (2016). *Engagement communication.* In R. Owens (Ed.), *Communication for consultants.* Business Expert Press.

Pligt, J. V. D., & De Vries, N. K. (1998). Expectancy-value models of health behaviour: The role of salience and anticipated affect. *Psychology and Health, 13*(2), 289–305. https://doi.org/10.1080/08870449808406752

Sallis, J. F., Owen, N., & Fisher, E. B. (2008). *Ecological models of health behavior.* In K. Glanz, B. K. Rimer, & K. Viswanath (Eds.), *Health behavior and health education* (4th ed., pp. 465–485). John Wiley & Sons.

Schein, E. H. (1978). The role of the consultant: Content expert or process facilitator? *The Personnel and Guidance Journal, 56*(6), 339–334.

Scott, B., & Barnes, B. K. (2011). *Consulting on the inside. A practical guide for internal consultants.* ASTD Press.

Sørensen, K., Van den Broucke, S., Fullam, J., Doyle, G., Pelikan, J., Slonska, Z., & Brand, H. (2012). Health literacy and public health: A systematic review and integration of definitions and models. *BMC Public Health, 12*(1), 1–13. https://doi.org/10.1186/1471-2458-12-80

Steinsbekk, A., Rygg, L. Ø., Lisulo, M., Rise, M. B., & Fretheim, A. (2012). Group based diabetes self-management education compared to routine treatment for people with Type 2 diabetes mellitus: A systematic review with meta-analysis. *BMC Health Services Research, 12*(1), 213. https://doi.org/10.1186/1472-6963-12-213

Stewart, M., Belle, B. J., Weston, W. W., McWhinney, I. R., McWillian, C. L., & Freeman, T. R. (2003). *Patient-centred medicine: Transforming the clinical method* (2nd ed.). Radcliffe Medical Press Ltd. https://doi.org/10.1016/s0031-9406(05)60508-1

Stoke-on-Trent City Council. (n.d.). *Presentations for health literacy event 17 June* [PDF document]. Retrieved July 2, 2023, from https://webapps.stoke.gov.uk/uploadedfiles/Presentations_for_health_literacy_event_17%20June.pdf

Titchener, J. (2014). A patient-centred clinical approach to diabetes care assists long-term reduction in HbA1c. *Journal of Primary Health Care, 6*(3), 195–202. https://doi.org/10.1071/hc14195

Whitaker, G. P. (1980). Coproduction: Citizen participation in service delivery. *Public Administration Review*, 240–246.

White, C., Baraniak, A., Bull, E. R., & Mahy, T. (2024). Trainee and qualified health psychologists' views and experiences of practice-based supervision. *Health Psychology Update, 33*(*1*), 8–13.

World Health Organization. (2023, April 5). *Diabetes*. https://www.who.int/news-room/fact-sheets/detail/diabetes

Zipursky. (2022). Proven consulting process: 4 steps to successful projects. Retrieved May 26, 2023, from https://www.consultingsuccess.com/consulting-process

17

Enquiry: Understanding High Antibiotic Prescribing Rates for Tailoring Public Health Campaigns

Lisa Hodges-Ballard and Nisha Sharma

Introduction

This chapter is in three sections. In the first section, we describe a consultancy project that involved providing expertise in qualitative data analysis and in health behaviour change to inform a project on antimicrobial resistance. We explain how the request for the work occurred, what the work involved, and the consultancy processes we engaged in. In the second section, we discuss the points at which we engaged in the process of enquiry in the project. In the third section, we reflect on the most striking elements of our analysis, our experience through other perspectives such as, Schein's expert consulting model (Schein, 1999) and the context surrounding the project.

The consultancy framework for health psychologists (Brady & Varkonyi-Sepp, 2025, see Chap. 3) contains five key processes: enquiry, building relationships, negotiating and contracting, planning and managing delivery, and evaluation. Although, in this chapter, we draw on all five processes, we focus particularly on enquiry. Enquiry is a foundation of successful consultancy involving continuous information-seeking and questioning from the early stages of engaging with clients to understand their needs, thoughts, and

L. Hodges-Ballard (✉) • N. Sharma
Cognitiva Consultancy Ltd, Southampton, UK
e-mail: l.ballard@soton.ac.uk; info@cognitivaconsultancy.co.uk

R. Brady et al. (eds.), *The Palgrave Handbook of Consultancy in Health Psychology*,
https://doi.org/10.1007/978-3-031-94529-8_17

desired outcomes, which guides the consultant through the other four elements of the consultancy process.

Our chapter is informed by Schein's expert consulting model (Schein, 1999) and 'humble inquiry' approach (2013) and is situated within the wider consultancy literature (e.g., client evaluation that goes beyond financial stability, and the characteristics of a successful consultancy project [Kometa et al., 1996]; quality in consultancy [McLeod & Schapper, 2020]; and, developing skills for consultancy [Sacks & Loon, 2016]). Schein's expert consulting model is underpinned by building 'helping' relationships with individuals, groups, organisations, and communities while humble inquiry is underpinned by an 'attitude of interest and curiosity'. Our approach was consistent with both as it incorporated an inclusive and person-centred approach, which recognises that no matter the problem or organisation you are working with, people are at the centre. This approach aligns with our professional experiences of working with patients, the public, and delivering behaviour change interventions in different settings. Schein also compares this helping relationship in humble inquiry with the therapeutic relationship in counselling, and also with more everyday relationships such as, with friends, family, and managers. Our reflections on the consultancy process align with Schein's perspectives.

The Case Study

In January 2021, we set up a health psychology consultancy (Sharma & Hodges-Ballard, 2025; see Chap. 11) and in this chapter we write about our first consultancy project. In this section, we describe the consultancy project. Firstly, a request for expressions of interest was circulated within a health psychology network of which the first author (LHB) was a member. The email originated from a health psychologist, whom we will refer to henceforth as 'the client'. The client worked at a behaviour change communications and marketing agency in England which developed behaviour change interventions for the National Health Service (NHS), local authorities, and similar organisations. The client was working on multiple projects requiring rapid turnaround times and wanted to build capacity by connecting with partners to work on selected projects. The email stated they were looking for Health Psychologists and Health Psychologists in Training and invited an expression of interest. The client described the type of work, which included literature reviews, designing topic guides and surveys, running focus groups and workshops, conducting interviews, and analysing data. LHB forwarded the email to the second author (NS). We submitted an expression of interest, and the client responded favourably by asking to meet us via video call.

Our initial meeting in April 2021 was organised by the client, and attended by the client, LHB, and NS. It is worth noting that we did no prior research about the client or company before the meeting, which we discuss below. During the meeting we asked questions about the client, the agency the client worked for, and the type of work the client had available. We also shared information on our skills and expertise so the client had a good understanding of what we could offer. The client had worked as a health psychologist for over ten years, specialising in public health. They had recently started work with the behaviour change communications and marketing agency where there was not enough work to employ another health psychologist, but enough to engage partners on an ad hoc basis. The agency had worked on a range of projects including wellbeing, criminal behaviour, prescribing rates, and the use of electronic health records.

In July 2021, the client contacted us via email to enquire about our capacity to conduct a thematic analysis (a systematic approach for identifying patterns [themes] within qualitative data sets [Braun & Clarke, 2021]) of data regarding antibiotic use and resistance that needed to be completed in the coming weeks. We asked for more information including how many hours the client thought the work would take, the number of transcripts, the length of interviews, the deadline, and the fee, in order to determine if we wished to pursue this project. This led to a further online meeting to find out more about the work. The client's aim was to provide research to inform a long-standing campaign that had been active for six years around antibiotic use and resistance for a local Clinical Commissioning Group (CCG). In the United Kingdom, a CCG is an organisation within the NHS which is responsible for planning and commissioning (buying) healthcare services for the local population of specific geographic areas. In this case, the CCG wanted the existing campaign messaging to be tailored towards individuals living in areas where prescribing rates for antibiotics were highest. This CCG campaign aimed to encourage taking the full course of antibiotics, to avoid sharing or stockpiling antibiotics, and to avoid requesting antibiotics for self-resolving illnesses such as the common cold or Influenza. The CCG wanted to ensure the information was accessible and appropriate to everyone, and that it was supportive, enabling, and educational. The geographic area targeted by the CCG contained people from Black, Asian, and Minority Ethnic (BAME) groups with multilingual skills. The client had conducted one-to-one, semi-structured interviews over the telephone through the English language with individuals who also spoke one of the following languages: Urdu, Polish, Czech, Pahari,

Punjabi, Bengali, Arabic, Kurdish, and African languages. To inform the topic guide, the client had used the Common-Sense Model of Illness and Health—Illness Perceptions (Leventhal et al., 2003), a psychological framework that examines how individuals form perceptions and beliefs about illness, and the COM-B Model (Michie et al., 2011), a theoretical framework used in behavioural science to understand behaviour as an interaction between Capability, Opportunity, and Motivation. All information was provided to us during the virtual meeting and through shared documents, such as their topic guide for the interviews and an insight brief.

There were several stakeholders involved in this consultancy project. Figure 17.1 includes each stakeholder along with the method and direction of communication between them and with us. The consultancy project involved the client, with whom we engaged in video conferencing and email correspondence, as well as the campaign manager, with whom communication was exclusively through email. The creative team from the CCG, representing the client's client, was provided with research to inform the customised campaign; no direct communication with the client's client was required.

It took 12 calendar days from the initial request for consultancy to agreeing a contract. Between meeting the client to discuss the consultancy project and signing the contract, we had a meeting with our mentor. Our mentor helped us feel confident with our fee (which was higher than the initial figure proposed), encouraged us to log all of our time (including time taken to complete administrative tasks and pricing them accordingly), and advised us to summarise conversations in emails to act as adjuncts to the contract. We started the work two days after the contract was signed and delivered the final report

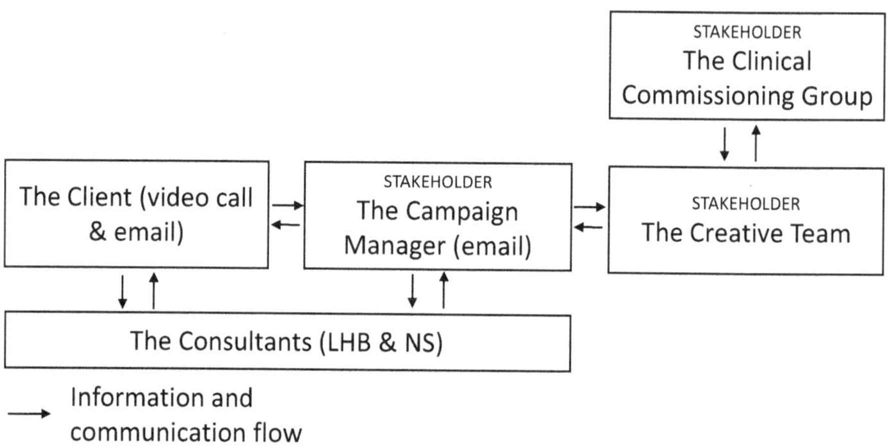

Fig. 17.1 Stakeholder communication flow

five days later. We recorded the time in a spreadsheet and kept the client informed of our progress. Completing the work took more hours than expected, which we communicated to the client. Despite this, we ensured it was delivered by the deadline. Due to the short timeframe, the client had predefined the objectives and we were asked for our agreement in one of our virtual meetings. We had no concerns, and an agreement was quickly reached. Following this discussion, a 'partner agreement' (the contract) was sent to us via email to read and sign. The partner agreement included details such as the parties involved, the summary of services (the objectives), the agreed rate of pay, the time scales (the work was to be completed within ten days), and terms and conditions. The agreed objectives and outcomes for the specific consultancy project included the following three components. First, we would produce a content analysis of the interview data, drawing out similarities and differences between groups (groups were defined by which language they spoke) based on the theoretical frameworks described above. Content analysis involves identifying words, themes, or concepts and allocating a quantitative value to them to examine frequency (Braun & Clarke, 2013). A thematic analysis was originally requested, however, during the consultancy process which is described below. The client agreed to a change in methods of analysis based on our recommendations. Second, we would advise on additional data collection. Finally, we would present findings in a report with clear sections for each area of analysis.

Due to the short turnaround time, we split the analysis into the two theoretical frameworks with one of us working on each. The findings were presented in a report format under the three sections specified by the client (COM-B, Illness Perceptions, and minor illness). We also used relevant literature to highlight and discuss the key findings. Due to the nature of the topic guide, and the way the data were recorded (notes verses verbatim), we recommended the use of content analysis. The campaign manager asked for our guidance on whether they should carry on with data collection. The client had completed ten interviews and was planning to conduct a further six, although they were having difficulty recruiting interviewees. We advised that provided the data was sufficiently detailed, ten interviews may be sufficient. We also took into consideration that the data were from a very small sample of individuals (the ultimate client or the ultimate beneficiaries of the work (Schein, 1999). We offered the client two options: to delay the analysis until the client had gathered more data, or to carry out the analysis in advance of their client's (the CCG) deadline. If we thought more data was needed, the client would have enough time to conduct further interviews to add more data to the existing analysis. The client went with the second option, optimising their resources and time.

Our report was structured in three layers of detail. The first presented key findings, the second delved into an extensive discussion of these findings, and the third provided a deeper analysis with quoted examples to illustrate significant points. While we delivered the report within the agreed timeframe, the extra effort to conduct a deeper analysis incurred costs for the client. After submitting the report, we requested feedback from the client and campaign manager who scheduled a virtual meeting 16 days later, providing valuable insights into the client's reception of our report and offering constructive feedback. Both the client and campaign manager were enthusiastic about the report's key findings, recognising their utility in shaping the forthcoming public health campaign. We were asked to amend the report to include a lay summary to highlight the main findings. Regrettably, we had overlooked this even though a lay summary would normally be included in our reporting. It is interesting to note that what we normally do can sometimes be forgotten in a novel setting. Our report was overly formal and academic, and we had not fully considered the needs of all the stakeholders. The campaign manager was not a health psychologist—another reason why a lay summary was requested. We were also asked to include a list of recommendations. While these were implicit in the report, they needed to be written in a clearer and more structured way.

Enquiry: Asking the Right Questions

Enquiry in consultancy is a collaborative activity to seek information and ask questions for the purpose of understanding the client's issues and then formulating solutions to address them (Hodges, 2021). In this section, we analyse our experience of conducting the above consultancy project using Schein's (1999) *expert model* of consultancy. The expert model describes a consultancy whereby the client purchases expertise from the consultant that they, or their organisation, do not possess. Through this lens, the client needs to have correctly identified their own expertise gap (Schein, 1999) as was the case in this project. The framework for consultancy in health psychology (Brady & Varkonyi-Sepp, 2025; see Chap. 3) will be used to structure this section, highlighting the aspects of enquiry we engaged in during each process in the framework, drawing on extant literature related to enquiry in consultancy and the wider consultancy literature.

Initial Request for Expertise

McLeod and Schapper (2020) recommend finding out the underlying reasons for a proposed consultancy project, giving an insight into the client's political stance and values through enquiry. Bloor and Pearson (2004) advise finding out about the client's guiding beliefs and principles and the purpose of the organisation the client sits within that grows from those beliefs. These enquiries will aid the consultant in reflecting on the wider public interest and how that fits with the consultant's values (McLeod & Schapper, 2020). When we agreed to this project, we were a new business and with that comes the temptation to say yes to anything that comes your way. With the help of our mentor, however, we spent time early in the development of our business pinning down our values and writing a mission statement. This can be used to check any offer of work against and to help guide declining potential opportunities that may not be a good match. For this case study, it was clear the work matched our values as it was an evidence-based public health campaign to help reduce antimicrobial resistance in under-served groups. This aligns with our values and guiding principles, especially with the health inequalities aspect, which is a key factor in our mission statement.

We did not consider, given the scale of the work (14 hours), conducting a detailed financial enquiry as recommended by Kometa et al. (1996), who describe this as a minimum enquiry task that reduces the risk to the consultant of carrying out works that cannot be financially compensated for. Kometa et al. offer a more detailed enquiry involving an evaluation of past performance, staff qualifications, team structures and current market conditions. In our work described here, the only check we carried out was to ensure the company had an online presence, and that it existed. What Kometa et al. describe is undoubtedly overly cautious for the project we undertook, but carrying out a small amount of due diligence regarding the likelihood of getting paid for the hard work you are going to put into a project is prudent. Reflecting on why we did not feel the need to be this cautious, we believe is a consequence of the client and the trustworthiness we perceived towards the client's client. The client reported to a local CCG and had a history of working with the NHS and local authorities. What we could have done in relation to financial enquiry is ask questions about company payment terms and policies in relation to faster payment for small businesses. In the contracting phase, we could have built in safeguards to mitigate against non- or late payment. For example, by asking for a percentage of the fee up front and specifying these terms within the contract.

Relationships

Effective consulting relies on strong relationships. Consultants, regardless of expertise, should work laterally with clients to drive change. Schein (1999) describes enquiry in building the helping relationship as one of the most important elements in the initial stages of the consultancy process. He emphasises the importance of active enquiry and open communication, advocating for clients and consultants to ask questions, listen actively, and seek to understand the underlying assumptions, values, and beliefs regarding the issues under discussion. Schein cautions that consultants, especially when employing the expert role, may fall into the trap of jumping in with possible solutions to the client's problem with the agenda of demonstrating particular expertise or knowledge. This use of active listening, enquiry, and leaving space for clients to contribute to solving their own problems is reminiscent of the conversational style of Motivational Interviewing (MI) (Miller & Rollnick, 2013), a skill we both trained in when working in health promotion services. Effective advice in MI is client-tailored and avoids repeating what the client has already considered. Curiosity and open questions enhance information-gathering about the client's actions.

Schein's concept of 'humble inquiry' is also useful to consider here and centres around the idea of asking questions with genuine curiosity and respect (Schein, 2013). It involves setting aside assumptions, being open to learning from others, and building relationships based on trust and empathy. This aligns with Acceptance and Commitment Therapy (ACT), another therapeutic approach we both practice in our client work. Adopting a curious attitude towards painful thoughts and feelings, rather than a judgemental one, is encouraged in ACT (Harris, 2019). We believe that being genuinely curious and seeing problems from the perspective of the client is an important part of enquiry. As described by Schein, building a helping relationship is not exclusive to consultancy. We found that in this project, we were using the therapeutic skills we have developed to build a relationship with the client, similar to what we would use with a friend who has a problem, when line managing employees, or dealing with a difficult boss. For example, it may have been difficult for the client to share that they did not have the qualitative research skills to complete the project. Through using our therapeutic skills outlined above, we created a safe and non-judgemental space for the client to share this and then be open to us using our expertise to complete the work.

Negotiating and Contracting

Before beginning work with a client, a negotiation process is essential to clarify the scope, objectives, and terms of engagement, resulting in a written agreement or contract that outlines the consultant's responsibilities and is subject to potential modifications (Brady & Varkonyi-Sepp, 2025; see Chap. 3). The contract is 'an explicit agreement of what the consultant and client expect from each other and how they are going to work together' (Block, 2011, p. 52). Block describes that to "contract flawlessly" involves behaving authentically (this is something our mentor would often mention) and employing skills in negotiation. Enquiry helps with the preparation phase before contracting starts; this involves asking questions about who the client is, who the key stakeholders are, the client's expectations of the consultant, and any underlying concerns the client might have. This stage requires the client to be able to communicate their needs and assess the consultant's expertise correctly (Schein, 1999). Our contract was in writing, which is often the case with an external client, and this should be seen with the view to aiding clarity rather than enforcement (Block, 2011, pp. 58–64). Block suggests the following elements should be included within a contract:

1. The boundaries of your analysis
2. Objectives of the project
3. The kind of information you seek
4. Your role in the project
5. The product you will deliver
6. What support and involvement you need from the client
7. Time schedule
8. Confidentiality
9. Feedback to you later

As mentioned previously, the partner agreement included details such as the parties involved, the objectives, agreed rate of pay, time scales, and terms and conditions. The objectives serve as a measure of whether the project was successful and the process of setting the objectives serves to keep realistic expectations (Block, 2011). Our objectives were set out in the partner agreement and negotiating these was a smooth process as the client communicated very clearly what they needed from us. There was little room or need to negotiate here, with the main discussions centring on how to meet the objectives methods-wise. Sacks and Loon (2016) recommend giving the client regular feedback regarding the objectives to ensure the client feels satisfied with your progress. This is reassuring and can highlight any issues early enough to make changes and manage expectations, it also allows the client to make their own contributions to any insights or changes.

Negotiating the fee was the most daunting part of the work, as we had almost no experience with this apart from lectures on consultancy during our health psychology training. In one of the meetings with the client we asked if they would share with us their expectations regarding payment for the work. It was significantly lower than the fee we had pitched previously. We discussed it between ourselves and with our mentor, keeping our learnings from training about valuing our skills in mind. We presented our offer to the client, even though it was 60% higher than what the client was expecting, with a justification regarding the skills we were offering. The client agreed with us and accepted our offer, which resulted in a fee that was acceptable to all and that valued our expertise.

One reason our enquiry was not as in depth as it should have been during the contracting and negotiating phase may have been due to how similar we felt to the client and how familiar we were with the work. The ingroup homogeneity effect describes the phenomena whereby individuals tend to develop assumptions and judgments about others based on perceived similarity or group membership (Simon & Pettigrew, 1990). In-group effects can lead people to assume that others within their own group are more similar to themselves in attitudes, beliefs, and behaviours. In this current example, our client was a health psychologist, and the topic area and theoretical framings were very familiar to us. If we had adopted a more active or humble enquiry stance (Schein, 1999, 2013), asked more questions, and given the client more space to answer, we may have enhanced our work and the end result. For example, avoiding making assumptions, such as what the client wants and needs to see in the final report.

Planning and Managing Delivery

Following initial negotiation and contracting, more detailed planning is necessary for consultancy projects with ongoing monitoring and potential contract revisions, ensuring the consultant fulfils their contractual obligations and facilitates effective problem-solving and solution implementation (Brady & Varkonyi-Sepp, 2025; see Chap. 3). The process of consultancy often has to be 'iterative and interdependent', which is when enquiry can be particularly of use (Kometa et al., 1996, p. 276). The iterative and interdependent nature of the process was highlighted through the client's own enquiry. The client asked us about the suitability of the data, the number of participants needed, and the method of analysis. Developing a suitable plan involved multiple email communications and for us to carry out some of the work and go back to the client for us to arrive at the end result. In our project, the client clearly stated what the main objectives were, and we were providing expertise on how to achieve those objectives. This was successful to the point of the report, and it is here that more enquiry and maybe moving out of expertise mode would have resulted in a workable outcome. We struggled with gauging how the client wanted the report to look, how much detail to include, and the length. But objectively, the planning and management of the consultancy project went well. We completed the work within the given timeframe and delivered the report in a timely manner.

Evaluation

In evaluating consultancy work, it is essential to assess both the outcomes of the project and the consultant's practice and development, with periodic planning and integration throughout the consultancy process (Brady & Varkonyi-Sepp, 2025; see Chap. 3). One evaluative measure is the objectives, which serve as an indicator of whether your consultancy project was successful (Block, 2011). We achieved the objectives in the agreed timeframe and the client sent a complimentary email about the findings in our report, indicating how useful they will be to informing the public health campaign. Given our values, this kind of impact was important to us.

Sacks and Loon (2016) outline an evaluation that takes place after the final report is delivered. This may include reviewing the successes and outcomes, how resources, such as time, have been used, any challenges that were overcome during the course of the project, and feedback to the consultants regarding future ways of working. We were informally carrying out evaluation throughout the whole project, especially during the managing delivery phase. Also, we requested a meeting with the client and the Campaign Manager for feedback on our performance as new health psychology consultants. The feedback from this is described above, but the overarching learning was that more enquiry was needed. However, the value from our expertise was also highlighted in this meeting. For example, we introduced a concept to the client that they had not encountered previously; loss and gain framed messaging (Rothman et al., 2003). In loss-framed messaging, the focus is on the potential negative consequences of not taking a particular action or not adopting a recommended behaviour and the opposite for positive-framed messaging.

The background reading we had completed to enable us to write up the findings of the analysis revealed that gain-framed messaging may be more appropriate when the outcome of the behaviour is more certain (i.e., to take the full course of antibiotics or do not take antibiotics for a self-solving illness) and when the behaviour is a prevention-focused one (i.e., preventing infection or antibiotic resistance. The client appreciated the evidence we had presented and felt it was particularly helpful to feed back to their client.

Reflections

In this final section, we write a reflective and reflexive account of our experience using Bolton's (2018) guidance for reflective and reflexive writing. Bolton does not recommend a prescriptive procedure or set of instructions for reflective and reflexive writing, rather a set of exercises that help question personal and professional actions. We have used a selection of questions posed by Bolton (2018) to guide our reflection. For Bolton, reflection involves reviewing what, who, when, where, and how of events, as well as your own and others' thoughts, feelings, and experiences. Reflection therefore aims to review these events from as many angles as possible, drawing on the wider context. Moreover, Bolton defined reflexivity as finding ways to question beliefs, assumptions, attitudes, values, and prejudices to foster responsible and ethical future action.

What Strikes Us About This Consultancy?

Two main thoughts struck us while writing this chapter. The first is that we did not do enough enquiry because we were still in the early stages of learning about consultancy processes. Prior to this project, we had not fully considered several aspects of consultancy practice. Once we had completed the project for the client, our mentor helped us identify elements of consultancy such as, providing expertise, developing rapport (relationship management), engaging with the client's needs, researching the company/asking questions, agreeing objectives, and negotiating our fee. This did not come easily to us and it highlights the importance of this book. Researching enquiry for this chapter and examining our approach to consultancy through the lens of Schein's expert and humble enquiry approach (Schein, 1999, 2013) has been a steep learning curve. In reality, rather than viewing the work explicitly as a consultancy project, we focused on using our expertise for the methods and analysis of the client's data, neglecting other elements of the consultancy process. Had we understood and engaged more in enquiry, for example, we might have understood more about our stakeholder's needs; we might have discovered key information regarding how the campaign messages were to be delivered to the ultimate client, and we might have better understood the client's expectations regarding the final report.

Our barriers to enquiry may have been personal ones. Imposter syndrome (Clance & Imes, 1978), and the thoughts and feelings that causes, may have stood in the way of curiosity, and therefore, prevented carrying out a full enquiry. Thoughts such as, 'I should know that. What will the client think if I ask them something I think I should already know?' may have prevented us from asking certain questions. It may also help if we think about it from the client's perspective. Questions can be asked in a way that conveys that curiosity, for example, 'I'm so interested to know more about…', 'I've been wondering about…', 'It would be great to get more insight into…'. This aligns with therapeutic skills in building up a trusting relationship and to the helping relationship highlighted by Schein (1999). Curiosity and humble inquiry (Schein, 2013) can help build a trusted relationship, allowing the client to communicate their needs and the consultant to ask the right questions.

The second realisation is that our expertise is valuable, and we can use it to be successful health psychology consultants. This, our first consultancy project, was a positive experience. As the client was a health psychologist, we did not need to argue the value that our expertise in health psychology and our knowledge of behavioural science would add to the work. The success of the consultancy was also facilitated by our experience of working on antimicrobial resistance training (NS), and by being experienced qualitative researchers who had applied the Common-Sense Model (Leventhal et al., 2003) (LHB) and the COM-B model (Michie et al., 2011) (LHB and NS) to qualitative research data. The project fitted well with our knowledge and skills and with a client who did not have the resources or expertise to fulfil the task (Schein, 1999).

Our expertise in qualitative research was the most significant element to our consultancy work and where we added the most value for the client. The client advised us that they were not a qualitative researcher and did not feel confident to analyse the data and also needed advice on the methodology. We brought expertise in qualitative research the client did not have in their organisation; we employed enquiry to design the analysis, and we used our findings from the analysis to inform further data collection. The aim of the research was specific, and the decisions made regarding data collection and analysis were pragmatic. For LHB, it also shone a light on how useful her research skills and university research experience could be to other agencies working to reduce health inequalities and the value health psychology consultants can bring to commercial and third sector work.

As well as our areas of expertise proving valuable to being successful health psychology consultants, they also help us to live our values. Working in academia (LHB) and healthcare (LHB and NS), we recognise the challenges of incorporating the voices of those from under-served groups; if a person or group is under-served from an accessing healthcare perspective, their voices will also be underrepresented in research (Dennison et al., 2022). The fact that the communications and marketing agency were able to recruit ten people from under-served groups deserves recognition and reflection from academics and health professionals on the methodologies we use. Accessing under-served voices may be challenging and require 'epistemic disobedience' (Mignolo, 2009) whereby well-used methods are not appropriate (Rai et al., 2022). If we do not take up this challenge, we add to the perpetuation of health inequalities. A recent review of Eurocentric health research practices highlighted the co-design element to inclusive research practices stating how individuals from under-served groups must be recognised as knowledge makers (Hardcastle et al., 2023). This is in essence what the client had achieved; co-designing a public health campaign to include the knowledge and the voices of under-served groups. Disappointingly, the findings produced from this work are not visible to the academic or practitioner communities or to wider audiences such as service commissioners who might use the findings when considering service design or resource utilisation. We believe it is an ethical issue that work such as this does not get published in academic literature.

What Have We Missed Out from This Account?

What is missing from our account is how we both felt about working together on this consultancy project. For example, what was it like to divide the work up and have to support each other when we needed help? We have never discussed this, which raises an interesting question in itself; why? It is because this is hard to talk about, but also because nothing adverse happened to prompt this discussion. However, reflecting here makes us think it would be a useful exercise to complete. Interestingly, whilst reading the literature regarding consultancy, we have not encountered much discussion regarding consultants working with other consultants. Lee and Jang (1998) mention this in their article identifying that consultants working collaboratively on a project will bring differing learning histories, attitudes, knowledge, perspectives, and preferred ways of working. The authors position this as a positive in that it enhances creativity; however, it is not difficult to imagine how these differences could cause tension, if not managed appropriately.

What Do We Feel Now, and How Did We Feel Then? Why?

During the consultancy project we felt that the work was not as challenging as similar work we had conducted in the past. This may have been an advantage, as it was not intimidating and was enjoyable. The enjoyable element may have come from being familiar with the way this work is conducted within an academic constraint where processes are slower. We also remember resisting the strong urge to do extra work without reporting the additional hours to the client. Where undertaking the work took more hours than expected, we communicated that to the client and that was reflected in the invoice. The main two reasons we managed to resist the urge was keeping in mind what we had learnt during our training and advice from our mentor about valuing our skills. We also feel proud about what we achieved in this consultancy project. Our account here details what could have gone better, which is a vulnerable action to commit to for our peers to read. However, we accept the feelings of vulnerability and uncomfortableness as this work is in the service of our values regarding giving back to the health psychology community and helping others learn from our experiences.

Different Perspectives?

Having our mentor to discuss the consultancy project with, especially how to negotiate the fee for the work, and to reflect on the whole process when it was done was invaluable. Having support and encouragement from our mentor prevented us from feeling alone. They saw the potential we had to start and maintain our consultancy and that encouragement went a long way towards the consultancy we have today. We imagine our former mentor would encourage us to feel proud of this consultancy project and for us to learn from what we have identified in this chapter.

Top Tips 1. Continuously assess and refine your enquiry approach.

2. If you have therapeutic experience, use skills such as active listening, reflection, and adopting a curious approach to help build rapport with clients.
3. Collaborate with an experienced health psychologist mentor to gain valuable guidance and support.
4. Align opportunities with personal values to help prioritise satisfying and meaningful work.
5. Embrace failure as a catalyst for growth.

Competing Interests The authors have no competing interests to declare that are relevant to the content of this chapter.

References

Block, P. (2011). *Flawless consulting: A guide to getting your expertise used* (3rd ed.). John Wiley & Sons.

Bloor, R., & Pearson, D. (2004). Brief solution-focused organizational redesign: A model for International Mental Health Consultancy. *International Journal of Mental Health, 33*(2), 44–53. https://doi.org/10.1080/00207411.2004.11043368

Bolton, G. (2018). *Reflective practice. Writing and professional development* (5th ed.). Sage.

Brady, R., & Varkonyi-Sepp. (2025). A framework for consultancy in health psychology. In I. R. Brady, J. Varkonyi-Sepp, & J. Smith (Eds.), *The Palgrave handbook of consultancy in health psychology*. Palgrave Macmillan.

Braun, V., & Clarke, V. (2013). *Successful qualitative research: A practical guide for beginners*. Sage.

Braun, V., & Clarke, V. (2021). *Thematic analysis: A practical guide*. Sage.

Clance, P. R., & Imes, S. A. (1978). The imposter phenomenon in high achieving women: Dynamics and therapeutic intervention. *Psychotherapy: Theory, Research & Practice, 15*(3), 241–247. https://doi.org/10.1037/h0086006

Dennison, L., Williamson, S., Greenwell, K., Handcock, M., Bradbury, K., Vennik, J., Yardley, L., Little, P., & Geraghty, A. W. A. (2022). Patient perceptions of vulnerability to recurrent respiratory tract infections and prevention strategies: A qualitative study. *BMJ Open, 12*(4), 1–11. https://doi.org/10.1136/bmjopen-2021-055565

Hardcastle, F., Lyle, K., Horton, R., Samuel, G., Weller, S., Ballard, L., Thompson, R., Trindade, L., Gómez Urrego, J., Kochin, D., Johnson, T., Tatz-Wieder, N.,

Redrup Hill, E., Robinson Adams, F., Eskandar, Y., Harriss, E., Tsosie, K. S., Dixon, P., Mackintosh, M., et al. (2023). The ethical challenges of diversifying genomic data: A qualitative evidence synthesis. *Cambridge Prisms: Precision Medicine*, 1–39. https://doi.org/10.1017/pcm.2023.20

Harris, R. (2019). *ACT made simple: An easy-to-read primer on acceptance and commitment therapy*. New Harbinger Publications.

Hodges, J. (2021). A framework for consulting. *Management Consulting Journal, 4*(2), 52–55. https://doi.org/10.2478/mcj-2021-0009

Kometa, S. T., Olomolaiye, P. O., & Harris, F. C. (1996). A review of client-generated risks to project consultants. *International Journal of Project Management, 14*(5), 273–279. https://doi.org/10.1016/0263-7863(96)84510-8

Lee, J., & Jang, Y. (1998). Factors influencing the success of management consulting projects. *International Journal of Project Management, 16*(2), 67–72. https://doi.org/10.1016/s0263-7863(97)00005-7

Leventhal, H., Brissette, I., & Leventhal, E. A. (2003). The common-sense model of self-regulation of illness and health. In L. Camerson & H. Leventhal (Eds.), *The self-regulation of health and illness behaviour*. Routledge.

McLeod, S., & Schapper, J. H. M. (2020). Understanding quality in planning consultancy: A review and synthesis of the literature. *Journal of Planning Education and Research*. https://doi.org/10.1177/0739456X20943928

Michie, S., van Stralen, M., & West, R. (2011). The behaviour change wheel: A new method for characterising and designing behaviour change interventions. *Implementation Science, 6*(42), 1–11. https://doi.org/10.1186/1748-5908-6-42

Mignolo, W. D. (2009). Epistemic disobedience, independent thought and decolonial freedom. *Theory, Culture & Society, 26*(8), 159–181. https://doi.org/10.1177/0263276409349275

Miller, W. R., & Rollnick, S. (2013). Motivational interviewing: Helping people change. In *Motivational interviewing: Helping people change* (3rd ed., pp. xii, 482). Guilford Press.

Rai, T., Hinton, L., McManus, R. J., & Pope, C. (2022). What would it take to meaningfully attend to ethnicity and race in health research? Learning from a trial intervention development study. *Sociology of Health and Illness, 44*(S1), 57–72. https://doi.org/10.1111/1467-9566.13431

Rothman, A. J., Kelly, K. M., Hertel, A. W., & Salovey, P. (2003). Message frames and illness representations: Implications for interventions to promote and sustain healthy behaviour. In L. Cameron & H. Leventhal (Eds.), *The self-regulation of health and illness behaviour* (1st ed., pp. 278–296). Routledge/Taylor & Francis Group.

Sacks, R., & Loon, M. (2016). Developing and using consultancy skills. In M. Loon (Ed.), *Professional practice in learning and development: How to design and deliver plans for the workplace* (pp. 151–206). Kogan Page.

Schein, E. H. (1999). *Process consultation revisited. Building the helping relationship*. Addison-Wesley Publishing Company.

Schein, E. H. (2013). *Humble Inquiry: The gentle art of asking instead of telling.* Berrett-Koehler.

Sharma, N., & Hodges-Ballard. (2025). Starting a health psychology consultancy. In I. R. Brady, J. Varkonyi-Sepp, & J. Smith (Eds.), *The Palgrave handbook of consultancy in health psychology*. Palgrave Macmillan.

Simon, B., & Pettigrew, T. F. (1990). Social identity and perceived group homogeneity: Evidence for the ingroup homogeneity effect. *European Journal of Social Psychology, 20*(4), 269–286. https://doi.org/10.1002/ejsp.2420200402

18

Consultant-Client Relationships: Increasing Awareness and Detection of Psychological Difficulties in People Undertaking Haemodialysis

Sarah A. Afuwape

Introduction

This chapter describes a consultancy project which involved the design and delivery of brief, accessible Cognitive Behaviour Therapy (CBT)-based teaching to nursing staff working on a haemodialysis unit. The aim of the teaching was to increase nurses' knowledge of and confidence in identifying common psychological presentations experienced by patients undertaking kidney dialysis treatment. Dialysis is the highly invasive life-sustaining treatment required by patients when they experience kidney failure (Bártolo et al., 2021). There are two main types of dialysis treatment; peritoneal dialysis (carried out at home) and haemodialysis. Haemodialysis is the treatment undertaken by most patients and for the majority, involves attending a dialysis centre three times each week for treatment that takes several hours (Swift et al., 2019).

S. A. Afuwape (✉)
Royal Free London NHS Foundation Trust, London, UK
e-mail: sarah.afuwape@nhs.net

R. Brady et al. (eds.), *The Palgrave Handbook of Consultancy in Health Psychology*,
https://doi.org/10.1007/978-3-031-94529-8_18

Psychological difficulties are common in people undergoing haemodialysis (Monaro et al., 2014) and patients can experience a high symptom burden including poor sleep, fatigue, anxiety, and depression (Al Naamani et al., 2021). In-centre haemodialysis can be particularly time-consuming for those less mobile who, in addition to the treatment time, are dependent on hospital transport for travel to and from the dialysis centre. In-centre dialysis is associated with lower self-reported quality of life than home dialysis (Antoun et al., 2023), However, psychological therapies can help alleviate symptoms of distress in patients on haemodialysis with varying effectiveness (Ling et al., 2020). A recent meta-analysis that included 15 studies of psychological interventions found significant improvements in mood, a reduction in anxiety, and improved quality of life following psychological interventions (Yan et al., 2025).

Uniquely, patients attending for treatment can see the same nursing staff several times per week sometimes for many years, creating an interpersonal relationship rarely seen in other medical settings. The busyness of these environments (which can treat over 80 patients per day in some of the larger units), combined with delayed transportation and monotony involved in dialysing, can contribute to feelings of frustration, irritability, and sometimes aggression which can put a strain on nursing staff. The intense and demanding nature of the nursing staff role in haemodialysis centres has been linked to staff burnout, particularly among younger and less-experienced nurses (Hayes et al., 2015, Karkar et al., 2015). Support through improving staff-patient communication, can be effective (Burns & Smyth, 2011).

In the Case Study section of this chapter, I describe a project that was eventually extended to all four of the hospital's kidney care centres with emphasis on the relationships between me as the 'consultant', the dialysis nurse manager who was the 'client' and the teams of highly skilled dialysis nurses and healthcare assistants who were the 'stakeholders.' I outline the need for the consultancy work and describe the teaching intervention and the role of the different players in setting up and delivery of the project. In the section on Building and Maintaining Relationships, I explore how the consultancy aligns with the principles of consultancy identified by social psychologist and consultancy expert Edgar Schein (Schein, 1999). The final section is a reflection on the consultancy process and looks at the successes and lessons learnt.

The Case Study

This internal consultancy case study took place in a National Health Service (NHS) Hospital Trust (henceforth, the Trust) in England. The Trust provides haemodialysis at four satellite dialysis centres close to the homes of the people they serve. Following a survey of haemodialysis patients I had conducted with my renal psychology colleague at the Trust (described below), I proposed an educational intervention for dialysis nursing staff with the overall aim of improving staff communication and awareness of patients' experience of dialysis. The intervention also aimed to support nurses to deliver more psychologically informed care given the known effectiveness of communication-based interventions for nurses (e.g., Salmani et al., 2020). The offer of very brief, readily accessible teaching that accommodated the nurses' working pattern was the key deliverable feature when consulting and contracting with the dialysis nurse manager to carry out this work.

In contrast to psychological practitioners' *direct* therapy work with patients which is not considered to be consultation, *indirect* work such as that through interventions with staff, can positively impact patients through changes in the approach taken by staff. Within mental health settings, 'indirect' or 'internal' consultation (Ghag et al., 2021) can support staff to develop therapeutic skills when working with clients/patients with challenging needs, and it can increase nursing staff confidence by enabling more skilful and competent work to support the delivery of compassionate and psychologically informed care (Ghag et al.; Murphy et al., 2013). For example, Murphy et al. delivered a 3-day CBT-based psychological training package to nurses on an older adult inpatient unit which increased staff members' opportunities to feel listened to and enabled space for reflection.

Other key intended beneficiaries of the consultancy work, therefore, included the Trust itself which, it was hoped, would benefit from staff who were more psychologically attuned to improve effective engagement with the patients for whom they cared. There was also an indirect benefit in that the teaching would help staff to better understand their own psychological well-being, which could support staff workplace resilience, enhance interpersonal relationships at work and increase helpful interactions with patients whilst reducing unhelpful or potentially harmful ones (Evans et al., 2011). For example, poor understanding of the underlying cause of a patient's behaviour whilst on dialysis could lead to the unhelpful labelling of this behaviour as 'challenging' rather than as an expression of the complex interaction of a patient's thoughts, feelings, and physical symptoms underlying the behaviour in question. The absence of this understanding is likely to prove less helpful to patients and could even be detrimental for the development of the nurse-patient relationship.

The renal psychologist colleague with whom I worked was also a stakeholder. As psychologists delivering therapeutic interventions to patients, we believed that compassionate, psychologically informed care delivered by nursing staff would improve the overall patient experience and that indirectly it could potentially reduce patient distress and the need for referrals to the service for direct renal psychology therapy (Dekker et al., 2023).

Identifying the Need for Consultancy

The consultancy was not directly requested by the client or the renal nurses. Rather, the teaching package was designed and delivered because, through my extensive work with patients and staff in renal services I recognised the need to better support the nursing team to improve their understanding of the patient experience. With the support of visiting psychology students, the Renal Clinical Health Psychology team and I had conducted the hospital's first renal Patient Experience Measures (PEM). The measure, designed by two consultant nephrologists and me, comprised 34-item mixed closed and open-ended questionnaires which were an amalgam of questions from the Kidney Disease Quality of Life—Short Form 1.3 (Kallich et al., 1995). The measure included several additional questions that captured the daily experiences of patients undertaking dialysis at the dialysis centres. Questions included the extent to which patients felt respected by staff, informed about various aspects of their care and felt supported to manage their life on dialysis.

The PEM survey findings were presented at a renal meeting for lead clinicians and managers and were then disseminated as a report to the senior management of the Trust. The PEM highlighted excellent care at the dialysis units and the presentation of findings showcased several aspects of care about which patients were extremely complementary. The findings differed for each dialysis unit although overall, results of the closed questions were good; most patients reported that they were treated with respect and that staff were friendly towards them. However, variation was found in results regarding whether patients felt involved in their treatment decisions and their reported psychological well-being. The report therefore also included areas in which improvements could be made.

Results of the open-ended questions indicated that where patients did express dissatisfaction with their dialysis experience, poor communication was a common theme and often, this (mis)communication was noted specifically between dialysis nursing staff and their patients. My clinical interactions with patients and relatives also indicated that staff struggled at times to either fully comprehend the patient experience and/or to identify patients' psychological distress to offer an appropriate response.

The Consultant

Throughout the consultancy, my role was a dual one. In terms of developing the teaching intervention for the nurses I was a Health Psychologist Consultant (HPC) although this occurred alongside my role as a Practitioner Health Psychologist (PHP) working directly with renal patients. Although employed in the role as PHP for several years, the HPC role was new and existed specifically for the purpose of the project. The benefits and challenges of the same individual occupying both roles will be discussed in the Reflections section later in this chapter.

The Doctor-Patient model of consultancy (Schein, 1999) which will be explored further in the next section, occurs where a consultant is invited into an organisation to 'diagnose' a problem and offer a 'treatment intervention'. As a PHP, I was in an ideal position to define the scope of the problem and to propose and deliver on feasible solutions, having access to all key stakeholders to enable suitable buy-in. Having an insider perspective can be an advantage for consultants although it is important to also retain a degree of objectivity. In this, we are guided by our professional standards which include the requirement to use our "skills, knowledge, expertise, and experience, and the information available ... to make informed decisions and/or take action where necessary" (HCPC, 2023, p. 8). Conducting the PEM had provided us with anonymous data directly from patients and highlighted areas for intervention, enabling me to 'diagnose' the problem and recommend a solution.

Based on the PEM findings and on issues raised by patients in therapeutic settings, I approached the matron to propose the development of a series of brief CBT-based interactive psychological teaching sessions for nurses. The aim of the sessions was to improve dialysis staff's understanding of patients' psychological distress and to increase staff confidence in their ability to respond to psychological distress appropriately. As an accredited CBT practitioner, it was evident to me that the interconnection between the potentially challenging dialysis situation and patients' thoughts, feelings, behaviours, and their physical presentations associated with the environment underpinned many of the clinical presentations and could be conceptualised within this evidence-based framework. CBT is associated with alleviating symptoms of depression in dialysis patients (e.g., Ling et al., 2020). A CBT approach was also more readily taught in the short timeframes available to the nursing staff to attend training.

It was hoped that an improved understanding of the dialysis patient experience would lead to better skills in communication and would foster a culture of compassionate, psychologically informed healthcare (Dekker et al., 2023). Although aimed at improving staff-patient communication, it is likely that the teaching would also enhance staff-to-staff relationships by providing informal opportunities for reflection and discussion.

The Intervention

The project objective agreed with the matron was to develop and deliver brief teaching to dialysis nurses on different psychological disorders, emotional states, and situations associated with psychological distress commonly observed in patients undertaking in-centre dialysis treatment. The framework and concept for the teaching was informed by an intervention delivered by psychological therapists for psychiatric staff in a psychiatric rehabilitative setting (Berry et al., 2016). Berry and colleagues' intervention comprised 26 one-hour sessions with nursing staff where CBT formulations about individual patients' needs were discussed and shared with the aim of improving staff-patient relationships. CBT formulations provide a framework for examining the interrelationship of patients' biological, societal, cultural, and psychological factors and how these factors interact to cause and maintain the psychological problem. Our work used the concept of CBT formulation but, unlike Berry's extended sessions with nursing staff to discuss individual patients, we adopted a more didactic teaching format to share ideas about patients' challenges more broadly, addressing the common psychological presentations observed on the dialysis unit. Teaching sessions were shorter (35 minutes), and formulations were briefer. We used the 5-Areas Model (Williams & Garland, 2002; Dale & Bull, 2022) which describes the five domains of a patient's experience and demonstrates the links and bidirectional relationship between (1) a challenging situation experienced by the patient (situation), (2) their difficult thoughts associated with the situation (thoughts), (3) the feelings accompanying the thoughts (emotions), (4) the associated behaviours related to the thoughts and feelings and (5) any physical sensations and symptoms triggered by the situation, thoughts, and feelings (physical). This approach lent itself well to five of the eight topic areas (see section 'The Agreed Objectives and Outcomes for the Work').

The nurses who received the bite-sized CBT-based teaching were of all grades from students and newly qualified NHS band 5 nurses to more experienced band 6 staff nurses, and band 7 senior dialysis nurses who manage the dialysis units. Although the teaching was considered the primary intervention, other elements involved in the process of delivering the intervention could themselves have influenced the intended change in confidence and acted as an unintended intervention. For example, the opportunity to learn about patients' psychological distress normalised distress and coping among nursing staff and thus facilitated a useful informal reflective space for them to share their own experiences.

Key Stakeholders and Their Needs/Priorities

Improving communication and crafting good relationships on the dialysis units is essential for many reasons. Haemodialysis can cause physical, psychological, and social challenges, with many patients frequently reporting feelings of fatigue, frustration, and helplessness (Al Naamani et al., 2021). The uniqueness of the staff-patient relationship in haemodialysis offers both benefits and challenges; the advantages are to be found in the continuity of care offered to these patients who undertake their dialysis at the same dialysis unit, on the same alternate-day-of-the-week shift, often for several years. Patients frequently describe the 'family-like' atmosphere of familiarity with fellow patients, nursing, and non-clinical reception and administrative staff. Yet this benefit can also be considered a challenge. *Dialysis burnout* (DB), often adopted in reference to the demands of diabetes care, is a term which relates to the biopsychosocial challenges that patients who undertake routine in-centre dialysis can experience (Bevin, 2024). Encountering the same patients and staff several times a week can put a strain on good working relations and act as a regular reminder to some patients that they require nursing care and are dependent on a machine to keep them alive. The psychosocial challenges that arise from DB can be similar to those identified in patients, educators, and therapists of patients with type 1 diabetes mellitus, and present as anger, sadness, stress, aggression, and interpersonal conflict which, if not understood and managed effectively, can increase tension and negatively impact working relations (Charman, 2000).

Like many other NHS Trusts serving dialysis patient populations, the reduction and management of violence and aggression directed towards their staff has been a top priority, the focus of which has been to channel efforts towards the use of body cameras with live monitoring as effective deterrents (Bruton et al., 2022). Violence and aggression in dialysis units has been of increasing concern and studies have demonstrated the significant impact on reduction in staff morale and job satisfaction and the intention to leave the organisation and/or profession (Sprigg et al., 2007; Sofield & Salmond, 2003). Brief staff education, it was thought, expand the opportunities for more helpful patient interactions and reduce the frequency of unhelpful or challenging ones.

The Agreed Objectives and Outcomes for the Work

The nature of the dialysis nurses' work and the set-up of the dialysis units presented several limitations around what could feasibly be delivered. It became apparent from discussions with the dialysis matron that there were few opportunities for nursing staff to leave the satellite dialysis unit for staff training. This was due to frequent staff shortages and the requirement for those remaining to maintain the appropriate patient-staff ratio and be available to connect and disconnect patients to and from their dialysis machine and answer the call bell if required. So, ensuring the teaching was brief, tailored, and readily accessible was paramount.

With these requirements in mind, time outside of the clinical setting was required to research, plan, and develop the brief teaching package, the content of which would be based in psychological theory yet readily digestible in the busy, compact space of the nurses' station. The specific goals, learning outcomes, and the ways these could be measured were determined. As described elsewhere in the chapter, the aim was to support nursing staff to better understand their patients' psychological distress and thus improve confidence and facilitate better recognition and response to patients' needs.

Academic databases PubMed, CINAHL, Medline, and Google Scholar were searched for any existing similar teaching packages. An extensive search produced no suitable literature reporting on training nurses in identifying psychological distress in dialysis. However, the theoretical work of Parle et al. (1997) who developed a staff training initiative aimed at improving health professionals' communication practices with patients with cancer, and the work of Berry et al. (2016) described earlier, were useful in informing the design of our teaching package.

Given the demands on nursing time and the need for staff to remain available for their patients, the sessions were designed to be delivered at the nurses' station. Presentation slides for each session were shown on a laptop; pre-and post-session data were collected on staff knowledge of the subject matter (using a quiz format or a 10-point Likert scale), their confidence in detecting the specific emotional states or symptoms in patients, and whether they would recommend the teaching to colleagues. The sessions were interactive, and staff were encouraged to participate by giving examples of their own experience with patients when and where appropriate.

There was an agreement with the matron that the teaching would be delivered initially in one of the four dialysis units with the intention to roll it out to the other three units over the subsequent months. The eight teaching sessions were entitled: Stress, Anxiety, Panic, Depression, Anger, Adherence, Communication, and The Renal Psychology Service. The eighth session, which described the purpose of the renal psychology service and how to make referrals, was merely informative and a suitable conclusion to the previous weeks' teaching. Sessions were delivered at a time designated by the senior nurse, which in most units was immediately after the nurses' handover in order to ensure that all staff were present and could engage in the discussion. All teaching sessions, bar The Renal Psychology Service, Adherence and Communication sessions, followed a similar outline in which (a) the topic was introduced and defined, (b) examples of the emotional state were presented (c) a 5-Areas CBT formulation was given demonstrating the maintenance factors and (d) simple, helpful intervention techniques were discussed. The Adherence session explored reason for treatment non-adherence focusing largely on the popular social cognition model of behaviour change, the Health Belief Model (Rosenstock, 1990), and the Communication session introduced and defined the topic with reference to various styles of communication as well as presenting examples of helpful and unhelpful or even harmful communication.

The first 8-week wave of teaching occurred at one dialysis unit with between 5 and 15 staff members in each teaching session depending on staff availability. In total, 70 post-teaching outcome measures were completed anonymously which reflected the responses of the different number of nursing staff who attended the sessions each week. A session register enabled us to determine which nurses attended each session although not who remained to the end and completed their outcome measure, as staff were often required to leave the teaching before the end to answer a patient call bell or attend to a patient needing to leave their dialysis session early.

Results showed that staff reported an increase in their post-teaching knowledge about all psychological states, and an increase in their confidence to detect them in their dialysis patients. Staff also reported an improvement in their decision to refer to the renal psychology service and improved knowledge about the referral criteria. Verbal feedback from managers showed that staff felt valued and appreciated the time out of their working day, albeit for the brief period, to reflect on emotions and behaviours from a different perspective.

Building and Maintaining Relationships: The Practitioner Health Psychologist as the In-House Health Psychologist Consultant

The role of Practitioner Health Psychologist (PHP) in the renal medical setting whilst also taking on the role of Health Psychologist Consultant (HPC) to undertake the work described in this chapter can be both challenging and rewarding. In this dual role, the psychologist is required to build and sustain credible and trusting relationships with patients by establishing oneself as a listener, advocate, and promoter of good mental health, whilst simultaneously supporting the needs of the organisation to ensure staff deliver excellent and compassionate patient care. Ultimately, each role is focused on the concept of *helping*, yet the nature of the help offered differs as does the process by which the help is given. In his book *Process Consultation Revisited*, Schein (1999) describes five key principles necessary for carrying out consultancy: (1) Always Try to Be Helpful; (2) Always stay in touch with the current reality; (3) Access your ignorance; (4) Everything you do is an intervention: and (5) It is the client who owns the problem and the solution (Schein, 1999). These concepts align well with the building and maintenance of relationships seen in the consultancy work described in this chapter.

Building on the models described by Schein (1999), Sacks and Loon (2016) highlight different models or *styles* of consultancy; the Expert Consultant model, the Doctor-Patient model, and the Process Consultancy model. The Expert Consultant model is suited to those consultants who are deployed on projects because of their specialised skills and knowledge in a specific area with the expectation that they will take ownership of the problem to be resolved using their own choice of solutions guided by the boundaries and remit of the client. Projects using this model of consultancy are bound by clearly identified beginnings and finite endings, and the client determines the nature of the problem and the outcome measures of success (Schein). Although a relationship that can potentially engender trust, use of such a model implies a short-lived consultant-client relationship and one that can lead to a dependence on the consultant for answers and limited engagement and ownership of the suggested solutions by the client.

In contrast, the Doctor-Patient model as described by Sacks and Loon (2016) is a more directive approach to consultancy and draws its metaphor from the relationship between a medical doctor and their patient. In this model, the consultant takes on the role of the 'doctor,' who possesses specialised knowledge, expertise, and skills in assessment, diagnosis, and treatment whilst the client or key stakeholder acts as 'patient,' and seeks guidance and support for a specific problem or need with less involvement in the decision-making process. Although this model of consultancy can offer a clear framework for engagement, it may produce an unhelpful power imbalance where the client may consider themself to have less agency or input into the decision-making process. Care needs to be taken to ensure a narrower focus on problems and issues rather than on exploring opportunities, does not arise.

Schein's (1999) Process Consultation Model highlights the role of the consultant as a process supporter who helps clients to better understand their organisational culture, improve communication and interactions, and solve problems collaboratively. The emphasis of the model is on the *process* of consultation instead of simply the provision of a solution, and there is significant weight placed on building and maintaining relationships with the stakeholders by using transparency, trust, and mutual respect. Each model can be adopted by both external and in-house consultants although the use of any one model is determined by the key stakeholder's understanding of consultancy, their expectation of the process, and the project outcome (Sacks & Loon, 2016).

The work described in the chapter aligns largely with the Process Consultancy model although I was also involved in the 'diagnosis' and 'prescription' elements of the Doctor/Patient model. The aim of the work was both remedial and preventative; staff were being taught to become more astute regarding patients' psychological needs and how to notice and intervene helpfully with patients in distress to improve their dialysis experience.

In the context of the eight general principles that govern the client-consultant relationship (Schein, 1999), I describe the first five below and highlight how I adopted them in both my role as PHP and HPC. Particular emphasis is placed on building and maintaining the different types of stakeholder relationship, all of which required nurturing, diplomacy, trust and a sophisticated understanding of the stakeholders' perspective and needs.

Principle 1: Always Try to Be Helpful

This first principle forms the bedrock of the objectives, all contacts, and activity carried out in this consultancy work. In every situation with all stakeholders, from actively listening to the concerns of patients to collating and disseminating the PEM results, approaching the senior managers with ideas about tackling the problems, to the design and delivery of the bite-sized teaching, the intention to be helpful was the dominant driver. However, 'helpfulness' in the role of a PHP engaging therapeutically with patients necessitates a different approach from that of HPC proposing an intervention to senior renal nursing staff to improve the delivery of services. For the PHP, discussions that occur during patient therapy sessions are bound by rules of confidentiality, and the relationship is both one of trust and collaboration. Patients are helped to feel safe in the therapeutic alliance to disclose their thoughts and feelings about their life which can include aspects of their treatment and interpersonal relationships with those both inside and outside of the dialysis unit. The former PHP role, although not considered consultancy by Schein, represents work at the *individual, direct level* whilst the HPC role targets work at the *face-to-face group* level (Schein, 1997).

Additionally, the role of the HPC was to deliver sensitive information of the outcome of the PEM regarding areas of service improvement. For the message to be well received, its delivery was important, with areas of identified good practice emphasised alongside aspects requiring improvement. Instruction and guidance on how these improvements could be made was discussed. The long-standing pre-existing relationship that I had with the renal management and staff teams facilitated a seamless change over to the HPC role; the stakeholders were accustomed to receiving help from me in my role as PHP and the relationship was already one built on trust. According to the Process Consultancy model (Schein, 1999), one could argue that I was in the best possible position to be able to offer help and to support the key stakeholders to think collaboratively how best to implement a feasible and sustainable solution given my permanent role within the Renal Health Psychology service. I was already simultaneously fulfilling roles of both consultant and client in that I had a vested interest as part of the wider organisation in the success of the project and in seeing an increase in the delivery of better psychologically informed care. I believe this aspect of the work helped to build and maintain a trusting relationship with the stakeholders as we had shared common long-standing patients who we all had a genuine desire to better support.

However, possible drawbacks of straddling both roles could have been my potential lack of objectivity and an overfamiliarity with the organisational culture, systems, and processes to generate a variety of fresh solutions. There was also the practical resource element of having to create time around my clinical PHP role to engage in the consultancy process which often led to me working beyond contracted hours.

Principle 2: Always Stay in Touch with the Current Reality

This principle relates to the need for the consultant to remain focused and to have a good grasp of the cultural context of the client system and to ensure this context is shared by the client. This can refer to having insight into up-to-date issues pertinent to the organisational culture which may impact on the process and outcome of the project. So, for example, having a shared understanding and awareness of the organisation's current financial situation will have affected the shared decision-making process between consultant and client with regard to what a feasible intervention might look like. Knowledge that is gained in the course of consultancy is not simply a one-way process but is knowledge that arises in the relational context with the client (Fincham, 2002). As the in-house HPC, I had the benefit of integrating knowledge in this way and the unique advantage of existing in a shared cultural reality and drawing on the strengths from pre-existing relationships within the organisation again, helping to build and maintain the client-consultant relationship beyond the initial implementation period of the project. A further challenge to the interconnectedness of the roles is an overfamiliarity with this shared reality, in that it prevents an unbiased perspective.

Principle 3: Access Your Ignorance

This principle relates to the state in which the consultant enters the process of consultancy with their need to better understand the problem and determine which is the most appropriate model of consultancy to adopt to best meet the needs of the client. It highlights the gaps in knowledge and the lack of wisdom to even know or enquire about what is not known. As the consultant in the work outlined in this chapter, I made some key assumptions about the solution to the problem without first seeking with the opinions of stakeholders including those of patients. For example, I made an assumption that nurses would have little or no pre-existing knowledge about the intervention and therefore pitched the teaching at a level to reflect this. On enquiry, this assumption was not correct as some nurses demonstrated that they were familiar with CBT. This aspect of the consultancy relationship is consistent with the more prescriptive, expert-led Doctor/Patient model of consultancy which fortunately did not negatively impact my relationship with my stakeholders who trusted my expertise.

Principle 4: Everything You Do Is an Intervention

The fourth principle suggests that all interactions, including the mechanism by which the problem is conceptualised, can be considered a change intervention in and of itself. In our work, the analysis and dissemination of the specific PEM results may have, for example, begun to impact staff's self-awareness of their own communication styles, causing them to alter or self-monitor what and how they communicated with others. There was some indication of this in their reaction when the PEM feedback for each specific dialysis unit was presented at the staff team meetings. It is unlikely that such an unintended consequence of simply distributing such results would, by themselves, have had a sustained effect on behaviour without the reinforcement of the teaching. However, it is important to accept that an unintended intervention like this can influence the production of the desired outcome. My role as consultant served to reassure staff that change was possible.

Principle 5: It Is the Client Who Owns the Problem and the Solution

This final principle suggests that it is the consultant's responsibility to foster a relationship in which the client can access help without the consultant taking full ownership and responsibility for the solution. Rather, the consultant empowers the client to remain proactive in creating lasting, workable, adaptable solutions.

In our work, the bite-sized teaching solution aimed at improving staff knowledge and confidence, was the creation of the consultant but owned by the client; the nature of the teaching sessions allowed me as the HPC to deliver material that required staff to interpret and translate the content into their own style of communication with patients. It was also the responsibility of the client to determine the utilization and sustainability of the teaching package beyond the period of the project, including whether to offer it as a rolling programme of teaching. To the advantage of the client, my role as in-house HPC has enabled the continuation of the teaching for several years and the expansion out to the other dialysis units within the trust. The client has remained proactive in determining the teaching frequency jointly, both around my team's availability to deliver it and the staffing ratios on the dialysis unit.

As a pilot project, the impact of the teaching was measured only on the effect of staff knowledge and confidence and no opportunity was created to formally assess the direct impact of the intervention on patient experience. For example, an immediate post-teaching PEM could have been designed to capture possible improvements in communication or overall patient experience for those patients identified with psychological difficulties requiring referral to the renal psychology service.

Reflection

In this section, I will explore some of the project strengths and areas for improvement and I will outline in more depth, the unique skills, knowledge, and expertise that I brought to the project to make it a success.

On reflection, the pre-existing, long-standing relationship that I had with the renal clinicians and staff stakeholder teams as the patients' renal psychologist facilitated the easy transition into the role of consultant. I had good oversight of the significant challenges, time pressures and insight into the potential stressors of the work of the staff. I was also aware of the camaraderie and excellent teamwork demonstrated by the nursing teams as a factor that would influence any successful intervention. These reflections echo those of Dyck (2002), who proposes that the internal consultant often has greater insight and knowledge of the organisation enabling them to "keep the organisation's best interest in mind" (Dyck, 2002, p. 113) and offer more tailored interventions. They have an in-depth understanding of the organisation's culture, processes, and goals, despite the lack of objectively often associated with external consultants.

However, as Wright (2009) points out in the context of describing the dual role of some managers as internal consultants, occupying the role of an internal consultant meant at times, that I inhabited two separate spaces; although the psychologist employee, my position and expertise as consultant could have identified me as the 'outsiders within'. This role ambiguity sometimes felt uncomfortable to navigate having to switch identities perhaps several times in one day. Largely, the 'dual subjectivities' as described by Meyerson (2003) offered a position of strength and advantage allowing familiarity with the organisational culture and the unique relationship that the renal dialysis nurses had with their patients. Moreover, with my detailed knowledge of the PEM results, I had the expertise to shape and tailor the content of the teaching package which on reflection, could have been developed in much closer collaboration with the stakeholders, including with a broader selection of patients.

The wider financial pressures of the NHS and the difficulty recruiting specialist dialysis nurses meant that renal dialysis teams across the capital experienced staffing pressures. The brief, inexpensive teaching delivered to the nurses in the dialysis unit space whilst their patients were still within sight was the project's unique approach, enabling the teaching to begin immediately after the nurses' handover meeting.

A significant drawback overlooked during the planning was the potential during the sessions, for distraction and interruption from patients requiring assistance. A teaching session could start with fifteen attendees and thirty minutes later, could end with only nine. The presence of the senior nurse to convene the nurses at the start of the teaching and buffer the distractions by attending to patients herself was extremely helpful. We therefore learnt quickly to adapt the structure to ensure sessions began with summaries of the previous teaching and that most sessions followed the recognisable CBT structure with the 5-area model formulation of the topic being taught. Flexibility around the frequency of the teaching was a requirement; although advertised to occur fortnightly, teaching was often cancelled to accommodate staffing pressures. This inevitably impacted the continuity of the sessions and the consolidation of the learning given a missed teaching session would mean a one-month gap. Although initially developed as a pilot, the bite-sized teaching was later delivered to all four hospital dialysis units on an annual basis to capture new staff joining the organisation and as a refresher for those having already received it. To avoid the long gaps between sessions, we have begun to offer weekly teaching in some dialysis units which is being successfully delivered by the trainee psychologist on placement.

The bite-sized psychology teaching continues today to be welcomed in dialysis units with discussions around extending a similar teaching package to other dialysis units across London.

Top Tips

1. Seek out named individual stakeholders who will help to drive the delivery of the objectives to enable shared accountability. For us, it was the matron/senior nurse and me as the consultant.
2. Ensure there is senior stakeholder buy-in to help develop and promote the project.
3. Think clearly about the available resources to deliver on the agreed objectives to avoid over-promising on objectives that are not deliverable. In the

NHS, time and financial resources are generally squeezed therefore creativity is useful.
4. Decide on efficient and effective methods of outcome data collection before the start of the work.
5. Allow room for flexibility, change, and pragmatic 'real world' consultancy.

Competing Interests The author has no competing interests to declare in relation to this chapter.

References

Al Naamani, Z. A. I., Gormley, K., Noble, H., et al. (2021). Fatigue, anxiety, depression and sleep quality in patients undergoing haemodialysis. *BMC Nephrology, 22*(1), 157. https://doi.org/10.1186/s12882-021-02349-3

Antoun, J., Brown, D. J., Jones, D. J. W., Clarkson, B. G., Shepherd, A. I., Sangala, N. C., Lewis, R. J., McNarry, M. A., Mackintosh, K. A., Mason, L., Corbett, J., & Saynor, Z. L. (2023). Exploring patients' experiences of the impact of dialysis therapies on quality of life and wellbeing. *Journal of Renal Care, 49*(1), 15–23. https://doi.org/10.1111/jorc.12416

Bártolo, A., Sousa, H., Ribeiro, O., & Figueiredo, D. (2021). Effectiveness of psychosocial interventions on the burden and quality of life of informal caregivers of hemodialysis patients: A systematic review. *Disability and Rehabilitation, 44*(26), 8176–8187. https://doi.org/10.1080/09638288.2021.2013961

Berry, K., Haddock, G., Kellett, S., Roberts, C., Drake, R., & Barrowclough, C. (2016). Feasibility of a ward-based psychological intervention to improve staff and patient relationships in psychiatric rehabilitation settings. *The British Journal of Clinical Psychology, 55*(3), 236–252. https://doi.org/10.1111/bjc.12082

Bevin, A. (2024). Diabetes and dialysis burnout—Is it any wonder? *Journal of Kidney Care, 9*(5). https://doi.org/10.12968/jokc.2024.9.5.229

Bruton, L., Johnson, H. et al. (2022). The impact of body-worn cameras on the incidence of occupational violence towards paramedics: A systematic review. *Journal of Aggression, Conflict and Peace Research, 14*(2), 133–142.

Burns, T., & Smyth, A. (2011). Reducing aggression in the haemodialysis unit by improving the dialysis experience for patients. *Renal Society of Australasia Journal, 7*(2), 79–89.

Charman, D. (2000). Burnout and diabetes: Reflections from working with educators and patients. *The Journal of Clinical Psychology, 56*, 607–617. https://doi.org/10.1002/(SICI)1097-4679(200005)56:5<607::AID-JCLP3>3.0.CO;2-A

Dale, H., & Bull, E. (2022). Formulation in health psychology clinical practice. In M. J. Forshaw (Ed.), *Health psychology in clinical practice* (1st ed., pp. 117–159). Routledge.

Dekker, J., Sears, S. F., Åsenlöf, P., & Berry, K. (2023). Psychologically informed health care. *Translational Behavioral Medicine, 13*(5), 289–296. https://doi.org/10.1093/tbm/ibac105

Dyck, D. (2001 [2002]). Internal and external consulting: Assisting clients with managing work, health, and psychosocial issues. *AAOHN Journal, 50*(3), 111–119. https://doi.org/10.1177/216507990205000305

Evans, K., Law, H., Turner, R., Rogers, A., & Cohen, K. (2011). A pilot study evaluating care staffs' perception of their experience of psychological consultation within a mental health setting. *Child Care in Practice, 17*, 205–219. https://doi.org/10.1080/13575279.2010.541423

Fincham, R. (2002). The agent's agent: Power, knowledge, and uncertainty in management consultancy. *International Studies of Management & Organization, 32*(4), 67–86. http://www.jstor.org/stable/40397549

Ghag, J., Kellet, S., & Ackroyd, K. (2021). Psychological consultancy in mental health services: A systematic review of service, staff, and patient outcomes. *Psychology and Psychotherapy: Theory Research and Practice, 94*, 141–172. https://doi.org/10.1111/papt.12264

Hayes, B., Douglas, C., & Bonner, A. (2015). Work environment, job satisfaction, stress and burnout among haemodialysis nurses. *Journal of Nursing Management, 23*(5), 588–598. https://doi.org/10.1111/jonm.12184

HCPC. (2023). Standards of proficiency. Practitioner psychologists. *Standard, 4*(3), 8. https://www.hcpc-uk.org/standards/standards-of-proficiency/practitioner-psychologists/

Kallich, J. D., Hays, R. D., Mapes, D. L., Coons, S. J., & Carter, W. B. (1995). The RAND kidney disease and quality of life instrument. *Nephrology News Issues, 9*(9), 29, 36.

Karkar, A., Dammang, M. L., & Bouhaha, B. M. (2015). Stress and burnout among hemodialysis nurses: A single-center, prospective survey study. *Saudi Journal of Kidney Diseases and Transplantation: An Official Publication of the Saudi Center for Organ Transplantation, Saudi Arabia, 26*(1), 12–18. https://doi.org/10.4103/1319-2442.148712

Liam Bruton, Hunter Johnson, Luke MacKey, Aaron Farok, Liz Thyer, Paul M. Simpson; The impact of body-worn cameras on the incidence of occupational violence towards paramedics: a systematic review. Journal of Aggression, Conflict and Peace Research 5 April 2022; 14(2): 133–142.

Ling, C., Evans, D., Zhang, Y., Luo, J., Hu, Y., Ouyang, Y., Tang, J., & Kuang, Z. (2020). The effects of cognitive behavioural therapy on depression and quality of life in patients with maintenance haemodialysis: A systematic review. *BMC Psychiatry, 20*(1), 369. https://doi.org/10.1186/s12888-020-02754-2

Meyerson, D. E. (2003). *Tempered radicals: How people use difference to inspire change at work*. Harvard Business School Press.

Monaro, S., Stewart, G., & Gullick, J. (2014). A 'lost life': Coming to terms with haemodialysis. *Journal of clinical nursing, 23*(21–22), 3262–3273. https://doi.org/10.1111/jocn.12577

Murphy, S. A., Osborne, H., & Smith, I. (2013). Psychological consultation in older adult inpatient settings: A qualitative investigation of the impact on staff's daily practice and the mechanisms of change. *Aging & Mental Health, 17*(4), 441–448. https://doi.org/10.1080/13607863.2013.765829

Parle, M., Maguire, P., & Heaven, C. (1997). The development of a training model to improve health professionals' skills, self-efficacy and outcome expectancies when communicating with cancer patients. *Social Science & Medicine (1982), 44*(2), 231–240. https://doi.org/10.1016/s0277-9536(96)00148-7

Rosenstock, I. M. (1990). The health belief model: Explaining health behavior through expectancies. In K. Glanz, F. M. Lewis, & B. K. Rimer (Eds.), *Health behavior and health education: Theory, research, and practice* (pp. 39–62). Jossey-Bass/Wiley.

Sacks, R and Loon, M (2016). 'Developing and using consultancy skills.' In: Loon, M, ed. Professional practice in learning and development: how to design and deliver plans for the workplace. Kogan Page, London, pp. 151–206. ISBN 9780749477424.

Salmani, Z., Shiri, H., Mofrad, M. N., & Nasiri, M. (2020). The effect of nursing communication skills training on satisfaction of patients undergoing hemodialysis. *Journal of Pharmaceutical Research International, 31*(6), 1–8. https://doi.org/10.9734/jpri/2019/v31i630383

Schein, E. H. (1997). The concept of 'client' from a process consultation perspective: A guide for change agents. *Journal of Organizational Change Management, 10*(3), 202–216. https://doi.org/10.1108/09534819710171077

Schein, E. H. (1999). *Process consultation revisited: Building the helping relationship.* Addison-Wesley.

Sofield, L., & Salmond, S. W. (2003). Workplace violence. A focus on verbal abuse and intent to leave the organization. *Orthopaedic Nursing/National Association of Orthopaedic Nurses, 22*(4), 274–283.

Sprigg, C. A., Armitage, C. J., & Hollis, K. (2007). Verbal abuse in the National Health Service: Impressions of the prevalence, perceived reasons for and relationships with staff psychological well-being. *Emergency Medicine Journal, 24*(4), 281–282.

Swift, O., Vilar, E., & Farrington, K. (2019). Haemodialysis. *Medicine, 47*(9), 596–602.

Williams, C., & Garland, A. A. (2002). Cognitive–behavioural therapy assessment model for use in everyday clinical practice. *Advances in Psychiatric Treatment, 8*(3), 172–179. https://doi.org/10.1192/apt.8.3.172

Wright, C. (2009). Inside out? Organizational membership, ambiguity and the ambivalent identity of the internal consultant. *British Journal of Management, 20*(3), 309–322. https://doi.org/10.1111/j.1467-8551.2008.00585.xr

Yan, S., Zhu, X., Huo, Z., Wang, Z., & Cui, H. (2025). Psychological intervention for depression and anxiety in hemodialysis patients: A meta-analysis. *Actas espanolas de psiquiatria, 53*(1), 154–164. https://doi.org/10.62641/aep.v53i1.1628

19

Consultant-Client Relationships: Supporting Development of a National Intellectual Disability Memory Service in Ireland

Marianne Fallon and Eimear McGlinchey

Introduction

This chapter outlines a consultancy project involving an inclusive approach to engaging with stakeholders in the development of service delivery indicators (SDIs) for a new National Intellectual Disability Memory Service (NIDMS) in Dublin, Ireland. Using the Public and Patient Involvement approach to health service delivery (Health Service Executive Research and Development, 2021), people ageing with intellectual disability were consulted, using accessible materials, regarding the development of this service.

This chapter will focus on the building relationships aspects of health psychology consultancy in the context of developing the SDIs. The importance of establishing credibility and trust when working with an expert team and meaningful and inclusive engagement with stakeholders will be discussed. It will outline how people ageing with intellectual disability in Ireland were co-creators of the new service, through involvement in designing the SDIs. Reflections on the evolution of my individual consultancy style to meet the opportunities and challenges of the role are included.

M. Fallon (✉) • E. McGlinchey
Trinity Centre for Ageing and Intellectual Disability, Trinity College Dublin, Dublin, Ireland
e-mail: fallonm7@tcd.ie; mcgline@tcd.ie

R. Brady et al. (eds.), *The Palgrave Handbook of Consultancy in Health Psychology*, https://doi.org/10.1007/978-3-031-94529-8_19

The first author, MF, is a Chartered Health Psychologist, with over 20 years of experience working within a community support service for people with intellectual disabilities. At the time of writing MF is a PhD candidate with the Trinity Centre for Ageing and Intellectual Disability (TCAID) in Ireland, investigating the longitudinal effect of a range of biopsychosocial risk factors for dementia in an ageing Irish population with Down syndrome. Through working together, TCAID were aware of the clinical, consultancy, and research-based skills that a health psychologist can offer. EMG is an academic psychologist specialising in dementia in people with Down syndrome, focusing on early biomarkers of Alzheimer's disease, prevention, and lifestyle intervention. Within this chapter, MF will write from her perspective as the psychologist using consultancy skills in the project, in collaboration with EMG as the research lead and the main contact person for the client, in this case the team at TCAID.

The Consultancy Project

Ageing with Intellectual Disability

Worldwide, people with intellectual disability are living longer than ever before due to improved health care and more inclusive community living (Lennox et al., 2015). Greater longevity brings an increased risk of developing the diseases of old age and a greater risk of inequity in access to preventative and therapeutic health care supports. One of the ageing-related conditions that people with intellectual disability are at greater risk of developing is dementia. People with Down syndrome have a genetic risk for Alzheimer's disease (AD), where virtually everyone with Down syndrome has the brain changes of AD by the age of 40 (Fortea et al., 2020). Down syndrome is caused by triplication of chromosome 21, where this chromosome produces the amyloid precursor protein (De França Bram et al., 2019), leading to overexpression of this protein and amyloid plaques—a hallmark of AD. Over 95% of people with Down syndrome develop dementia (McCarron et al., 2017), with the mean age of dementia onset 53.8 years (Iulita et al., 2022). People ageing with intellectual disability of other aetiology have also been shown to be at increased risk of developing dementia compared to their peers in the general population (Strydom et al., 2020).

Diagnosing dementia in people ageing with intellectual disability is complex. Establishing a deterioration from the person's best level of functioning can be difficult due to a pre-existing intellectual disability, significant inter-individual variation in cognitive ability, and patterns of normal daily functioning. Other common conditions that can mimic dementia also need to be ruled out, for example, depression and low thyroid functioning. Specialist assessment instruments administered by experts are required for comprehensive dementia assessment for this population. Dementia may present atypically (Sheehan et al., 2015). There may be a floor effect even with specialised objective memory tests (i.e., the test items are too difficult for respondents to score on) for people with severe to profound intellectual disability (Wissing et al., 2022).

The National Intellectual Disability Memory Service

The Irish National Dementia Office was established in 2015 to oversee the implementation of the National Dementia Strategy (Department of Health, 2014), one of whose aims was to establish a network of Memory Clinics accessible for all ageing Irish residents. Given the complex nature of memory assessment requirements for those ageing with intellectual disability, a specialised memory clinic was required. A multidisciplinary team from Tallaght University Hospital (TUH), Dublin, TCAID, and AVISTA CLG service provider, collaborated on the development of a new National Intellectual Disability Memory Service (NIDMS) in TUH. This service addresses an inequity in access to dementia assessment for people with an intellectual disability in Ireland, where previously access to specialist memory assessment was limited to a few intellectual disability service providers. NIDMS is funded by the Irish National Dementia Office. Professor Sean Kennelly, Consultant Geriatrician, is the Clinical Director of NIDMS. Professor Mary McCarron, Director of TCAID, is the Executive Director of NIDMS.

Consultancy Negotiations/Scope of Consultancy

I (MF) was asked by the Director of TCAID to work within the NIDMS team to support development of the SDIs for NIDMS. This was not a formal consultancy contract, rather it was a part-time secondment into the team to support the development of this new service, using my health psychology clinical, consultancy, and research-based skills. Other strands of this role involved education and training to support service development. This chapter will cover the consultancy skills used within the role and will focus on the collaborative work done in supporting the SDIs.

The role was overseen by the TCAID team on behalf of NIDMS. A period of negotiation took place between my employers and TCAID to draw up a formal contract of secondment of two days per week to work with TCAID for a period of one year initially, with option to extend. I was consulted regarding the development and terms of this agreement. This contract covered the aims of the role within NIDMS, the hours per week for the secondment, renumeration, and the name of the key liaison people within TCAID and NIDMS. This contract was signed by me, my employers, and TCAID for NIDMS. TCAID would oversee my work in developing the SDIs, but ultimate reporting would be to NIDMS.

I undertook discussions with the Director of TCAID and with EMG to determine the scope of the project; this is vital to ensure client expectations can be met within an agreed timeframe (Sacks, 2016). Core values of NIDMS informing the SDIs were respect and meaningful inclusivity of the ultimate clients (i.e., people with an intellectual disability and their carers), academic rigour, transparency, and international best practice. These SDIs would then inform the development and ongoing evaluation of the NIDMS in terms of clinical governance, academic research, and education and training outcomes. The further development, use, and evaluation of the developed SDIs in guiding these outcomes over the medium to longer term was agreed to be 'out of scope' for this project.

Why a Health Psychologist?

Historically, clinical and educational psychologists have been the key professionals to work with people with intellectual disability. However, a health psychologist's skillset is in many ways ideally suited to the needs of those ageing with an intellectual disability. Despite gains in longevity in recent decades (Dolan et al., 2021; García-Domínguez et al., 2020), people ageing with intellectual disability continue to present with higher levels of multimorbidity, chronic illness and mental health support needs than their ageing peers in the general population (McCarron et al., 2013; Sheerin et al., 2022). Health psychologists are uniquely positioned to promote health and quality of life in this population through assessment of the broader determinants of health, development of treatment interventions, and reducing health inequalities (Clarke, 2011; Hilton & Johnston, 2017). With an additional focus in Irish health psychology training on research competence within a scientist-practitioner model and policy development skills (Corbett, 2013; Hevey & Hickey, 2013), I was well suited to the broad range of competencies required for this consultancy role.

Stakeholders

During the period of contract negotiations, I became familiar with the agencies associated with the new Memory Service and the prospective client base for the Service. The NIDMS was identified as the key stakeholder in this consultancy work, given that this would be the new service development. Other stakeholders were identified as Tallaght University Hospital and Avista CLG as partners in developing the new service, sharing its core values. TCAID is a multidisciplinary academic research centre examining key issues in the lives of people ageing with ID, with the aim of influencing national policy and service provision to this population. Tallaght University Hospital (TUH) has an Institute for Memory and Cognition which was able to support the set-up of the NIDMS on-site. Avista CLG is a large voluntary/NGO service provider for people with intellectual disability throughout their lifespan. The ultimate beneficiary stakeholders of the work would be the community of Irish people ageing with intellectual disability and their families/carers.

Management of Reporting Obligations

Reporting obligations on this project were complex given the multiple stakeholders. Regular formal and informal reporting was undertaken to the TCAID team, as they were the main drivers of the initial work on the project. Regular reporting was also necessary to the NIDMS team with this being a more formal meeting utilising PowerPoint presentations summarising the main SDI development findings as they progressed. This reporting was important in terms of promoting communication and trust in the project progress. EMG and I were responsible for working with team members to ensure surveys were developed, interviews were undertaken, data was collated and analysed and formal presentations then developed to inform on progress. My involvement in the project ended with the development of the resources to measure the SDIs. Since then, the SDIs have been used to evaluate the delivery of the service and the experience of those attending it.

Building Relationships Within the Consultancy Process

Model of Consultancy

This section will focus on the importance of the relationship-building aspect of the consultancy process as working effectively with all stakeholders was crucial to the development and success of this project. Through conversations with TCAID, it became clear that a *process consultancy* approach would be the most suitable (Schein, 1990). This would involve close collaboration and trust on an equitable basis with other expert team members in a discovery process to develop appropriate SDIs for the new NIDMS model. Each team member brings their own unique perspective and professional background to this collaborative discovery process. Process consultancy, to be successful, demands a high level of credibility, demonstrated competence, and interpersonal skills in relationship building from the consultant (Sacks, 2016).

Process consultancy requires advanced communication and facilitation skills from the consultant, applying structure and focus to delivering project objectives, whilst respecting the talents and experience of individual team members and existing group dynamics. The process consultant works with the team to explore, encourage, and facilitate movement towards achieving project objectives (Newton, 2019). Being integral to the development of outcomes gives a team more ownership of, and buy-in to, these outcomes. Given the multidisciplinary and expert background of team members within NIDMS, respect for their contributions, and facilitating a team discovery process towards the development of the SDIs was deemed to be the most suitable consultancy approach.

Establishing Trust

The project team consisted of the two Directors of the Memory Service, a Consultant Psychiatrist, an Advanced Nurse Practitioner, a Clinical Nurse Specialist, a Strategic Development Officer, and EMG. As I was unknown to most of the project team, it was essential to establish trust as the foundation of the client-consulting relationship (Maister et al., 2000). I needed not only to establish my credibility as an experienced clinician and health psychologist working in intellectual disability and dementia, but also my ability to develop and deliver on the agreed project aims. This process is characterised in the literature as showing ability and integrity, aligning to client expectations to demonstrate benevolence and establishing an emotional connection. This enables the client(s) to make a 'leap of faith' into a trusting relationship (Nikolova et al., 2015). These dimensions of trust are often cited in the literature as the ABI (Ability, Benevolence and Integrity) model of perceived trustworthiness (Mayer et al., 1995). An important aspect of this model is the process perspective, which is the recognition that trust building takes time and is a dynamic social learning process between consultant and client (Nikolova et al.).

I began my work on this project with a focus on building relationships with team members. Initial meetings, mostly online, were undertaken with team members to introduce myself and my professional background. I also aimed to obtain their perspective on the aims of the project and to identify any issues they perceived might arise. It was important to clearly identify who the various stakeholders were, given the multiagency nature of the NIDMS set-up, and to establish who within the team was the most appropriate advocate/link for each stakeholder. It was important for me to clarify my role in the team also. This development of an online social space contributed to building a feeling of safety and relational connectedness between team members and myself. Establishing trusting professional relationships is central to fostering a feeling of safety in meeting online (Waldman, 2018).

Another important aspect of these initial discussions was to identify the skill set of each team member in order that there be maximum utilisation of, and respect for, the available expertise as part of the process consultancy. There was also a need to agree the available time each team member might have to work with me on the project. This would depend on their existing professional commitments and the extent that their current role overlapped with project aims. The time spent on this initial introductory discussion process was very valuable in terms of establishing strong interpersonal relationships built on credibility, trust, and respect. It demonstrated my ability to be flexible in synchronising my work style with the team's existing work style. A shared working style gave confidence to the team members that I would be easy to work with and fit within the pre-existing culture of the team, further building trust (Collina, 2021; Nikolova et al., 2015).

This clarification/alignment of expectations phase is vital to provide confidence to team members that the project will be moved forward in a credible coherent fashion (Nikolova et al., 2015; Sacks, 2016). I was able to demonstrate my skills in interpersonal relating and group process management, important competencies for a successful consultancy engagement (Appelbaum & Steed, 2005). This was a "relational and developmental" process of trust-building with the team (Nikolova et al.)

Organising the Project

I spoke with all team members initially to clarify and align their expectations of what the outcomes of the consultancy work would be. A small core team of people were identified as being available for regular meetings and work on project aims. The wider group were kept regularly updated on progress or consulted as the need arose. The core team consisted of myself, EMG, the Strategic Development Officer, the Advanced Nurse Practitioner, and the Clinical Nurse Specialist. In the planning stage with the core team, we specified project aims and the break-down of the work into smaller, measurable goals with achievable agreed deadlines. I regularly met online with team members to discuss progress and help them to resolve any issues arising that were hindering progress. Small regular successes within the project contributed to a sense of achievement, confidence, and trust in the process and the consultant. It also fostered a sense of positive ownership within the team for project progress, as these were highlighted in the regular wider team updates.

There was a focus by the members of the core team on proactively resolving issues ahead of deadlines in order that positive results were regularly achieved, minimising stress and maximising morale. This focus on 'getting ahead of issues' also minimised the potential for negative interpersonal interactions. I cannot remember there being any significant negative interpersonal issues that arose during the process within the team. This is also a tribute to the professionalism and mutual respect already existing within the TCAID and NIDMS teams; it is their normal way of working.

My approach to this consultancy project maps well onto the high-impact consulting model proposed by Schaffer (2002) for successful consultant-client engagement. He recommends that there be a focus on results at the start of the project, with the overall output aims broken down into 'rapid-cycle subprojects' leading to quick positive results for the team. The importance of clear consistent communication of project aims and outputs and fostering a sense of ownership with all stakeholders is also emphasised.

Inclusive Engagement with Stakeholders

It was agreed that the development of the stakeholder SDIs would be informed by stakeholder consultation, including meaningful consultation with people with intellectual disability (prospective NIDMS clients), using an accessible interviewing format. These participants would be consulted on what they felt would be important for them in attending a national memory service. The questions would be framed using an accepted model of health service delivery, covering clinic structure, process, and outcomes (Donabedian, 1988). The results of this consultation would further inform the development of the SDIs.

This consultation process links to the overarching NIDMS principle of patients and their families being valued in shaping memory service delivery. Patient and public involvement (PPI) is a key tenet of current Irish health service development and delivery (Health Service Executive Research and Development, 2021). PPI can be defined as current or potential end users of a health service being involved in the design and undertaking of research into development/delivery of a health service. PPI involvement is now a central pillar of health service development in many countries; however, recent reviews have found considerable barriers to inclusion of people from more marginalised communities with issues related to health literacy and lack of supports for ability, cultural, and language diversity identified (Ocloo et al., 2021).

Inclusive engagement also links to the related concept of co-production in healthcare services whereby patients are integrally involved in the design of their healthcare service and delivery, and in monitoring of its quality and management of their own health condition (Elwyn et al., 2020). The disability rights movement, emerging in the second half of the twentieth century, has emphasised the central importance of people with disabilities being involved in decisions about their lives; 'nothing about us without us' (Scotch, 2009).

An inclusive consultation process was chosen as it is a unique initiative in this field and it aligned well with the overall values and ethos of the NIDMS, the self-determination of people with disabilities and the emphasis on PPI involvement within the broader Irish health service.

Necessary Adjustments to the Scope of the Project

As the project work coincided with the onset of the Covid-19 pandemic, in-person focus groups and interviews with people with intellectual disability were not possible. This posed an unexpected challenge that had not been envisaged during the drawing up of the consultancy contract and a change to the scope of the process. Previous research undertaken by TCAID had shown that level of engagement with technology was low for Irish people with an intellectual disability (McCarron, 2017; McCausland et al., 2023). It was therefore necessary to devise and agree a procedure for engaging with these stakeholders remotely in an accessible way to maximise their meaningful participation. To guide this process, I consulted the recently published guidelines issued by the Irish regulating body for psychologists in response to necessary remote working practices during the Covid-19 pandemic (Psychological Society of Ireland, 2020). Although these guidelines focus on online therapy, they offer a set of good practice principles for psychologists for remote engagement that was suitable to inform the development of an online protocol around consultation with stakeholders and informed consents for interviews.

The change in approach was successful in engaging with the stakeholders and enabling them to give their opinions on SDI development. However, this necessary process of remote engagement with stakeholders did lead to some limitations overall in the engagement process which will be discussed in more detail below. My ability to proactively adjust the project scope in an unexpected environment of restrictions added to my credibility with the team.

Limitations of Remote Interviewing People with ID: How Does This Impact on Relationship Building?

An initial focus group with participants with intellectual disability to establish the suggested SDIs of memory service structure, process, and outcome from participants' direct suggestions could not be held. Given the Covid-19 pandemic regulations in force at that time, it was not possible to meet in a group setting. The core team had to develop the suggested SDI statements for the interviews with people with intellectual disability, based on their expert knowledge and experience of the issues important to people with intellectual disability who visited for memory assessments and other appointments in a clinic setting. This leads to the SDIs having been 'expert-led' in their initial development which is not wholly in keeping with the 'bottom-up' PPI process approach.

Other limitations arose with the remote interview process itself, interviewing participants with intellectual disability about the relative importance they placed on each SDI within the suite of suggested SDIs. Remote interviewing limits the opportunity for more creative direct engagement and communication with participants with intellectual disability, as communication may need to be enhanced with concrete pictorial or object references that can be exchanged between parties. Remote interviewing led to a less nuanced communication with each participant. If the interviews had been in person, the SDIs could have been arranged on a tabletop in front of each participant, with supported discussion to facilitate the rank ordering of SDIs, with participants being encouraged to point to those they felt to be important and physically moving them around to indicate relative importance. However, those who did participate in the online interview process were very positive about being included in it, as were the staff who supported them to participate. There did not appear to be issues with participants understanding the SDIs, as evidenced by the amount of spontaneous qualitative comments on the SDIs collected from participants. The development of accessible materials to support the interview process and the person being supported to review these materials with a supporter before the interview was an adaptive way to support meaningful communication with participants.

In Summary

Viewing this process through a consultancy lens, I worked mainly as a 'friendly co-pilot' and 'capability builder' with the team, facilitating progress and change rather than directing it, using the clients' and stakeholders' existing resources and expertise (Carucci & Tetenbaum, 2000; Nees & Greiner, 1985). I supported the building of consensus around what actions to take, and SDIs were developed in an atmosphere of respect and collaboration. This is in sync with the emerging consensus in consultancy literature in recent years, recommending consultants and clients work together in a dynamic and responsive way, characterised by high levels of trust and respect on both sides (Appelbaum & Steed, 2005).

Reflection on Practice

Choice of Consultancy Model

The process consultancy model proved to be a good fit for the needs of the project and the existing skillset of the team. The team was composed of highly experienced and skilled academics, administrators, and multidisciplinary health professionals who already had the skills to achieve project deliverables but required a structure and focus to be placed upon the process along with a project management component. At times, however, this approach did lead to time lags in the project, due to the consensus-based approach and the difficulty in gathering team members together, owing to conflicting and busy work schedules. However, flexibility of consultancy approach is important in terms of being responsive to the needs of the project at different stages. Occasionally I moved into a more expert consultancy stance (Silacheva,

2019), where I had gained a more in-depth knowledge of the topic; for example, the recommendations on SDI development made to EMG and the NIDMS team following my initial literature review of SDI development for health services.

My Individual Consultancy Style: Moving Beyond the Model

I found that my approach to the consultancy was strengths based and solution focused. I tended to seek to work to each person's strengths in the team and where necessary, subtly backfill for any limitations. I was also open and honest about my own limitations and welcomed other team members' solutions to backfill my own limitations! This type of approach requires self-knowledge and continuous reflective enquiry by the consultant. It fits into the 'reflective practitioner' model of consultant-client interactions (Schön, 1987), whereby both sides have knowledge and skills related to problem solving, with a balanced power relationship based on regular communication (Nikolova & Devinney, 2012). Client and consultant work to co-create outcomes of value (Becker et al., 2015).

Fostering a Culture of 'Psychological Safety'

A significant new project such as setting up the NIDMS can generate feelings of anxiety in team members, which can reduce their ability to tolerate uncertainty and ambiguity (West, 2000). The term 'psychological safety' has been used to explain the concept of people feeling comfortable with taking creative risks and asking for help and feedback within the workplace (Edmondson, 2002). Research in health service teams has found that the crucial elements of fostering psychological safety within a team include: the belief that the team is safe to take interpersonal risks (such as asking for help or feedback, suggesting new ideas), and team members feeling able to admit to mistakes and to give and receive constructive feedback on performance, along with a more relational than transactional style of interacting (Edmondson, 2002). Creativity is enhanced when team members feel safe to suggest ideas without fear of criticism (Collina, 2021). Psychological safety within a team both arises from, and creates a high level of, trust within team members, forming a virtuous circle. The core team NIDMS members had an already established high level of psychological safety and trust and so it was important that I respect and support this on entering the team.

Supporting and promoting psychological safety within teams in order to enhance relationships, confidence, and creativity has always been a strong focus in my clinical work, and I continued to support the existing culture within NIDMS team. This approach of supporting psychological safety within a consultancy role requires patience and emotional intelligence to meet each team member 'where they are' rather than trying to fit people into predefined boxes. It requires open-mindedness and curiosity about people's skills and a tolerance for ambiguity, particularly at the start of the process, when relationships are evolving. It also requires a lack of defensiveness and confidence on the part of the consultant. The consultant needs to be open to correction and feedback and to welcome ideas of a better way of doing things. It is an approach that requires continuous self-reflection and a sense of humble and appreciative enquiry (Gordon, 2008; Mohr & Watkins, 2002; Watkins et al., 2011).

Challenges

The Covid-19 pandemic posed unique challenges to this project as it meant that in-person meetings were not possible. I found that I had to be responsive and flexible in meeting these challenges to trust- and relationship-building, interviewing, and overall communications. This change in scope led to some limitations in the project. The first limitation was a slightly lessened ability to communicate with people with intellectual disability in an engaging and imaginative way. The second limitation was the necessary inclusion of more able rather than less able people with intellectual disability in the focus groups due to the meetings being online in nature. There was also a longer time span in undertaking engagement with all stakeholders due to adaptation to and use of remote technologies and processes.

The Patient Voice at the Heart of Service Development and Delivery

The model of co-production in healthcare services design presented in this chapter proved to be a very positive experience, with optimal buy-in from all stakeholders during the process, despite the challenge posed by ever-evolving pandemic restrictions on in-person engagement. Historically, people with an intellectual disability have encountered additional marginalisation and inequalities in many areas of life, including access to general and specialist health service provision. This project proves that many people with intellectual disability can and will take the opportunity to advocate for themselves in terms of what they want from a health service. It also shows the ability of people with intellectual disability, even those living with early stage dementia, to adapt to new technologies and to meaningfully contribute to an online interview with the aid of accessible materials and appropriate preparation and supports.

People with intellectual disability are capable of engaging in PPI and meaningful co-production in the design of their healthcare services. Inclusive engagement of these stakeholders is aligned with the disability rights movement of 'nothing about us without us' (Scotch, 2009) and proves that people with intellectual disability can and must be consulted in any healthcare initiatives that concern them.

Final Reflections on Practice

Reflecting on practice involves higher-order thinking on three elements of the experience: content reflection (an analysis of the situation/presenting issue), process reflection (evaluating what strategies to use and the effectiveness of those chosen), and premise reflection (reflecting on the impact of practitioners' own assumptions on their approach to the situation and why the situation exists) (Mezirow, 1990). Premise reflection can often be the most difficult aspect of reflecting on practice as it involves an ability to recognise one's own biases and assumptions and an ability to take a wider focus regarding the reason the situation exists, beyond the immediate presenting issue (Plack & Greenberg, 2005). Reflecting on practice is an essential step in developing critical thinking and new perspectives and approaches to ongoing practice (Plack & Greenberg).

Reflecting back on my own input into this project through the consultancy lens of this chapter, I drew on many of the consultancy skills that I had developed through my training and clinical practice as a health psychologist. These were ideally suited to working with an expert team within a health services context, comprising a pre-existing good knowledge of Irish health services delivery and many years of clinical experience in working with people with intellectual disability and their families, including those living with dementia. This enabled me to analyse the presenting issues quickly and with confidence, and to present as a credible member of the core team. I feel that I was able to choose correct interpersonal approaches with other team members, respecting their pre-existing expertise and experience. I was able to demonstrate my ability to 'add value' to the team with the addition of my health psychology skillset. I strove always to be open-minded in my approach in order to minimise the effect of any bias or assumptions on my behalf that might interfere with the working of the team.

My experience in this process was aided by the team itself being very professional and dedicated and having a strong ethos of inclusion and PPI engagement underpinning all of their work. I found it to be a very positive and enriching experience to work within this project supporting the development of SDIs for a new memory service dedicated to the needs of those ageing with intellectual disability and dementia.

Top Tips

1. Develop accessible engagement materials and protocols to maximise understanding and participation by all stakeholders.
2. As a health psychology consultant, be clear on the overall consultancy approach you are using and respect the existing expertise, skillset, and dynamics of the team.
3. Remain fluid and dynamic in your approach to unexpected challenges.
4. Embed a PPI approach when working within a health services consultancy context.

Acknowledgments With thanks to Professor Sean Kennelly, Clinical Director, and Professor Mary McCarron, Executive Director, NIDMS, for their vision and support throughout the project. Thanks to the NIDMS team members and to June O'Reilly and Gavin Dann, TCAID. Finally, a special thanks to the people ageing with intellectual disability and their families and staff for advising and collaborating on the project.

Competing Interests The authors are unaware of any competing interests relating to this chapter.

References

Appelbaum, S. H., & Steed, A. J. (2005). The critical success factors in the client-consulting relationship. *Journal of Management Development, 24*(1), 68–93.

Becker, S. V., Aromaa, E., & Eriksson, P. (2015). Client-consultant interaction: The dynamics of and conflicts in value co-creation and co-destruction. *International Journal of Services Technology and Management, 21*(1–3), 40–54.

Carucci, R. A., & Tetenbaum, T. J. (2000). *The value-creating consultant: How to build and sustain lasting client relationships.* .
Clarke, H. (2011). Learning disabilities—Calling more health psychologists. *Psychologist, 24*(7), 540–543.
Collina, L. (2021). What are the implications of virtualisation for building trust during the management consultancy lifecycle? *Management Consulting Journal, 4*(2), 82–101.
Corbett, T. (2013). Health psychology in the UK and Ireland. *European Health Psychologist, 15*(4), 82–89.
De França Bram, J. M., Talib, L. L., Joaquim, H. P. G., Carvalho, C. L., Gattaz, W. F., & Forlenza, O. V. (2019). Alzheimer's disease-related biomarkers in aging adults with Down syndrome: Systematic review. *Current Psychiatry Research and Reviews, 15*(1), 49–57. https://doi.org/10.2174/1573400515666190122152855
Department of Health. (2014). *The Irish National Dementia Strategy*. Department of Health.
Dolan, E., Lane, J., Hillis, G., & Delanty, N. (2021). Changing trends in life expectancy in intellectual disability over time. *Irish Medical Journal, 112*(9), 1006–1010.
Donabedian, A. (1988). The quality of care: How can it be assessed? *Journal of the American Medical Association, 260*(12), 1743–1748.
Donabedian, A. (2002). *An introduction to quality assurance in health care*. Oxford University Press.
Edmondson, A. C. (2002). *Managing the risk of learning: Psychological safety in work teams*. Division of Research, Harvard Business School Cambridge, MA.
Elwyn, G., Nelson, E., Hager, A., & Price, A. (2020). Coproduction: When users define quality. *BMJ Quality & Safety, 29*(9), 711–716.
Fortea, J., Vilaplana, E., Carmona-Iragui, M., Benejam, B., Videla, L., Barroeta, I., Fernández, S., Altuna, M., Pegueroles, J., & Montal, V. (2020). Clinical and biomarker changes of Alzheimer's disease in adults with Down syndrome: A cross-sectional study. *The Lancet, 395*(10242), 1988–1997.
García-Domínguez, L., Navas, P., Verdugo, M. Á., & Arias, V. B. (2020). Chronic health conditions in aging individuals with intellectual disabilities. *International Journal of Environmental Research and Public Health, 17*(9), 3126.
Gordon, S. (2008). Appreciative inquiry coaching. *International Coaching Psychology Review, 3*(1), 17–29.
Health Service Executive Research and Development. (2021). *Knowledge translation, dissemination, and impact: A practical guide for researchers. Guide No 8: Patient and public involvement in HSE Research*. Health Service Executive Research and Development. https://hseresearch.ie/wp-content/uploads/2021/12/Guide-no-8-Patient-and-Public-Involvement-in-HSE-Research.pdf
Hevey, D., & Hickey, A. (2013). Health psychology in Ireland: A healthy prognosis. *The Irish Journal of Psychology, 34*(3–4), 147–155.

Hilton, C. E., & Johnston, L. H. (2017). Health psychology: It's not what you do, it's the way that you do it. *Health Psychology Open, 4*(2). https://doi.org/10.1177/2055102917714910

Iulita, M. F., Garzón Chavez, D., Klitgaard Christensen, M., et al. (2022). Association of Alzheimer disease with life expectancy in people with down syndrome. *JAMA Network Open, 5*(5), e2212910. https://doi.org/10.1001/jamanetworkopen.2022.12910

Lennox, N., Van Driel, M. L., & van Dooren, K. (2015). Supporting primary healthcare professionals to care for people with intellectual disability: A research agenda. *Journal of Applied Research in Intellectual Disabilities, 28*(1), 33–42. https://onlinelibrary.wiley.com/doi/abs/10.1111/jar.12132

Maister, D. H., Green, C. H., & Galford, R. M. (2000). What is a trusted advisor? *Consulting to Management, 11*(3), 36–41.

Mayer, R. C., Davis, J. H., & Schoorman, F. D. (1995). An integrative model of organizational trust. *Academy of Management Review, 20*(3), 709–734.

McCarron, M., Swinburne, J., Burke, E., McGlinchey, E., Carroll, R., & McCallion, P. (2013). Patterns of multimorbidity in an older population of persons with an intellectual disability: Results from the intellectual disability supplement to the Irish longitudinal study on aging (IDS-TILDA). *Research in Developmental Disabilities, 34*, 521–527. https://doi.org/10.1016/j.ridd.2012.07.029

McCarron, M., Haigh, M., McCallion, P., Carroll, R., Burke, E., McGlinchey, E., O'Donovan, M., McCausland, D. & Sheerin, F. (2017). Health, wellbeing and social inclusion: Ageing with an intellectual disability in Ireland. *Evidence from the first ten years of The Intellectual Disability Supplement to The Irish Longitudinal Study on Ageing (IDS-TILDA).*

McCausland, D., McCarron, M., & McCallion, P. (2023). Use of technology by older adults with an intellectual disability in Ireland to support health, wellbeing and social inclusion during the COVID 19 pandemic. *British Journal of Learning Disabilities, 51*(2), 175–190.

Mezirow, J. (1990). *Fostering critical reflection in adulthood.* Jossey-Bass Publishers San Francisco.

Mohr, B. J., & Watkins, J. M. (2002). The essentials of appreciative inquiry. *A Roadmap for Creating Positive Futures.*

Nees, D. B., & Greiner, L. E. (1985). Seeing behind the look-alike management consultants. *Organizational Dynamics, 13*(3), 68–79.

Newton, R. (2019). *The management consultant.* Pearson UK.

Nikolova & Devinney. (2012). *The nature of client-consultant interaction: A critical review.* Oxford University Press.

Nikolova, N., Möllering, G., & Reihlen, M. (2015). Trusting as a 'leap of faith': Trust-building practices in client–consultant relationships. *Scandinavian Journal of Management, 31*(2), 232–245.

Ocloo, J., Garfield, S., Franklin, B. D., & Dawson, S. (2021). Exploring the theory, barriers and enablers for patient and public involvement across health, social care

and patient safety: A systematic review of reviews. *Health Research Policy and Systems, 19*, 1–21.
Plack, M. M., & Greenberg, L. (2005). The reflective practitioner: Reaching for excellence in practice. *Pediatrics, 116*(6), 1546–1552.
Psychological Society of Ireland. (2020). *Guidelines on use of online or telephone therapy*. Psychological Society of Ireland. Retrieved May 29, 2023, from https://www.psychologicalsociety.ie/source/PSI%20Guidelines%20on%20use%20of%20Online%20Therapy.pdf
Sacks, R. L. M. (2016). Developing and using consultancy skills. In M. E. Loon (Ed.), *Professional practice in learning and development: How to design and deliver plans for the workplace* (pp. 151–206). Kogan Page.
Schaffer, R. H. (2002). High-impact consulting: Achieving extraordinary results. *Consulting to Management, 13*(2), 12.
Schein, E. H. (1990). Organizational culture: What it is and how to change it. In *Human resource management in international firms: Change, globalization, innovation* (pp. 56–82). Springer.
Schön, D. A. (1987). *Educating the reflective practitioner: Toward a new design for teaching and learning in the professions*. Jossey-Bass.
Scotch, R. K. (2009). "Nothing about us without us": Disability rights in America. *OAH Magazine of History, 23*(3), 17–22.
Sheehan, R., Sinai, A., Bass, N., Blatchford, P., Bohnen, I., Bonell, S., Courtenay, K., Hassiotis, A., Markar, T., McCarthy, J., Mukherji, K., Naeem, A., Paschos, D., Perez-Achiaga, N., Sharma, V., Thomas, D., Walker, Z., & Strydom, A. (2015). Dementia diagnostic criteria in Down syndrome. *International Journal of Geriatric Psychiatry, 30*(8), 857–863. https://doi.org/10.1002/gps.4228
Sheerin, F., Fleming, S., Burke, E., Byrne, K., Cleary, M., Doyle, C., & Keenan, P. (2022). Exploring mental health issues in people with an intellectual disability. *Learning Disability Practice, 25*(4), e1999.
Silacheva, M. (2019). Exploring skills and competencies for consultants. *Management Consulting Journal, 2*(2), 35–42.
Strydom, A., Dodd, K., Uchendu, N., & Wilson, S. (2020). *Dementia and other disorders associated with ageing in people with intellectual disability*. Oxford University Press.
Waldman, A. E. (2018). Safe social spaces. *Washington University Law Review, 96*, 1537.
Watkins, J. M., Mohr, B. J., & Kelly, R. (2011). *Appreciative inquiry: Change at the speed of imagination*. John Wiley & Sons.
West, M. A. (2000). Reflexivity, revolution and innovation in work teams. In *Product development teams* (pp. 1–29). Jai Press.
Wissing, M. B. G., Fokkens, A. S., Dijkstra, R., Hobbelen, J. S. M., Van Der Putten, A. A. J., De Deyn, P. P., Waninge, A., & Dekker, A. D. (2022). Dementia in people with severe/profound intellectual (and multiple) disabilities: Practice-based observations of symptoms. *Journal of Mental Health Research in Intellectual Disabilities*, 1–30. https://doi.org/10.1080/19315864.2022.2061092

20

Consultant-Client Relationships: Group Intervention for Post-bariatric Surgery Patients

Gillian Smith

Introduction

This case study describes a consultancy project carried out in the Clinical Health Psychology department of a United Kingdom (UK) National Health Service (NHS) Trust, hereafter referred to as the Trust. The aim of the project was to develop an evidence-based intervention to improve motivation, confidence, and self-efficacy in post-bariatric surgery patients in relation to adherence to dietary regimes and behavioural goals. Following delivery and evaluation of a bespoke teaching programme, I carried out a separate evaluation of the existing Bariatric Surgery Support Group (BSSG) to assess patient perceived effectiveness of the group and to highlight any unmet needs. The consultancy took place over a nine-month period. An account of processes involved in the case study will be followed by an in-depth focus on building and maintaining relationships with the client and key stakeholders. Finally, I will reflect on the consultancy and my learning from it.

G. Smith (✉)
Healthy You Ltd, Huddersfield, UK
e-mail: gill@healthyyoultd.co.uk

R. Brady et al. (eds.), *The Palgrave Handbook of Consultancy in Health Psychology*,
https://doi.org/10.1007/978-3-031-94529-8_20

The Case Study

Conducting Enquiry

In 2016, as a trainee health psychologist, I was invited by a member of the Clinical Health Psychology Department at the Trust to discuss a potential consultancy project. This would be my first formal experience of providing consultancy. The invitation led to a face-to-face meeting with a consultant clinical psychologist working in the complex eating department to explore ideas on how to improve aspects of their post-bariatric surgery services. During this meeting, it was clear there was no specific project in mind. Nor was the client aware of how a health psychology approach might be helpful. I gave a brief overview of the competencies required in health psychology and explored with the client how these competencies might help in general in a clinical health psychology service by giving examples. In order to understand how I might help with specific issues in the complex eating service, I asked about the bariatric surgery pathway and what might benefit from change. The client identified a specific group of patients who, two years after their bariatric surgery, were struggling to avoid unwanted weight gain. The client was keen to know if and how I might help with this group.

Seeking information and asking questions at the beginning and throughout consultancy work is paramount to its success (Saks & Loon, 2016). Through asking further questions, I learned how the department functioned within the Trust and also, about the existence of a patient support group, the bariatric surgery support group (BSSG). The BSSG was originally set up by the Trust to provide opportunity for pre- and post-operative patients to meet and share experiences and information about their weight loss journey. The group, which was run by patients and facilitated by a dietitian, held regular meetings across three Trust sites. The BSSG was regarded by members of the complex eating department multidisciplinary team (MDT) as being popular, with many patients continuing to attend two years post-surgery. Attendance at the BSSG meetings was encouraged by the MDT.

Following that first meeting, and prior to making a proposal, I reviewed the intervention literature on outcomes for bariatric surgery patients. This revealed that post-bariatric patients were a psychologically vulnerable client group requiring significant behaviour change support and improved coping skills (Ratcliffe et al., 2014). Psychological issues impacting on motivation for this group of patients had been identified as low self-esteem, low self-efficacy, and negative self-stigmatisation (Lazzerretti et al., 2015). The evidence suggested that improving psychological functioning is associated with higher success rates in interventions for weight loss. Consequently, it has been suggested that inclusion of interventions that address psychological factors may improve weight loss outcomes (Kalarchian & Marcus, 2015). Despite this evidence, psychosocial interventions are not common in bariatric surgery programmes (White et al., 2010).

Following the literature review, I suggested a programme of evidence-based teaching sessions to address the psychological issues identified in the research. The client expressed interest in exploring this further. After I described my background in nursing and my expertise in health psychology teaching and group work, the client invited me to draw up a proposal for the intervention which outlined the aims and objectives, action plan, project time frame, and plans for evaluation, which would form the basis of a contract.

Negotiation and Contracting

The negotiation and contracting stage of consultancy work relates to the iterative process of negotiating the contract and planning the work (Earll & Bath, 2004). In this case, it involved discussion of a written proposal with the client. We agreed on a programme of group sessions as the key intervention for the project which I would design and implement. We agreed a timeline of six months based on my estimate of the time needed. Following agreement on the proposal, I prepared a contract documenting the finer details of the project and providing more clarity about roles and expectations of both client and myself as advised by Block (2011). The client read, agreed, and signed the contract in my presence. I did not ask for a fee for this work and I will reflect on the issue of *pro bono* work later in the chapter.

Many factors influence the feasibility of a project, including the anticipated timeframe, access to information, skills and experience of the consultant, and support of the client (Crowther & Lancaster, 2008). The initial timeframe was extended for two reasons: (1) due to staff shortages there was a delay in receiving an honorary contract from the Trust which was needed to enable me to work with patients; (2) following completion of the group intervention, additional work to assess the effectiveness of the BSSG was commissioned by the client. This resulted in a revised contract.

The consultancy literature highlights the importance of understanding organisational context and clarifying desired outcomes when assessing consultancy requests from clients (e.g., Martinez et al., 2016). To understand more about the weight management services and the BSSG, I attended a departmental MDT meeting which discussed patients' physical and psychological readiness for surgery. I also attended a clinician-led seminar for prospective bariatric surgery patients focusing on preparedness for surgery, including managing expectations. Following this, in collaboration with the client and the dietitian, I planned two introductory meetings with the BSSG to explore their needs. At the meetings, I presented on emotional eating which had been highlighted as problematic for bariatric surgery patients in the literature review. Emotional eating has been described as a tendency to eat in response to stressful or negative emotions and has been associated with both pre- and post- bariatric surgery patients (Ames et al., 2022). I provided information about the proposed programme of sessions which was called 'Time for Change' and I invited patients to complete evaluation forms which asked about interest in the programme, and requested suggestions for topics which they would wish to explore. Eight patients expressed interest in attending the sessions although only seven did so.

Planning and Implementation

In the programme there would be emphasis on individual weekly action-focussed goal setting and group support, shown to be effective with post-operative bariatric surgery patients (Weineland et al., 2011). I used an Acceptance and Commitment Therapy (ACT) (Hayes, 2004) approach, which had been used successfully with post-bariatric patients in the Weineland interventional study. ACT is an evidence-based 'third wave' behavioural therapy that uses strategies that focus on increasing valued actions rather than reducing 'problem' behaviour, and on a mindful approach of 'being in the moment' (Weineland et al.). These strategies have been found to be effective in addressing psychological issues commonly encountered by bariatric surgery patients before and after surgery (Lillis et al., 2009; Forman et al., 2009). I delivered five group sessions in the education centre of the Trust details of which can be seen in Table 20.1. The themes for each session were related to the main ACT principles and how they applied to the group objectives: mindfulness, emotional eating, self-esteem, body image, and barriers to progress.

During the first session, issues of confidentiality were discussed, and the patients signed a document indicating agreement to participate by way of consent. The additional work to evaluate the effectiveness of, and patient satisfaction with, the BSSG which was commissioned after the group intervention is described in the following section.

Table 20.1 Outline of group sessions

Session	Aims	Exercise samples/ handouts	Application to bariatric surgery (BS)
Session 1 Overview of emotional eating and presentation of ACT model	• Individual behavioural assessment • Socialisation into programme • Set weekly/final goals	• External eating quiz • Willingness and action plan[a] • Bull's eye[a]	• Awareness of the function of emotional eating • Learning to discriminate between behaviours and where they are leading
Session 2 Mindfulness and Defusion	• Goal progress/set weekly goal • Introduction to core values • Introduction to mindfulness	• Mindfulness exercise[a] • Magic Wand metaphor[a] • Hands as Thoughts metaphor[a]	• Awareness of how negative feelings interfere with healthy behaviours
Session 3 Self-esteem	• Goal progress/set weekly goal • Reminder of goals and underlying issues	• Drop Anchor mindfulness exercise[a] • Simple Ways to Get Present handout[a] • Self-esteem Booklet: Helpful Facts • 10 Positive Things About Myself exercise	• Considering the importance of self-esteem in motivating goal achievement
Session 4 Barriers to success ... moving forwards	• Goal progress/set weekly goals • Problem-solving • Establishing core values	• Participant-led mindfulness exercise • Choice Point activity[a] • Writing exercise: imagine you are 80 years old[a]	• Examining barriers to progress such as negative feelings and rules about the body
Session 5 Self-concept and body image Acceptance and willingness	• Goal progress • Explore self-identify and relationships with body image	• Hero mindfulness exercise	• Committing to a direction of self-compassion, addressing previous patterns of self-criticism • Preparing for barriers to change

[a] Exercises and handouts are from Harris (2009)

Evaluation

A key process in consultancy is evaluation of impact. This is because best practice in consultancy is to build in continuous evaluation from the beginning of a consultancy project (Brady & Varkonyi-Sepp, 2025; see Chap. 3). To evaluate the group sessions, I used three measures used in the Weineland (2011) study to assess eating behaviour, psychological flexibility, and self-efficacy pre- and post-intervention (within a week of the final session). The measures, which were linked to the consultancy aims, were: The Acceptance and Action Questionnaire for Weight (AAQ-W) (Lillis & Hayes, 2007); The General Self Efficacy Scale (Schwarzer & Jerusalem, 1995); The Eating Disorder Examination Questionnaire (EDE-Q) (Fairburn & Beglin, 1994). All patients reported increased self-efficacy relating to achieving their behavioural goals following the intervention. The EDE-Q scores indicated that eating, weight, and body image concerns were lower than pre-intervention. AAQ-W scores were lower for six of the participants suggesting less experiential avoidance and more psychological flexibility, which is the desired outcome following an ACT programme.

In addition, I used a standardised Trust form to gather 'satisfaction' feedback from the patients who participated in the teaching programme, although I adapted the form to correspond to the programme objectives. On a 5-point Likert scale (1 = poor, 5 = excellent), all seven patients attending rated their experience of the programme and of the facilitator as excellent. Patients also agreed the programme had helped them meet their individual weekly behavioural goals and that their life was better after the programme than before. Following completion of the taught programme, and with the client's agreement, I also used a brief patient satisfaction questionnaire to assess if patient needs were being met in the monthly BSSG meetings. This followed comments raised by two members of the group regarding some intra-group hostility which they had experienced. In consultation with the client and the dietitian, and after reviewing some existing satisfaction questionnaires, I designed a questionnaire comprising nine questions and using a 5-point Likert scale and free text options for responses. The questionnaire focused on satisfaction with support pre- and post-surgery, the content of the meetings, and the welcoming atmosphere of the group. Twenty-eight completed forms were returned with results indicating high levels of satisfaction with the BSSG, with seventy-five percent of patients strongly agreeing that their needs were being met by attending the meetings. Two patients indicated dissatisfaction with the organisation and structure of the meetings in their feedback and suggestions for improvement were to include more specialist talks.

On completion of the project, I delivered a written report describing the processes and outcomes, what I had learned, and recommendations for practice. The report was shared with the departmental team. Overall, the client was pleased with the outcomes of the consultancy work and acknowledged the recommendations, including the cost implication of conducting a similar type of group intervention delivered by health psychology trainees in the future. Following this, I was invited to present the work to the clinical and health psychology department at the next Trust governance meeting. I prepared a short presentation summarising the project and recommendations which was followed by questions and comments, all of which were positive and indicated interest in the project. To obtain client feedback on my performance I used a consultancy evaluation form which assessed professional competency, knowledge, and skills; the feedback indicated 'excellent' in all areas. The reliability and validity of feedback forms used will form part of my reflections in the final section.

Building and Maintaining Collaborative Relationships

Relationships with Whom?

In consultancy it is important to be clear about who we will be working with in addition to the client, and how their roles might impact the consultancy outcomes. For example, Applebaum and Steed (2005) remind us that different types of clients may well have different needs, expectations, and levels of participation in the consultancy. In this project, the overall approach with the client and main stakeholders was a collaborative one. I identified what Schein (1999) categorises as the 'contact client', the person with whom I contracted; in this project the contact client was the consultant clinical psychologist. I also considered that other stakeholders would include the clinical health psychology team in the Trust, and the patients participating in the project. The clinical health psychology team would be ultimately responsible for implementing any changes outlined in the report recommendations. According to Schein's client categories, the patients in this project were 'unwitting' as they were unaware of their involvement in a consultancy project, even though they would be the main beneficiaries. Post-surgical bariatric patients at the Trust could fit Schein's category of 'ultimate clients' since the group sessions, if successful, could have wider consequences for the Trust's service improvement agenda. In this project, the dietician was a key stakeholder due to her close involvement with the BSSG and MDT meetings. It was, therefore, important to establish a collaborative relationship with her, to value her knowledge and input, and to include her in key programme communication.

Trust

Fostering a good and collaborative relationship with client and stakeholders in a consultancy project is paramount and is discussed extensively within the literature (e.g., Fullerton & West, 1996). For example, as well as the consultant demonstrating a real understanding of contextual issues at enquiry stage, success factors for an ideal client-consultant relationship include an authentic partnership based on clear communication, clear objectives, and expectations, and trust (Solomson, 2012). Being trusted as a consultant can influence effective communication throughout the project (Saks & Loon, 2016). This view is consistent with Schein's (1990) *process consultancy model* which highlights the importance of building a strong relationship and developing trust between client and consultant. In the process consultancy model, the relationship is collaborative throughout the project and the client and consultant learn from and support one another (Saks & Loon, 2016). This approach best describes the relationship between me and the client for this project.

Relationship with the Client and Stakeholders

Clear communication with the client could also be described as a fundamental precursor to establishing trust. A communication strategy from the beginning of the consultancy project is helpful in ensuring all communication is timely, consistent, and impactful, and a check list can help with this (Applebaum & Steed, 2005). In the NHS England stakeholder analysis document (NHS England, n.d.), matrix tables which identify key stakeholders, their roles, and their readiness for change are considered useful tools to use in the consultancy process. Although I did not undertake a formal stakeholder analysis, in hindsight it would have been helpful. I was, however, clear about who I would be communicating with. Since my main contacts were the client and the dietician, I considered frequency of communication and what format would work best for them. At the second face-to-face meeting with the client, following discussion of the proposal and contract, we agreed that we would communicate mainly by email with interim face-to-face meetings to be arranged at significant intervals during the project; for example, the meetings would follow completion of the group programme sessions, and would take place after BSSG evaluation, and after the final report. Similarly, I agreed with the dietician to communicate mainly by email during the course of the consultancy project. We also agreed that if there were any delays in the client or dietician responding, or if situations arose which were not expected or which needed further clarification, it would be acceptable to communicate by text or phone.

During the first meeting with the client, in exploring the nature of the work in the complex eating department, and given the uncertainty about project specifics, I shared my health psychology experience and the skills I could bring to the consultancy project. By doing so, I wanted to demonstrate my potential for contributing to improving outcomes for patients. For example, the client was interested to learn about a teaching session I had carried out with a weight management service user support group in the community on the impact of stress on eating behaviour. She was also interested to learn about my previous nursing and management experience in the NHS. At this stage of the consultancy project, the level of interest by the client indicated confidence in my expertise and a willingness to consider a proposal to work with the BSSG patients, whom she described as a vulnerable group of adults. This felt to be a reassuring start to this collaborative process.

Both sides of the consultant-client relationship are important when it comes to establishing and maintaining trust. From a consultant's perspective, the client must be able to take responsibility for following through on agreements made during the contracting and planning phase (Applebaum & Steed, 2005). It is also helpful if the client is committed to remaining engaged with the project generally by responding to communication and being willing to accept changes recommended by the consultant. Fundamentally, the client should have the organisational leverage to do so in terms of following through on agreements (Fullerton & West, 1996). For this consultancy project, there was a protracted period between the first and second meeting with the client, owing to the client's other work commitments, which impacted on delays in response to my emails. However, I felt comfortable enough to prompt the client from time to time and she responded by text message. During this period, I was conscious of the need to balance my priority to secure a contract for the consultancy work with the need to avoid pushing too hard when the client had more pressing priorities. Some of the delays were outside the client's control and involved administrative issues in securing an honorary contract which would allow me to work as an external consultant within the Trust supporting governance requirements such as data protection and patient confidentiality. The client and I copied each other into email correspondence as a way of documenting active engagement with the consultancy process and of maintaining consistent communication.

Relationship with Other Stakeholders

For this project, while the planned intervention was discussed and agreed mainly with the client, the dietician member of the MDT was a key stakeholder. I had learned through enquiry that her role was central to the BSSG because of involvement in the patients' bariatric surgery pathway, and her facilitation of the group meetings. I wanted to consider how the dietician might feel about and react to the proposed project; this is described below. I was keen to know her thoughts and opinions and saw this as a first step in building a successful relationship with the dietitian.

Saks and Loon (2016) remind us how vital it is to keep our key stakeholders involved in the project throughout. The initial contact with the dietician was made by phone and was an opportunity to explain the background to the project, the proposal itself, and the importance of her involvement. I wanted to acknowledge the value of her role from the outset to avoid causing any feelings of exclusion. I did this by involving her in the arrangement of the group sessions and by collaborating with her on the questionnaire design for the BSSG evaluation. Together with the client, she suggested two additional questions for inclusion in the patient satisfaction questionnaire. Collaborating on this enabled us to create a questionnaire which would sensitively gather information and ultimately inform the client and dietician, as well as satisfying the consultancy objectives. Other collaboration with the dietitian included planning for practicalities regarding venue and resources, such as access to technical equipment which was needed for the group sessions. We agreed that the sessions should be held on the Trust site and the dietician booked the venue and organised the resources we had agreed would be required. She also helped to arrange temporary passwords to enable me to sign-in to the hospital computer system.

During implementation of the teaching programme, I wanted to incorporate a motivational interviewing (MI) approach (Rollnick & Miller, 1995) in communication with the patients. MI is a non-judgemental, non-directive counselling approach developed by psychologists which is widely used for eliciting behaviour change. Although commonly used in face-to-face settings,

MI can be used successfully in small group settings where the same principles apply. The four processes used involve engaging the group, evoking member perspectives, broadening perspectives and building momentum for change and moving into action (Wagner & Ingersoll, 2012). For the teaching programme, this meant that as facilitator I would be speaking less and listening more, allowing the group to 'shape and drive itself'. This approach helped to encourage interaction and open reflection within the group. I was conscious of vulnerabilities some members of the group may have, as disclosed by the client, and reminded myself about issues to be aware of when developing and maintaining positive relationships. For instance, working within the professional boundaries required for health psychologists in the UK (British Psychological Society, 2021), it is important to recognise the possibility of power imbalance and to foster a climate of trust and respect (Knapp, 2015). It was possible that the patients in this group invested power in the facilitator's perceived capacity to make a real difference in their lives (Boyd, 1996). It was important therefore to consider this and to manage patient expectations by clear and open communication. It was also possible that all members of the group might feel some power imbalance between each other relating to individual demographics (Chung et al., 2020). With this in mind, I tried to create a welcoming and informal atmosphere at all the meetings, emphasising the importance of confidentiality, and one in which the patients would be more likely to engage and benefit from the programme. The group would need to be a psychologically safe place where patients felt comfortable sharing their stories and interacting with one another. The group was small and the resulting intimacy seemed to enhance group dynamics. At the first session a short mission statement was drawn up highlighting the overall aim of the sessions, the values of respect for one another and the importance of confidentiality within the group.

Boundaries

When considering client relationships within the consultancy process, it is helpful to think about consultant boundaries. As an external consultant, I had an honorary contract to work within the Trust for the duration of the contracted period of consultancy. On one occasion the organisational boundaries became a little blurred between me and the project stakeholders. This relates to the evaluation of the BSSG group and the plan to promote the patient satisfaction questionnaire to members of the group. Although the BSSG groups were linked to the Trust's complex eating department via the dietician who helped facilitate meetings, they were independently run by the patients themselves. To respect the independence of the group, rather than my contacting them directly, the client and dietician both recommended a sensitive and ethical approach by contacting the BSSG patient lead directly to request permission to attend a meeting together with the dietician and to circulate questionnaires.

Overall, this section has examined some key factors which help to build and maintain healthy collaborative relationships in the consultancy process. The examples shared of my own experience highlight how this is often complex and requires a sensitive response to ensure the consultancy outcomes are not compromised.

Reflection

The reflective process involves challenging and developing our existing professional knowledge base and avoiding past mistakes. It also clarifies our thinking and maximises our opportunities for learning (Bolton, 2014); Bolton suggests the need to be a critical observer of oneself, considering the limits of our knowledge and capabilities; our values, and any prejudices we may implicitly hold. This can be hard to do and can involve some personal discomfort as we expose our own vulnerabilities as professionals, acknowledging our limitations in knowledge and competence. This aligns with the guidance laid out in the British Psychological Society's Code of Ethics which includes working within the boundaries of our knowledge and skills (British Psychological Society, 2021).

For this consultancy project I found Schön's (1983) reflective practice model particularly useful and one which I still value in my work today. Schön considers the importance of *reflection in practice/action* and *reflection on practice/action* (Schön, 1983); reflection *in* action involves reflecting on something while it is happening, whereas reflection *on* action is reflecting on something after it has happened. From a practitioner perspective, this suggests that the more knowledge and experience we have to draw on, the speedier we can enable this in our actions. This process then facilitates a greater reflective response after an event (Bolton, 2014).

My experience of the consultancy process, which required me to navigate new and uncertain situations, is described by Schön as 'trial and error learning' (Schön, 1987). I used my existing experiential knowledge to problem-solve while dealing with issues (*thinking-in),* following which I was able to reflect later and learn from the associated problems and anxieties I held at the time *(thinking-on)*. Prior to starting out on my health psychology journey, I had longstanding professional experience working in the healthcare sector, in both public and private sector environments. Having prior knowledge of the organisational and hierarchical structure of an NHS Trust, and an understanding of some barriers to progress within an organisation, such as financial and resource limitations, helped my understanding of the contextual background for this project. For example, the client had mentioned at the enquiry stage of the project that additional support for the post-bariatric surgery patients was limited due to inadequate resources and financial input. Indeed, this was a factor I considered when planning the project.

Using an ACT Intervention for the First Time in a Group Setting

Having recently completed training in ACT, I was conscious throughout of conveying confidence in the ACT intervention despite being new to it. I had described the principles of ACT in the first group session, after which I planned to use ACT techniques. For example, I prepared a mindfulness exercise to open subsequent sessions. This was an example of Schön's (1987) trial and error learning, or 'entering a place of not knowing' as outlined in Bolton's work (Bolton, 2014) and was for me *reflection in practice*. I also sought professional supervision throughout the implementation of this intervention.

Managing Complex Psychological Issues in a Group Setting

From the first session of the group programme, discussions revealed some profound psychological issues about self-esteem, which I had not anticipated. These were related to negative body image and its impact on self-esteem. Although as a health professional I had experience of dealing with vulnerable people in a range of situations, I hadn't anticipated the intensity of the feelings of low self-esteem in one member of the group. It caused me to reflect on whether I could have probed more deeply about self-esteem with the client during the initial enquiry. Fortunately, as a trainee health psychologist at the time, I was able to discuss this with my university supervisor, and I also asked for advice from the client, a clinical psychologist, who was aware of the patient's psychological history. In hindsight, I think it would have been prudent to include a formal risk assessment when seeking consent from the programme participants during the first session.

During my reflections at the time, I considered the British Psychological Society (BPS) (2021) and Health and Care Professions Council (HCPC) (2023) guidelines which outline the need to work within the limits of one's knowledge and skills. Although I had experience of working with groups through my work and during my professional training, the group setting felt more intimate, as the group was smaller, and the participants were more vulnerable than I had anticipated. I could see how identifying and seeking appropriate input in advance from MDT members would have enabled me to better anticipate psychological risks and to seek specialist support for individual members of the BSSG group if needed. This is integral to my practice now.

Working Pro Bono

Pro bono work is defined as work provided voluntarily and without payment by a professional (Goupil & Kinsinger, 2020). My trainee status at the time of the consultancy project meant that I felt it was inappropriate to charge remuneration fees for the work, although I accept that others might not share this view. It was important to make the pro bono aspect of the work clear during enquiry and to include it within the contract details. Having worked on other consultancy projects since then, I have considered the value of the time and expertise usually expended in a period of consultancy work. Indeed, my reflections on pro bono work have highlighted how it could compromise the perceived professional value of one's work in some situations. In my view there are benefits to pro-bono work; in addition to the altruistic element, whereby there is a sense of being helpful and useful to others, pro bono work can help in marketing your services and creating a favourable impression. On the other hand, one needs to consider the personal demands of working pro bono as well as the potential to perpetuate exclusion of people who cannot afford to offer services on this basis from opportunities to develop their practice (Zilvinskis et al., 2023).

What Professional Skills, Knowledge, and Expertise Did I Bring?

In my prior experience in healthcare, including management roles, I had learned to think on my feet to work under pressure and to deadlines. I was also fortunate to have worked alongside many clinicians and health care professionals in a collaborative way, for example, in my nursing career and later as a multidisciplinary team co-ordinator and care and well-being manager in the private sector. These experiences proved to be especially helpful when undertaking this first consultancy project. As well, by this stage in my professional training, I was already accumulating and consolidating specific skills and knowledge which were to define all my future professional roles. These skills included planning and delivering teaching and behaviour change sessions to individuals and groups, undertaking training and becoming an ACT practitioner, and using my knowledge of research skills to carry out literature reviews and evaluations.

What Difference Did This Consultancy Work Make to the Client and Stakeholders?

Evaluating the impact of the project and providing feedback to the client and stakeholders is a vital part of the consultancy process. Sharing feedback provides an opportunity to give evidence in support of the project outcomes by outlining what has been learned, what still needs to be learned, and by making recommendations to facilitate any required changes (Saks & Loon, 2016). Conversely, the client and stakeholders should also have opportunity to provide their own feedback as a measure of their satisfaction with the process. Client and stakeholder feedback was reassuring for me in my role as trainee health psychologist and helped to validate my abilities. The feedback confirmed that the project had led to positive change. For example, the patients reported improvements in their lives following the group sessions, and the client felt that she had a better understanding of the BSSG and its needs going forward.

Although it was encouraging to receive positive feedback, I did reflect on the reliability and robustness of the standardised measures used. I was aware that there are a number of factors which might influence feedback, including personal characteristics, individual perception and timing. Literature in this area reminds us that well-designed evaluation tools and self-evaluation should be part of the overall consultancy process (Annan et al., 2013). Although I completed a reflective log throughout the consultancy project period, in hindsight I can see the value in using a validated self-evaluation measure for future projects.

Supervision

Since this was my first formal consultancy project, and I was a BPS Stage 2 trainee health psychologist at the time, supervision was a professional requirement and proved particularly valuable. During supervision I was able to explore the iterative processes involved in consultancy, where each stage informs the next (Earll & Bath, 2004), enabling me to get reassurance that I was on the right track. For example, creating a consultancy contract is important in order to formalise the arrangement between consultant and client. I sought guidance from the consultancy module leader regarding some of the clauses, and also from my professional doctorate peers who had already completed the consultancy competency. Completing the contract made me aware of how it improved my understanding of the consultancy process and the expectations of all parties. It was also helpful to have developed a more concrete project timeline to guide the process.

Summary: What I Learned

I can now look back at this first formal consultancy experience which left me feeling more confident and competent both as a consultant and as a health psychology practitioner. I felt fortunate to have had the opportunity to expand my learning into weight management services and deliver a psychologically informed group intervention for the first time. I also felt pleased to have carried out my first consultancy project for the NHS, an organisation where I had previously been employed for many years and one for which I have a great respect and admiration. Knowing that this was achieved as part of a successful consultancy relationship made the experience even more satisfying. Overall, I was able to identify some key personal strengths in this first experience of consultancy which have been valuable in my consultancy work since then.

Top Tips

1. Make sure you and your client(s) share the same objectives and expectations.
2. Understand the organisational and specialist background in which you practice consultancy.
3. Be prepared to revise your contract if needed.
4. Take time to build and maintain professional and authentic relationships with client(s) and stakeholders.

Competing Interests The author has no competing interests to declare in relation to this chapter.

References

Ames, G. E., Koball, A. M., & Clark, M. M. (2022). Behavioural interventions to attenuate driven overeating and weight regain after bariatric surgery. *Frontiers in Endocrinology, 13*, 934680. https://doi.org/10.3389/fendo.2022.934680

Annan, S. L., Tratnack, S., Rubenstein, C., Metzler-Sawin, E., & Hulton, L. (2013). An integrative review of student evaluations of teaching: Implications for evaluation of nursing faculty. *Journal of Professional Nursing, 29*(5), e10–e24.

Applebaum, S. H., & Steed, A. J. (2005). The critical success factors in the client-consulting relationship. *Journal of Management Development, 24*(1), 68–93.

Block, P. (2011). *Flawless consulting: A guide to getting your expertise used* (3rd ed.). Pfeiffer.

Bolton, G. (2014 [2009]). *Reflective practice 4th edition: Writing and professional development.* Sage.

Boyd, K. K. (1996). Power imbalances and therapy. *Focus, 11*(9), 1–4.

Brady, R., & Varkonyi-Sepp, J. (2025). A framework for consultancy in health psychology. In R. Brady, J. Varkonyi-Sepp, & J. Smith (Eds.), *The Palgrave handbook of consultancy in health psychology*. Palgrave Macmillan.

British Psychological Society. (2021). Code of Ethics and Conduct. https://doi.org/10.53841/bpsrep.2021.inf94

Chung, M. H., Ko, Y., & Kim, J. Y. (2020). Group power structure, inter-subgroup cross-dependency, and work group performance. *Asia Pacific Journal of Management, 37*(1), 297–323.

Crowther, D., & Lancaster, G. (2008). *Research methods: A concise introduction to research in management and business consultancy* (2nd ed.). Elsevier Ltd.

Earll, L., & Bath, J. (2004). Consultancy: What is it, how do you do it, and does it make any difference? In S. Michie & C. Abraham (Eds.), *Health psychology in practice*. Blackwell Publishing.

Fairburn, C. G., & Beglin, S. J. (1994). Assessment of eating disorders: Interview or self-report questionnaire? *International Journal of Eating Disorders, 16*, 363–370.

Forman, E. M., Butryn, M. L., Hoffman, K. L., & Herbert, J. D. (2009). An open trial of an acceptance-based behavioural intervention for weight loss. *Cognitive and Behavioural Practice, 16*(2), 223–235.

Fullerton, J., & West, M. A. (1996). Consultant and client working together? *Journal of Managerial Psychology, 11*(6), 40–49.

Goupil, K., & Kinsinger, F. S. (2020). Pro bono services in 4 health care professions: A discussion of exemplars. *Journal of Chiropractic Humanities, 7*(27), 21–28. https://doi.org/10.1016/j.echu.2020.10.001

Harris, R. (2009). *ACT made simple: An easy-to-read primer on acceptance and commitment therapy*. New Harbinger.

Hayes, S. (2004). Acceptance and commitment therapy, relational frame theory, and the third wave of behavioural and cognitive therapies. *Behaviour Therapy, 35*, 639–665.

Health & Care Professions Council. (2023). *Standards of proficiency: Paramedics.* https://www.hcpc-uk.org/globalassets/standards/standards-of-proficiency/reviewing/paramedics%2D%2D-new-standards.pdf

Kalarchian, M. A., & Marcus, M. D. (2015). Psychosocial interventions pre and post bariatric surgery. *European Eating Disorders Review, 23*(6), 457–462.

Knapp, H. (2015). *Therapeutic communication: Developing professional skills.* Sage Publications Ltd.

Lazzerretti, L., Rotella, F., Pala, L., & Rotella, C. M. (2015). Assessment of psychological predictors of weight loss: How and what for? *World Journal of Psychiatry, 5*(1), 56–67.

Lillis, J., & Hayes, S. C. (2007). Measuring avoidance and inflexibility in weight related problems. *International Journal of Behavioral Consultation and Therapy, 4*(1), 30.

Lillis, J., Hayes, S. C., Bunting, K., & Masuda, A. (2009). Teaching acceptance and mindfulness to improve the lives of the obese: A preliminary test of a theoretical model. *Annals of Behavioural Medicine, 37*(1), 58–69.

Martinez, L. F., Ferreira, A. I., & Can, A. B. (2016). Knowledge transfer in small and medium sized enterprises change processes. *Psychological Reports, 118*(2), 608–625.

NHS England. (n.d.). Stakeholder analysis: Online library of quality service improvement and redesign tools. https://www.england.nhs.uk/wp-content/uploads/2022/02/qsir-stakeholder-analysis.pdf

Ratcliffe, D., Ali, R., Ellison, N., Khatun, M., Poole, J., & Coffey, C. (2014). Bariatric psychology in the UK National Health Service: Input across the patient pathway. *BMC Obesity, 1*(20), 2–7.

Rollnick, S., & Miller, W. (1995). What is motivational interviewing? *Behavioural Cognitive Psychotherapy, 23*, 325–334.

Saks, R., & Loon, M. (2016). Developing and using consultancy skills. In M. Loon (Ed.), *Professional practice in learning and development: How to deliver plans for the workplace.* Kogan Page.

Schein, E. H. (1990). Organizational culture. *American Psychologist, 45*(2), 109–119.

Schein, E. H. (1999). *Process consultation revisited: Building the helping relationship.* Addison-Wesley/Pearson.

Schön, D. A. (1983). *The reflective practitioner: How professionals think in action.* Basic Books.

Schön, D. A. (1987). *Educating the reflective practitioner.* Jossey-Bass.

Schwarzer, R., & Jerusalem, M. (1995). Generalized self-efficacy scale. In I. J. Weinman, S. Wright, & M. Johnston (Eds.), *Measures in health psychology: A user's portfolio. Causal and control beliefs* (pp. 35–37). NFER-NELSON.

Solomson, W. L. (2012). Trust and the client-consultant relationship. *Performance Improvement Quarterly, 25*(3), 53–80.

Wagner, C. C., & Ingersoll, K. S. (2012). *Motivational interviewing in groups.* Guilford Press.

Weineland, S., Arvidsson, D., Kakoulidis, T. P., & Dahl, J. (2011). Acceptance and commitment therapy for bariatric surgery patients, a pilot RCT. *Obesity Research & Clinical Practice, 6*, e21–e30.

White, M. A., Kalarchian, M. A., Masheb, R. M., Marcus, M. D., & Grilo, C. M. (2010). Loss of control over eating predicts outcomes in bariatric surgery patients: A prospective, 24-month follow-up study. *The Journal of Clinical Psychiatry, 70*(2), 10844.

Zilvinskis, J., Kinzie, J., Daday, J., O'Donnell, K., & Zande, C. V. (Eds.). (2023). *Delivering on the promise of high-impact practices: Research and models for achieving equity, fidelity, impact, and scale*. Taylor & Francis.

21

Consultant-Client Relationships: Hearts and Minds - Psychological Consultancy in Cardiac Rehabilitation

Eleanor Whittaker

Introduction

This case study outlines a project undertaken over a period of three years within a community cardiac rehabilitation (CR) service which operates under the umbrella of a specialist cardiothoracic National Health Service (NHS) Trust in the United Kingdom (UK). Behaviour contributes to the cause of much current mortality and morbidity and, therefore, attempts to change behaviour are essential in prevention (Michie & Johnston, 2012). Behaviour change techniques (BCTs) are integral to CR design, aiming to assist patients to improve adherence to health-related behaviours to deliver changes in different modifiable vascular risk factors (Heron et al., 2016). The project aimed to appraise the use of behaviour change techniques within the existing CR service, and how confident healthcare professionals felt to deliver them. I then designed and delivered a training package that aimed to provide a multidisciplinary team of healthcare professionals with the skills to deliver behaviour change interventions as part of their routine work. The training package comprised two sessions, introducing principles in behaviour change and why it was important within CR. The training package was based around Self-Determination Theory (SDT; Ryan & Deci, 2000) which is a theory of

Supplementary Information The online version contains supplementary material available at https://doi.org/10.1007/978-3-031-94529-8_21.

E. Whittaker (✉)
Public Health Team North Yorkshire Council, North Yorkshire, UK
e-mail: eleanor.whittaker@northyorks.gov.uk

R. Brady et al. (eds.), *The Palgrave Handbook of Consultancy in Health Psychology*,
https://doi.org/10.1007/978-3-031-94529-8_21

motivation. Within SDT, there are three basic psychological needs (autonomy, competence, and relatedness), which need to be satisfied to develop more intrinsic forms of motivation. These forms of motivation exist along a continuum from intrinsic motivation (doing something for its inherent enjoyment), to amotivation (a lack or absence of motivation). The training package centred on how healthcare professionals could use SDT principles to satisfy patients' basic psychological needs within CR. To contextualise these psychological needs, I defined them in terms of characteristics of patients we had seen within clinics. Patient characteristics are each assigned a letter in Fig. 21.1. Figures can be found in the supplementary material for this chapter (ESM_21.1). Each of these patient characteristics is then evident within Fig. 21.2, which demonstrates how each of them might be evident within the CR pathway. Once the healthcare professional had diagnosed the patient in terms of these characteristics, Figure 21.3 demonstrates the techniques that could be used to satisfy each of these psychological needs. This was based on systematic review evidence. Further information on the training package can be found in my PhD thesis (Whittaker, 2021).

The outcome of this consultancy project was to develop and deliver a bespoke behaviour change training package for healthcare professionals working in CR. Involving the multidisciplinary team of healthcare professionals was central to the consultancy process. As I will explain later in this chapter, enquiry, in this case attempting to understand the client and the culture of the organisation, acted as a first step in allowing me to understand how to help my client achieve a desired outcome. In this project, enquiry allowed me to understand how the service operated, and how psychological principles and knowledge could be applied to improve practice. This collaborative and integrative approach with the multidisciplinary team as both client and end user was essential for establishing a behaviour change intervention that had real-world significance and influence. To achieve this, I embraced evidence-based practice (Greenhalgh et al., 2014) and practice-based evidence approaches, by ensuring that the work was theoretically grounded, and closely attuned to the needs of those who might use it. Therefore, rather than trying to revolutionise the rehabilitation service by starting from a blank slate, my focus on enquiry and relationship building allowed the client and key stakeholders to agree on the priorities for the project, while being guided by academics with expertise in intervention development and behaviour change.

I led the project as a PhD researcher, supported by a multidisciplinary supervisory team comprising a psychologist, a physiologist, and an epidemiologist who was also the Director of Clinical Trials for the NHS Trust in question. I will briefly describe the health context for the work before describing the case from the initial invitation to completion. I will then, through a consultancy lens, explore how I developed and nurtured key relationships and how these relationships helped to improve the real-world applicability of the project's outcomes. I will then reflect upon my role as a consultant within this project and make recommendations for professionals aiming to conduct similar work in the future, particularly if they are spanning NHS and academia and if they are new to professional practice.

Cardiac Rehabilitation

A nurse-led service, CR is delivered by a multidisciplinary team of healthcare professionals including cardiac nurses, physiotherapists, exercise physiologists, and healthcare assistants. CR is defined as:

> The coordinated sum of activities required to influence favourably the underlying cause of cardiovascular disease, as well as to provide the best possible physical, mental and social conditions, so that the patients may, by their own efforts, preserve or resume optimal functioning in their community and through improved health behaviour, slow or reverse progression of disease. (British Association for Cardiovascular Prevention and Rehabilitation (BACPR), 2023, p. 3)

According to this definition, CR aims to improve the health outcomes for people following a cardiac event, surgery or diagnosis by ensuring they are supported in their return to a full an active life as possible through lifestyle support clinics and comprehensive cardiovascular rehabilitation. Specifically, this service comprises information and education covering topics such as healthy eating, stress management, medication, and relapse prevention. Alongside education, CR provides eight to twelve weeks of structured physical activity sessions, in line with BACPR protocols, allowing patients to safely build their physical fitness as well as developing their confidence to increase or maintain their levels of physical activity. The 2018 National Audit of Cardiac Rehabilitation (NACR, British Heart Foundation, 2019) highlighted that only around 10% of CR services within the UK included a practitioner psychologist as part of their staffing model. Health-related behaviour change, such as increasing levels of physical activity, is a central component of the BACPR definition of CR (Cowie et al., 2019), and there has been an increase in CR patients experiencing psychological distress (British Heart Foundation, 2019; Hinde et al., 2019). For these reasons, there appears to be a need for healthcare professionals working within CR to have expertise in behaviour change and the psychological elements of rehabilitation and illness.

The focus on enquiry and relationship building, driven by a desire to understand the service I was attempting to influence, allowed me to identify the project's key stakeholders, and their priorities in their work. The main client was the multidisciplinary team of healthcare professionals. Key stakeholders were the Trust's research unit, CR patients, and a multidisciplinary academic supervisory team. A key priority for the healthcare professionals was ensuring that their work was based on the best available evidence to enable them to change patients' health-related behaviour in a manner that would empower patients to exercise a greater degree of autonomy over their recovery. Patients wanted to be supported to establish a *new-normal* level of functioning, and to prevent a secondary cardiac event. The NHS research unit priority was to deliver research into new and improved therapies and techniques, and to maximise the potential of innovation to improve patient care. A key feature of the research was design, delivery and reporting of single- and multi-centre clinical trials focusing on applied health research. This project was a deviation from the research unit's traditional work. As I will explore below, the success of the project required development of strong relationships and trust between stakeholders.

The request for consultancy arose through a partnership between the NHS Trust and a local university. The university had a pre-existing research collaboration with the NHS Trust and wanted to explore how behaviour change was being utilised within CR. As a PhD student, I had a developing understanding of the application of psychology to health, providing expertise in research, intervention design, and theories such as self-determination theory (Ryan & Deci, 2000), the theory of motivation chosen as the theoretical basis for the project. Throughout the project, I attempted to understand the CR service in question and had a central aim of ensuring the outcomes of the consultancy were useful for healthcare professionals and bespoke to the needs of the service. To do this, I drew on the Theoretical Framework of Acceptability (Sekhon et al., 2017, 2018), to determine whether my work, and the proposed intervention, was acceptable to the multidisciplinary team, and if it was feasible for them to deliver within the constraints of their service. Assessing acceptability is important as if a training package has low acceptability, it may not be delivered as intended by healthcare professionals, which may limit its overall effectiveness (Sekhon et al., 2017, 2018). I chose to include this approach as it was important to me to undertake work that was useful for the healthcare professionals' practice, and therefore an assessment of acceptability prior to an impact evaluation felt like it better aligned with the ethos of the work. I was advised by my supervisory team that a traditional impact evaluation would not be necessary for the purpose of my thesis, and therefore the focus of the thesis was on intervention development and how this was undertaken with healthcare professionals' views at the core.

Needs assessment is a core aspect of enquiry in the consultancy framework (Brady & Varkonyi-Sepp, 2025; see Chap. 3). Within this project, a needs assessment was integral to this project and allowed strong relationships between the client and stakeholders to be developed and maintained. As I had never worked in CR prior to this project, I chose to spend most of the first year of the project shadowing clinics, attending team meetings, speaking to patients and their families, and attempting to understand how the service was delivered to get a sense of what could be changed or improved. I also conducted interviews with the multidisciplinary team of healthcare professionals and with patients, and consulted the clinical physical activity literature to understand how SDT had been previously utilised in healthcare settings (Gillison et al., 2019). I spoke to other CR services and national organisations to understand how behaviour change was evident within CR. During the needs assessment, stakeholder interviews and clinic shadowing highlighted a large knowledge gap in terms of healthcare professionals' explicit knowledge of behaviour change. Healthcare professionals largely perceived behaviour change to be synonymous with Motivational Interviewing (MI), which is a "person-centred therapeutic style to enhance readiness for change by helping people explore and resolve their ambivalence" (Rollnick et al., 2010, p. 91). Healthcare professionals were able to access training in MI from the NHS Trust, but any wider competence or understanding of behaviour change was largely perceived to be based upon experiential learning. There were no previous examples of how healthcare professionals within CR can be supported to deliver behaviour change interventions. In addition, healthcare professionals within the service I was undertaking the consultancy with perceived training programmes that aimed to fill this gap to be inaccessible (Whittaker et al., 2022).

By drawing on Medical Research Council guidance on developing complex interventions (Medical Research Council, 2008; Moore et al., 2015; Wight et al., 2015), I developed a theory-based intervention that allowed healthcare professionals to deliver physical activity behaviour change interventions in their routine work. Throughout the project, I used CR team meetings to sense check my ideas and plans to make sure they were acceptable to the healthcare professionals and that they were aligned with the needs of the service. For example, I delivered presentations on SDT, showing how it had been used previously in healthcare settings as a basis for behaviour change interventions, and justifying why it had been selected. These discussions allowed me to feed back in a manner that allowed healthcare professionals to understand how their views and experiences had shaped the project. The project then culminated in delivering a bespoke training package to the multidisciplinary team of healthcare professionals and assessing whether they could use it in their routine work. The training package was perceived to represent a different way of approaching conversations with patients by using information already collected in their assessments in a different way.

Negotiation and initial contracting were not, on reflection, a focus in this work and I will comment further on this later in the chapter. From my perspective as the lead of the project, this meant that although it was unclear initially what I was contracted to do, through enquiry I learned that the CR health professionals did not understand how to deliver behaviour change interventions in relation to physical activity or other health behaviours. They had not received any training in this nor had they access to psychology expertise in the service. A key finding from the enquiry work was that CR was perceived by the team as a holistic service and they defined their service as 'not just the exercise programme', as it was perceived by healthcare professionals who did not work in CR. This enabled me to ensure that this was reflected in the aims and objectives of the training package. I will describe how I achieved this in the next section.

Building Relationships: Navigating Boundaries and Arriving at a Shared Understanding

In this section, I will discuss how I developed and maintained relationships in a manner that placed my client at the centre of my project so that they, supported by academia, largely determined the direction of my work. This approach presented challenges, particularly in academic circles, which will be discussed. For this chapter, I consider enquiry (Brady & Varkonyi-Sepp, 2025; see Chap. 3) in the sense of seeking information and asking questions to assess the needs of the client, to be integral to relationship building. Whilst leading this work, I did not consider the consultancy literature. Doing so retrospectively, however, has helped me to understand my consultative stance, and the project demonstrates that enquiry and relationship building are complementary.

According to Kitay and Wright (2003) analysis of different consulting roles, I took a *partner* role with the multidisciplinary team, which "emphasises building social ties with the client beyond a simple market relationship, with the result that the boundaries between client and consultant become somewhat blurred" (Kitay & Wright, 2003, p. 25). This approach was critical as I was new to professional practice in consultancy with no experience of working in CR and was tasked with leading the project. Shadowing CR staff in the clinic was a form of partnering which allowed me to understand their practice and the challenges they faced in helping patients to engage with and maintain healthy behaviours. This, in turn, helped me to see the opportunities to embed psychological approaches in their practice, which would be the focus of the training I went on to develop. To adopt this partner role, I was interested in understanding how psychology could improve the CR service, and this informed my interviews with them. They regarded me as a 'known quantity' and they were open, honest, and willing to be challenged on their practice or provide answers to my interview questions that drew on experiences we had seen in clinics.

At the end of the project, some of the feedback I obtained to evaluate the training included an understanding that I had asked valuable questions and that they felt listened to. I realised in writing this chapter that my practice aligned with principles of process consultation (Schein, 1999) which at its core has the tenets that the consultant should try to be helpful and should work with, and not for, the client. My approach allowed me to become the 'known quantity' as described by Kitay and Wright (2003). This, in turn, deepened my understanding of the service I was trying to influence, which I believe was integral to developing an intervention that was useful for them. Critically, I showed I had listened to the healthcare professionals and placed their opinions and experiences at the heart of the project to effect meaningful change. Operating as a partner allows tacit knowledge held within the client organisation to be gathered, confidential information to be shared over a long period of time, and provides opportunities for healthcare professionals to talk to the consultant as an outsider, but one who has made an effort to know and understand the system (Kitay & Wright) and was therefore trusted.

The potential risks of taking a partner role are described by previous literature focusing on experienced psychologists working with high-performance multidisciplinary teams (McDougall et al., 2015). This work suggests that the practitioner should be both "a part and apart" (p. 269) within the context they are working within, so that a relationship with one group of stakeholders is not prioritised over another. This approach is imperative in establishing the kind of relationship that enables the psychologist to gain the trust of multiple clients and work more broadly across the environment. In these settings, for optimal work it is necessary to remain distinct, detached, and not clearly affiliated with any one specific group (McDougall et al.).

In this project, I was balancing the needs of two key stakeholders: the multidisciplinary team (the client) and the academic team who needed to ensure that the project was a rigorous piece of research. When applied to this project, my approach allowed me to be 'a part' of the CR service, positioning myself as someone who tried to understand how it operated, and the challenges faced by each of the multidisciplinary team that psychological theory might be able to address. As a practitioner with no prior experience of working in CR, this was a particularly important, and daunting, undertaking. However, I was also 'apart' from the team, meaning I needed to maintain a detachment so that I could work objectively across the service, as well as conducting work that drew on best practice in terms of research and academia. This was a constant balancing act which required me to consider how I could be 'a part' of the service, generating the necessary depth of relationship to build trust with healthcare professionals so they engaged with and maintained interest in the work, whilst remaining 'apart' so that the work could be completed optimally and objectively. I will reflect on how effectively I believe I did this later in the chapter.

So, What Did I Do?

Health psychology can demonstrate how to layer theory, evidence, and practice onto challenges in health services to generate change. In discussions with the healthcare professionals, they asked me about the evidence base behind any changes to practice. I understood that this was because they wanted to be able to understand and interrogate the evidence themselves. Including theory within the training package served two purposes. It assured the academics that my research was academically rigorous, and assured healthcare professionals that what I was proposing was underpinned by the best available evidence. When building relationships with academic stakeholders, I was aware as a PhD student that they would need reassurance that I was aware of and using appropriate theory to inform the work. Previous work by Kislov helped me shape this use of theory, by advocating for "theoretically informative improvement research which, although guided by existing theory, would be able to yield new theoretical insights applicable to a broader range of settings" (Kislov, 2019, p. 177).

An advantage of choosing SDT was that it has common philosophical underpinnings with MI, which from the perspective of the healthcare professionals, was synonymous with behaviour change. Using SDT and explaining the overlap with MI provided a tangible starting point for demonstrating how psychology was relevant in CR. Although there is not space to describe the full training package here, SDT allowed me to contextualise psychological concepts in terms of CR (e.g., relatedness being achieved by healthcare professionals providing reassurance and comfort to the patient; Whittaker, 2021). This increased healthcare professionals' understanding of SDT and how it could be used to change behaviour and allowed them to identify how they could build on their MI skills. This approach is supported by previous literature, where clients felt that it was important that both the client and the consultant found a tailor-made solution rather than the consultant simply giving an off-the-shelf solution (Fullerton & West, 1996). The theoretical basis of the training package is outlined in supplementary material (ESM_21.1) and further detail can be found in my PhD thesis (Whittaker, 2021).

The relationship I developed with the healthcare professionals over the first year had an important impact on the way I approached the development of the training. Hodges (2021), writing about the stages of consultancy, highlighted that consultants may assume they know what is important in a project without first undertaking any groundwork, a common pitfall in consultancy. Initially, my supervisory team and I proposed a randomised control trial (RCT) with an intervention group and a control group (standard care). This would allow us to assess the training package's effectiveness in terms of patients' levels of health-related behaviour change. When I presented the proposed RCT to the healthcare professionals, it was not well-received, as they said this would not work for them, and was not ethical or logistically feasible to randomise. This feedback led to the first challenge in balancing relationships between my client and key stakeholders.

I was acutely aware that to complete this consultancy project, I needed to develop and maintain a positive relationship with both the healthcare professionals and my academic supervisors. The feedback from the CR team that the proposed RCT was perceived as a waste of time and unworkable, meant that I could alienate them if I attempted to continue with it and it would be impossible to implement. To address I adjusted my approach by reflecting on a key question: *I am here for three years—how can I be as useful as possible to you as healthcare professionals?* This was a critical shift in terms of consultancy because I was now engaging with the client, the CR team, to understand the issues from their perspective to enable me to design an intervention that would address their needs. This was based on my view that I was someone who needed to get the healthcare professionals onside, I had a skillset in a discipline that was not immediately apparent within their service, and I had an opportunity to make a difference if I made every effort to understand them and their service. By using the question as a cornerstone of my project, I became more interested in how I could undertake a programme of work that would be beneficial for healthcare professionals' practice and placed their experiences at the forefront of my work. This impacted the expectations of the academic supervisory team, and I will explore this further later in the chapter.

But I'm a Busy Healthcare Professional, Why Should I Bother?

Shadowing clinics and joining team meetings allowed me to listen to the concerns that patients were raising, identify patterns of behaviour that prevented health-related behaviour change, and allowed me to try and understand how patients were attempting to make sense of, in some cases, risk of dying. I tried to understand the tens of medical acronyms, joined the team huddle before clinics, spoke to patients and their family members about how life had changed, and then in the car back to our base would ask (what one of the nurses described as) 'thousands' of questions as we reflected on the patients we had seen that day.

As well as this, I saw people who lived alone who were motivated to come to CR as it was the only social contact they would have that week. On numerous occasions patients told me that I looked like their granddaughter, and I heard stories about their often-remarkable lives. Sometimes, patients who were deeply grateful for the healthcare professionals who had saved their lives, wept during interviews. Healthcare professionals also expressed emotion during interviews about their work with patients and expressed the desire to make a difference to patients' lives.

Those experiences were the most humbling parts of this project. To this day I am extremely grateful to everyone who I was able to spend time with, even if just for a couple of hours. As a consultant and psychology practitioner, I listened carefully to understand the issues that most affected people attending CR. As Schein (1999) explains, this approach underpins process consultation, where "the creation of a situation in which learning, and change can take place by individuals and groups" (p. 3) was established through my development of these relationships. On completion of the project, the healthcare professionals reflected that I had grown so much as a person and a practitioner, and they were proud and very grateful for what I had done. Without those experiences of asking questions, allowing me to develop relationships as far as possible, I do not believe I would have received this feedback. On reflection, however, I would recommend that consultants engage in meaningful enquiry work to create strong relationships with their client and key stakeholders while also establishing boundaries, so that the consultant does not end up overwhelmed with the volume of work, or the complexity of services. This was not a consideration I made at the time.

Reflection

Writing this chapter has enabled me to reflect on my work through a consultancy lens. The project demonstrates interdependencies between the enquiry and relationship processes of the consultancy framework (Brady & Varkonyi-Sepp, 2025, see Chap. 3) and the development of trust. Developing a middle ground between academic stakeholders and healthcare professional clients and communicating in a manner that did not alienate either party was critical for developing trust (Avakian et al., 2010). With the CR team, I invested time in understanding the CR service and their challenges. When encouraging the CR team to consider how psychology could inform their practice, I adopted a performance narrative in my conversations with healthcare professionals such as "*your trust is already outstanding, your service is hitting its key performance indicators, but what would an extra 1%, 5% do for you, and what would it look like?*" Asking open questions such as these, based on my own experiences of making psychology more accessible to non-psychologists, showed that I saw my role as using my slightly different, but complementary, skill set as a psychologist to help enhance practice. Reflecting on the consultancy literature, I can see now that I took an approach that aligns with process consultation, with its emphasis on being a helper by "engaging the client in a process that will in the end be perceived as helpful to the client by both consultant and client" (Schein, 1999, p. 2).

With a background in academic health psychology, I had expertise in a discipline that was not formally included in the CR service. However, as someone who was new to professional practice, this was my first project as lead consultant, so much of it felt like trial and error. As I was not in training as a professional health psychologist, consultancy was not a core element of my PhD and, therefore, I was not exposed to the consultancy literature or to consultancy mentoring at the time of the project. On reflection, in relation to the proposed consultancy framework for health psychologists (Brady & Varkonyi-Sepp, 2025; see Chap. 3), relationship building based on enquiry was a key focus of my project. Reflecting on the consultancy overall, the opportunity to evaluate the impact of the project was limited. My focus was on doing something useful and, given the large focus on enquiry and qualitative research, there was not time, nor was it within the scope of a PhD, to assess the impact on behaviour change. Assessments of this sort would follow if funding could be secured, although I acknowledge that in consultancy practice, evaluation is ideally built in from the beginning of a project, rather than being added at the end. Reflecting on my performance as a consultant, the importance I placed on adopting a partner role with the multidisciplinary team of healthcare professionals may have clouded my objectivity, and in McDougall's terms I was probably more *a part* and less *apart*, as I wanted to demonstrate my worth and be useful within the service (McDougall et al., 2015). By doing so, as the project progressed, I placed the healthcare professionals' views at the heart of my work, and prioritised ensuring the project would help my client.

My approach to the work looked unlike other PhD projects that were happening in my academic institution, which were largely lab-based and used quantitative data. Within my department, there were no health psychologists other than my supervisor, and no NHS-based research taking place. A key factor in my PhD was the way I positioned psychology as a central, yet, complementary, discipline amongst others within healthcare settings such as CR. I found publications on intervention development particularly informative (Croot et al., 2019; Duncan et al., 2020; Hoddinott, 2015; O'Cathain et al., 2019; Rousseau et al., 2019), alongside a consideration of the merits of evidence-based practice versus practice-based evidence and how theory could be used (Kislov, 2019; Kislov, Pope, et al., 2019a; Kislov, Wilson, et al., 2019b). Considering this body of evidence, none of which sat within 'traditional' health psychology journals, alongside the theoretical framework of my work (SDT: Ryan & Deci, 2000), allowed me to position the work in the wider applied health research domain. I believe that this approach is a real strength of my project as it is more reflective of the service I was looking to influence. Even so, this approach presented significant challenges for some academic audiences, and I was reminded that for the purposes of academic circles, my work had to be a Psychology PhD "*not health research*".

My approach to the project presented a key challenge to my relationship with my host academic department and institution. As part of my PhD researcher role, I was invited to present a seminar to academics and healthcare professionals that outlined my work and progress made after eighteen months, focusing on the developmental approach, and demonstrating how it drew on the wider health services research domain to make a tangible difference to healthcare professionals' practice. I understood that this work deviated greatly from usual research in my department.

My presentation attracted several critical questions as to how I would demonstrate that the work would have any measurable impact and why I was not using a randomised design to evaluate its effectiveness. The academic feedback was critical of the value of qualitative research. However, when questioned by healthcare professionals and my academic supervisors, who had supported me to develop this approach that considered psychology alongside several other disciplines, the work was praised for attempting to make a tangible difference to practice. It was praised for being an approach that placed the client's needs at its core. Receiving these two vastly different pieces of feedback within the same seminar demonstrates the challenges of conducting this interdisciplinary research in an academic psychology department, whilst trying to satisfy the demands of my NHS Trust. This challenge was also reflected at my PhD viva, where much of the discussion focused on the theoretical basis of my thesis, with limited focus on the work's interdisciplinary and practical focus. Whilst leading this project, I felt supported by my supervisory team, and worked with them to ensure my project was commensurate with PhD level, although I struggled with balancing the demands of academia with ensuring my work was useful to my client. I am not sure how I could have approached the project differently to satisfy academia to a larger extent, but I feel it is a key consideration that future consultants, and their supervisory teams if it is in the context of a PhD, need to contemplate. I would encourage anyone in similar positions to understand, from an early stage in the project, how different stakeholders would define success within the project, and identify what is most important for the consultancy to achieve from their perspective. Doing so may help to avoid the tensions between academia and practice that I faced.

A key learning point from this project is simply that as a consultant we are trying to help people, a service, or an organisation to achieve change that benefits them (and patients or service-users). However, without properly engaging the population and groups we are trying to impact, how can we understand their needs? The enquiry phase of this project, and the strength of the relationships it allowed me to develop, meant that I had a safe space where academia and practice in health could challenge each other with an aim of maximising their effectiveness through collaboration. Without this enquiry, I simply would not have had this environment and would not have been able to do this work. Therefore, future work that aims to impact healthcare professionals' practice should make every effort to properly understand the service they operate within, before working with the client to shape what the involvement of a consultant should be.

Top Tips

1. Understand the context
   (a) Shadow, join meetings, have informal conversations, conduct interviews, and make observations.
   (b) Use interviews and observations as formal data collection methods, ensuring ethical and professional compliance.
2. Take your time
   (a) Focus on the enquiry and relationship building stages of the consultancy framework.
   (b) Understand what a successful project looks like from different perspectives.
3. Refine communication skills
   (a) Articulate why different audiences should care about your work.
   (b) Identify priorities for your client and other stakeholders.
   (c) Adapt communication techniques and key messages for different audiences.
4. Integrate disciplines
   (a) Consider health psychology evidence alongside other disciplines.
   (b) Recognise that psychology rarely works in isolation in healthcare settings and seek to understand how it can be complementary to other disciplines.
5. Leverage student placements
   (a) Use placements to bring together key stakeholders to exchange ideas and expertise.

Competing Interests The author has no competing interests to declare that are relevant to the content of this chapter.

References

Avakian, S., Clark, T., & Roberts, J. (2010). Examining the relationship between trust and culture in the consultant-client relationship. In *Organizational trust: A cultural perspective* (Vol. 1, pp. 129–155). Cambridge University Press. https://doi.org/10.1017/cbo9780511763106.006

Brady, R., & Varkonyi-Sepp, J. (2025). A framework for consultancy in health psychology. In R. Brady, J. Varkonyi-Sepp, & J. Smith (Eds.), *The Palgrave handbook of consultancy in health psychology*. Palgrave Macmillan.

British Association for Cardiovascular Prevention and Rehabilitation. (2023). Cardiovascular disease prevention and rehabilitation 2023. *British Association for Cardiovascular Prevention and Rehabilitation, 2023*, 1–26.

British Heart Foundation. (2019). The national audit of cardiac rehabilitation: Annual statistical report. Retrieved December 20, 2019, from https://www.bhf.org.uk/informationsupport/publications/statistics/national-audit-of-cardiac-rehabilitation-quality-and-outcomes-report-2019

Cowie, A., Buckley, J., Doherty, P., Furze, G., Hayward, J., Hinton, S., Jones, J., Speck, L., Dalal, H., & Mills, J. (2019). Standards and core components for cardiovascular disease prevention and rehabilitation. *Heart, 105*(7), 510–515. https://doi.org/10.1136/heartjnl-2018-314206

Croot, L., O'Cathain, A., Sworn, K., Yardley, L., Turner, K., Duncan, E., & Hoddinott, P. (2019). Developing interventions to improve health: A systematic mapping review of international practice between 2015 and 2016. *Pilot and Feasibility Studies, 5*(1), 1–13. https://doi.org/10.1186/s40814-019-0512-8

Duncan, E., O'Cathain, A., Rousseau, N., Croot, L., Sworn, K., Turner, K. M., Yardley, L., & Hoddinott, P. (2020). Guidance for reporting intervention development studies in health research (GUIDED): An evidence-based consensus study. *BMJ Open, 10*(4), 1–12. https://doi.org/10.1136/bmjopen-2019-033516

Fullerton, J., & West, M. A. (1996). Consultant and client—Working together? *Journal of Managerial Psychology, 11*(6), 40–49. https://doi.org/10.1108/02683949610129749

Gillison, F. B., Rouse, P., Standage, M., Sebire, S. J., & Ryan, R. M. (2019). A meta-analysis of techniques to promote motivation for health behaviour change from a self-determination theory perspective. In *Health psychology review* (Vol. 13, Issue 1, pp. 110–130). Routledge. https://doi.org/10.1080/17437199.2018.1534071

Greenhalgh, T., Howick, J., & Maskrey, N. (2014). Evidence based medicine: A Movement in crisis? *British Medical Journal, 348*, g3725–g3725. https://doi.org/10.1136/bmj.g3725

Heron, N., Kee, F., Donnelly, M., Cardwell, C., Tully, M. A., & Cupples, M. E. (2016). Behaviour change techniques in home-based cardiac rehabilitation: A systematic review. *British Journal of General Practice, 66*(651), e747–e757. https://doi.org/10.3399/bjgp16X686617

Hinde, S., Bojke, L., Harrison, A., & Doherty, P. (2019). Improving cardiac rehabilitation uptake: Potential health gains by socioeconomic status. *European Journal of Preventive Cardiology, 26*(17), 1816–1823. https://doi.org/10.1177/2047487319848533

Hoddinott, P. (2015). A new era for intervention development studies. *Pilot and Feasibility Studies, 1*(1), 36. https://doi.org/10.1186/s40814-015-0032-0

Hodges, J. (2021). A Framework for Consulting. *Management Consulting Journal, 4*(2), 52–55. https://doi.org/10.2478/mcj-2021-0009

Kislov, R. (2019). Engaging with theory: From theoretically informed to theoretically informative improvement research. *BMJ Quality and Safety, 28*(3), 177–179. https://doi.org/10.1136/bmjqs-2018-009036

Kislov, R., Pope, C., Martin, G. P., & Wilson, P. M. (2019a). Harnessing the power of theorising in implementation science. *Implementation Science, 14*(1), 1–8. https://doi.org/10.1186/s13012-019-0957-4

Kislov, R., Wilson, P., Cummings, G., Ehrenberg, A., Gifford, W., Kelly, J., Kitson, A., Pettersson, L., Wallin, L., & Harvey, G. (2019b). from research evidence to "evidence by proxy"? Organizational enactment of evidence-based health care in four high-income countries. *Public Administration Review, 79*(5), 684–698. https://doi.org/10.1111/puar.13056

Kitay, J., & Wright, C. (2003). Expertise and organizational boundaries: The varying roles of Australian management consultants. *Asia Pacific Business Review, 9*(3), 21–40. https://doi.org/10.1080/13602380312331288610

McDougall, M., Nesti, M., & Richardson, D. (2015). The challenges of sport psychology delivery in elite and professional sport: Reflections from experienced sport psychologists. *Sport Psychologist, 29*(3), 265–277. https://doi.org/10.1123/tsp.2014-0081

Medical Research Council. (2008). *Developing and evaluating complex interventions: New guidance, 337*. https://doi.org/10.1136/bmj.a1655

Michie, S., & Johnston, M. (2012). Theories and techniques of behaviour change: Developing a cumulative science of behaviour change. *Health Psychology Review, 6*(1), 1–6. https://doi.org/10.1080/17437199.2012.654964

Moore, G. F., Audrey, S., Barker, M., Bond, L., Bonell, C., Hardeman, W., Moore, L., O'Cathain, A., Tinati, T., Wight, D., Baird, J., O'Cathain, A., Tinati, T., Wight, D., & Baird, J. (2015). Process evaluation of complex interventions: Medical Research Council guidance. *British Medical Journal, 350*, h1258. https://doi.org/10.1136/bmj.h1258

O'Cathain, A., Croot, L., Duncan, E., Rousseau, N., Sworn, K., Turner, K. M., Yardley, L., & Hoddinott, P. (2019). Guidance on how to develop complex interventions to improve health and healthcare. *BMJ Open, 9*(8), 1–9. https://doi.org/10.1136/bmjopen-2019-029954

Rollnick, S., Butler, C. C., Kinnersley, P., Gregory, J. W., & Mash, B. (2010). Motivational interviewing. *British Medical Journal, 340*, c1900. https://doi.org/10.1177/026455059904600413

Rousseau, N., Turner, K. M., Duncan, E., O'Cathain, A., Croot, L., Yardley, L., & Hoddinott, P. (2019). Attending to design when developing complex health interventions: A qualitative interview study with intervention developers and associated stakeholders. *PLoS ONE, 14*(10), 1–20. https://doi.org/10.1371/journal.pone.0223615

Ryan, R., & Deci, E. (2000). Self-determination theory and the facilitation of intrinsic motivation. *American Psychologist, 55*(1), 68–78. https://doi.org/10.1037/0003-066X.55.1.68

Schein, E. H. (1999). *Process consultation revisited: Building the helping relationship.* Addison Wesley.

Sekhon, M., Cartwright, M., & Francis, J. J. (2017). Acceptability of healthcare interventions: An overview of reviews and development of a theoretical framework. *BMC Health Services Research, 17*(1), 1–13. https://doi.org/10.1186/s12913-017-2031-8

Sekhon, M., Cartwright, M., & Francis, J. J. (2018). Acceptability of health care interventions: A theoretical framework and proposed research agenda. *British Journal of Health Psychology, 23*(3), 519–531. https://doi.org/10.1111/bjhp.12295

Whittaker, E. M. (2021). *A self-determination theory approach to embedding physical activity behaviour change in cardiac & pulmonary rehabilitation: Intervention development and optimisation* (Doctoral thesis, Edge Hill University). Edge Hill University Research Archive. https://research.edgehill.ac.uk/en/studentTheses/a-self-determination-theory-approach-to-embedding-physical-activi

Whittaker, E. M., Levy, A. R., Matata, B., Kinnafick, F. E., & Midgley, A. W. (2022). Using behavior change interventions in cardiac and pulmonary rehabilitation: Perspectives from healthcare professionals in the United Kingdom. *International Journal of Environmental Research and Public Health, 19*(4), 1980. https://doi.org/10.3390/ijerph19041980

Wight, D., Wimbush, E., Jepson, R., & Doi, L. (2015). Six steps in quality intervention development (6SQuID). *Journal of Epidemiology and Community Health, 70*(5), 520–525. https://doi.org/10.1136/jech-2015-205952

22

Negotiation and Contracting: Delivering Healthcare Differently

Liz Edwards-Smith

Introduction

This chapter explores the negotiation and contracting element of the consultancy framework proposed by Brady and Varkonyi-Sepp (2025; see Chap. 3) with a focus on balancing the informal and relational aspects of consultancy work. Using a case study about an innovation project in the UK that piloted the use of shared medical appointments as an alternative to ten-minute General Practitioner (GP) consultations, I bring to life the realities of negotiating and contracting during complex consultancy work. I illustrate how four independent parties collaborated to successfully bid for funding to deliver the project. I describe how negotiation and (re)contracting took place before and during the planning and delivery of the project, both formally and informally. I reflect on the importance of getting the balance right between formal and informal contracting to enable innovation, and on how strong and open relationships are key to this when delivering consultancy work. I write from the perspective of a psychology-informed consultant in health so there will, naturally, be differences in emphasis and approach than if written by a health psychologist.

L. Edwards-Smith (✉)
Evalesco Consulting, Plymouth, UK
e-mail: liz@evalesco.org.uk

R. Brady et al. (eds.), *The Palgrave Handbook of Consultancy in Health Psychology*,
https://doi.org/10.1007/978-3-031-94529-8_22

The Case Study

As a consultant with expertise in organisational development, change and transformation, I have worked with health clients in the United Kingdom (UK) for over eight years and before this, with a breadth of non-health clients for 15 years. During this time, I developed strong professional relationships with those I worked with. Prior to the project described in this chapter, I worked with a Clinical Commissioning Group (CCG; responsible for commissioning healthcare services within a geographic area) in England reviewing chronic pain services. The project was seeking to address high levels of spend on opioid medication for the management of chronic pain. At the time, guidance from the National Institute for Health and Care Excellence (NICE) was clear that opioids were not indicated for chronic pain (reaffirmed in 2021 guidelines: NICE, 2021).

A key learning from that work was the difficulty within a ten-minute GP consultation, to provide the support needed by people living with chronic pain such as, education to support self-management or signposting to interventions like group exercise. The impact of that was felt not just by patients who described feeling unheard and misunderstood, but also by GPs themselves, who described 'heart sink' moments as medication and other interventions, such as secondary care pain management programmes, had little effect for some people. Stellman and Ellis (2024) recognise and describe this 'heart sink' dilemma, advocating for personalised care.

One particular GP, working on the CCG project, described an alternative approach to consultations: shared medical appointments (SMA: Hayhoe et al., 2017). The Kirsh et al. (2017) realist review of SMAs described key benefits: creation of a social support base for patients; improved uptake of health knowledge; creative problem solving by providers, and improved trust in the doctor–patient dynamic. During SMAs, patients come together to have a consultation as a group, led by a medical doctor with nursing and administrative support. Patients, typically with the same medical condition, receive healthcare including physical examination, clinical support and education, and are able to listen and contribute to each other's consultation. Whilst there was not the opportunity to try this alternative within the scope of the CCG project, the idea was lodged firmly in our minds.

With that context in mind, in 2018 I became aware of a new innovation funding call by a UK-based national health charity (the funder). The call was to develop and test innovative ideas and approaches to improve health and social care delivery or the way people managed their own health care, through redesign of processes, practices, services and models of delivery. I saw this as relevant to pain management and to address high usage of primary care services. With my consultancy experience in pain management projects, this presented an opportunity to shape a project around SMAs.

I approached an existing client, the Chief Executive Officer (CEO) of a social enterprise that managed GP practices. I had in mind an outline pilot project and I had looked at literature to better understand shared medical appointment models in other countries. The systematic review by Edelman et al. (2015) described the potential for SMAs to be a more efficient way to offer chronic disease care, whilst also improving staff satisfaction and patient outcomes. This initial, informal pre-bid meeting was an opportunity to persuade the client to collaborate on shaping a bid for funding, to negotiate and agree that an SMA pilot be located within one of their GP practices, and to secure commitment that resources would be made available to support the project. I describe my approach to this meeting later in the chapter.

Securing commitment from the CEO was an important first step. This paved the way for the development of a joint bid. Table 22.1 details the stakeholders involved at each stage of the project.

I approached three collaborators to jointly develop the funding bid (using capacity within their day jobs), each known to me from the CCG project: first, a GP with a special interest in pain management and SMAs; second, a professor of health and well-being with applied expertise in non-pharmacological interventions delivered in group settings, and in the evaluation of such approaches; third, an independent clinical psychologist with expertise in mindfulness and reflective practice. The professor brought expertise in physical movement to help manage pain; nutrition and diet to promote strength and healing; relaxation techniques; patient activation (understanding a person's level of knowledge, skills and confidence to manage their own health and care) and engagement.

The funders were interested in how and what successful applicants would learn through the process of delivering an innovation project, and we wanted reflexivity to be part of our learning approach, alongside supported reflection using Gibb's model (Bassot, 2016). Over two months, we worked to develop and submit a joint bid, using two meetings and email exchanges to negotiate between ourselves and agree the details. I describe this in more detail later in the chapter.

The project would pilot SMAs for patients with chronic (non-cancer) pain who were prescribed over 120 mg of morphine equivalent pain relief daily. The risk of harm increases substantially at doses above an oral morphine equivalent of 120 mg/day, with no increased benefit (Faculty of Pain Medicine of the Royal College of Anaesthetists, n.d.). With a biopsychosocial focus

Table 22.1 Stakeholders involved in shared medical appointments (SMA) pilot project

			Stages of project and stakeholder involvement						
			Pre-award		Post-award				
Stakeholder	Organisation	Project role	Pre-bid	Bid development (2 months)	Project planning (3 months)	Project delivery (12 months)	Collaborators	Core project team	Wider project team
CEO	Social enterprise	Senior responsible officer	✓	✓					
GP	Social enterprise	SMA clinical lead		✓	✓	✓	✓	✓	✓
Professor of health and wellbeing	Higher education institute	Advisor, subject matter expert		✓	✓	✓	✓	✓	✓
Clinical psychologist	Independent	Advisor, reflective practice lead		✓	✓	✓	✓	✓	✓
Project consultant	Independent	Advisor, chair, bid and project lead, facilitator	✓	✓	✓	✓	✓	✓	✓
Health and wellbeing practitioner	Higher education institute	SMA health and wellbeing lead			✓	✓		✓	✓
GP administrator	Social enterprise	Administrator			✓	✓		✓	✓
GP practice manager	Social enterprise	Administrator			✓	✓			✓
Expert patient	Independent	Lived experience expert			✓	✓			✓
Pharmacist	Social enterprise	SMA pharmacist lead			✓	✓			✓

(Gatchel et al., 2007), our SMA model would be led by a multidisciplinary team (MDT) combining medical and non-medical expertise in pain management, which was, as far as we knew, a novel approach. A systematic review by Edelman et al. (2015) found that MDTs typically included a person skilled in patient education or in facilitating patient interaction, and a prescribing practitioner. In line with this, our core MDT included the following: a GP (medical, prescriber, educator); a health and well-being practitioner (exercise coach, educator, facilitator); an administrator (facilitator); supported occasionally by the clinical psychologist (mindfulness) and practice-based pharmacist. Our aim was to achieve reduced use of opioid-based medication whilst encouraging self-management and peer-to-peer support. We wanted SMAs to positively impact the well-being of individuals within the MDT, exploring this through reflective practice and a focus group.

Each SMA would last for two hours, would occur six-weekly and would involve groups of eight patients. The duration, frequency and patient numbers were based in part on Edelman et al. (2015) systematic review and, more practically, on the capacity of the core MDT. Patients would be encouraged to attend as many, or as few, of the SMAs as they felt they needed. Each SMA would start with group conversation facilitated by the GP or health and well-being practitioner to agree discussion topics. Then, each patient would have their GP consultation in front of the group to facilitate shared learning. An adjoining clinic room was available if needed. This was followed by discussion of the agreed topics, which included medicines management, an introduction to the pain cycle, nutrition and diet to help healing, and sleep hygiene. The group discussions, facilitated by the GP and health and well-being practitioner, encouraged peer support, problem solving and goal setting. On occasion, to support the group discussions, informal education was provided by the GP or the health and well-being practitioner or clinical psychologist or pharmacist. This depended on a joint decision between patients and professionals on whether informal education was wanted and was thought to be of benefit. Each SMA would finish with optional gentle exercise, to show how movement can help manage pain, and would introduce techniques for relaxation. Led by the health and well-being practitioner, exercises were personalised to suit individual capabilities. Patients completed a physical activity readiness questionnaire that we developed, and they assumed responsibility for flagging any adverse effects. This combination of medical and non-medical approaches to managing pain in primary care in a group setting, where patients each had a GP consultation and took the lead in generating and prioritising discussion topics, met with the requirements of the funding call for innovation in healthcare delivery and were aligned with NICE guidelines for the management of chronic pain.

Following submission of the joint bid we were shortlisted and, after a successful interview with the funder, awarded £75,000 to deliver the project. The formal funding contract was between the social enterprise and the funder and was based on the details we had submitted in the bid. This was deemed sufficient by all parties to proceed to delivery, and we relied on this as the sole contracting mechanism together with the audit trail of emails in which each collaborator had confirmed their role, responsibilities and commitment to the project. The project took place over 15 months. A three-month planning period marked the beginning of a new phase of negotiation with the wider project team. During project design workshops, we reality-tested the assumptions underlying the funding bid. I discuss this in more detail later.

During the 12-month delivery phase, we created different spaces within which stakeholders could discuss and monitor progress and reflect on the work. These spaces were the project steering groups, core project team reflective sessions, and the SMAs themselves, which included patient contracting at the beginning and reflective pauses at the end of the sessions. The spaces enabled informal negotiation and contracting about the work we were doing and how we were doing it. They continued throughout the delivery phase and were ways in which we managed change. I discuss these spaces and how they related to negotiation and contracting in more detail later.

We held 24 SMAs, engaging 20 patients who each attended on average 4.6 SMAs. Quantitative data analysis showed that, on average, clinical contact reduced by 73% during the SMA project period, compared to the previous 12 months. When SMA attendance was taken into account, clinical contact overall reduced by 35%. Reductions were seen in medication queries, out-of-hours contacts and emergency department attendances by 67%, 14% and 63%, respectively. Furthermore, one-third of patients reduced medication levels over the project period.

We were equally interested in patients' and core project team's experiences of the SMAs. To gain independent insights we commissioned a researcher to conduct two focus groups; one for patients who had attended SMAs and one for the core project team including the expert patient. A paper discussing our qualitative findings is currently in preparation (Kordowicz et al., 2025, manuscript in preparation). The end of the project coincided with the beginning of the coronavirus (COVID-19) pandemic and the first UK COVID-19 lockdown. Due to COVID-19 restrictions, we had to stop the SMAs. Interest in them is being revived and we are exploring opportunities to deliver them again.

Negotiation and Contracting: Creating Intentional Spaces to Facilitate Change

Negotiation, in its broadest sense, is an interactive, dynamic human process where we seek agreement with others to do that which we cannot do alone (Menkel-Meadow, 2022). It does not happen in a social vacuum. Fisher et al. (1991) point out that negotiation and contracting rely on processes of back-and-forth communication until agreements are reached and decisions are taken, and negotiation continues throughout a (consultancy) project (Adams & Tovey, 2012). Negotiation is an important part of complex problem solving (Richardson & Anderson, 1995) and was a feature of the SMA project.

Context is important when it comes to negotiating. The purpose of the negotiation, the people involved, the issues at stake, all have an impact on how negotiation happens (Menkel-Meadow, 2022). The SMA pilot was an innovation project, with existing relationships between collaborators, and a wider project team where some people were meeting for the first time. Whilst there was a formal contract in place between the funder and the social enterprise (the client) outlining the proposed project, none of us had delivered SMAs before and this meant dealing with uncertainty and ambiguity. We were learning by doing, working in an agile and emergent way, accumulating new knowledge and reflecting on this to decide next steps. To support this way of working, we created spaces at different stages of the project within which negotiation and contracting could take place (see Table 22.2) as we

Table 22.2 Stages of project, negotiation and contracting spaces, and stakeholders

Stages of project		Negotiation and contracting spaces	Stakeholders involved
Pre-award	• Pre-bid	• Meeting with CEO	• CEO, project consultant
	• Bid development (2 months)	• Meetings with collaborators	• GP, professor of health and wellbeing, clinical psychologist, project consultant
Post-award	• Pilot planning (3 months)	• Project design workshops	• Wider project team
	• Pilot delivery	• Shared medical appointments	• GP, health and wellbeing practitioner, GP administrator, patients (and on occasion clinical psychologist, pharmacist)
		• Project steering group meetings	• Core project team (with open invite to wider project team)

navigated our way through the work. Here I describe what happened in those spaces.

Pre-award: CEO Meeting

My relationship with the CEO of the social enterprise enabled me to have an 'informal' conversation about the project idea. I took time (unpaid) to thoroughly prepare for this meeting. I read the funder's documentation, which included the aims of the programme, application form and guidance, budgeting template, submission process and timescales, so I was prepared for questions the CEO may have. My research enabled me to share knowledge about the potential benefits of SMAs for healthcare professionals and patients. I formulated a list of questions that would help us to explore the potential of an innovation project. In addition to my reading of the funder's documentation, these questions were informed by my research into SMAs, my understanding of what might be important to the CEO, and my prior consultancy experience. I documented this knowledge and the questions into a brief presentation to take to the meeting and, whilst I didn't use this, it proved a useful tool as the bid progressed.

During this meeting, I was clear about the expertise I could bring: organisational development, facilitation, communication and stakeholder engagement, coaching and project governance. Together, we identified expertise in medical and non-medical management of pain, mindfulness and facilitated reflexive practice, and expertise in patient group facilitation, patient activation and engagement as necessary for the pilot project. Based on previous work, I had ideas about potential partners to collaborate with to develop a bid proposal.

Worthy of note here is the approach I took to this initial meeting. An innovation project such as this, by its very nature, had many unknowns, depending equally on knowledge from the CEO as well as myself. Nikolova et al. (2009) describe three models of client–consultant interaction: the expert model, the critical model and the social learning model. The latter emphasises the role of the client as well as the consultant in problem solving, suggesting that jointly finding solutions leads to a balanced form of interaction. Through open dialogue, the client took an active role in exploring the potential SMAs. Furthermore, I took the role of a partner as described by Carucci and Tetenbaum (2000) where I positioned myself as taking equal accountability for the project's objectives, process and outcomes.

The CEO agreed to a pilot being located within one of the social enterprise's GP practices (where the GP collaborator worked), and that resources within the practice would support the project. They also agreed to the Head of Finance supporting me with costings for the budget. Following the meeting, I documented our discussion, decisions and next steps and sent this via email to the CEO. Without this initial commitment there would have been no joint bid.

Pre-award: Collaborator Meetings

The next challenge was to negotiate and agree the scope of the project and write a successful joint bid. I invited potential collaborators to two face-to-face meetings, which took place at the GP surgery where the SMAs would be delivered. I facilitated conversations with a focus on listening to different perspectives and ideas for what the project could include. Hogan (2003) explores different facilitation techniques describing four types of questions as central to all facilitation work: Objective, Reflective, Interpretative and Decision questions (ORID). During these meetings I used the presentation I had prepared for the CEO meeting and took responsibility for documenting the proposed pilot approach as it emerged through our conversations. This was the beginning of negotiating an agreed approach for the innovation project.

Coming to a consensus about the outline proposal and the scope of the project was an important step and acted as a north star to guide the grittier aspects of our bid development or as Cope (2010, p. 96) describes, "the point when the undiscussable has to be discussed ... such as responsibilities, remuneration, risks and results". Having previous experience of bid writing, I agreed to take responsibility for writing the bid response. Our outline proposal clearly identified where the main high-level responsibilities would lie, which was sufficient for the bid, and this was straightforward to agree via email with all collaborators. My role as project consultant included developing and facilitating design workshops, chairing the project steering group, being the key contact with the funder and producing reports and any funder requested documentation. I engaged individually with each stakeholder to agree their costs and worked with the Head of Finance to cost the resources within the GP practice where the SMAs would take place. We also agreed the number of SMAs we would aim to deliver over 12 months, and this was built into the budget with some contingency. The bid rules and budget template determined the financial envelope we needed to work with (£75,000). All collaborators were aware of it, making this aspect of negotiation much easier. I developed a high-level project plan which showed the timeline, the main tasks month by month and who was responsible for them, key milestones and key deliverables.

Our existing relationships, based on trust and a track record of delivering good work together, enabled us to tackle these, sometimes trickier, aspects of negotiation relatively easily and enabled smooth passage of the bid proposal through due diligence and financial sign-off processes at respective collaborator organisations. The consultancy framework proposed by Brady and Varkonyi-Sepp (2025; see Chap. 3) references the importance of trusting relationships between consultant and client. Karantinou and Hogg (2001) explore the key factors in successful client–consultant relationships with Solomonson (2012), also focusing on trust. We were particularly concerned about the SMAs reliance on key personnel and what would happen if they were absent. To mitigate this, the professor of health and well-being agreed to a substitute health and well-being practitioner being available who would shadow one of the early SMAs. We also agreed to invite GPs from the practice to observe the SMAs and we included contingent budget to backfill the SMA clinical lead if necessary. We used a risk register throughout the project to capture and monitor risks. Williams (2017) describes how a risk register can be a starting point for mapping risks that feature in complex projects.

It took roughly two months (elapsed time) to develop, agree and submit the bid to the funder. During this period, I worked at risk, in other words with no formal contract or payment. Whilst I viewed this as business development and investment of time in my client relationships, we did agree, as collaborators, to include some costed time in the budget to cover my work on the bid, should we be successful. This was likely possible because of our existing relationships. It is not always possible to cover bid costs in this way; working at risk, on occasion, can be part of consultancy work. Menkel-Meadow (2022) describes four different orientations to negotiation; one of these is integrative-collaborative-problem solving negotiation. This is a collaborative approach where parties have shared interests. As collaborators we shared common interests: that people with chronic pain needed a holistic approach that supported them to self-manage and to reduce reliance on opioid-based medication and to live well with pain (Hoover, 1986; Kress et al., 2015). This was a sound foundation, from which to start planning and delivering the project.

Post-award: Project Design Workshops

The first three months of the project, post funding award, were dedicated to planning. The stakeholder landscape had become more complex and now included the wider team who would support and deliver the SMAs (see Table 22.1). My role was to facilitate two project design workshops to negotiate and agree the detail of how we would deliver the SMAs. These workshops were important negotiation spaces for the wider project team. Most had not been involved in the bid development, so we took time to explain and to discuss the outline proposal, establishing a common understanding. We then focused on discussing and agreeing the details of delivery: identifying the target patient population and the criteria for inviting patients. In planning the format of the SMAs, we specified what happens in the group and what happens outside the group, roles and responsibilities, the process of running the SMAs and the inputs and outputs. We considered the physical environment; where would SMAs take place, how that would affect the clinic schedule, health and safety risks within the SMA room, and room layout. We identified potential training needs within the core MDT; for example, motivational interviewing and managing group dynamics and how to create a safe group space. And we discussed and agreed how we would measure outcomes and evaluate impact.

There was substantial discussion and negotiation before we reached agreement about how we would do these things. The reality of the operational environment where SMAs would be delivered was brought to life by the GP Practice Manager and the GP Practice Administrator. Valid concerns were raised about how to deliver SMAs alongside other clinics and how to manage the additional administrative workload. The Expert Patient sensitively described some of the challenges the layout of the SMA room and the duration of the sessions may present for some patients.

Whilst finances were not discussed during the design workshops (the budget had already been agreed with the Head of Finance), additional risks relating to delivery of the SMAs emerged and these were captured with mitigations and owners on the risk register. One concern was about breaches of confidentiality outside the SMAs. This risk was owned by the GP Practice Manager who put in place a consent and confidentiality process for patients before they joined the SMAs.

All of the different perspectives added to the richness of debate and negotiation and resulted in an agreed approach to delivery. Beers et al. (2006) framework brings together complex problem solving and multidisciplinary teamwork and describes the importance of negotiating meaning and position in order to reach such common ground. My role as consultant leading the project was to hold the design workshop space and facilitate the negotiations. We agreed simple ground rules for discussions; respectful listening, no interruptions or talking over others, each voice needs to be heard and is valued, there are no 'stupid' questions. I summarised individual discussion points, sought clarifications, gave space for reflection and asked for general agreement before moving on to the next topic. Hartnett (2010) explores facilitation skills required for participatory decision-making and reaching consensus within group problem solving. I took responsibility to document the decisions and agreements, which were shared and agreed formally via email. The outputs from the design workshops provided a baseline plan, our common ground, from which to start delivering the SMAs.

Post-award: Shared Medical Appointments

The SMAs were delivered over 12 months. Before taking part, each patient was supported through a formal contracting process, typically called consent process. The SMAs were deemed enough of a departure from traditional GP consultations that formal contracting was needed. This contracting process committed patients to confidentiality, to respecting others in the group consultation, to taking joint responsibility for their safety during any exercise and provided the opportunity to opt out at any time.

Informal negotiation and contracting took place during the SMAs: agreement on the topics for discussion, the timing of the rest breaks, and the general rules of engagement for the group. At the end of each group consultation patients were encouraged to make suggestions for changes that would improve their experience. One significant change was to increase the frequency of the SMAs to monthly rather than six-weekly. This change was brought to the project steering group.

Post-award: Project Steering Group Meetings

My role as consultant was to chair the project steering group meetings. This was a space where we discussed and agreed any major changes to the delivery plan and any potential impact on the budget and resources. We reviewed the risk register for the project which detailed potential risks and mitigating actions. The request from patients to change the frequency of the group consultations was considered at the project steering group. We discussed the availability of the GP and the health and well-being practitioner, whether the budget could accommodate additional sessions, the impact on administrative staff and the practicalities of clinic room availability. We negotiated and agreed the release of additional time for the GP, the GP Administrator and health and well-being practitioner, all covered within the contingent budget. The clinic room was also secured through these group meetings. Our shared ambition to deliver a successful pilot and a good patient experience underpinned these discussions and agreements.

Reflection

Consultancy work is not just about skills, knowledge and expertise. It is as much about social practices and the ability to build strong relationships through which you can mutually learn (Nikolova et al., 2009). The approach to the SMA project was actively participatory. I did not have all of the answers, nor did anyone else involved in the project. Together, we constructed a way of working in which we could all contribute to generating a shared approach to delivering the project. Moving away from a traditional expert model of consultancy toward a social learning model (Nikolova and Reihlen) was a particularly freeing experience. To be thought of, and to act as, a thinking and doing partner enables a different kind of relationship to develop; one of equipoise. It removes the constraint of having to have an answer and it acknowledges the uncertainty and ambiguity that comes with innovation. Being able to sit with that, in the company of others, and to be curious about what is possible was a much more authentic place to be. It gave permission to embrace the messiness and dive right in—and we achieved much more because of it.

The Schein (2016) model of 'humble consulting', recognises that being a consultant does not necessarily mean having all the answers, or indeed, at times, any answers. Humble consulting is a different way of relating to clients that is founded on a commitment to be helpful, to be honestly curious and to genuinely care about your client and what is on their mind (Schein, 2016, p. 13). Sitting with the uncertainty and ambiguity that was the SMA project, was made possible because I genuinely cared about my collaborators, and I wanted us to enjoy the project and the experience. Whilst I could bring expertise to the project, for me, it was as much about *how* we did the work together as it was about successfully delivering SMAs. I enjoyed learning with my collaborators. I think this way of working is possible even without pre-existing client relationships. I think that as consultants we can choose to work in a relational way with others and to centre relationship as the context for our work. With new clients this may take time and effort as we get to know each other. Getting comfortable with 'not knowing' is also a personal journey, even for experienced consultants. We purposefully used reflection sessions to help us learn and remain open and curious throughout the SMA project.

At regular points, the clinical psychologist led reflection sessions for the core project team. To our knowledge at the time, there was no guidebook on how to deliver SMAs, on how to successfully blend medical and non-medical interventions and expertise, on how to work with a group of patients with diverse needs in the same room at the same time, as distinct from group pain management programmes. The reflection sessions provided a safe space to negotiate our way through the challenges of working differently and our individual and collective experience of doing that. Reflection was useful as it moved us away from the technicalities of delivery and brought a focus on feelings and emotional responses. Working within a multidisciplinary team that was actively developing a different way to deliver health care was inspirational. The collective reflection enabled us to share our anxieties, hopes and aspirations for the work and each other and it was fascinating to see how each of us had come to the work with different expectations and assumptions. The strength of the reflective sessions, in some way, was that they set the tone for how we would work together—relationally and with care—as we negotiated our way through the innovation project.

Alongside my agreed consultancy role, which included roles as project and bid lead, developing and facilitating design workshops, chairing the project steering group, being the key contact with the funder and producing reports and any funder requested documentation, I found myself coaching team members, writing operational processes and patient facing documents, completing environmental risk assessments and managing the budget. At face value this was scope creep (see Brady & Varkonyi-Sepp, 2025; Chap. 3 where they describe the potential causes of scope-creep). Some of the tasks I took on because team members were struggling with capacity. For tasks which we had not anticipated, I took them on because they needed doing, because I had the expertise, and because we had enough contingency in the budget. Even without a budget I would have taken on the additional tasks because I felt a deep sense of responsibility for and ownership of the project and was acutely aware of the 'ultimate client' (Schein, 1997: cited in Applebaum & Steed, 2005)—patients living with chronic pain.

That said, stepping outside of what I had agreed to do did feel unsettling. Not because I was not capable, but because it felt awkward that I had apparently not anticipated all these extra tasks and responsibilities. This mindset came from years of previously working within a traditional expert model of consultancy, where the expectation from seniors was to have the answers because 'that's what the client is paying for'. To even contemplate, let alone accept, that I might not have thought of everything was internally disconcerting. The reflection sessions helped to work this through as it reminded me that I was learning by doing alongside my client and others, and that I was necessarily managing different roles in response to the work we were doing. This process of reflection enabled me to learn more about myself and those I was working with, particularly as it helped us to create a shared set of assumptions and a common sense-making language.

This combination of a social learning model of consultancy (Nikolova et al., 2009) and embedded reflective practice brought relational working to the fore. It felt important that we, as a wider project team, worked in a way that modelled and acknowledged the value of relational endeavour, recognising that this would be a large part of the actual group consultations as patients and health practitioners re-negotiated interpersonal boundaries. This re-negotiation of how to 'be' within a group consultation was a theme that came up during the project reflection sessions as it became clearer that the social context of delivering health care within a group setting was psychologically resourcing for all involved. Peer support between the healthcare practitioners and between patients, together with the emergence of a new status quo based on sharing knowledge and group problem solving, shone a light on the deficits of the traditional ten-minute GP appointment.

Throughout the project we, as collaborators, relied on one formal contracting mechanism, which was the contract between the funder and the social enterprise. Our decision to rely solely on this and the email trail of agreements leading up to the bid, without an associated formal contract for the work we had agreed to do, was based on two things: the strength of relationship between the parties and our acceptance of the inherent risk with this approach. Whilst it was a risk to work without a formal contract, I was comfortable relying on the email trail that detailed the decisions and agreements that shaped the final bid response. Furthermore, I was reassured with the agreement to cost time into the bid that covered my efforts during the writing and submission process. This wasn't just an 'internalised' state of mind, however. I was transparent with the team that I was working on that contractual basis and once that was shared and agreed I did not spend any further time thinking about it. Had I not had such strong relationships, developed through previous work, I may have considered putting in a more formal agreement alongside the funder contract.

Having existing relationships with the client and others involved in the project was helpful. We were known to each other and therefore time wasn't taken up by ego and jostling for position. Our values were aligned particularly when it came to patient centredness and our decision making focused on the patient experience; what would make group consultations easy to engage with, how we could support patients to be part of the pilot. This attitude prevailed across the project and was the foundation for how we approached the work.

Negotiation and contracting are not just about legal documents and paperwork. They are inherently human processes that benefit from a relational lens. They are ongoing processes of dialogue, discussion, adjustment and agreement as you work alongside clients to learn and deliver together. Greenhalgh and Chapman (1995) describe a model where relationship and negotiation are inseparable, viewing relationship as the context within which negotiation occurs and through which it is given meaning. By acknowledging that we were learning by doing and that the learning was as much a part of the work as delivering the shared medical appointments, we were able to set aside the false notion of 'having all the answers'. This approach meant that we could focus on the process of negotiation as a way to explore delivery options and ways of working. Creating intentional spaces to navigate these inevitable changes can be a useful way to address the messy realities of consultancy.

Top Tips

When thinking about negotiating and contracting in consultancy work, I offer three tips:

1. First, think of negotiating and contracting as simply discussion, debate and agreement with others
2. Second, these are human processes that benefit from trusting relationships—take time to get to know your client
3. Finally, consultancy projects are rarely delivered according to plan. Negotiating and contracting, formally and informally, are ways to manage change.

Acknowledgements To those I worked alongside and learned from—we embraced the uncertainty together and are wiser for it.

Competing Interests The author has no competing interests to declare that are relevant to the content of this chapter.

References

Adams, R., & Tovey, W. (2012). *Consultancy in public services*. Policy Press. https://doi.org/10.51952/9781847429445

Applebaum, S. H., & Steed, A. J. (2005). The critical success factors in the client-consulting relationship. *Journal of Management Development, 24*(1), 68–93. https://doi.org/10.1108/02621710510572362

Bassot, B. (2016). *The reflective practice guide: An interdisciplinary approach to critical reflection*. Routledge. https://doi.org/10.4324/9781315768298

Beers, P. J., Boshuizen, H. P. A., Kirschner, P. A., & Gijselaers, W. H. (2006). Common ground, complex problems and decision making. *Group Decision and Negotiation, 15*, 529–556. https://doi.org/10.1007/s10726-006-9030-1

Brady, R., & Varkonyi-Sepp, J. (2025). A framework for consultancy in health psychology. In R. Brady, J. Varkonyi-Sepp, & J. Smith (Eds.), *The Palgrave handbook of consultancy in health psychology*. Palgrave Macmillan.

Carucci, R. A., & Tetenbaum, T. J. (2000). *The value creating consultant: How to build and sustain lasting client relationships*. AMACOM.

Cope, M. (2010). *The seven Cs of consulting* (3rd ed.). Pearson.

Edelman, D., Gierisch, J. M., McDuffie, J. R., Oddone, E., & Williams, J. W. (2015). Shared medical appointments for patients with diabetes mellitus: A systematic review. *Journal of General Internal Medicine, 30*, 99–106. https://doi.org/10.1007/s11606-014-2978-7

Faculty of Pain Medicine of the Royal College of Anaesthetists. (n.d.). *Opioids aware*. https://www.fpm.ac.uk/opioids-aware

Fisher, R., Ury, W., & Patton, B. (1991). *Getting to yes: Negotiating agreement without giving in* (2nd ed.). Random House Business Books.

Gatchel, R. J., Peng, Y. B., Peters, M. L., Fuchs, P. N., & Turk, D. C. (2007). The biopsychosocial approach to chronic pain: Scientific advances and future directions. *Psychological Bulletin, 133*(4), 581–624. https://doi.org/10.1037/0033-2909.133.4.581

Greenhalgh, L., & Chapman, D. I. (1995). Joint decision making: The inseparability of relationships and negotiation. In R. M. Kramer & D. M. Messick (Eds.), *Negotiation as a social process* (pp. 166–185). Sage.

Hartnett, T. (2010). *Consensus oriented decision making: A CODM model for facilitating groups to widespread agreement*. New Society Publishers.

Hayhoe, B., Verma, A., & Kumar, S. (2017). Shared medical appointments. *BMJ, 358*. https://doi.org/10.1136/bmj.j4034

Hogan, C. F. (2003). *Practical facilitation: A toolkit of techniques*. Kogan Page.

Hoover, D. (1986). A holistic approach to pain management. *Journal of Holistic Nursing, 4*(1), 16–19. https://doi.org/10.1177/089801018600400105

Karantinou, K. M., & Hogg, M. K. (2001). Exploring relationship management in professional services: A study of management consultancy. *Journal of Marketing Management, 17*(3–4), 263–286.

Kirsh, S. R., Aron, D. C., Johnson, K. D., Santurri, L. E., Stevenson, L. D., Jones, K. R., & Jagosh, J. (2017). A realist review of shared medical appointments: How, for whom, and under what circumstances do they work? *BMC Health Services Research, 17*(113), 1–13. https://doi.org/10.1186/s12913-017-2064-z

Kordowicz, M., Moss, D., Bloxham, S., Edwards-Smith, E., Parry-Jones, C. E., Rayment, J., & Vaughan, S. (2025). *Shared medical appointments for multimorbidity: Harnessing the relational.* Qeios. https://doi.org/10.32388/J42BCH

Kress, H., Aldington, D., Alon, E., Coaccioli, S., Collett, B., Coluzzi, F., Huygen, F., Jaksch, W., Kalso, E., Kocot-Kepska, M., Mangas, A. C., Ferri, C. M., Mavrocordatos, P., Morlion, B., Muller-Schwefe, G., Nicolaou, A., Hernandez, C. P., & Sichere, P. (2015). A holistic approach to chronic pain management that involves all stakeholders: Change is needed. *Current Medical Research and Opinion, 31*(9), 1743–1754. https://doi.org/10.1185/03007995.2015.1072088

Menkel-Meadow, C. (2022). *Negotiation: A very short introduction.* Oxford University Press.

National Institute for Health and Care Excellence. (2021). *Chronic pain (primary and secondary) in over 16s: Assessment of all chronic pain and management of chronic primary pain.* https://www.nice.org.uk/guidance/ng193

Nikolova, N., Reihlen, M., & Schlapfner, J. F. (2009). Client–consultant interaction: Capturing social practices of professional service production. *Scandinavian Journal of Management, 25*(3), 289–298. https://doi.org/10.1016/j.scaman.2009.05.004

Richardson, G. P., & Anderson, D. F. (1995). Teamwork in group model building. *System Dynamics Review, 11*, 113–137. https://doi.org/10.1002/sdr.4260110203

Schein, E. H. (2016). *Humble consulting: How to provide real help faster.* Berrett-Koehler Publishers Inc.

Solomonson, W. L. (2012). Trust and the client–consultant relationship. *Performance Improvement Quarterly, 25*, 53–80. https://doi.org/10.1002/piq.21123

Stellman, S., & Ellis, B. (2024). Making chronic pain less painful—For everyone. *British Journal of General Practice, 74*(738), 30–31. https://doi.org/10.3399/bjgp24X736017

Williams, T. (2017). The nature of risk in complex projects. *Project Management Journal, 48*(4), 55–66. https://doi.org/10.1177/875697281704800405

23

Planning and Managing: Consultancy for Establishing a Multidisciplinary Rehabilitation Outpatient Clinic

Avital Gershfeld-Litvin

Introduction

In Israel, as in several other countries, the title *medical psychologist* refers to clinicians working with people with medical physical conditions, who are specifically trained to work within the general health system. This interdisciplinary area bridges the discipline of psychology and the medical profession and also bridges research and practice in the areas of health and illness. The field of *medical psychology* includes the specialties of *health psychology, rehabilitation psychology, pediatric psychology, neuropsychology,* and *psychopharmacology,* psychosomatics, as well as subspecialties in consultancy within medical settings, such as preparation for intrusive medical interventions. The term medical psychology encompasses the multiple specialties that make up *healthcare psychology,* embracing the *biopsychosocial paradigm* of mental/physical health and extending that paradigm to clinical practice through research and the application of *evidence-based* diagnostic and treatment procedures. Thus, medical psychologists share several characteristics with those of health psychology, behavioural medicine, and clinical psychology, and are licensed to practice psychotherapy (Jacoby, 2001, 2005; Moore & Muse, 2012).

A. Gershfeld-Litvin (✉)
The Academic College of Tel Aviv-Yaffo, Tel Aviv, Israel
e-mail: avitalgr@mta.ac.il

R. Brady et al. (eds.), *The Palgrave Handbook of Consultancy in Health Psychology*,
https://doi.org/10.1007/978-3-031-94529-8_23

The leadership at the Department of Neurological Rehabilitation (NRD) at a hospital in Israel asked me, as the medical psychologist working in the rehabilitation inpatient unit, to develop a proposal for an enhanced outpatient service. The idea was to establish a specific outpatient service for patients discharged from inpatient care who needed further multidisciplinary rehabilitation. This would enable patients to improve their motor functioning using cutting-edge technology physiotherapy (PT) and occupational therapy (OT). Patients would also receive the psychological treatment they needed while transitioning back to their home life. Although no formal written contract was involved, these aims informed the proposal, and the development of the new service. The assessment, or enquiry, phase of this internal consultancy programme, lasted around two months. In the initial phase of a programme, consultants may choose to rely in their enquiry solely on information provided by the client, in this case, the doctor heading the NRD and the physiotherapist heading the outpatient clinic. I expanded my enquiry, speaking with others within the organisation before submitting a proposal (Lalonde, 2011).

Assessing Clinic Functioning and Needs, Setting Goals

According to the guidelines and principles of clinical psychology in medical settings it is essential to recognise and study both the external and internal expectations and requirements of the healthcare system (American Psychological Association APA, 2013). I acquainted myself, therefore, with a variety of contextual factors, cultural dynamics, and systemic aspects, to develop an outpatient clinic service that would effectively address the demands and needs of my client stakeholders both at the NRD and at the existing outpatient clinic. I also had to consider the *ultimate clients* (Schein, 1997): the patients who would ultimately benefit from the programme. For a comprehensive approach to the consultancy, I outlined three distinct subobjectives: (1) familiarising myself with the characteristics of the existing outpatient clinic; (2) identifying the requirements for transitioning the existing clinic into an enhanced outpatient service; and (3) acquiring an in-depth understanding of patient needs within the framework for the service (Hodges, 2021).

Familiarisation with the Existing Outpatient Clinic

My initial enquiry focused on the needs of the existing clinic team and patients. Over a period of two months, I conducted meetings to gather information and insights. These meetings included several joint sessions with the clinic manager, the head of NRD, and managers of the hospital general outpatient unit. I asked them to describe the day-to-day operation of the clinic, and their views of the patients' experience. I also wanted to know their opinions on changes needed to improve the functioning of the clinic. I met with the staff and spent days in the clinic as an observer to deepen my understanding of their needs. I also drew upon my previous experience in treating post-discharge patients, which allowed me to gain insights into the unique requirements of the clinic from a medical psychology perspective.

The existing outpatient clinic was located a 15-minute walking distance from the hospital main building and offered separate and individual PT and OT sessions. Patients with a variety of conditions were treated at the clinic, including people with spinal cord injuries, brain injuries, neurological disorders, head injuries, orthopedic injuries, cerebral palsy, and more. The clinic offered innovative and advanced technologies, including the use of robot-assisted therapy to facilitate mobility even for individuals with complete paralysis. Patients treated at the clinic had to be referred by a specialist rehabilitation physician or another specialist physician based on a need to improve rehabilitation using technological means.

The clinic provided individual treatments or a combination of two consecutive therapies: PT along with hydrotherapy (HT) or OT. The clinic team included a full-time manager (a physiotherapist), three part-time physiotherapists, one part-time occupational therapist, and two additional occupational therapists available for two to three hours twice a week. Collaboration between the physiotherapists and occupational therapists occurred solely for the purpose of coordinating the appointment schedule. There were no psychological services at the clinic. Therefore, the existing clinic was not offering a full-day rehabilitation programme outpatient clinic.

Typically, patients who were discharged from hospital with a recommendation for outpatient intensive rehabilitation care would require two to four days per week of multiple and diverse rehabilitation therapy as well as ongoing medical follow-up by both nurses and physicians and social support provided by a social worker. Patients would have been referred to a general rehabilitation clinic in the hospital, which had three primary limitations. First, long waiting periods, sometimes several months, for admission to outpatient care. Second, the clinic did not have high-tech equipment to improve motor function. Third, the clinic did not offer the option to maintain therapy with the treating medical psychologist. This last limitation was significant for me as a medial psychologist, as it meant discontinuing psychotherapy with patients I had been treating all through their inpatient hospitalisation period, and with whom I had formed a therapeutic alliance. The transition from inpatient to outpatient care is psychologically challenging; continuing the therapeutic continuum is one of the strategies to ease the reintegration to life, and adjust to the disability (Rimmer & Henley, 2013).

Clinic and Staff

Since the outpatient team was multidisciplinary, I took both intra- and inter-team aspects into consideration. I learned that the staff consisted of people from different disciplines that were intended to cooperate. Staff members were in contact with other teams daily: monodisciplinary teams (e.g., the HT team) and multidisciplinary teams (e.g., the NRD team). I reflected on writings by Korner (2008, 2010) on multi- and interdisciplinary team approaches in rehabilitation clinics and I comment below on important insights from this. I met with current clinical staff and non-clinical staff members with whom we would collaborate daily (e.g., pool staff, external OT team), as well as with the rehabilitation specialist physician who would later become an attending physician of the outpatient unit.

These meetings helped me to acquaint myself with staff members and with the formal and informal work procedures of the clinic. I became familiar with the technology used and I observed a variety of treatments provided to patients with different illnesses or injuries. I was impressed by how the long-standing collaboration between team members from different fields fostered strong and informal personal relationships. I learned that the working model within this multidisciplinary clinic was characterised by a centralised type of management (Korner, 2010), where the clinic manager was responsible for receiving patients referred to the clinic by other physicians. In terms of therapist–patient relationships, I learned that rapport between staff members and patients was mostly informal. Staff members did not wear hospital uniform, both therapists and patients addressed one another by their first names, and coffee stations and lavatories were shared between staff and patients.

Identifying Requirements for Transitioning the Existing Clinic into an Outpatient Unit

Based on this work to familiarise myself with the clinic's daily functioning, its patients' needs, and the general requirements of an outpatient unit, I identified several issues that would require careful consideration and further intervention as part of my consultancy.

Logistical Issues

The clinic was located in an old structure, situated outside the main hospital grounds. The 15-minute walk to the hospital could take longer for patients with physical disabilities. The geographical distance could pose a significant challenge in all aspects of multidisciplinary teamwork (such as the arrival of physicians for regular patient examinations and joint staff sessions), as well as for patients, limiting their access to other therapeutic services (art workshops, hydrotherapy), and even catering services. While initially the new outpatient service would be based at the existing site, these issues were expected to be resolved through the relocation of the service to the new, spacious hospital wing within the NRD at a later date.

Setting and Ethical Issues

The building consisted of one room where PT sessions could take place, which simultaneously served as the clinic manager's office and as a storage space. I realised that holding joint staff meetings without disturbances, given the lack of appropriate space, could prove to be a challenge. Conducting psychological sessions in privacy in this setting would not be possible.

Objectives for Consultancy with Staff Members

Staff members were not trained in psychological aspects of rehabilitation, particularly regarding post-discharge emotional impact, nor were they experienced in working in a collaborative interdisciplinary way. Two of the objectives, therefore, were to provide psychoeducation to staff members regarding the psychosocial needs of patients post-discharge, and to implement an interdisciplinary team model.

Identifying Patient Needs

Transitions of care have emerged as an important point of vulnerability in the healthcare system (Josephson, 2016). Hospital discharge and transition involve unique psychological aspects that differ from those typical of the hospitalisation period. First, discharge itself can be a stressful event. After an extended period away from home, patients are then required to readjust to relationships; family life and work life may entail dealing with new expectations and demands. Drastic changes inherent to discharge after a long period of inpatient care can be experienced as personal, marital, and familial stressors (Neeman et al., 2011). Second, discharge highlights gaps between the patient's actual functional states and what they hoped to achieve. Most patients are discharged in a functional state that is different from their pre-illness or pre-injury state, and they face the need to reconcile changes in their bodies with their expectations for role engagement in the real-life world (Rumble et al., 2013; Wood et al., 2010).

In my professional experience, this holds particularly true for patients who still require ongoing outpatient care and hope to achieve complete recovery. Discharge accelerates meaning construction processes of the illness or injury, grief over multiple losses, and any potential effects on one's self-perception and identity (Neeman et al., 2011). Patients struggle to come to terms with the consequences of their illness and functional challenges, while simultaneously maintaining hope for improvement. Thus, the constant anticipation of continued improvement could potentially lead patients to "put everything else on hold, solely continue working on recovery", as a patient of mine once described.

Another gap exists between life during and post-hospitalisation. As an inpatient, the person lives in a controlled environment in conditions that cater to their every need in terms of accessibility, nursing care, medical supervision, provision of food and medication, and a structured routine for daily treatments. Upon discharge, they are faced with the challenge of organising all these elements themselves, grappling with issues of accessibility, mobility, bureaucracy, and a perception of system abandonment (Guilcher et al., 2013).

These aspects represent the most prominent psychological challenges of the post-discharge period and emphasise the need for continuous uninterrupted psychological treatment. In a period characterised by dynamic shifts and changes, the psychological treatment that began in the hospitalisation period may serve as a stabilising factor.

Planning and Managing after Initial Enquiry

Getting acquainted with the requirements for establishing a new outpatient service within an existing clinic helped me develop a comprehensive interdisciplinary medical psychology programme. As a medical psychologist, it was a unique opportunity to recommend a service that would essentially integrate the biopsychosocial approach (Engel, 1977) which would consider biological, psychological, social, and interpersonal factors related to health and illness. Collaboration between the psychological service and the outpatient service would also be in line with one of the goals of modern medicine—developing a holistic treatment programme led and operated by a multidisciplinary team (Korner, 2010).

The consultancy programme encapsulated both administrative and psychological principles. First, transitioning from a multidisciplinary working model to an interdisciplinary working model. Second, developing the administrative framework of the outpatient service. Third, patient care coordination. Fourth, providing consultations, training, and psychoeducation to multidisciplinary team members. Fifth, providing psychological treatment for patients. The initial enquiry work had effectively laid the groundwork for establishing the outpatient clinic which was opened a few months later.

Planning and Managing Delivery: Implementing the 'Psychologist Case Manager Model'

The new outpatient service opened its doors in 2012 for a one-year trial period. A decision had been made to assess, throughout this period, whether the clinic could effectively operate as an outpatient unit in terms of organisation, management, and its capacity to handle the treatment workload.

Assessing Needs and Setting Goals

The new outpatient service relied on existing clinic staff, without any changes except for my joining the team as the head of the service and as its chief psychologist. Simultaneously, the service continued to operate as a facility that also served patients seeking individual therapies. In my new role, I was responsible only for patients who were referred to the intensive care programme within the framework of the outpatient service.

A primary need for real-time flexibility was identified throughout this trial period. Due to the swift establishment of the service and the fact we were going through a trial period, we had to continually reassess its performance and adjust as needed. In practice, I had weekly meetings with the head of the clinic to discuss problems with patients, staff, scheduling, and to evaluate changes needed. In addition, based on needs identified during the pre-establishment stage, I adopted the five previously mentioned principles of the programme (transitioning to an interdisciplinary working model; developing administrative framework; patient care coordination; providing consultations to team members; and providing psychological treatment for patients) as the objectives for the systemic consultancy.

Another need that emerged was to identify patients among those hospitalised in the NRD who were eligible for discharge, and who were well-suited from a psycho-medical perspective, to receive further treatments at the outpatient unit. This was established by coordinating with the psychology team at the inpatient ward. Together we discussed the psychological needs for each patient who were recommended for further rehabilitation before discharge.

Implementing the Psychologist Case Manager Model

In the planning and managing phase of the intervention, I chose to implement the psychologist case manager model (Clark, 2011). The definition of the role of a case manager (CM) is to facilitate the integration of assessment, planning, implementation, coordination, and supervision processes of all available services necessary for and in agreement with the medical needs of the patient (Clark, 2011). All of this is achieved using communication and available resources to promote cost-effective results (Roggenkampa et al., 2005). Thus, the CM role is to align the patient's needs with systems while minimising unnecessary waste of time and resources for both parties.

The principles of case management include ensuring continuity, accessibility, focusing on patient–staff relationships, tailoring the programme to the patient's needs and capabilities, and aiming to improve self-sufficiency (Clark, 2011). For example, a patient with spinal injury and fecal incontinence who requires a couple of hours to get ready in the morning due to their condition, may find it beneficial if they could start their rehabilitation programme at the clinic later in the day. Another example is a patient who would like to end their treatment session at 13:00 so they could pick up their children from school (this was particularly significant for one patient who had been hospitalised for 10 months straight).

Another responsibility of the CM is to monitor the treatment plan and the mental health of the patient and, should the need arise, to adapt it accordingly (Mas-Expósito et al., 2013). The reality of my dual role compelled me to consider the ethics of holding two positions that are interconnected in terms of how they relate to the patient. Among other things, in my capacity as CM I evaluated whether I should also serve as each patient's therapist on a case-by-case basis. Could the information I had regarding the patient, in my capacity as CM, affect therapy and how? Should I share the fact that I know certain things about the patient with the patient or not?

The literature (Clark, 2011) on case management suggests that psychotherapy and case management can be combined. It is stated that the evolving relationship between the CM and the patient contributes to the cultivation of the therapeutic alliance. Consequently, integrating an individual with psychological training into the CM role enhances the effectiveness of the CM, as a psychologist can better comprehend the patient's needs, facilitating appropriate interventions and improving adherence to psychological and medical treatments. In my time as the head of the unit, I followed this case manager-psychologist (CMP) model (Clark, 2011) whenever I worked on cases, both as a CM and as a therapist. In some cases, patients continued to receive treatment from the psychologist who treated them during inpatient rehabilitation owing to the importance of therapeutic continuity. In other cases, it was deemed inappropriate for the CM to also provide therapy for a specific patient. In such cases, whenever ethical issues arose, I would refer the patient to another psychologist and act as a liaison between the therapist and other staff members. In any case, the continuation of a therapeutic relationship that began during hospitalisation would require adaptations in terms of the treatment goals, therapeutic contract, and therapeutic setting.

Assembling a Team Operating on an Interdisciplinary Team Model

The existing clinic staff operated on a multidisciplinary team model (Korner, 2008, 2010), which consisted of staff members from multiple disciplines with no formal collaboration. The model I aimed to develop was an interdisciplinary model, in accordance with The World Health Organization (World Health Organization, 2006) definition of neuro-rehabilitation. According to this interdisciplinary model, each sub-team would work collaboratively, meet regularly, conduct discussions about each patient, and thus would be able to create an integrative treatment plan together. This team-based model is characterised by high-quality cooperation and communication. In line with APA guidelines for the integration of medical psychologists in the healthcare system (APA, 2013), I introduced the following measures.

Joint Staff Sessions

Before the establishment of the outpatient service there had been no joint staff sessions. When I joined the staff as head of the unit, I initiated the practice of monthly or bi-monthly joint staff sessions, where members from all sub-teams would conduct discussions on each patient together. These sessions also included discussions about new patients and whether they were well-suited for the outpatient clinic framework, as well as decisions regarding discharges. I took great care in leading these discussions and contributing to the development of admission and discharge policies, assigning particular emphasis to providing equal significance to psychological factors in the formulation of treatment plans, admissions, and discharges.

Methods of Team Communication and Data Transference

Communication between staff members was conducted both formally and informally. First, I organised a system for transferring information to staff via email and phone messages consisting of weekly itineraries, updates about schedule changes, topics for weekly staff sessions, and reminders regarding treatment summary reports which are required for the preparation of requests for extension of outpatient care. All the information was compiled and conveyed to the staff by me. Second, patient medical records were updated to include sections dedicated to psychological treatments, alongside other sectors which already exist in the system. I ensured that documentation guidelines were followed with respect to treatment sessions, phone conversations with patients, and recommendation letters in preparation for discharge.

Integrating Team Formulation as a Consultancy

I took great care to familiarise staff with the contribution of psychosocial components to the medical perspective, and with integrating formulation into the work of the team by establishing joint meetings and discussions on each patient. Each staff member would describe their interaction with the patient, and they shared perceptions about the patient's progress and difficulties. I used these meetings to gently and respectfully enhance understanding of patients and to suggest different views based on my psychological insights when needed.

Team formulation can be seen as a type of staff consultation or supervision and is likely to focus on allowing space for understanding and processing staff feelings such as frustration, stuckness, or hopelessness (Johnstone, 2013, 2018). I provided in-depth descriptions of the psychological aspects of transitioning from inpatient care to outpatient care as well as the characteristics of various illnesses staff members had yet to encounter when they were required to provide more intensive care. In this way, I was also able to demonstrate my own contribution as a medical psychologist to the betterment of patient motivation and health, and to the development of treatment plans tailored to each patient.

In the normal course of operations at the service, additional staff needs were identified. As patients with more complex conditions were admitted to the clinic for treatment, team members encountered and reported new challenges. Team case formulations helped staff members to understand their patients' behaviour as well as establishing a more coherent rehabilitation plan. Among my responsibilities as the head of the unit, I regularly advised and supported staff members in matters related to adherence to treatment, managing expectations based on medical treatment plans, dealing with patients' disappointments, personal behavioural issues, and liaising with patients' families. For example, one patient arrived at the clinic believing she would relearn to walk. The staff believed, however, that she would not be able to take more than a few steps on her own and would otherwise need support equipment to walk.

A new challenge emerged whenever staff needed to notify patients of their imminent discharge from the outpatient service. Due to the hospital-based framework of the service, it was necessary to establish clear treatment goals. Once treatment objectives were met, the patient could be discharged from outpatient care at the hospital and continue treatment in an outpatient care framework in their community. Patients would sometimes meet these notices of discharge with dissatisfaction and disappointment. The physiotherapists, led by the head of the clinic, struggled to deal with these reactions and, in some cases, refrained from addressing the expected discharge with the patient (Wiles et al., 2004). This resulted in patients expressing reluctance to be discharged and feeling confused and abandoned. I also supported members of staff in dealing with personal issues that came up in their encounters with patients' illnesses and disabilities. In the previous multidisciplinary framework, such issues were mostly unaddressed, as there were no onsite psychologists at the clinic.

Identifying Patients from Within the Department Before Discharge

Since I had worked in the NRD before assuming the role of head of the outpatient rehabilitation service, I believed it was important to identify eligible patients as early as their admission to inpatient care. In fact, this goal served as the fundamental rationale for the establishment of the outpatient rehabilitation service. The idea was to ensure therapeutic continuity in all aspects of treatment. I collaborated with the chief psychologist in the NRD and the attending physician from the service (who was also a physician in the NRD), to evaluate the prognosis of new patients in the department. We also sought the professional opinion of a social worker regarding coverage for medical expenses. We developed criteria for early identification of patients with a greater potential to benefit from the outpatient rehabilitation service treatment programmes upon their eventual discharge. We agreed on the following criteria: first, patient history of impaired physical functioning or spinal injury; second, prognosis based on rehabilitative medical measures; third, preparedness to enter psychological treatment based on pre-intake conversations during the initial days of hospitalisation; fourth, place of permanent residence in relative proximity to the hospital within the district as required for insurance coverage of outpatient hospital care by the health maintenance organisations. These criteria enabled me to begin treatment with patients during their hospitalisation, thereby fostering the therapeutic alliance prior to their discharge from the department. In general, whether a patient in the department was treated by me or by another therapist, if they were expected to continue treatment at the outpatient service, they received notification of the fact directly from me as liaison between inpatient and outpatient phases. During these conversations, which occurred prior to discharge, I described the outpatient service, provided an overview of the treatment programme, and obtained important personal information (distance from hospital, time estimation to arrive each morning, difficulties in waking up in the morning and getting ready for rehabilitation, medication, and mental state that should be taken under consideration) that would later be used to tailor the treatment programme to the patient's needs. I believe this process facilitated the transition between the department and the outpatient service.

Reflection and Evaluating Intervention Effectiveness

After a one-year trial period, the new outpatient service became permanent. It had successfully provided rehabilitation for six patients who received intensive day care three times a week on a regular basis. In fact, for the first time, the establishment of the outpatient rehabilitation service allowed for psycho-medical therapeutic continuity, beginning with hospitalisation, through out-patient hospital care at the new service, and onward to outpatient care in the community. As far as the department was concerned, the outpatient service achieved its goals, since the capacity to provide outpatient care doubled and tripled gradually from the initial five to eight patients weekly. However, my evaluation took additional quantitative criteria into consideration.

Interdisciplinary Cooperation

First and foremost, I examined whether I was able to reach interdisciplinary cooperation, where the psychologist and the physician determine the combined biopsychosocial-based treatment plan together. The intervention would be deemed effective indeed only when this goal was achieved (Sinclair et al., 2009). Following an adjustment period of several months, staff members' workflow fully transitioned to an interdisciplinary model guided by teamwork and regulated by a routine of collaborative staff sessions. Every patient was admitted following a joint discussion between me, the head of the clinic, and the attending physician, taking into consideration both the physical and psychological aspects as equally important factors. Additionally, in some cases patients who did not meet the full medical criteria for admission were admitted to the unit. For example, when a patient's chances of improving their motor functions were slim but they required intensive psychological treatment.

Assessing Patient Satisfaction

Patient satisfaction is another significant factor in assessing the effectiveness of systemic interventions (Sinclair et al., 2009). Conversations with patients revealed that the possibility of therapeutic continuity was a crucial factor in deciding to attend the clinic and in boosting their confidence during the transition from inpatient to outpatient care. For patients, the possibility of therapeutic continuity was a source of peace and solace following inpatient care.

Furthermore, patients reported that having to connect and build trust with a new therapist, who knew nothing of their struggles or achievements prior to discharge, was an intimidating notion. The fact that I also served as a CM made it easier for patients to transition to the outpatient unit, because they needed someone who would be attentive to and aware of their psychological needs (Emerich et al., 2012). Patients shared with me the comfort they felt knowing I also worked at the inpatient unit. They felt they were seen by someone who understood the journey they had gone through and who acknowledged their accomplishments as well as their challenges. From their perspective, I served as a bridge to the world of the discharged patient, so to speak. The question of patient feedback was complex, since I deliberated what kind of questions to ask: Were they satisfied with the new clinic rehabilitation programme? With their personal rehabilitation process? With me as their CM? With the therapeutic process? I assessed their satisfaction by observing their attendance and by identifying themes relating to the rehabilitation process that I identified during our conversations. In retrospect, the use of formal qualitative and quantitative measures to assess satisfaction from various aspects would have been useful.

Assessing Staff Satisfaction

The final factor in assessing the effectiveness of the intervention was staff satisfaction (Sinclair et al., 2009). Though not measured quantitatively using questionnaires, satisfaction was evident in the way the staff and I functioned as one cohesive unit: we had regular staff meetings and discussions regarding admission and discharge, we consulted on patient adherence to rehabilitation activities, we shared insights regarding psychological coping and difficulties affecting the rehabilitation process. Staff members shared with me and with management that they felt that the support they needed was finally available to them. For me, the evidence for the successful intervention was when staff members initiated conversations with me about their challenges with patients. I seamlessly assimilated with my team and together we developed an informal relationship, cultivating a relaxed professional atmosphere.

The most unambiguous vote of confidence in the effectiveness of the intervention was the fact that at the end of the one-year trial, I was offered a permanent position as the head psychologist of the outpatient service. I worked at the service from the end of my residency until recently. The service has since moved to a new building within the main rehabilitation building, where a room is specifically allocated for a psychologist, and several other psychologists have been integrated to the service. I consider these moves proof of the idea that the presence of a medical psychologist can be vital and integral to the system (Jacoby, 2001, 2005).

The number of patients gradually increased in the following years and, currently, 20 to 30 patients attend for rehabilitation. Following the success of the model of operation, three new specified sub-clinics were established within the service, each offering a rehabilitation outpatient programme, including a psychological component, for specific conditions: Parkinson's and movement disorders, Neuro-oncology; and Ehlers-Danlos syndrome. Accordingly, the psychology staff has grown in order to provide the necessary assessment and psychotherapy.

The integration of psychologists within the healthcare system essentially represents an application of the biopsychosocial model (Engel, 1977). Integrating psychologists as part of the medical treatment team, where psychological services are provided concurrently and in coordination with medical and paramedical services, contributes to the promotion of health and treatment of patients based on both physical and mental aspects (Gatchel & Oordt, 2003; Suls & Rothman, 2004). A medical psychologist in the healthcare system should be able to apply clinical abilities (diagnosis and assessments of psychological distress) and provide diverse therapeutic interventions in terms of type and duration. Thus, they should integrate seamlessly in the system, demonstrate their presence in the clinic, and implement an interdisciplinary team model (Auxier et al., 2011). Additionally, the psychologist should become familiar with the therapeutic setting and be able to work as part of a collaborative team (Tovian, 2006).

Psychology consultancy in medical settings is the use of psychological skills and knowledge to facilitate, develop, or enhance the effectiveness of others in the maintenance and improvement of human health. This case study describes a consultancy aimed at improving rehabilitation services for people living with disabilities, post-hospitalisation. As a medical psychologist, I have been trained to deal with the full spectrum of health and illness and to focus on biopsychosocial and systemic aspects (Jacoby, 2001, 2005). I believe my training meets the requirements for establishing and operating the outpatient rehabilitation service (APA, 2013).

Another related skill of a medical psychologist is a significant degree of flexibility, which is required in order to be able to do the job well (Tovian, 2006). Such flexibility could be observed through my ability to offer therapeutic interventions to staff members as well as patients, and to provide integrative psychotherapy combining different therapeutic approaches (psychodynamic, existential, narrative, cognitive-behavioural, and psycho-educational).

In establishing a new outpatient clinic, I acted both as a consultant and as an implementor as the consultancy progressed from inquiry through planning and to managing delivery, and evaluation. The opportunity to lead the efforts behind the establishment of an outpatient rehabilitation service proved a challenge in my dual role as an administrator and a psychologist. At the outset, a great responsibility was placed upon me, and I saw it as an opportunity to highlight the significant contribution of a medical psychologist within the healthcare system. Furthermore, the prospect of providing psychological treatment to patients, following their discharge, resonated with me. After an extended period of tending to patients who were hospitalised in the department until their discharge, I now had the chance to accompany them during another significant period of their rehabilitation. I viewed it as a profound calling. Up until then, patients with whom I cultivated a supportive and empathetic therapeutic relationship would not have been able to continue treatment with me post-hospitalisation, even when they expressed their willingness to do so.

The establishment of the outpatient clinic meant that I was finally able to meet patient needs through a continuous treatment process that would allow patients to continue to rely on our established relationship, particularly at a time when they needed it most. In addition, I felt that my experience of treating patients during hospitalisation enhanced my understanding of the experience, challenges, and needs of patients who had recently been discharged. Consequently, the perspective I gained during residency has not only helped me diagnose and treat patients then, but also continued to serve this purpose when I transitioned into my new role at the outpatient service

In retrospect, as I reflect on my experience, I wish I had an external co-consultant to reflect in real time on the consultancy process and implementation. The combination of roles—interdisciplinary staff member, CM, and psychotherapist—was challenging and hindered my ability to fully assess the consultancy. In many ways, once the consultancy was implemented, I was assimilated in the new clinic, and as such no longer a consultant.

Top Tips

1. Familiarise yourself with the setting and staff on a personal and professional level so that you are accepted as a consultant.
2. Psychoeducation is a fundamental intervention explaining the psychologist's role within the rehabilitation and medical domains to both patients and staff.

3. Follow the steps suggested in this chapter to begin with assessment, observation, and planning. The medical system may request a swift solution, but consultancy requires time and thought for long-lasting changes.

Competing Interests The author has no competing interests to declare that are relevant to the content of this chapter.

References

American Psychological Association (APA). (2013). Guidelines for psychological practice in health care delivery systems. *American Psychologists, 68*(1), 1–6. https://doi.org/10.1037/a0029890

Auxier, A., Farley, T., & Seirert, K. (2011). Establishing an integrated care practice in a community health center. *Professional Psychology: Research and Practice, 42*(5), 391–397. https://doi.org/10.1037/a0024982

Clark, S. (2011). Integration of supportive psychotherapy with case management for older adults with borderline personality disorder. *Journal of Gerontological Social Work, 54*(6), 627–638. https://doi.org/10.1080/01634372.2011.585391

Emerich, L., Parsons, K. C., & Stein, A. (2012). Competent care for persons with spinal cord injury and dysfunction in acute inpatient rehabilitation. *Topics in Spinal Cord Injury Rehabilitation, 18*(2), 149. https://doi.org/10.1310/sci1802-149

Engel, G. L. (1977). The need for a new medical model: A challenge for biomedicine. *Science, 196*, 129–136. https://doi.org/10.4135/9781446221129.n3

Gatchel, R. J., & Oordt, M. S. (2003). *Clinical health psychology and primary care: Practical advice and clinical guidance for successful collaboration*. APA. https://doi.org/10.1037/10592-000

Guilcher, S. J., Craven, B. C., Lemieux-Charles, L., Casciaro, T., McColl, M. A., & Jaglal, S. B. (2013). Secondary health conditions and spinal cord injury: An uphill battle in the journey of care. *Disability and Rehabilitation, 35*(11), 894–906. https://doi.org/10.3109/09638288.2012.721048

Hodges, J. (2021). A framework for consulting. *Management Consulting, 4*(2), 52–55. https://doi.org/10.2478/mcj-2021-0009

Jacoby, R. (2001). Medical psychology in Israel. *Journal of Clinical Psychology in Medical Settings, 8*, 45–50.

Jacoby, R. (2005). Psychology in Israel. In *The handbook of international psychology* (pp. 419–435). Routledge.

Johnstone, L. (2013). Using formulation in teams. In *Formulation in psychology and psychotherapy* (pp. 216–242). Routledge. https://doi.org/10.4324/9780203380574-18

Johnstone, L. (2018). Psychological formulation as an alternative to psychiatric diagnosis. *Journal of Humanistic Psychology, 58*(1), 30–46. https://doi.org/10.1177/0022167817722230
Josephson, S. A. (2016). Focusing on transitions of care: A change is here. *Neurology: Clinical Practice, 6*(2), 183–189. https://doi.org/10.1212/cpj.0000000000000207
Korner, M. (2008). Analysis and development of multiprofessional teams in medical rehabilitation. *GMS Psycho-Social Medicine, 5.*
Korner, M. (2010). Interprofessional teamwork in medical rehabilitation: A comparison of multidisciplinary and interdisciplinary team approach. *Clinical Rehabilitation, 24*, 745–755. https://doi.org/10.1177/0269215510367538
Lalonde, C. (2011). Challenging universal criteria in management consulting: When practices meet prescriptions. In A. F. Buono, R. Grossmann, H. Lobnig, & K. Mayer (Eds.), *The changing paradigm of consulting: Adjusting to the fast-paced world* (pp. 279–308). Information Age Publishing, Inc.
Mas-Expósito, L., Amador-Campos, J. A., Gómez-Benito, J., & Lalucat-Jo, L. (2013). Depicting current case management models. *Journal of Social Work*, 1–14. https://doi.org/10.1177/1468017313477296
Moore, B. A., & Muse, M. (2012). Medical psychology: Definitions, controversies, and new directions. In M. Muse & B. A. Moore (Eds.), *Handbook of clinical psychopharmacology for psychologists* (pp. 1–15). John Wiley & Sons, Inc.
Neeman, D., Porat, O., Shraga, E., Rotem, Z., & Poran, R. (2011). Psychological rehabilitation following physical injury: Theory and practice. In A. Ohry, A. Lazary, & R. Heruti (Eds.), *Principles of rehabilitation medicine*. Dyonon.
Rimmer, J. H., & Henley, K. Y. (2013). Building the crossroad between inpatient/outpatient rehabilitation and lifelong community-based fitness for people with neurologic disability. *Journal of Neurologic Physical Therapy, 37*(2), 72–77. https://doi.org/10.1097/npt.0b013e318291bbf6
Roggenkampa, S. D., White, K. R., & Bazzoli, G. J. (2005). Adoption of hospital case management: Economic and institutional influences. *Social Science & Medicine, 60*, 2489–2500. https://doi.org/10.1016/j.socscimed.2004.11.010
Rumble, S., Noggle, C. A., Dean, R. S., & Barisa, M. T. (2013). Transitioning into neurorehabilitation. In C. A. Noggle, R. S. Dean, & M. T. Barisa (Eds.), *Neuropsychological rehabilitation* (pp. 291–301). Springer.
Schein, E. H. (1997). The concept of "client" from a process consultation perspective: A guide for change agents. *Journal of Organizational Change Management, 10*(3), 202–216. https://doi.org/10.1108/09534819710171077
Sinclair, L. B., Lingard, L. A., & Mohabeer, R. N. (2009). What's so great about rehabilitation teams? An ethnographic study of interprofessional collaboration in a rehabilitation unit. *Archives of Physical Medicine and Rehabilitation, 90*, 1196–1201. https://doi.org/10.1016/j.apmr.2009.01.021
Suls, J., & Rothman, A. (2004). Evolution of the biopsychosocial model: Prospects and challenges for health psychology. *Health Psychology, 23*(2), 119–125. https://doi.org/10.1037/0278-6133.23.2.119

Tovian, S. M. (2006). Interdisciplinary collaboration in outpatient practice. *Professional Psychology: Research and Practice, 37*(3), 268–272. https://doi.org/10.1037/0735-7028.37.3.268

Wiles, R., Ashburn, A., Payne, S., & Murphy, C. (2004). Discharge from physiotherapy following stroke: The management of disappointment. *Social Science & Medicine, 59*(6), 1263–1273. https://doi.org/10.1016/j.socscimed.2003.12.022

Wood, J. P., Connelly, D. M., & Maly, M. R. (2010). 'Getting back to real living': A qualitative study of the process of community reintegration after stroke. *Clinical Rehabilitation, 24*(11), 1045–1056. https://doi.org/10.1177/0269215510375901

World Health Organization. (2006). Neurological disorders: Public health challenges. https://www.who.int/publications/i/item/9789241563369

24

Planning and Managing: Co-developing a Framework Addressing Self-stigma in People Living with HIV

Ashlee Mulimba and Puja Patel

Introduction

In this chapter, we describe a consultancy project to co-develop an empowerment framework to address self-stigma in people living with HIV. The framework we co-developed was published (Fast-Track Cities London, 2021), part of a global effort to end HIV by 2020 (United Nations, n.d.), and has since been widely adopted in London, England. We then focus particularly on the consultancy processes involved in planning and managing delivery in the context of working closely with stakeholders. Finally, in our reflection we discuss what we learned from our delivery of this project and from taking a retrospective view of our role as consultants.

A. Mulimba (✉) • P. Patel
Healthy Dialogues, London, UK
e-mail: ashlee@healthydialogues.co.uk; info@drpujapatel.com

R. Brady et al. (eds.), *The Palgrave Handbook of Consultancy in Health Psychology*,
https://doi.org/10.1007/978-3-031-94529-8_24

The Case Study

Tackling HIV Stigma in London

London aims to be the leading city across the world to end new cases of HIV through achieving the following ambitions: zero new HIV infections, zero preventable deaths, and zero stigma by 2030 (Fast-Track Cities, n.d.). This ambition is led by Fast-Track Cities London, which is a partnership of organisations, including the Mayor of London, NHS England, United Kingdom (UK) Health Security Agency, Integrated Care Systems, London Councils (a collective of local government in London) and the members of the HIV voluntary sector and community.

Stigma is a major hurdle for people with HIV, leading to discrimination and barriers in healthcare and biomedical prevention access (Hedge et al., 2021). Fast-Track Cities London has collaborated with over 100 individuals and organisations to combat HIV stigma and discrimination in the capital, beginning with healthcare settings and self-stigma. Self-stigma can have a tremendous impact on a person's health and well-being outcomes. For someone living with HIV, self-stigma can manifest in feelings of shame, guilt, low self-esteem, or feeling unlovable (Fast-Track Cities London, 2021). Not addressing self-stigma can result in individuals avoiding necessary care or treatment or withdrawing from societal opportunities.

Our company, Healthy Dialogues, is a health psychology consultancy that specialises in public health and behaviour change. At Healthy Dialogues, we had previously worked with colleagues from Fast-Track Cities London on other large-scale behaviour change initiatives, and we had established ourselves as authorities in the field of self-management for long-term health conditions. In April 2021, we were invited by a commissioner at Fast-Track Cities London, our client for this project, to participate in a tender to co-develop an empowerment programme framework with people with lived experience of HIV and those with experience in delivering such programmes for people living with HIV. An empowerment programme framework is a structured guide that defines the methods, strategies, and resources required to deliver training aimed at enhancing the capacity of individuals or groups to gain control over their lives and influence the decisions that affect them (Fetterman et al., 1996). This framework would be designed to provide guidance and tools for facilitators to deliver training to people living with HIV to help them to tackle self-stigma. The framework would help address one of the key strands of the client's HIV prevention work which was tackling stigma in HIV communities. Fast-Track Cities London wished to have a tangible and published framework that could be easily accessed and adapted to suit any voluntary, community and social enterprise organisation serving different populations with diverse cultures of people living with HIV.

Responding to an Invitation to Tender

In their tender, Fast-Track Cities London asked us to submit a proposal based on their specification of requirements which included three proposed activities:

1. Creation and development of a generic training empowerment programme framework with inbuilt evaluation that others can use to train people living with, affected by, and at risk of HIV, to develop resilience, confidence, and other skills to tackle self-stigma.
2. Creation and development of a framework with additional components to support the further growth and development of a group of HIV ambassadors. These ambassadors will be visible voices, sharing their stories with both people with lived experiences of HIV and the broader public community.
3. The work must be fully designed and delivered with input from the HIV community and stakeholders with the regular organisation and facilitation of focus groups expected.

Before writing a proposal, we reviewed literature on empowerment and training programmes addressing HIV-related stigma. We learned that this was a new and developing field both across the UK and internationally (Hempel et al., 2021). We found that existing empowerment programmes drew on principles and approaches of health psychology and other psychology disciplines. They included, for example, the use of cognitive behavioural therapy (Pantelic et al., 2017), motivational interviewing (Rongkavilit et al., 2015) and peer support (Tam et al., 2012). We learned that intersectionality is a major factor for many people living with HIV (Logie et al., 2011)—that is, many people who are living with HIV belong to more than one marginalised group in the UK (such as gender identity, faith-based identity, sexuality, ethnicity, immigration status, drug use or sex work), compounding the stigma and trauma they are living with. Yet, how to address it is still largely unknown (Pantelic et al., 2019). Ultimately, our research found that no one approach was effective on its own and that a combination of the above approaches was most effective (Pantelic et al., 2019; Dunbar et al., 2019).

As health psychologists, we were excited for the opportunity to deliver this work as it was innovative, and it presented a new challenge for us. We particularly value and enjoy participatory approaches to development work such as these, as they enable us to translate research evidence and health psychology practice into a programme that draws on local experiences, language and tools, and which is valued by people on the ground delivering it. We also felt that we had the expertise and experience to do this well, drawing on our practices of developing public health and community-based programmes for self-management and resilience to empower people to take steps that would enhance their quality of life, self-esteem and self-efficacy.

Our written proposal included our understanding of the programme of work, our methodology and approach, proposed outputs, and timelines and costings. We proposed a six-month programme of work utilising two health psychologists (AM and PP). Our proposal also offered assurances that the empowerment framework would recognise intersectionality and the pre-existing vulnerabilities and co-morbidities that came with it so that those who are most marginalised are able to participate. We highlighted that the empowerment framework would be co-produced from a range of voices and led by people living with HIV collaborating in a Community of Practice (CoP). A CoP is

> composed of two or more individuals who (a) exist to perform organisationally relevant tasks, (b) share one or more common goals, (c) interact socially, (d) exhibit task interdependencies (i.e., workflow, goals, outcomes), (e) maintain and manage boundaries, and (f) are embedded in an organisational context that sets boundaries, constrains the team, and influences exchanges with other units in the broader entity. (Kozlowski & Bell, 2003, p. 334)

The undertaking would be participatory, creative, trauma sensitive, and would draw on skills already in the community, an approach we consistently employ when developing behaviour change interventions. As required by the specification, we would also include training for HIV ambassadors who would work with local organisations using the empowerment framework. The HIV ambassadors would later be employed by Fast-Track Cities London to support the promotion and delivery of the empowerment programme. The ambassadors would be visible voices for Fast-Track Cities London, tackling stigma by sharing their stories and issues affecting the community both with the HIV community itself and through work targeted at the wider public.

The Plan

When submitting the proposal, we created a four-stage project plan (explained below) to highlight how we would achieve the aims and objectives of this framework based on the client's wants and needs. We included objectives, tasks, responsibilities, timelines, and risks for each stage. We will explore each of these in more detail later in the chapter. Ultimately, our plan and proposal were accepted, and we were awarded the contract to carry out the work in the summer of 2021.

Output and Evaluation

Meeting the aims of the commissioner and drawing on the expertise of the CoP, the empowerment programme framework was developed to enable delivery of key outcomes presented in Box 24.1.

Box 24.1 A Framework for Empowerment Programmes to Tackle Internalised Stigma (Fast-Track Cities London, 2021)

A set of competencies, case studies and relevant resources, and further reading materials for facilitators tackling self-stigma through an empowerment programme for people living with HIV. It includes:

1. Peer support competencies (for recruiting peer supporters to help facilitate the programme)
2. Key competencies for the empowerment programme
    - Developing a support network
    - Understanding self-stigma
    - Understanding what HIV is, U=U (undetectable-untransmittable)[1] and living well with HIV
    - Building self-acceptance, self-esteem and an individual's sense of power
    - Developing skills: including self-advocacy, public advocacy and ambassador skills
3. Evaluating your programme

[1] Undetectable = untransmittable: Effective treatment reduces the level of HIV (the viral load) in the blood of a person living with HIV. When the viral load is very low (less than 200 copies/ml of blood measured), it is called an undetectable viral load. This is also medically known as virally suppressed. At this point, HIV cannot be transmitted sexually.

In January 2022, six London organisations were commissioned by Fast-Track Cities London to deliver empowerment programmes for people living with HIV, using the framework we co-created. They delivered the programmes to different community groups, including women, mothers, gay and bisexual men, men who have sex with men, black African adults, people from Spanish and Portuguese speaking communities and people who experienced internalised stigma to the extent that it negatively impacted engagement in medical care or confidence in accessing additional external HIV support. Three of the organisations measured the impact of their programmes before, after and at three-month follow-up. They found marked improvements in all competencies of the empowerment programme framework. Qualitative feedback captured from the programmes demonstrated that participants had an improved ability to articulate their HIV status, better self-confidence, and resilience following attending the programme (Fast-Track Cities London and Healthy Dialogues, 2023). Due to these positive results, some organisations were developing plans to collaborate to continue the work on reducing stigma, whilst another had secured funding to undertake monthly peer support sessions.

Planning and Facilitating Co-Creation of the Empowerment Framework

When writing our proposal in response to the commissioner's specification we felt that our four-stage plan showed a strong, systematic approach that drew on our health psychology skills and expertise, and it defined a clear structure for achieving our goals. The first stage involved developing a project initiation document which included a communications plan, identifying risks that may interfere with the work, and conducting desk-based research to update our knowledge of the subject area. We also established that the work would be governed by the Fast-Track Cities London leadership group. During the second stage, we anticipated that the CoP would support us in reviewing any previous training frameworks and evidence that would assist in the development of the HIV empowerment framework. For the third stage, timelines were devised for fortnightly meetings with the CoP group to discuss and begin to co-develop various aspects of the empowerment framework. We anticipated this to be the longest stage of the process as co-development of any product may take some time, with discussions going back and forth until all parties are satisfied. The final stage was then presenting findings and a draft framework to the leadership group for final comments and incorporating their comments into the final empowerment framework.

Smith (2002) found that when delivering a consultancy project, consultants should clearly define the strategy, structure and process for accomplishing the change. This is an approach we begin all our consultancies with, so that both we and our clients have a clear vision on what will be achieved and how. Nevertheless, when we began the work, we felt it was important for us to re-clarify, at an inception meeting with the client, the requirements, aims and objectives of the project. We wanted to identify anything we might have missed or that had changed since the original specification. This would also provide the leadership group at Fast-Track Cities London with an opportunity to describe their priorities for the work and to ensure that we were on the same page for the co-development of the framework.

We first engaged with the Fast-Track Cities London's own *advisory group* (see Fig. 24.1). The advisory group was made up of people with lived experiences of HIV and was set up by Fast-Track Cities London to support their strategic planning. There is tremendous value in involving people with lived experience in the co-design of programmes aimed at them; it ensures that the programmes are rooted in real-life experiences and insights and address their genuine needs (Davidson et al., 2012). We invited the advisory group to take part in an interactive workshop to establish the CoP's objectives as well as the desired outcomes of the final empowerment programme training framework. The advisory group met online where we facilitated a discussion on their views about what we needed to consider, and the challenges involved in living with HIV and related stigma. This helped with our enquiry to understand the nature of the problem we were trying to address. For example, the depth of the impact of self-stigma on a person's life. In the planning phase, we assumed

Fig. 24.1 Key relationships in co-production and delivery of the Empowerment Programme Framework

that most of the development work would be completed by us, drawing on research evidence and our experience on what works well. We assumed we would then be working closely with the CoP who bring their wealth and breadth of knowledge and expertise to refine the work and make it relevant to their experiences. We had estimated that we would need to allocate two to three weeks of initial development work at the onset, then follow up with one to two days a fortnight until the framework was complete, over the period of six months.

With that in mind, we began our desk-based research by looking at the evidence of what makes an effective empowerment programme framework, and what makes a good empowerment programme framework for people living with HIV. We gathered ideas by looking at empowerment programme frameworks for other conditions, and we settled on developing a guide for facilitators delivering empowerment programmes for people living with long-term conditions. We recognised that we could use our experience of self-care and confidence building programmes for people with long-term conditions, and we also believed that a facilitator guide would be best suited for organisations with varying levels of experience in delivering such programmes.

Collaborating with a Community of Practice

The CoP was composed of participants from eight organisations and voluntary groups. They were brought together by our client, Fast-Track Cities London. The CoP members were established within the field of HIV prevention work and brought together evidence, best practice, and their passion to empower those people living with HIV. They came with a range of expertise in understanding and addressing self-stigma. Some came from academia and had developed advanced empowerment programmes for populations across the world. Others were more experienced in delivering localised empowerment programmes addressing intersectionality with different population groups. Some had recently completed an empowerment programme as a participant for the first time. Most had experience of living with HIV and self-stigma and understood what was important for the journey towards empowerment.

During the period of May to July 2021, we planned six online fortnightly CoP meetings where we brought together evidence of best practice and where members shared their experiences and knowledge of how to successfully support and improve the quality of life for those living with HIV. The first CoP meeting was an introduction to the agreed aims and objectives of the project including approving the Terms of Reference and clarifying expectations of being members of the CoP. Next, we presented our four-step project plan to the CoP. To further refine the project objectives and outcomes, we used this meeting to present what we had already learned from the advisory group and understand the following using an online interactive white board exercise:

- What makes a good empowerment programme?
- What competencies would they want to achieve from the framework?

Enquiry is a process that should continue throughout a project including planning, management and delivery (Brady & Varkonyi-Sepp, 2025; see Chap. 3). We wanted to ensure we understood the expectations of CoP members regarding what we would achieve together and to have their buy-in for the project. The results from this exercise not only allowed us to understand what was important to the CoP, it also made us realise that the CoP had strong ideas on how the empowerment framework would be delivered. The CoP understood that there were challenges to living with HIV that were different to living with other long-term conditions, something we needed to learn about. For example, the biggest challenge to living with HIV is the stigma attached to the condition. While HIV is now easy to manage, early views of the disease being contagious, along with existing discrimination on minority groups where prevalence of HIV was higher, such as men who had sex with men, migrant communities and people who injected drugs, prevailed. This was consistent with findings of Swendeman et al. (2006) as the demographic characteristics and context of a person living with HIV can contribute to the level of stigma they feel, and that stigma can impact on psychological well-being. Addressing self-stigma was much more central to the empowerment framework from the CoPs perspective than we had originally accounted for.

We also realised that the CoP members had clear ideas on what the empowerment framework should look like, drawing on their experiences of what is needed and what works for people living with HIV. It was at this point we realised that the CoP did not share our view of our role in the project. Having a clear understanding of roles and responsibilities within a project is key to successful delivery of a project (Nikolova & Devinney, 2009). We re-evaluated how we saw our role, understanding the need to shift from expert to a facilitator or helper role. We also understood at this point that while we were commissioned by Fast-Track Cities London, the CoP represented those who would be using the framework and were therefore our de facto client. We discussed this with our commissioner who agreed, and we highlighted that it was important that the CoP members were happy with the resulting empowerment programme framework and would have a sense of ownership of it, as they would be the ones implementing it.

Having negotiated this change, we moved away from positioning ourselves as the experts (in what was needed for this particular empowerment framework) to a *process consultation* model (Schein, 1999). Process consultation is a philosophy by which the consultant is not the expert, but rather the helper that starts from a position of ignorance as to what is going on in the client's situation and discards the expert role (Schein, 1999). We set out to collaborate with the CoP to establish a joint ownership of the development of the framework. This allowed us to let go of the need to be more knowledgeable than our clients in their area of expertise, and instead to draw on their expertise while bringing in our skillsets as appropriate. For example, instead of bringing our proposals to the CoP for discussion, we brought our research and curious, explorative questions to them, and guided them to shape the product we were developing together.

Following this initial meeting, we began to devise a plan for the next five sessions based around the recommendations from the CoP. This involved changing our approach to project planning. In our original proposal, we had begun with a PRINCE2 framework to our project planning. PRINCE2 is a linear management approach that includes set of processes and principles that enables us to plan, execute and control projects in a structured and efficient way (Bentley, 2010). It originated in the UK in the 1980s as a solution to common project delivery problems and is now the de facto standard used by UK Government organisations. With PRINCE2 we can divide our project into manageable and controllable stages, with clear start and end points. However, for this consultancy work, we felt that the PRINCE2 approach might not provide the flexibility needed in our collaborative approach to working with the CoP. We instead adopted the Agile approach (Denning, 2015), which allowed us to embrace the changes and flexibility involved in process consultancy (Greenhalgh et al., 2016). The Agile approach was developed in the United States in the early 2000s by a team of software developers who were looking for a project management system that was less document-led and more adaptable than available systems at the time. The Agile approach promotes frequent, transparent communication, and continuous feedback exchange which we felt was a better fit for the CoP, joint ownership of the work, and the enquiry approach we adopted throughout the consultancy.

Drawing on principles of co-creation and effective partnership strategies discussed in Greenhalgh et al. (2016), we approached each session with a plan of action and set of questions to explore, knowing that these plans could often be reformed, adapted, or discarded within minutes of the meeting beginning, based on new insights or priorities raised by CoP members. At times, we faced concerns about completing the framework on time, but these interruptions were valued by the CoP, reflecting their culture of inclusivity and respect. As consultants, we embraced this dynamic environment, co-developing session plans and continuously adapting them to ensure that the framework we were developing was jointly owned by each member of the CoP. Before each session, we sent an agenda and outline for the next meeting to the CoP for review and feedback. Given that all CoP sessions were conducted online, we utilised a shared cloud-platform folder for disseminating relevant materials, ensuring that all parties had access to the latest versions of slides, brainstorming sessions, and reading materials at any point in the process.

For the second session, we began to define the themes for the empowerment programme training framework drawing on existing literature and evidence that would support these themes. Early themes included: peer support; understanding internal stigma; stress management and coping; education on HIV and treatment; and skills building. To prepare to address these themes we conducted a literature review of the evidence on empowerment programmes for people living with HIV and compiled a summary on what worked, what has been shown to not work and gaps in research. For the following four sessions we focused largely on developing and refining the themes through discussion, debate and with reference to research evidence. Through time we developed our themes into competencies and included a guide for recruiting peer supporters to help facilitators to deliver the programme, and a guide on developing an evaluation framework to measure the impact of the empowerment training programmes on self-stigma.

Our process, in embracing the Agile approach, was one of ongoing review and adaptation. We were attuned to our own knowledge and expertise in the area, knowledge gaps, the dynamics and expertise within the group, and our impact on those dynamics. We were able to draw on our skills as researchers, enquirers, and listeners to develop each learning outcome of the framework into something that was based on CoP experiences, research evidence and best practice. Our role in the group was constantly evolving as the project progressed and as the group's confidence and culture evolved. This worked very well with our Agile approach, and did not impact on the amount of time and resource we budgeted for the project which we had set under the PRINCE2 framework. It did impact on how we used our time and focus, with a shift from development and writing to facilitation.

The mix of expertise in the world of HIV empowerment among members of the CoP brought with it different viewpoints as to what to realistically to expect from organisations who would be delivering the empowerment programme. This led to much discussion drawing on evidence-base from academic literature and personal experiences. Puutio et al. (2009) discuss asymmetry as one of the pitfalls to consultancy, whereby asymmetry is an imbalance of knowledge and power when providing advisory services. To resolve such asymmetry and to enhance the usefulness of advice offered, a question-answer format to the consultancy should be applied, with an active involvement of the different recipients. We recognised this asymmetry early on in our work with the CoP and adopted that question-answer format to ensure all viewpoints were heard and respected. In applying the process consultation approach, we developed an alliance with the CoP to jointly define what the empowerment programme framework was to achieve, for whom and why.

Over the subsequent CoP meetings, we jointly developed an approach to meeting the specification. We used the outcomes and competencies aimed for in the empowerment framework (see Box 24.1), to shape the meetings, researching and presenting evidence to inform the questions and discussions to enable CoP members to explore how our research connected with their own views on how the outcomes should be presented. We employed a coaching approach to guide the group to come to a consensus that was respectful of the different expertise in the room while meeting their intended objectives (Schein, 1999). We found that this approach brought a solidarity within the group and pride in the outcomes of the work, which was ultimately what we wanted to achieve.

Reflection

In respect of this work, we considered ourselves to be 'outsider researchers' (Gaillet & Guglielmo, 2014), that is, we were not members of the researched population, nor did we have any lived experience relating to the population of interest. As consultants, we faced two potential scenarios: our lack of lived experience could hinder our ability to truly understand the experiences of those living with HIV, or we could acknowledge our lack of lived-experience, alongside our desire to reduce any potential bias by exploring the implications and impact of stigma. We wanted to ensure the second scenario was true. Although we had extensive experience of working with a diverse range of clients and population groups, the strength and impact of the stigma associated with living with HIV was something we had not come across before professionally. While the time we had spent researching the literature to understand self-stigma was helpful, it was not until we spoke to those with lived experience in the advisory group and in the CoP that we truly began to understand the impact of self-stigma, the journey of empowerment as described by the CoP, and what our role was in this contract.

We adopted a pragmatic stance in planning and conducting this work. Pragmatism is a philosophical perspective that emphasises finding effective solutions to real-world challenges. It asserts that knowledge comes from experience, and that our views of reality are influenced by our social interactions. Much of this knowledge is socially constructed, meaning that it is shaped by the shared experiences of people in a community (Dewey, 1905). This perspective allowed us to be flexible and reflective as psychologists in this consultancy. We recognised that we might have different goals from the members of the CoP. Our goal, as required by the client, was to deliver a final product (the empowerment programme framework) that met the client's expectations. The CoP, on the other hand, wanted to use their personal experiences and knowledge to create positive change for their communities. Although these goals were not identical, they were both necessary for the successful completion of the consultancy. We acknowledged this difference to ourselves and our client, who hired us.

Whilst our commissioner did not change through the development of this programme of work, our understanding of the governance that was in place did. We answered to the Fast Track Cities-London leadership group, who were also supporting the CoP. The CoP had the expertise on the ground in terms of addressing self-stigma in HIV, and they would be the ones delivering the empowerment programmes. We understand that the client would consider it a satisfactory outcome if our CoP was happy with the final product. This meant we had a community of clients to collaborate with and answer to. Our role changed from bringing our expertise in the world of developing empowerment frameworks for long-term conditions, to becoming a 'humble enquirer' (Schein, 2013) facilitating a group of experts to bring together their expertise to create the framework. With our change of role, came a change in our style of project management. Once we embraced the Agile approach, we were better able to respond to the continuous changes and improvements that were necessary in this co-development work, and we still completed the work within the originally agreed timeframe. The Agile approach is one we have taken forward in our practice following this project as our preferred method for project management, especially for collaborative projects.

Collaborating with individuals from diverse professional backgrounds necessitated us to apply our skills as health psychologists in research, advanced communication, and facilitation, as underscored by Manley and Titchen

(2017). The Manley and Titchen study highlights that effective facilitation acts as a catalyst for collaborative problem-solving, fostering innovation, and enhancing outcomes. Initially expecting to focus on research and product development, we transitioned to facilitating this consultancy, relying on facilitation skills to understand the topic area, negotiate, establish and maintain trust, and manage realistic expectations regarding timelines and project scope. We also navigated the dynamics of a diverse group, including those with lived experiences and professional expertise.

Co-developing or collaborating with individuals who have lived experiences can be immensely valuable but may also present challenges if personal assumptions are not carefully managed. Dowding (2020) explores the initial assumptions made by researchers and those with lived experiences. For example, people with lived experiences often assume that the researchers are purely objective in the co-production of work, and researchers often assume that the contributors or the lived experience groups offer only subjective accounts with no formal research training, and therefore it may be difficult to manage group biases. In addition, the role of researcher can bring a power dynamic that can create barriers or opportunities for meaningful dialogue, especially as researchers are the ones to set the agenda and steer the conversation. It can affect how people communicate, listen and understand each other (Gaillet & Guglielmo, 2014). We sought to avoid such biases and imbalances as we felt they were unhelpful in drawing out the experiences, knowledge and the wealth of information from the CoP that we as researchers were seeking to learn about.

We drew on the principles of psychological safety (Kahn, 1990) to ensure that the advisory group and CoP felt comfortable and confident to express their ideas, questions and concerns. We did this by establishing a clear and shared purpose for the group, so that everyone understood the goals and expectations of the meetings, encouraging open and honest communication, and actively listening to others' perspectives and feedback, showing respect and appreciation for each group member's contributions and diversity, and admitting our own fallibility and limitations, and willingness to learn from others.

After the initial CoP meeting, we felt it was important to acknowledge the diversity of opinions and experiences surrounding the same issue. For example, whilst many of the CoP members had lived experiences of HIV, there were representatives from differing backgrounds, education levels, genders and age, all of whom were bringing different stories. It was important that we ensured all contributions were equally heard and valued. We wanted to ensure that those with more experience in articulating their views were not overpowering the workshops. We used interactive and creative methods to engage all members to ensure they are all heard. For example, using an interactive whiteboard and virtual post-it notes which have been shown to promote more inclusive discussions and improved communication (Li et al., 2021). We utilised these tools to encourage participants to present their views without needing to wait for their turn to speak. We spent time on each individual's view, asking each person to provide more information. We then used reflective listening, reflecting the idea back to the speaker, to make sure the idea has been understood correctly and that the individual felt comfortable to elaborate further, a key tool for demonstrating empathy (Braillon & Taiebi, 2020).

We learned a great deal from the CoP and the advisory group. For example, we learned that the nuances of language can have an enormous impact on how we present ourselves, think about ourselves, and how we see others. Simple changes such as 'sharing' rather than 'disclosing' an HIV status and 'living with' rather 'infected with' HIV reduces the stigma attached to having HIV. We learned how intersectionality brings with it an additional level of self-stigma and can compound and increase an individual's sense of feeling like an outsider which must be addressed head on to build empowerment. As affirmed by the CoP, we learned that it is the journey to empowerment that is important, rather than the end goal. The journey helps people to connect with others, learn to think differently about their HIV status and connect better with their treatment options. For some, this journey might be short-lived, for others it is a life-long commitment. Finally, we learned that there is a community of people living with HIV in London that are hugely empathetic, supportive and proactive in addressing stigma and self-stigma and helping people through their own empowerment journey.

As health psychology consultants we learned that we do not have to be the experts in the room. Rather, we can be just as effective when drawing on the expertise of others using the many tools we have developed in our training and practice.

Top Tips

Here are our top tips for co-development work:

- Use creative methods to ensure all voices are heard and valued.
- Create an environment of psychological safety and actively listen to every opinion.
- Define roles and responsibilities early, remaining flexible as work evolves.
- Discuss any changes to your approach with stakeholders and maintain regular communication.
- Have a wealth of knowledge and openly acknowledge and learn from others' expertise.

References

Bentley, C. (2010). PRINCE2: A Practical Handbook (3rd ed.). Routledge.

Brady, R. & Varkonyi-Sepp, J. (2025). A framework for consultancy in health psychology. In R. Brady, J. Varkonyi-Sepp & J. Smith (Eds.), *The Palgrave Handbook of Consultancy in Health Psychology*. Palgrave Macmillan.

Braillon, A., & Taiebi, F. (2020). Practicing 'reflective listening' is a mandatory prerequisite for empathy. *Patient Education and Counselling, 103*(9), 1866–1867.

Davidson, L., Bellamy, C., Guy, K., & Miller, R. (2012). Peer support among persons with severe mental illnesses: A review of evidence and experience. *World Psychiatry, 11*(2), 123–128.

Denning, S. (2015). How to make the whole organization Agile. *Strategy & Leadership, 43*(6), 10–17. https://doi.org/10.1108/SL-09-2015-0074

Dewey, J. (1905). The realism of pragmatism. *Journal of Philosophy, Psychology & Scientific Methods, 2*, 324–327.

Dowding, K. (2020). Co-producing research with people who have experienced severe and multiple disadvantages. *Social Research Practice*, (9).

Dunbar, W., Labat, A., Raccurt, C., Sohler, N., Pape, J. W., Nathalie, M., & Coppieters, Y. (2019). A realist systematic review of stigma reduction interventions for HIV prevention and care continuum outcomes among men who have sex with men. *International Journal of STD & AIDS, 31*(8), 712–723.

Fast-Track Cities London. (2021). A framework for empowerment programmes to tackle internalised stigma. https://fasttrackcities.london/a-guide-to-tackling-internalised-stigma-for-people-with-hiv/

Fast-Track Cities London. (n.d.). Roadmap to zero. https://fasttrackcities.london/about-us/roadmap-to-zero/

Fast-Track Cities London, & Healthy Dialogues. (2023). Reflections from the HIV Empowerment Programme. https://fasttrackcities.london/wp-content/uploads/2024/03/Reflections-from-the-HIV-Empowerment-Programme-1.pdf

Fetterman, D. M., Kaftarian, S. J., & Wandersman, A. (1996). *Empowerment evaluation: Knowledge and tools for self-assessment and accountability*. SAGE Publications.

Gaillet, L. L., & Guglielmo, L. (2014). The role of the researcher. In *Scholarly publication in a changing academic landscape: Models for success* (pp. 85–102). Palgrave Macmillan. https://doi.org/10.1057/9781137410764_5

Greenhalgh, T., Jackson, C., Shaw, S., & Janamian, T. (2016). Achieving research impact through co-creation in community-based health services: Literature review and case study. *Milbank Quarterly, 94*(2), 392–429.

Hedge, B., Karrish, D., Catalan, J., Cheshire, A., & Ridge, D. (2021). HIV-related stigma in the UK then and now: To what extent are we on track to eliminate stigma? A qualitative investigation. *BMC Public Health, 21*, 1022.

Hempel, S., Ferguson, L., Bolshakova, M., et al. (2021). Frameworks, measures, and interventions for HIV-related internalised stigma and stigma in healthcare and laws and policies: Systematic review protocol. *BMJ Open, 11*, e053608. https://doi.org/10.1136/bmjopen-2021-053608

Kahn, W. A. (1990). Psychological conditions of personal engagement and disengagement at work. *Academy of Management Journal, 33*(4), 692–724.

Kozlowski, S. W. J., & Bell, B. S. (2003). Work groups and teams in organizations. In W. C. Borman, D. R. Ilgen, & R. J. Klimoski (Eds.), *Handbook of psychology: Industrial and organizational psychology*, Vol. 12, pp. 333–375). John Wiley & Sons, Inc.

Li, Q., Zhang, J., Xie, X., & Luximon, Y. (2021). How shared online whiteboard supports online collaborative design activities: A social interaction perspective. In *Advances in Creativity, Innovation, Entrepreneurship and Communication of Design: Proceedings of the AHFE 2021 Virtual Conferences on Creativity, Innovation and Entrepreneurship, and Human Factors in Communication of Design, July 25–29, 2021, USA* (pp. 285–293). Springer International Publishing. https://doi.org/10.1007/978-3-030-80007-9_5

Logie, C. H., James, L. L., Tharao, W., et al. (2011). HIV, gender, race, sexual orientation, and sex work: A qualitative study of intersectional stigma experienced by HIV-positive women in Ontario, Canada. *PLoS Med*, 8. https://doi.org/10.1371/journal.pmed.1001124

Manley, K., & Titchen, A. (2017). Facilitation skills: The catalyst for increased effectiveness in consultant practice and clinical systems leadership. *Educational Action Research, 25*(2), 256–279.

Nikolova, N., & Devinney, T. M. (2009). Influence and power dynamics in client-consultant teams. *Journal of Strategy and Management, 2*(1), 31–55.

Pantelic, M., Boyes, M., Cluver, L., et al. (2017). HIV, violence, blame and shame: Pathways of risk to internalized HIV stigma among South African adolescents living with HIV. *Journal of the International AIDS Society, 20*, 21771–21779. https://doi.org/10.7448/IAS.20.1.21771

Pantelic, M., Steinert, J. I., Park, J., et al. (2019). 'Management of a spoiled identity': Systematic review of interventions to address self-stigma among people living with and affected by HIV. *BMJ Global Health, 4*, e001285. https://doi.org/10.1136/bmjgh-2018-001285

Puutio, R., Kykyri, V.-L., & Wahlström, J. (2009). The process and content of advice giving in support of reflective practice in management consulting. *Reflective Practice: International and Multidisciplinary Perspectives, 10*(4), 513-528.

Rongkavilit, C., Wang, B., Naar-King, S., et al. (2015). Motivational interviewing targeting risky sex in HIV-positive young Thai men who have sex with men. *Archives of Sexual Behavior, 44*, 329–340.

Schein, E. H. (1999). *Process consultation revisited: Building the helping relationship*. Addison-Wesley Publishing Company, Inc.

Schein, E. H. (2013). *Humble inquiry*. Berrett-Koehler Publishers.

Smith, M. (2002). What client employees say about consultants. *Leadership & Organization Development Journal, 23*(2), 93–103.

Swendeman, D., Rotheram-Borus, M. J., Comulada, S., Weiss, R., & Ramos, M. E. (2006). Predictors of HIV-related stigma among young people living with HIV. *Health Psychology, 25*(4), 501.

Tam, V. V., Larsson, M., Pharris, A., et al. (2012). Peer support and improved quality of life among persons living with HIV on antiretroviral treatment: A randomised controlled trial from Vietnam. *Health and Quality of Life Outcomes, 10*. https://doi.org/10.1186/1477-7525-10-53

United Nations. (n.d.). Countries commit to action to end AIDS by 2030. https://www.un.org/en/academic-impact/countries-commit-action-end-aids-2030

25

Planning and Managing: Providing Health Psychology Expertise in a Local Co-produced Wellbeing Service

Debbie M. Smith

Introduction

This case study will outline the experience of planning and monitoring the delivery of an evolving consultancy project, with a focus on the role of the health psychologist as part of a team of experts. The consultancy project began by developing and supervising placements for psychology students and evolved into the co-production and co-facilitation of well-being courses. Prior to my involvement, the service had no health psychology input so I will outline how I addressed this and fostered a strong relationship with the client. I will reflect on the planning and management of the consultancy project and more widely reflect on me as a health psychologist following this experience. Key learnings from this consultancy experience will be shared.

The Context: Recovery Colleges

The Recovery College (RC) model applies an educational approach which aims to equip people with the necessary skills to feel in control of their personal mental health recovery journey and achieve physical and mental

D. M. Smith (✉)
University of Manchester, Manchester, UK
e-mail: Debbie.smith-2@manchester.ac.uk

R. Brady et al. (eds.), *The Palgrave Handbook of Consultancy in Health Psychology*,
https://doi.org/10.1007/978-3-031-94529-8_25

well-being (Perkins et al., 2012). The first RC opened in the United Kingdom (UK) in 2009 following the successful delivery of RCs in the United States of America (Anfossi, 2017). According to *Implementing Recovery through Organisational Change* (ImROC), the number of RCs has increased yearly in the UK, with around 75 in 2017 (Perkins et al., 2018). The concept of an RC is consistent, but the commissioning and funding is individual to each RC, with some hosted in the UK National Health Service (NHS) and others within charity organisations or local authorities. Anyone can refer themselves into an RC to select from a range of educational courses that they feel meet their individual needs (Perkins et al., 2012). Courses for the public cover awareness and well-being (e.g., building self-confidence and self-esteem), and courses for staff include well-being training. Individuals can select and enrol on as many courses as they wish as the RC experience is personal to them. Courses can consist of one-off short workshops through to accredited courses delivered over several weeks. A central element of RCs is co-production with several experts involved in each course design and delivery. Co-production is viewed by NHS England as important for service design and delivery that sees several experts work together in a team with a shared outcome, clear roles and equal power (NHS England, 2023). All RC courses are co-produced and co-facilitated by various experts including clinical psychologists, charity representatives, and people with lived experience of mental health and well-being recovery. Wilton (2021) argues that co-production needs to be embedded into all health care to reduce social inequality and to improve healthcare for all. Within the RC, a small group of experts work together to design and deliver educational workshops, each bringing an element of skill and knowledge to the process. The process of planning and managing delivery whilst working in a co-production team will be discussed in the next section of this chapter. Research has shown that RCs can have both a positive short-term impact on attendees (Sommer et al., 2018; Zabel et al., 2016) and a long-term impact on attendees (Thompson et al., 2021). In these qualitative research studies, the co-production element of the RC featured as a positive influence on the attendees. Likewise, the impact on NHS staff attending an RC has been explored in a mixed-methods paper which found a positive impact on the care that they offered following this to others (Perkins et al., 2017).

The Role of a Health Psychologist in a Recovery College

The focus on feeling in control of one's life and well-being as part of the recovery journey was emphasised as a requirement for mental health services to support physical and mental health (Department of Health, 2011). As such, the term 'recovery' was defined in this UK cross-government mental health outcomes strategy as

> a deeply personal, unique process of changing one's attitudes, values, feelings, goals, skills and/or roles. It is a way of living a satisfying, hopeful and contributing life, even with limitations caused by the illness. Recovery involves the development of new meaning and purpose in one's life. (Anthony, 1993, p. 15)

Health psychologists' primary focus is on physical health, illness and health care, but as the *No Health Without Mental Health* strategy document (Department of Health, 2011) outlines, physical health is closely entwined with mental health and thus often a health psychologist's work will overlap with mental health support or recovery journeys. A discussion regarding professional boundaries is covered further in the later reflection section.

As a health psychologist situated in academia, most of my (teaching, research or consultancy) work builds on the *teachable moment* concept and thus supports associated behaviour change, increased understanding, healthcare professionals' well-being and provision of care (e.g., Flocke et al., 2014; Lawson & Flocke, 2009). Teachable moments are highlighted in education and health as a time in one's life when something happens (e.g., health event like surgery or interaction with healthcare services such as midwifery appointments) that encourages the assessment of the risk and outcomes of behaviours which, along with changes in opportunities and capability, often lead to increased motivation to make positive changes (McBride et al., 2003; Olander et al., 2016; Phelan, 2010). In the case of the RC, the recovery journey following a period of poor mental health or well-being could act as a teachable moment with an opportunity for health psychologists to support positive changes to health behaviours. Such an approach has been taken for example, in Lee et al. (2016) a proof-of-concept pilot study, and in pregnancy research by Rockliffe et al. (2021, 2022). Behaviour change theory and techniques can be used to support behaviour change in these teachable moments and thus, there is a clear role for a health psychologist within the co-production team to bring their expertise and knowledge in behaviour change and well-being to support healthy living in RC attendees.

In this case study, the external consultancy project was established due to an existing relationship with a local RC. Initially, the relationship with the RC was based around my role as an academic supervising psychology undergraduate student, before it developed into an external consultant role. To understand the consultancy project and the process of planning and management of delivery, both steps to the relationship between me and the RC will be outlined.

The RC and Psychology Placements

In my capacity as a senior university lecturer in health psychology, I was initially put in touch with a local RC to explore the potential for educational placements for psychology undergraduate students. A face-to-face introductory meeting was set up with the manager of the RC to start discussions about placement suitability and to hear more about the local RC. In preparation for the initial meeting, I read widely about the RC model and researched existing courses offered by the local RC. After reading about the RC focus on mental health and well-being recovery, I was excited about a possible larger role for health psychology and was eager to explore this opportunity as part of their co-production model. This enquiry approach to consultancy work is important as it sets the base for the whole consultancy project. The second stage (of seven) in Hodges' consultancy cycle for change framework is 'inquiry and analysis' (Hodges, 2017). In this initial meeting, my priority was to explore the placement opportunity within the local RC objectives and priorities. However, I was also keen to outline the role of a health psychologist and the expertise we hold in relation to these objectives, and I was particularly reflexive at this early stage. Specifically, I thought deeply about the way I communicated who I was as a health psychologist to the RC manager, as part of my practice which was in line with Oliver's framework of reflexive inquiry (Oliver, 2005). The skills employed at this stage were similar to the skills I employ as a qualitative researcher collecting and analysing data. It was agreed at this meeting that the RC would offer several student placements under my supervision the following year. My professional role in these negotiations involved advising of suitable placements within the expertise and knowledge of the undergraduate psychology student cohort. Due to the co-production element of the RC model, objectives for the placement included several placement students supporting the co-production and co-facilitation of an RC course that they felt comfortable with and for which they had an appropriate level of expertise (e.g., lived experience, knowledge of target group, or training delivery skills). I also facilitated contact between the University and RC to complete relevant risk assessments and curriculum-related requirements. Development meetings were agreed in this initial meeting with the RC manager to continue the discussion of my long-term involvement as a health psychologist within the RC. I viewed my role as a consultant in this stage helping both my students and the RC towards their end goals (e.g., placement and co-produced courses). This idea of helping clients to reach their goals was found in a qualitative study of business consultants and was one I still believe in terms of my role as a consultant (Kakabadse et al., 2006).

Health Psychology Input into a New Recovery College Educational Course

At regular meetings with the client, in addition to reviewing student placements, we discussed the evolving needs of the RC and the possible contribution of health psychology expertise. These discussions built on the openness and honesty about priorities that were initiated in my first meeting with the local RC manager. Through the placement supervision and delivery of the placement objectives, trust, which is key to any co-production relationship (Redman et al., 2021) and to consultancy relationships (Williams, 2022), grew between me and the RC manager. Trust was developed through the professionalism and expertise that I and the students demonstrated, and the added value we brought to the service in terms of our role in the co-production teams for individual courses; in a few cases this led to the students staying on with the RC after the placement in a volunteering capacity. Furthermore, as our development meetings continued, it became evident to me that the RC manager began to understand my expertise as a professional due to open dialogue including asking questions of one another (Schein, 2013). My expertise as an educator (particularly relevant at the time of this work as online education provision was rapidly growing due to the COVID-19 pandemic) and in behaviour change were recognised over this time through the questions I asked, and the questions the RC manager asked of me. These led to discussions about ways to engage learners on a virtual platform which was new to the RC and to many academics at the time. For example, I had been working hard to develop a sense of community amongst my students whilst learning online, which was something the RC wanted to create on their online courses to enable attendees to feel comfortable to share their experiences. This was a challenge for most educators during the COVID-19 pandemic when all educational provision was online (e.g., Greenhow et al., 2022).

This appreciation of expertise led to the RC manager asking me to join a newly formed co-production team for a proposed online eight-week course to support behaviour change in times of uncertainty. The aim of the new course was to enable people to deal with change, the uncertainty that can come with change, and to help them build personal resilience to deal with future change and select healthy behaviours. As this course ran during the COVID-19 pandemic, change during this time was both enacted by choice and forced due to government restrictions and thus was unsettling for many and had become a priority area for RC. This newly formed co-production team consisted of myself contributing behaviour change expertise, a clinical psychologist contributing mental health expertise, and four experts with lived experience of mental health recovery and lifestyle changes. It is important to state that the COVID-19 pandemic was new to all of us and that we each brought an aspect of lived experience to the work. The RC manager wanted me to bring a health psychology perspective to the new course and it was agreed that I would contribute behaviour change theory and techniques (e.g., using goal setting and goal review in the course to encourage behaviour change) to support the uncertain feelings of change in attendees during the new course. Goal setting as a behaviour change technique can be effective in supporting behaviour in a number of behaviours (Epton et al., 2017). Behaviour change techniques (BCTs) are the tools that health psychologists use to help people change behaviours and have been described as the 'active ingredients' of interventions (Michie et al., 2011, p. 11). As a health psychologist, I introduced BCTs to the RC co-production team to support changes around uncertainty.

I agreed with the RC manager that my involvement in this course would be twofold. First, I applied my health psychology knowledge of health behaviour change to the design of this new course. Second, I would apply my expertise and experience in teaching and training, one of the core competencies of the British Psychological Society (BPS) health psychology training (BPS, 2020) to the design of materials; I would also apply my communication and delivery skills to co-facilitate with the clinical psychologist the delivery of this online course. The clinical psychologist and I met weekly initially to conceptualise the content of the eight-week course. The clinical psychologist and the experts with lived experience all had designed and delivered RC courses before, but the online environment was new to them too so my expertise in online teaching was valuable. The proposed course content was then discussed with the experts with lived experience to ensure that they had the opportunity at this early stage to input their knowledge and ideas. As COVID-19 was an uncertain and ever-changing situation for all, a tailored and rolling approach was taken which saw the co-production team weekly assess the needs of the course attendees and design the materials accordingly. This approach worked well as we were able to respond to emerging behavioural changes due to the COVID-19 pandemic regulations as raised in sessions, many of which were associated with physical health or health care including, for example, mask-wearing. Mask-wearing was deemed difficult by many during the COVID-19 pandemic. Psychologists trialled numerous interventions to support people to use masks frequently (e.g., self-imagery; Conroy et al., 2022).

The course was well-received, with most attendees attending regularly across the eight-weeks. Attendee evaluations were collected by the service and were all positive about the course including enjoying the mix of science and activities including goal setting and review. The RC manager was happy with my health psychology expertise being shared in the design and delivery and I was asked to contribute my health psychology expertise to more sessions. Having additional psychological input from a health psychologist on physical health behaviours such as physical activity and sleep as opposed to purely mental health as previously was deemed a benefit.

The consultancy project developed over time in terms of planning and managing delivery; this evolving process will be the focus of the remainder of the chapter. However, it is important to note that the consultancy journey with RC is still ongoing as are the regular meetings with the RC manager.

Planning and Managing Delivery in an Evolving Relationship

Planning as a Consultant

As a health psychologist in academia, it was refreshing to be involved in this applied work with the RC, especially as it continually adapted to the needs of the attendees and the scope for my involvement was ever evolving. I felt that I was having a direct impact on individuals at a time where health behaviours changes were being enforced due to the COVID-19 pandemic. Having the flexibility and allowing creative space to adapt plans and associated actions are important in the planning stages of any project (Thompson & Thompson, 2008) and were particularly true here due to the evolving nature of the work which was situated in the co-production team.

There are many definitions of a consultant in the literature with no agreement due to variation of the role. For me, I feel most comfortable with the first part of the Earll and Bath working definition of consultancy which states "a formal relationship where one party seeks help from another" (Earll & Bath, 2004, p. 230). I feel consultancy is about helping to reach a goal and I like the idea of a consultant being a helper as described by Schein in the 'humble consulting model' (Schein, 2016). The humble consulting model outlines the need for humility in the relationship with the client and also in terms of the situation being presented. Schein outlines the need to act in a humble manner in response to the client's needs and the multifaceted situations they present. In the work with the local RC, I wanted to help by contributing my expertise to the RC to support people in the local area to have healthy lifestyles; the 'help' I could offer was my health psychology expertise in behaviour change and my training/teaching skills to help the RC meet the emerging needs of the course attendees. I adopted a humble approach by taking time to listen to the unique situation of the RC, and by building the trust between myself and the RC manager through open and honest communication, something Schein identifies as being important for the consultant to be fully viewed as the helper by the client. We spent in the early stages getting to know each other in a professional capacity and increasing mutual understanding through dialogue.

As well as my behaviour change knowledge and my expertise in teaching and behaviour change techniques being required in the eight-week course, my skills as a trainer/teacher were also required. Being able to impart knowledge in a learning and teaching environment is not a skill all professionals have. As a health psychologist, I view learning as an active process influenced by one's cognitive ability, cultural background and social interaction. I believe learning is a personal experience in which we construct knowledge through attributing meaning to all of our interactions and observations. In a teaching and training environment, the individual's *lived experience* of learning must be recognised and responded to in the design of the environment (Jehangir, 2010, p. 56). This aligns with a constructivist approach which has a base in Vygotsky's sociocultural theory of cognitive development where cultural and social influences are recognised (Vygotsky & Kozulin, 2012; Zinkiewicz et al., 2003). In practice, this meant I was able to suggest the use of different learning and teaching techniques to provide an environment where interaction with the material and others could occur. For example, working alongside the clinical psychologist, we prepared interactive sessions including breakout rooms with one lived experience attendee in each to facilitate discussion. Likewise, the concept of 'recovery' as a teachable moment to encourage behaviour change in the recovery journey, aligns well with my expertise in health and educational settings. My knowledge of learning and teaching was drawn upon in the planning stages to suggest ways to encourage attendee online engagement which I monitored during the eight-week course. I suggested moderations based on observations, such as the use of features like including break-out rooms being led by experts-by-experience to enable a safe space to encourage engagement.

Management of Delivery as a Consultant

Due to the evolving nature of the work, it was important to communicate clearly with the client in order to effectively plan and adapt well in order to avoid *scope creep*. Scope creep is when a consultant goes beyond the initially agreed scope of a project, and it has been reported as one of the main causes of failure in consultancy projects (Ajmal et al., 2020). My role was clearly defined both in placement supervision and in the design and delivery of the eight-week online course. The pre-defined student projects and course content made it easier to manage the length of time of my input. The concern for me in relation to scope creep was taking on more RC courses, but I was aware of my time commitments and was guided by these throughout. The requirement to input behaviour change knowledge into the eight-week course was agreed by me and the RC manager before the work commenced. My role in the co-production group was treated as equal with the other 'experts', each of us working together on the same goal of producing a course that met the needs of the attendees. The measure of the success of the course was discussed in early meetings with the RC manager, with the main objective being that the course met the attendees' needs in terms of supporting their ability to cope with the uncertainty that can assist change, and in attendance numbers, which remained constant, and the end of course evaluation. It was important for us to be aware at the start of the outcome measures of success for the course so we could ensure we measured our behaviour and delivery against this throughout the project.

Asking questions and listening. Not being aware of the RC before my initial contact with the local RC manager was an advantage as it encouraged me to do research in advance of the first meeting to explore specific questions such as *'What is the RC?'*, *'What does the RC offer to local people?'*, *'Who is involved in the delivery of the RC?'* and *'What role does psychology play in the RC?'*. As well as more specific questions such as *'What can I bring to the RC?'* and *'What can I learn from the RC?'*. I then took the questions and answers along to my meeting with the RC manager. I also spent time exploring and understanding the key stakeholders in the RC. Asking questions and listening to the answers is an important step in the planning process of any consultancy project and helps both the consultant and client to find out information about each other and plan the project with all key facts (Schein, 2013). Asking these questions helped to identify where my involvement was most productive.

Due to the co-production element of the RC, it was vital at the start of the consultancy project that I met all the different people involved in the design and delivery of the new course. Meeting all relevant people and having the opportunity to ask questions and learn more from them about their role in the course and RC was important as it allowed for more knowledge to be gathered and gave a solid base for the building of strong relationships and thus planning of the consultancy work (Sacks & Loon, 2016). A published case study found that models of consultancy that included the client-consulting relationship and process issues were the most useful in predicting project outcomes (Appelbaum & Steed, 2004).

In the ongoing development meetings with the RC manager, we still discuss questions when we meet that include the recurring *What are the current priorities?* and *What can I do to help meet these?*. The answers to these questions inform plans for future work. The RC manager and I agreed a clear plan for the course and my role in achieving that verbally in meetings and through emails. The lack of a formal written contract may have been influenced by the fact that I was not receiving any payment for this work. Moving forward, I plan to include a written contract in future work as it protects both parties legally.

Co-production. Understanding my contribution and role in the co-production team was a key part of the planning and delivery management. As a health psychologist in academia, much of my research and teaching is conducted within a multi- or interdisciplinary team. Therefore, I was easily able to identify my expertise as an educator and in health behaviour change as relevant contributions to the RC team. I achieved this by meeting with the team individually initially to learn more about them and their personal and professional expertise. While the eight-week course was running, we met as a team pre- and post- the weekly online session to ensure all views and experiences were being included and everyone was adequately debriefed to ensure the effective delivery. We also gave the attendees of the sessions the opportunity during every session to highlight things they would like to cover in future weeks on the course to ensure the delivery of the material was tailored to them (this was essential due to the changing situation of COVID-19 as outlined above). My reflections of being part of a co-production team are presented in the next section.

Reflection on This Consultancy Experience

Being a Socially Responsible Health Psychologist

Being a 'reflective' professional is very important to me to enable me to continue to develop as a health psychologist and practitioner psychologist. It is also part of our social responsibility to those we are working with as it enables us to ensure we are meeting their needs and allows for us to take responsibility for our actions (Bolton, 2005). I have kept a diary since doing my PhD and stage 2 health psychology training to enable me to be 'reflective' of my actions and I use Gibbs' model of learning to guide my reflection on an event and consider actions (Gibbs, 2013). These are practices I encourage with all of my students from an early point so that they become habitual.

Being reflective is not easy and requires time and effort as well as self-awareness (Thompson & Thompson, 2008), which can be challenging as we need to acknowledge both the helpful and less helpful things we do. Being self-aware allows us to self-monitor and regulate our behaviour and influence future behaviours (Bandura, 1986). Over the last few years, I have become aware of compassion-focused therapy and the idea of the compassionate mind which has led me to be more self-compassionate when conducting reflection as well as when receiving feedback from others (Gilbert, 2010). Gilbert's compassion focused therapy informed the approach taken by the clinical psychologist on the eight-week course and I have since attended compassion focused therapy training to understand the applicability to my practice as a health psychologist as I found it a useful technique to support behaviour change and well-being. I have included this approach in both my research, teaching and consultancy projects since that point. Taking a compassion focused approach has helped me to pay attention to what I do well. In this example, I was impressed with my ability to build a strong relationship with the local RC and, through this, to have the confidence to develop a consultancy opportunity. I was also impressed with my ability to bring warmth and humour to my delivery in these sessions, this was a skill the clinical psychologist pointed out to me. Before my adoption of a compassionate mindset, I would have felt uncomfortable with a compliment but I have learnt to accept them and feel pride.

However, I do not think being reflective is always enough. I think we must work hard to be 'reflexive'. Being reflexive takes place in real time and is more active than reflection as reflexivity acknowledges the current situation and the influences on us and the influences we may be having on the situation (Schön, 1991). To enable reflexivity, I use self-talk and mindfulness methods in situations to enable me to step back from myself and consider how others are viewing me and what impact I am having. In this case study, these methods were useful in both the training session and co-production meetings as they allowed me to consider my role in the wider team and to ensure that my own personal experience of change and uncertainty in the context of COVID-19 was not influencing my practice. Self-talk was particularly helpful in preparation for, and following, the training sessions as it allows me to reassure myself by saying out loud what I am doing, and why, to remind myself of my professional role in this context.

Teaching/Training Skills

As a health psychologist who works in academia, delivering educational training to people on a personal recovery journey has been really rewarding as I have had the opportunity to apply both my psychological and educational knowledge and share their journey. Whilst writing this case study, I have reflected on the importance of my teaching and training skills.

In the initial planning stages of this consultancy project, I spent a long time considering how relevant my learning and teaching experience in Higher Education was in the context of the RC. The success of an online course in terms of attendance and feedback was influenced by the content and the delivery. My expertise of behaviour change contributed to the content and my expertise in teaching and training contributed to the delivery of the content of the sessions, the activities and the behaviour change techniques used in these activities. This amalgamation of expert skills is reflected below in a quote from a member of the co-production team on my input to the RC courses.

> Debbie brought her vast knowledge to participants at a level and in an interactive way that they understood, and importantly, although people knew her as the expert, in her field, her mannerisms and delivery, meant that each individual including myself, felt understood and included.

Promoting Health Psychology

On numerous occasions in my career, I have had to explain the role of a health psychologist, and the expertise and knowledge we hold, to a multidisciplinary team. The promotion of the health psychology discipline is important as there is still a lack of understanding of the role (Hart et al., 2023). I am always keen to promote health psychology and to ensure I have a template description of what health psychology is and what I do as a health psychologist that I can adapt for each audience in terms of their needs. In some situations, I find it useful to compare health psychology to other psychologists who the client may be familiar with. For example, in this instance, the local RC worked with clinical psychologists so was aware of their professional skills and expertise; I found that a comparison with their role was a useful way to explain my discrete health psychology expertise and knowledge. The importance of promoting health psychology in this current case study is highlighted in the quote from the RC manager when reflecting on this work and my role in it in terms of identifying relevant behaviours and support change:

> The experience of working with a health psychologist has been a truly rewarding one. It has encouraged us as Recovery College to think about psychological theories, and how these can be brought into our course content and delivery and has helped us in taking a wider view of our course curriculum and how we can better support behavioural change.

Mental Health and Health Psychology

Writing and receiving feedback on this chapter, made me re-consider my role as a health psychologist and my professional boundaries in terms of supporting mental health in my work. The focus of health psychology is on physical health, but we cannot entirely exclude mental health when supporting someone's physical health. As a Practitioner Psychologist, I adhere to the Health and Care Professionals Council (HCPC) standards of proficiency which includes the statements to "practise safely and effectively within the scope of practice" and "practise as an autonomous professional, exercising their own professional judgement" (HCPC, 2023, p. 6 and p. 8). While my training as a health psychologist does not give me skills and expertise to diagnose or treat mental health conditions, it does give me an understanding of the complex relationship between mental and physical health in the wider context which I acknowledge in my work. On reflection, my decision to work closely with clinical psychologists in most of my work supports my confidence in that I follow professional standards. Discussions with clinical psychology colleagues also help to clarify the often-blurred line between mental and physical health as it reaffirms the expertise of our professions. Making time with colleagues to have these academic discussions is important and helps with the standard of proficiency to "look after [their] health and wellbeing, seeking appropriate support where necessary" (HCPC, 2023. p. 8). In this particular case, a clinical psychologist and I worked together on content delivery with me focusing on behaviour change, and the clinical psychologist focusing on the management of mental health.

Being Curious

Not being scared to ask questions and to be asked questions is how my interest in psychology originated. However, it was not until this case study and reading the work of Schein (2013) that I realised this was an important skill in consultancy and a strength of mine. For me it was a key ingredient in the success of this project. My curiosity and my behavioural science background led me to research the local RC before I met with the client; this meant that in advance of meeting, I had an idea of the potential role of health psychology in the RC; this shaped my questions and may have led to the development of work. Schein's humble enquiry model informed me in terms of how and why I asked questions (Schein, 2013).

Co-production

I was immediately drawn to the co-production element of the RC as I had just completed a research programme in Type-1 diabetes research with experts with lived experience (Smith et al., 2018) and believe the concept of co-production is relevant to every aspect of my role as a health psychologist; research, teaching and consultancy. Co-producing and co-facilitating the sessions with experts with lived experience of mental health and well-being recovery was a wonderful experience as we worked as a team to ensure we had a good mix of activities and science. On reflection of this experience and reviewing the current literature (e.g., Redman et al., 2021), I have learnt to *always* gather the views of people with lived experience of the topic I am researching, teaching or consulting.

Conclusion

As a health psychologist, I am confident I have knowledge and skills to offer to a variety of consultancy projects, but it is the part of my role I engage in the least. I acknowledge that I have a lot to learn about consultancy from the consultancy literature which up to now has been alien to me. I hope that reading about this project has shown that consultancy projects can evolve from existing relationships and can be dynamic and exciting to be involved in. I made myself a promise whilst writing this chapter to learn more about ways to combine health psychology and consultancy and to ensure that I continue to support and recognise the role health psychology can have on the workplace and more widely on society.

Top Tips

1. Prepare a standardised description of the expertise you bring as a health psychologist to take to initial meetings.
2. During new experiences, build in time to make a note of reflexive thoughts to return to at times of uncertainty, for example, keep a professional diary.
3. Be honest and kind to yourself when reflecting on your practice.
4. Have open and honest discussions with colleagues to explore your professional boundaries and expertise.
5. Trust is vital to the success of any consultancy project; spend time building it.

Competing Interests The author has no competing interests to declare that are relevant to the content of this chapter.

References

Ajmal, M., Khan, M., & Al-Yafei, H. (2020). Exploring factors behind project scope creep–stakeholders' perspective. *International Journal of Managing Projects in Business, 13*(3), 483–504. https://doi.org/10.1108/ijmpb-10-2018-0228

Anfossi, A. (2017). *The current state of Recovery Colleges in the UK: Final report.* ImROC.

Anthony, W. (1993). Recovery from mental illness: The guiding vision of the mental health system in the 1990s. *Psychosocial Rehabilitation Journal, 16*(4), 11–23. https://doi.org/10.1037/h0095655

Appelbaum, S. H., & Steed, A. J. (2004). The critical success factors in the client-consulting relationship. *Journal of Management Development, 24*(1), 68–93. https://doi.org/10.1108/02621710510572362

Bandura, A. (1986). *Social foundations of thought and action: A social cognitive theory.* Prentice Hall.

Bolton, G. E. J. (2005). *Reflective practice: Writing and professional development.* Sage Publications Inc.

British Psychological Society (BPS). (2020). *Qualification in health psychology (stage 2): Handbook for candidates.* https://cms.bps.org.uk/sites/default/files/2022-07/QHP%20Candidate%20Handbook.pdf

Conroy, D., Smith, D. M., & Armitage, C. J. (2022). Very small effects of an imagery-based randomised trial to promote adherence to wearing face coverings during the COVID-19 pandemic and identification of future intervention targets. *Psychology and Health, 38*(10), 1288–1308. https://doi.org/10.1080/08870446.2021.2012574

Department of Health. (2011). *No health without mental health: A cross-government mental health outcomes strategy for people of all ages.* Department of Health.

Earll, L., & Bath, J. (2004). *Consultancy: What is it, how do you do it, and does it make any difference? Health psychology in practice.* BPS Blackwell.

Epton, T., Currie, S., & Armitage, C. J. (2017). Unique effects of setting goals on behavior change: Systematic review and meta-analysis. *Journal of Consulting and Clinical Psychology, 85*(12), 1182–1198. https://doi.org/10.1037/ccp0000260

Flocke, S. A., Clark, E., Antognoli, E., Mason, M. J., Lawson, P. J., Smith, S., & Cohen, D. J. (2014). Teachable moments for health behavior change and intermediate patient outcomes. *Patient Education and Counseling, 96*(1), 43–49. https://doi.org/10.1016/j.pec.2014.03.014

Gibbs, G. (2013; online version). *Learning by doing: A guide to teaching and learning methods.* Online edition. https://stephenp.net/wp-content/uploads/2015/12/learning-by-doing-graham-gibbs.pdf

Gilbert, P. (2010). *The compassionate mind: A new approach to life's challenges.* New Harbinger Publications.

Greenhow, C., Graham, C. R., & Koehler, M. J. (2022). Foundations of online learning: Challenges and opportunities. *Educational Psychologist, 57*(3), 131–147. https://doi.org/10.1080/00461520.2022.2090364

Hart, J. K., Michael, P., Hawkins, R., Bull, E. R., Farrar, A., Baguley, C., Turner, R. R., & Byrne-Davis, L. M. T. (2023). 'We just need to find space for them to practice so that we can help to make a stronger society': Perceived barriers and facilitators to employing health psychologists in UK public health and clinical health settings. *British Journal of Health Psychology, 28*, 1206–1221. https://doi.org/10.1111/bjhp.12680

Health & Care Professional Council (2023). *The standards of proficiency for practitioner psychologists.* Practitioner psychologists | (hcpc-uk.org).

Hodges, J. (2017). *Consultancy, organization development and change.* Kogan Page.

Jehangir, R. R. (2010). *Higher education and First-Generation Students*. Palgrave Macmillan.

Kakabadse, N. K., Louchart, E., & Kakabadse, A. (2006). Consultant's role: A qualitative inquiry from the consultant's perspective. *Journal of Management Development, 25*(5), 416–500. https://doi.org/10.1108/02621710610666268

Lawson, P. J., & Flocke, S. A. (2009). Teachable moments for health behavior change: A concept analysis. *Patient Education & Counselling, 76*(1), 25–30. https://doi.org/10.1016/j.pec.2008.11.002

Lee, A. S., Ozakinci, G., Leung, S., Humphris, G., Dale, H., & Hamlet, N. (2016). Lifestyle change in the cancer setting using 'the teachable moment': Protocol for a proof-of-concept pilot in a urology service. *Pilot and Feasibility Studies, 2*, 1–13. https://doi.org/10.1186/s40814-016-0102-y

McBride, C. M., Emmons, K. M., & Lipkus, I. M. (2003). Understanding the potential of teachable moments: The case of smoking cessation. *Health Education Research, 18*(2), 156–170. https://doi.org/10.1093/her/18.2.156

Michie, S., Abraham, C., Eccles, M. P., Francis, J. J., Hardeman, W., & Johnston, M. (2011). Strengthening evaluation and implementation by specifying components of behaviour change interventions: A study protocol. *Implementation Science, 6*, 10. https://doi.org/10.1186/1748-5908-6-10

NHS England. (2023, July 6). *Co-production: An introduction*. https://www.england.nhs.uk/long-read/co-production-an-introduction/

Olander, E. K., Darwin, Z. J., Atkinson, L., Smith, D. M., & Gardner, B. (2016). Beyond the 'teachable moment'—A conceptual analysis of women's perinatal behaviour change. *Women and Birth, 29*(3), e67–e71. https://doi.org/10.1016/j.wombi.2015.11.005

Oliver, C. (2005). *Reflexive inquiry: A framework for consultancy practice*. Routledge.

Perkins, R., Repper, J., Rinaldi, M., & Brown, H. (2012). *Briefing: Recovery college*. https://imroc.org/wp-content/uploads/2022/04/1.Recovery-Colleges.pdf

Perkins, A. M., Ridler, J. H., Hammond, L., Davies, S., & Hackmann, C. (2017). Impacts of attending recovery colleges on NHS staff. *Mental Health and Social Inclusion, 21*(1), 18–24. https://doi.org/10.1108/MHSI-11-2016-0035

Perkins, R., Meddings, S., Williams, S., & Repper, J., (2018). *Recovery colleges 10 years on*. https://static1.squarespace.com/static/65e873c27971d37984653be0/t/668c0c17506df25c98d01377/1720454168113/ImROC-Recovery-Colleges-10-Years-On.pdf

Phelan, S. (2010). Pregnancy: A 'teachable moment' for weight control and obesity prevention. *American Journal of Obstetrics & Gynaecology, 202*(2), 135.e1–135.e8. https://doi.org/10.1016/j.ajog.2009.06.008

Redman, S., Greenhalgh, T., Adedokun, L., Staniszewska, S., Denegri, S., et al. (2021). Co-production of knowledge: The future. *British Medical Journal, 372*. https://doi.org/10.1136/bmj.n434

Rockliffe, L., Peters, S., Heazell, A. E. P., & Smith, D. M. (2021). Understanding pregnancy as a teachable moment for behaviour change: A comparison of the

COM-B and Teachable Moments models. *Health Psychology and Behavioral Medicine, 10*(1), 41–59. https://doi.org/10.1080/21642850.2021.2014851

Rockliffe, L., Peters, S., Smith, D. M., Heal, C., & Heazell, A. E. P. (2022). Investigating the utility of the COM-B and TM model to explain changes in eating behaviour during pregnancy: A longitudinal cohort study. *British Journal of Health Psychology, 27*(3), 1077–1099. https://doi.org/10.1111/bjhp.12590

Sacks, R., & Loon, M. (2016). Developing and using consultancy skills. In M. Loon (Ed.), *Professional practice in learning and development: How to design and deliver plans for the workplace* (pp. 151–206). Kogan Page.

Schein, E. H. (2013). *Humble inquiry*. Berrett-Koehler.

Schein, E. H. (2016). *Humble consulting*. Berrett-Koehler.

Schön, D. (1991). *The reflective practitioner: How professionals think and act*. Avebury.

Smith, D. M., Donnelly, P. J., Howe, J., Mumford, T., Campbell, A., Ruddock, A., Tierney, S., & Wearden, A. (2018). A qualitative interview study of people living with well-controlled Type 1 diabetes. *Psychology and Health, 33*(7), 872–887. https://doi.org/10.1080/08870446.2017.1423313

Sommer, J., Gill, K., & Stein-Parbury, J. (2018). 'Walking side-by-side': Recovery colleges revolutionising mental health care. *Mental Health and Social Inclusion, 22*(1), 18–26. https://doi.org/10.1108/MHSI-11-2017-0050

Thompson, S., & Thompson, N. (2008). *The critically reflective practitioner*. Palgrave Macmillan.

Thompson, H., Simonds, L., Barr, S., & Meddings, S. (2021). Recovery colleges: Long-term impact and mechanisms of change. *Mental Health and Social Inclusion, 25*(3), 232–242. https://doi.org/10.1108/MHSI-01-2021-0002

Vygotsky, L. S., & Kozulin, A. (2012). *Thought and language: Revised and expanded edition*. MIT Press.

Williams, M. (2022). Consulting and the pyramid of trust. *Management Consulting Journal, 5*(1), 62–65. https://doi.org/10.2478/mcj-2022-0007

Wilton, C. (2021). Coproduction and partnership with people and communities. *BMJ Leader, 5*(2), 1–4. https://doi.org/10.1136/leader-2020-000424

Zabel, E., Donegan, G., Lawrence, K., & French, P. (2016). Exploring the impact of the recovery academy: A qualitative study of Recovery College experiences. *The Journal of Mental Health Training, Education and Practice, 11*(3), 162–171. https://doi.org/10.1108/JMHTEP-12-2015-0052

Zinkiewicz, L., Hammond, N., & Trapp, A. (2003). *Applying psychology disciplinary knowledge to psychology teaching and learning: A review of selected psychological research and theory with implications for teaching practice*. The HE Academy Psychology Network.

26

Planning and Managing: Consultancy for Local Government - Behavioural Science in Self-management of Well-being

Rachael Thorneloe, Abigail Millings, and Madelynne Arden

Introduction

This case study details a consultancy project with a United Kingdom (UK) local authority (LA), a form of local government responsible for providing services to a geographical region, that was commissioned through an invitation to tender (ITT). We have changed some details of the case study to maintain the anonymity of the client, stakeholders, and service users. The project involved three stages of contracting: (1) responding to the ITT which formed the basis of the initial contract; (2) inception and early planning meetings with the client, and (3) review and subsequent (re)contracting with the client. We first explore these three stages and consider how they impacted on the planning and delivery of the project and second, we reflect on our learnings and changes in working practice as consultants in health psychology and behavioural science.

R. Thorneloe (✉) • A. Millings
Sheffield Hallam University, Sheffield, UK
e-mail: rachael.thorneloe@shu.ac.uk; a.millings@shu.ac.uk

M. Arden
Manchester Metropolitan University, Manchester, UK
e-mail: m.arden@shu.ac.uk

R. Brady et al. (eds.), *The Palgrave Handbook of Consultancy in Health Psychology*,
https://doi.org/10.1007/978-3-031-94529-8_26

The Case Study

First Stage of Contracting: Responding to the ITT

The client issued an ITT in 2020 via a procurement portal. The project aims and objectives were somewhat vague. The client wanted a supplier to co-design a website for and with members of the general public which would include behavioural science expertise (described later in this chapter). The website would promote well-being for community residents in three key areas: physical activity, social isolation, and COVID-19 management and prevention. The website would triage users with additional support needs (e.g., those managing complex issues) to a face-to-face support service to be commissioned separately by the client.

Opportunity to engage in enquiry to explore the context for the project was limited to submission of questions via the procurement portal. The client collated and responded to all questions received, sharing responses with all suppliers that had registered interest.

Our proposal. Reviewing the ITT and client responses to questions, we identified areas where our expertise in behavioural science could bring significant value to the project. We wrote a project bid which outlined our planned methodology, timeline and costings, the parameters of our input, and the assumptions that we made: our 'best guess' (McLeod & Schapper, 2020) about what we could deliver in the time and budget allocated. We proposed to co-design aspects of the website to support two service user behaviours important for optimising effectiveness of the website: engagement with website functions, and engagement with target self-management behaviours (e.g., accessing local support services) that would contribute to health and well-being (e.g., improved physical activity). We would do this by:

1. Working with stakeholders—public health team members, healthcare professionals, community group volunteers, and people from the target population (community members in the LA area) to co-design aspects of the website
2. Advising on the website content (tools), structure (tailoring and features to encourage engagement) and measures (triaging and evaluation).

Based on the ITT, we assumed the website would be created by web-designers (commissioned separately by the LA) who would participate in the co-design and who would translate our recommendations into the design and features of the new website.

Our approach for this project was informed by the Capability, Opportunity, and Motivation model of Behaviour (COM-B) and the Behaviour Change Wheel (BCW) (Michie et al., 2011, 2014), which are models recommended for use within LA public health teams when designing or adapting public health interventions (West et al., 2019). By establishing which capability (i.e., knowledge, skills), opportunity (i.e., physical and social environment), and motivation (i.e., reflective and habitual processes) factors need to change to facilitate the behaviour, the BCW can be used to identify matching interventions and behaviour change techniques (BCTs; Michie et al., 2013).

Our methodology was informed by the 4-stage Double Diamond co-design model (Design Council, 2005). *Discovering* the nature of the issues would involve discussing and prioritising the barriers and facilitators to engagement with the website functions, and engagement with the target self-management behaviours. *Defining* the nature of the problem would require defining the barriers for each target behaviour and generating ideas and solutions to address those barriers. *Designing* potential solutions would involve exploring what people like or dislike about potential solutions and how they could be improved. *Delivering* solutions required a focus on what would be likely to be acceptable, feasible, and effective. In this final stage, and based on our interpretation of the ITT, we planned to consult with web designers to deliver a prototype website and seek community member input to refine that prototype. Our proposal was based on some unknowns (e.g., how many co-design sessions the client was expecting) and assumptions (e.g., that the client had commissioned web designers). We reflect on challenges in this regard later in the chapter.

Second Stage of Contracting

Having won the contract, we set up planning meetings to undertake enquiry (Brady & Varkonyi-Sepp, 2025; see Chap. 3) negotiation, and contracting. Our assumption that the client had commissioned web designers was incorrect. In response to our questions about the timescales of future commissioning of the web designers, the client indicated that not only would commissioning web designers be informed by the outcomes of our project, but so too would the overall budget and timescale for website development. This meant that web designers would not be available to participate in the co-design sessions. We raised concerns that this could have a negative impact on the delivery of a website prototype. As behavioural scientists we could make recommendations about what to include in a website but were unable to appraise what website design and functionality was possible within the client's budget and timescales. We felt it was also unlikely that the web designers would have the knowledge and understanding of behavioural science to ensure fidelity to our recommendations in the absence of opportunity to engage with us.

During this enquiry process we learned that the client had previously undertaken work with stakeholders from local community and voluntary organisations to identify the key health and wellbeing domains on which they wanted the website to focus. The client was keen to examine whether service users would identify the same key domains.

We contracted to undertake the following work. We would plan and facilitate two co-design sessions with people working with intended service users within LA and voluntary sector organisations to identify their needs regarding the website structure, content, and tools. We would also undertake three co-design sessions with intended service users (recruited by the LA) to identify how they would prefer to access and navigate the website, and the content they would like to see included. We would produce a report and recommendations to inform the future design of the website. The client would commission web designers to create website prototypes, informed by our recommendations. We would undertake further co-design sessions to develop and refine the website using those prototypes and produce a final report with our recommendations.

Delivering the agreed work. In the initial co-design sessions, we found that representatives of community and voluntary organisations agreed with the client's planned areas of focus, while service user representatives identified broader aspects of health and well-being (e.g., communication, empowerment, and learning opportunities). Service users expressed scepticism about whether their voices would be heard by the LA through this process of co-design, having been asked to input into previous consultations without feeling that they had any influence on outcomes. We fed this back to the client to and highlighted the risk that focusing solely on LA priorities could reinforce service users' scepticism about co-design and tokenistic engagement (Moll et al., 2020).

We also discussed our concerns with the client regarding the intended assessment tool to triage service users with additional support needs to a face-to-face support service. We were unable to identify a theoretically informed and validated triage tool that would be effective, fair, and work across all three well-being areas. Service users might be unwilling to complete an online measure of this nature. We agreed to develop a way to triage users within each key area separately and explained that we were unlikely to find validated measures with established cut-offs to inform this. We reflect on this process of negotiation later in the chapter.

We reported the findings from the co-design work, and our recommendations that service users should navigate a tailored journey in line with COM-B, with tools and support to address identified barriers. Since web designers had not been appointed, we provided three optional pathways for web content and navigation to reflect different levels of complexity and likely cost:

1. simple with focus on information only (capability),
2. more complex involving self-navigation through content divided into issues of capability, opportunity, and motivation,
3. tailored involving assessment of the service user's current situation and barriers to change, with the content tailored accordingly.

Informed by the co-design sessions, our report commented on the likely acceptability of each of these pathways for service users. Whilst the first pathway was likely to be the easiest to develop (and might be more acceptable to commissioners), service users reported a reluctance to navigate through a range of content that might not meet their needs (e.g., if their challenge was a motivational one). We recommended optional online assessment tools available to all users as well as face-to-face support for all those requesting it. This was an alternative to the 'triage tool' originally requested by the client that would triage only those service users with additional support needs to a face-to-face support service. We reflect on these issues later in this chapter.

Third Stage of (Re)Contracting

Meeting with the client to discuss the report, it became clear that while we had delivered what we were contracted to do, our report did not match the expectations of the client. We reflect on this later in this chapter. The client had expected a blueprint of the functions and pathways and mechanisms of engagement that the website needed to enable a detailed specification to be written for the yet-to-be commissioned web designers. We enquired further about the client's exact requirements for commissioning web designers. We explained that as behavioural scientists we did not have the expertise to write a detailed specification for the website. We could, however, suggest methods to maximise engagement and pathways (including tools and functions) that would meet the recommendations of our work. The client agreed with this solution. We provided flow diagrams with notes on recommended content, questions, tailoring options, and behaviour change tools, for two content areas on the website (physical activity and social isolation, as requested by the client). These were informed by the co-design sessions and our behavioural science knowledge and expertise. We detailed the pathways and the questions and responses that would lead to different tailored tools and content for service users. For example, those who selected an option to find out more about local groups and projects relevant for supporting physical activity (a capability need) would be directed to a page with relevant information and hyperlinks to service providers' websites. This additional work required some additional staff time that was not costed into our bid, but we felt an obligation to deliver the work required for the client to progress the project.

Delays with the client commissioning processes for the web designers meant we would not have a prototype for use in the next co-design sessions, so we adapted our methods accordingly and used static images of potential web content. We highlighted the limitations of this approach to the client, who agreed the changes. We were able to conclude the co-design work and write our final report, incorporating feedback from service users about the proposed website.

Challenges in evaluation. Because our role in the project ended before development of the website, we were unable to explore its usability, accessibility, and helpfulness of content, and whether it improved well-being as intended. We sought client feedback on the report. They were satisfied that we had delivered on the contract.

Planning and Managing Delivery: (Re) Negotiating Changes

In this section, we focus on planning and managing delivery of the project, particularly in light of the restrictions to enquiry involved in tendering, and the need to renegotiate and re-contract throughout. Planning a project involves a range of activities at the pre- and post-contract stage: resource allocation, timescales, meetings, and deliverables.

Pre-contract Planning

When responding to an ITT, there are limited opportunities for enquiry pre-contract. Consultants rely on the information provided in the ITT. Proposals are based on a 'best guess' with limited knowledge of clients' needs and underlying drivers (Cicmil, 2000; Sturdy et al., 2009). Planning a project in sufficient detail to enable proper costing within the required timescales, as well as being appealing to the client and meeting their assessment criteria, poses risks to the consultant. Any misunderstanding of the ITT could make the project undeliverable or result in a low-quality project. According to McLeod and Schapper (2020) quality in consultancy can relate to: (1) inputs or conditions (quality of planning systems and competencies of planners); (2) process (quality of consultancy, project management success); (3) project/consultancy deliverables (plan and product quality, client satisfaction); and (4) performance in realising benefits (implementation, effectiveness). We focus here on three important implications of planning limitations for this project: first, negotiating changes to maintain professional standards; second, shared understandings of health psychology competencies and language; and third, negotiating shifting requirements.

Negotiating Changes to Ensure Professional Standards are Maintained

To address the requirement in the ITT to recommend or develop an online triage tool, we drew on our professional knowledge of existing tools. The Patient Activation Measure (PAM, Hibbard et al., 2004; Hibbard & Gilburt, 2014) measures knowledge, skills, and confidence to self-manage. Although widely used in the United States, Europe (Rademakers et al., 2016), and the UK National Health Service, we had reservations about its suitability for triaging. The PAM has a health/illness focus, whereas the client wanted to include self-management of social isolation. The PAM is also not designed for people living with multiple co-morbidities whose responses might vary depending on which condition they are thinking about when they complete it (see Armstrong et al., 2017; Gao et al., 2019). Furthermore, there are also different factors affecting self-management of COVID-related behaviours (e.g., Thorneloe et al., 2022; Wright & Fancourt, 2021) social isolation (e.g., De Koning et al., 2017), and physical activity (e.g., Howlett et al., 2019; Ige-Elegbede et al., 2019). Being able to self-manage in relation to physical activity would not necessarily mean that a person could self-manage COVID-19 related behaviours. Despite these issues, we were aware that finding an alternative existing measure that would meet the requirements was unlikely.

We therefore included identifying a triage tool in our plan, aware that we would need to negotiate. As health psychologists, our standards of proficiency require that we practise within the legal and ethical boundaries of the profession (Health and Care Professions Council [HCPC], 2015). These include that we *"understand the need to act in the best interests of service users at all times"* and *"understand the need to respect and uphold the rights, dignity, values and autonomy of service users including their role in the assessment, treatment and intervention process and in maintaining health and wellbeing"* (Health and Care Professions Council). Advising wrongly with regard to the triage tool would not be acting in the best interests of service users, and this could impact on the rights of service users to receive an appropriate intervention to effectively support their health and well-being. The HCPC standards required that we did not take this client requirement at face value, hence we needed to negotiate to ensure that we could arrive at a solution which both met the client's and service users' needs. Although there was the risk that the client would be unwilling to negotiate an alternative solution, we decided to take this risk and bid for the project, confident that we would find a way to steer the client towards an ethical solution. We planned to explore the acceptability and feasibility of a triage tool within the stakeholder and service user co-design sessions and present the findings back to the client for negotiation.

In the discovery and define co-design sessions, service users reported reluctance to complete questionnaires, or to register their personal details unless they saw a clear personal benefit. This is consistent with research showing that people are more willing to disclose personal data if they think that they will benefit (Degutis et al., 2023). This posed a problem for an online triage tool where most would be asked to disclose personal data, but not all would gain access to face-to-face support. When discussing these findings with the client, we discovered that resource limitations meant that face-to-face support could not be a universal offer and needed to be targeted to the most needy. We needed to negotiate a solution that met this requirement in a different way, satisfying both the client and our professional standards (UK Health and Care Professions Council, 2015), by identifying and directing only service users who had a genuine need for additional support to the face-to-face service.

We drew on our understanding of theory and behaviour change to recommend web-based tailored pathways that would triage based on the specific choices and experiences of the individual. If service users struggled to navigate the website pathway or self-identified that the tools (e.g., goal setting) and links provided (e.g., local community groups) did not sufficiently meet their needs, they would be invited to sign up for access to the additional support service. Web-based interventions are well-placed to offer this kind of tailoring based on user input (Noar et al., 2011). The service user would not be asked to register until the additional benefit to them (access to additional support) was apparent. This met the reciprocation needs highlighted by service users in the co-design sessions (Degutis et al., 2023), and the triage needs of the client who was satisfied with this solution.

Shared Understandings of Health Psychology Competencies and Language

Our role as consultants was to co-design aspects of the website with stakeholders, including target service users. We ensured that the content of the website provided people with the capability, opportunity, and motivation for self-management in the context of three target areas. The client agreed with our aims and methodologies at the pre-contract stage and our approach specified in early meetings. Following the planning and delivery of the co-design sessions, we produced a report of our findings and our recommendations for the website. We made recommendations about the look and feel of the website by drawing on the EAST model (Behavioural Insights Team, 2014) which recommends that behaviour change interventions are Easy, Attractive, Social and Timely with the inclusion of simple intuitive navigation, engaging and attractive content, and making use of videos showing 'people like me'. Our recommendations regarding behaviour change tools, and the BCTs (Michie et al., 2013) underpinning them, were based on the barriers and facilitators to engaging in self-management behaviours that we identified in the discovery, define and design co-design, as well as existing literature (e.g., Michie et al., 2008). These included: a decisional balance tool that supported users to consider the pros and cons of behaviour change; a goal setting template that supported users to write SMART goals (Specific, Measurable, Achievable, Relevant, and Time-bound, Michie et al., 2008) and, an action planning and implementation intention (if-then plan) template (Gollwitzer & Sheeran, 2006) to support detailed planning of the performance of the behaviour.

It became apparent that the client had expected a website prototype or blueprint, rather than recommended behaviour change interventions. This partly reflected misunderstanding from the client about what we do as behavioural scientists, the differences between behavioural science and web design, and our neglecting to explore the client's expectations in sufficient depth in the early meetings.

Ojasalo (2001) identifies three types of client's expectations: fuzzy expectations, (the client does not know exactly what they want), implicit expectations (the client believes that the objectives are self-evident), and unrealistic expectations (the client's expectations do not match the consultant's roles and responsibilities). In this project, the client was not clear about whether they wanted behaviour change interventions, a website prototype, or both. This meant that the objectives were not clearly defined in the ITT, nor in the subsequent contracting stage, resulting in a mismatch between what we delivered (intervention recommendations) and what was expected (website prototype).

During the initial contracting stage, sufficient time needs to be spent to determine the client's expectations and to establish a clear division of roles and responsibilities (Nikolova & Devinney, 2009). On reflection, we could have spent more time establishing the client's precise requirements. It is the consultant's responsibility to ask questions to the client to find out what they want, and why they think they need this before the consultant can explain what they can offer to address those needs. Schein (2016) discusses the need for genuine curiosity from the consultant in asking the right questions, listening carefully to the client's description of their problem and using open and trusting communication to get to the (sometimes hidden) underlying issues. In this case, we would have benefited from asking about the rationale that led to the specification outlined in the ITT, and what resources were available from the client to support their contributions to the project. While this latter point may seem unintuitive given that the client is hiring external expertise for a given project, much of the work we do as behavioural scientists necessarily interfaces with the client's own staff teams and capabilities, hence it is important to secure access to the requisite 'insider' knowledge, skills, processes, and resources (e.g., data) via relevant staff's time. We find this particularly salient when consulting for LAs, when the ambition of commissioners is not always supported by sufficient resourcing of operational staff.

In the context of behavioural science consultancy, we need to know what assumptions the client is making about the parameters of behavioural science and how it intersects with other fields, such as web design. This can be particularly challenging when this other field uses similar methodologies or frameworks, such as the Double Diamond co-design model (Design Council, 2005), and the same terminology to describe different things (e.g., a prototype intervention vs. a prototype website). Our assumption (based on the ITT) that web designers would be involved in the co-design sessions meant we did not develop a shared understanding of how our role differed from web designers, with the client. We had intended to use the APEASE criteria (Acceptability, Practicability, Effectiveness, Affordability, Side Effects, Equity) (Michie et al., 2014) to help evaluate the likely practicality and feasibility of the interventions from the perspective of the web designers and the client. Because the web designers had not been appointed, we could not evaluate the extent to which our intervention recommendations could be implemented within the website. In order to maintain quality and client satisfaction in the consultancy deliverables (McLeod & Schapper, 2020), subsequent to our report's lukewarm reception by the client, we provided further detail in the form of the flow diagrams and outline of how our intervention recommendations could be translated into a website prototype, at no additional cost to the client. The relatively minimal staff time this incurred was absorbed by our team.

Negotiating Shifting Requirements

Co-creation is described as a collaborative process, involving stakeholders in co-design (of a new solution) and co-production (implementing a predetermined solution) (Vargas et al., 2022). These terms are often used interchangeably (Masterson et al., 2022). Managing client requirements can be challenging as clients' needs might not be evident early on and can change rapidly (Barkley & Saylor, 1994). A major challenge we had to navigate was a shift in the client's requirements. What had started out as *co-design,* (and we adopted the Double Diamond approach) necessarily turned into *co-production.* The client requested an open-ended approach (co-design), confident that service users would generate a list of website content areas that matched their own. There can be a considerable mismatch between service users and health professional's preferences for self-management of health and well-being (e.g., Jones et al., 2000), hence we questioned this decision, but the client was immovable. We agreed to proceed to preserve our relationship with the client although we recognised that we would not be able to fully utilise the stages of the Double Diamond approach to do so.

Schein (2016) argues that the consultant's role is to help the client see the complexity and messiness of a particular problem, and to help them consider more adaptive solutions rather than 'quick fixes'. The consultant needs to make clear to the client the anticipated consequences of certain decisions, so they are fully informed and can make joint decisions on what actions to take. Despite the different priorities of service users' self-management of health and well-being, the client requested that we utilise their pre-specified content areas. This generated a challenge to our relationship with the service users, with whom we needed to continue collaborative design activities. Balancing service user sensibilities against the requirements of the project involved circumventing some service user anger towards the client for the shift in direction. It posed a risk for the consultancy team's ability to retain the trust of the service users (who wanted assurance that their input was worthwhile), which was necessary to deliver the work. Previous studies have highlighted the importance of establishing realistic expectations at the start of co-design to avoid people feeling dissatisfied with the pace of progress and their impact within the project (Bowen et al., 2013). The success of any project depends not only delivering the requirements for the client, but also on working successfully with other key stakeholders who may have competing needs and priorities (Karlsen, 2002). We discussed these issues and negotiated a way forward that enabled service user input with the parameters set out by the client thus maintaining good relationships with both the client and service users and were able to deliver the project to their satisfaction.

Reflection

One of the challenges for health psychologists in responding to an ITT is knowing exactly where and how our skills can be utilised to best effect within the planned project. The tendering process can pose specific challenges to acquiring a clear understanding of a project, which impedes the ability to discern and sell the fit of health psychology skills to the brief. Schein (2016) argues that it is the consultant's responsibility to understand what the client wants (or thinks they want), in order for the consultant to then determine how best they can offer their expertise to address the client's issue. In the context of responding to an ITT, there are limited opportunities to explore with the client where health psychology can (and cannot) be utilised. We may need to rely heavily on what is provided in the ITT in order to determine what we as health psychologists can offer to the project. Clients may have limited understanding and awareness of health psychology competencies, skills, and approaches and this is a barrier to being able to draw up a suitable specification with which to commission work (Curtis et al., 2018; Moffat et al., 2022). The client might miss key areas where health psychology expertise could bring significant value, and this lack of awareness can be reflected in the ITT. The nature of responding to an ITT means that it is not always possible to have a sufficient period of 'joint diagnosis' at the pre-contract stage, whereby a jointly agreed action plan is drafted, based on the consultant understanding the nature of the problem, and the client understanding the kinds of expertise that might be relevant to their problem (Schein, 1999). Insufficient opportunities for enquiry at the pre-contract stage can put consultants in a position of risk. An ITT that is unclear can result in a bid which does not sufficiently meet the client's requirements and risks the consultant not winning the work. Another risk is that if the consultant scopes out the work and wins the contract with gaps in their understanding of client requirements, later enquiry may reveal a poor fit with the requirements of the project. Subsequent re-negotiating risks rendering the project undeliverable if it produces a project that is substantially different in terms of professional competencies and staff required, timescales, and budget. It is important that consultants who respond to ITTs take full advantage of opportunities for enquiry at the pre-contract stage, however limited in scope. Asking the right questions is crucial, both to explore the client's requirements and to check the accuracy of their own assumptions. Doing so can help ensure that the consultant is able to clearly explain in their proposal how their expertise as health psychologists can help to solve the client's problem.

Our specific learnings from this project are numerous. First, we are more aware of ambiguity in ITTs as a potential indicator of risk. Where ITTs are missing key details that enable us to have confidence in our project plan, and when we cannot clarify ambiguity by the pre-bid questions and responses, we choose not to bid. If consultants decide not to submit a project proposal due to a lack of clarity in the ITT, they may wish to consider informing potential clients that this is their reason why they are not bidding for the project.

Second, we are now more aware of potentially differing interpretations of outcomes, and of the need to alert clients to potential problems and risks in unambiguous ways. With the benefit of hindsight, we could have alerted the client explicitly in writing via email about the risks of not having a web designer on board at the beginning of the project and what that would mean for the outcomes of the project and what we could deliver and not deliver. This could have avoided the need for negotiation and additional work on our part at a late stage.

Third, to ensure that we fully understand client expectations, we also now ask clients in the pre-contract and early planning meetings to advise on the exact format they require for reports. Knowing what is expected early on allows us to plan the reporting and to better understand the clients' expectations. Where clients do not have a standard reporting template, we create one and ask the client for feedback to ensure that it meets their expectations. With the benefit of hindsight, this could have alerted us to the differing expectations of the recommendations that we could make, according to our skills and competencies, and what was expected, and we could have renegotiated the outcomes earlier in the process, saving time, effort, and costs.

Fourth, misunderstandings of what co-design is and is not is a key area of learning from this project. We frequently see this term in ITTs, and we now recognise that this usually means some kind of co-creation (Masterson et al.,

2022) undertaken between researchers, stakeholders, and service users (target population). We don't make assumptions about what kind of collaborative activities these are. While co-design in which service users, stakeholders and researchers work together to design the solution (Vargas et al., 2022) is our preference, and in our view fits best with the BCW approach to intervention development (Michie et al., 2014), some projects require different co-creation methods to meet timeframes, costs, and pre-specified outcomes.

Lastly, we observe that consultancy such as the project we have described often works in the opposite direction to how we, as behavioural scientists, would choose to work. This project was already defined as one focused on development of a website before we commenced our activities. Ideally, if we were to follow the BCW approach to intervention development (Michie et al., 2014), we would not pre-specify the mode of delivery of an intervention (i.e., a website) because this limits the kinds of barriers that can be addressed, and the type of intervention functions and behaviour change techniques (Michie et al., 2013) that can be included. Theoretical approaches from the discipline suggest working from the target behaviour, through a period of insight gathering, before identifying key barriers and potential solutions, and then using the APEASE evaluation criteria to guide decision making (Michie et al., 2014). Clients often seem to work from the opposite end—deciding on a mode of delivery (e.g., new service provision, a website, communications/messaging) at the start of the project and commissioning the work to design and deliver it. This can be a common challenge for health psychologists working in behaviour change and intervention design and something we see when we run training sessions in behavioural science for LAs and government organisations. There is a strong tendency to jump to the solution before properly understanding the problem. While the value of the BCW approach is clear, in that it enables solutions that best match the specific needs of the target population in relation to capability, opportunity and motivation, it poses a challenge for commissioners because the budgets and timescales needed are unknown until part way through the work. An intervention could be anything from messages to a website, support service or environmental change, and this is not known until after evidence reviews, insight gathering, and analysis and intervention development take place.

Working as a consultant in behaviour change therefore requires some flexibility and pragmatism when it comes to the application of intervention development frameworks. Based on our experience, we make the following recommendations for health psychologists using the BCW or similar intervention development frameworks in consultancy projects. If the client wants to deliver an intervention to support behaviour change, and they have a preferred mode of delivery (e.g., a website) for delivering that intervention, we suggest that the consultant:

1. Explores the barriers and facilitators for the target population to engage in the particular behaviour, using the COM-B model (Michie et al., 2011, 2014).
2. Explores service users' perceived acceptability of delivering interventions using the preferred mode of delivery, using the Theoretical Framework of Acceptability (Sekhon et al., 2017).
3. Uses the APEASE criteria in consultation with the client and wider stakeholders (e.g., web designers) to explore the extent to which the preferred mode of intervention delivery could be adapted or revised to target and address the needs identified in points 1 and 2.

The bid needs to explain the value of this approach and how it enables the intervention to have the best chance of success. Providing examples from previous work of how this approach has been used successfully is always helpful if the requirements for the format response to tender have sufficient flexibility to do so.

Conclusion

We were commissioned as consultants to provide behavioural science expertise to inform the development of a self-management website. We worked with stakeholders and service users through a process of co-creation to explore how people would access and engage with a website designed to support self-management, the kinds of content and tools that people would like to see on that website, and how to identify people who needed additional face-to-face support. We used these findings to make recommendations about the website. Some differences in interpretation of the brief and project plan led to us renegotiating aspects of the work and adjusting our approach. This enabled us to deliver as promised while maintaining good relations with both the client and service users and meeting our professional competencies. Our learnings from the project include the need to glean as much information as possible about the needs for the project and the rationale for its commissioning at the beginning of the project and ensuring that there is shared understanding about the outcomes.

Top tips

1. Explore shared meanings with client at earliest opportunity, for example, by explaining what we as health psychologists understand by a term they have used and checking that their understanding matches ours.
2. Be clear on the boundaries of your expertise and competencies so that expectations about process and outcomes are shared between the consultant and client.
3. Negotiation requires some flexibility, but you don't have to say yes to everything. The project needs to remain deliverable for the allocated time and budget, as well as being within competence and ethical boundaries.
4. Agree reporting requirements early. Find out exactly what they are looking for, in what format, and whether they want to see and comment on a draft before the report deadline.

Competing Interests The authors have no competing interests to declare that are relevant to the content of this chapter.

References

Armstrong, N., Tarrant, C., Martin, G., Manktelow, B., Brewster, L., & Chew, S. (2017). *Independent evaluation of the feasibility of using the Patient Activation Measure in the NHS in England-Final report*. University of Leicester and The Health Foundation. https://www.england.nhs.uk/wp-content/uploads/2015/11/pam-evaluation.pdf

Barkley, B., & Saylor, J. H. (1994). *Customer-driven project management: A new paradigm in total quality implementation*. McGraw-Hill Companies.

Behavioural Insights Team. (2014). *EAST: Four simple ways to apply behavioural insights*. Behavioural Insight Team. https://www.bi.team/wp-content/uploads/2015/07/BIT-Publication-EAST_FA_WEB.pdf

Bowen, S., McSeveny, K., Lockley, E., Wolstenholme, D., Cobb, M., & Dearden, A. (2013). How was it for you? Experiences of participatory design in the UK health service. *CoDesign, 9*(4), 230–246. https://doi.org/10.1080/15710882.2013.846384

Brady, R., & Varkonyi-Sepp, J. (2025). A framework for consultancy in health psychology. In R. Brady, J. Varkonyi-Sepp, & J. Smith (Eds.), *The Palgrave handbook of consultancy in health psychology*. Palgrave Macmillan.

Cicmil, S. (2000). Quality in project environments: A non-conventional agenda. *International Journal of Quality & Reliability Management, 17*(4/5), 554–570. https://doi.org/10.1108/02656710010298599

Curtis, K., Fulton, E., & Brown, K. (2018). Factors influencing application of behavioural science evidence by public health decision-makers and practitioners, and implications for practice. *Preventive Medicine Reports, 12*, 106–115. https://doi.org/10.1016/j.pmedr.2018.08.012

De Koning, J. L., Stathi, A., & Richards, S. (2017). Predictors of loneliness and different types of social isolation of rural-living older adults in the United Kingdom. *Ageing & Society, 37*(10), 2012–2043. https://doi.org/10.1017/S0144686X16000696

Degutis, M., Urbonavičius, S., Hollebeek, L. D., & Anselmsson, J. (2023). Consumers' willingness to disclose their personal data in e-commerce: A reciprocity-based social exchange perspective. *Journal of Retailing and Consumer Services, 74*, 103385. https://doi.org/10.1016/j.jretconser.2023.103385

Design Council. (2005). *The 'double diamond' design process model.* Design Council. https://www.designcouncil.org.uk/our-resources/the-double-diamond/

Gao, J., Arden, M., Hoo, Z. H., & Wildman, M. (2019). Understanding patient activation and adherence to nebuliser treatment in adults with cystic fibrosis: responses to the UK version of PAM-13 and a think aloud study. *BMC Health Services Research, 19*, 1–12. https://doi.org/10.1186/s12913-019-4260-5

Gollwitzer, P. M., & Sheeran, P. (2006). Implementation intentions and goal achievement: A meta-analysis of effects and processes. *Advances in Experimental Social Psychology, 38*, 69–119. https://doi.org/10.1016/S0065-2601(06)38002-1

Health and Care Professions Council. (2015). The standards of proficiency for practitioner psychologists. Retrieved September 18, 2023, from https://www.hcpc-uk.org/standards/standards-of-proficiency/practitioner-psychologists/

Hibbard, J., & Gilburt, H.. (2014). *Supporting people to manage their health. An introduction to patient activation.* Kings Fund. Retrieved February 12, 2025, from https://policycommons.net/artifacts/1716007/supporting-people-to-manage-their-health/2447678/

Hibbard, J. H., Stockard, J., Mahoney, E. R., & Tusler, M. (2004). Development of the Patient Activation Measure (PAM): Conceptualizing and measuring activation in patients and consumers. *Health Services Research, 39*(4p1), 1005–1026. https://doi.org/10.1111/j.1475-6773.2004.00269.x

Howlett, N., Schulz, J., Trivedi, D., Troop, N., & Chater, A. (2019). A prospective study exploring the construct and predictive validity of the COM-B model for physical activity. *Journal of Health Psychology, 24*(10), 1378–1391. https://doi.org/10.1177/1359105317739098

Ige-Elegbede, J., Pilkington, P., Gray, S., & Powell, J. (2019). Barriers and facilitators of physical activity among adults and older adults from Black and Minority Ethnic groups in the UK: A systematic review of qualitative studies. *Preventive Medicine Reports, 15*, 100952. https://doi.org/10.1016/j.pmedr.2019.100952

Jones, A., Pill, R., & Adams, S. (2000). Qualitative study of views of health professionals and patients on guided self management plans for asthma. *BMJ, 321*(7275), 1507–1510. https://doi.org/10.1136/bmj.321.7275.1507

Karlsen, J. T. (2002). Project stakeholder management. *Engineering Management Journal, 14*(4), 19–24. https://doi.org/10.1080/10429247.2002.11415180

Masterson, D., Areskoug Josefsson, K., Robert, G., Nylander, E., & Kjellström, S. (2022). Mapping definitions of co-production and co-design in health and social care: A systematic scoping review providing lessons for the future. *Health Expectations, 25*(3), 902–913. https://doi.org/10.1111/hex.13470

McLeod, S., & Schapper, J. H. (2020). Understanding quality in planning consultancy: A review and synthesis of the literature. *Journal of Planning Education and Research, 44*(1). https://doi.org/10.1177/0739456X20943928

Michie, S., Rumsey, N., Fussell, A., Hardeman, W., Johnston, M., Newman, S., & Yardley, L. (2008). *Improving health: Changing behaviour. NHS health trainer handbook*. Department of Health and British Psychological Society. https://core.ac.uk/download/pdf/18619054.pdf

Michie, S., Van Stralen, M. M., & West, R. (2011). The behaviour change wheel: A new method for characterising and designing behaviour change interventions. *Implementation Science, 6*(1), 1–12. https://doi.org/10.1186/1748-5908-6-42

Michie, S., Richardson, M., Johnston, M., Abraham, C., Francis, J., Hardeman, W., et al. (2013). The behavior change technique taxonomy (v1) of 93 hierarchically clustered techniques: Building an international consensus for the reporting of behavior change interventions. *Annals of Behavioral Medicine, 46*(1), 81–95. https://doi.org/10.1007/s12160-013-9486-6

Michie, S., Atkins, L., & West, R. (2014). *The behaviour change wheel. A guide to designing interventions* (1st ed.). Silverback Publishing. www.behaviourchangewheel.com

Moffat, A., Cook, E. J., & Chater, A. M. (2022). Examining the influences on the use of behavioural science within UK local authority public health: Qualitative thematic analysis and deductive mapping to the COM-B model and Theoretical Domains Framework. *Frontiers in Public Health, 3742*. https://doi.org/10.3389/fpubh.2022.1016076

Moll, S., Wyndham-West, M., Mulvale, G., Park, S., Buettgen, A., Phoenix, M., Felisig, R., & Bruce, E. (2020). Are you really doing 'codesign'? Critical reflections when working with vulnerable populations. *BMJ Open, 10*(11), e038339. https://doi.org/10.1136/bmjopen-2020-038339

Nikolova, N., & Devinney, T. M. (2009). Influence and power dynamics in client-consultant teams. *Journal of Strategy and Management, 2*(1), 31–55. https://doi.org/10.1108/17554250910948695

Noar, S. M., Grant Harrington, N., Van Stee, S. K., & Shemanski Aldrich, R. (2011). Tailored health communication to change lifestyle behaviors. *American Journal of Lifestyle Medicine, 5*(2), 112–122. https://doi.org/10.1177/1559827610387255

Ojasalo, J. (2001). Managing customer expectations in professional services. *Managing Service Quality: An International Journal, 11*(3), 200–212. https://doi.org/10.1108/09604520110391379

Rademakers, J., Maindal, H. T., Steinsbekk, A., Gensichen, J., Brenk-Franz, K., & Hendriks, M. (2016). Patient activation in Europe: An international comparison of psychometric properties and patients' scores on the short form Patient Activation Measure (PAM-13). *BMC Health Services Research, 16*(1), 1–7. https://doi.org/10.1186/s12913-016-1828-1

Schein, E. H. (1999). *Process consultation revisited: Building the helping relationship*. Addison-Wesley. https://lccn.loc.gov/98024926

Schein, E. H. (2016). *Humble consulting: How to provide real help faster*. Berrett-Koehler Publishers.

Sekhon, M., Cartwright, M., & Francis, J. J. (2017). Acceptability of healthcare interventions: An overview of reviews and development of a theoretical framework. *BMC Health Services Research, 17*(1), 1–13. https://doi.org/10.1186/s12913-017-2031-8

Sturdy, A., Werr, A., & Buono, A. F. (2009). The client in management consultancy research: Mapping the territory. *Scandinavian Journal of Management, 25*(3), 247–252. https://doi.org/10.1016/j.scaman.2009.05.008

Thorneloe, R. J., Clarke, E. N., & Arden, M. A. (2022). Adherence to behaviours associated with the test, trace, and isolate system: An analysis using the theoretical domains framework. *BMC Public Health, 22*(1), 1–11. https://doi.org/10.1186/s12889-022-12815-8

Vargas, C., Whelan, J., Brimblecombe, J., & Allender, S. (2022). Co-creation, co-design, co-production for public health: A perspective on definition and distinctions. *Public Health Research & Practice, 32*, 2. https://doi.org/10.17061/phrp3222211

West, R., Michie, S., Atkins, L., Chadwick, P., & Lorencatto, F. (2019). *Achieving behaviour change: A guide for local government and partners. Public Health England*. https://assets.publishing.service.gov.uk/media/5e7b4e85d3bf7f133c923435/PHEBI_Achieving_Behaviour_Change_Local_Government.pdf

Wright, L., & Fancourt, D. (2021). Do predictors of adherence to pandemic guidelines change over time? A panel study of 22,000 UK adults during the COVID-19 pandemic. *Preventive Medicine, 153*, 106713. https://doi.org/10.1016/j.ypmed.2021.106713

27

Planning and Managing: Everything Due an Hour Ago - Consultancy with a Government Department

Daniella Watson, Wendy Lawrence, and Mary Barker

Introduction

During the COVID-19 pandemic, governments looked to research for evidence-based recommendations. So, how did we as consultants ensure that we were conducting rigorous, ethical but rapid research in line with our professional guidelines and regulations? This chapter will describe a case study illustrating the strategies and challenges involved in delivering high-quality research at the speed demanded by the rapidly changing conditions during the pandemic and conclude with top tips for future consultancy teams working under similar constraints. The chapter has three sections: a description of the consultancy from initial contact to evaluation; an analysis of planning and delivery, including managing scope creep; and a reflection on lessons learnt and considerations for future consultancies.

Supplementary Information The online version contains supplementary material available at https://doi.org/10.1007/978-3-031-94529-8_27.

D. Watson (✉)
Imperial College London, London, UK
e-mail: daniella.watson@imperial.ac.uk

W. Lawrence • M. Barker
University of Southampton, Southampton, UK
e-mail: wtl@mrc.soton.ac.uk; meb@mrc.soton.ac.uk

R. Brady et al. (eds.), *The Palgrave Handbook of Consultancy in Health Psychology*,
https://doi.org/10.1007/978-3-031-94529-8_27

The Consultancy Project

Client and Consultants

The client, a United Kingdom (UK) government department, approached a medical research team at the University of Southampton to pilot a COVID-19 screening programme during the first lockdowns of the COVID-19 pandemic between April and November 2020. The client was working with local and national public health departments to develop options for screening for COVID-19 infection. The university was chosen because it was already working on a screening programme with a local authority, had well-developed laboratory facilities, information technology (IT) systems and existing relationships with local government and schools. The client requested a qualitative evaluation of the programme to explore the acceptability of the programme to those who took part and to understand why others declined to participate. The medical research team recognised they had neither the capacity nor the expertise to conduct this evaluation. They therefore approached experienced qualitative researchers for support, that is, the authors of this chapter. There was no time available to draw up a formal contract for the consultancy; the urgency of the pandemic meant that the client expected an immediate start. MB, a Professor of Psychology and Behavioural Science, was approached to supervise a small team to conduct this evaluation because of her extensive qualitative experience and close relationships with stakeholders within the university and the city. MB asked her PhD student (DW) to lead this on the ground. DW had been working with MB and WTL on qualitative research since 2014. Alongside her PhD, DW worked as a Senior Research Assistant coordinating three qualitative studies in South Africa, Ghana and Burkina Faso. She was also a UK Stage 2 trainee health psychologist at the time, under the supervision of WTL. WTL has worked at the university as an Associate Professor of Health Psychology, conducting qualitative research locally and internationally for 20+ years. She runs a consultancy delivering behaviour change communication training (Healthy Conversation Skills) to health professionals and volunteers around the world (Lawrence et al., 2016).

In this project, the consultant-client relationship was complex. The *'Basic Type of Clients Model'* (Schein, 1997; see ESM_27.1 for details of the model) is helpful in illustrating this consultant-client complexity, so we adopt their terminology to use with clients and consultants alike. The government department in this case study is the 'primary client', as they owned the problem being addressed and paid the consultancy bills. Consultancies often have one or more specialists (Nicolescu & Nicolescu, 2016); in this consultancy, there were two levels of consultants. The first was the research team, the 'contact consultants' who were originally contracted by the client and who then asked us to conduct the qualitative evaluation. The second level of consultants is the qualitative evaluation team, the authors of this chapter, the 'intermediate consultants'. The contact consultants had direct communication with both the primary client and the intermediate consultants, so they managed communication between us. Schein (1997) also describes 'ultimate clients', normally members of the public whose interests the client wishes to serve. In this case, the ultimate clients were members of our local community, whom we aimed to protect from contracting and spreading COVID-19.

Consultancy Objectives

The contact consultants negotiated the objectives of the evaluation with the client. Agreed objectives were to conduct a qualitative evaluation to explore participants' and decliners' experiences of the COVID-19 screening programme. The client wanted to know if the programme was acceptable to participants and how it could be improved. Outputs from the evaluation would help to modify the programme to improve recruitment and retention of participants and would shape local and national strategies for COVID-19 screening programmes, restrictions on freedom of movement and infection protection measures. The consultancy was carried out in two phases. In Phase One, we conducted a small-scale qualitative evaluation over a month. The client valued the insights provided and modifications were made to the programme. This led to an additional month's funding to conduct further qualitative evaluation in Phase Two. The aims of the evaluation were broadly the same but with a higher number of interviews and an expansion to include a more diverse range of participants. The client also wished to explore experiences of the modified programme.

As the contact consultants had limited qualitative research experience, no specific objectives were agreed upon with the client about the consultancy's scope and methodology. This later became an issue as we discuss below. In Phase One, on behalf of the intermediate consultants, MB and DW set specific objectives for the qualitative evaluation: to conduct 30 telephone interviews in one month with participants and decliners of the programme and to feed back the findings. In Phase Two, specific objectives were abandoned as the urgency of responding to the pandemic increased. Each week, the contact consultants expected us to be talking to more participants. In order to meet these demands, we hired a further 11 experienced qualitative researchers to support DW to conduct the interviews and focus groups. They became affectionately known as the 'Qual Army'.

Choosing the Method

Readers can access a full description of the methodology and lessons learnt from this evaluation by accessing the two publications on this work (Watson et al., 2022; Anil et al., 2023). The focus of this chapter is on explaining the work through the lens of consultancy.

DW and MB chose to adopt a 'rapid qualitative evaluation' method, previously used when UK government departments required real-time feedback on a programme designed to shape national policy at speed (Nunns, 2009). Rapid qualitative evaluation involves conducting interviews and focus groups over a short space of time, where the analysis involves summarising key points and producing 'real-time' feedback (Beebe, 2014; Neal et al., 2015; Taylor et al., 2018). These are then added to a shared report, known as a rapid assessment procedure (RAP) sheet, which is edited by the research team and updated continuously as new data and insights are generated (Lewis et al., 2003; Vindrola-Padros et al., 2020; Vindrola-Padros & Johnson, 2020).

Carrying Out the Consultancy

We developed semi-structured discussion guides which were informed by the needs of the client as defined by the research team. From our previous experience of conducting telephone interviews (Lawrence et al., 2020; Strömmer et al., 2018) and of online public consultations (Barker et al., 2022; Gbesemete et al., 2020), we knew that remote methods could be used when face-to-face interactions were not possible. We conducted telephone interviews in the smaller-scale Phase One evaluation. In Phase Two, we conducted online focus groups to increase the number of participants alongside telephone or online one-to-one interviews with participants testing positive for COVID-19, those who declined to take part in the programme and senior staff working on the programme. For these groups, one-to-one interviews allowed more privacy for discussion of potentially sensitive topics such as testing positive, reasons for declining or complaints about their experience of the screening programme.

Every week at research team meetings, DW presented a short report of key findings from the RAP sheet, which was then emailed to the client. In the weekly meetings, the research team also discussed the client's priorities for the

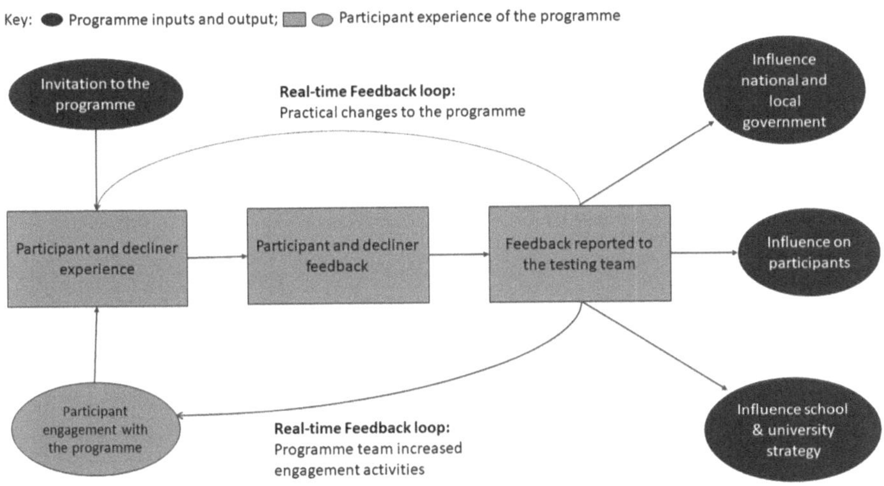

Fig. 27.1 The way that participants' experiences informed the COVID-19 programme. (Watson et al., 2022)

following week. We worked flexibly and adapted to accommodate these. Our reports and updates enabled the research team to make modifications to the running of the screening programme and the client to pass on insights from our evaluation to those developing other national screening programmes. Figure 27.1 illustrates the way in which real-time feedback from the rapid qualitative evaluation fed into modifications to the way the programme ran which in turn influenced levels of participation. There was also a pathway along which evaluation data might flow to influence national and local government policy, and university and school strategies, in ways of working with communities and improving the delivery of COVID-19 programmes.

By the end of the consultancy, we had conducted 77 telephone interviews and 20 online focus groups, which gave us a combined total of 223 participants and those people who declined to take part. The client was satisfied with these numbers and with participant diversity, which included those who had tested positive, those who declined to take part and senior university, general practice and school representatives responsible for delivering the programme in their organisations.

Stakeholders

We were aware of the importance of distinguishing between the participants, stakeholders and community groups when building relationships during this consultancy (McLeod & Schapper, 2020). To maximise recruitment for our evaluation, it was essential to work with different stakeholders across the city. We worked collaboratively with the COVID-19 Test and Trace team to share data on positive COVID-19 cases, kept the City Council updated with our evaluation findings, and communicated with schools, general practices and the university to help recruit participants. The range of stakeholders involved can be seen in supplementary material (ESM_27.1).

Deliverables

At the beginning of the consultancy, the only agreed outputs were to summarise our findings for the government department in interim and final reports (Godfrey et al., 2020). In the final report, we used themes from the RAP sheet to structure recommendations, organised under sub-themes extracted from additional qualitative analysis undertaken for a research publication. As academics, it was important to publish our evaluation in an open-access journal to be able to share our findings and lessons learnt with other research teams. Although not a required deliverable, the client was supportive and paid for an additional two weeks of time to conduct this analysis. We justified our desire as a consultancy team to publish by persuading the research team that publishing would give the findings greater credibility and would support the wider research community in designing more effective screening programmes. The research team negotiated with the client to secure permission for us to publish the data (Watson et al., 2022; Anil et al., 2023).

Following the completion of data collection in Phase Two and prior to writing the reports, findings were presented to a group of public and patient involvement contributors in an online meeting hosted by the university. Their feedback helped us to write the reports and publications in an accessible, focused format. This was a strength of this consultancy as it provided reassurance that our interpretation of the data, collected using rapid evaluation techniques, reflected participants' experience. Other outputs included oral presentations to the client and to another government department which found our findings relevant to their work. This meant COVID-19 programme designers across the country were able to learn from our work in a timely fashion, which was useful given the urgency of the situation. The findings were also presented at three conferences: the Behavioural Science and Public Health Network, the British Psychological Society Division of Health Psychology and the International Congress of Psychology, enabling us to explore with our peers the challenges and benefits of providing health psychology consultancy.

Evaluation

No formal evaluation of the consultancy was conducted, mainly due to the fast-paced nature of the pandemic. We delivered interim and final reports according to the client's requirements. Although we had no formal feedback from the client, the informal feedback that we received via the research team was that the qualitative insights and recommendations were invaluable. We will reflect further on this in the final section of this case study.

Planning and Managing Delivery of the Consultancy

In this section, we focus on planning and managing the delivery of the consultancy project and on addressing the challenges of 'scope-creep'. Scope creep is where a project gradually expands beyond its original objectives (Ajmal et al., 2020).

Managing Scope Creep

If the project plan is not set out clearly from the beginning, scope creep can set in. Factors influencing scope creep include lack of understanding of the specifications and requirements of the client, change in tasks required by the client, lack of consultant's technical expertise, lack of risk management plans, change in context, complexity of consultancy and lack of a formal communication plan (Ajmal et al., 2020). Documenting and communicating the goals, roles and boundaries at the beginning of a project can prevent scope creep (Wulf, 2020). In our rapid qualitative evaluation, scope creep largely arose from a lack of specific objectives. In Phase One, DW conducted 28 telephone interviews under MB's and WTL's supervision. However, in Phase Two, the client wanted more interviews and focus groups from a larger, more diverse group. We understood the rationale for this but had to consider resources and time. We decided to conduct focus groups to access multiple perspectives as rapidly as possible. We decided to hire one more qualitative researcher so we could have one moderator and one observer working together. More investment of time in project management was needed for the increased number of interviews and focus groups being undertaken. This required additional recruitment, meetings with gatekeepers to access participants, increased scheduling of interviews and focus groups, more writing up of observation notes and data management.

Rapid qualitative approaches rely heavily on the use of a team to collect data from multiple sources at speed. This adds to the administration and coordination of research tasks (Vindrola-Padros et al., 2020). The client had allocated one month per phase to collect the data; two months in total. This was a short amount of time but clearly appropriate during the height of the pandemic. DW knew that she did not have the capacity to meet the client's needs alone, so she asked a senior member of the research team if there was a budget to hire more qualitative researchers. She was told to hire whoever she needed. Because of the urgency of the pandemic, this consultancy was perhaps unusual in that there were no budgetary constraints as long as the spend was justified. We were given funds for more researchers, online meeting accounts and second computer monitors to conduct the focus groups. DW recruited the 11 qualitative researchers, the Qual Army, through an open invitation across her professional network and employed them on short-term casual contracts with the university. DW kept track of payments to the Qual Army by being the middle person between them and the programme finance manager.

Who Does the Planning?

Aware that there was a lot of work to do in very little time, DW adopted a transformational leadership approach (Bass & Riggio, 2006), where she motivated the team with a shared vision and belief in the project to get the best out of them under pressure. The advantage of this leadership style is that it encourages freedom and openness. DW emphasised the importance of the project findings for improving the uptake of the screening programme, which would keep more people safe from COVID-19 in the community; she made the point that they were doing their 'bit' during the pandemic. DW consciously used an empowering communication style, based on Healthy Conversation Skills developed by WTL and MB (Lawrence et al., 2016), to negotiate, influence and facilitate team meetings, which was well received by the team.

Being organised is an important part of leading any consultancy, as is knowing the availability, skillset, and strengths of your team. In the first week, DW asked the Qual Army to document their qualitative experience and skillset in a shared online document. She also asked them to add their availability each week to a shared calendar. DW used the calendar and skillsets to decide who should be conducting interviews or focus groups. DW ensured each researcher observed one or two focus groups with DW or someone else that DW had trained, before they started facilitating focus groups. This boosted the confidence and competence of each researcher and enhanced the quality of the focus groups.

Communication within the team is important for any consultancy work as it ensures that the team members know what they are doing, feel supported and that the work is being conducted efficiently and to a high standard. To keep all team members up to date and feeling supported, DW arranged online weekly meetings. The meetings consisted of updates from the previous week, insights from each team member about how the focus groups and interviews were going, any interesting findings or technical issues and plans for the following week. DW listened to the opinions and concerns of all team members, which made the Qual Army feel valued. This encouraged shared learning but also facilitated team building and confidence. If team members were unable to attend the meeting, they were encouraged to read the follow-up email summarising key points from the meeting or meet separately with DW. Meetings lasted no longer than an hour, which was important as everyone was very stretched at the time.

Monitoring

Monitoring recruitment progress was vital in order to achieve the required number and diversity of participants quickly. To do this, DW used separate online shared spreadsheets for each recruitment method that were accessible to all team members in real time. The team also recorded interviews and focus groups completed and noted observations on a shared real-time spreadsheet. This allowed DW to keep track of the tasks that the Qual Army had completed and chase those who had not completed their task.

It is important to check in with your client throughout the consultancy to ensure that the work is meeting their needs and to adapt the deliverables if required to do so by the client. Delivery of an interim report at the midway point of data collection and attending weekly online meetings with the research team provided opportunities to communicate progress to the client and to ask for help when necessary. The regularity of contact often meant adapting plans at the last minute and being flexible. The research team indicated with whom DW should meet in the following week and changed the timing of tasks depending on the priority and timescale over which the task needed to be done. DW wrote herself to-do lists, planned the changes and then communicated them to her team as quickly as she could to keep the work on track.

After the consultancy, the Qual Army reflected on the lessons they had learnt from conducting a rapid qualitative evaluation during the pandemic and published a paper outlining their learning (see Table 27.1) (Anil et al., 2023). The table shows actions for both a leader and a team member in the rapid qualitative evaluation that could help consultants to plan, set up and deliver their consultancy projects. Some of the actions were developed at the start of the consultancy, such as DW preparing for the rapid virtual environment, whereas other actions, such as leading a large team and creating a supportive culture, became necessary later, when scope creep set in and we suddenly needed to hire a team of qualitative researchers. Part of effective project planning and management is the ability to adapt to changing circumstances (Too et al., 2017).

Reflection

To provide structure for our reflection on the experience of providing consultancy services for a government department, we used Gibbs' reflective cycle, consisting of description, feelings, evaluation, analysis, conclusion and action plan (Gibbs, 1988). We chose this approach as we felt it gave a suitable framework to examine and learn from our experiences of delivering a rapid qualitative evaluation.

Description

In summary, the research team contacted MB as a specialist consultant because of her expertise, and MB asked DW to lead a team of qualitative researchers in delivering the rapid qualitative evaluation. DW planned and monitored the data collection to keep up with deadlines and built relationships with stakeholders who acted as gatekeepers to the participants and the client. We adapted to the client's additional requirements and rapid timelines, delivering above and beyond what was agreed by the client in terms of data collection and dissemination. We negotiated resources via the research team to keep up with the client's new requests. We evaluated the work continuously, shared key findings in weekly team meetings and provided interim and final reports to the client.

Table 27.1 Actionable points for each lesson learned

Lesson	Specific actions for a leader	Specific actions for a team member
Novelty of a large team with varied backgrounds	Identify skill gaps among your team and provide support/training to address those gaps	Familiarise yourself with your team members' skills to identify opportunities to assist your own work and/or improve your own and their skills
	Be prepared to listen to opposing opinions and make the final decisions on any discrepancies; this can be done by being clear on your project goals	
Having a shared vision	Clearly communicate the project's goals and its importance early on and throughout the project to maintain team motivation	Ensure you know why the project is needed and its goals early on to inform your tasks
Effective project management	Plan the project in-depth as early as possible; this includes the following: • Preparing timescales for each step of the project • Deciding deadlines • Building the team • Deciding task delegation to the team based on skill	Familiarise yourself with project timescales and deadlines
	Create regular meeting spaces with team members to communicate the following: • Project goals • Deadlines • Update on project outputs and next steps	Ensure you know how to access project information and learn to use any required project-related technology
	Consider using a platform (such as Microsoft Teams) as a central location to store and share real-time project information and documents with the team	
	Build a confident team by identifying individuals with the right skills for the project	
	Actively involve all team members by asking and listening to their opinions	
	Following each meeting send a summary and action points to all team members	
Creating a proactive and supportive work culture	Listen to the opinions of your team and allow for the potential for their opinions to influence the project plans	Listen to the opinions of other team members and communicate problems with each other to work collaboratively
	Implement a shared vision and efficient project management using the points above	Offer support to other team members where needed and if you have the capacity
	Approach your senior colleagues for support and advice when needed	
	Recognise and show appreciation of team members for their efforts by providing positive feedback	

(continued)

Table 27.1 (continued)

Lesson	Specific actions for a leader	Specific actions for a team member
Developing leadership skills	Reflect on your leadership skills by recognising your concerns and identifying ways to overcome them; use strategies such as Gibb's Reflective Cycle for reflection	Noting the leadership skills of your project lead may help you vicariously develop your own leadership skills; look out for the following to help you: • Methods used to communicate information • Storage of information • How they use technology to support the project • How they interact with team members and the type of support they offer
Preparing for a rapid approach and a virtual setting[a]	Clearly communicate deadlines and expectations of work timescales to your team early on by: • Storing deadlines and timescales on a central storage system that is easily accessible • Ensuring every team member knows where and how to access this information • Emphasising task expectations by outlining specific task details and workload involved • Outlining expectations of the work schedule by setting working hours dependent on your team's availability	Ensure you are prepared to reply to communications from your project lead and team members quickly to ensure task deadlines are met
	Balance your rapid project with your other projects by setting specific hours and days to work on specific projects	Communicate your specific working hours to your project lead to set communication expectations
	Match your rapid project timescales to your work schedule to ensure deadlines are met	
	Update project information as soon as possible and communicate these updates to your team; having a real-time report (e.g. on Microsoft Teams) will greatly assist this communication	
	Prepare to be flexible in the project work schedule in case of unexpected project challenges, such as sickness within your team or a resource becoming suddenly disrupted/unavailable	
	Create a plan that can be flexible, based on your deadlines, your team's working hours and skills of team members	

[a]Lessons learned from a rapid approach and remote working were combined as many of the suggested actions overlapped
Based on Anil et al. (2023)

Feelings

Although providing consultancy is a core competency of health psychologists (British Psychological Society, 2025), nothing had prepared us for such an intense consultancy with a government department. Before starting the evaluation, it is fair to say we felt nervous and doubted our ability to effectively deliver to a client outside academia and working in government. We were also very excited and proud to be part of the COVID-19 effort. Once we started, we felt more confident that the rapid qualitative evaluation could produce findings that would be useful for the client. There were times when we felt overwhelmed, as there was so much time pressure alongside the ever-changing context of the pandemic. When we had completed the evaluation, we felt a sense of relief as it had somewhat taken over our lives. We felt immensely proud that our qualitative work could potentially have such an impact on the client, the general population and national policy. We were honoured when DW was invited to present to two UK government departments, received 'Employee of the Month' and 'Shine a Light' awards from her university department, and the programme team were awarded the University of Southampton's Vice-Chancellor's award for 'Public Good'.

Evaluation

The generation of a set of shared beliefs and values amongst the team was important to the success of this consultancy. DW emphasised the importance of this work in contributing to the pandemic effort, which seemed to resonate with the team and give them a sense of common purpose. Open communication throughout the project and explicitly encouraging everyone to contribute and valuing everyone's opinions were also important in creating cohesion and good working relationships within the team. Communication strategies included weekly online catch-ups, follow-up emails and documents with task instructions. These encouraged team members to proactively engage with the project, respond to communications quickly and offer help to each other (Greenwood et al., 2017; Hofstede, 2011; Savage, 2019). The Qual Army were positive about their experience of this approach in the paper published on lessons learnt (Anil et al., 2023). MB and WTL provided advice and support throughout.

The contracting arrangements for this consultancy were not ideal, however. The urgency created by the pandemic meant that a formal, detailed contract was not in place before the work started. On reflection, this was a mistake made by us as naïve consultants; we learnt that the time taken to set up a contract is not wasted, even in desperate circumstances, as it can avoid other, more time-consuming challenges later on, such as issues with payment. We also felt honoured and privileged to be doing necessary work for a government department in this time of crisis. This made it easier to overlook the fact that the contract was not finalised when we started the work. The power dynamics between client and consultant can create risk for the consultant who might agree to compromising contracts and scope creep because the client is the paymaster and may, as in this case, be an important national or global body (Kometa et al., 1996). Our take-home message from this experience is that health psychologist consultants should know their worth and ensure proper contracting arrangements regardless of the urgency of the work, who the client is or how important they perceive them to be.

Health psychologist consultants need to think very carefully about the national or global context when taking on a consultancy, as there could be reputational risks associated with the work (McLeod & Schapper, 2020). Science is political and can be used as a weapon to create different national and global narratives. If, for example, a participant had been injured through participation in the programme, we might have been held responsible by the government department for whom we were working and had to deal with damaging publicity.

Analysis

Looking back on the experience, when any of us were feeling stressed or overwhelmed, we found that a good coping mechanism was to acknowledge that we were at our limit and to ask for help. This was especially true for DW, a health psychology trainee and PhD student at the time. Although DW had led teams before, it still felt quite overwhelming to manage a team of 11 researchers with such high-stake clients at her career stage. DW never felt she was working outside her professional boundaries in terms of ethics, data management or skillset but did sometimes feel like she had taken on too much. This was because DW was a full-time research assistant on an international project, completing her PhD and her Health Psychology Stage Two professional training, as well as working on other COVID-19 consultancies, which were demanding in terms of short deadlines and additional requests from the client. DW sought advice and supervision from MB and WTL, where they discussed what DW could do to reduce these feelings to better manage the situation. DW was initially reluctant to ask for help; she was so overwhelmed that she found it difficult to imagine what could help and was just concerned that this might require her to do even more work. This proved to be the case since when she did ask for help, she was asked to find and lead a team of additional researchers to support the completion of the work. Hiring and training a new team did increase DW's workload in the short term but decreased it in the long run. DW learnt a lot very quickly about how to manage teams, how to adapt and be flexible in response to changing client needs and perhaps most importantly, how and when to ask for help.

Conclusion

A clear contract of work established at the beginning of employment is vital to protect consultants from financial risk and scope creep. When leading a consultancy team delivering to short deadlines, we found it helpful to inspire the team with a shared vision, understand their availability and skillset and communicate effectively with them. In this case study, the communication skills that we brought as health psychologists and as Healthy Conversation Skills trainers supported us to build relationships and rapport quickly with stakeholders who were gatekeepers to community groups, participants and the client. We found it important to plan ahead, to be adaptable in the face of the client's changing demands and to have processes in place, such as the real-time spreadsheets we used to monitor the work in order to keep on top of the client's expectations.

A key learning from this experience of consultancy is that the team really enjoyed the ever-evolving nature of their work and the variety this brought with it; the rapid timelines resulting from working in a pandemic meant we were constantly adapting to the changing situation. As consultants, we can work rapidly and flexibly and provide immediately useful feedback to our clients when required, perhaps not possible when working under traditional academic constraints. Consultancy gives health psychologists the opportunity to stretch the boundaries of their working practice, but it is our job to ensure that we maintain our scientific rigour throughout this process, whilst relishing the challenges this brings.

Action Plan

As consultants, it is important to have a plan from the outset, with clear and detailed steps for how the required work and outputs will be achieved. In this case, everything had to happen at speed to provide real-time feedback and recommendations to the client, so it felt like there was minimal time to plan. In future, we would aim to establish more direct contact with the client following the initial approach to better plan timelines, outputs and funding from the beginning. This could be inspired by the 'level two relationship' approach suggested by Schein (2016) of having informal relationships with clients, which build trust and honesty. This can be done by learning together and getting to know the client holistically. It is also important to plan risk mitigation with the client, effective communication strategies and to record the client's requirements and expectations (Ajmal et al., 2020; Wulf, 2020).

ABC of Top Tips

- **A**sk for help from your team, supervisors or mentors … or anyone you feel you can get support from whenever you start to feel overwhelmed.
- **B**uild relationships and trust with stakeholders, ideally utilising existing networks and contacts, as this helps establish rapport faster.
- **C**reate an empowering culture and shared vision within your team to maximise their motivation to provide the agreed deliverables within the expected timeframe.
- **D**raw up a contract from the outset to define and agree with all aspects of the project to avoid later problems with timelines, deliverables, funding and scope creep.
- **E**stablish shared documents that update in real time to monitor and track progress with large teams working to tight deadlines.

Competing Interests The authors have no competing interests to declare that are relevant to this chapter.

References

Ajmal, M., Khan, M., & Al-Yafei, H. (2020). Exploring factors behind project scope creep–stakeholders' perspective. *International Journal of Managing Projects in Business, 13*(3), 483–504. https://doi.org/10.1108/ijmpb-10-2018-0228

Anil, K., Watson, D., Alagil, J., Dewar-Haggart, R., Fearn, S., McGrath, C., Meagher, C., Muir, S., & Barker, M. (2023). Narrowing the gap between research and policy: Using rapid evaluation during the COVID-19 crisis. *Perspectives in Public Health, 143*(1), 14–17. https://doi.org/10.1177/17579139221138449

Barker, C., Collet, K., Gbesemete, D., Piggin, M., Watson, D., Pristerà, P., Lawerence, W., Smith, E., Bahrami-Hessari, M., & Johnson, H. (2022). Public attitudes to a human challenge study with SARS-CoV-2: A mixed-methods study. *Wellcome Open Research, 7*, 49. https://doi.org/10.12688/wellcomeopenres.17516.1

Bass, B. M., & Riggio, R. E. (2006). *Transformational leadership*. Psychology Press. https://doi.org/10.4324/9781410617095

Beebe, J. (2014). *Rapid qualitative inquiry: A field guide to team-based assessment*. Rowman & Littlefield.

British Psychological Society. (2025). Qualification in Health Psychology (Stage 2). Retrieved January 5, 2025, from https://www.bps.org.uk/qualification-health-psychology-stage-2

Gbesemete, D., Barker, M., Lawrence, W., Watson, D., De Graaf, H., & Read, R. (2020). Exploring the acceptability of controlled human infection with SARSCoV2—A public consultation. *BMC Medicine, 18*(1), 1–8. https://doi.org/10.1186/s12916-020-01670-2

Gibbs, G. (1988). *Learning by doing: A guide to teaching and learning methods*. Further Education Unit.

Godfrey, K., Bagust, L., Baird, J., Barker, M., Batchelor, J., Bryant, S., Colbain, C., Everest, H., Flockhart, A., & Glyn-Owen, K. A. (2020). Evaluation of the expanded Southampton pilot study (Phase 2) for use of saliva-based lamp testing in asymptomatic populations: Final report. https://eprints.soton.ac.uk/445622/1/Evaluation_of_the_expanded_Southampton_pilot_study_Phase_2_for_use_of_saliva_based_lamp_testing_in_asymptomatic_populations_eprints.pdf

Greenwood, R., Oliver, C., Lawrence, T. B., & Meyer, R. E. (2017). *The Sage handbook of organisational institutionalism*. Sage.

Hofstede, G. (2011). Dimensionalising cultures: The Hofstede model in context. *Online Readings in Psychology and Culture, 2*(1). https://doi.org/10.9707/2307-0919.1014

Kometa, S. T., Olomolaiye, P. O., & Harris, F. C. (1996). A review of client-generated risks to project consultants. *International Journal of Project Management, 14*(5), 273–279. https://doi.org/10.1016/0263-7863(96)84510-8

Lawrence, W., Black, C., Tinati, T., Cradock, S., Begum, R., Jarman, M., Pease, A., Margetts, B., Davies, J., & Inskip, H. (2016). 'Making every contact count': evaluation of the impact of an intervention to train health and social care practitioners in skills to support health behaviour change. *Journal of Health Psychology, 21*(2), 138–151. https://doi.org/10.1177/1359105314523304

Lawrence, W., Vogel, C., Strömmer, S., Morris, T., Treadgold, B., Watson, D., Hart, K., McGill, K., Hammond, J., & Harvey, N. C. (2020). How can we best use opportunities provided by routine maternity care to engage women in improving their diets and health? *Maternal & Child Nutrition, 16*(1). https://doi.org/10.1111/mcn.12900

Lewis, J., Ritchie, J., & Ormston, R. (2003). Generalising from qualitative research. *Qualitative Research Practice: A Guide for Social Science Students and Researchers, 2*, 347–362.

McLeod, S., & Schapper, J. H. (2020). Understanding quality in planning consultancy: A review and synthesis of the literature. *Journal of Planning Education and Research*. https://doi.org/10.1177/0739456x20943928

Neal, J. W., Neal, Z. P., VanDyke, E., & Kornbluh, M. (2015). Expediting the analysis of qualitative data in evaluation: A procedure for the rapid identification of themes from audio recordings (RITA). *American Journal of Evaluation, 36*(1), 118–132. https://doi.org/10.1177/1098214014536601

Nicolescu, O., & Nicolescu, C. (2016). Specificity of managerial consultancy for SMEs and its status in Romania. *Procedia-Social and Behavioral Sciences, 221*, 39–48. https://doi.org/10.1016/j.sbspro.2016.05.088

Nunns, H. (2009). Responding to the demand for quicker evaluation findings. *Social Policy Journal of New Zealand, 34*, 89–99.

Savage, M. (2019). Sociology, class and male manual work cultures. In *British trade unions and industrial politics* (pp. 23–42). Routledge. https://doi.org/10.4324/9780429453526-2

Schein, E. H. (1997). The concept of "client" from a process consultation perspective: A guide for change agents. *Journal of Organizational Change Management, 10*(3), 202–216. https://doi.org/10.1108/09534819710171077

Schein, E. H. (2016). *Humble consulting: How to provide real help faster.* Berrett-Koehler Publishers.

Strömmer, S., Lawrence, W., Rose, T., Vogel, C., Watson, D., Bottell, J. N., Parmenter, J., Harvey, N. C., Cooper, C., & Inskip, H. (2018). Improving recruitment to clinical trials during pregnancy: A mixed methods investigation. *Social Science & Medicine, 200*, 73–82. https://doi.org/10.1016/j.socscimed.2018.01.014

Taylor, B., Henshall, C., Kenyon, S., Litchfield, I., & Greenfield, S. (2018). Can rapid approaches to qualitative analysis deliver timely, valid findings to clinical leaders? A mixed methods study comparing rapid and thematic analysis. *BMJ Open, 8*(10). https://doi.org/10.1136/bmjopen-2017-019993

Too, E., Le, T., & Yap, W. Y. (2017). Front-end planning- The role of project governance and its impact on scope change management. *International Journal of Technology, 8*(6), 1124–1133. https://doi.org/10.14716/ijtech.v8i6.708

Vindrola-Padros, C., Chisnall, G., Cooper, S., Dowrick, A., Djellouli, N., Symmons, S. M., Martin, S., Singleton, G., Vanderslott, S., & Vera, N. (2020). Carrying out rapid qualitative research during a pandemic: Emerging lessons from COVID-19. *Qualitative Health Research, 30*(14), 2192–2204. https://doi.org/10.1177/1049732320951526

Vindrola-Padros, C., & Johnson, G. A. (2020). Rapid techniques in qualitative research: A critical review of the literature. *Qualitative Health Research, 30*(10), 1596–1604. https://doi.org/10.1177/1049732320921835

Watson, D., Baralle, N. L., Alagil, J., Anil, K., Ciccognani, S., Dewar-Haggart, R., Fearn, S., Groot, J., Knowles, K., & Meagher, C. (2022). How do we engage people in testing for COVID-19? A rapid qualitative evaluation of a testing programme in schools, GP surgeries and a university. *BMC Public Health, 22*, 1–11. https://doi.org/10.1186/s12889-022-12657-4

Wulf, S. A. (2020). Successful project consulting. *IEEE Engineering Management Review, 48*(2), 12–14. https://doi.org/10.1109/emr.2020.2978797

28

Evaluation: Improving Employee Health and Wellbeing

Joe Gaunt and Lisa Newson

Overview

This case study summarises our consultancy, which, in collaboration with the client—a rapidly expanding marketing automation technology firm in the United Kingdom (UK), aimed to enhance the client's employee retention by addressing their employees' health and wellbeing needs. Our innovative *Consultancy-to-Practice Model*, detailed in this chapter, highlights the significance of preparatory work via a *Discovery Needs Assessment*, which underpinned the success of the consultancy implementation and subsequent evaluations. We identified key priorities by engaging with the client to understand their goals and scrutinising data. In this chapter, we take the reader through our implementation of the Consultancy-to-Practice Model. We recommended a comprehensive range of services to support the client's employees' physical, mental, social, and financial health and suggested operational improvements. The success of this consultancy was measured by strategic impacts, knowledge transfer, and client satisfaction. The latter part of this chapter focuses on the evaluation of the consultancy, which included process

J. Gaunt
Zeno Health Group, Bardsey, Leeds, UK
e-mail: joe@zenohealth.co.uk

L. Newson (✉)
Liverpool John Moore University, Liverpool, UK
e-mail: l.m.newson@ljmu.ac.uk

R. Brady et al. (eds.), *The Palgrave Handbook of Consultancy in Health Psychology*,
https://doi.org/10.1007/978-3-031-94529-8_28

evaluation, outcome evaluation, for which all recommendations were adopted, and finally, reflective evaluation, for which we sought feedback from the client and evaluated our project management, performance, and capabilities. At the end of the chapter, we provide some top tips to embed evaluation into future consultancy work.

The Consultants

Health psychology consultancy is "the use of specialist health psychology skills and knowledge to provide a service to an external business client" (British Psychological Society, BPS, 2020, p. 40) and is a defined piece of work that is negotiated and conducted by the consultant directly with the client. In this context, Joe Gaunt (JG), a trainee health psychologist, and Lisa Newson (LN), a health psychologist, are the consultants. JG is the Chief Executive Officer (CEO) of Zeno Health Group, United Kingdom. This digital, holistic, and person-centred health start-up company uses consultancy and data to design company-specific health strategies; conduct gap analysis programmes (assessment of an organisation's discrepancies between the current and desired states and action to reduce the gap between these two components); and provide individual services (to promote health and wellbeing and to create healthy workplace culture) to support organisations. Lisa Newson (LN) is the lead author of this chapter, a health psychologist, and Professor of Health Psychology and Behavioural Medicine at a UK University, and was one of JG's supervisors for his professional training. In addition, Professor Helen Poole (HP), a health psychologist at the University, also provided supervision support to JG. Together, JG, LN, and HP engaged in supervision and reflective practice, during which health psychology and evidence-based approaches were integrated to improve JG's model of consultancy within his company and to enhance the outcomes achieved for a client.

The Client

We were recommended to the client based on our health and wellbeing consultancy expertise. The client was facing challenges in retaining staff. The international technology industry offered competitive packages to attract staff, making it challenging to retain people. The client wanted to improve their offer to staff by focusing on staff health and wellbeing to attract new staff and improve overall job satisfaction.

Preliminary and Exploratory Meetings

We, the authors, arranged preliminary and exploratory meetings to establish a strong relationship with the client and gain key insights from their perspective. These sessions helped us collect valuable information and assess the project's feasibility and compatibility with our consultancy services. Rather than immediately proposing solutions, our discussions focused on exploration and enquiry, aligning with a process consultancy style (Schein, 2016), which emphasises collaboration with clients to diagnose their needs and co-develop solutions rather than offering pre-determined advice. As consultants, we engaged in "humble inquiry" (Schein & Schein, 2021), acting as supportive partners by being curious, caring, committed, and authentic (see examples of questions below and in Table 28.1). Given our approach to enquiry, we needed to understand the client's specific workforce needs without imposing our assumptions or advocating for existing approaches that might not suit their situation. For example, while we were familiar with evidence suggesting that organisational interventions are crucial for improving employees' health and wellbeing (European Agency for Safety and Health at Work, 2016; Nielsen & Randall, 2013, p. 1030), we recognised that intervention success

Table 28.1 Examples of questions asked throughout to engage in formative and process evaluation

Questions we asked ourselves, as the consultants	Questions we asked the client
Are we using questioning and curiosity rather than giving solutions? Are we jointly exploring different perceptions of the problem? Are we being supportive and non-judgemental? Are we creating an even balance of power? Have we created rapport and trust? Are we considering different perspectives and interpretations and actively listening to client concerns/explanations? Have we triangulated data from different sources to enhance validity? Have we considered the client's readiness for change; to hear analysis and implement change; and do we need to support skill development?	Which features of a project are working and which are not working so well? Are there identifiable obstacles or design features that are getting in the way of the work progressing? Which project components do you or your staff say could be strengthened? Will our approach reach and engage with all staff? Is the Discovery Survey appropriate in length and clear in language? Have we provided you with opportunities to explore challenges and discuss various approaches to the problem? Are you clear on roles and expectations and the activities we will engage in?

varies (Montano et al., 2014). We assessed the organisation's readiness to change, considering the client's commitment and capacity to enact change (Weiner, 2009).

This exploration involved understanding their needs, experience with health-related strategies, and desire to impact employees' health positively. We asked questions such as "*What key challenges do you address through your health strategies?*" and "*Could you share insights into your employees' health needs?*". We also inquired about past health initiatives and lessons learned. To grasp the client's approach to employee wellbeing comprehensively, we explored physical, social, mental, and financial health strategies, asking questions such as "*How do you measure the impact on employee wellbeing?*". To aid our engagement with employees, we wanted to understand which communication channels employees preferred: email, in-person meetings, or other methods. We also asked how employees interacted with existing health initiatives and identified any challenges hindering engagement. Throughout this process, we asked ourselves, within supervision, reflection, internal meetings, and meeting notes, if we had answered all our exploratory questions and provided opportunities for the client to express their challenges fully. Based on our enquiry, we believe the client genuinely wanted to prioritise staff health and wellbeing rather than solely focusing on organisational productivity (for further exploration of this specific issue, see Guest, 2017). Feedback from current and former employees emphasised the need for structured and continuous support in areas including sleep, nutrition, physical activity promotion, stress reduction, and fostering a positive organisational culture. We collaborated with the client, listening and learning without making assumptions, to define the project's key aims.

After the preliminary and exploratory meetings, we outlined our services, emphasising our consultancy philosophy, which focuses on health psychology and holistic health. We believed the client was a good fit for building a productive, positive working relationship, and providing consultancy services tailored to their needs. While others may start contractual negotiations at this stage, we took additional time to explore the consultancy opportunity thoroughly. As this was our first engagement with the client, we recommend conducting a comprehensive Discovery Needs Assessment before formalising any contracts or beginning negotiations (see Consultancy-to-Practice Model, Fig. 28.1). This evaluation approach was previously described as a process assessment (Stetler et al., 2006). The Discovery Needs Assessment allowed us to delve deeper into the client's needs and situation, while establishing trust in our consultant role. Moreover, it allowed us to establish trust with our clients

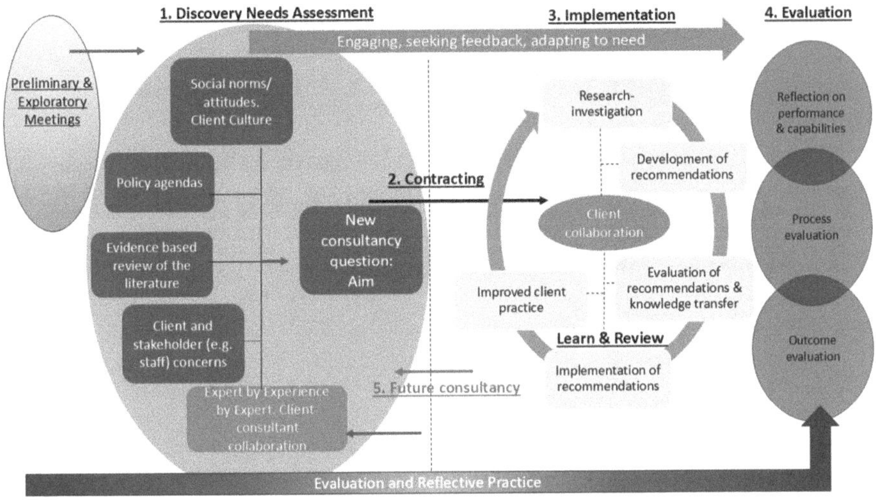

Fig. 28.1 A Consultancy-to-Practice Model

as their consultants and demonstrate that they would receive value and quality from the proposed work. We explore this further below.

Adopting a Tailored Consultancy Approach

For this consultancy, we reflected on a research-to-practice integration model (Sterling & Weisner, 2006, p. 13). Research-to-practice integration models focus on bridging the gap between academic research and its application in real-world settings. Although Sterling and Weisner's model has been devised to promote the integration of health-based research into clinical healthcare practice, it was helpful for us to reconsider this model in our consultancy process, for which we created a new Consultancy-to-Practice Model (Fig. 28.1). Instead of research, the focus is on consultancy, and we have added additional components, such as "Expert by Experience" (to acknowledge our prior skills and knowledge as experienced consultants and health psychologists). We include adding arrows to represent the ongoing, continuous feedback and collaborations between the consultant and the client. Our model distinguishes between the Preliminary and Exploratory meetings, which are considered the introductory meetings, and then a more comprehensive investigative phase, which we term the Discovery Needs Assessment, which precedes the Contracting process. Subsequently, this is followed by an Implementation component, which includes a Learn and Review feedback element with the client. Finally, we incorporated an evaluation component, emphasising the value of evaluation to the consultancy as a whole. By adopting this holistic consultancy model, evaluation becomes integral to the planning stage, and therefore, evaluation processes are embedded throughout.

The model assumes continuous interaction between the consultant and the client, with ongoing communication and feedback integral to the consultancy process. This collaborative approach involves developing project questions and aims, agreeing on recommendations, and integrating them into the client's organisational practice.

Consultancy in Practice

Discovery Needs Assessment

Before this consultancy, we conducted an evidence review on wellbeing interventions in organisations. We had conducted consultancies in other organisations adopting a similar approach. We dedicated significant preparation and time to conducting the Discovery Needs Assessment to fully explore this client's needs, concerns, and client/company culture. Although this phase was unpaid, it facilitated a comprehensive understanding of the project, and established a collaborative partnership between us, the consultants, and the client.

Contracting

The next step was to formalise the consultancy project through contracting. Together with the client, we defined the project scope and outlined specific objectives. As specified within the details of the contract, the agreed aim of this work was to help the client consider and build their strategic approach to promoting staff health and wellbeing. The consultancy activity was specified, for which this consultancy would seek to develop a full assessment of staff health and wellbeing needs, develop recommendations to support the development of an employee health strategy, and provide the client with a clear plan of recommendations for improving their practice. We agreed to investigate the client's organisational strategy, policies, and procedures, for example, through documentary evaluation and observational approaches. Furthermore, we planned to conduct research with staff through quantitative (survey-based) and qualitative data collection. We would assess the relevant evidence on employee health and wellbeing interventions, analyse the organisation's staff data with reference to this evidence base, and benchmark the client against national and comparative (similar organisations) statistics.

The client needed to allocate time for discussions and negotiation decision-making, ensuring relevant staff participation. The client provided access to necessary information, such as company strategies and data on staff wellbeing. Survey distribution and completion were the client's responsibility. We confirmed terms, price, and finalised contracts, which detailed services to be provided by whom and when; Client Obligations; Intellectual Property; Data Protection; Service Level Agreements; Pricing and Payment; Term and Renewal; Termination; Suspension of Services; Warranties and Compatibility; Force Majeure; Liability; Partnership, Agency, and Rights of Third Parties; Severance; Dispute Resolution; Governing Law; Notices; Waiver. It is important to note that while these terms were agreed upon for the consultancy, this text does not represent legal advice, and the client and consultant should seek independent legal counsel for legal matters related to the contract.

As stated within the contract, we planned to present our findings and recommendations in a written report with an executive summary and recommendations for implementation. Additionally, we proposed an interactive Review and Learn session with the client to collectively agree on recommendations (see further details below). Clarifying expectations for this session was essential in our contracting process. We agreed to create an implementation plan and annual review procedure to help the client implement our recommendations. Finally, we agreed on the details of our evaluation procedures, and who, what, and when feedback was required from the clients for us as consultants.

Implementation

With input from the client and the insights we gathered during the discovery phase, we adapted an existing (Zeno Health Group, United Kingdom) health and wellbeing survey. We engaged in proof-of-concept testing with a sample of staff to ensure the acceptability and feasibility of the survey before full distribution. To maximise employee participation, we designed a concise and user-friendly online questionnaire consisting of 17 questions. The questionnaire covered areas comprising the following: physical health, mental wellbeing, manager support (examining manager engagement with employee wellbeing), and perceptions of the company's focus on wellbeing, which included exploring the organisational environment and cultural commitment to wellbeing. Additional questionnaire topics included assessments of staff's smoking habits, alcohol consumption, happiness, and sleep. Some questions were aligned with the UK Office for National Statistics data for future benchmarking, such as "*How happy did you feel yesterday?*" (Office of National Statistics, 2022). In addition to collecting quantitative data, the survey encouraged employees to provide qualitative feedback through open-text comments and invited employees to contact us directly to provide additional information. The survey prioritised staff anonymity as it was the client's inaugural health and wellbeing assessment. We analysed the data and compiled a draft Discovery Report with an executive summary. These outputs were presented during a Learn and Review session with the client, where we explained the consultancy findings, outcomes, and our draft recommendations.

Learn and Review

The Learn and Review session began with us stating our objectives, including addressing sensitivities associated with exploring employees' wellbeing needs, such as respecting privacy and acknowledging potential stigma associated with discussing mental health and wellbeing issues. We encouraged the client to foster an open and understanding culture to reduce stigma and encourage employees to seek support without fear of judgement. Following this discussion, we presented our investigation and findings.

We compared the client data against workplace, health promotion, and health psychology evidence to create baseline data on employees' health and wellbeing. Benchmarking their data against comparable local companies in the United Kingdom, national statistics showed that the client's staff generally exceeded national physical activity, diet, and sleep standards, which was positive. However, the client's data indicated below-average employee satisfaction regarding senior-level prioritisation of staff wellbeing. Compared to UK national standards, there was also notably lower reported happiness and financial wellbeing among employees, and many staff members were smokers. Anonymous quotes from the qualitative data were provided to the client to help create a context for how employees felt. The client recognised the value of this evidence, welcomed the creation of baseline data, and acknowledged that seeking direct input from employees through surveys and other measures provided invaluable insights into understanding the staff's needs. The client's realisation of their below-UK average employee satisfaction regarding the senior management's prioritisation of staff wellbeing signalled a need for strategic intervention. The client recognised the necessity of improving the perception and reality of staff wellbeing within the organisational hierarchy.

The Learn and Review session focused on enhancing the visibility and communication of health and wellbeing initiatives at the senior management level. It was agreed that the client should allocate staff time and resources to improve employee wellbeing, offering a package of health initiatives championed by leadership at all levels of the organisation. Simultaneously, there was consensus on developing a robust training and communication strategy to increase employees' awareness of the organisation's commitment to wellbeing. This could include regular updates, establishing a champion network, and conducting training sessions led by senior leadership to emphasise the importance of staff health.

We engaged in *knowledge transfer*, as defined by the Canadian Institutes of Health Research (2004, p. 4) as "the exchange, synthesis and ethically sound application of knowledge within a complex system of relationships among researchers and users", researchers here being the consultants, and users being the organisation's employees. For instance, we discussed findings using the Capability-Opportunity-Motivation-Behaviour (COM-B) model of behaviour change (Michie & Abraham, 2008; Michie et al., 2014) and the Behaviour Change Wheel and associated Taxonomy (D'Lima, et al., 2020). The goal was not to train the client to deliver health psychology interventions themselves but to help the client understand the relevance and importance of such an approach in addressing staff health and wellbeing issues and to use this new knowledge for informed decision-making. We collaborated in a guided discussion to co-develop solutions, reviewing and selecting suitable behaviour change interventions for their employee health and wellbeing strategy. Specifically, we discussed examples from client data to help the client understand how individuals may engage in behaviour change interventions to modify health behaviours. For example, since many staff members were smokers, we guided the discussion towards the client's role in supporting staff who may wish to quit and to promote workplace smoking cessation. We introduced strategies for utilising behaviour change techniques (Michie & Abraham). For instance, we suggested creating a supportive social environment and using health promotion interventions and personalised goal setting to motivate staff to quit smoking (Michie et al.).

To finalise this consultancy and aid co-development, our draft recommendations were discussed with the client, using the APEASE criteria (Acceptability, Practicability, Effectiveness, Affordability, Side-effects, and Equity) (Public Health England, 2019) to assess the interventions, and together, we agreed on the final consultancy recommendations, which are set out in Box 28.1.

Box 28.1 Recommendations for Client

Recommendation one: Promote and support all employees' health and wellbeing by implementing a digital technology product (created by Zeno Health Group) tailored to the company's tech-oriented approach. To ensure equal access and to consider all employees' needs, digital support should focus on improving physical and psychological capability and opportunities to change health behaviours.

Recommendation two emphasised the company prioritising employee health and wellbeing. This involved establishing a health champions network to foster camaraderie, motivation, and social support for positive employee health. The client agreed to implement a Continuous Professional Development (CPD) accredited Wellbeing Champions programme, where staff could engage in bespoke training to become champions and participate in an implementation plan focusing on modelling behaviour, peer support, transparency, and promotion of positive company culture.

Recommendation three focused on retaining staff and providing CPD, incorporating health and wellbeing initiatives to foster a positive and health-promoting organisational culture. This included implementing "Mindset" sessions, webinars, and seminars accessible to all staff through digital and in-person delivery formats.

Recommendation four acknowledged that the client sought to create a positive environment that fosters opportunities and motivates employees to prioritise their health and wellbeing. However, providing adequate health support remains a long-standing challenge for organisations, especially as they adapt to an ever-changing landscape. For instance, since the COVID-19 pandemic, evidence continues to be reviewed on concepts such as working from home (see Oakman et al., 2020). Recognising that recommendations may change, we proposed developing an annual intervention delivery plan. This strategic document would outline the schedule, resources, and actions needed to implement the recommended interventions throughout the year. It would act as a roadmap for executing strategies effectively to achieve the client's goals.

Recommendation five: Lastly, we recommend conducting an annual follow-up Discovery Survey to monitor and review employee wellbeing.

Evaluating Consultancy Outcomes and Impact

We regard consultancy evaluation as an approach to systematically assess and analyse the consulting services' effectiveness, efficiency, and overall impact. It involves thoroughly examining the outcomes, results, and value generated during the consultancy engagement to determine its success and pinpoint areas for improvement. The consultancy framework proposed by Brady and Varkonyi-Sepp (2025; see Chap. 3) recommends that evaluation be planned at the project's outset and integrated throughout the work. As described above, the Consultancy-to-Practice Model promotes continuous communication between us, the consultants, and the clients. The model promotes ongoing process evaluation and seeking client feedback throughout the process. Engaging in a comprehensive Discovery Needs Assessment phase before contracting allowed us to develop a comprehensive understanding of the client's needs, and, as such, we could plan and agree on clear aims and objectives. The contract included specific requirements regarding our evaluation needs and processes.

We evaluate our consultancy in three parts: process evaluation, which examines how it was conducted, accepted, and implemented; outcome evaluation, which assesses whether it achieved its proposed aims and objectives; and reflective evaluation, which examines our performance and capabilities and, explores areas such as our professional development, skills, strengths, and areas for improvement as consultants (see Fig. 28.1).

Process Evaluation

As Stetler et al. (2006) described, in applying research to clinical practice, formative evaluation ensures that a research programme's activities are feasible, appropriate, and acceptable prior to implementation. In our experience, formative process evaluation also creates opportunities to build trust and rapport with the client, fostering an open, honest environment that strengthens as the consultancy progresses. Throughout the consultancy, we continued with this formative evaluation process, asking questions of ourselves and the client (see Table 28.1). We asked these questions formally and informally through various channels, such as emails, verbal feedback, scheduled meetings, and written reports summarising our discussions and agreed actions. We conducted self-reflection and questioned our approach towards the consultancy. Asking questions in this way helped us ensure the project remained focused, prevented scope creep, and enabled us to respond, be supportive, and have a transparent communication process with the client.

In designing the Discovery Needs Assessment, we aimed to maximise staff engagement to have a meaningful picture of staff health behaviours and perceptions. To achieve that, we collaborated with the client to explore effective ways of communicating with their staff. While email emerged as the most efficient means of reaching all staff, we also employed various promotional strategies. These included sharing a link to the online survey, conducting briefings for internal communication, and sending out reminders to encourage survey completion. A key part of this communication was reiterating the protection of anonymity for individual feedback, encouraging employees to share their personal experiences and needs, and giving reassurance of the relevance and importance of this work to their future work environment. We urged the client to emphasise the survey's importance to their staff, allotting dedicated time for completion. Over 80% of staff participated fully in the survey, surpassing the client's expectations and showcasing a remarkable level of acceptance and engagement.

Outcome Evaluation

In this consultancy, we embarked on an exploratory journey, engaging with the client to enhance the corporate offer and improve their employees' health and wellbeing. Our initial findings regarding the consultancy's outcomes reflect positively on our recommendations' acceptability and successful implementation. We consider these outcomes, firstly regarding strategic impacts, for which we helped the client assess their staff health and wellbeing needs. We used this insight to create an implementation plan for change and improvements throughout the organisation. Secondly, as the client confirmed, our consultancy process enhanced their understanding of their employees' health and wellbeing. Thirdly, a core outcome of this work was client satisfaction, as observed through their ongoing engagement with us as consultants, their desire, and willingness to learn from us, seek guidance, and collaborate with us.

As part of the planning and proposal of this consultancy, we purposely did not agree to engage in a lengthy ongoing process to monitor the implementation of the recommended interventions or assess the impact of the interventions on the employees themselves. We acknowledged this as a potential issue for our consultancy when negotiating the contract. We communicated clearly within the contract and in discussions with the client about where this consultancy project started and ended. Indeed, the consultancy framework proposed within this book (Brady & Varkonyi-Sepp, 2025; see Chap. 3) highlights challenges when not including the implementation of recommendations into the consultancy project. We attempted to mitigate this by viewing any implementation as a future consultancy opportunity. In the contract, we specified implementation as potential additional work, which we would review for discussion on completion of the initial agreement. A key part of our consultancy approach was developing a strong collaborative relationship with the client to be re-contracted to implement recommended interventions. We were mindful that at the end of this consultancy project, the client could have ended our relationship and commissioned another consultancy to implement the suggested recommendations. Indeed, *all* the recommendations proposed from the outputs of this consultancy were agreed to with the client and subsequently implemented. So, the outcome of this consultancy was establishing a long-term relationship with this client, since, subsequently, a three-year contract to roll out the recommended interventions was secured.

The consultancy outcomes and impact were highly positive, achieving the project aims. Furthermore, the client also agreed to an annual review and follow-up. The consultants revisited the client one year later to conduct a Discovery Survey to assess and evaluate the impact of the intervention implementation. Good practice here will be to fully evaluate the effect of the interventions on, and measure changes to, the employees' health and wellbeing and to consider a broader evaluative approach considering individual factors of the employees' experiences, such as living with a long-term condition or being a carer.

Reflection

Reflective and evidence-based practice are integral to the modern health psychologist's role and significantly influence how health psychologists approach evaluation. The BPS considers evaluating outcomes a crucial skill in professional practice cycles (BPS, 2017). This is reinforced by the UK Health & Care Professions Council (HCPC), which states that, in the United Kingdom, practitioner psychologists must be capable of evaluating interventions using recognised outcome measures and making necessary revisions in collaboration with the service user (client) (HCPC, 2015). We engaged in enquiry, a research and evidence-based approach towards understanding the client's issue, and we used the consultancy as an opportunity to promote organisational change. The reflection of our consultancy performance consists of two components: first, a reflection on the project's success; second, a personal reflection on self-development and the use of supervision throughout this consultancy project.

Reflection on Project Success

Drawing on expertise from health psychology meant that this consultancy drew from the latest research and best evidence-based practices relevant to employee health, wellbeing, and behaviour change. This approach informed the implementation of this consultancy and the subsequent recommendations provided, ensuring that the interventions were grounded in scientific evidence and likely to yield positive outcomes. Leveraging our knowledge of behavioural science, we recommended interventions to target the underlying factors influencing the health behaviours of the client's employees. We offered tailored solutions to fit the specific needs of the client's organisation. As psychologists, we are skilled in engaging empathetically with clients and employees. Effective communication, for example, through Socratic questioning (Clark & Egan, 2015) and fostering collaboration, was key in understanding the client's and employees' needs, aligning with the client's objectives, and gaining support for the proposed strategies.

The client has acknowledged the success of this consultancy, firstly in terms of accepting and implementing the recommendations, commissioning future consultancy, and including a health psychology approach. Through a formal evaluation survey, and ongoing written and verbal feedback, the client confirmed their satisfaction with the consultancy project, the outcomes achieved, and the conduct of the consultancy itself. The client particularly valued our transparent communication style, which involved discussing their challenges and navigating complex internal and external data to ensure a thorough understanding of their issues. They acknowledged the dedication and time invested during our Discovery phase, highlighting our non-judgemental and adaptable approach throughout the consultancy process. This positive experience has resulted in continued and new consultancy opportunities, highlighting their satisfaction with our methods as a new client-consultancy partnership.

Recognising Change

We must consider the evolving environment and context in which we live, work, and conduct consultancy. In the United Kingdom, the HCPC standards for Proficiency of Practitioner Psychologists (2015) state that we must remain up-to-date in our practice and manage and adapt to change. This organisational health-based consultancy was initiated during the coronavirus (COVID-19) pandemic in 2022, and care was taken to consider changing work-based practices throughout this period. In hindsight, employee health and wellbeing may have been further impacted by COVID-19 in ways unknown at the time of this project. Published evidence on the COVID-19 pandemic reported significant challenges to workplaces worldwide, and acknowledging and addressing these issues is paramount to effective organisational health projects (de Waal et al., 2021). We have considered various professional issues relevant to these changes, some of which were accounted for within this consultancy. However, other aspects could be strengthened for the follow-up consultancy with this client. The COVID-19 pandemic highlighted the importance of promoting equality in the workplace. For example, the pandemic exacerbated the need for employee wellbeing support and, in part, triggered the client's recognition of the need, hence the commissioning of this consultancy project. As the client navigated the challenges posed by the pandemic, it was crucial to ensure that our recommendations and the client's subsequent decisions considered the diverse needs of employees. This included supporting employees who were more vulnerable to the impacts of the pandemic, such as caregivers, individuals with pre-existing health conditions, or those facing economic hardships (Blundell et al., 2020). As evidenced by employee feedback in the Discovery Survey, there was a perception that support from their employer was not equitable for all staff. The recommendations we proposed for interventions were considerate of these varied staff needs, for which we intended to help the client promote parity in their offer to all employees. However, we recognise that further investigation focusing on the needs of these potentially vulnerable staff groups could have been conducted during the Discovery Needs Assessment of this consultancy.

JG Personal Reflection and Use of Supervision

Supervision was an invaluable aspect of professional development during this consultancy. Supervision provided a safe space to explore ideas in presenting and challenging concepts of health psychology consultancy in practice. As I (JG) am an experienced business CEO offering organisational change, health psychology proposed an alternative approach, challenging me to formalise my consultancy methods and ensure evidence-based practice, embedding psychological behaviour change theories and models into the way that I work, and the recommendations for which I make with clients. Regular supervision with experienced health psychologists provided a safe and supportive space to discuss experiences, challenges, and insights. Previously, I had not considered a process consultation approach as proposed by Schein (1969, 1999) or, indeed, a research-to-practice integration model (Sterling & Weisner, 2006), an approach subsequently adapted by Dr Newson into a Consultancy-to-Practice Model (see Fig. 28.1). I planned to use the business model outlined via the Seven C's of consulting (client, clarify, create, change, confirm, continue, close) (Cope, 2010) as a framework to plan, design, implement, and evaluate this project. The seven Cs was a business-consultancy model I was familiar with and had used successfully within my consultancy business. However, whilst these seven Cs (Cope) provided a basic framework for considering steps within consultancy, these steps were more of a tick-box exercise than a guiding process for conducting the consultancy. Dr Newson encouraged me to reevaluate my approach. Going back to reconsider my consultancy style was an important learning process. It allowed me to expand my knowledge and implement new consultancy approaches, helping to articulate my methods. Adopting a process and cyclical model of continuous feedback and formative evaluation through the Consultancy-to-Practice Model allowed me to ensure the project remained on track whilst also providing space for me to be a reflective practitioner and seek guidance from my supervisors—in essence, building in space within the consultancy to learn, grow, and adapt.

Supervision allowed us to pause, reflect on our consultancy approach, review the evidence base that informed our decisions, and agree on initial evaluation plans. It served as a space to promote self-reflection, enhance self-awareness, and assess our strengths, limitations, biases, and areas for growth in consultancy. As part of the performance evaluation, we discussed applying Schein's (1999) ten principles of consultant behaviour in supervision.

These principles were central to our consultancy approach, ensuring it remained practical and relevant to the client's real-world context (principle 2). We prioritised aligning our solutions with the client's needs, offering feasible and applicable outcomes rather than overly theoretical concepts. While we acknowledged that we might not have all the answers (principle 3), we embraced openness and proactivity (principle 1) and fostered continuous dialogue and feedback (principles 9 and 10). For example, we presented our data analysis clearly and sensitively, highlighting strengths and improvement areas. We recognised that every action was an intervention (principle 4) and consistently centred the client in decision-making (principle 5). This included discussing strategies for communicating effectively with their staff to encourage participation in the health and wellbeing survey, an aspect the client had not previously considered in detail. We worked at the client's pace (principles 6 and 7), understanding that while we did not have all the answers individually, collaboration enabled us to develop effective strategies. Our Discovery meetings and Review and Learn sessions were crucial for refining this process (principle 8).

Discussing these principles within supervision provided a forum to explore alternative ideas, perspectives, and approaches to progressing the consultancy itself. Of relevance, supervision discussions explored the reach and inclusivity of the consultancy, whereby the project was being implemented during the COVID-19 pandemic, and workplaces were in rapid adjustment. Supervision helped to consider how we could change employee health and wellbeing, which paved the way for the collaborative development of agreed-upon recommendations with the client.

Having previously conducted various consultancy projects, approaching this consultancy through a health psychology lens was refreshing. It validated our evidence-based practice approach, allowing us to sell the consultancy more as a unique proposition to the client, which promoted an investigatory method. Writing this case study chapter in light of the new consultancy framework presented in this book (developed after the consultancy was completed), re-reading the consultancy literature, and receiving feedback from the book's editors has prompted deeper self-reflection. Questions such as "*Why did you do that?*" and "*Can you explain the reasoning behind your approach?*" have further catalysed continuous learning, growth, and skill development in health psychology consultancy.

Conclusion

This consultancy employed a comprehensive approach to address the client's health-related challenges. Health psychology practitioners' skills, knowledge, and expertise informed evidence-based strategies tailored to the organisation's unique context. By focusing on employee wellbeing and engagement, the interventions aimed at fostering a healthy and thriving work environment. The collaboration with the client throughout and our application of a Consultancy-to-Practice Model ensured that the recommended strategies were effective and aligned with the client's goals, positively impacting the organisation and its workforce.

Top Tips

1. Use a Consultancy-to-Practice Model that integrates reflective practice and process evaluation.
2. Conduct a Discovery Needs Assessment to ensure a transparent, well-planned consultancy and establish a positive client relationship.
3. Agree on communication and evaluation processes during contracting to support successful consultancy outcomes.
4. Ensure comprehensive evaluation: process (how consultancy was conducted), outcome (whether aims were met), and reflective (self-assessment of performance and development).

Competing Interests Joe Gaunt is CEO of Zeno Health. The authors have no other competing interests to declare in relation to this chapter.

References

Blundell, R., Costa Dias, M., Joyce, R., & Xu, X. (2020). COVID-19 and inequalities. *Fiscal Studies, 41*(2), 291–319. https://doi.org/10.1111/1475-5890.12232

Brady, R., & Varkonyi-Sepp, J. (2025). A framework for consultancy in health psychology. In R. Brady, J. Varkonyi-Sepp, & J. Smith (Eds.), *The Palgrave handbook of consultancy in health psychology*. Palgrave Macmillan.

British Psychological Society. (2017). *BPS practice guidelines*. https://doi.org/10.53841/bpsrep.2017.inf115

British Psychological Society. (2020). Qualification in health psychology (Stage 2). In *Handbook for candidates 2020*. The British Psychological Society. https://www.bps.org.uk/qualification-health-psychology-stage-2

Canadian Institutes of Health Research. (2004). *Canadian Institutes of health research knowledge translation strategy: Niche and Focus 2004–2009*. Ottawa. www.cihr-irsc.gc.ca/e/documents/kt_strategy_2004-2009_e.pdf

Clark, G. I., & Egan, S. J. (2015). The Socratic method in cognitive behavioural therapy: A narrative review. *Cognitive Therapy and Research, 39*(6), 863–879. https://doi.org/10.1007/s10608-015-9707-3

Cope, M. (2010). *The seven Cs of consulting* (3rd ed.). Financial Times/Prentice Hall.

de Waal, A., Linthorst, J., & Hetterschijt, C. (2021). Lessons learned by organisations during the COVID-19 pandemic. *International Journal of Management and Applied Research, 8*(1), 72–90. https://doi.org/10.18646/2056.81.21-00

D'Lima, D., Lorencatto, F., & Michie, S. (2020). The behaviour change wheel approach. In *Handbook on implementation science* (pp. 168–214). Edward Elgar Publishing. https://doi.org/10.4337/9781788975995.00014

European Agency for Safety and Health at Work. (2016). *Second European Survey of Enterprises on New and Emerging Risks (ESENER-2). Overview report: Managing safety and health at work*. Publications Office of the European Union. https://op.europa.eu/s/n7Wt

Guest, D. E. (2017). Human resource management and employee well-being: Towards a new analytic framework. *Human Resource Management Journal, 27*(1), 22–38. https://doi.org/10.1111/1748-8583.12139

Health and Care Professionals Council (HCPC) (2015). *Standards of proficiency: Practitioner psychologists*. http://www.hpcuk.org/assets/documents/10002963sop_practitioner_psychologists.pdfHC

Michie, S., & Abraham, C. (Eds.). (2008). *Health psychology in practice*. John Wiley & Sons.

Michie, S., Atkins, L., & West, R. (2014). The behaviour change wheel. In *A guide to designing interventions* (1st ed., pp. 1003–1010). Silverback Publishing.

Montano, D., Hoven, H., & Siegrist, J. (2014). Effects of organisational-level interventions at work on employees' health: A systematic review. *BMC Public Health, 14*(1), 135. https://doi.org/10.1186/1471-2458-14-135

Nielsen, K., & Randall, R. (2013). Opening the black box: Presenting a model for evaluating organizational-level interventions. *European Journal of Work and Organizational Psychology, 22*(5), 601–617. https://doi.org/10.1080/1359432X.2012.690556

Oakman, J., Kinsman, N., Stuckey, R., et al. (2020). A rapid review of mental and physical health effects of working at home: How do we optimise health? *BMC Public Health, 20*, 1825. https://doi.org/10.1186/s12889-020-09875-z

Office of National Statistics. (2022). *Personal wellbeing in the UK: April 2021 to March 2022. Estimates of life satisfaction, feeling that the things done in life are worthwhile, happiness and anxiety at the UK, country, regional, county, local and unitary authority level.* https://www.ons.gov.uk/peoplepopulationandcommunity/wellbeing/bulletins/measuringnationalwellbeing/april2021tomarch2022#personal-wellbeing-in-the-uk

Public Health England. (2019). *Achieving behaviour change: A guide for local government and partners.* https://assets.publishing.service.gov.uk/government/uploads/system/uploads/attachment_data/file/875385/PHEBI_Achieving_Behaviour_Change_Local_Government.pdf.

Schein, E. H. (1969). *Process consultation: Its role in organization development* (1st ed.). Addison Wesley.

Schein, E. H. (1999). Empowerment, coercive persuasion and organizational learning: Do they connect? *The Learning Organization, 6*(4), 163–172. https://doi.org/10.1108/09696479910280622

Schein, E. H. (2016). *Humble consulting: How to provide real help faster.* Berrett-Koehler Publishers.

Schein, E. H., & Schein, P. A. (2021). *Humble inquiry: The gentle art of asking instead of telling.* Berrett-Koehler Publishers.

Sterling, S., & Weisner, C. (2006). Translating research findings into practice: Example of treatment services for adolescents in managed care. *Alcohol Research and Health, 29*(1), 11–18.

Stetler, C. B., Legro, M. W., Wallace, C. M., Bowman, C., Guihan, M., Hagedorn, H., et al. (2006). The role of formative evaluation in implementation research and the QUERI experience. *Journal of General Internal Medicine, 21*, S1–S8. https://doi.org/10.1111/j.1525-1497.2006.00355.x

Weiner, B. J. (2009). A theory of organisational readiness for change. *Implementation Science, 4*, 67. https://doi.org/10.1186/1748-5908-4-67

29

Evaluation: Consultancy to a Health Project in Soweto, Johannesburg

Delan Naidoo

Introduction

Commissioned by a government development finance institution in South Africa (SA), the project I outline in this chapter aims to train youth (ages 18–30) for sustainable health employment, while providing free health services to impoverished communities. The health project in question is affiliated with a leading research university in Johannesburg and focuses on health and employment in Soweto, Johannesburg, as detailed by Stoutenberg et al. (2023). The project trains Health Advocates (HAs) in health interventions and research, growing their employment skills. The HA training is founded on a health industry-approved course awarded by the SA national health sector training authority. The health project is considered disruptive in a positive sense, as it aims to train and support youth into employment within a sustainable sector (health), while researching the health effects on the trained youth. This chapter presents the consultancy that I delivered as a qualified counselling psychologist involved in implementing health provision within under-resourced communities. The chapter takes an evaluation stance when describing the consultancy that I offered. Firstly, I describe the health project, including the client, origins, aims, objectives, impact, stakeholders, and

D. Naidoo (✉)
Mindsightful, Jersey, UK
e-mail: del@mindsightful.com

R. Brady et al. (eds.), *The Palgrave Handbook of Consultancy in Health Psychology*,
https://doi.org/10.1007/978-3-031-94529-8_29

consultancy delivery. I then discuss the evaluation phase of the project. Reflective insights are provided, followed by consultancy tips.

The Case Study

The Client

The client is an independent organisation housed within a non-profit research entity that forms part of the university, and the project aims to improve education, employment, health, and community engagement in Soweto over five years. Stoutenberg et al. (2023) detailed the HA community-based home visits to offer health screening and health education to individuals, as well as the integration of youth training and health education with preventive interventions for the trainees themselves. These activities counter the fragmentation of health and education interventions that exist. As a founder and consultant for the initial year, I contributed to the health project's conceptualisation, design, implementation, and evaluation.

The project aims to broaden funding for health and social initiatives. The funder, an SA government development finance institution, traditionally focuses on civil infrastructure projects to support economic development. Schein (1999) clarified that funding organisations often have a clear purpose (e.g., this funder's economic development infrastructure aims), yet applying this purpose to health contexts poses a challenge for some organisations. The funder's support for the project marked a leap into health and community care funding. The project arose after the project's co-founders pitched the concept to the funder's senior executives following development funding networking events.

Rationale for the Project

The unemployment rate in SA is 32.9% (Statistics SA, 2023a), with youth unemployment at 46.5% (Statistics SA, 2023b). Townships like Soweto experience low economic activity and high unemployment; these townships were historically designed to house Black African people, segregating them from the White South African population under apartheid (United Nations General Assembly, 1974) before democratic changes in 1994. These segregated environments remain the norm for the majority of residents, reflecting past political legacies.

Hasumi and Jacobsen (2014) note poor-quality healthcare experiences for township service users. The project innovatively combined health employment and training for township unemployed youth, and the delivery of health education/screening in townships (Stoutenberg et al., 2023). The project envisions economic opportunity and empowering youth to build healthier communities, guided by their 'Help, Understand, Behave, and Become' (HUBB) values. As part of the outcomes, there is provision for meaningful work experience, youth training, and healthcare qualifications, which fosters health consciousness in HAs and helps expand community healthcare access.

The Origins of My Involvement in the Project

My work as a counselling psychologist serving Soweto university students revealed to me the complex needs of this community's youth. The experience provided exposure to the Soweto psychosocial/health context, including how mental health risk factors are often impediments to Sowetans' health behaviours (Draper et al., 2022). Challenges experienced have led to poor education, limited access to health services, and exacerbated issues during the Coronavirus (COVID-19) pandemic (Ware et al., 2022). Poverty, nutrition, education, employment, and safety concerns make abstract concepts like non-communicable disease (NCD) education less prominent (Pretorius, 2013).

My experience, combined with other project co-founders' research, grounded in over two decades of Soweto health research (Richter et al., 2018), ensured that the activities in this project were relevant to the community. One co-founder/consultant, an established health researcher, focused on NCDs and health behaviour. Her expertise in preventative health interventions and rigorous research ensured evidence-based interventions. Combined with my in-practice health experience and the community-based stakeholder experience of the third co-founder, the project interventions were informed by peer-reviewed research, such as the Pretorius (2013) study of Soweto residents and heart disease.

The Stakeholders

The consultancy focused on health training, employment, and community-based interventions in Soweto. Initial discussions between founders and Soweto residents highlighted a lack of proactive healthcare in Soweto, and this aligned with research by Ware et al. (2019, 2022). Echoing the emphasis on stakeholder significance by Sacks and Loon (2016), stakeholder identification was critical. Table 29.1 details the stakeholders and their relevant aims.

Table 29.1 Stakeholders and aims

Stakeholder	Level of support for the project	Aims	Evidence that stakeholder's aims were met
The project funder (an infrastructure development bank)	Strongly supportive	Economic development that positively impacted the community within which the client operated	Regular planned reporting indicating the project's contribution to local economy
The client (and their health project)	Strongly supportive	Soweto-based education, employment, community health intervention and research initiatives	Measured goal achievement in each domain through regular planned reporting
Training provider	Strongly supportive	Academic development of the HAs	Academic assessments and qualitative feedback on HA progress
Health sector training authority	Neutral	Industry vocational training standards	Trainees' successful completion of national exam
Health advocate trainees	Strongly supportive	Training, employment and personal development aims (improved health, nutrition, mental resilience)	Completion of academic training; activities supporting successful entry into sustainable employment
Community members and organisations	Neutral	Community development through relevant, in-depth community engagement	Community leaders' engagement and feedback through forums attended by the project's staff and consultants
The university	Strongly supportive	Ethical, sustainable, relevant evidence-based research-ready interventions implemented from project activities	Annual reporting of interventions in the project's reports; peer-reviewed journal articles
The university	Strongly supportive	Legal, fiduciary and ethical business operations to facilitate the project's operations	Monthly reporting of activities and interventions to ensure compliance with legal, financial and business best-practices

I used my psychological skills of empathy, active listening, and open-ended questioning to engage with community leaders during meetings. This helped bridge the gap between community expectations for higher local resident recruitment, while also ensuring that academic criteria for entry onto the programme were maintained.

Project Aims

The client aimed to effectively impact health, education, and youth socio-economic empowerment in Soweto. The complexity of these aims, the relevant stakeholders, and how my skills as a psychologist facilitated this consultancy are summarised in Table 29.2.

The following section considers aspects of how the consultancy was delivered.

Delivery of the Consultancy

My initial unpaid role as a co-founder on the project transitioned to a paid consultancy due to increased project demands. The expanded consultant role covered planning, evaluation, focusing on stakeholder partnerships, HA well-being, and evaluation planning, for one day each week. Shifting to a fee-based model paid for my time during office hours but affected my private practice availability. I was comfortable with this shift in time focus because I had a commitment and passion for the project activities. As consultant, I facilitated academic training and guided the integration of diverse expectations, stakeholder needs, health imperatives, and trainee onboarding during COVID-19. Maintaining a position as a consultant (Block, 2011), I was involved in advising on health initiatives and respecting psychologist professional boundaries, while steering clear of implementing these activities, which was not my role.

Project Outcomes

Over five years, some of the outcomes included 90,000+ individuals seen for health screening and health promotion in Soweto, almost 100 unemployed youth completing health-related qualifications, seven full-time staff employed, and 12 health research projects. The project created over 50 employment and training opportunities during the COVID-19 pandemic, crucial for Soweto's economy, which was heavily impacted. The pandemic worsened pre-existing

Table 29.2 Project aims with psychologist input

Project aim	Target stakeholder	Consultant role
Employment (fixed-term, one-year contracts) and sustainable, industry-accredited training	Youth who were not in education, employment or training (NEET) from Soweto. These were the youth that were to be trained as HAs	Used health-profession regulations knowledge to research industry qualifications; select academic training provider; support recruitment and selection campaign design and delivery; support orientation and induction processes for HAs
Initial psycho-social support	HAs who were enrolled on the programme	Student psychosocial support and wellbeing experience to support HA wellbeing and achievement. Referral to counselling support services when/if necessary
Conceptualise and design a sustainable psychosocial wellness programme	HAs who were enrolled on the programme	Experience as a psychologist of designing and deploying student wellness services in further/higher education settings to conceptualise and design the psychosocial support offering beyond the initial year of the client's project programme
Supporting Soweto youth into sustainable employment	HAs who were enrolled on the programme	Deployed career development and health industry knowledge to support HA employment for their first post-project transition
Health screening and education initiatives within the larger Soweto community	Soweto residents	Supported the consultancy and delivery teams in the conceptualising and design planning through deployment of health-industry regulatory and local health provision knowledge (e.g. deploying knowledge of the local Soweto primary care/hospital networks and inter-agency/ referral procedures)

economic disadvantages prevalent in South African townships like Soweto (Mathibe et al., 2022; Schotte & Zizzamia, 2023). The NCD co-founder colleague was a health research consultant and facilitated the project's goals by merging researched Soweto health outcomes with practical, evidence-based solutions. This included devising screening protocols, kits, and training for HAs in Healthy Conversation Skills. This technique, previously deployed with National Health Service staff in the United Kingdom and with healthcare staff in Australia, is based on motivational interviewing and has been shown to reduce the barriers for healthcare staff to engage in person-centred,

Table 29.3 Significant project outcomes

Health intervention	Outcome	Measurement method
Studying psychological and behavioural impacts of the programme on the health advocates	Improvements in HA physical health and emotional resilience	Six monthly measurements of physical and emotional coping
Training youth in evidence-based health interventions	Greater awareness among the youth; increased qualifications and knowledge; taking their learning into their communities, families and social spaces	Health Promotion Officer national qualification composed of exam and portfolio of evidence
50,000 health interventions with individuals in Soweto over three years	Screening for NCDs, health education in homes, clinics, malls, religious spaces; workshops, presentations for awareness	HA practical experience logs that served as evidence portfolios for the Health Promotion Officer qualification award
Increasing access to NCD screening during COVID-19 lockdowns/ restricted movement/ grouping of individuals	Offering in-home screenings, referrals amid reduced healthcare access due to COVID-19 transmission fears in households	HA practical experience logs and portfolios of evidence for the Health Promotion Officer qualification award

supportive health behaviour change conversations (Hollis et al., 2021). Key health impacts can be seen in Table 29.3.

Evaluation: Managing Constant, Consistent, and Multiple Evaluation Imperatives

In this section, through the *evaluation* lens of the framework for consultancy in health psychology (Brady & Varkonyi-Sepp, 2025; see Chap. 3), I explore the evaluation of the project throughout all stages and not just at project end. A final reflection includes the acknowledgement that such projects are complex and often involve various changing and conflicting priorities. The skills to manage complex or conflicting priorities are regularly called upon in psychologists' daily role activities. Psychologists are thus well-placed to manage the competing variables and to integrate these skills to facilitate project consulting.

Mapping the *purchase-of-expertise* (the consultant provides expertise to address an identified problem) and *doctor-patient* (the consultant diagnoses a

Table 29.4 Models of consultancy mapped to my consultancy for the client

Consultant model (Schein, 1999)	Example in the consultancy engagement
Purchase-of-Expertise Model Clients seek consultants for an independent perspective on specific challenges. The focus is on detached expertise rather than the client relationship itself	I was part of a team of co-founders and consultants on the project who leveraged knowledge and experience of working in healthcare provision and researching health in Soweto
Doctor-Patient Model The consultant diagnoses the organisation's issues, using expertise to identify strategic problems, emphasising building a trusting client-consultant relationship	My role here was to synthesise my understandings of environmental/psychological/ social factors with research into the health outcomes in Soweto and to collaborate with consultant colleagues to design and implement a HA programme to alleviate health-related challenges experienced by Sowetans
Doctor-Patient Model The consultant diagnoses organisational issues, leveraging expertise to identify strategic problems, emphasising a strong, trust-based client-consultant relationship	Consultants on the project leveraged knowledge and experience of working in healthcare provision and researching health in Soweto to change the ways in which health training was delivered and engage with Soweto residents around health-related issues in their natural environments (homes, community spaces, etc.)

problem and suggests a solution) models of consultancy (Schein, 1999) with my experience during project engagement helps to situate the context of the necessary roles that I fulfilled. Table 29.4 details this by using Schein's models of consultancy and describing specific instances of my consultancy relevant to each aspect of the model.

Considerations Regarding Evaluation Timelines

In many undertakings, evaluation activities are discrete steps that follow at the end of the project (Hodges, 2021). With this project's context, however, evaluation was embedded within ongoing project activities. This included quarterly strategy meetings, where the senior operational team in the project, which included me and other co-founders, explored the project activity relevance, as well as informal feedback discussions with the HAs. These activities were intentional actions planned during the conceptual phases of the project to ensure continuous improvement from learnings derived from evaluative actions. I also derived much personal satisfaction in hearing the HA trainees' experiences of the various phases of their project involvement.

Integrating evaluation activities early on in implementation of this project enabled consistent and sustainable quarterly reporting (according to predetermined funder criteria). Wainwright (2022) notes that the complexities of quality assurance in the health sector are ongoing. The varied project deliverables, which included training, community health interventions, and research imperatives, necessitated ongoing, consistent project evaluation to ensure that the project was fit for purpose. Such an approach to evaluation also facilitated the project's funding conditions, namely, regular, consistent project outcome reporting. For this reason, monthly, quarterly, and annual evaluation processes were intrinsic to the project's implementation. These reports detailed specifics such as the numbers and demographics of trainees on the project, the number of community members reached through health activities, and entrepreneurial activities created.

Two aspects of my activities as a consultant inform this chapter: first, a continuous evaluation of the impact and outcomes of the project; second, a reflective evaluation of my practice as a consultant.

Continuous Evaluation Activities

The Affordability, Practicality, Side Effects/Safety, and Equity (APEASE) model (Michie et al., 2014) informs the evaluation of the consultancy I delivered. The model specifies vital aspects of consultancy to ensure project robustness. Table 29.5 shows how the APEASE criteria map to examples of my contracted consultancy activities.

Embedded within the project were four-monthly trainee data-gathering activities. These offered the project team an opportunity to assess the ongoing effectiveness of the programme in the lives of the HAs. We also tracked any behaviour change interventions targeting, for example, nutrition and exercise with the trainees themselves, and whether the approaches were yielding positive change in trainees' health outcomes (i.e., improvements in health, nutrition, and mental resilience). While analysis of research findings around this is still in progress, anecdotal evidence indicates that HAs show positive changes in health, economic, and social outcomes.

Table 29.5 Mapping APEASE criteria (Michie et al., 2014) to significant agreed consultancy activities

Criterion	Description	Consultancy activities
Affordability	Budget constraints are significant. Interventions must be affordable, effective and accessible to all relevant beneficiaries	I helped plan and formulate project activities for cost-effective delivery, acquiring specialised equipment (e.g. non-communicable disease screening kits) from select suppliers. Calculating expenses for equipment and academic services guided the project's planning
Practicability	An intervention is practical if it can be effectively delivered as intended to the target population, considering real-world limitations and resources	Conceptualised activities to align with township realities (e.g. high population density, limited access to services, prevalent crime). Merging real-world experience and Soweto health research informed decisions
Effectiveness and cost-effectiveness	Effectiveness evaluates achievement in real-world scenarios while efficacy measures ideal outcomes. Cost-effectiveness compares impact to cost, aiding selection. If equally effective, it guides choice; otherwise, affordability and other factors weigh in	I guided decisions in planning the 12-month HA training programme, considering factors like equipment availability, provider timelines, cost-effectiveness and branding for effective recruitment campaigns. Effectiveness assessments tracking HA health and resilience were planned quarterly
Acceptability	The intervention's acceptability refers to its appropriateness as evaluated by the relevant stakeholders	I used research skills to integrate feedback from health intervention activities (e.g. feedback conversations with service users), community forum meetings and HA debrief sessions to increase acceptability in further activity planning and conceptualisation
Side-effects/ safety	Considerations that indicate that an intervention may be effective and practicable but have unwanted side-effects or unintended consequences	I ensured that health regulations guiding interventions were appropriately followed
Equity	Assessing the level that an intervention impacts inequalities in wellbeing, health or living standards of various populations	The research-focused consultant co-founders' work supported the embedding of equity in contrast to the health inequalities highlighted by previous research (e.g. mother-to-child determinants of health conditions due to lowered access to service in Soweto)

Adaptations Necessary to Accommodate Real-World Challenges

Considered, planned, and robust approaches to evaluation are susceptible to real-world challenges, even with risk mitigation measures integrated into the plan. The health project was no exception to this, as challenges occurred within the early implementation phases. During the early assessment and reporting periods (pre-determined by the funder), two significant issues adversely affected the project's deliverables and outcome evaluation. One challenge was the delayed construction of the training facilities, and the other was the impact of the COVID-19 pandemic on project delivery.

The project, based within a community hub (which was still under construction on project launch date), initially launched operations at a large public hospital in Soweto due to the designated site's construction delays. Construction delays arose due to a combination of socio-political and labour-related challenges in a complex economic environment, which included construction-industry disputes, conflicting expectations of local-area service providers, and the property owner's and developer's imperatives. Workplace limitations due to COVID-19 safety legislation also impacted construction delays. Many of the challenges were borne by the property owner and developer, which fortunately mitigated the risk to the health project.

These delays adversely impacted the deliverables that could be achieved in the first year of the project. I helped by assisting in the planning, guiding, and sourcing of alternative training facilities and community health engagement activities but these nonetheless reduced the project delivery team's effectiveness towards outcomes. Revised targets for some of the early evaluation periods were necessary in order to conform to COVID-19 regulations. I was part of the team of consultants who translated the government regulations for safe COVID-19-approved interactions into operational activities to ensure that the HAs and members of the public were safe during interactions. The negotiations around the revisions were easily achieved through electronic communications to the HAs and other relevant stakeholders. There was a general consensus among stakeholders at this time that revised arrangements were often needed to ensure that operations continued during the COVID-19 pandemic and its aftermath.

A significant example of adjusted arrangements included transferring all learning online initially. This necessitated the provisioning of mobile internet data for the HAs to continue their training online. Another example related to the sourcing of larger academic training venues to facilitate social distancing when permitted by regulations. The financial implications meant that electronic delivery and submission of learning material, and learner management system access, were new items that needed to be budgeted and accounted for. This reduced the number of HAs that could be recruited within the budget. Under the circumstances of the pandemic, adjustments to the project deliverables were accepted by the funder.

My role in this phase of revised operations centred on facilitating the programme's activities: researching online learner management systems; supporting the pivot to distance learning; and negotiating with academic training partners reprogramme provision during the altered training delivery methods. Interim and continuous evaluation of the consultancy, along with Schein's (1999) guidance about being grounded in reality of the context of the project, helped strengthen my consulting activities in these rapidly changing circumstances.

Features of the framework for consultancy in health psychology proposed by Brady & Varkonyi-Sepp (2025; see Chap. 3) reflect the way in which the consultancy activities were delivered. In the framework, the authors emphasise, for example, the external perspective of consultancy, the requirement for expertise and contracting, and, in the context of health psychology, the need for evidence-based practice. As part of my evaluation of the consultancy delivered, I retrospectively reviewed my practice in the context of these key features. Included in this overview is Saad's (2017) description of *knowledge transfer* and how this was handled during the consultancy.

External Perspective. The consultancy clarified for me a boundary between consultant and operational staff. This consultant role involved strategic conceptualisation rather than direct service delivery. This posed challenges during events like poorly attended health awareness days, when I would have loved to have been involved in marketing outreach. Balancing my passion for community health with consultant-level detachment from implementation was intricate.

Contract. An explicit contract with the university was concluded by the other co-founder consultants. I was not involved in negotiating or finalising this contract. From this university contract flowed the individual engagement contract that governed the consultancy that I provided. The consultancy contract ensured a clarity of role, as well as the requisite legal, human resources, financial, and time-related stipulations. Details, such as consultant timesheets, reporting expectations/deadlines were clarified in this contract.

Expertise. It is notable that the application of psychology-grounded knowledge to shape initiation of the project was distinct from my experience of psychological therapy/counselling provision. Such counselling service provision was outside the purview of my consultancy engagement. Consistent with the consultative stance approach (Block, 2011), I drew upon specialist expertise and past experience of providing community-based psychological interventions to shape the activities that the project intended to deliver. These experiences included my past interactions as a psychologist within community-based substance misuse counselling services, foster care counselling services, and rape crisis support centres. Psychological therapy, if needed, was facilitated through a referral to organisations, which included statutory community health clinics, district hospitals, and voluntary counselling services.

Evidence-Based. As psychologists, grounding our work in a robust, relevant and real-world evidence base is central to our professional practice. Within the context of this consultancy project, the evidence base for psychosocial interventions (Duncan, et.al., 2021), such as mental health awareness activities at community level, was a guiding principle in the strategic planning of project activities.

Knowledge Transfer. The framework proposed by Brady et al. (2025; see Chap. 3) explicitly clarifies that psychological expertise in a professional sense is not transferred. I acknowledge that while providing psycho-education related to health-related behaviour change is helpful, it is distinct from transferring professional psychology expertise, which can only be gained through professional training and practice. Other authors (e.g., Saad, 2017) discuss knowledge transfer as a key element of, for example, management consultancy. Appelbaum and Steed (2005) also write that there is sometimes a need for consultants to transfer competencies to personnel. Regarding the delivered consultancy activities, it was important to transfer specific knowledge and skills (e.g., I was responsible for ensuring clear communications and guidance to the project implementation and delivery team regarding boundaries of their interventions). This was crucial, for example, as the team handled patient health data governed by SA data protection regulations. As such, extreme care and professionalism on the part of the HAs in relation to patient privacy were vital.

Health profession regulations mandate specific interventions by licensed practitioners, as is the case in SA. My consultancy focused on guiding the delivery team in respecting boundaries, referring service users appropriately, and maintaining professionalism. This included signposting community members to counselling services and assisting in navigating health services. For example, the HAs needed to support community members by guiding them through statutory health provision, which could include starting at primary health clinics, then district hospital out-patient clinics, and attending scheduled appointments.

Reflection

As a psychologist, I integrated reflective practices, such as journal writing and participation in peer supervision groups, to improve and develop my work. These actions enhanced the effectiveness of the consultancy I offered to the client. Thompson and Pascal (2012) guide that human challenges cannot often be solved by technical solutions or knowledge application alone, and that reflective practice is imperative. Discussions in my clinical supervision sessions after the fact, akin to reflection-on-action (Schön, 1991), also contributed to my growth and effectiveness in consulting to the project. Examples of issues discussed in peer supervision groups and clinical supervision include: navigating community forum meetings respectfully, yet assertively, and reconciling my initial need to affect change on a systemic level, while also boundaried in my role as a consultant to the project, and accepting that I could be of more use as a facilitator of HAs as change agents. I also learned a great deal about project development within very rapidly changing dynamics, which included regulations changing as COVID-19 realities persisted and fluctuated. This included my ability to remain focused on the task at hand and work through varying possibilities with fellow consultants to arrive at pragmatic solutions.

The integration of theory and practice during my professional training as a counselling psychologist enabled me to develop consultancy skills, which I applied in supporting the training provider's programme delivery within project-designed frameworks. For example, I used my knowledge of statutory and regulatory issues in healthcare to advise the training provider on compliance, which coincides with the SA psychologist registration that includes an exam on healthcare laws and the country's constitution. As a professionally registered counselling psychologist, I used my knowledge in planning and delivering psychosocial wellness support for HAs, ensuring compliance with SA regulatory guidance around psychological health. My expertise in supporting student clients in higher/further education was indispensable in devising a robust and relevant HA support strategy.

Social justice imperatives necessitate a holistic, multi-dimensional, and evidence-based approach to health care solutions for populations, and psychologists are ideally positioned to capitalise on their skills in pursuit of aims such as these (Kasket, 2012). In Soweto, and integral to the client's values, the project approach aimed to be part of a solution to social injustice, for example, health/empowerment inequalities. This informed the consultancy with psychology, public health, and community building being foundational elements that the consulting team leaned upon. The team's consultants leveraged their individual expertise in relation to psychology provision, NCD public health research, and community/governance to formulate an integrative approach that informed the project's activities. Financial and budgetary management skills, which were often part and parcel of psychology training and research grant funding, were critical to the approval of the project. My inputs into supporting the founding team's strategic budget planning included costing and negotiating costs of academic training provision, various health equipment options, as well as supporting the budgeting for unplanned expenses.

Reflecting on Psychology Professionals in Consultancy

Real-world problems often require real-world, pragmatic solutions. In the context of this project, my experience of working in substance use services supported the conceptualisation of the health promotion activities. Maphumulo and Bhengu (2019) document the precarious state of healthcare in SA. Psychologists serving in a consulting context often have an insight into such a 'real world' that is frequently characterised by health inequalities. During counselling psychology training, we engage in practical placements that immerse us in the realities of societal and individual dysfunction. The reality for the communities that the client operates in is characterised by dysfunction in healthcare access and service delivery, with socio-economic challenges related to poverty, low economic activity, elevated exposure to trauma, among other issues.

Furthermore, my experience of the realities around counselling both survivors and perpetrators of gender-based violence in Soweto gave me an insight into the subjective world of clients' realities in these cases. This insight helped me foreground HA safety when supporting the planning of project activities (such as HAs visiting residents' homes). As psychologists, we often confront the realities of social experiences/systems that are meant to promote well-being, but do not always succeed. Integrating this knowledge into the consultancy that I offered around conceptualising HA community and home visits was imperative to implementing robust solutions.

The consultative guidance that I offered to the implementation phases of the project ensured that the foundations of communications deployed by project staff were service-user focused and fit for purpose. I deployed the psychologist's skills of implementing communications and interventions to facilitate change, valuing meaningful, sensitive, contextually appropriate communications to the specific needs and circumstances of our audience(s). In this consultancy's context, my psychology-informed approach supported the integration of '*both-and*' solutions. For instance, designing a unique HA programme that paid academic fees and provided a stipend catered to economic needs and enhanced programme completion.

Being a psychologist with an advanced postgraduate doctoral-level education implied an engagement with research questions that often extend the boundaries of an existing evidence base. These academic endeavours advocate the creation of new ways of conceptualising and solving challenges (at the intra-, inter-personal, or systemic level) or novel applications of existing knowledge in varied contexts. My psychological understanding of best-practice health service delivery in clinical settings helped me strengthen the HAs' health screening and education activities.

These are some of the skills that I leveraged during the consultancy to support the project in its implementation phase. The unique interplay of these skills required a deftness and flexibility to be able to craft an approach and solution offering. Such solutions ensured community buy-in, stakeholder engagement and continue to meet the client's expectations.

Psychologists' Experiences of Multi-Disciplinary Team Working

Psychological training equips professionals with diverse real-world skills applicable to client scenarios and communities. Within the project, the consultant founders' professions spanned psychology, governance, health research, and corporate experience. Functioning within high-pressure environments while juggling health, medical, psychosocial, and socio-political priorities is the nature of the work environments within which psychologists function. These experiences prepare psychological professionals to function within environments such as the client's ecosystem with the various stakeholders, their diverse, and often very specific needs.

Tackling Soweto's training and health disparities requires innovative approaches. Psychologists' abilities in open-ended conversations helped to refine the project's processes with stakeholders. Psychologists inhabit spaces and roles where they are exposed to facilitating solution-building in often limited resource environments. This chapter exemplifies one such response, while this book organises thinking and fosters an integrated approach to address similar calls to action. Writing this chapter has affirmed for me the importance of bearing a structured approach to health consulting in mind when engaging in consultancies of this nature. Go Forth and Consult!

Top Tips

1. Evaluation is not a discrete step at project's end—embed it throughout the project.
2. Ensure clarity around client and stakeholder boundaries and expectations.
3. Get multi-disciplinary (multi-disciplinary consulting teams are strong teams)!

Competing Interests The author has no competing interests to declare that are relevant to the content of this chapter.

References

Appelbaum, S. H., & Steed, A. J. (2005). The critical success factors in the client-consulting relationship. *Journal of Management Development, 24*(1), 68–93. https://doi.org/10.1108/02621710510572362

Block, P. (2011). *Flawless consulting* (3rd ed.). Wiley.

Brady, R., Varkonyi-Sepp, J. (2025). A framework for consultancy in health psychology. In R. Brady, J. Varkonyi-Sepp, & J. Smith (Eds.), *The Palgrave handbook of consultancy in health psychology*. Palgrave Macmillan.

Draper, C. E., Cook, C. J., Redinger, S., Rochat, T., Prioreschi, A., Rae, D. E., Ware, L. J., Lye, S. J., & Norris, S. A. (2022). Cross-sectional associations between mental health indicators and social vulnerability, with physical activity, sedentary behaviour and sleep in urban African young women. *The International Journal of Behavioral Nutrition and Physical Activity, 19*(1), 82. https://doi.org/10.1186/s12966-022-01296-6

Duncan, F., Baskin, C., McGrath, M., Coker, J. F., Lee, C., Dykxhoorn, J., et al. (2021). Community interventions for improving adult mental health: Mapping local policy and practice in England. *BMC Public Health, 21*(1), 1691. https://doi.org/10.1186/s12889-021-11741-5

Hasumi, T., & Jacobsen, K. H. (2014). Healthcare service problems reported in a national survey of South Africans. *International Journal for Quality in Health Care, 26*(4), 482–489. https://doi.org/10.1093/intqhc/mzu054

Hodges, J. (2021). A framework for consulting. *Management Consulting, 4*(2), 52–55.

Hollis, J. L., Kocanda, L., Seward, K., et al. (2021). The impact of Healthy Conversation Skills training on health professionals' barriers to having behaviour change conversations: A pre-post survey using the Theoretical Domains

Framework. *BMC Health Services Research, 21*, 880. https://doi.org/10.1186/s12913-021-06893-4

Kasket, E. (2012). The counselling psychologist researcher. *Counselling Psychology Review, 27*(2), 64–73.

Maphumulo, W. T., & Bhengu, B. R. (2019). Challenges of quality improvement in the healthcare of South Africa post-apartheid: A critical review. *Curationis, 42*(1), e1–e9. https://doi.org/10.4102/curationis.v42i1.1901

Mathibe, M., Muchenje, T., & Masonta, M. T. (2022). Smart township digital framework: Growing the township economy post-COVID-19 pandemic. In A. Eniola, C. Iwu, & A. Opute (Eds.), *The future of entrepreneurship in Africa*. Routledge.

Michie, S., Atkins, L., & West, R. (2014). *The behaviour change wheel: A guide to designing interventions*. Silverback Publishing.

Pretorius, S. (2013). The impact of dietary habits and nutritional deficiencies in urban African patients living with heart failure in Soweto, South Africa—A review. *Endocrine, Metabolic & Immune Disorders Drug Targets, 13*(1), 118–124. https://doi.org/10.2174/18715303130102

Richter, L. M., Naicker, S. N., & Norris, S. A. (2018). Birth to Twenty Plus: Early health and development from a longitudinal perspective. In *Child and adolescent development: An expanded focus on public health in Africa* (pp. 114–138). UCT Press.

Saad, Y. G. (2017). Deliverable accountability, change management and breach in consultancy contracts: A comparative study of World Bank versus EuropeAid funded projects. *Journal of Public Procurement, 17*(4), 525–571. https://doi.org/10.1108/JOPP-08-2016-0020

Sacks, R., & Loon, M. (2016). Developing and using consultancy skills. In M. Loon (Ed.), *Professional practice in learning and development: How to design and deliver plans for the workplace* (pp. 151–206). Kogan Page.

Schein, E. H. (1999). *Process consultation revisited: Building the helping relationship*. Addison-Wesley.

Schön, D. A. (1991). *The reflective practitioner*. Ashgate Publishing.

Schotte, S., & Zizzamia, R. (2023). The livelihood impacts of COVID-19 in urban South Africa: A view from below. *Social Indicators Research, 165*(1), 1–30. https://doi.org/10.1007/s11205-022-03011-3

Statistics South Africa. (2023a). *Quarterly employment statistics (QES)*. https://www.statssa.gov.za/publications/P0277/P0277March2022.pdf

Statistics South Africa. (2023b). *Quarterly labour force survey (QLFS) – Q1:2023 media release*. https://www.statssa.gov.za/publications/P0211/Media%20release%20QLFS%20Q1%202023.pdf

Stoutenberg, M., Crouch, S. H., McNulty, L. K., Kolkenbeck-Ruh, A., Torres, G., Gradidge, P. J., et al. (2023). Acceptability and feasibility of home-based hypertension and physical activity screening by community health workers in an under-resourced community in South Africa. *Journal of Public Health*, 1–12. https://doi.org/10.1093/pubmed/fdab017

Thompson, N., & Pascal, J. (2012). Developing critically reflective practice. *Reflective Practice, 13*(2), 311–325. https://doi.org/10.1080/14623943.2012.657795

United Nations General Assembly. (1974). *International Convention on the Suppression and Punishment of the Crime of Apartheid.* https://www.un.org/en/genocideprevention/documents/atrocity-crimes/Doc.10_International%20Convention%20on%20the%20Suppression%20and%20Punishment%20of%20the%20Crime%20of%20Apartheid.pdf

Wainwright, S. (2022). Perspectives on quality and quality assurance in the management consulting sector. *Management Consulting Journal, 5*(2), 111–121.

Ware, L. J., Prioreschi, A., Bosire, E., Cohen, E., Draper, C. E., Lye, S. J., & Norris, S. A. (2019). Environmental, social, and structural constraints for health behavior: Perceptions of young urban Black women during the preconception period—A healthy life trajectories initiative. *Journal of Nutrition Education and Behavior, 1*(8), 946–957. https://doi.org/10.1016/j.jneb.2019.06.007

Ware, L. J., Maposa, I., Kolkenbeck-Ruh, A., Norris, S. A., Soepnel, L., Crouch, S., et al. (2022). Are cardiovascular health measures heritable across three generations of families in Soweto, South Africa? A cross-sectional analysis using the random family method. *BMJ Open, 12*(9), e059910. https://doi.org/10.1136/bmjopen-2021-059910

30

Evaluation: Including Experiences of Transgender People in Health Care

Kevin Turner

Introduction

In this chapter, I describe, discuss, and reflect on a consultancy project that I undertook to help improve health and wellbeing outcomes for people from Lesbian, Gay, Bisexual, and Transgender (LGBT) communities through the design and delivery of workshops for student nurses in the United Kingdom (UK). In the first section, The Case Study, I describe how the consultancy came about and my approach to the co-development and co-delivery of workshop content with transgender people. This is followed in the section, Evaluation: adopting a multi-modal approach to help assess the impact of consultancy practice, by a more detailed description of the evaluation of the workshop, as well as my evaluation of my practice as a consultant. In the final section, Reflection, I explore what I learnt about consultancy practice from the project, and how this will help to inform the way I do consultancy in the future.

K. Turner (✉)
Dorset HealthCare University, NHS Foundation Trust, Poole, Dorset, UK
e-mail: kevin.turner6@nhs.net

R. Brady et al. (eds.), *The Palgrave Handbook of Consultancy in Health Psychology*,
https://doi.org/10.1007/978-3-031-94529-8_30

The Case Study

In 2019, when invited to undertake this consultancy, I was working on placement as a Senior Health Advisor at a National Health Service (NHS) Health and Wellbeing service for LGBT communities (hereafter referred to as the H&W service) as part of my training to become a chartered health psychologist. The purpose of the H&W service was to respond to the health and wellbeing needs of local LGBT people, a community that continues to experience reduced health outcomes and encounter stigma and discrimination when accessing health care services (Bachmann & Gooch, 2018). Amongst LGBT people, the stigma of sexuality can lead to depression, anxiety, substance misuse, and engagement in high-risk sexual behaviours that increase susceptibility to HIV and Sexually Transmitted Infections (STIs) (The Lancet, 2016).

To address these health inequalities, the H&W service provided a range of specialist services, including a screening and treatment clinic for STIs, targeted Hepatitis B vaccination programmes, one-to-one support around gender identity and sexual orientation, as well as hosting a range of social support groups. Alongside regular health promotion events, the H&W service frequently delivers teaching and training sessions to schools, colleges, health services, and public sector organisations to increase awareness of LGBT communities and to help improve the experiences of LGBT people when accessing them.

Invitation to Provide Consultancy

The client e-mailed the H&W service using contact information available on the H&W website to enquire about the teaching and training services provided by the H&W service. Within the e-mail, the client introduced themselves as a lecturer who was responsible for the delivery of the undergraduate nursing degree programme at a UK-based university. A key focus of the teaching curriculum they were responsible for was to help and support nurses in developing services that were person-centred, and which responded to the individual needs of patients under their care (Department of Health, 2010). To assist students on the course in developing an understanding of the individual needs of transgender people, the client was interested in running a workshop on transgender health for second-year nursing students. The client did not have the expertise to do this within their organisation, so they contacted the H&W service about the possibility of outsourcing this work.

Having previously delivered training to health care professionals on the health and wellbeing needs of transgender people, I was initially confident in my abilities to fulfil the request from the client. However, given that I had not previously delivered this work to student nurses, nor had I prior experience of working with the client's organisation, I decided to undertake some initial background research to assess my suitability at fulfilling the request before replying to the client's e-mail. Using publicly available information on the internet, I began by researching the client organisation, with a focus on the nursing degree programme. From the university website, I learnt that the undergraduate nursing degree programme was delivered through a combination of placements, lectures, and seminars. Previous teaching experience in delivering lectures and seminars to university students enrolled on undergraduate psychology degree courses elsewhere gave me confidence in being able to design and deliver a workshop tailored for student nurses. On the university website, the course was advertised as being accredited by the Nursing and Midwifery Council (NMC); that prompted me to undertake additional research into the NMC to ensure that any recommendations I might make to the client encompassed their aims to 'act with kindness, in a way that values people, their insights, situations and experiences' (Nursing & Midwifery Council, 2020, p. 8). The emphasis by the NMC on inclusivity and respect for diversity mirrored the value of inclusivity within the client organisation. This helped to provide an insight into the approach required by the client to educate nurses on how to deliver care that met the individual needs of transgender people.

In response to the client's e-mail, I outlined my initial interest in the work and suggested a face-to-face meeting to further assess the client's needs and to agree on my suitability for the work. Several consultancy experts outline recommendations to best approach the first meeting with the client. For example, Crucini and Kipping (2001, p. 583) advise 'not to scare clients with an uninterrupted flow of words or ideas' and instead recommend taking time to listen to the client. By using active listening, I was able to achieve a shared understanding of the client's main needs, which were focused on providing nursing students with learning to improve their professional practice based on the lived experience of transgender people. The following open-ended questions supported the initial discussions: 'What do you hope students will gain from the workshop?'; 'What has worked well when delivering teaching in the past?'; 'What are the areas you would like me to prioritise most in the session?' It was also helpful to summarise and reflect back responses from the client; for example, 'My understanding is that you would like…' and 'I can see that … is important to include'.

Stakeholders

With the aim of supporting nurses to deliver person-centred care, it was important for me to include transgender people in a 'nothing about us, without us' approach (Jackson & Moorley, 2022, p. e75). Contacting local organisations supporting transgender people helped me to reach individuals who would be willing to contribute to the design and delivery of the workshop. Those who were interested in taking part in the project were invited to a meeting at the H&W service. At the meeting, a brief overview of the aims of the proposed workshops was presented to the attendees, who welcomed the efforts of the client organisation in providing opportunities for student nurses to learn how to provide person-centred care to transgender people. To ensure that the workshop would reflect the actual, rather than perceived, needs of transgender people, those attending the meeting were asked to reflect on a series of questions. These questions included: 'What are the unique health needs of transgender people?'; 'What are the barriers to accessing health care in the UK?'; 'Have you had any negative or positive experiences when accessing health care?'; and 'What recommendations would you give to health care professionals to improve the quality of care you receive?'

In response to these questions, the transgender people in the meeting emphasised the importance of including information in the workshop on the role of language and the correct use of pronouns when working with transgender individuals. Recommendations were also made to include information about referral and care management pathways for hormone treatment and gender reassignment surgery, in addition to providing real-life insights around the psychological issues often experienced by transgender people, such as stigma, discrimination, and isolation. The group also made recommendations about the best way to deliver this information to student nurses during the workshops. Suggestions included the use of slide presentations to present information about treatments and surgery clearly, and the use of publicly available video clips from the internet to highlight wider experiences of transgender people, including other perspectives such as those of parents whose children were transgender. Finally, three members of the group volunteered to co-deliver the sessions: a transgender man (female-to-male), a transgender woman (male-to-female), and a person who identified as non-binary (an umbrella term used to define several gender identity groups, including, but not limited to: '(a) an individual whose gender identity falls between or outside male and female identities, (b) an individual who can experience being a man or woman at separate times, or (c) an individual who does not experience or rejects having a gender identity' (Matsuno & Budge, 2017, p. 116). Their involvement provided opportunities for student nurses to ask direct questions about their lived experiences.

Contracting

Based on the discussions with transgender people, I e-mailed the client with a proposed lesson plan that included recommendations for the design and delivery of the workshop sessions. The lesson plan clearly outlined what would be covered in the workshop, and how it would be presented; for example, slide presentation, video clips, or face-to-face verbal accounts from those with lived experience. I presented these initial plans with provisional timings to highlight how the workshop could be delivered within the allocated time required by the client. A copy of the slide presentation, co-developed with transgender people, was also included. This enabled the client to see whether the information included met both their expectations and requirements.

A follow-up meeting was arranged with the client, who agreed to the proposed plan, approved the slide presentation, and asked me to complete the work. A contract was drawn up between me and the client, outlining mutually agreed conditions for delivering the work. The contract helped to act as a guide that we could both refer to throughout the course of the consultancy project.

Delivery

Four, 90-minute workshops were delivered to small groups of 10 to 15 student nurses across two scheduled face-to-face teaching days at the university. On each day, one workshop session was delivered in the morning, followed by a second workshop in the afternoon. Each of the workshops was delivered by me along with three transgender people, who volunteered to discuss their lived experiences. At the beginning of each workshop, I facilitated a discussion with student nurses about what they wanted to get out of the session. These learning aims were recorded on flip chart paper and revisited with students at the end of the session to make sure that I had met their individual learning goals. I then introduced each of the three transgender people who talked openly about their transition and their experiences of accessing health care services. This prompted a question-and-answer session, which enabled student nurses to ask direct questions to people with lived experience.

Examples of these questions included 'What was it like for you coming out as transgender to your partner/family?' and 'What could we do as student nurses to help look after you when accessing health care services?' Further information about hormone treatments and surgeries was presented using presentation slides to help give students an insight into the medical processes available and undertaken by transgender people in the United Kingdom.

Outcomes

The client measured attendance using a register at each of the four workshops. In total, 51 students attended. Students were asked to provide feedback to the client about each workshop using standardised evaluation forms provided by the university. A formal assessment of learning was undertaken by the client through the submission of a written assignment by students on the importance of personalising care to the individual needs of patients.

Evaluation

I worked with the client to evaluate not just the workshops themselves, but also my effectiveness in providing expertise as a trainee health psychologist and as a consultant with specialist knowledge and experience in working with transgender people in the context of health and wellbeing. In their evaluation forms, the student nurses reported increased confidence in providing care, which included using language preferred by transgender people. The students valued the opportunity to hear first-hand about people's experiences of transitioning gender and accessing health care services; the students said that the opportunity to discuss transgender patient care with people with lived experience would improve their patient care in the future. Keen to also evaluate my performance as a consultant, I asked the client to complete a client satisfaction evaluation form. Feedback provided helped to confirm that I had met the client's expectations of the consultancy. Producing a final report for the client enabled me to summarise collected feedback and demonstrate the success of the workshop sessions. This led to future bookings being made by the client for the delivery of the workshops in the following academic year. I will discuss my approach to evaluation in greater detail in the next section, before reflecting on my practice as a consultant in the final section of this chapter.

Evaluation: Adopting a Multi-Modal Approach

The process of evaluation in consultancy is sometimes overlooked and is regarded as an underdeveloped area of practice (Motamedia, 2015). Health psychologists have a range of options available to them to evaluate their interventions; for example, the APEASE criteria, which encompass Acceptability, Practicability, Effectiveness, Affordability, Side-effects, and Equity (West & Michie, 2019). However, there is little guidance available for consultants in general about *what* to evaluate, *when* to evaluate, and the best methodological and systematic approaches to do so (*how*). The approach to evaluation in this case study was guided by the client and the information they needed to collect to be able to report on the success of the consultancy to their organisation. As I was keen to assess my abilities as a trainee health psychologist undertaking consultancy work, the client also agreed to record feedback on my performance.

Several consultancy models are based on a staged or linear approach to consultancy that often begins with engagement or contact between client and consultant and ends with evaluation or termination of the contract (Hodges, 2021; Nickols, 2003). Whilst these models offer a familiar and systematic approach to consultancy, they appear to assume that evaluation is best positioned at the end of a consultancy. However, by the end of the consultancy, it can often be too late to design and implement relevant monitoring frameworks to measure success (Davidson et al., 2009). Similarly, leaving evaluation to the end of a project limits opportunities to make adjustments that could have otherwise helped to improve outcomes.

Evaluation in this case study was instead approached as a continuous process (Taylor et al., 2005) that ran throughout the entire lifespan of the project. This approach was largely informed by my abilities and experience of using validated wellbeing measures (depression: PHQ-9, Kroenke & Spitzer, 2002; anxiety: GAD-7, Spitzer et al., 2006) to continuously monitor the effectiveness of psychological interventions during their delivery to patients or research participants. An ability to review the effectiveness of interventions during delivery in the past had enabled me to make suitable adjustments so that the interventions were more helpful and meaningful to those to whom they were being delivered. To ensure that the work in the current consultancy met the needs of the client, I decided to adopt a similar approach that would enable me to modify the delivery of my work if needed; therefore, I monitored all aspects of the project from the outset.

Creating an opportunity to discuss evaluation with the client from the outset is important, as successful outcomes can hold different meanings and values for both the consultant and the client (Curuksu, 2018). This challenges misconceptions that consultants are solely responsible for designing and undertaking project evaluations and instead acknowledges that both the client and consultant may require a range of information to report on the success of a consultancy project. In discussing evaluation with the client in the first contact meeting, I became aware that the client preferred to use standardised evaluation forms, developed by the university, and used these across the nursing degree programme, to measure student satisfaction with the wider content delivered to them in other lectures and seminars.

Course evaluation forms are the most used evaluation tools to obtain feedback about learning experiences (Anderson et al., 2005) and typically provide important insights into the learning process and how future delivery can be improved. In this case study, paper evaluation forms were distributed to student nurses at the end of each of the delivered workshop sessions. Open-ended in nature, the forms contained three questions: First, 'What did you learn from this session that you will take into your future practice?'; second, 'What could have been done differently in terms of the content and delivery of the session?'. Finally, there was a free-text option inviting student nurses to provide feedback about the workshop session they had attended.

Alongside evaluation forms, I used open-ended questions throughout the delivery of the workshop to check that students understood the information being presented to them (Fisher & Frey, 2014) and to make sure that the pace of the workshop suited them. This approach helped me to realise that student nurses were having trouble differentiating between gender identities (such as transgender and transsexual) and the preferred use of 'they', 'them', 'their' pronouns by non-binary people who did not like to use 'he', 'him', 'his', or 'she', 'her', 'hers' pronouns that were used by people who identified solely as either male or female. Based on this feedback, I decided to spend some more time on this subject to help support the student nurses' understanding of these terms. I invited the transgender people co-delivering the workshop to share their own experiences of being misgendered to help highlight the importance for health care workers to use correct terminology when providing personalised care to transgender people. Checking in with the student nurses again towards the end of the sessions helped me to realise that rather than a question-and-answer session, the student nurses preferred to use the remaining time to discuss with the transgender co-facilitators things they could do to improve their future practice and experiences for transgender people when accessing health care services.

The client attended all the teaching sessions and provided valuable observations on the delivery of the workshop and on my performance as a consultant. Immediately following each session, the client and I used each other's experiences of the session to reflect on the delivery. Together, we reviewed the evaluation forms, which had been completed by the student nurses. Looking at student feedback helped us to check what we believed had worked well and to identify successes we had not considered, in addition to discussing potential adjustments to the remaining sessions to help improve outcomes. For example, in one session, a student used question-and-answer sessions with the co-facilitators to start developing recommendations to help improve experiences of transgender people accessing health care services. These discussions included how to approach transgender people about what pronouns to use, and how to best carry out physical examinations when this was clinically indicated. This process of joint problem-solving between the student nurses and transgender people was not something that I had considered within the original workshop design but was introduced as an activity in the remaining sessions. This change helped to enhance the project in several ways. First, it helped to further engage student nurses in their learning and provided them with opportunities to directly demonstrate their abilities to personalise the care given to transgender people. Second, it helped to demonstrate to the client the benefits of using a process of evaluation to monitor and improve the performance of the consultancy. Finally, it helped to demonstrate my abilities as a consultant to adapt the work to the needs of the client.

Gathering feedback about the workshop delivery from the student nurses was important for assessing their learning experience and for identifying how future workshop sessions could be improved (Benton & Ryalls, 2016). I recognised, however, that the student nurses were only able to assess part of my role as a consultant. Whilst they could observe my competence as an implementor in delivering the workshops, they were not able to evaluate other aspects of my practice as a consultant, such as the interpersonal skills used to develop a good relationship with the client, or the planning skills that I had used to organise the workshop. For this, I needed more feedback from the client. I could not find any examples or templates of evaluation forms for clients to fill in about the performance of consultants. Instead, I decided to create one that would help me to understand whether I had met the expectations of the client, as well as learning about the strengths and weaknesses I could build on to help me in future consultancy work.

I structured my evaluation form into five sections: evaluation of aims and objectives, role expectations, consultancy skills, client satisfaction, and informing future practice. In the first section, as recommended by Earll and

Bath (2004), I evaluated whether I had met the aims and objectives of the project. To do this, I listed each of the aims and objectives individually using a four-item Likert scale (Likert, 1932) that was rated from *strongly agree* to *strongly disagree*. I then asked the client to score on the scale whether I had met each of the aims and objectives. I decided to use Likert scales to help reduce the amount of time needed by the client to answer each question (Medina et al., 2019). To capture any additional feedback, I also included free-text comment boxes for the client to complete.

In the second section, I used information about my role that had been included in the contract agreed upon with the client. I listed each of my agreed responsibilities, again with a Likert scale, and comments box for the client to provide feedback about my performance. In the third section, I listed professional competencies for consulting skills in health psychology (The British Psychological Society, 2020) and used Likert scales and comment boxes to collect feedback from the client about my consultancy performance.

In the fourth section, I used a validated quantitative questionnaire to measure client satisfaction with the services I had provided as a consultant. I chose the Client Satisfaction Questionnaire (CSQ-8) (Attkisson & Zwick, 1982) for its wide use as a service evaluation tool. Including this measure within the evaluation form helped to remove bias in the design of the questions. The flexibility of this questionnaire in evaluating a range of services meant that I would also have a resource that I could use in future project evaluations, enabling me to monitor my performance across a range of consultancy work. With the aim of collecting responses from the client to help inform my future practice, the final section included the same open-ended questions requested by the client for inclusion in course evaluation forms, adapted to consultancy performance. This enabled the client to report on the success of the consultancy using the standard feedback used in the university. The questions included, 'What went well with the consultancy?', 'Were there any aspects of the consultancy that could have been improved upon?', and 'Were there any areas that the consultant could develop for future practice?'

I presented the findings from both the student and client evaluations in a report for the client on completion of the consultancy (Barasa Kabeyi, 2019). The report had four sections. To begin, Section 1 included a summary of the consultancy to help set the scene of the project for anyone reading it who was not directly involved in the work. Next, Section 2 outlined the aims and objectives to help outline the focus and goals of the project. Responses from student evaluations, grouped together into themes and supported with direct quotes, followed in Section 3. Section 4 included feedback from students on how to improve the session, which informed my recommendations, along with suggestions on implementation to further improve the delivery of future sessions.

Reflection

Practitioner health psychologists in the United Kingdom are expected by their professional and regulating bodies to reflect on the work that they undertake (The Health & Care Professional Council, 2023). To reflect on my performance as a consultant, I used Gibbs' Reflective Cycle (Gibbs, 1988). This model provides a way to examine experiences and allows you to learn and plan from things that went well or did not go well. It includes six stages designed to help the process of reflection on a particular experience: description, feelings, evaluation, analysis, conclusion, and action plan. The first stage of Gibbs' Reflective Cycle, description, has already been provided. I focus below on the remaining five stages. While my reflection on this project was based on Gibbs' Reflective Cycle, I acknowledge the work of Bolton and Delderfield (2018) on *reflexivity,* which goes beyond reflection by not only examining past experiences but also considering the influence of individual beliefs, values, and biases on actions and decisions. Reflecting more deeply in this way will inform my approach to future consultancy work.

Feelings

I went into the consultancy feeling confident. This was largely based on my previous experiences of receiving positive feedback when delivering teaching and training as part of my work at the H&W service. As a trainee health psychologist, I was especially keen to use the experience to demonstrate the competencies required by my professional training, which included consultancy practice. In thinking about the requirements of my course, I placed additional pressure on myself to get it right the first time, especially since I would be assessed on my performance. This had a big impact on how I thought about my role as a consultant, which was as someone who was solely responsible for the success of a consultancy project. My identity as a trainee also impacted the way I perceived myself as someone who was not yet 'professional' enough to do the work.

Thinking in this way meant that I started to view myself through a deficit-based lens. However, my status as a trainee was a forgiving backdrop, and one that I decided to embrace throughout the consultancy as an opportunity to explore, discover, and further refine my skill set. Although not yet qualified as a health psychologist, I had specialist knowledge and experience that an organisation wished to benefit from. Under the safety of my trainee status, I decided to embrace the consultancy by taking all of myself, strengths and weaknesses, into it in order to showcase my abilities while gaining new skills to support my future consultancy practice.

Thinking about how I felt about the consultancy encouraged me to consider my motivations for engaging in this work and the impact that had on my approach. From the outset, the proposed consultancy 'spoke to me' and to my experience and abilities. In the past, transgender people accessing the H&W service had presented with accounts of negative experiences in health care and often felt unable or powerless due to the concern that speaking out would negatively impact on the care they may receive in the future. The consultancy presented a safe environment to draw upon that lived experience as a way to bring about positive change for transgender people.

My own experiences of being misunderstood in health care led me to empathise with the three transgender people involved in the consultancy project and the ways in which assumptions from health care professionals had resulted in negative experiences when accessing health care services. That reflection encouraged me to draw upon my identity as a health care worker with experience of working with transgender people to help bridge the gap of 'us and them' that transgender people described as a challenge when deciding not to raise their concerns with health care professionals in the past. In some ways, these connections I felt to the project encouraged me to take on the work. It felt as though I was at the right place, at the right time, and could be the right person to do this work.

Thinking about my experiences as a student also helped me to consider what opportunities somebody in a 'learning' capacity might want from the workshops. I thought about training I had found enjoyable or useful, and how I could bring this to the current project. In the past, I had always welcomed the opportunities to hear first-hand from patients about their experiences. I was always motivated to use those experiences to help navigate improvements to my own individual practice or service delivery, which encouraged me to create a similar opportunity for the student nurses within the workshops.

Evaluation

Looking back at the consultancy through the proposed framework for consultancy in health psychology (Brady & Varkonyi-Sepp, 2025; see Chap. 3) has enabled me to consider specific incidents that have helped to improve my understanding and learning for future consultancy practice.

Enquiry. Meeting with the client face-to-face provided me with an opportunity to understand the reasons why I had been chosen as someone who could support them with expert knowledge and experience. The opportunity to ask the client questions helped me to further clarify my interpretation of the brief, enabling both of us to assess my suitability to accept the role.

Relationships. In thinking about when I felt most connected to the consultancy, it would have to be when I was 'with the client'. Meeting regularly with the client and keeping sustained contact with them through e-mails helped me to keep pace and to feel both engaged and connected with the work. My relationship with the client existed not as a singular phase, but rather as a continuum across all stages of the consultancy process.

Contracting. I worked with the client to develop a contract that was mutually agreeable. This helped to provide clarity around the scope of the work and understanding of each other's roles and responsibilities. Having a formal contract made me feel secure and confident in the consultancy, as it offered a shared framework to guide the work. Having a signed written contract meant that both of us had something to refer to throughout the project.

Planning and Managing Delivery. Planning the consultancy with the client helped to resolve feelings of being solely responsible for the success and delivery of the consultancy. Taking the time to plan the consultancy collaboratively enabled me to formulate practical steps that would help me to meet the project goals, which made the consultancy feel 'lighter' and achievable.

Evaluation. Collecting feedback from the students and from the client helped to further enrich my own perspective and interpretation of my performance in the consultancy. Providing opportunities for free-text responses enabled the client to feedback freely about how pleased they were with the partnership approach to the work, the safe and flexible space that I had created for student nurses, and the opportunity for personal reflection by student nurses within the workshop sessions.

Analysis

Feedback from the client, coupled with my own reflections, has enabled me to think about the consultancy and make sense of what was going on throughout the project. The key success of this consultancy was the relationship that I had built up with the client. This supports the literature on consultancy practice, which highlights the interaction between clients and consultants as being central to the success of a consultancy project (Nikolova, 2007). Being honest and open with the client from the outset helped to build the necessary trust (Nikolova et al., 2015) needed to discuss expectations and concerns about the project. Being transparent in this way enabled me to feel more authentic and secure in my role as a consultant and made me feel like the client was able to better connect with who they were working with (Bamford et al., 2013).

Developing a contract helped to further support the client-consultant relationship. Working collaboratively with the client to produce a written contract resulted in a shared interpretation and mutual agreement around the parameters of the work (Holtz, 1985), which further contributed to a transparent and trusting relationship in which the work could be delivered. Mobilising the contract into a plan of action, again developed in collaboration with the client, gave me more confidence that I was delivering what was expected to fulfil the brief and meet the client's needs.

Talking about evaluation from the onset enabled both the client and me to understand what success would look like, and the best way to collect evidence of achieving it. Adopting a multi-modal approach, which aimed to collect a range of feedback both formally through student evaluation forms and the client satisfaction questionnaire, and informally through the use of open-ended questions with students during the delivery of workshops, helped in collecting feedback throughout the consultancy, so that changes could be made to improve outcomes during delivery. Designing an evaluation form for the client to complete alongside student feedback helped in understanding my performance from a range of perspectives.

Conclusion

Central to my learning from this project has been the importance of embracing consultancy practice as a springboard for new and continued learning. By responsibly taking 'all of myself' into this consultancy, I have been able to create a trusting and transparent relationship with a client, which has helped me to develop into an authentic and successful consultant who is able to plan, deliver, evaluate, and reflect on their professional practice.

Overall, the consultancy has provided me with a positive experience of sharing my knowledge and skills with others and has encouraged me to consider that my expertise as a health psychologist will be of benefit to other clients. In addition to teaching, training, and intervention design, developing my skills in consultancy processes will enable me to seek out opportunities to improve health outcomes for underserved communities, something that I have learnt through reflexive thinking is important to me, both personally and professionally. Understanding the consultancy process, in addition to my knowledge and skills in health psychology, will enable me to support the development and delivery of interventions to improve health outcomes for others, while also raising the profile of health psychology with health care providers.

Action Plan

For future consultancy projects, my practice will benefit from drawing upon my feelings of learning and sense of accomplishment from the current consultancy, to seek out more opportunities to further refine my skills, and recognise my abilities within consultancy practice. The transparent and honest nature of my approach in this case study has encouraged 'authentic me' to arrive early at the hypothetical front door of the client's office, and to value the importance of the client-consultant relationship and the opportunities this creates to safely explore and discover my potential. Onward practice will continue to benefit from a multi-modal approach to evaluation that, in future, would be improved by collecting feedback from those with lived experience who contribute to the design or delivery of this work. Integrating feedback from people with lived experiences will help to further understand their experiences of being involved in efforts intended to bring about positive change in health care.

Finally, reaching out to other consultants in practice, to listen and learn about their experiences, will help to inspire confidence and creativity in the opportunities that we, as health psychologists, have to extend our work through consultancy and to make a difference in health care. This handbook is timely and will encourage much discussion and help to create new opportunities for its readership.

Top Tips

1. Do not leave evaluation to the end of your consultancy; make it an ongoing process throughout.
2. Talk about evaluation with your client from the beginning.
3. Remember to evaluate your consultancy performance along with the outcomes or deliverables of the project.
4. Take time to reflect on what you have done and to deepen your understanding through reflexivity.
5. Embrace the opportunities that consultancy can offer to refine and develop your skill set.

Competing Interests The author has no competing interests to declare that are relevant to the content of this chapter.

References

Anderson, H. M., Cain, J., & Bird, E. (2005). Online student course evaluations: Review of literature and a pilot study. *American Journal of Pharmaceutical Education, 69*(1), 34–43.

Attkisson, C. C., & Zwick, R. (1982). The client satisfaction questionnaire: Psychometric properties and correlations with service utilization and psychotherapy outcome. *Evaluation and Program Planning, 5*(3), 233–237. https://doi.org/10.1016/0149-7189(82)90074-X

Bachmann, C. L., & Gooch, B. (2018). *LGBT in Britain: Trans report.* Stonewall. https://files.stonewall.org.uk/production/files/lgbt_in_britain_-_trans_report_final.pdf

Bamford, M., Wong, C. A., & Laschinger, H. (2013). The influence of authentic leadership and areas of worklife on work engagement of registered nurses. *Journal of Nursing Management, 21*(3), 529–540. https://doi.org/10.1111/j.1365-2834.2012.01399.x

Barasa Kabeyi, M. J. (2019). Project and program evaluation process, consultancy and terms of reference with challenges, opportunities and recommendations. *International Journal of Scientific and Research Publications, 9*(12), 171–194. https://doi.org/10.29322/IJSRP.9.12.2019.p9622

Benton, S. L., & Ryalls, K. R. (2016). *Challenging misconceptions about students ratings of instruction.* The Idea Centre. https://files.eric.ed.gov/fulltext/ED573670.pdf

Bolton, G., & Delderfield, R. (2018). *Reflective practice: Writing and professional development* (5th ed.). Sage.

Brady, R., & Varkonyi-Sepp, J. (2025). A framework for consultancy in health psychology. In R. Brady, J. Varkonyi-Sepp, & J. Smith (Eds.), *The Palgrave handbook of consultancy in health psychology*. Palgrave Macmillan.

Crucini, C., & Kipping, M. (2001). Management consultancies as global change agents? Evidence from Italy. *Journal of Organizational Change Management, 14*(6), 570–589. https://doi.org/10.1108/EUM0000000006143

Curuksu, J. D. (2018). The client-consultant interaction. In J. D. Curuksu (Ed.), *Data driven; An introduction to management consulting in the 21st century* (pp. 43–59). Springer International Publishing. https://doi.org/10.1007/978-3-319-70229-2_4

Davidson, P., Motamedia, K., & Raia, T. (2009). Using evaluation research to improve consulting practice. In A. Buono (Ed.), *Emerging trends and issues in management consulting: Consulting as a Janus-faced reality* (p. 61.73). Information Age Publishing.

Department of Health. (2010). *Person centred planning: Advice for professionals..* https://www.base-uk.org/sites/default/files/%5Buser-raw%5D/11-07/dh_115245_pro.pdf

Earll, L., & Bath, J. (2004). Consultancy: What it is, how do you do it, and does it make any difference? In S. Michie & C. Abrahams (Eds.), *Health psychology in practice* (pp. 230–250). BPS Blackwell.

Fisher, D., & Frey, N. (2014). *Checking for understanding: Formative assessment techniques for your classroom* (2nd ed.). ASCD.

Gibbs, G. (1988). *Learning by doing: A guide to teaching and learning methods*. Further Education Unit.

Hodges, J. (2021). A framework for consulting. *Management Consulting Journal, 4*(2), 52–55. https://doi.org/10.2478/mcj-2021-0009

Holtz, H. (1985). *Utilizing consultants successfully: A guide for management in business, government, the arts, and professions*. Quorum Books.

Jackson, D., & Moorley, C. (2022). 'Nothing about us without us': Embedding participation in peer review processes. *Journal of Advanced Nursing, 78*(5), e75–e76. https://doi.org/10.1111/jan.15122

Kroenke, K., & Spitzer, R. L. (2002). The PHQ-9: A new depression diagnostic and severity measure. *Psychiatric Annals, 32*(9), 509–515. https://doi.org/10.3928/0048-5713-20020901-06

Likert, R. (1932). A technique for the measurement of attitudes. *Archives of Psychology, 22*, 5–55.

Matsuno, E., & Budge, S. L. (2017). Non-binary/Genderqueer identities: A critical review of the literature. *Current Sexual Health Reports, 9*, 116–120. https://doi.org/10.1007/s11930-017-0111-8

Medina, M. S., Smith, W. T., Kolluru, S., Sheaffer, E. A., & DiVall, M. (2019). A review of strategies for designing, administering and using student ratings of instruction. *American Journal of Pharmaceutical Education, 83*(5), 753–764. https://doi.org/10.5688/ajpe7177

Motamedia, K. (2015). A framework to evaluate consulting efforts. *Graziadio Business Review, 18*(1), 1–9.

Nickols, F. (2003). *The consulting process: A 'bare bones outline'*. Distance Consulting. https://www.nickols.us/consulting_process.pdf

Nikolova, N. (2007). *The client-consultant relationship in professional business service firms*. Springer Gabler. https://doi.org/10.1007/978-3-658-24376-0

Nikolova, N., Möllering, G., & Reihlen, M. (2015). Trusting as a 'leap of faith': Trust-building practices in client-consultant relationships. *Scandinavian Journal of Management, 31*(2), 232–245. https://doi.org/10.1016/j.scaman.2014.09.007

Nursing & Midwifery Council. (2020). *NMC Strategy 2020–2025*. https://www.nmc.org.uk/globalassets/sitedocuments/strategy/nmc-strategy-2020-2025.pdf

Spitzer, R. L., Kroenke, K., Williams, J. B. W., & Löwe, B. (2006). A brief measure for assessing generalized anxiety disorder: The GAD-7. *Archives of Internal Medicine, 166*(10), 1092–1097. https://doi.org/10.1001/archinte.166.10.1092

Taylor, M., Purdue, D., Wilson, M., & Wilde, P. (2005). *Evaluating community projects: A practical guide*. Joseph Rowntree Foundation. https://evaluationsupportscotland.org.uk/wp-content/uploads/2020/08/evaluating-community-projects.pdf

The British Psychological Society. (2020). *Qualification in health psychology (Stage 2) handbook for candidates*. https://cms.bps.org.uk/sites/default/files/2022-07/QHP%20Candidate%20Handbook.pdf

The Health & Care Professional Council. (2023). *Standards of proficiency: Practitioner psychologists*. https://www.hcpc-uk.org/globalassets/resources/standards/standards-of-proficiency%2D%2D-practitioner-psychologists.pdf

The Lancet. (2016). Meeting the unique health-care needs of LGBTQ people. *The Lancet, 387*(10014), 95. https://doi.org/10.1016/S0140-6736(16)00013-1

West, R., & Michie, S. (2019). *UBC Briefing 7: Evaluating behaviour change interventions using APEASE*. Unlocking Behaviour Change. https://www.unlockingbehaviourchange.com/pdfs/5c766be7b6281890464249.pdf

Part IV

Concluding Chapter

31

Conclusion

Roseanna Brady, Judit Varkonyi-Sepp, and Jan Smith

The purpose of this book is to help to fill a gap in resources for training and professional development of health psychologists in consultancy practice. It does so by including several chapters on topics of relevance to practice (Part II of the book). Those chapters illustrate opportunities and challenges available to health psychologists to make a positive difference in a wide range of health conditions through consultancy that is guided by professional and ethical standards. The book also includes a framework for consultancy in health psychology (Chap. 3; henceforth referred to as 'the framework'), providing a guide to the various processes involved in seeking, engaging in and evaluating consultancy. In addition, there are 16 separate case studies (Part III of the book) illustrating consultancy in practice and focusing on a specific consultancy process in some depth.

R. Brady (✉)
Psychology for Health Associates, Bedford, UK
e-mail: bradykbs@msn.com

J. Varkonyi-Sepp
Department of Adult Health Psychology, Hampshire and Isle of Wight Healthcare NHS Foundation Trust, Southampton, UK
e-mail: j.varkonyi-sepp@soton.ac.uk

J. Smith
Glasgow Caledonian University, Glasgow, UK
e-mail: jan.smith@gcu.ac.uk

R. Brady et al. (eds.), *The Palgrave Handbook of Consultancy in Health Psychology*,
https://doi.org/10.1007/978-3-031-94529-8_31

The case study authors have varying levels of experience and expertise in consultancy. The case studies presented in this book show clear benefits both to clients and stakeholders and to the consultants themselves. Prior to writing chapter contributions, case study authors were asked to describe their work through the lens of the framework; they were invited to draw on the wider consultancy literature and to select one of the processes in the framework to analyse in depth. This approach has provided a rich vein of learning, both for the authors themselves as they discuss in their reflections on their practice, and for readers. It is important to note that none of the case studies are presented as 'perfect' examples of consultancy practice. Authors faced and responded to a variety of challenges, sometimes altering their planned approach to projects while working within the boundaries of professional and ethical standards. Some authors also reflect on missed opportunities to enhance the consultancy work, for example, through deeper levels of pre-contract enquiry or through negotiating with clients to enable evaluation of the impact of their work following implementation. These reflections are strengths of those chapters, and we commend the authors for exploring those issues with candour and humility. Rarely, if ever, do practitioners work on real-world problems without encountering obstacles that require them to compromise and adapt. The 'swampy lowlands', described by Schön (1995) as the place where practitioners strive to apply theories and models to what are often messy problems, is where the work of consultancy is conducted. Health psychologists adapt to real-world challenges in consultancy, knowingly demonstrating commitment to scientific rigour and being mindful of the importance of best practice.

This book came into existence primarily in response to the unmet need for a comprehensive, practical guide to consultancy which had been expressed by health psychologist colleagues. The need for, and impact of, health psychology consultancy at scale was clearly recognised during the COVID-19 pandemic. For example, as Arden et al. (2020) outline, health psychologists provided expertise in behavioural science to the United Kingdom government, while others offered consultancy to several organisations through the Health Psychology Exchange, a collaborative of health psychology professionals who volunteered their expertise and time to assist in the COVID-19 pandemic response. That multidisciplinary and collegial attitude enabled us to compile this book which we believe will become a core resource for health psychology practitioners, trainees, supervisors and academics, providing them with detailed, practical, hands-on information in consultancy processes and examples from varying contexts.

What We Have Learned from Editing This Book

Engagement in Consultancy

First and foremost, we have learned that consultancy in health psychology is 'alive and well'. To our knowledge, this book contains the largest collection of examples of consultancy practice in health psychology. In editing it, we have answered the call from more than 25 years ago to publish examples of consultancy in health psychology (Michie, 1998). The variety of consultancy projects described across private, public and third sectors shows the wide applicability of health psychology expertise to problems in health in varying degrees of scale and complexity. We welcomed chapters from health psychologists and other professionals with consultancy experience working exclusively in consultancy from their own independent practice or company. The richness and depth of those authors' experience illustrate that it is possible to build a sustainable independent practice in consultancy (Chaps. 8, 12 and 24).

The work described in the book may well be the tip of the iceberg since much of consultancy in health psychology is not published. We could not find a peer-reviewed journal or periodical devoted specifically to consultancy in health psychology. Incentives to publish in private practice are not the same as for people in academia, where the 'pressure to publish' may be a feature (Hyland, 2016). In practitioner settings such as public health organisations and private consultancy practices, consultants need to weigh up the potential benefit of publishing without direct funding if they cannot persuade their employers or clients to fund publication and dissemination. Clients may also be concerned about confidentiality, and consultants need to be sensitive to that. A key benefit of publication to consultants, however, is that it showcases their expertise in a specific field and therefore helps them become attractive to potential clients (e.g., Chaps. 7 and 12). Clients sometimes do support publication, particularly when the project is publicly funded (e.g., Chaps. 24 and 27).

In the absence of substantial literature on consultancy in health psychology or the availability of robust data, we cannot confidently estimate the number or proportion of health psychology professionals who are active in consultancy practice. Indeed, it is possible, even likely, that health psychologists are engaged in consultancy without naming their work as consultancy. It is important to find out who is engaging in consultancy practice in order to learn how best to support those practitioners and to learn from their experience and expertise.

The Framework for Consultancy in Health Psychology

We have learned that the framework appears to be a good 'fit' for consultancy in health psychology. Case study authors reflected in some depth on their practice in one of the processes in the framework. In addition, several contributors to the 'Perspectives' in Part II have also explored their main topic through the lens of one or more of the processes in the framework (Chaps. 4, 6, 7, 8, 10, 12 and 14). While the framework is not yet tested by research, some reflections from authors suggest that prior knowledge of the framework might have enhanced their work, and they expect it to do so in future.

Enquiry. Of the five processes in the framework, enquiry emerges as perhaps the most fundamental. Often described as a 'stage' (Hodges, 2021; Block 2011), enquiry underpins all aspects of consultancy; that is why in the framework we describe enquiry as a *process* rather than a stage. Our approach is closely aligned with that of Schein (2016) in his description of 'humble inquiry', where he advocates for genuine curiosity in the pursuit of understanding the client's needs. While three authors chose to explore enquiry in depth in their case studies (Chaps. 15, 16 and 17), most of the case study authors also reflect on the process of asking questions and learning about client and stakeholder needs. Authors who developed successful independent consultancies describe enquiry in the context of preparing to approach prospective clients, write proposals and negotiate contracts (Chaps. 7, 10 and 12). A particularly detailed explanation of enquiry in the pre-proposal stage of consultancy is included in Chap. 7. The chapter highlights the importance of asking questions and carefully considering the needs of the client, the assumptions being made, and the resources needed to deliver the objectives agreed upon with the client. In several chapters, authors reflect particularly on how they might have conducted enquiry differently and more productively, which readers will find helpful.

Consultant-Client Relationships. Building effective relationships with clients requires "humility in the face of the complexity of the problems, and humility in the relationship with the client in the sense that I am here to help work things out together, not to take over the problem and run with it" (Schein, 2016, p. 17). This attitude is clearly visible across the case studies, for example in Chaps. 21, 22 and 24, rather than assume they had (or needed to have) all the answers, the authors embraced uncertainty and worked with others in defining both the problems presented and the solutions or interventions they offered. We agree with the authors of Chap. 5 who state that it is a balance of expertise, confidence and humility that enables consultants to work effectively with others; this aligns closely with Schein's process consultancy model (Schein, 1999) where consultants create relationships that enable the clients to own the problem and the solution to the problem. Health psychologists possess an understanding of behaviour and they have available to them practical tools such as the Behaviour Change Wheel (Michie et al., 2011; D'Lima et al., 2020) which can help clients to define problems and ensure that solutions are effective. To do this, health psychologists need to balance their expertise in health psychology and behavioural science with the confidence to ask questions and to discuss potential solutions with clients and stakeholders, and with the humility to recognise the expertise and contributions of others.

We saw in the case studies that the client with whom the consultant initially contracted was not always the person with whom the consultant worked on a day-to-day basis. Other stakeholders - staff, leadership teams, consultants from other disciplines, and the ultimate beneficiaries of the consultancy work including the public, service users and patients - needed to be considered. Stakeholders were often involved in co-design, in the implementation of interventions, and in the evaluation of consultancy. Failure to identify and engage with stakeholders who need to be involved and consulted (Eskerod et al., 2015) can either make or break a project. Where authors took particular care to identify and build relationships with stakeholders, the results appeared positive in terms of outcomes and the work was satisfying for the consultants. This was illustrated in those case studies which involved co-design or co-production, enabling the consultants to shape their interventions in response to input from key stakeholders (e.g., Chaps. 16, 19, 21, 24, 25, 28 and 30).

Boundaries in relationships with clients are also important to understand and maintain. Regardless of whether a consultant is internal or external to the client organisation, the consultant also has either an 'insider' or 'outsider' role in consultancy. Being an 'insider', in the sense of having an insider view of the organisation through working with the client over time, can confer advantages such as understanding internal facilitators and barriers that may impact effective practice. On the other hand, the blurring of boundaries could contribute to further challenges. For example, the consultant may become more like a 'surrogate manager' and be expected to take responsibility for aspects of the work over which they have no control, potentially losing the objectivity that is the hallmark of a consultant. This concept is explored in several chapters citing Kitay and Wright (2004) and is explored in depth in Chap. 8.

Negotiation and Contracting. This topic was explored in great depth in three of the Perspectives chapters (Chaps. 7, 10 and 12) where experienced consultants shared their expertise in preparing to bid for consultancy work.

Careful enquiry and research prior to making a proposal are needed, and negotiation requires confidence. Health psychologists do not always possess the skills to negotiate effectively, and this may be a barrier to securing consultancy work. Only one of the contributors we contacted offered to write a case study focusing specifically on negotiation and contracting. Speaking with potential contributors, several expressed concerns about writing on such a 'sensitive' topic and about a potentially negative impact on clients who might read their chapter; others said they did not feel they were 'expert' enough in negotiation and contracting to write about it in depth. The author who agreed to focus on negotiation and contracting had a successful career in professional consultancy prior to undertaking postgraduate study in psychology, and evidence of that experience is visible in the chapter (Chap. 22). One other case study discusses re-negotiation and re-contracting in the context of planning and managing a project (Chap. 26) which is helpful in illustrating how to deal with challenges while maintaining scientific rigour as well as how processes in the framework overlap. In addition, to our knowledge, this book contains a chapter which is the first publication to explore the pricing of consultancy work in health psychology in depth (Chap. 9). While some of the contributing authors offered their services on a pro bono basis, we were reminded of the potential pitfalls in doing so. For example, we were alerted to a potential devaluing of our expertise through under-pricing our work as well as the increased stress involved in an unbalanced effort/reward equation (Siegrist, 2016, cited in Chap. 10). We should also be mindful that offering or agreeing to work unpaid might exclude people from financially disadvantaged backgrounds from gaining experience, developing their skills and building their reputation.

Several skills are needed to prepare to negotiate and to contract effectively; for example, identifying potential risks, calculating the resources that will be required, evaluating the input from and impact of varied stakeholders, and so on, all of which need to be considered in contracting. In addition, consultants need to present their proposals in a way that persuades clients to place their trust in them (e.g., O'Mahoney & Markham, 2013). It is possible that negotiation and contracting skills are not always well developed for several reasons. For example, internal consultants, who provide consultancy to departments or functions with which they are not involved on a day-to-day basis within their employing organisation, might not be required to formally contract with internal clients. Instead, they may willingly offer their specialist knowledge and skills to improve services, as several of the contributing authors have acknowledged. We would strongly recommend negotiating and contracting in internal consultancy. Clarifying the scope of work and the outcomes to be delivered is always important (Ajmal et al., 2020) and agreements in writing ensure that the consultant and client have a record of roles, responsibilities, assumptions, agreements and outcomes.

Health psychologists who offer consultancy from academic institutions or large consultancy businesses may rely on business teams to cost and price work and to formally contract with clients, such that the health psychologists do not have the opportunity to develop contracting skills. Nevertheless, regardless of where consultants work *from*, they need to negotiate and agree on a scope of work. Failure to do so can lead to scope creep (Wulf, 2020), unpaid work, and unhappy clients. Negotiation and contracting were also highlighted as a training need for the profession by the experienced health psychologists who contributed to Chap. 2.

We also learned about how consultants find new clients through health psychology networks (Chap. 11), publishing on topics of interest to clients (Chap. 12) and establishing themselves as 'thought leaders' (Chap. 7). New clients are also found through responding to open tenders or responses to requests for proposals (Chaps. 10 and 12).

Planning and Managing Delivery. Planning and managing delivery of a consultancy project is a process where the scientist-practitioner model, emphasising as it does the role of research and scientific practice underpinning practice (Lane & Corrie, 2007), enables health psychologists to shine. Although usually applied to clinical practice (e.g., Shapiro, 2002), the scientist-practitioner model also applies to health psychology consultancy, where the application of scientific principles distinguishes health psychologists from many other consultants. Using scientifically rigorous methods in planning and delivery, for example through clearly defining the problem to be addressed and identifying evidence of the effectiveness of prior interventions, can reduce the risk of waste from applying interventions/solutions that evidence has shown to be ineffective (e.g., Chap. 26). The health psychologist's role in "providing proportionate evidence-based claims, accounting for confounding explanations, caveating around generalisability or transferability of interpretations, and advising on process and outcome or impact evaluation" can differentiate health psychologists from competitors (Lunt, 2025; see Chap. 7).

Depending on the complexity of the project, management of delivery might include careful and considered positioning of the consultant in relation to others. Examples presented in this book include delineation of roles between consultant and manager in internal consultancy (e.g., Chap. 23); working with other consultancy providers (e.g., Chap. 12); working with a variety of stakeholders with varying levels of understanding of the role of the health psychology consultant (e.g., Chap. 24) and working in other cultural and geographical contexts (Chap. 14). A skilled health psychology consultant will be able to identify these and other relevant issues through enquiry to enable careful preparation in the planning phase. Where projects sometimes overrun and consultants experience scope creep (Ajmal et al., 2020), it is usually because consultants have not planned the time and resources needed to deliver the work for a variety of reasons. Several of the case studies focusing on planning and managing delivery of consultancy discuss scope creep and ways to avoid it (e.g., Chaps. 26 and 27) as well as the use of project management tools to assist with planning (Chap. 24).

Evaluation. Evaluating the effectiveness of interventions is central to health psychology research and practice. In the framework, we propose that this process be integrated from the very beginning of a consultancy project. What needs to be evaluated is both the interventions themselves *and* the way we conduct consultancy. In other words, we need to know if the way we are conducting the processes in consultancy—enquiry, relationship building, negotiation, and so on—is effective in meeting the needs of clients and stakeholders. The book includes three quite different case studies with differing approaches to evaluation from which we learn about how the authors approached evaluation, in each case building evaluation into the work through the various stages of the projects (Chaps. 28, 29 and 30).

Evaluation can be challenging in practice for health psychology consultants. Firstly, consultants are not always involved in implementing their recommendations and evaluation is restricted to the outcomes agreed in the contract (e.g., delivering a set of recommendations or delivering an education intervention aimed at changing health professional behaviour). While some contributing authors had access to reliable and valid methods for measuring interventions, others found it difficult to identify measures to evaluate their performance as consultants. Research suggests that clients base their decisions on engaging consultants on several factors relating to the personal qualities of the consultant themselves (Maister, 2010). In several of the case studies, although health psychologists were able to collect quantitative and qualitative data on the agreed outcomes, they did not always have the opportunity to evaluate the changes resulting from implementation. Health psychology consultants are not always involved in implementation; their contract often ends with a report and recommendations. Consultants may measure the delivery of the intervention and the immediate response to it (e.g., an educational intervention), but not the impact that intervention has on changing the behaviours of health professionals or patients. If we are to produce robust practice-based evidence, we will need as a profession to address this. Evaluating outcomes of implementation is always important in consultancy (Nicolescu & Nicolescu, 2021), and it is vital that this issue is addressed when scoping projects and negotiating contracts. Wherever possible, we need to seek agreement to collect reliable data to help evaluate the impact of consultancy work on the 'ultimate' beneficiaries of the work: patients, service users or members of the public.

Transferable Skills

An important learning from the book is that in addition to technical or scientific expertise, a variety of skills such as negotiation and planning for example, are required for consultancy practice (Block, 2011). Health psychologists do not, however, come to consultancy with an empty toolbox. Embarking on consultancy might feel like a daunting prospect. The health psychologist new to consultancy might perceive that they lack consultancy skills or that they do not know or understand the business world. On the contrary, as health psychologists, we are trained in a variety of robust skills. For example, we are able to assess the needs of individuals and groups and to formulate an evidence-based hypothesis on what might address these needs (enquiry); we are able to build non-prejudiced, non-judgemental rapport and relationships with individuals, groups, colleagues and clients—for example patients, health care professionals or students (consultant-client relationship); we adjust communication styles to a variety of audiences depending on their needs and levels of understanding to reach a shared objective (negotiating and contracting); we are able to develop and deliver interventions for individuals and groups and to transfer knowledge that could support training and teaching that is applicable to planning and managing delivery in consultancy; finally, as health psychologists, we are able to identify and apply appropriate evaluation methods in our intervention or teaching and training activities (evaluation). These are core skills in our health psychology professional training.

Similarities between psychology and consultancy are explored by Berendsen (2022). For example, both consultants and psychologists are involved in the sequential processes of diagnosis (identifying the 'problem' to be tackled), construction (creating a formulation) and changing (intervention to achieve a desired outcome) (interpretation in parentheses is authors' own). In some consultancy settings, different terms are used for these skills, and health psychology consultants sometimes lack familiarity with the language rather than with the skills as such. What we advocate, therefore, is to think outside of the limiting 'box' of terminology, identify skills that health psychologists already possess and find opportunities to develop them in practice. Health psychology consultants also need to develop new skills, for example, in project management (e.g., Chap. 24), in working with clients in specific business sectors (e.g., Chap. 13), in pricing and budgeting (e.g., Chaps. 9 and 22), in running a business (Chap. 11) or in working with international partners (Chap. 14).

Learning from Other Professions

A key learning from this book is that health psychologists in consultancy practice work with professionals from a wide range of professions. Clients are often professional managers, and stakeholders often include specialists from other professions. In effective consultancy, collaboration with clients and stakeholders is required to achieve a desired outcome. In doing this, each has the opportunity to learn from one another and to share their own expertise since no one person needs to have all the answers (e.g., Chap. 22). Resolving problems in health requires collaboration across disciplines (Peet & Middleton, 2025) and each profession can learn from working with others, a point well made by contributors to Chap. 2. Consultancy, therefore, provides an opportunity to learn how problems in real-world settings can be resolved through collaboration with a wide range of stakeholders.

For many contributors to this book, researching the wider consultancy literature was a new experience. The need to do so was based on the dearth of literature on consultancy specific to health psychology. A substantial body of literature in management and organisational consultancy, which includes empirical data as well as reviews and expert opinion, has been built over many decades. We have much to learn from it and from other professions engaged in consultancy. We are trained to read and review with a critical eye to identify robust evidence that can be applied to our own practice. Just as we cite the medical literature when writing about our work with people living with long-term conditions, for example, we research and cite from wider consultancy literature to inform our learning, our practice and our writing. The degree to which consultancy literature was considered helpful by contributors varied; it is positive that contributors accessed and evaluated the literature, and it is clear from the chapters that many contributors learned a great deal about consultancy processes from doing so. We encourage fellow health psychology professionals to continue to engage with the wider literature and to contribute to it. Other professions can also learn from health psychologists' approach to consultancy, particularly in terms of methodology and evidence-based practice.

Implications for Practice

It is clear from the contributions to this book that there is a need to focus on acquiring and developing consultancy skills to equip health psychologists to work in a variety of different contexts while delivering work that is scientifically robust and produces practice-based evidence. Professional standards for health psychologists, such as those of the British Psychological Society and the Health Care Professions Council in the United Kingdom, have laid a foundation for developing skills and those foundations need to be built upon. Training providers have a responsibility to ensure that training and supervision are delivered in a consistent way by health psychology professionals with practitioner expertise in consultancy. Health psychologists who are established as consultants have much to offer in sharing their expertise with others. Health psychology consultants working independently and in their own consultancy practices usually fund their own professional development from their earnings. While many of them have contributed generously to this book, we need to recognise that if we are to engage them to support training and development of others in other ways, their input needs to be remunerated.

Since we do not yet know how many health psychologists are actively engaging in consultancy, it would be helpful to learn more. For example, knowing where consultancy is practised (client sectors and health domains) as well as *from where* consultants practise (e.g., independent consultants, owners of consultancy practices, employees in consultancy practices, in academia and so on) would help us to understand the breadth of practice as well as gaps that might potentially be filled through consultancy. It would also be helpful to know what proportion of consultants in health psychology are members of professional bodies and, for those who are not, what would encourage them to become members. If we learn about who is practising, where and how, we will be in a better position to support skills development, networking, mentoring and continuous professional development. Professional bodies are more likely to invest in supporting these activities if they are aware of existing and potential levels of engagement.

As yet, there are few opportunities for health psychologists in consultancy practice to disseminate their work. Health psychologists can do more to disseminate their work both within and outside the health psychology community. It is possible to obtain funding from clients to publish as we have seen in this book. For health psychologists with available resources and support, it is also sometimes worthwhile to self-fund publication and dissemination. For example, publishing in peer-reviewed medical and public health journals can attract attention from potential clients and collaborators. Attendance at conferences may enable promotion of consultancy work outside of peer-reviewed scholarly journals. However, consultants need to balance the time and cost of writing for publication against the potential reputational benefits and the revenue it will generate either directly or indirectly over time. Publication outside health psychology journals can prove lucrative for consultants, as we have seen in this book (e.g., Chap. 12).

Professional bodies could support the development of consultancy by creating dedicated resource libraries for consultancy practice. More opportunities to present at health psychology conferences could also attract consultancy practitioner attendees who are in a position to fund attendance; this could enable practitioners and academics to work together to strengthen methods and bridge the research-evidence gap. Practitioners themselves could consider publishing their consultancy work in journals, periodicals and blogs that potential clients are likely to read; for example, in public health or medical journals and in business journals aimed at leaders in the health sector.

We must be wary of preaching to the choir. To resolve problems in health, we need to engage with the wide range of organisations involved in health. Conferences can provide opportunities to present our work and generate interest in behavioural science. Several of our contributing authors have taken advantage of professional networking opportunities at health conferences. Not only would this bring health psychologists into contact with potential clients (and research partners), it could also help to showcase the health psychology profession amongst those who would benefit from learning about how health psychology theory, evidence and tools could make a difference to their own work. Collaboration between groups of practitioners, academic institutions, and professional bodies to fund this might be a way forward.

It is clear from the contributions to this book that there is a need to focus on acquiring and developing consultancy skills to equip health psychologists to work in a business context. Professional standards for health psychologists have laid a foundation for developing skills, and those foundations need to be built on. Training providers have a responsibility to ensure that training and supervision in consultancy are delivered in a consistent way by health psychology professionals with expertise in consultancy. Health psychology professionals themselves have a responsibility to continually develop their skills as they practise consultancy.

Final Thoughts

Consultancy enables health psychologists to work with real-world challenges and to make an impact at scale. It involves direct contact with clients and often with beneficiaries of our work. We enjoy the benefits and learning opportunities of working with professionals from other disciplines. We draw on our knowledge from training and the body of evidence created within our health psychology profession. Consultancy is often intellectually stimulating, challenging and is professionally and personally rewarding and enjoyable.

Consultancy in health psychology is a relatively new area of practice in a relatively new health psychology profession. In our Calls to Action below, we recognise there are resource implications in terms of time and funding. We also believe that the valuable input of consultancy practitioners in efforts to upskill and develop the profession should be remunerated. If we are to encourage and support more health psychologists to engage in effective consultancy and make a difference in health at scale, further dialogue needs to happen within our community, and these Calls to Action are intended to start that dialogue.

Calls to Action

Health Psychology Practitioners

Practice and Skills

1. Seek and create (more) opportunities to engage in consultancy in order to make a positive difference in health at scale.
2. Network with other health psychology practitioners to share learning and knowledge.
3. Develop and offer training in consultancy skills to support continuous professional development for health psychologists and trainee health psychologists.
4. When consulting, seek opportunities to collaborate with academic and research health psychologists to build the evidence base for health psychology in practice.

Dissemination

5. Create (more) opportunities to co-publish with clients.
6. Publish in journals likely to be read by potential clients (i.e., other than health psychology journals).
7. Collaborate with other practitioner health psychologists and professional bodies to share consultancy findings where potential clients such as businesses, health organisations and policy makers can easily access them.

Academic and Research Organisations

1. Increase collaboration with practitioners to create opportunities to test theories and models and to generate practice-based evidence.
2. Engage more practitioners with expertise in consultancy to support the learning and application of consultancy skills for health psychology trainees.
3. Conduct exploratory research to test the utility and effectiveness of the framework for consultancy in health psychology.

Professional Bodies Supporting Health Psychology Professionals and Trainees

Practice and Skills

1. Establish the number of health psychologists (members and non-members) engaged in consultancy practice across sectors.
2. Use existing member communication channels to demystify consultancy (e.g., by publishing a 'Day in the Life' series from practitioner consultants).
3. Provide more consultancy skills training delivered by practitioners who have expertise in consultancy practice.
4. Establish and publicise a network of consultancy mentors (and supervisors) to provide guidance, encourage continuous learning and support psychological safety for independent practitioners working alone.
5. Develop collaborative opportunities with health-related businesses through, for example, (paid) internships to develop mutual understanding of different experiences and realities, challenges and priorities and of the terminology used in business and sector-specific environments.

Dissemination

6. Increase the opportunities for practitioner consultants to disseminate their work within the health psychology community (e.g., through a consultancy journal or periodical, through a dedicated programme at health psychology conferences, and through local health psychology professional networks).
7. Create a professional health psychology presence at conferences attended by potential clients and research collaborators.
8. Develop international collaboration and networking opportunities for health psychologists working or wishing to work in consultancy, for example, at international health psychology conferences.

We welcome opportunities to engage with our professional community to respond to these Calls to Action.

Competing Interests The authors have no competing interests to declare that are relevant to this chapter.

References

Ajmal, M., Khan, M., & Al-Yafei, H. (2020). Exploring factors behind project scope creep–stakeholders' perspective. *International Journal of Managing Projects in Business, 13*(3), 483–504. https://doi.org/10.1108/ijmpb-10-2018-0228

Arden, M. A., Byrne-Davis, L., Chater, A., Hart, J., McBride, E., & Chilcot, J. (2020). The vital role of health psychology in the response to COVID-19. *British Journal of Health Psychology, 25*, 831–838. https://doi.org/10.1111/bjhp.12484

Berendsen, T. (2022). The role of psychology in consulting-some considerations. *Management Consulting Journal, 5*(1), 43–50. https://doi.org/10.2478/mcj-2022-0005

Block, P. (2011). *Flawless consulting*. Pfeiffer.

D'Lima, D., Lorencatto, F., & Michie, S. (2020). The behaviour change wheel approach. In *Handbook on implementation science* (pp. 168–214). Edward Elgar Publishing. https://doi.org/10.4337/9781788975995.00014

Eskerod, P., Huemann, M., & Ringhofer, C. (2015). Stakeholder inclusiveness: Enriching project management with general stakeholder theory. *Project Management Journal, 46*(6), 42–53.

Hodges, J. (2021). *Consultancy, organizational development and change*. Kogan Page.

Hyland, K. (2016). *Academic publishing: Issues and challenges in the construction of knowledge*. Oxford University Press.

Kitay & Wright. (2004). Take the money and run? Organisational boundaries and consultants' roles. *The Service Industries Journal, 24*(3), 1–18. https://doi.org/10.1080/0264206042000247731

Lane, D. A., & Corrie, S. (2007). *The modern scientist-practitioner: A guide to practice in psychology*. Routledge. https://doi.org/10.4324/9780203624616-10

Lunt, J. (2025). The sustainable consultant. In R. Brady, J. Varkonyi-Sepp, & J. Smith (Eds.), *The Palgrave handbook of consultancy in health psychology*. Palgrave Macmillan.

Maister, D. (2010). Professionalism in consulting. In *Management consulting today and tomorrow*. Routledge.

Michie, S. (1998). 8.06 Consultancy. *Comprehensive Clinical Psychology, 8*, 1530169. https://doi.org/10.1016/B0080-4270(73)00276-5

Michie, S., Van Stralen, M. M., & West, R. (2011). The behaviour change wheel: A new method for characterising and designing behaviour change interventions. *Implementation Science, 6*, 1–12. https://doi.org/10.1186/1748-5908-6-42

Nicolescu, O., & Nicolescu, C. (2021). *Stakeholder management and social responsibility*. Routledge. https://doi.org/10.4324/9781003217701

O'Mahoney, J., & Markham, C. (2013). *Management consultancy*. Oxford University Press.

Peet, J., & Middleton, R. (2025). Multi professional consultant practice—What is it and how does the role contribute systems transformation? *Journal of Evaluation in Clinical Practice, 31*(1), e14235. https://doi.org/10.1111/jep.14235

Schein, E. H. (1999). *Process consultation revisited: Building the helping relationship*. Addison-Wesley.

Schein, E. H. (2016). *Humble consulting: How to provide real help faster*. Berrett-Koehler Publishers.

Schön, D. A. (1995). Knowing-in-action: The new scholarship requires a new epistemology. *Change*, Nov–Dec, pp. 27–34. https://doi.org/10.1080/00091383.1995.10544673

Shapiro, D. (2002). Renewing the scientist-practitioner model. *The Psychologist, 15*(5), 232–234. http://cognaction.org/cogs105/readings/scientist-practitioner.pdf

Wulf, S. A. (2020). Successful project consulting. *IEEE Engineering Management Review, 48*(2), 12–14. https://doi.org/10.1109/emr.2020.2978797

Index

A

Acceptability, Practicability, Effectiveness, Affordability, Spillover effects, Equity (APEASE), 49, 51, 508, 512, 513, 547, 567, 568, 585
Acceptance and Commitment Therapy (ACT), 320, 324, 338, 390, 392, 399, 401
Accessibility, 243, 244, 248, 314, 315, 448, 450, 504
Accommodations, 101, 102, 104–110, 116
Active listening, 130, 319, 338, 346, 563, 581
Adherence, 108, 164, 222, 223, 225, 243, 246, 249, 357, 387, 451, 453, 456
Adherence to health-related behaviours, 407
Adoption and engagement, 247
Advisor, 46, 143, 146–151, 154, 155, 158, 214
Assessment, 32, 44, 62, 101, 123, 125, 136, 148–150, 153, 157, 158, 162, 172, 174, 176, 194, 195, 250, 273, 277, 282, 283, 294, 297, 315, 359, 371, 372, 378, 400, 410–412, 418, 438, 444, 450, 457, 459, 483, 485, 502, 503, 505, 506, 522, 540, 542, 544, 546, 569, 584
Assessment of risks, 48
Associate (noun. as in associate consultant), 124, 130, 131
Assumptions, 8, 13, 29, 32, 41, 44, 65, 91, 95, 103, 133, 136, 155, 169, 175, 189, 193, 231, 234, 254, 257, 258, 318, 338, 340, 342, 361, 382, 383, 430, 438, 439, 476, 500, 501, 508, 511, 512, 541, 542, 590, 602, 605
Awareness raising campaigns, 82

B

Barriers, 6, 21, 22, 26, 27, 29, 30, 33, 38, 65, 86, 91–93, 152–154, 174, 186, 205, 223, 246, 252, 270, 271, 274, 275, 278, 280, 296, 301, 302, 304, 314, 316, 343, 377, 390, 399, 464, 476, 501, 503, 507, 510, 512, 513, 564, 582, 603, 604

R. Brady et al. (eds.), *The Palgrave Handbook of Consultancy in Health Psychology*, https://doi.org/10.1007/978-3-031-94529-8

Barrier to engagement, 247
Baseline costs, *see* Costs
Behavioural insights, 125, 127, 259, 318
Behavioural prompts, 249
Behavioural regulation, 280
Behavioural science, 5, 6, 8–10, 12, 23, 24, 30, 31, 43, 82, 90, 101, 102, 114–116, 243, 246, 251, 252, 254, 255, 257, 259, 260, 268–274, 280, 282, 311, 312, 317, 319, 334, 343, 494, 499–514, 524, 552, 600, 603, 610
Behaviour change, 10, 21, 23, 27, 29–31, 50, 66, 67, 82, 93, 125, 152, 206, 222–224, 243, 244, 249, 252, 257, 259, 268, 271, 274, 275, 278–282, 321, 331–333, 357, 388, 396, 401, 407–411, 415, 416, 418, 464, 483–486, 488–492, 494, 504, 506, 507, 512, 513, 520, 547, 551, 565, 571
Behaviour change intervention, 23, 152, 204, 251, 268, 271, 278, 332, 407, 408, 411, 412, 466, 507, 508, 547, 567
Behaviour change techniques (BCTs), 246, 249, 252, 270, 273, 407, 486, 488, 492, 501, 507, 512, 547
Behaviour change theory, 246, 247, 252, 271, 274, 483, 486, 553
Behaviours, 8, 9, 21–24, 26–28, 30, 31, 43, 61, 67, 72, 82, 86, 124, 126, 127, 152, 153, 162, 163, 172, 223, 224, 246, 248–250, 268, 270–272, 278–281, 283, 292, 293, 295, 304, 305, 313, 316, 317, 319–321, 333, 334, 340–342, 351, 353, 354, 358, 362, 390, 392, 395, 407, 409, 410, 412, 413, 415, 416, 453, 483, 486, 487, 489, 491, 493, 500, 501, 505, 507, 512, 513, 547–549, 552, 554, 561, 603, 606
Benchmarking fees, 177
Best interests decision-making, 292, 295, 301
Bid, 38, 185, 187, 188, 190, 193, 227–229, 425, 427, 430, 432–435, 438, 439, 500, 504, 506, 510, 511, 513, 603
Biopsychosocial, 124, 127, 355, 370, 427, 443, 449, 457
Bite sized teaching, *see* Teaching
Boundaries, 7, 8, 31, 43, 61, 66, 84, 89, 93, 111, 127–129, 137, 143–159, 172, 175, 176, 179, 191, 208, 209, 258, 277–278, 304, 305, 318, 322, 324, 339, 358, 397–398, 412–416, 439, 466, 483, 493, 495, 505, 514, 525, 532, 533, 563, 570, 571, 574, 575, 600, 603
Boundary Model of Relationships, 7, 143
Budget, 94, 130, 133–135, 163, 165, 166, 177, 186, 187, 189, 190, 192, 194, 211, 214, 228–230, 233, 236, 237, 256, 258, 275, 304, 305, 433–438, 500–502, 511, 512, 514, 526, 570, 573
Budgetary constraints, 5, 38, 526
Building relationships, *see* Relationship building
Business acumen, 163
Business case, 133, 137, 187
Business landscape, 83
Business models, 51, 126, 137, 553
Business partner, 48, 209
Business start-up, 129
Business sustainability, 124, 138

C
Capability Opportunity Motivation and Behaviour (COM-B), 4, 9, 12, 15, 21, 22, 24–27, 29–34, 41, 45, 65, 67, 82, 83, 91, 94, 96, 112, 113, 127, 128, 130, 131, 133, 153, 155, 162, 163, 166, 173, 174, 179, 185–188, 190–192, 194, 199, 200, 203–207, 209, 214, 215, 222, 223, 225–228, 232, 235, 237, 243, 245, 249, 252–259, 270, 271, 273, 282, 300, 304, 316, 322–324, 334, 335, 337, 343, 346, 351, 354–356, 359, 363, 369, 378, 382, 387, 388, 396, 398, 400–402, 408, 410, 413, 416, 417, 426, 427, 429, 430, 436, 449, 450, 453, 458, 464, 466, 469, 476, 483, 484, 486, 490–492, 500–504, 507, 508, 510–514, 527, 533, 534, 540, 542, 547–552, 561, 563, 567, 582–587, 590, 591, 593, 599, 600, 605, 606, 608–613
Capability, *see* Capability Opportunity Motivation and Behaviour (COM-B)
Capacity (decision-making), 208, 291, 293, 301
Cardiac rehabilitation (CR), 407–419
Case Manager model (CM), 449–454, 456, 458
Case studies, 4, 11, 13, 14, 102, 116, 125, 126, 130, 133, 134, 137, 195, 232, 282, 310, 316–318, 321, 324, 325, 332–337, 350–358, 387–393, 407, 425–430, 457, 464–465, 467, 481, 484, 490, 492–494, 499–513, 519, 520, 525, 533, 539, 555, 560–565, 579–586, 593, 599, 600, 602–604, 606
Choice architecture, 127
Chronic pain, 206, 426, 430, 434, 438
Client, 4–9, 11–13, 19, 25–34, 37–47, 49–52, 60, 63–66, 69–72, 82, 83, 85, 86, 89–96, 101, 123–138, 143–150, 152–158, 163, 165–168, 171–173, 175–177, 186, 188–194, 196–199, 207, 211, 214–216, 225, 226, 228, 229, 231–233, 235–237, 250, 254, 258, 259, 268, 279, 291, 293, 296–299, 303, 305, 311, 315–317, 320, 322, 323, 332, 333, 335, 337, 339, 341, 343, 360, 362, 372, 387–389, 392, 393, 395, 401, 418, 485, 500, 502, 506–510, 512, 513, 520–522, 532, 533, 542, 546, 549, 551, 552, 581, 584, 588, 592, 606, 607
Client-centred, 128, 129, 138
Client classification, 132
Client expectations, 31, 132, 166, 167, 173, 177, 256, 372, 374, 511
Client motives, 32, 130–132
Client obligations, 545
Client rapport, 125
Client satisfaction, 126, 171–173, 505, 508, 539, 550, 584, 587, 588, 592
Clinical evaluation, 247
Clinical trial, 222–225, 231, 410
Clinical validation, 247
Co-create, 123, 125, 127, 380, 468–470, 472, 509, 511–513
Code of practice, 61, 62
Co-design, 250, 259, 344, 469, 500–504, 506–512, 603
Cognitive Behaviour Therapy (CBT), 312, 349, 353, 354, 357, 361, 364

Collaboration
collaborative relationship, 91, 393–398, 550
collaborators, 12, 318, 427, 430, 431, 433–434, 437, 439, 610, 613
Commissioner, 4, 89, 148, 187, 194, 212, 226, 344, 464, 467, 468, 471, 475, 503, 508, 512
Common Sense Model of Health and Illness, 334
Communication, 8, 32, 43, 47, 51, 67, 70, 86, 88, 89, 91, 128, 134, 162, 169, 171, 173, 190, 191, 208, 209, 213, 215, 227, 236, 254, 269, 277, 282, 297, 301, 313–317, 320, 322, 325, 332–334, 338, 341, 344, 350–352, 354–357, 359, 362, 363, 373, 374, 376, 378–381, 394–397, 420, 431, 432, 450, 452, 472, 475–477, 486, 488, 502, 508, 512, 520, 521, 526, 527, 531, 542, 544, 547, 549, 552, 555, 569, 571, 573, 574, 607, 612
Communication plan, 47, 65, 235, 268, 394, 525, 531, 534, 547
Communication skills, 32, 38, 43, 88, 163, 302, 319, 420, 533
Community of Practice (CoP), 466–477
Co-morbidities, 107, 466, 505
Competence, 6, 7, 10, 23, 32, 33, 42, 61, 62, 66–67, 115, 163, 188, 194, 197, 268, 316, 317, 372, 374, 398, 408, 411, 514, 527, 587
Competition, 43, 63, 187, 188, 191, 199
Competition-based pricing, *see* Pricing
Competitive procurement, 187
Competitive tender, 45, 186, 187
Complementary relationships, *see* Relationships
Complex eating service, 388
Confidence, 9, 25–29, 32–34, 49, 81–96, 115, 138, 158, 175, 197, 259, 313, 314, 320, 322, 349, 351, 353, 355–357, 362, 363, 375, 376, 381, 382, 387, 395, 399, 409, 427, 455, 456, 465, 468, 470, 473, 491, 494, 505, 511, 527, 581, 584, 592, 593, 602–604
Confidentiality, 46, 63, 106, 107, 213, 216, 234, 235, 339, 360, 390, 396, 397, 435, 436, 601
Conflict between ethical principles, 70–71
Conflict of interest (CoI), 69, 70
Confounding explanations, 126, 605
Consent, 60, 64, 65, 109, 112, 252, 300, 378, 390, 400, 435, 436
Consultancy, 3–15, 19–35, 37–52, 59–78, 81–96, 101, 143–159, 161–179, 185–187, 189–191, 194–197, 199, 200, 203–217, 221, 227–229, 234, 237, 243–260, 267–283, 291–299, 302–306, 310–325, 331, 332, 334–338, 340–345, 349–353, 358–361, 365, 369–371, 374, 379–383, 387–389, 392–398, 400–402, 407–420, 425, 427, 431, 432, 434, 437–440, 443–459, 463, 464, 469, 472, 474–476, 481, 483–485, 487–495, 499–514, 519–534, 539–555, 559–575, 579–581, 583–594, 599–613
Consultancy model, 38, 49, 254, 268, 270, 379–380, 544, 585, 603
Consultancy practice, 4–6, 11–13, 30, 32–34, 37, 39, 105, 203–214, 216, 217, 342, 418, 579,

589–593, 599–601, 607–610, 612
Consultancy skills, 5, 6, 10, 26, 30, 33, 39, 88, 126, 370, 372, 382, 572, 587, 607, 609–612
Consultancy-to-Practice Model, 539, 542, 543, 548, 553–555
Consultant, 4–12, 14, 19, 20, 22–25, 29–34, 37–46, 70, 81–84, 86–88, 90, 91, 93, 95, 96, 102, 104, 107, 123, 143–146, 150–151, 156–158, 163–166, 171, 172, 174–177, 179, 186–189, 193, 196, 198, 216, 221, 223, 226–227, 235–237, 254, 256, 257, 260, 268, 269, 271, 274, 277, 283, 297–299, 310, 317, 318, 321–323, 338, 341, 343, 344, 353–354, 358–363, 376, 379–381, 394–397, 402, 413, 415, 418, 458, 489, 504, 513, 520, 528, 533, 560, 571, 587, 601, 605–607
Consultant-client relationships, 7, 42, 48, 358, 380, 395, 520, 602, 607
Contact client, 132, 232, 393
Content analysis, 313, 335
Contingency, 44, 112, 136, 137, 155, 168, 169, 171, 177, 188, 195, 196, 433, 438
Contract, 6, 8, 9, 13, 14, 26, 27, 29, 31, 32, 34, 38–46, 48–50, 68–71, 74, 78, 84, 89, 91, 93, 102, 111, 123, 129–138, 146, 150, 155, 158, 166, 169–171, 175, 185–187, 205, 208, 214–216, 221, 227, 228, 231–236, 255, 256, 258, 275, 278, 296, 299, 303, 325, 331, 334, 335, 337, 339–340, 351, 371–373, 377, 389–390, 395, 397, 400, 402, 412, 425–440, 444, 451, 467, 475, 490, 499–504, 508, 511, 520, 521, 526, 531–534, 542–545, 549–551, 555, 570, 583, 585, 588, 591, 592, 602–607
Co-production, 251, 304, 317, 377, 381, 382, 469, 476, 481–487, 489, 490, 492, 494, 509, 603
Core competence, *see* Competence
Cost assessment, 107, 167, 168, 174, 176
Cost-based pricing, *see* Pricing
Cost-plus-value-based pricing, *see* Pricing
Costs, 10, 27, 41, 45, 48, 93, 94, 107, 112, 113, 133–135, 161, 165–177, 185–188, 190, 194, 195, 198, 199, 204, 208, 210–213, 216, 217, 231, 233, 234, 244, 246, 258, 275, 336, 393, 433, 434, 439, 503, 509, 511, 512, 573, 605, 610
Critical thinking, 38, 88, 134, 382
Cross-functional teams, 256
Cues to action, 249
Customer satisfaction, 49

D

Data protection, 213, 234, 245, 318, 396, 571
Decision-making, 6, 23, 28, 31, 62, 71, 87, 110, 113, 114, 124, 196, 204, 208, 291–306, 359, 361, 436, 440, 512, 545, 547, 554
Decision-making capacity, 291
Decision-making support, 293, 297, 301, 303, 305
Dementia, 12, 60, 101, 102, 106, 107, 110–114, 370, 371, 374, 382, 383
Design aesthetics, 248
Design thinking, 250–251

Determinants of behaviour, 279, 280
Diagnostic work, 127, 134, 244, 370
Digital health, 13, 47, 225, 243–260
Digital health apps, 245, 246
Digital health innovation, 246
Digital health interventions (DHIs), 246–249, 251–253, 255–257, 259
Digital health technologies (DHTs), 48, 244–246
Digital literacy, 247
Digital therapeutics (DtX), 225, 245, 247
Direct costs, 134, 135, 168–170
Disabilities, 65, 101, 102, 104, 105, 108–111, 114–116, 291, 299, 369–383, 446, 447, 453, 457
Discovery Needs Assessment, 539, 542–544, 549, 553, 555
Disease awareness campaigns, 223
Disease burden, 106
Disparities, 65, 105, 111, 244, 574
Doctor-patient model (of consultancy), 353, 361
Domains model, 84–86
Double Diamond, 501, 508, 509

E

EAST model, 507
Economic disadvantages, 564
Educational interventions, 7, 163, 351, 606
Effectiveness, 10, 31, 32, 192, 246, 247, 249, 251, 252, 259, 276, 295, 303, 350, 351, 382, 387, 389, 390, 410, 415, 419, 451, 455–458, 500, 505, 548, 567, 569, 572, 584, 585, 605, 606
Efficacy, 224, 245, 246
Empowerment framework, 463, 466, 468–472, 474, 475
Empowerment programme, 464–467, 469, 470, 472–475
Engagement (with health apps), 243
Enquiry, 13, 14, 26, 31, 39–42, 51, 73, 78, 90, 92, 102, 106, 110, 111, 115, 129–133, 143, 154–158, 189, 190, 192, 221, 225–232, 255–258, 270, 271, 291, 294, 296–302, 310, 315, 323–325, 331, 333, 336–343, 346, 361, 380, 381, 388–389, 394, 396, 399, 400, 408, 410–412, 417–419, 444, 445, 449, 469, 471, 472, 484, 494, 500–502, 504, 510, 511, 541, 542, 551, 591, 600, 602, 604, 606, 607
Equality, 205, 207, 298, 305, 317, 553
Ethical guidelines, 60, 61
Ethical implications, 60
Ethically prepared, 71
Ethical practice, 13, 31, 60–78, 129, 165
Ethical responsibilities, 114
Ethical safeguards, 70
Ethics, 59–78, 127, 233, 252, 259, 451, 532
Ethnicity, 64, 102, 105–107, 206, 465
Evaluation, 5, 23, 28, 39, 40, 47–52, 60, 77, 90, 102, 104, 105, 113, 115, 126, 130, 162, 196, 221, 231, 235–237, 245–247, 251, 252, 255, 267, 268, 273, 275, 278–282, 296, 303, 304, 315, 331, 332, 337, 341–342, 372, 387, 389, 390, 395–397, 401, 410, 411, 418, 427, 455, 458, 465, 467, 473, 487, 489, 500, 504, 512, 519–525, 528, 531–532, 539–555, 559, 560, 563, 565–571, 579, 584–589, 591–593, 600, 603, 605–607
Evidence-based, 5, 9, 30–32, 37–39, 41, 43, 45, 50, 52, 69, 82, 115,

125–127, 130, 131, 137, 162–164, 172, 205, 243, 246, 247, 251–253, 260, 270, 295, 300, 324, 337, 354, 390, 408, 418, 443, 540, 551, 553, 555, 561, 564, 571, 572, 605, 607, 608
Evidence-based interventions, 172, 205, 243, 387, 561
Evidence-synthesis, 127
Expert by experience, 543
Expert consultant, 12, 223, 226–227, 234, 358, 379
Expertise, 4–6, 8, 9, 11, 12, 21, 23, 25, 27, 28, 31, 33, 38, 39, 41–43, 45, 47, 49, 51, 59, 64, 66–68, 81–96, 101, 111, 114, 125, 126, 128, 129, 134, 137, 144, 145, 152, 155, 156, 158, 162–165, 167, 171–173, 175–177, 179, 186–188, 191, 192, 194, 196, 197, 200, 206–208, 210, 211, 214, 215, 225–227, 229, 232, 235–237, 246, 247, 251–255, 257, 259, 272, 278, 279, 295, 298, 304, 314, 317–319, 321, 331, 333, 336–344, 353, 359, 362, 363, 375, 379, 383, 389, 395, 400–401, 408, 410, 412, 417, 426, 427, 429, 432, 437, 438, 466–468, 470, 472–477, 481–495, 500, 503, 504, 508, 510, 511, 513, 520, 525, 528, 540, 551, 555, 561, 565, 570–573, 580, 584, 593, 600–604, 607–610, 612
Expert patient, 430, 435
External consultant, 8, 10, 32, 47, 93, 144, 146, 163, 257, 260, 271, 297, 318, 319, 363, 396, 397, 484
External verification, 132

F

Facilitation, 8, 127, 173, 374, 396, 432, 433, 436, 465, 473, 475, 476
Focus group, 123, 135, 144, 193, 250, 273, 332, 377, 378, 381, 429, 430, 465, 522, 523, 525–527
Formulation(s), 39, 68, 125, 127, 134, 162, 297, 354, 357, 364, 452–454, 607
Framework, v, 3, 5, 11, 13, 22, 23, 25, 28, 33–35, 37–52, 60, 62, 63, 65, 70, 72–77, 86, 89, 92, 102, 110, 116, 127, 130, 143, 154–158, 166, 189–191, 194, 206, 221, 222, 227, 229, 245, 246, 248, 252, 255, 256, 259, 280, 281, 291, 296, 303, 305, 315, 316, 331, 334–336, 354, 359, 411, 417, 418, 425, 434, 435, 444, 449, 450, 452–454, 463–477, 484, 508, 512, 528, 548, 550, 553, 555, 565, 570–572, 585, 591, 599, 600, 602–607, 612
Framework for consultancy in health psychology, 3, 11, 13, 34, 37–52, 72–77, 130, 221, 255, 291, 305, 336, 565, 570, 591, 599, 602–607, 612
Functionality, 248, 502
Funding bid, *see* Bid

G

Gamification, 249
Gap analysis, 125, 540
Generic consultancy processes, 38, 39
Generic consultancy skills, 5, 6, 8, 10, 39
Goal setting, 249, 252, 390, 429, 486, 487, 506, 507, 547
Governance and planning, 47

Group intervention, 387–402
Guidelines, 60, 61, 65, 223, 270, 277, 282, 314, 378, 400, 426, 430, 444, 452, 519

H

Habit formation, 249
Haemodialysis, 349–351, 355
Health, 3, 5, 19–35, 37–52, 59, 82, 101, 123, 143, 161–179, 185, 203–217, 221, 243–260, 267–283, 309, 331–346, 351, 369, 388, 408, 425, 443, 464, 481–495, 499, 520, 539–555, 559–575, 579–593, 599
Health Advocates (HAs), 559, 561, 564, 566, 567, 569–574
Health and safety (H&S), 124–128, 130, 131, 435
Health and wellbeing, 23, 222, 494, 502, 506, 539–555, 580
Health and wellbeing practitioner, 429, 434, 437
Healthcare, 5, 9, 22–24, 26, 28–30, 32, 34, 42, 48, 59, 60, 104, 115, 125, 161, 162, 164, 173, 175, 196, 206, 222–224, 243–247, 249–251, 254, 257–259, 269–275, 277–279, 282, 291–293, 295, 296, 298, 300–302, 304, 310, 333, 344, 350, 354, 377, 381, 382, 399, 400, 409, 411, 418, 425–440, 443, 444, 448, 452, 457, 458, 464, 482, 483, 543, 560, 561, 564, 572, 573, 580, 584, 590, 593
Healthcare professional(s), 23, 28, 115, 196, 223, 224, 246, 247, 269–274, 277, 278, 407–419, 432, 483, 500, 590
Health disparities, 244, 574
Health education, 90, 272, 560, 561, 563
Health inequalities, 102, 103, 115, 205, 207, 320, 324, 337, 344, 372, 573, 580
Health literacy, 112, 127, 247, 313–315, 320, 324, 325, 377
Health outcomes, 24, 103, 237, 246–248, 253, 260, 273, 305, 409, 483, 564, 567, 580, 593
Health partnership, 268–278, 281–283
Health promotion, 21, 162, 164, 175, 338, 546, 547, 563, 573, 580
Health psychologist, 3–13, 19–34, 37–39, 42, 43, 47–52, 59–63, 65–67, 69, 71, 72, 78, 83, 93–96, 101, 102, 104, 110, 114–116, 124, 129, 130, 132, 135, 137, 138, 143, 152, 158, 162, 164, 167, 169, 172, 174–177, 185, 189–192, 194, 203–206, 221–224, 235, 243, 247–248, 251–260, 268, 272–274, 282, 292, 295, 300, 303, 305, 306, 312, 318, 321, 331–333, 336, 340, 343, 346, 358–363, 370, 372–374, 382, 388, 397, 399, 401, 402, 417, 418, 425, 466, 475, 481, 483–488, 490–495, 505, 510–512, 514, 520, 531–533, 540, 543, 551, 553, 580, 584, 585, 589, 590, 593, 599–601, 603–613
Health psychology, 3–14, 19–35, 37–52, 60–62, 66, 68, 69, 72–77, 82–83, 85, 86, 88, 123, 124, 126–128, 130, 134, 144, 152–154, 161–179, 185, 187, 189, 192, 195, 203–217, 221–224, 227, 236, 237,

243–260, 267–283, 291, 295, 303–305, 316, 322, 332, 336, 340, 341, 343–345, 369, 371, 372, 383, 388, 389, 393, 395, 399, 402, 414, 417, 418, 420, 443, 464–466, 468, 477, 481–495, 499, 505, 507–510, 524, 532, 540, 542, 546, 547, 551–553, 555, 565, 570, 588, 591, 593, 599–613
Health psychology consultancy, 20, 27, 28, 34, 38, 39, 61, 62, 161–179, 187, 203–217, 243–260, 267–283, 295, 305, 332, 369, 464, 524, 540, 553, 555, 600, 605
Health psychology training, 123, 126–127, 134, 340, 372, 486, 491
Health technology, 222, 225, 255
Honorary contract, 389, 395, 397
Human error, 124, 128
Human factors, 124
Humble consulting, 299, 437, 488
Humble inquiry, 92, 104, 270, 271, 332, 338, 340, 342, 343, 494, 541, 602
Humility, 11, 33, 81–96, 488, 600, 602, 603

I

Implementation, 6, 7, 23, 25, 28, 29, 43, 51, 52, 70, 72, 86, 88, 131, 133, 146, 149, 150, 162, 169, 258, 280, 294, 296, 297, 300–302, 304, 318, 340, 361, 371, 390, 396, 399, 450, 458, 505, 507, 539, 543, 545–546, 548–551, 560, 567, 569–571, 573, 574, 589, 600, 603, 606, 607
Implementation planning, 270
Imposter syndrome, 33, 115, 128, 137, 139, 343
Independent consultancy, 78, 123, 127, 602
Independent practice, 162, 601, 612
Indirect costs, 134, 165, 169, 170, 174
Informed decision(s), 85, 134, 233, 295, 314, 353
Inpatient, 351, 444, 446, 448, 450, 453–456
In scope, 47, 52, 236, 381, 511
Insider, 6, 7, 144–146, 148–150, 154–157, 318, 353, 508, 603
Institutional power, *see* Power
Insurance, 210, 212, 231, 233–235, 277, 454
Integrity, 28, 50, 51, 61, 62, 69–78, 132, 167, 177, 186, 254, 258, 259, 316, 317, 374, 375
Intellectual disability (ID), 65, 71, 72, 109, 110, 198, 291, 292, 369–383
Intellectual property, 45, 46, 70, 186, 216, 234, 235, 545
Interdisciplinary working model, 449, 450
Internal consultancy, 6, 10, 41, 46, 125, 144, 291, 297, 299, 303, 304, 306, 310, 312, 315, 318, 322, 323, 351, 444, 604, 605
International clients, 12
International consultancy, 268
International Health Partnership(s) (IHPs), 12, 267–283
Interpersonal boundaries, 439
Interpersonal skills, 6, 43, 84, 90, 144, 146, 374, 587
Intervention design, 6, 49, 153, 162, 197, 251, 410, 512, 593
Intervention functions, 269, 512

Intervention(s), 5, 7–9, 12, 23, 24, 27, 28, 30–32, 38, 39, 41, 43, 46, 47, 60, 64, 71, 72, 83–85, 88, 90, 92, 94, 101, 105, 108, 125, 147, 150, 152–154, 162–164, 166, 168, 172, 173, 192, 195, 203–205, 243, 244, 247, 251, 252, 268–271, 275, 278–281, 294–296, 298, 303, 305, 311–314, 316–318, 320, 321, 323, 325, 332, 350–355, 357, 358, 360–363, 370, 372, 387–402, 407, 408, 410–413, 415, 418, 426, 427, 438, 443, 447, 450, 451, 455–458, 466, 486, 487, 501, 506–509, 512, 513, 541, 544–548, 550–555, 559–561, 567, 571, 573, 585, 593, 602, 603, 605–607
Intrapersonal, 146, 154, 156, 158
Intrinsic motivation, *see* Motivation
Invitation to Tender (ITT), 45, 188, 465–466, 499–501, 504, 505, 508, 510, 511

K

Key deliverables, 351, 434
Key relationships, *see* Relationships
Knowledge sharing, 91
Knowledge Transfer Partnership (KTP), 162

L

Learning disability, 105
Legislative and policy framework, 86
Legislative context, 86, 297, 299–300
Literacy, *see* Health literacy
Literature review, 230, 231, 332, 380, 389, 390, 401, 473

M

Management, 5–7, 10, 21, 22, 25, 32, 33, 38–40, 42, 47, 50, 51, 64, 67, 82, 84, 87–89, 93, 94, 96, 125, 127, 129, 134, 136, 143, 144, 146, 147, 156, 161, 163–165, 168, 172, 173, 187, 191, 193, 195, 196, 216, 221, 222, 224, 230, 252, 254, 256, 277, 298, 310, 317–319, 341, 342, 352, 355, 360, 373, 375, 377, 379, 389, 395, 400, 402, 409, 426, 427, 429, 430, 432, 438, 446, 449–451, 456, 471–473, 475, 481, 484, 489–491, 494, 500, 505, 525, 528, 532, 540, 546, 547, 570, 571, 573, 582, 605, 606, 608
Management consultant(s), 5–7, 10, 32, 39, 84, 143, 146, 156, 163, 165, 168, 221, 317–319, 571
Marginalised, 105, 377, 465, 466
Marketing, 129, 137, 175, 208, 209, 214–216, 224, 225, 228, 256, 259, 332, 333, 344, 400, 539, 570
Medical devices, 48, 222, 244–246
Medical psychologist, 12, 443–459
Mentor, 90, 158, 206, 208, 214–215, 334, 337, 339, 340, 342, 345, 612
Methodology, 23, 28, 31, 35, 50, 89, 133, 134, 138, 165–178, 195, 199, 246, 250, 251, 259, 280, 281, 343, 344, 466, 500, 501, 507, 508, 521, 522, 608
Microbial resistance, 331
Mitigating actions, 436
Mixed-methods research, 163
Mobile health apps, 243–245
Motivation, 408
See also Capability Opportunity Motivation and Behaviour (COM-B)

Motivational Interviewing (MI), 319, 338, 396, 397, 411, 414, 415, 435, 465, 564
Multidisciplinary team(s) (MDT), 89–93, 274, 275, 371, 388, 390, 394, 396, 400, 401, 407–414, 418, 429, 435, 436, 438, 446, 447, 449, 451, 493
Multi-modal, 579, 585–589, 592, 593
Multiple levels of enquiry, *see* Enquiry
Multiple stakeholders, *see* Stakeholder(s)

N

Negotiating, 4, 6, 13, 14, 29, 31, 32, 34, 38, 40, 43–47, 74, 78, 84, 102, 106, 111, 123, 129–132, 134–136, 138, 146, 149, 165, 167, 169, 171, 177, 192, 221, 227, 228, 231–235, 255, 256, 258, 275, 304, 331, 339–340, 342, 371–373, 389–390, 412, 425–440, 484, 501, 503–507, 509–511, 514, 542, 545, 550, 569, 570, 573, 600, 603–607
Networking, 25, 29, 32, 33, 40, 207, 225, 226, 255, 560, 609, 610, 613
Non-pharmacological intervention(s), 427
Nudge, 127, 128

O

Occupational disease, 124
Occupational health, 127
Opportunity, *see* Capability Opportunity Motivation and Behaviour (COM-B)
Organisational consultancy, 126, 608
Organisational environment, 81, 83, 87, 545
Outcome evaluation, *see* Evaluation
Outcome measures, 357, 358, 489, 551
Outcomes, 9, 24, 25, 27, 29, 40–42, 44, 46–52, 68, 69, 71, 82, 83, 85, 90–92, 96, 102, 103, 126, 132, 137, 147, 149, 157, 158, 163, 167, 171, 172, 174, 186, 188, 190, 192, 193, 195–197, 214, 223, 237, 244, 246–248, 251, 253, 257, 260, 273, 277, 293–295, 297–298, 305, 310, 313, 314, 317, 321–323, 332, 335, 341, 342, 356–362, 365, 372, 374, 376–378, 380, 388, 389, 392, 393, 395, 398, 401, 408–410, 427, 432, 435, 464, 466, 467, 469, 471, 473–476, 482, 483, 489, 490, 501, 502, 511–514, 540, 546, 548–552, 554, 555, 561, 563–565, 567, 569, 579, 580, 584–587, 592–594, 603–608
Out-of-scope, 49, 236
Outpatient, 12, 443–459
Outsider, 41, 145–150, 154, 155, 157, 363, 413, 474, 477, 603

P

Partner agreement, 335, 339
Partnership, 12, 13, 65, 147–149, 164, 208, 209, 211–213, 227, 229, 235, 246, 254, 259, 267–283, 312, 317, 323, 394, 410, 464, 472, 544, 552, 563, 591
Patient advocacy, 223
Patient and public involvement (PPI), 369, 377, 378, 382, 383, 524
Patient outcomes, 223, 231, 244, 427
Patient pathways, 82
Patient satisfaction, 390, 392, 396, 397, 455–456

Peer support, 113, 207, 388, 429, 439, 465, 467, 468, 473, 548
Performance indicators, 90, 172, 237, 417
Personal autonomy, 153
Personal power, *see* Power
Personalisation, 247, 249
Person-centred, 148, 247, 317, 319, 332, 411, 540, 564, 580, 582
Pharma, *see* Pharmaceutical
Pharmaceutical, 48, 221–225, 228, 234, 237, 238, 245
Physical activity, 22, 86, 246, 310, 409, 411, 412, 429, 487, 500, 504, 505, 542, 546
Planning, 4, 13, 14, 38, 44, 46–48, 86, 104–106, 108, 109, 112, 130, 131, 165, 187, 191, 195, 199, 209, 217, 230, 256, 257, 268, 270, 273, 275–278, 281, 294–296, 321, 333, 335, 340, 341, 364, 376, 389, 390, 395, 396, 399, 401, 425, 430, 434, 435, 449, 450, 458, 459, 468–472, 475, 481, 484, 487–490, 492, 499, 501, 504–505, 511, 519, 525–528, 544, 550, 563, 569, 571–573, 587, 591, 604–607
Planning and managing delivery, 40, 46–49, 76, 102, 113, 221, 255, 277, 331, 340–341, 449–454, 463, 482, 487–491, 504, 525–528, 591, 605–607
Post-bariatric patients, 388, 390
Power, 7, 46, 61, 63–65, 67, 86, 92, 111, 134, 135, 208, 317, 380, 397, 467, 474, 476, 482, 532
Power imbalance, 49, 64, 106, 108, 130, 137, 208, 359, 397
Practice-based evidence, 32, 38, 408, 418, 606, 609, 610, 612
Practitioner health psychologist (PHP), 12, 291, 353, 358–363, 589, 612
Preferred supplier, 188
Presumption of capacity, 300
Pricing, 13, 129, 133–138, 161–179, 194, 195, 210, 211, 334, 604, 608
Pricing strategies, 161, 165, 166, 171, 173, 211
Primary client, 125, 131, 132, 228, 232, 235, 520, 521
Principles, 10, 20, 60–78, 96, 107, 162, 163, 177, 196, 213, 223, 233, 234, 243, 250, 252, 259, 272, 274–278, 282, 292, 299–301, 304, 316–318, 321, 337, 350, 358–363, 377, 378, 390, 397, 399, 407, 408, 413, 444, 449, 450, 465, 472, 476, 554, 571, 605
Privacy and confidentiality, 63
Privacy concerns, 247
Private sector, 13, 21, 46, 82, 84, 164, 221–238, 399, 401
Problem solving, 91, 132, 164, 192, 254, 323, 340, 380, 426, 429, 431, 432, 434–436, 439, 476, 587
Pro bono, 161, 165, 166, 174–176, 179, 389, 400, 604
Process consultancy, 125, 270, 278, 358–360, 374, 375, 379, 394, 472, 541, 603
Process evaluation, *see* Evaluation
Procurement portal, 500
Professional accountability, 67
Professional development, 66, 67, 88, 114, 152, 322, 549, 553, 599, 609, 611
Professional distance, 297
Professional integrity, 28, 50, 132, 186, 254, 259

Professional networking, *see* Networking
Professional power, *see* Power
Professional standards, 32, 78, 353, 494, 505–507, 609, 610
Professional training, 6, 67, 88, 129, 143, 152, 156, 400, 401, 532, 540, 571, 572, 589, 607
Profit, 133, 137, 167, 168, 171, 192, 210, 230, 231, 236
Progress tracking, 249
Project goals, 48, 268, 319, 591
Project management, 47, 51, 88–89, 93, 94, 96, 127, 129, 134, 136, 144, 147, 163, 173, 195, 224, 230, 379, 472, 475, 505, 525, 540, 605, 606, 608
Project milestones, 256
Project outcomes, 85, 137, 186, 322, 359, 401, 490, 563–565, 567
Project plan, 236, 434, 467, 471, 511, 513, 525
Project scope, 166, 232–233, 476, 544
Proof of concept, 483, 545
Proposal(s), 11, 24, 45, 85, 92, 129–136, 138, 163–166, 169, 176, 185–200, 227–230, 232, 233, 293–294, 298, 313, 388, 389, 395, 396, 432–435, 444, 465–468, 472, 500, 501, 504, 511, 550, 602, 604, 605
Prospective clients, 130–132, 134, 136, 225, 228, 232, 237, 373, 602
Protected characteristics, 65, 103
Protective factors, 103, 158
Psychological functioning, 389
Psychological safety, 42, 380–381, 476, 477, 612
Psychological therapies, 350
Psychologist case manager model, *see* Case Manager model (CM)
Public funds, 45, 211
Public health interventions, 205, 501
Public sector, 10, 45, 83, 164, 185, 186, 188, 196, 317, 580
Purchase-of-expertise model of consultancy, 336, 565

Q

Qualitative data, 127, 193, 280, 320, 331, 333, 544, 546, 606
Qualitative research, 190, 205, 260, 338, 343, 418, 419, 482, 520, 521
Quality improvement (QI), 90, 271, 279, 319
Quality of life, 128, 143, 148, 149, 350, 372, 466, 470

R

Randomised controlled trial (RCT), 247, 415
Rapid assessment procedure (RAP), 522, 524
Rapid qualitative evaluation, 522, 523, 525, 528, 531
Rapport, 125, 167, 173, 190, 215, 229, 297, 298, 342, 346, 446, 533, 534, 549, 607
Recommendations, 5, 7, 10, 11, 25, 26, 29, 46, 51, 64, 68, 83, 94, 129, 133, 138, 143, 146, 149, 150, 208, 224, 231, 250, 255, 257, 258, 268, 273, 278, 294, 296, 297, 299, 302, 310, 318, 335, 336, 380, 393, 401, 409, 445, 452, 472, 500–503, 507–509, 511–513, 519, 524, 525, 534, 540, 544–548, 550–553, 555, 581–583, 587, 589, 606
Recovery College (RC), 481–494

Reflection(s), 13, 14, 30–34, 110, 114, 124, 143, 161, 166, 195, 198, 203, 206, 237, 281, 302–305, 310, 319–323, 325, 332, 342, 344, 350, 351, 353, 354, 363–364, 369, 379–383, 393, 397–402, 412, 417–419, 427, 436–440, 455–458, 463, 474–477, 483, 491–494, 508, 510–513, 519, 528–533, 542, 551–555, 565, 571–574, 579, 589–592, 600, 602
Reflection-in-action, 398
Reflection-on-action, 398, 491, 572
Reflective practice, 13, 43, 51, 52, 95, 137, 380, 398, 427, 429, 439, 540, 554, 555, 572
Reflective process, 281, 398
Reflective questions, 271
Reflexivity, 51, 115, 342, 427, 492, 589, 594
Regulated healthcare, 222
Regulatory landscape, 246
Regulatory oversight, 245
Regulatory review, 245
Rehabilitation psychology, 443
Relationship building, 32, 51, 75, 89, 96, 111, 145, 149, 174, 192, 255, 257, 274, 275, 283, 299, 316, 323, 325, 331, 338, 369, 374–379, 381, 408, 410, 412–417, 420, 523, 606
Relationships, 4, 10, 20, 38, 64, 83, 102, 130, 143, 163, 186, 207, 221, 255, 268, 269, 297, 316, 332, 350, 369, 387, 408, 409, 425, 446, 469, 481, 509, 520, 541, 587, 602
Report, 10, 21, 27, 29, 33, 35, 44, 51, 63, 65, 72, 88, 92, 103, 111–114, 127, 129, 150, 163, 195, 206, 231, 236, 273, 277, 303, 334–336, 340, 341, 343, 352, 393, 395, 433, 438, 452, 502–504, 507, 509, 511, 514, 522–525, 527, 528, 545, 549, 567, 584–586, 588, 606
Reputational benefits, 132, 610
Reputational risk(s), 41, 259, 532
Request for Proposal (RfPs), 45, 188–191, 228, 229
Resource allocation, 504
Resources, 3, 4, 7–9, 20, 27, 30, 38, 41, 46–48, 68, 69, 78, 86, 87, 89, 90, 93, 94, 96, 102, 129, 133, 136, 137, 144, 146, 147, 149, 150, 155, 165, 168, 169, 173, 177, 186, 191, 192, 194, 208, 209, 216, 222, 225, 230, 231, 235, 244, 248, 251, 254, 256, 257, 269, 278, 279, 293–296, 300–306, 313, 336, 341, 343, 344, 361, 364, 365, 373, 379, 396, 399, 427, 433, 436, 450, 464, 467, 473, 506, 508, 525, 528, 547, 548, 570, 574, 588, 599, 600, 602, 604, 606, 609–611
Respect, 61–66, 70, 72, 78, 96, 106, 131, 275, 316, 317, 338, 352, 359, 372, 374–376, 379, 381, 383, 397, 398, 402, 452, 473, 474, 476, 506, 581
Responding to tenders, *see* Tender(s)
Responsibility, 7, 8, 31, 43, 44, 46–48, 61, 62, 64, 67–70, 72, 78, 89, 91, 114, 115, 176, 208, 224, 235, 255, 258, 277, 304, 316, 317, 322, 339, 362, 395, 429, 430, 433, 435, 436, 438, 451, 453, 458, 467, 471, 477, 491, 507, 508, 510, 545, 588, 591, 603, 605, 609, 610
Review and Learn, 545, 554
Rights-based approach, 291–306
Risk, 8, 32, 40, 41, 43–45, 48, 68, 69, 81, 89, 92, 93, 103, 107, 109,

126, 127, 132, 133, 136–138, 153, 155, 157, 169, 171, 179, 186, 188–197, 199, 204, 208, 209, 212, 230, 233, 234, 236, 247, 250, 256, 257, 259, 274, 277, 337, 370, 380, 400, 407, 413, 416, 427, 433–436, 438, 439, 465, 467, 468, 483, 485, 502, 505, 506, 509–511, 525, 532–534, 561, 569, 604, 605
Risk management, 127, 525
Risk register, 434–436
Roles and responsibilities, 46, 68, 89, 235, 435, 471, 507, 508, 591

S

Safeguarding, 63, 253
Safeguards, 70, 245, 337
Scientific method, 28, 31, 32, 69, 126
Scientist-practitioner, 6, 39, 129, 130, 139, 163, 605
Scope change, 48, 49
Scope creep, 43, 48, 89, 135, 137, 138, 257, 304, 306, 438, 489, 519, 525–526, 528, 532–534, 549, 605, 606
Scope of competence, 66, 67, 317
Scope of knowledge, 66
Scope of practice, 6, 8, 34, 66, 493
Screening programme, 520–524, 526
Self-awareness, 144, 146, 154, 157–158, 362
Self-determination theory (SDT), 407, 408, 410, 411, 414, 415, 418
Self-efficacy, 271, 281, 387, 388, 392, 466
Self-esteem, 388, 390, 399, 464, 466, 467, 482
Self-management, 23, 244, 310, 317, 426, 429, 464, 466, 499–514
Self-monitoring, 158, 252
Self-stigma, 320, 463–477
Semi-structured discussion guides, 190, 522
Service Level Agreement, 545
Seven Cs, 553
Shared medical appointment (SMA), 425–438, 440
Situational determinants, 128
Social isolation, 152, 500, 504, 505
Social learning model, 432, 437, 439
Social stories, 293, 294, 301, 302
Social support, 249, 273, 426, 445, 548, 580
Sole practitioner, 208
Specification, 48, 94, 129, 465, 466, 468, 469, 474, 503, 508, 510, 525
Staff health and wellbeing, 540, 542, 544, 545, 547, 548, 550, 552
Stakeholder analysis, 87, 89, 394
Stakeholder engagement, 87, 94, 293–294, 432, 574
Stakeholder management, 40, 87, 88
Stakeholder mapping, 43
Stakeholder needs, 291, 315, 563, 602
Stakeholder(s), 5, 8, 13, 30–34, 38, 40–44, 46, 48–52, 64, 68, 70–72, 86–92, 94, 102, 104, 106–108, 110, 114–116, 138, 163, 166, 171, 195, 222, 224, 225, 233, 248, 250, 256, 257, 268, 274, 275, 291, 293–294, 297–299, 306, 310, 312, 315–318, 320, 334, 339, 343, 350, 352, 353, 355–356, 359–364, 369, 373–379, 381–383, 387, 393–397, 401, 402, 408, 410, 411, 413–415, 417, 419, 420, 427, 428, 430–433, 435, 444, 463, 465, 477, 490, 499, 500, 502, 506, 507, 509, 510, 512, 513, 520, 523–524, 528, 533, 534, 559, 561–563, 569, 574, 575, 582–583, 600, 602–606, 608

Start-up costs, 204
Stigma, 103, 105, 106, 108, 464–469, 471, 473, 474, 477, 546, 580, 582
Strengths/asset-based, 317
Structured education, 311
Subcontracting, 129, 135
Submission (proposal), 186, 188, 198, 228, 232
Supervision, 4, 33, 51, 65, 67, 68, 114, 115, 127, 158, 275, 320–322, 325, 399, 402, 448, 450, 453, 484, 485, 489, 520, 525, 532, 540, 542, 551, 553–555, 572, 609, 610
Support needs, 110, 322, 372, 426, 500, 502, 503
Sustainable, 13, 23, 28, 30, 33, 86, 93, 123, 124, 138, 163, 175, 179, 187, 245, 272, 273, 275, 276, 317, 360, 362, 559, 567, 601
SWOT analysis, 206
Systems thinking, 124

T

Tacit knowledge, 126, 128, 302, 303, 413
Tailored solutions, 164, 552
Teaching, 4, 6, 7, 12, 23, 33, 88, 203, 206, 349–357, 360–364, 387, 389, 392, 395–397, 401, 483, 486, 488–492, 494, 580, 581, 583, 587, 589, 593, 607
Technical credibility, 129
Technical skills, 6, 34, 38
Template for Intervention Description and Reputational Framework (TIDieR), 130
Templates, 129, 209, 215, 225, 229, 233–235, 293, 295, 296, 301, 432, 433, 493, 507, 511, 587
Tender(s), 13, 45, 167, 185–188, 198, 214, 464–466, 513, 605
The Change Exchange (TCE), 272–275, 277–283
Theoretical Domains Framework (TDF), 49, 127, 280
Theoretical framework, 280, 303, 316, 334, 335
Theoretical Framework of Acceptability, 410, 418, 513
Think aloud methodology, 249, 251
Think tanks, 125
Third sector, 5, 20, 25, 45, 60, 104, 111, 147, 211, 344, 601
Thought leadership, 127–128, 227, 232, 255
Training, 4, 6–12, 20, 23, 24, 26, 27, 30–33, 38, 41, 66, 67, 83, 88, 90, 96, 104, 115, 123, 124, 126–130, 134, 143, 148, 152, 156, 162, 163, 171, 172, 195, 203, 204, 206, 211, 214, 221, 223, 224, 230, 253, 269–271, 273, 275, 280–282, 291–294, 296, 299, 300, 312, 321, 340, 343, 345, 351, 354, 356, 371, 372, 382, 399–401, 407, 408, 410–415, 417, 435, 449, 451, 457, 464–466, 468, 469, 473, 476, 477, 482, 485, 486, 488, 491–493, 512, 520, 532, 533, 540, 547, 548, 559–561, 563, 564, 567, 569–574, 580, 581, 589, 590, 593, 599, 605, 607, 609–612
Training interventions, 12, 41, 125
Transferrable skills, 88
Transformational leadership, 526
Transgender health, 580
Transitions of care, 448
Triage, 500, 502, 503, 505–507

Trust, 42, 47, 52, 64, 67, 85, 91, 92, 94, 105, 106, 111, 114, 146, 157–158, 166, 171, 173, 177, 190, 192, 205, 225, 236, 247, 257, 258, 298, 318, 338, 358–360, 362, 369, 373–376, 379–381, 394, 395, 397, 410, 413, 414, 417, 426, 434, 456, 476, 485, 488, 495, 509, 534, 542, 549, 592, 604
Trust equation, 128
Type 2 Diabetes (T2D), 310, 311

U

Ultimate beneficiaries, 102, 335, 373, 603, 607
Ultimate client(s), 102, 105, 108–110, 114–116, 132, 335, 343, 372, 394, 438, 444, 521
Unethical, 71, 112
Unintentional discrimination, 65
Unintentional harms, 60
Unique selling point, 129, 232
Usability, 28, 30, 245, 248, 251, 252, 259, 504
Usability testing, 248, 249, 251, 256
User experience (UX), 49, 229, 243, 247–250, 252, 254–256, 258, 260
User experience principles, 243
User friendliness, 245
User research, 251, 253–258

V

Value-based pricing, *see* Pricing
Value proposition, 172, 177, 227
Values, 3, 13, 14, 20, 25, 27, 28, 31, 33, 34, 40–42, 50, 51, 60, 63–66, 70, 78, 90, 95, 111, 114, 128–129, 131, 137, 139, 153, 155, 157, 161–179, 185, 190, 191, 194, 195, 198, 199, 204–207, 209, 211, 213, 215, 217, 228, 243, 246, 249, 251–254, 257, 259, 260, 274, 292, 298, 300, 304, 305, 312, 315–318, 321, 323, 325, 335, 337, 338, 341–346, 372, 373, 377, 380, 394, 396–398, 400, 401, 419, 438–440, 466, 469, 483, 485, 500, 506, 510, 512, 513, 531, 543, 544, 546, 548, 561, 572, 581, 586, 589, 593
Vulnerability, 42, 101–103, 105–111, 114–116, 248, 345, 397, 398, 448, 466
Vulnerable clients, 101, 110–114, 116, 388
Vulnerable service users, 101

W

Website, 115, 131, 191, 205, 209, 212–216, 225, 314, 500–504, 506–509, 512, 513, 580, 581
Wellbeing, 21, 23, 27, 28, 60, 68, 69, 86, 115, 125, 131, 132, 137, 146–148, 155, 157, 158, 162, 167, 187, 205, 206, 222, 260, 333, 351, 352, 401, 427, 429, 434, 437, 464, 471, 481–495, 499–514, 539–555, 563, 573, 579–581, 584, 585

FSC
www.fsc.org
MIX
Papier | Fördert
gute Waldnutzung
FSC® C083411

Kolibri 360 GmbH
Ferdinand-Jühlke-Straße 7
99095 Erfurt, Deutschland
produktsicherheit@kolibri360.de